The Official Government Auction Guide

****

The Official Government Auction Guide

★★

GEORGE C. CHELEKIS

Foreword by **SONNY BLOCH**

CROWN PUBLISHERS, INC.

NEW YORK

This publication is designed to provide accurate information on the subject matter covered. Procedures and addresses may vary in local areas and are subject to change. All information provided is effective as of September 1991.

The author is not engaged in rendering legal or accounting advice. Use of a competent and recognized attorney is advised when making real estate or other substantial investments.

The author assumes no liability for anyone making investments in real estate or purchasing personal property or real estate at any auctions. Attendance, participation, bidding, and/or purchase of personal property or real estate at auctions or through other methods should be done with discretion and with the full and complete understanding that one is responsible for the decisions he or she makes or does not make.

Advice, tips, and strategies given by the author should be understood as having come from what are generally considered to be reliable or authoritative sources. The author assumes no liability for the inaccuracy of these sources or subsequent errors or losses that may result from such advice.

Past performance at auctions or in real estate investments does not guarantee current or future comparable performance.

Copyright © 1989, 1992 by George Chelekis

All rights reserved. No part of this book may be reproduced or transmitted in any form or by any means, electronic or mechanical, including photocopying, recording, or by any information storage and retrieval system, without permission in writing from the publisher.

Published by Crown Publishers, Inc., 201 East 50th Street, New York, New York 10022. Member of the Crown Publishing Group.

CROWN is a trademark of Crown Publishers, Inc.

Manufactured in the United States of America

Library of Congress Cataloging-in-Publication Data
Chelekis, George C.
    The official government auction guide : a complete directory of government agency auction programs for personal property and real estate / by George C. Chelekis. — 1st ed.
        p.   cm.
    1. Government sale of real property—United States. 2. Surplus government property—United States—Purchasing. 3.   Auctions—United States. 4.   Auctioneers—United States—Directories. I. Title.
    JK1661.C566   1992
    353.0071'3045—dc20   91-42573
                                                            CIP
ISBN 0-517-58938-9
10 9 8 7 6 5 4 3 2 1
First Crown Edition

This book is dedicated to my father and mother, who helped provide me with an education and skills; and to Ron, who showed me what it takes to be a writer and gave me the know-how and inspiration to write.

Contents

★★★

Acknowledgments

★★★

This book would never have been possible without the valuable assistance of the hundreds of government agency employees and auctioneers who were interviewed. Many gave tips and advice so you could benefit from both government and private auctions.

I would like to thank many senior officials and other employees in the General Services Administration, U.S. Marshals Service, Internal Revenue Service, Department of Defense, U.S. Customs, Department of Housing and Urban Development, Bureau of Land Management, Department of Veterans Affairs, Farmers Home Administration, Federal Deposit Insurance Corporation, Resolution Trust Corporation, Fannie Mae, Freddie Mac, and the many sheriffs and police departments for providing us all with the real "inside scene" in the government auction business.

Additionally, a great deal of historical and current information on the auction business was provided by the Executive Staff of The National Auctioneers Association (NAA); Anita Faddis, curator of the NAA's Hall of History; and Ann Wood of the Certified Auctioneers Institute (CAI).

Special thanks to these auctioneers: Dick DeWees, President of the Missouri Auction School, who provided behind-the-scenes information about the evolution of several government agency auction programs, historical auction infor-

mation, suggestions on how some government agencies can improve their auction programs, and numerous advice on what bidders should know before attending auctions; Kurt Kiefer should be thanked by anyone who ever finds an incredible deal at a state university auction (he is the auctioneer who brought them to my attention) and for his inside information on RTC auctions and many other government agency auctions; G. Robert Diero for his analysis and comments on IRS auctions; Richard Keenan for his comments and assistance on the Small Business Administration, and bank and real estate auctions; Robin Marshal for his instructive advice on farm auctions and the Farmers Home Administration; John Dixon, of Hudson and Marshall, for his assistance and insights into the Federal Deposit Insurance Corporation and the Resolution Trust Corporation; Bernard Brzostek for his inside knowledge of automobile auctions and other government agency auctions; T. Eddie Haynes for help with a variety of government agency auction programs; Robert Steffes for an overview of current auctions; and William Landau for many strategies and tactics auctioneers use, as well as valuable tips on negotiated sales.

Attorneys Steven Hayes and Lance Roger Spodek helped me with practical information on legal practices and procedures. Another author, Sonny Bloch, has been over the years a great source of information on buying and selling real estate.

There were several individuals who not only made this book professional but also made my job easier to complete. Thelma Sharkey provided many of the directory entries herself. Patricia Prince, Maaret Schnier, and Victor Burton researched several important areas at the beginning of this project. Maria Larsson pulled the entire book together at the very end, even when it meant many sleepless nights slaving away at her computer; she also greatly assisted me with the revisions.

Of course, without Jane Gelfman, my agent, and Richard Marek, senior editor at Crown, this book would never be in your hands.

Finally, I would like to deeply thank my wife, Gwen, and my daughter, Katie, for having completely supported me throughout everything that led to creating this book.

Today, books are the products of many unnamed individual contributions. Without the help and guidance received from all of these individuals, this vast amount of knowledge would never have been provided to you, the reader.

Foreword

★★

There has never been a better time for an auction book with the tremendous depth and scope of this one. Because our economy has gone through overexpansion, overmanufacture, and overbuilding, there is an excess of merchandise and marketable goods, which has made auctions one of the most exciting ways to purchase what you need at pennies on the dollar and purchase what you can for resale at a profit.

Auctions are a fun way to buy, but they can be tricky, sometimes even deceiving. With this road map, *The Official Government Auction Guide*, you will, in fact, be given the way to the end of the rainbow. Follow it carefully, and keep it as a reference book, because you will be referring to it constantly.

This book will lead you through the intricacies of the everyday auction, and even take you into auction arenas that you never knew existed. From the practical to the exotic, *The Official Government Auction Guide* has arrived on the scene, just in time. The author, George Chelekis, leaves no auction unturned.

This book will take you through the history of auctions and the types of auctions and introduce you to the players in the auction arena. You will learn how to participate in every auction known to man. Most auction books fail to show you how to buy an item *prior* to the actual auction sale itself.

This book will show you how to negotiate a sale prior to auction.

It will teach you all of the auction terms. It will show you how to compare auction values so that you're not overpaying because of the emotional aspects of the auction. It will teach you how to do your homework prior to the auction.

If you read this book, you'll know how to utilize all the bidding strategies: setting your limits, low bids, piggybacking with other professionals, and more. This book will teach you how to price and buy vehicles, computers, electronics, antiques and collectibles, art, jewelry, coins, real estate, and much much more.

The Official Government Auction Guide will take you through the steps of reselling for a profit, including how to find and sell to international buyers, which is the biggest market in today's world. It will show you how to finance what you are purchasing and sell it, sometimes before you even take delivery.

Also, you'll learn about bid-rigging and rings and what recourse you have if you've been cheated, how to void a sale after it has been made, and where to complain.

The Official Government Auction Guide is a virtual supermarket of auction information about the various public agencies that hold auctions. Not only will you find a very complete guide on the intricacies and idiosyncrasies of each of these agencies, you'll also have a directory of, and learn how to work with, each of them.

Anyone who has ever purchased or thought about purchasing something at an auction will have a copy of this book in his or her library. I am very pleased that George Chelekis is sharing with the public his expertise in the field of auctions. No one in the country could do a better job in putting together this book.

SONNY BLOCH

Preface

★★★

Auctions are already a vital and essential part of your life. Even if you have never been to an auction, you benefit from them every single day. In fact, your life would be quite disrupted if all auctions throughout the world came to an abrupt halt. And so would the worlds of commerce, banking, agriculture, and manufacturing.

The food you ate today—eggs, bacon, toast, and orange juice—passed through one or more auctions on their way to your breakfast table. So did the gas that fuels your car. So did the money in your pocket or in the pockets of a German, Briton, or Australian.

The metal and plywood of which your house is made passed the auctioneer's gavel. More than likely, so did the land beneath your house or even the house itself.

Some of the books you read, movies you saw, and prints of the art on your walls made a trip to auction before you could enjoy them.

Many cars that pass by your home have been sold through one or more auctions. Much of the materials in those cars was auctioned several times before that car could be made.

Athletes are leased by wealthy owners to play professional sports for a few seasons. And they pass through an auction, but it's euphemistically called a sports draft. This practice is so old it dates back to Roman times.

The interest you pay on a mortgage or on your debts is daily set at auction. Interest paid on your bank deposits is determined by auction. The value of the dollar against foreign currencies is decided many times each day through a series of ongoing auctions, held in the United States and in financial capitals around the world. Throughout the business day common stocks and corporate debt are sold using auctions. The rise and fall of the Dow Jones Average is established, minute to minute, by auctions. So are the prices we will eventually pay for bread, meat, beans, and a host of other commodities that we eat, wear, or simply admire.

The price of the gold in the jewelry you wear, as well as the diamonds you dream of, are both set by auctions. The fish or meat you ate last night was sold at auction before reaching your supermarket. Even how much inflation we will have is determined by the outcome of auctions.

The entire world revolves, not around the sun each day, but around auctions. Without auctions, life would be very different. Since the beginning of recorded history, auctions have been a major part of the woof and warp of business, love, war, art, and civilization.

Although U.S. government auctions did not officially start until the middle of the Civil War, government and other auctions have played a major role in the society we have inherited. From economics to interpersonal relationships to breakfast, the federal government plays a dominating role in our daily lives. Auctions are tools that have been used, thus far, to demand compliance with laws or as an outcome of noncompliance (drug seizures and voluntary income tax).

The current character of government auctions and U.S. economic conditions suggest that government auctions and real estate sales programs must now take the next evolutionary step to the private sector. Is the private sector ready for this? Can private auctioneers resolve the morass of a disjointed government auction program? Many say that they can.

By the way, "disjointed" correctly defines the state of government auctions. Today, this book is not only necessary to understand and fully participate in government auctions, but it is also required just to find out about all the diverse offerings from the government. Personal property and real estate have either failed to sell at government auctions or, instead, have sold at bargain prices because the government agency in question did not act in a professional manner. Many professional auctioneers privately hold government agency auction employees in contempt.

Many people find it difficult to get on one or more of the various government agency mailing lists, let alone all of them. Getting notified well in advance of a government auction is not always easy. Instructions sent to potential auction customers by, for example, the General Services Administration, are misleading, inaccurate, and contain out-of-date information. And many consider the GSA to be the premier auction arm of the U.S. government!

Using this book, it is now possible to rapidly acquire auction notices, keep oneself abreast of upcoming auctions, and fully understand where and how one can participate. It was quite a feat compiling this information into a readily grasped format for immediate usage. Researchers for this book found many government agencies (with disconnected telephone numbers) mailing out-of-date auction information, issuing incorrect instructions or misleading statements, and sometimes even discouraging auction attendance. When reading this book you will find out more about the details of government-auction programs than some of their own agencies know! That's how confused some government agencies are about their own auction and sales programs. Fortunately, contradictory information has been ironed out so you won't have that obstacle working against you.

This book is written to satisfy both the bargain hunter and the consumer advocate. Government auctions provide enough excitement and controversy to delight either. Please use it to benefit yourself and the government. For better or for worse, auctions are here to stay and will play an increasing role in determining our very lives for the rest of this century and beyond.

How to Use This Book

★★

Just because this is a very big book does not mean it should be difficult to use. This publication is designed to gradually introduce you to government and private auctions. What could be simpler than shopping in stores and markets? That's all auctions are, except the price tags are missing. People, many like yourself, go to auctions to find a great bargain. You haggle among yourselves, with the auctioneer as an emcee urging each of you on, until a final sales price has been reached.

Obviously, the less people know about these sales, the greater the deals. Most newcomers have gone to the wrong government auctions. The ones that are given gigantic headlines in the local newspaper or featured on the television evening news are hardly the ones to attend, if you wish for a good deal.

But first things first. Going to an auction without having learned a few of the basic principles would be like jumping into a car without ever having learned the first thing about driving. Sure, most of us would say, "No problem, I can drive a car," but how many would volunteer to commandeer a Boeing 747 on a transatlantic flight? Not many, is my guess. So, the entire first section of the book has been laid out to gently bring you the guidelines and procedures of participating at auctions. Each of the chapters slowly but carefully gives you a bit more knowledge until you have a full grasp of the subject.

Now, many will jump to Section Two or Three of this book and expect instantly to find the steal of the century. Well, the book is rigged to help even those individuals. It's better to work your way through the first section first, though.

Section Two investigates each of the government agencies that mainly sell merchandise, equipment, and other things you could pick up and carry home with you (either in your car or with a professional moving company). Because there has been so much inaccurate and incomplete information about government agencies—and wild promises about auction giveaways—I took the liberty of rating each of the government agencies. At most auctions, while you might not find the steal you always dreamt of, you should be able to get a good deal. There are a few government agencies that still insist on giving things away. You'll find out about those in the ratings system at the end of Section Two.

For auction bargains that you don't carry away, Section Three explains the spectrum of government real estate. You live in what you buy. Sometimes real estate is sold at auction and other times it is not. With luck, that will change so that all government real estate can soon be sold at auction. That should liven up the American real estate picture!

In Section Four, you will find a mammoth compilation of private auctioneers. Just about anyone you ever wanted to contact about auctions should be in one of those chapters. Private auctioneers now stand an excellent chance of taking over the lion's share of the government auction program. That's why their section is the largest portion of this book.

Special care has been devoted to providing you with the latest developments in the government auction business. It *is* a business. You should be interested in it because taxpayer money finances the purchases that later appear as bargains at government auctions. And, since you do pay taxes, you owe it to yourself to attend these government auctions.

Much has been written about government auctions. Most of the media attention has been inaccurate or incomplete, telling only a very small part of the entire story. Books written on the subject have either contained false and misleading information or omitted a good number of government agencies and others who hold auctions. Mail order firms, for example, have promised BMWs, Jaguars, and Porsches for $100. They have probably never been to a government auction. The only jeeps you'll be able to buy for $49 are of the crushed and mutilated variety, hardly the kind you can drive if you want to cruise down the interstate. Homes do sell for $1, but the program is so restrictive that many readers would never qualify . . . and to top it off, you would have to win the lottery before anteing up your dollar bill. That's how such house sales are conducted. For those who bought homes for $1, congratulations! You found a great deal, but not as good as the deals, with no strings attached, professional auction-goers regularly find.

This book should answer practically any question you ever had about government auctions and even the auction business. To write a book about government auctions and not bring up the private sector is to exclude the fastest-growing segment of the government auction business.

Using this book has been made as simple and easy as possible. At the end of those chapters describing each of the government agencies, you will find a telephone and/or address directory.

After you read about that government agency's auctions, you can immediately call and get further information about their auctions, have your name placed on their auction mailing list, or find out when the next one is being held and go to it.

All phone numbers and addresses have been thoroughly verified. Some government agencies frequently change their telephone numbers. With the information in each chapter, you can correct this potential problem by either writing to that government agency or asking the assistance of the directory information telephone operator.

One of the prime uses of this book is to have your name and address placed on the various government and private auction mailing lists. While many of these are free, please don't abuse that privilege. General Services Administration (GSA), one of the mammoth players in the government auction business, estimates that it costs about 50 cents to print an auction catalog. If everyone in America called tomorrow and asked for their sales catalogs, there in one mailing would go GSA's annual auction income.

Read and *use* the professional insider tips found throughout Section One and in other parts of the book. I wish these had been available when I first started going to auctions. It would have saved me thousands in bad deals. Don't pay the price that I did of letting the good deals get away or buying junk.

There is a mini-glossary at the beginning of each of the first three sections that exists to familiarize you with the basic terms appearing in the chapters of that section. These are but a few of the many new words that you should learn to become proficient in this subject. Learning new subjects requires an understanding of what the special words of that subject mean. Use the glossary at the end of the book so you don't arrive at an auction and can't figure out what is going on.

One of the best ways to go through this book is to read Section One first, then read about one of the government agencies in Section Two or Three. Just choose one of the agencies in Chapters 9 through 27 and read about that agency. Decide if that government agency's auctions interest you. If not, pick another agency and read about theirs. Search around until you finally locate a government agency that has the type of merchandise or real estate that appeals to you, the style of auction that you can live with, or conducts their auctions to your tastes.

A shortcut is to go right to the conclusion of either of those sections and review their ratings. Don't stop there, though. Go back and read about the government agency that you favor and confirm that you would like to start with them.

Give that agency a call or write them a letter asking for auction notices, fliers, catalogs, or brochures, depending on what they have available. While you're waiting for mail to arrive, flip through the chapters in Section Four. From this directory call a few local auctioneers and ask them about upcoming auctions. If any have merchandise, equipment, or real estate that interests you, ask them to send you their auction notices.

That is how most professionals would use this book. If you want to sit back and read it cover to cover, go ahead. It's interesting to read, but the purpose of this book is to get you to succeed at auctions. There is no quiz when you finish reading it. Your final exam grade on how well you read and understood this book is determined entirely by your performance at auctions. If you get a good bargain, you passed. Should you get an incredible bargain, go to the head of the class. When you hit gold and get a bona fide auction giveaway, drop me a line. I'd like to hear about it. Write to me anytime. All letters will be answered.

George Chelekis
Author of *The Official Government Auction Guide*
% Crown Publishing
201 East 50th Street
Fifth Floor
New York, NY 10022

Successful Bids

★★★

The bids that follow were prices paid by auction-goers at a variety of government auctions over a period of several years for vehicles, aircraft, and vessels. These are being presented here to demonstrate that prices vary widely at such auctions. There are no guarantees that one can always get a fantastic deal or that one will always overpay. Final sales prices are determined by the judgment and skill of the auction participants. Occasionally, luck plays a factor in the results of auctions.

Final bid prices were supplied courtesy of:

The National Auction Bulletin, Inc.
4419 West Tradewinds Avenue
Fort Lauderdale, FL 33308-4464

To order The Info Pack, containing complete listings of auction prices on vessels, aircraft, and vehicles, send $7.50 to the above address or call toll-free and order with a major credit card: 1-800-327-2049.

The following key should be used for some of the abbreviations in the listings:

FBG   Fiberglass

O/F   Open Fisherman

Sp/F   Sportfisherman

Fly/B   Flybridge

O/B   Outboard

LCP   Personnel Landing Craft

LCM   Mechanical Landing Craft

B/D   Bird Dog

C/C   Cabin Cruiser

F/V   Fishing Vessel

L/B   Lobster Boat

I/O   Inboard/Outboard

I/B   Inboard

MOTOR VEHICLES

1975	Mercedes	$	3,350
1977	Lincoln Continental	$	800
1982	Toyota Celica	$	6,000
1968	Corvette	$	2,000

MOTOR VEHICLES

1984	Lamborghini Countach	$ 68,000	
1981	DeLorean	$ 14,300	
1978	Cadillac Seville	$ 2,000	76,000 miles
1977	Ford LTD	$ 222	
1980	Olds	$ 30	A Gem!
1973	Motorhome	$ 1,550	
1985	BMW 745i	$ 23,500	
1979	BMW 320i	$ 3,100	
1960	Firetruck	$ 225	
1976	Rolls-Royce	$ 12,500	
1981	BMW 733i	$ 18,500	
1979	Mercedes 450SEL	$ 16,800	
1980	Corvette	$ 48,000	
1971	Corvette	$ 4,300	
1982	Mazda	$ 4,500	
1980	Thunderbird	$ 1,300	
1985	Maserati Quattroporte	$ 40,000	Like New!
1980	BMW 320i	$ 3,100	
1970	Mercedes 250	$ 1,000	For Export Only
1968	Pontiac LeMans	$ 25	
1969	Oldsmobile Cutlass	$ 25	
1975	Lemans	$ 5	True Story!
1984	Porsche 944	$ 13,300	Only 9,000 miles
1983	Lincoln Town Car	$ 6,400	Signature Edition
1971	Rolls-Royce	$ 15,000	
1977	Porsche 911S	$ 9,500	
1971	Rolls Silver Wraith	$ 13,300	
1987	Volkswagen Jetta	$ 8,600	
1956	Rolls Silver Cloud	$ 18,500	
1986	Acura Integra	$ 8,650	
1961	Corvette	$ 20,000	Red & white: beautiful
1978	Mercedes SEL	$ 16,500	Custom
1981	Porsche 928S	$ 20,500	30,000 miles
1979	Mercedes 450 SLC	$ 6,500	For Export Only
1980	Mercedes 450 SLC	$ 10,500	For Export Only
1979	Winnebago Chevy Van	$ 2,300	
1978	Landrover Ranger	$ 4,100	For Export Only
1974	Rolls Silver Shadow	$ 30,000	
1980	BMW 320i	$ 800	
1975	Corvette	$ 12,500	Nice!
1986	Lotus Esprit	$ 27,500	Beautiful
1971	Corvette	$ 6,100	
1987	Cadillac Deville	$ 13,700	Good buy!

MOTOR VEHICLES

1981	Jaguar XJ6	$ 1,300	Deal!
1984	Ferrari Mondial	$ 43,000	Export Only
1977	Mercedes 280SE	$ 350	
1986	Isdera Imperator	$ 50,000	Export Only
1987	Mercedes 560SL	$ 44,500	
1977	Panther J-72 Roadster	$ 14,250	Export Only
1979	Fruehauf 40' Trailer	$ 1,000	
1967	Corvette Stingray	$ 37,500	
1979	Dodge Van Ram	$ 1,050	Fair Condition
1986	Excalibur Phaeton	$ 43,500	Excellent Condition
1984	Rolls Silver Spur	$ 26,500	
1987	Isuzu pickup	$ 2,300	
1988	Alfa Romeo Spider	$ 9,300	

AIRCRAFT

1979	Bell206B Jet Ranger Helicopter	$ 170,000	
1965	Piper Aztec	$ 14,000	
Bell	47G3B1 Helicopter	$ 50,000	
1978	Cessna Skymaster 337	$ 40,000	
1977	Cessna Skywagon T207A	$ 25,000	
1979	Piper Turbo Arrow IV	$ 25,000	
1980	Cessna 414A	$ 170,000	
1942	Douglas DC-3	$ 16,778	
1969	Mitsubishi MU 2B	$ 75,000	
1976	Piper Navajo 31-350	$ 42,000	
1981	Cessna 172 Skyhawk II	$ 111,500	
1972	Beech Queen	$ 19,500	
1969	Cessna 310	$ 17,000	
1980	Cessna 172XP Hawk	$ 35,000	
1982	Aero Commander 980/695S	$ 420,000	
1965	Cessna 172	$ 8,100	
1978	Lear 24	$ 148,000	
1967	Beechcraft King Air A-90, TT 9100	$ 182,000	
1980	Turbo Commander	$1 million	Only 200 hours
1982	Bell Jet Ranger III Model 208B	$ 240,000	
1982	Piper Seneca 3 N81687 Twin Continental	$ 91,000	
1965	Cessna 411	$ 17,000	
1973	Piper Navajo N7496L S/N 31-7300916	$ 101,501	No Log Books
1965	Beech Queen Air Twin Engine	$ 8,615	No Log Books, inoperable

VESSELS

Year	Description	Price	Notes
1980	25' Four Star Boat	$ 5,920	
1964	Schooner	$ 8,306	
1969	Mini-Cigarette	$ 2,400	
1973	26' Formula	$ 5,000	
1980	20' Regal with 1984 260 HP Merc.	$ 1,300	With 79' Trailer
	200 Foot Coaster Freighter	$ 7,000	
1965	62' St. Augustine Shrimper	$ 300	
1979	36' Cigarette	$ 26,000	
1977	32' Excalibur	$ 24,000	
1973	21' Sea Ray Runabout	$ 2,600	
1978	44' Double Cabin Cruiser	$ 12,000	Fiberglass
1978	23' Make	$ 3,150	
1978	18' T Bird	$ 1,650	
1974	36' Trojan	$ 27,500	
1979	25' Allman Cabin Cruiser	$ 6,500	
1943	135' Mine Sweeper	$ 2,200	
1978	36' Cigarette	$ 26,000	
1974	28' Cigarette	$ 9,500	
	269' Submarine	$ 38,666	For Scrap
1984	26' Sailboat	$ 11,000	
1982	28' Gulfstream with 2 Merc V6	$ 12,400	
1985	18' Thompson Bowrider with 170 HP	$ 3,850	Fiberglass
1982	29' Wellcraft 2 235 Evinrude	$ 16,500	Myco trailer
1970	17' Tarpon Runabout	$ 1,000	
1978	28' Manta Jaguar	$ 16,050	
1969	26' Motor Whale Boat	$ 3,510	
1962	36' Personnel Landing Craft	$ 5,188	
1974	18' T-Bird 250HP Commander	$ 3,100	
1983	Gulfstream Longliner Trawler 12V71	$ 92,000	
1985	37' Midnight Express with 4 Merc	$ 38,500	
1979	24' Aquasport	$ 5,500	
1985	40' Scarab 2 Merc 400HP	$ 43,000	
1979	18' Checkmate	$ 2,100	
1978	36' Cigarette 2 V8 Mercs	$ 18,500	
1972	58' Hatteras FlyB 2 8V71 Detroits	$ 145,000	

Section One

★★★

Mini-Glossary

★★

Below are some of the important words you should understand before reading Section One. This book contains several specialized words that, when not completely understood in their context, could prevent you from becoming skilled in this subject.

These are only a few of the basic terms. A full glossary of specialized words and terms appears at the end of this book. Please use this glossary when you encounter unfamiliar terms in this subject. Use a regular dictionary for other words that you do not understand.

Bid   This means an offer. Someone who makes a bid at an auction is making an offer to purchase the merchandise being sold.

Auction   A sale where bids are accepted from prospective buyers. These bids are usually vocal offers made by prospective buyers to an auctioneer, who attempts to get participants to compete against each other. Specifically, an auction is a sale of merchandise or real estate made by public outcry, where a series of increasing bids are made to the auctioneer. When no bidder goes higher, the sale is complete.

Minimum Bid   The lowest offer an auctioneer will accept to start the auction. A minimum bid can be the first bid to start the auction.

Reserve Price   This is the lowest selling price that an auctioneer will accept to finalize the sale. If no one makes this bid, the auctioneer will withdraw the auction item.

Auction with Reserve   A sale conducted with a reserve price; or, minimum or asking price.

Absolute Auction   A sale conducted by an auctioneer that does not have a minimum bid or a reserve price. No matter what the highest bid is, that is the winning bid.

1

Blame It on the Romans!

★★★

It could be on a Saturday afternoon, or even a Monday morning, that hundreds, perhaps thousands, of hammers slam down across America, followed by auctioneers shouting "SOLD" into their microphones. At that moment one auction-goer, at any of these auctions, may feel like he or she has just won the lottery. Mark Lewis did when he purchased a $50,000 boat for only $10 at a U.S. Marshals auction. The anonymous individual who purchased a home in Fulton County, Georgia, at a sheriff's sale for only $15 savored that instant success. So did the man who bought over $100,000 worth of land at a government tax sale in Florida for only $120.

The world of government auctions can be filled with wonders and surprises. Not everyone walks away the proud owner of a drug dealer's eye-popping Lamborghini for a handful of spare change. Nor does every auction-goer necessarily get the "steals" Dick Textor finds when he goes to a military surplus auction and buys a fax machine for only $10, a computer for $60, or a truck for $120. But with the increased popularity of auctions and the rise of auction attendance across America, you can bet that thousands of great bargains are being uncovered every month.

When an auctioneer slams down his gavel and shouts "SOLD TO BIDDER NUMBER 632," he's following a routine dating back to the cradle of our civilization. Today's U.S. government auction system owes its heritage primarily to the Romans. Government auctions trace their ancestry back more than 2,000 years. While the ancient Babylonians and Greeks were known mainly for auctioning slaves, the Romans were responsible for broadening the auction world and making it popular and appealing to the general public. But first . . .

What Is an Auction?

While translating a comedy by the Roman playwright Plautus, a respected (at the time) British poet, William Warner, coined the word "auction." The word "auction" came into the English language in the year 1595 simply because Warner knocked off the suffix from the Latin word *auctionem*. If he hadn't, we might all be going to an *auctionem* instead of an auction.

"Auction," itself, originally comes from another Latin word, *augere*, which means "to increase." An auction is really "a sale concluded by an increase of bids." That tells you basically what goes on at an auction and what an auction is all about. Something is finally sold to one lucky auction-goer after he and others have made a series of increasing offers to the auctioneer for that property or merchandise.

Sounds simple. But then, something as simple as auctions can get awfully complex, especially when the government starts holding them. Because auctions and auctioneers have been known to sometimes confuse the first-time participant, let's discuss a few of the more famous auctions held down through history. You'll find all the tricks of auctions and auctioneering by looking closely at ancient Roman and other auctions. You might even pick up a few tips along the way!

Don't Lose Your Head at an Auction

Crowds usually gather around the auctioneer, drawn by the excitement of the big moment. Auction fever can set in, just as gambling fever sets in around a craps or blackjack table in a casino. Auction fever is a contagious disease that strikes many who get carried away while making bids. Bidding at an auction is not a time to lose one's head, as did Didius Julianus, a Roman Emperor who once reigned for all of sixty-six days. Julian's big day came in March, AD 193, when he outbid another for ownership of the entire Roman Empire.

The Praetorian Guard murdered their emperor, Pertinax, and were parading his head on a stick in the streets of Rome. In the middle of this coup, the emperor's father-in-law was giving everybody the idea that he should take the throne. One bright Praetorian guardsman, who wanted to make some money on this deal, shouted on the ramparts that the Roman Empire was up for sale to the highest bidder. (Sounds like what the federal government has been slowly doing each time it offers U.S. Treasury Bonds to the Japanese!)

Because of their large numbers, the Praetorian Guard normally had the final say on who would be emperor. On this occasion they instead held a public auction. All they did was sell their "protection and allegiance" to the new emperor. Sounds like the Mafia selling "insurance." Even the bids were made on a per-soldier basis, which shows to whom the guards owed their loyalty.

The previous emperor's father-in-law, Sulpicianus, started the auction off with a bid of 5,000 drachms per guardsman, or about $11 million total in today's money. Didius Julianus, a wealthy

senator, was urged on by his wife, daughter, and friends. He went over the top at 6,250 drachms. In essence, for about $14 million, Senator Julian bought the empire lock, stock, and barrel, or at least he thought he did. At least the Praetorian Guard were thrilled. They got about ten years' worth of salary in one swoop.

Julian didn't fare well. His reign was short-lived because the Roman army disagreed with the Praetorian Guard's choice of emperor. Septimus Severus, the nearest head general, returned from the Danube to Rome with his legions. The bodyguards, now a little richer, got smart fast and had Julian quietly beheaded. General Severus got the throne and Rome, after that, went down the tubes.

So, don't do what Julian did—don't lose your head at an auction. This is the *most important rule* of auction-going: don't get caught up in auction fever. As a side note, when you buy something at an auction, make sure you have clear title (undisputed ownership) to your purchase, something Julian didn't really have. He just thought he owned it. Big mistake.

Caligula Makes Auctions the "In Thing"

Ordinary people, like you and me, got their first chance to bid at Roman auctions. With this breakthrough came the necessity of learning the rules of auction-going. In dealing with amateurs instead of slave dealers, auctioneers really got started pulling the wool over people's eyes. Many of the tricks of the auction trade can be learned by studying some of the lessons of that period. You'd be surprised how little difference there is between a government auction today and one held in Rome during the year AD 39.

Emperor Gaius Caesar Germanicus, better known by his famous nickname, Caligula, used every opportunity he could to hold auctions—at a time when Rome sorely needed cash. During his reign Rome suffered a deficit, and Caligula desperately tried to raise revenue. Some of his schemes were bizarre. For example, he tried to produce gold from the sulphur of arsenic. He opened a brothel in one of his residences, staffing it with the wives and children of noble families and sending pimps throughout Rome to drum up business. Caligula even panhandled at the palace entrance to raise money. But his most popular solution to the cash crunch was holding auctions.

Imagine the president of the United States frantically trying to raise money to eliminate the deficit by playing auctioneer. That's what Caligula did! In Gaul, now known as France, Caligula personally auctioned off some of his sisters' possessions to raise cash. Accounts have it that he behaved in such a way as to make today's auctioneers proud.

He chewed out the crowd for being so stingy, teased the auction-goers for being richer than himself, and hyped the quality of the merchandise being auctioned. Here was the Emperor of Rome selling off family heirlooms, badgering the crowd into buying, and moaning about how ordinary guys like the auction-goers could now own such fantastic luxuries. What a showman!

In the last paragraph, you will see the key ingredients found in many of today's successful auctioneers: they are loud, brimming with hoopla, brash, sometimes a bit wacky, and may have an added dash of self-deprecation. Remember, it's showtime when the auction starts. Just like any TV game show host, he's in the spotlight, but only there so he can point the spotlight on the contestants. And auction-goers *are* the contestants. Never forget that auctions are also entertainment. That's one of the reasons people get auction fever. It's an electrifying experience one gets, like being in front of a TV camera or seeing your photograph in the local newspaper.

Scared of Nodding Your Head at an Auction?

A few of the darker tricks of the auction business emerge from Emperor Caligula's antics. Did you ever wonder about those guys at an auction who "assist" the auctioneer? Or how about some of those guys who put in bids but never seem to buy anything? What about nodding your head at an auction or twitching? Where did that come from?

You guessed it. Rome. Caligula did everything necessary to get the highest price for whatever he sold at auction. His hobbyhorse was selling off gladiators. Those were the slaves who beat each other to death in the colosseum with swords, chains, and clubs. Selling gladiators isn't too removed from our professional football drafts. The highest bidder buys the athlete for a few seasons. Caligula had everything but television and stopped at nothing to get the highest price.

He'd auction the winning gladiators off as the finale to a show. He'd use his shills to drive up the bidding—of course as shills nearly always do, they'd conveniently drop out when the price got too high. Since the gladiator shows were prime-time entertainment in ancient Rome, the stadium was packed. If you wanted to skip them, you'd have to find a sub to represent your "house" and save face. Bidding was fierce, especially since Caligula had a few agents working the sidelines with "puff bids," bids that aren't serious and drive up the price of the goods.

Auctions were also a time for merriment and this meant that quite a few bidders got drunk. At one auction, a nobleman, Aponius Saturninus, slumbered in a stupor, jerking his head as he slept. His snoozing didn't stop the auctioneer, who took each twitch as a serious bid. When Saturninus woke up, he was the proud new owner of 13 gladiators, which cost him 9 million sesterces (translation: about $1.5 million), nearly wiping him out.

As you can see, bidding signals could be misinterpreted, such as in that example. Take into consideration, though, that Caligula's auctioneer was probably under orders to get the highest price. So the drunken Aponius Saturninus was an easy mark. I've found that auctioneers don't want to force you into buying something you don't want. Often, the auctioneer may give you a chance to get out before he slams down the gavel.

Newcomers to auctions often have the misconception that you should stick your hands in your pockets while standing around at an auction. Look around the auction area and notice how many people are holding their hands down or have them in their pockets. I guess the fear of ending up with an unwanted and expensive tractor trailer filled with three-penny widgets still persists. It's just a fallacy.

Shills

Although Caligula used shills, don't talk to auctioneers about this subject unless you want the same reaction you'd get by passing wind in church. Shills are those guys at auctions who are placing bids against you or others, but who are really on the auctioneer's payroll. In various parts of the country, they might be called straws, sticks, or puffs. You might find shills at carnivals, at cheap gambling halls, and, yes, even at auctions. Talking about shills to an auctioneer is worse than insulting his mother. Most get defensive about shills if you mention them. Others get angry. Some get pretty argumentative and say it's beneath them or it's not professional. Besides, using shills is illegal.

Most present-day auctions are unlikely to have shills, although you will find them popping up occasionally. Some auctioneers may use them but not quite as blatantly or as frequently as Caligula once used them. Most will, instead, use other clever tricks, which we'll discuss in subsequent chapters.

"Hey, General: Have We Got a Deal for You!"

(THE FIRST MILITARY SURPLUS AUCTIONS)

Auctions, in ancient times, were primarily used to raise money quickly by selling off slaves, furniture, artwork, pottery, and other household goods. Sort of like having a garage sale today. But during this time period, the Romans were also the first to popularize military auctions.

They held them throughout the Roman Empire, which was huge; at Rome's peak the empire stretched from England down to Morocco and across the Danube and Europe to present-day Iran and Saudi Arabia. The Pentagon has obviously taken a clue from the Romans since the Department of Defense's military surplus auctions are held around the world, not just in the United States.

In Rome, the problem was what to do after they'd conquered the country and robbed the natives of whatever wealth was to be had, including their women and children. The Romans figured out a way to auction off the slaves and property seized by their soldiers while defeating the local tribes around Europe, North Africa, and the Near East. Since hard money, like gold and silver, was, indeed, hard to come by, soldiers got paid in booty that had been confiscated during their conquering and was then auctioned off.

Keep in mind that soldiers back then weren't even paid until around the 4th century BC. They got to fight for free. Even when they finally did get paid, it only amounted to about $200 a year. If you wanted the big payday, you stuck it out with your legion (about the size of a modern day battalion) and got some land and a good pension to live on after your army years. The generals doled out the goods, so it was important to be loyal to the big boss.

To get themselves some spending money out in the hinterlands, there were smaller auctions held by the soldiers among themselves, as the battle was ending. The fleetest of the warriors would kill his foe, thrust a spear into the ground next to his victim, and then hold a quickie auction to dispose of that guy's possessions. A mini-version of today's police auction. And there were probably some good deals on sandals and swords.

The citizens of Rome heard about these great deals and soon business agents would tag along with the legions and attend these auctions. This practice, of following an army to sponge off the spoils of war, also happened during the U.S. Civil War. Auctioneers would follow the Union Army as it was capturing territory in the Deep South. They'd then hold auctions, right on the plantation site, selling off the landowner's personal property.

The Auction Block Makes Its Appearance

Military auctions caught on back in Rome proper. Business agents got smart and figured they could resell their purchases for a profit back home. The quick-footed soldier was replaced by a *magister auctionarium,* a licensed auctioneer. The Romans realized that by licensing auctioneers the government could tax buyers; Caesar Augustus came up with a 2% tax on all auction purchases around the year zero.

The tradition of throwing a spear into the ground to start an auction continued and was given a Latin name, *sub hasta,* meaning "under the spear," and that later became "at auction." If you were in ancient Rome and wanted to find an auction, you'd look for a spear in the ground.

At the major auctions the personal possessions of the captured village, and even the captives themselves, were put on a big rock and auctioned off. This is how we got the "auction block." It was just a big rock on which goods and people were placed and sold off to the soldiers or business agents. Whenever the soldiers needed a place to hold their auction, they would just find the biggest rock and hold it there. That's all the auction block was.

Later, the Romans would use a raised platform or stage from which to sell their slaves or personal property. It was called the *atrium auctionarium,* and there auction-goers could preview samples of the merchandise before the auction.

Nowadays, the auction block is just a term. It doesn't have the tangible, physical reality that it did then. Amazingly, some people still get shivers and dread thinking about having all their personal possessions put on the auction block. A pretty grim thought, indeed, but at least *you* won't be sold at an auction. At many auctions, you won't even see an auction stage, let alone the auction block. The term *auction block* is now just part of the auction nomenclature.

The auction block has been reduced to an auctioneer on a small platform or taking bids from a podium. Or on a low-bed trailer being driven around the auction grounds. Don't be surprised, at many auctions, to find the auctioneer standing in the middle of a crowd with or without a microphone and portable PA system. The grandeur that was Rome isn't always found at today's auctions, but the thought is still there.

Bankruptcy Auctions

Rome was also responsible for bringing us bankruptcy auctions, although some Roman bankruptcy auctions were worse than today's farmer losing his farmland. The word bankruptcy also comes from Latin and means a "wrecked bench." It became a wrecked bench because the angry creditors broke it up when they found they weren't going to get their money.

The same places where we cash our paychecks owe their roots to these benches. From their benches, traders bought and sold in the bazaars, the marketplace. Entire businesses evolved around "the bench." That's where the moneylenders did their business too. In fact, most of the broken benches came about from failed moneylenders. (Perhaps forerunners to our savings and loan institutions.)

If the Roman trader spent more than he made, his creditors didn't hire lawyers and sue his pants off. Instead they wrecked his bench (literally) and seized his assets. Creditors, then as now, aren't too happy about a debtor declaring bankruptcy.

The family was sold into slavery by auction and the proceeds were turned over to satisfy the creditors. No protection of the "corporate veil" for a Roman merchant as there is for today's businessman.

Later it became more civilized. The creditors would go to the courts and get a *vendito bonorum,* a compulsory sale. Then, the property would get auctioned off to the highest creditor. One catch: the successful bidder also got *all* of the guy's debts. These bankruptcy auctions were also where we first got the term *caveat emptor,* let the buyer beware. The *emptor* was the successful bidder at an auction. Because the *emptor* got stuck with the trader's debts when he won the guy's property at auction, there was a lot he should be careful of. After all, he might be the next one torn to shreds.

It's amazing how even our modern bankruptcy and credit-reporting systems are still tied into this time period. Debtors would work as slaves for their owners for seven years and then be freed . . . though not with a full restoration of rights. The seven-year term actually goes back to the Old Testament and was a widespread practice throughout that part of the world. Now, we have credit reports in which a bankrupt individual has a black mark on his or her credit report for, you guessed it, seven years! Of course, many banks and other lenders jump on these people to lend them money, since the U.S. bankruptcy code says that you can only file bankruptcy every seven years.

Creating the Auction Format

The Romans were always big on formality, as the British and some Europeans are today. Known for their organized military, they were the first to give auctions a structure that still survives to this day. Until the Romans, about the only things auctioned were slaves and food. Then, with the vastly increased variety of merchandise and property offered at auction, the auctions became less spontaneous events. No more, "Here's the spear, so come and get it."

The guy who sold his property at auction was the *dominus;* this translates into "master" and gives you an idea of what he was often selling. The *dominus* was the auctioneer's client.

Auctions require preparation and organization, whether yesterday or a few thousand years ago. The gentleman who financed, organized, and regulated the auction was the *argentarius.* That was also the Roman term for moneylender. So, when the banker wasn't getting his bench wrecked and torn to shreds or tearing someone else up and sending their family into slavery, he was also putting together an auction deal. He also was there to make sure the *emptor* (the highest bidder) paid up.

An auction that isn't well promoted inevitably fails to get the best prices. (Humble advice for some of our government agencies!) The Romans had someone who did the marketing. He was called the *praeco.* Not only did he run through the streets and tell everybody there was an auction coming up, but the *praeco* also called out the bids at the smaller auctions, working also as an auctioneer.

The larger auctions were conducted by the *magister auctionis,* which translates literally to master of the auctions. He presided over the auction, occasionally handling the bid-calling, as Caligula did.

So the next time you're at an auction, realize that it's not just the auctioneer holding an auction. Auctioneers consider the actual bid-calling to be about 10% of what goes on at a successful auction. That may be all you see, but it's all the things that you didn't notice which got you there.

Slavery and Roman Auctions

Auctions from the beginning of time drip with gloom, hardship, and misery. Where else would you buy slaves if you were a Roman or Babylonian? You'd go to an auction or send a purchasing agent. Slavery and auctions have gone hand in hand down through the ages. As one country clobbered another, its natives would be sold into slavery . . . by auction.

Both the Greeks and Romans even had a central trading site for slave auctions, just as America has predominant locations for commodities trading: New York, Chicago, and Kansas City. Slave auctions were held on the Greek Island of Delos, located in the south Aegean sea near Athens. The Greeks also held corn auctions and festivals worshipping Apollo, the god of music, healing, and prophecy, but slave trading was the big business. Now Delos is a popular tourist spot.

The Romans capitalized on misfortune, and their legacy lasted through 19th-century Europe and America. The prime candidates for auction, a conquered nation or an incompetent businessman, passed by the auction block on their way to slavery. Fortunately, none of these practices continue today, yet the modern-day auctioneer still cringes at auction history. And many buyers stay away from auctions because of the bad connotations associated with them.

That's on a par with not going to your local medical doctor for an exam just because doctors once used to be barbers with leeches. Auctions have changed too! Auctions now are held to help both the buyer and the seller. And with our next example you'll see how they could also help the U.S. government!

Auctions for the Public Good

As Rome became more civilized and the merchant class grew, the auction process was borrowed from the slave traders; creditors and the Roman justice system used auctions to resolve financial misfortunes. Auctions were still a first cousin to bad news if you didn't pay your bills or got yourself conquered. Until Caligula's time, auctions were only used to dispose of property that came either when Roman legions captured new territory or as incompetent traders failed.

As with any other major developments in the history of auctions, you'll find the Romans were also the first to put the auction process to use entirely for the public benefit! Caligula turned to auctions (as well as other unusual solutions) to raise money for the treasury when he abolished some forms of taxes. Romans had been complaining about taxes being too high. Some things never change, do they?

Tiberius, the Emperor before him, had already reduced taxes and Caligula went even further. Having no steady taxes rolling in, he resorted to auctioning his surplus government property: gladiators, furniture, jewelry, and art. This worked for a while.

It was Marcus Ulpius Traianus, also known as Emperor Trajan, who finally found a higher purpose for auctions about fifty years later. Trajan, a Spaniard by birth, was a Roman general whose military successes took the Empire to its widest boundaries. His armies drove north into modern-day Czechoslovakia, southern Poland, and the

Ukraine, as well as east into Persia and the southwestern USSR. Probably experienced in the auction process during his military campaigns as a means of quick property disposal, Trajan used auctions to balance the budget. (Is Congress listening?)

Rome enjoyed not only one of the more peaceful times in her history under Trajan, but it was also a more productive period. A few years earlier, Emperor Nero (the famous fiddler) suffered through Rome's burning down. Who rebuilt it? Trajan.

How did he do it? Trajan used auctions. Auctions were already part and parcel of the Roman lifestyle. But no one before Trajan figured out how to efficiently use auction proceeds to help finance the government. Trajan sold off whatever wasn't needed. There were buyers and that balanced the Roman budget.

Trajan took the auction proceeds and built new buildings, giving Romans a beautiful city to be proud of. Trajan charitably sponsored programs to help the poor and was remembered for being a top-notch administrator, not just another emperor swathed in purple imperial robes and pretending to be a god, like Caligula or Nero.

As a result, Rome was pretty calm for the next 100 years. These years have even been referred to as the Golden Age of Rome, which probably came about because Trajan reduced taxes and balanced the budget by using auctions (a cue for Congress?). Trajan was so highly admired that a column dedicated to him still stands in his own forum in present-day Rome. His statue remained in Rome for almost 1,500 years after his death, before it was replaced by one of St. Paul. (Imagine what would happen if the president and congress teamed up to actually reduce the deficit by making the existing auction programs actually work! Especially for all the foreclosed real estate!)

Longest Auction on Record

Emperor Marcus Aurelius Antoninus, the famous philosopher-king, needed to finance his war campaigns on the Danube against the Germanic tribes. In order to pay off his war debts and balance the budget, he held an auction of household goods: furniture, art, sculpture, jewelry, and slaves. He waged eight long winter campaigns across the Danube. These wars ran up huge debts, which he settled by having the auction. To get the price he needed, Aurelius just held out. The auction took months, but he got the funds he needed to balance the Roman budget.

A glance at military and economic history will show you that wars are just too expensive. Military expenditures run up debts and bankrupt every treasury, from ancient Chaldea to Russia and the U.S. If one lesson could be learned from history, it would be that wars cost too much and skilled diplomacy can always avoid them. Following every war throughout history, you can expect a major economic recession, whether the war takes place in Vietnam or the Persian Gulf.

The U.S. government should do what the Romans did to balance the budget: hold a series of really big auctions that are well promoted and are held by professional auctioneers, not government bureaucrats. There's plenty of surplus merchandise and foreclosed real estate to sell.

When Did the First Auction Take Place?

(SEX AND THE SINGLE GIRL)

Three thousand years ago they didn't have singles bars or personal ads. Even then, families had problems with their female offspring—how to get them out of the house and into someone else's chow line. Before we had matchmakers, the Babylonians had auctions . . . for single women who needed husbands. Maybe, because of these auctions, yentas (Yiddish for matchmakers) were the natural evolution.

Before the Romans, village tribes in ancient Babylonia (now called Iraq) had yearly bridal auctions. The earliest recorded auctions, around the 5th century BC, appeared in the first book of Herodotus' histories.

The way Herodotus describes one bridal auction shows you how modern-day auctioneers

sometimes operate when selling off merchandise. Auctions haven't changed that much over the past few thousand years. It's what is being auctioned off that has changed.

Each year all the young maidens who were old enough to be married off were gathered up into one place. The Babylonian bachelors would form a circle around the bachelorettes with the auctioneer in the middle. The herald, a pitchman of sorts, would call up the lasses one by one. He'd start off with the most beautiful one, the woman-of-your-dreams whom everyone wanted. That would get a bidding war going. Getting the gorgeous trophy was big even back then. Of course, that young lady would also get the highest price at the auction.

The pitchman would work his way down, with the next most beautiful going second, until he got to the also-rans. Bachelors who couldn't care less what their future wife looked like, paid the least. After they were sold off, the herald would auction the ugly and crippled women by paying bidders to take them off his hands for as little as he could.

Some car auctions I've seen have been run this way: start with the real cream puff at the beginning and get auction fever going hot and heavy, then work down to the lemons. Most present-day auctions usually start with junk and save the good stuff for later. Today's auctioneers use different tactics in laying out their merchandise for sale: some start off with the luxury items, others work their way up to it, and still others sell it in the middle of the auction. It depends on the auctioneer and his strategy.

Always Inspect the Merchandise Before You Buy

(THE BABYLONIANS DID!)

It's always a good idea to inspect the merchandise before buying at any auction. That's one of the golden rules of auction-going. The Babylonians had an odd way of examining the "merchandise" before these annual auctions.

According to Herodotus, there was this old Babylonian law that forced all native-born women to make a single trip to the Temple of Venus. She would have to wait there until a man came along and threw a silver coin into her lap.

The law was sacred about what followed: she would be required to sleep with him. The young maiden couldn't refuse and would have to accept the first man who tossed a silver coin into her lap.

Again, the tall and beautiful ones didn't have to stay there long. Those less well-endowed were said to spend quite a while waiting for someone to throw a coin. This was said to have satisfied the goddess of love, and it's also the earliest example of inspecting before buying at an auction.

Even though Babylonian brides were treated on the same level as slaves and accorded no leeway in choosing their husbands, the anecdote still serves to illustrate the importance of carefully inspecting merchandise at an auction. The lesson is a hard one to forget, isn't it? I'll bet there are more than a few car buyers who, not having been allowed a chance to test drive them first, bought clunkers at some government auctions and then cursed the auctioneer. Failure to inspect before buying can leave you with a bitter aftertaste. Think of the Babylonians before buying at your next auction.

Auctions after Rome Fell

By the time the Roman empire fell to its invaders in the 5th century AD, all but slave auctions had ceased. For hundreds of years civilized commerce throughout Europe bottomed out. Possessions were just seized by brigands, their victims murdered. Auctions were unnecessary except for trading slaves. The Arabs, for instance, had a thriving slave auction business in Seville, Spain, while the rest of the continent coped with the Dark Ages. In the 9th century slaves were imported from eastern Africa for auction and ended up as slave farmers working the fields in southern Iraq.

Bankruptcy and other commercial auctions were pointless in the absence of civilized laws. Nomadic tribes, bandits, invaders, and despots set their own legal procedures for a millennium, usually with pikes, swords, and bows. It was not until 1542 that King Henry VIII established the first English bankruptcy laws. Ironically, he passed them after having, himself, nearly bankrupted the royal treasury. Soon after that, bankruptcy auctions began anew.

Commercial auctions re-emerged as cargo ships sought out exotic ports and brought back trade. Beginning around 1100 AD, Jewish merchants in Cairo and throughout the western Mediterranean traded with merchants in India. As ships returned home loaded with gemstones, spices, and silk, auctions returned from their hiatus. Many captains of those vessels were among the first modern-day auctioneers. Auctions were held at sea aboard the ship or on the pier upon returning to port.

Such auctions became a vital part of commerce throughout the Renaissance and into the modern era. Keep in mind that trade was slow without letters of credit, fax machines, and Federal Express. It might have taken two years or more before a ship returned home with cargo, if it ever returned at all. Auctions provided an efficient means for selling inventory and quickly raising vital cash to repay impatient moneylenders. Trade and banking might never have evolved beyond simple bartering or plunder. Even the exploration of new lands would never have become financially practical. Because they were fast and efficient, auctions greased the wheels of commerce.

As trade routes opened and commerce grew, auctions became more commonplace. Even Christopher Columbus visited an English public auction on his way to the New World. Find any key point, during the Renaissance or later, where a country's economy underwent a surge in growth and you will find auctions played a major role. Without auctions we might all still be in the Dark Ages.

The Great Tulip Craze

With trade coming in from the East, Europeans went into ecstasy over what we consider ordinary things. One item that absolutely drove the Dutch mad with greed was tulips. Although the Dutch went crazy over these flower bulbs, they did bring us the best lesson we can learn on auction fever. Auction fever describes that wide-eyed, palm-sweating, throat-tightening, stomach-clenching feeling one gets in moments of feverish excitement. Your temperature probably reads at 99.9°F. If you still can't picture it, then take a rollercoaster ride or go fall in love. Auction fever is the exact moment when you lose your senses—when you go out of your mind. Which is exactly what the Dutch did between the years 1633 and 1637.

Tulips had such a powerful stranglehold over the Dutch that Holland went into an economic spin as a result of wild speculating by any Dutchman who had a bagful of gold guilders. It all started innocently enough when the Austrian ambassador to Turkey sent tulip bulbs back home. But when a cargo of Turkish tulip bulbs arrived in Antwerp, Holland, in 1562, they might as well have lit a fuse to a warehouse of dynamite. Europe went wild with tulips.

Within a few years tulips became so prized someone exchanged a single tulip bulb for a prosperous French brewery. The tulip could be used as the dowry for a bride. Then, the Dutch really went overboard. Until tulip auctions came along, the Dutch were only into auctioning wines and pottery . . . nothing big. Tulips changed all that. Over a four-year period, tulips started costing more than homes. Throughout Holland, homeowners were mortgaging their estates, selling off entire businesses, borrowing against their firms' net worth, and more just to own a little tulip bulb.

Finally, even the Dutch realized how enormously fragile their investment was . . . come springtime of 1637. By then, nearly everyone who had money was holding tulips. Prices were so high that no one had any money left to buy them. Auction fever had burst and tulips just about wiped out Holland. So remember this: if it can happen to a whole country, auction fever could bite you.

Oh, but that was the Dutch and that was over 300 years ago. What's happened in recent years? Gold prices took a jump in mid-1979 from less than $300 an ounce way up to more than $800 an ounce. Silver prices increased about tenfold during that same time period. Those, too, were auctions. Step into a commodity ring, sometime, in Chicago or New York and say you don't see auction fever.

What about the Japanese real estate boom? That spilled over into the art auction market and brought tens of millions for paintings that the original artists could barely trade for room and board in their own lifetimes. That real estate boom first gushed into the stock market and took the Nikkei Stock Index to deadly heights. It got absurd when real estate investors began taking 100-year mortgages! Now, the Japanese are setting new records . . . for bankruptcies!

Auction fever is the deadliest disease you can get at an auction. It's the easiest to get. The cure is usually an empty wallet or a drained bank account. Unfortunately, auction fever is quite contagious. When excitement spreads through the crowd, that's auction fever. If you're at an auction and you feel like getting carried away (oh, why not? what the heck?), take a break and go smell a few flowers. Remember, the Dutch once mortgaged their homes to buy one little tulip bulb.

End of History Lesson

Auctions comprise the fabric of commerce as they have since the beginning of recorded history. Business and auctions have gone down through time hand in hand. There are hundreds of interesting auction anecdotes that could amuse readers for another few chapters. However, the previous ones were selected solely to show you the roots of auctions and auctioneers.

The central lessons to be learned about auctions are evident in the preceding pages. They also make up several of the important points about auction attendance and participation. Later, at the end of Chapter 3 you'll find the golden rules of auctions. Meanwhile, here are the history lessons that you should remember at any future auction you attend.

1. *Always* know what it is you are buying and what its real value is. Emperor Didius Julianus didn't when he "bought" the Roman Empire. And it cost him his head. *Caveat emptor* (Be careful, bidder).

2. *Never* get auction fever. The Dutch did with tulips and it wrecked Holland's economy.

3. *Always* inspect the merchandise. If the Babylonians did, you should too.

4. *Never* forget that an auctioneer is a *Salesman* and he is *Selling* you something. Remember Caligula and his tricks. It's showtime when the auction starts and that auctioneer may well be the best salesman you will ever meet.

2

Is the Circus in Town?

★★

When you step onto the auction site, you are going to find a "big picture." It may be confusing. Throughout this chapter that picture will be broken down into its basic elements so you will know what is going on, who is doing what, and why. By understanding these elements, auction-going should be a breeze. And a lot of fun.

If you haven't already been to one, your first encounter with an auction could make you think you were at the carnival or a flea market, depending on the quality of the auction and the auctioneer holding the event. Government auctions, like most auctions, are not subtle little affairs with neat rows of folding chairs lined up in a perfect rectangle, well-groomed bidders, and tea served from bone china.

Sure, art auctions are like that. So are some real estate auctions, as is the occasional U.S. Marshals Service auction conducted by a prestigious auction house for the luxurious trappings of a drug lord. But, for the most part, expect to find the local Joes and Janes in rolled-up shirt sleeves, suspenders, and loafers.

Some auctions are crowded, a testimony to the wise government agency that keeps a mailing list (and sends auction notices regularly and in advance) or the usually competent private auctioneer who does a good marketing job. Many government auctions, though, are not overflowing to capacity. At these, only a few people hear about

them in time to get motivated enough to attend; or, that government agency has someone answering the telephone who discourages attendance. That's right! It does happen. Some government bureaucrats, unlike private auctioneers, get upset when people want to find out about their auctions. Imagine that! Of course, the best auctions to attend are the most poorly promoted.

Types of Auctions

Government auctions are a peculiar breed of horse. While most auctioneers stick primarily to the public auction method, many government agencies mess around with the different auction styles available. With all auctions, you're going to find four basic types. They are:

1. *Public Auction.* Crying out a series of increasing bids to the auctioneer until someone yells out the highest price with no one else challenging and increasing it.

2. *Sealed Bid Auction.* Mailing in your bid and having it secretly opened up, the winning bid being the highest offer. The bidder is notified by return mail.

3. *Spot Bid Auction.* Attending the auction and bringing your secret bid to the auctioneer, who

opens each of the bids up at the auction site and announces the winning bid at the auction.

4. *Negotiated Sales*. Written and telephone offers are taken by the government agency or auctioneer off the auction site and before the actual auction takes place. The highest offer is accepted.

Why So Many Different Types of Auctions?

This is a good question. Why don't the government agencies just have one type of auction and simplify everything? Is it because they're the government and that's that? No, it would be too easy to just blame the government bureaucracy. There's plenty of room left in this book to do that.

One of the primary reasons for the different auction methods is that the government doesn't really want to be in the auction business, and especially not in the real estate business. Most government agencies would rather just turn over property and merchandise to private auctioneers and go on with their business. Unfortunately, these same agencies are also scared to death that some auctioneer is going to do what they already did: sell a $50,000 boat for $10, sell a fax machine for $10, sell a house for $15, etc. And then, that government agency will take the heat! The government is trying its best to make do within the available auction framework. Auction styles themselves have changed over the years.

Other Types of Auctions

(INCH OF CANDLE)

The deep, hidden reason for such a variety of auction methods is that the auction system has been played around with over the years, and we should be happy to have just *four* basic methods instead of 16 or 20. Auctions, over the years, have gone through various transformations.

For instance, throughout the 17th century, auc-

tions were timed to the burning of a candle. Entire ships were sold this way. The auctioneer would light a candle and then start taking bids. These were called "auction by inch of candle," since they only burned one inch per auction. The winning bidder was the guy who put in the last offer before the candle flame expired. King William the 3rd of England even made it a law that all goods and merchandise from the East Indies would be sold by "inch of candle" or else the property would be confiscated by the government.

How would you like to buy a drug dealer's Porsche if you had to wait around for a candle to go out? Thank goodness, our government didn't adopt that technique. French wine is still sometimes sold by "inch of candle" at the vineyards; they've been doing that since about the 1400s. But it's not a practical or speedy method of holding a government auction.

Dutch Auctions

Thank our lucky stars that government auctions are not done the *Dutch* way. Millions of auctions throughout the centuries have probably been held Dutch-style. That's where the auctioneer starts high and works downward. The lowest bid is the winning bid.

The practice started with sea captains who wanted to get the most out of their cargo and started their auctions at outlandish prices. Then the captain would keep dropping his price until someone accepted.

It's also been called Mine-ing. That's because the guy who wanted to buy the merchandise would shout "MINE." It sounds pretty simple, but inflation has taught us to think in terms of things going up, not down.

You'll still find the Dutch Auction method used in parts of England, in Holland, and in Israel. Dutch auctions are used to sell some commodities. Remember, these boys with the wooden shoes were the same ones who brought us "dutch treat"!

Even Stranger Types of Auctions

If you visited the Tokyo fish market and were allowed to bid, there would be quite a surprise waiting for you. Everyone puts in their bid at the same time. It's like the spot-bid method. Fish buyers, at the moment the auction is started, give hand signals describing the price they want to pay for a particular load. The auctioneer glances across the crowd and picks the guy with the hand signal making the highest bid. A little room for error, don't you think?

Fruit and vegetable auctions are often conducted this way electronically. Buyers put in their bids by pushing buttons and numbers appear on the auctioneer's screen. Again the highest bidder wins, just like in the spot-bid method. Remember that next time you have a salad.

In some parts of China, you will find the auctioneer has gnarled hands instead of auctioneer's laryngitis. That's because he conducts "handshake auctions." Bidders reveal their offers with their fingers under a cloth. The auctioneer shakes their hands and feels how many fingers the guy is willing to bid. The number of fingers the auctioneer can grab and the number of squeezes the bidder makes with those fingers determines the bid. Of course, it's open to fraud and favoritism, just like the next method.

Whispering bids into the auctioneer's ear is how fish is sold in parts of the Far East, particularly in Singapore and Manila. You can also find it done this way in Venice. The bidders just whisper their bids into the auctioneer's ear. It's peaceful and quiet, unlike most auctions, but can you imagine the sore losers?

Over the years there've been a number of amusing ways auctions have been held. One of the more memorable ones was accepting bids on an item until the sand in an hourglass ran out; or, speaking of running, the auctioneer might take offers from the audience for as long as it took a young boy to run from some distant point to the auction site. Winning bids were determined when the last sand grain reached bottom or when the boy arrived at the end of his race. If nothing else, the tempo of the auction picked up at the very end.

These types of auctions are not held by government agencies. However, in case they get any strange ideas, you'll be prepared.

The Public Auction

This is the most common form of auction and is the kind that nearly everyone thinks is always held everywhere and anywhere. It's not, but it is the one you'll see most often. There are different ways to conduct a public auction, but that is covered in the next chapter. If you go to enough auctions, you'll also see a broad assortment of environments in which auctions can be conducted: from vacant lots to warehouses, from fairgrounds to catering halls, on courthouse steps, in storefronts, on television, on the radio, behind locked Cyclone wire fences, inside tomblike basements, inside restaurants, outside farmhouses, outside storage units, and so on. You get the picture. Practically anywhere three people can stand or sit an auction can be held—and possibly already has been.

Public auctions may also go by other names. One person might call it an oral auction. Another might call it an open-bidding auction. These more clearly define the public auction but mean the same thing. Bids are made vocally, not in writing, as in the case of spot- or sealed-bid auctions. They are made openly, which again is different from the other auction methods.

Typically, when you walk into an auction area or site, it will either be indoors or outdoors, unless an in-between place has been discovered that I don't know about yet. Your first stop will be to register with the auctioneer's representatives. Usually, they have a large folding table with chairs at the entrance to greet you upon arrival.

At the registration table, you'll be expected to show some identification to prove who you are. Bring a valid driver's license. That's the common passport to registration. If you don't have a driver's license, bring a passport or some official identification that has your address and photograph on it.

Registration is simple and painless. You show your identification, then fill out a slip of paper giving your name, address, and telephone number. You'll be given a card with a bidder's number on it. At some auctions you might be given a Ping-Pong paddle with a number on it. You wear the card on your chest or protruding from your shirt pocket. Obviously, you carry the paddle. There may be a deposit or registration fee at some auctions, usually minimal, to ensure that the bidder returns the paddle or to discourage spectators who aren't buying.

In any event, don't lose that bidder's card. If you leave the auction before it's over, take the card home with you or tear it into tiny shreds. Your bidder number identifies the buyer for the auctioneer. Should someone bid with that card *and*

buy something, you might be held responsible. It rarely happens, but it could. If a stranger makes a bid with your number and then leaves the auction site, the auctioneer will have your address. While it might not stick in court, or the auctioneer might not pursue the case, why get an unnecessary headache when a simple precaution will avoid the whole problem?

Conditions of Sale

While at the registration booth there might be a large sign posted. You might be given an auction flier or catalog describing the merchandise or property for sale. Often there will be both a large sign and a pamphlet given concerning the auction. On that sign or pamphlet you'll find something that tells you the Conditions of the Sale. That means that the following merchandise is being

```
                    PROSPECTIVE BUYER'S APPLICATION
 ┌──────────────┐                                    ┌──────────────┐
 │ PLEASE PRINT │                                    │              │
 └──────────────┘                                    └──────────────┘
       INVOICE TO: _____

        YOUR NAME: _____

          ADDRESS: _____

             CITY: _____  COUNTY: _____

            STATE: _____  ZIP CODE: _____  PHONE: (____) _____

   YOUR EMPLOYER: _____  PHONE: (____) _____

       YOUR BANK: _____  ADDRESS: _____

    RESALE TAX #: _____  DEALER #: _____

        ** NO EQUIPMENT RELEASED ON AUCTION DAY IF PAID FOR BY CHECK **

 ┌─────────────────────────┐   I UNDERSTAND THIS IS A PUBLIC AUCTION, AND THAT ALL
 │                         │   ITEMS ARE SOLD "AS IS" THERE ARE NO WARRANTIES ON
 │ *** OFFICE USE ONLY *** │   ANY ITEMS.  I AGREE THAT IF I AM HIGH BIDDER ON ANY
 │                         │   ITEM, I WILL PAY FOR THAT ITEM ON AUCTION DAY.  I
 │ D/L# _____ │   UNDERSTAND THAT I HAVE 15 DAYS TO TO REMOVE ANY
 │                         │   ITEM I PURCHASE FROM THESE PREMISES BEFORE STORAGE
 │ D.O.B. ____/____/_____ │   CHARGES BEGIN.
 │                         │
 └─────────────────────────┘   SIGNATURE _____
```

IMPORTANT - PLEASE READ BEFORE BIDDING

SPECIAL TERMS AND CONDITIONS OF SALE

BIDDERS INDEBTED TO THE GOVERNMENT: Purchasers of surplus personal property must make arrangements to pay promptly all amounts administratively found to be due the United States Government arising out of their prior purchase of surplus personal property. Failure to pay any such amount upon demand may be cause for rejection of all future bids until such time as the debt is paid.

SALE TO GOVERNMENT EMPLOYEES: To the extent not prohibited by the regulations of any executive agency, an employee of such agency (either as a civilian or as a member of the Armed Forces of the United States including the U. S. Coast Guard, on active duty) may be allowed to purchase Government surplus personal property. The term "EMPLOYEE" as used in this statement includes any agency or immediate member of the household of the employee. GSA EMPLOYEES ARE INELIGIBLE TO BID. Other Federal employees should check their own agencies as to their eligibility to bid.

FORMS OF PAYMENT: ACCEPTABLE FORMS OF PAYMENT INCLUDE CASH, CASHIER'S CHECKS, OFFICIAL CREDIT UNION CHECKS (Federal/state chartered), MONEY ORDERS, TRAVELER'S CHECKS AND GOVERNMENT CHECKS (Federal, State or Local Government). PERSONAL OR COMPANY CHECKS WILL BE ACCEPTED ONLY IF ACCOMPAINED BY AN INFORMAL BANK LETTER GUARANTEEING PAYMENT. BANK LETTERS NEED NOT BE IN ANY SPECIFIC FORMAT BUT STATE IN ESSENCE THAT THE DEPOSITOR IS IN GOOD STANDING AND THE BANK WILL GUARANTEE CHECKS UP TO A SPECIFIC AMOUNT THROUGH A SPECIFIC DATE AND SHOULD STATE THAT THEY COVER THE PURCHASE OF U. S. GOVERNMENT PROPERTY ONLY.

REMOVAL RESPONSIBILITIES: PROPERTY CUSTODIANS ARE NOT RESPONSIBLE FOR AND WILL NOT MAKE ANY REMOVAL ARRANGEMENTS. THE SUCCESSFUL BIDDER MUST MAKE THESE ARRANGEMENTS, INCLUDING LABOR FOR PACKING, CRATING, REMOVAL, AND TRANSPORTATION. TO RELEASE PROPERTY TO ANYONE OTHER THAN THE SUCCESSFUL BIDDER, WRITTEN NOTIFICATION MUST BE FURNISHED TO THE PROPERTY CUSTODIAN.

CONSIDERATION OF BIDS: Qualified bids, bids specifying order of choice or UNSIGNED BIDS may not be considered. The Government reserves the right to reject any and all bids. TELEPHONIC AND TELEGRAPHIC BIDS ARE NOT ACCEPTABLE AND WILL NOT BE CONSIDERED.

The bidder warrants that he is not under 18 years of age. For breach of this warrant the Government shall have the right to annual any contract without liability. Identification may be required.

DISPUTES: Any contract resulting from this offering is subject to the Contract Disputes Act of 1978, Public Law 95-563 and is hereby incorporated by reference. A copy of the clause is available upon request from the GSA Sales Office conducting this sale.

RESULTS OF SALE: Bid results are not furnished by telephone. A bidder may request sale results by enclosing a stamped, legal size or larger, self-addressed envelope along with his/her bid. This action is necessary due to current budgetary limitations.

Condition of property is not warranted.

DESCRIPTION WARRANTY

THE GOVERNMENT WARRANTS TO THE ORIGINAL PURCHASER THAT THE PROPERTY LISTED IN THE INVITATION FOR BIDS WILL CONFORM TO ITS DESCRIPTION. IF A MISDESCRIPTION IS DETERMINED BEFORE REMOVAL OF THE PROPERTY, THE GOVERNMENT WILL KEEP THE PROPERTY AND REFUND ANY MONEY PAID. IF A MISDESCRIPTION IS DETERMINED AFTER REMOVAL, THE GOVERNMENT WILL REFUND ANY MONEY PAID IF THE PURCHASER TAKES THE PROPERTY AT HIS OR HER EXPENSE TO A LOCATION SPECIFIED BY THE CONTRACTING OFFICER. NO REFUND WILL BE MADE UNLESS THE PURCHASER SUBMITS A WRITTEN NOTICE TO THE CONTRACTING OFFICER WITHIN 15 CALENDAR DAYS OF THE DATE OF REMOVAL THAT THE PROPERTY IS MISDESCRIBED AND MAINTAINS THE PROPERTY IN THE SAME CONDITION AS WHEN REMOVED. AFTER PROPERTY HAS BEEN REMOVED, NO REFUND WILL BE MADE FOR SHORTAGES OF PROPERTY SOLD BY THE "LOT."

THIS WARRANTY IS IN PLACE OF ALL OTHER GUARANTEES AND WARRANTIES, EXPRESS OR IMPLIED. THE GOVERNMENT DOES NOT WARRANT THE MERCHANTABILITY OF THE PROPERTY OR ITS FITNESS FOR ANY USE OR PURPOSE. THE AMOUNT OF RECOVERY UNDER THIS PROVISION IS LIMITED TO THE PURCHASE PRICE OF THE MISDESCRIBED PROPERTY. THE PURCHASER IS NOT ENTITLED TO ANY PAYMENT FOR LOSS OF PROFIT OR ANY OTHER MONEY DAMAGES, SPECIAL, DIRECT, INDIRECT, OR CONSEQUENTIAL. CLAUSE NO. 2 OF STANDARD FORM 114C IS DELETED.

DEFICIENCIES, WHEN KNOWN, HAVE BEEN INDICATED IN THE ITEM DESCRIPTION. HOWEVER, ABSENCE OF ANY INDICATED DEFICIENCY DOES NOT MEAN THE ITEM MAY NOT HAVE DEFICIENCIES. BIDDERS ARE CAUTIONED TO INSPECT BEFORE BIDDING. CONDITION OF PROPERTY IS NOT GUARANTEED.

This property is being offered in accordance with the exchange/sale provision of Section 201(C) of the Federal Property and Administrative Services Act of 1949, 63 STAT 384 as amended, except items, 1,6,7,8,9,15,17,18 thru 34, 37,38,40 thru 45, 50 thru 66, 69,70,71,74,75,102,103,107, 108,109,110,111,113,114,115,116,128,129,130,131,132,136,137,138,139,140,141,142,143,144,145, 146,147,152,153,154,155,156,157,158,162,175.

offered for sale on a certain basis. The sale is based upon certain conditions being met. If you don't read the terms and participate in the auction, tough luck. Read the terms.

The large sign might say: PAYMENT IN FULL IN CASH ON THE DAY OF THE AUCTION. AS IS/WHERE IS. This can be a disappointment to those who only brought a checkbook or just their credit cards. Unless you happened to see a big auction sign and wandered into an auction, you'll probably have found out about the auction some other way: a newspaper ad, an auction notice mailed to you, or even a radio or television commercial.

When you discover an auction is going to take place, *always* find out what the conditions of the sale are. Finding out can be just a telephone call away. Ask the auctioneer or government agency what the accepted forms of payment are. Normally, cash, money orders, certified or cashier's checks, and business checks with letters from your bank guaranteeing payment are suitable. Nevertheless, find out in advance and avoid disappointment.

Most government agencies will list the conditions of the sale right on the auction flier or pamphlet. Read them carefully and make sure you can comply with their rules before you make a bid. How would you like to find yourself buying a late-model Mercedes-Benz for a mere $3,400 and then discover that it's for export only? Worse yet, you have 36 hours to get it out of the U.S. or you forfeit the purchase *and* your money! This is an actual example and there are many more where that came from. U.S. Customs Auctions frequently have that condition of sale.

The condition of sale will list each of the special characteristics of that auction. The main characteristics are form of payment and removing the merchandise. You will probably also read on the condition-of-sale sheet whether or not mailed, telegraphed, or hand-carried bids will be accepted by the auctioneer. There might be other important points for that particular auction, but how you're paying for it and when you're taking it away should be your main concerns.

Inspection

Would you like to buy the Brooklyn Bridge? Without seeing it? Many amateurs will buy something at auction without ever having it inspected. This is what separates the professionals from the turkeys.

Inspections are not only allowed but encouraged at nearly all auctions. Inspection periods vary from an hour before the auction up to a week prior to the sale. You'll have ample opportunity to look carefully at the merchandise or property. Most novices omit this step or do it carelessly. That gives auctions a bad name because the results are shocking. Sort of like buying the Brooklyn Bridge with your life savings.

After you've registered and read the conditions-of-sale terms, you must inspect the merchandise. On every condition of sale I've read, you will find: "as is, where is." You might also find a clause with this phrase: "no warranty expressed or implied." These refer to the merchandise or real estate. Anything you are likely to buy at an auction is going to be sold to you in the condition it's in. Similarly, moving the merchandise is up to you.

There are exceptions to the above rule and certain protections, but again these involve unnecessary headaches and other complications. It is far easier to understand that when you buy something at auction, the merchandise won't have a 90-day or extended-service contract. If the vehicle, boat, airplane, computer or house needs repairs, you pay for them. The auction house or government agency does not provide a delivery service. Carting away your purchase is solely your responsibility . . . often the day of the auction.

I've been amazed to see many bidders actually place serious offers on cars and other goods to which they've never given more than a brief glance. Just a quick check of the odometer, a once-over on the exterior, and the novice makes bids. That's dangerous. Inspection and appraisal tactics are covered in Chapter 3. Don't leave this step out.

The Auction Takes Place

Public auctions can happen any day of the week but generally are held on the weekends in order to attract a large crowd. So, at this point, you're registered, have a bidder's number, should have inspected the merchandise or property you wish to buy, and want to get started.

At this point it's not hard to find where the auction itself is taking place. Just look for the auctioneer. More often than not, his voice will be booming through a public-address system. He'll either be in the front of a crowd or surrounded by one. You might find him on a raised platform or at ground level. In any event, you'll find the auction where the crowd is.

A word about the auctioneer's voice. In case you've never been to an auction, you'll hear him talking at hyperspeed. It may even sound incomprehensible, words and numbers running together in a fast jumble. No, he didn't take a gulp of helium. That's the way he encourages bidders to make offers, by making them feel rushed. This is called the auction chant or bid-calling. The way he calls out bids is the auctioneer's trademark. It sets the tempo of the auction. When he speeds it up, the auction goes faster. When he slows the bid-calling down a bit, the auction pace slackens. That's just one of the many strategies he employs, which you'll find out about in the next chapter.

What separates the public auction from any other style of auction is the public outcry of increasing bids. Nothing is hidden. Everything is out in the open. At any given moment, both the auctioneer and the bidders know exactly what the going offer is on that particular item, be it a Jaguar or a duplex apartment. Public auctions stir up crowds because there is an expectancy that something *big* is about to happen.

There may be just two bidders or a whole flock of them chasing the same item. Unlike other auction methods, you are not likely to find one bid high and the others very low. Bids successively increase from one price to a higher one. Except for the oddball bid, from time to time, bids gener-

ally go up uniformly in price. Bids might increase in increments of $10, $50, $100, $1,000 or more depending on the property or merchandise being auctioned. The final price is almost always going to be slightly higher than the previous bid. Surprises are few and far between, unlike the other auction styles.

Ringmen

The auctioneer has help in getting you to make a bid. He'll employ ringmen who scurry about the crowd trying to drum up business. These are the auctioneer's assistants. They were hired entirely to get activity going from the bidders. The ringman's duty is to get you to make a bid.

You'll be surprised at how provocative they can act: friendly, cajoling, encouraging, badgering. One might put his arm around you and implore you to make a bid, another might just scowl and say: "Come on. Do it." Auctioneers find them useful. They do get slow auctions moving.

The term "ringman" comes from livestock auctions where bidders would, and still do, view the animals for sale from a ring. The ringman would move the herd in and out of the ring. In some areas he might be called a floorman. He'll be pacing the floor looking for a live one to make bids. Best way to get rid of them if you aren't bidding is to shake your head from side to side and then look away. They'll be off to their next mark.

Auctioneer's Other Assistants

When you make the winning bid, that moment of success, the auctioneer's clerk will write your bidder's number down in a logbook along with the item number and the price you bid. In many cases, the clerk will also tape-record the auction for legal purposes.

A runner will take the winning bids, the bidder numbers, and the corresponding numbers identifying the merchandise to the cashier. You'll pay at the cashier and then arrange to pick up your merchandise. Any arrangements regarding removal of your purchase should be made at that time. Occasionally, buyers make the purchase but don't remove the merchandise. This irritates the auctioneer and the seller, since it now has to be resold.

Those are the major players at the auction, aside from the seller of the merchandise or the property. You, of course, are the most important person at the auction because you are the potential buyer. Don't forget that. Auctioneers and government agencies pay a closetful of marketing and advertising money to get buyers to come to their auctions. Without you, the auction participant, an auction doesn't take place at all.

Sealed-Bid Auctions

These are secretive affairs, sort of like a midnight rendezvous to meet someone you've never encountered before. You have the feeling you don't know what you've gotten yourself into until it is too late. A sealed-bid auction is like this. It is usually done almost entirely through the mail. Sometimes, the government agency will permit a faxed sealed bid. All sealed bids are made in writing. The main drawback to these is that absolutely no one knows what is going on. Bidders don't know whether they've won, sometimes for many days after the sealed bids were opened.

A sealed-bid auction, according to some auctioneers, isn't really even an auction. By definition, they are correct. An auction, as defined by nearly all dictionaries, is a competitive sale conducted by a series of increasing bids. Sealed-bid sales don't have increasing bids. They may be competitive in that many have more than one bidder sending in a written bid; however, it is not uncommon to find a single bidder on a piece of equipment or real estate at these auctions. Sometimes, no bids at all are made on a property or merchandise.

Additionally, the mood and atmosphere of an auction are lost when a government agency or auctioneer insists on using the sealed-bid method. Gone is the "horse trading" ambience, the friendly get-together of a public auction, and the one-upmanship skill needed to win big at an auction. Sealed-bid auctions could even be held without an auctioneer. All you need is a clerk who opens up the envelopes and picks the highest bidder.

Sealed-bid auctions are not fun, unless, of course, you are the highest bidder. Instead of an auction climate, you have the spirit of a lottery. Sealed-bid auctions closely resemble lotteries. When participating in them, the frame of mind is "pick a number and hope it wins." That's how most amateurs participate in a sealed-bid auction. In the next chapter, you'll find a strategy to intelligently place a sealed bid.

How to Participate in a Sealed-Bid Auction

There are a few government agencies and auctioneers who will use the sealed-bid method when auctioning real estate and merchandise. These government agencies are covered in Sections Three and Four of this book. At this point, let's go over some basics about the sealed-bid method, information you need to know before participating in one.

A few government agencies print catalogs of what will be sold by sealed bid. They are called Invitations for Bids (IFB). Contact the applicable government agency and ask for a catalog or the IFB on an upcoming auction. Refer to the directories in Section Three of this book for the current telephone numbers.

Some are scheduled regularly, such as every few weeks or every month, while others are arranged irregularly. Each government agency does things differently so don't expect each agency to have a sealed-bid auction on a certain date. It doesn't work like that.

You will find that the Department of Housing and Urban Development (HUD) advertises their sealed-bid auctions in the classified section of your local weekend newspaper. HUD will list the real estate up for sale, but doesn't have a catalog, as such. However, in the Denver, Colorado, area,

IFB 27-1079
RETURN WITH BID TO DRMR COLUMBUS

FORM APPROVED OMB. NO.
29-R0022

SALE OF GOVERNMENT PROPERTY-BID AND AWARD	INVITATION FOR BIDS NO.	PAGE NO.

ISSUED BY
Defense Reutilization & Marketing Region
Post Office Box 500
Blacklick, OH 43004-0500

ADDRESS YOUR BID TO
SALES CONTRACTING OFFICER
Defense Reutilization & Marketing Region
Post Office Box 500
Blacklick, OH 43004-0500

FOR INFORMATION CONTACT (Name & tel. no.)

See Inside Front Cover

BIDS WILL BE OPENED AT (Place, date and time)

Defense Reutilization & Marketing Region
926 Taylor Station Road
Blacklick, OH 43004-9615 23 **MAY** 91 - 9:00 **A.M.**

Sealed bids in __one__ copy(ies) for purchasing any or all items listed on the accompanying schedule, will be received at the place designated above until the date and time specified above and at that time publicly opened, subject to: (1) The General Sale Terms and Conditions, SF 114C, 6-86 edition; and Special Sealed Bid Conditions SF 114C-1, Jan 1970 ed. |X|; Special Sealed Bid-Term Conditions SF 114C-2, Jan 1970 ed. | |; all incorporated herein by reference; and such other special terms and conditions |X| attached or |X| incorporated herein by reference and identified as (See Page 14 thru 17 of this IFB)-(Copies of these forms, unless attached hereto, are on file at the issuing office and will be made available upon request.)
(2) BID DEPOSIT | | IS NOT REQUIRED; |X| IS REQUIRED IN AN AMOUNT NOT LESS THAN __20%__ OF THE TOTAL BID, MADE PAYABLE TO: U.S. TREASURY.
(3) Bidder is required to pay for any or all of the items listed on the Item Bid page(s) as part of this Bid, at the price set opposite each item, and to remove the property within (See Loading Table) Pages 18 & 19 calendar days after date of award by the Government.

BID (This section to be completed by the bidder)

In compliance with the above, the undersigned offers and agrees, if this bid is accepted within_____calendar days (60 calendar days if no period is specified by the Government or the bidder, but not less than 10 calendar days in any case) after date of Bid opening, to pay for and remove the property. The total amount of the Bid(s) is #_____ and attached is the bid deposit, when required by the Invitation, in the form(s) of_____, in the amount of #_____.

BIDDER REPRESENTS THAT: (Check appropriate boxes)
(1) He/She | | has, | | has not, inspected the property on which he is bidding.
(2) He/She | | is, | | is not, an individual or a small business concern. (See CFR, Title 13, Chapter 1, Part 121   Sec. 121.3-9, for the definition of small business.)(Complete the following only if the total amount of the bid(s) exceeds $25,000.)
(3) (a) He/She | | has, | | has not, employed or retained any company or person (other than a full-time, bona fide employee working solely for the Bidder) to solicit or secure this contract, and (b) he/she | | has, | | has not, paid or agreed to pay any company or person (other than a full-time, bona fide employee working solely for the bidder) any fee, commission, percentage or brokerage fee, contingent upon or resulting from the award of this contract; and agrees to furnish information relating to (a) and (b) above as requested by the Contracting Officer. (For interpretation of the representation, including the term 'bona fide employee', see CFR, Title 41, Subpart 101-45.3.)

NAME AND ADDRESS OF BIDDER (Street, city, state & ZIP Code) (Type or print) (MUST BE SAME AS ON ENVELOPE)	SIGNATURE OF PERSON AUTHORIZED TO SIGN THIS BID
TELEPHONE NUMBER: BIDDER IDENTIFICATION NO.(If applicable):	SIGNER'S NAME & TITLE (Type or print) DATE OF BID

ACCEPTANCE BY THE GOVERNMENT (This section for Government use only)

ACCEPTED AS TO ITEM(S) NUMBERED (FOR ACCEPTANCE INFORMATION SEE DPDS FORM 1427 ATTACHED)	UNITED SATES OF AMERICA BY _____ (Contracting Officer)	DATE OF ACCEPTANCE
TOTAL AMOUNT	CONTRACT NUMBER(S)	NAME AND TITLE OF CONTRACTING OFFICER

114-109

STANDARD FORM 114 (Rev. 5-76)
Prescribed by GSA FPMR (41 CFR) 101-45.3

COMPUTER GENERATED FORM

* GPO : 1982 O - 361-526 (7343)

the listing can be so large that its own multipage insert is included in the newspaper.

When you receive the catalog, your first task will be to remove those annoying staples punched right into the pamphlet. They come in various sizes and colors, so be on the lookout for them when they hit your mailbox. It may even look like junk mail at first glance.

In this catalog you will find a brief description of the merchandise or property for sale. Often, the condition of the merchandise will be described. For instance, in one government agency's sealed-bid catalog, the General Services Administration's, the description of the equipment may state next to it, "repairs required." These descriptions are brief and give you a summary of what you might be buying. In the Department of Defense's military surplus catalog you might find "poor" or "fair."

The catalog will generally have a large number of items for sale. It looks like a shopping list without prices. Not only will you find the description of the equipment, but you will also read the quantity of the merchandise being offered. That refers to the number of *that* particular item being sold. You can't just bid on a single item in that description. You have to bid on the whole lot, which means all of them. For example, there might be five typewriters, 4,000 staplers, or 30 army tents. Your single bid is for all those typewriters, staplers, or army tents, not just one of them. Be sure to look at the quantity next to the description. Yes, there are many lots that only have one of the item offered. And there are just as many that have dozens, hundreds, or thousands of that same item up for sale.

Some sealed-bid auctions, such as those held by the Department of Defense, are held in this way to discourage the ordinary consumer; small businesses, dealers, and other professionals are welcomed. (This doesn't mean that *You* can't bid at these auctions. You are very much allowed to place bids. It's just the way that this government agency behaves.) This attitude has actually worked against this particular government agency, as dealers have a wide-open playing field.

Now, you can join the dealers and cash in on these deals too.

Often, the catalog will also tell you where the property is located. For instance, while the brochure may have been sent from Atlanta to your home, the merchandise might be located in Alabama. This will happen with both Department of Defense and General Services Administration sealed-bid auctions. Newspaper advertisements for HUD sealed-bid properties are almost always right in your city. It's easier to move equipment than it is to truck a house around the country.

While looking through the catalog you will also find the conditions of sale. As described earlier, in the public-auction section, it is imperative that you read the conditions of the sale. Otherwise, you risk investing in something you can't cart away in time or the payment terms could be different from what you expect. Or you might discover a clause that could adversely affect your purchase. No one should make a bid without first reading the conditions of sale.

Making the Bid

The catalog will include a bid form, which looks like an ordinary order form. Usually, it's found on the last page of the catalog or toward the end of the pamphlet. On that sheet you will find the instructions necessary for placing your bid. Within that pamphlet, there could be as many as several pages of instructions or merely a few paragraphs. Read them carefully so you understand what actions must be taken.

Each catalog represents a specific sealed-bid auction. As mentioned earlier, these auctions may have thousands of items for sale. On the front page of the catalog and also on the bid form there is a sale number. This refers to that auction. If the sale number is #92FBPS-91-241, that's the name of that particular sealed-bid auction. Please keep a written note of the number.

Either on the front page of the catalog or on the bidding sheet (order form), you will find the address where this sheet must be mailed. There will also be a deadline date and time when your bid sheet must be received. As with all sealed-bid auctions, it helps to or may be required that you print the following information on your mailing envelope, along with the specific address to which you are mailing your bid: the sealed-bid auction # (insert the sale number of this auction) and the deadline date and time (insert this from the catalog).

Fill in the bid sheet, sign it, and return it by the deadline date. In some cases, you may need to send the bid with an overnight service. Either be sure the government agency will receive your bid by the deadline date and time or just forget about making your bid at all. Any bids that arrive after the deadline won't be accepted. At least one government agency allows bids to be sent by fax.

You may also be required to send a deposit with your bid at some sealed-bid auctions. This varies among government agencies. Some require a 20% deposit. Others ask that you *don't* send one. Money orders, cashiers checks, and certified checks are the standard methods of paying a deposit. At one government sealed-bid auction, I was permitted to fax my bid and make my deposit by credit card. Eventually, other government agencies will catch on to this idea and make it easier for all of us.

Inspecting Before a Sealed-Bid Auction

Just as with public auctions, you'll have a preview period at sealed-bid auctions, during which you can personally inspect the merchandise or hire someone else to do so. The inspection periods are usually longer than those before a public auction, just as the lead time before the auction is often greater. It is important that you inspect the merchandise in some way, either personally or by hiring someone, prior to placing your bid.

A big disadvantage of sealed-bid auctions is that they are frequently distant from home. You might be living in Cincinnati and the inspection site is in South Carolina. That may knock out many would-be bidders and possibly reduce the sale price. This is a great opportunity for the ambitious.

One way of getting a general idea of the quality of the merchandise before wasting further time or money is found inside some of these sealed bid catalogs. Under some of the groupings is a telephone number with a contact name. This contact is the custodian for that property. Telephone this person and inquire about the equipment or item that caught your eye. You're only getting an opinion, but it may save you wasted time, expense, and effort.

If you do wish to place a sealed bid without inspecting the merchandise, make a very small one. For example, if you're willing to pay $500 for the merchandise, you might consider bidding half of that amount or $250, in case there is something wrong. Personally, I would bid even less, but that's up to you.

Spot-Bid Auctions

A spot-bid auction is a hybrid auction. It resembles a public auction in that a crowd shows up and an auctioneer conducts the proceedings. At the same time, auction-goers don't shout out bids. They write them down on a bid sheet secretly and give them to the auctioneer. These auctions are relatively new to government agencies, but their popularity may continue to grow.

The spot-bid auction is conducted like a public auction. The auctioneer describes the merchandise or property to the audience and then asks for bids to be placed. After the bids are opened and the winning bid announced, the auctioneer moves on to the next item at the auction.

You attend these auctions as you would a public auction. You write your bid on the official bid sheet, sign it, and turn it in to the auctioneer. If your bid wins, you'll go through the same procedure of claiming your auction prize and taking it away.

Spot Bids at Public Auctions

Spot-bid auctions evolved from the common practice of sending a sealed bid to the auctioneer. Someone who couldn't attend a public auction for one reason or another would mail or telegraph a bid to the auctioneer with instructions to have it opened at the auction or entered into the bidding. As this practice continued, auctioneers got the idea of having auctions in this way. Remember, auctions have gone through many changes over the past 3,000 years.

You will find a clause in the conditions of sale for the auction noting whether or not telegraph, facsimile, or mail bids will be permitted. The auctioneer may mention, at the beginning or during the auction, that he has sealed bids or written bids placed on the property being auctioned.

Review your conditions of sale to determine if it is possible to place a written bid in this way. The rule of inspecting the merchandise or property applies with spot bids placed in your absence.

You may also hire a proxy to attend the auction for you and place a written bid. The government agency may require that this individual have a written letter of authorization from you before allowing your bid.

Again spot-bid auctions are not pure auctions because there is no public outcry and the competition is seen but not heard, making your bidding skills of little use. In many cases, the government agency holding the spot-bid auction is counting on a wiseguy to place an unusually large bid on the merchandise, beating the other bidders. This can discourage the professionals at the auction because they will know what the merchandise is really worth. Someone craving a particular item of the merchandise has a tendency to overbid for it.

Negotiated Sales

A negotiated sale often takes place between a bankruptcy auctioneer and active buyers he has listed. There have been notices placed by U.S. marshals asking for negotiations on merchandise. These can also occur with real estate. Auctions, by definition, require competition and a series of increasing bids. Negotiated sales are not auctions as we know them. But they do occur with government property that is up for auction.

The negotiated sale takes place *before* the auction date. From the point when it is announced that merchandise or real estate is going to be sold at auction until the actual auction takes place, negotiations do occur. I know this because I have participated in them.

Negotiated sales are not usually advertised. Finding out about a negotiated sale requires some phone calls to auctioneers. Most will play ball and talk to you. Many won't sell to you directly like this. Others will sell because it eliminates for the auctioneer the risky part of auctions. In you he may have an immediate buyer. On the other hand, he's not going to let you steal the merchandise from him.

When doing a negotiated sale the auctioneer is really wearing the hat of a broker. Brokers sell things that aren't theirs and get a fee or commission for their work. Auctioneers, among themselves, call this brokering. Essentially, that's what he is doing. He's holding merchandise or preparing real estate for auction and you come along. Now, he's got a ready and willing buyer. Should he or shouldn't he take you up on your offer?

If he gets a good price, chances are he will sell you the merchandise. Auctioneers are often astute appraisers of their goods. They have a ballpark idea of what it will fetch at auction. The prices you will be quoted, when attempting a negotiated sale, are the *top bid*. That means you are going to pay more to buy the merchandise or real estate than the auctioneer thinks he will get for it at auction. Additionally, you will have no idea whether or not there are competitors. In some cases, the auctioneer may be creating your competition out of thin air.

The method he'll use to take bids is a close cousin to the Dutch auction method. The auctioneer will start high, as high as he can. You shouldn't get discouraged, since he expects you to come lower. His make-break point on accepting your deal is whether or not he thinks he can get that price at auction. The auctioneer will only go lower if he has doubts about the auction. He's sitting on the pulse and knows whether his advertising has worked, whether he's likely to draw a good crowd, the market conditions for that merchandise, and a rough estimate of what he thinks it's worth.

As a buyer you are working against his knowledge in trying to determine a fair negotiated sale price for the merchandise you want to buy. Closing a negotiated sale can be a tense matter. Success doesn't always come to beginners, but

then again you can't just say no to the auctioneer's price and try your luck at his public auction.

You don't physically attend a negotiated sale, as you would a public auction. No written bids are secretly placed as with sealed-bid or spot-bid auctions. All of your work is done over the telephone and by fax.

Generally, auctioneers like to wrap it up, if a negotiated sale is going to close, a few days before the auction. Few auctioneers are ecstatic about withdrawing merchandise from the auction the day before. Bidders who've spent the time to inspect the merchandise get awfully upset with auctioneers who make this a steady practice.

The amount of time available to you to participate in a negotiated sale may be a few hours to a few months, depending on the merchandise or property and the auctioneer. An employee once told me about a negotiated sale he had with a local sheriff. The sheriff was repossessing personal property from someone's home for nonpayment of rent. The employee was passing by and asked the sheriff if he could buy the merchandise. The sheriff said: "Give me a price." He did, and he bought the merchandise for next to nothing. Deals like this do happen.

Conclusion

Now you know the four different methods that government agencies and auctioneers use in conducting an auction. If auctions were cut and dry like this, everyone attending them would walk away a winner. But real life isn't like that. Mistakes are made and some of them can be costly. The next chapter will discuss the auctioneer and auctions, in depth, with the various strategies you need to be successful. Don't be shy. Step right up. The fun's about to begin. . . .

3

Secrets Revealed
How to Succeed at Auctions

★★

One of my favorite auctioneers often repeats this saying: "At any given auction, on any given day, you can expect someone to walk away with a great deal." Many people find great bargains at auctions. Some are ordinary people, others are hard-nosed professionals. There are certain rules these winners follow that the losers don't.

Unfortunately, there are many auctions where a winner will be more upset than a loser. That is because that winner overpaid on his auction purchase. One or more of the golden rules of auction participation was either not known or ignored. At the end of this chapter you'll find the complete list of the golden rules of auction participation. Stick to them and you will never fail at an auction.

The Basic Auction Terms

Before we discuss the strategies for successful participation at an auction, let's go over a few of the basic ways nearly all auctions are held and some of the common auction words. These terms apply to public auctions, sealed bids, spot bids, and, in most instances, negotiated sales. You must know and understand these auction conditions before bidding at an auction.

Auction with Reserve

At any type of auction that has a reserve, the property or merchandise being offered for sale must be sold at or above a specific price. No merchandise may be sold for less than the reserve price. The term "reserve" means having a limitation. While many auctions are free-form events where the highest bidder walks away with the merchandise, an auction with reserve must reach that price point before the sale will go through.

Unfortunately, many government agencies demand that auctions for their property be held with the reserve clause. While some private auctioneers announce the reserve price before the merchandise is open to bids, government agencies typically keep the reserve price a secret. In the conditions of sale in many sealed-bid catalogs you are likely to find this exclusionary clause: "If none of the bids received represents a fair price commensurate with the market value of the property, an award is not made and the item or lot may be reoffered for sale at a later time." This is the standard clause, but the wording may vary.

At government public auctions, the agency will try to get as close to the fair-market value as possible for the merchandise or property. However, in most sealed-bid sales, very low prices have been accepted for equipment and property. This exclusionary clause only serves a public-relations function, to make the agency look good in the eyes of its peers, congress, consumer advocates, and the taxpayer.

However, at public auctions the government or private auctioneer is well aware of the reserve price and may withdraw the merchandise from the auction if he's not getting a high enough bid for it. The auctioneer will either say, "I can't accept that price," or he will just stop taking bids on that item and move on to the next lot up for sale. You will know then that the reserve price wasn't reached.

Experienced auction-goers don't like reserve auctions. Many auctioneers know this and try to persuade their clients to sell their merchandise without reserve. Publicizing an auction as being one with reserve can be the kiss of death for that auction. People enjoy the free-for-all that goes on at an auction. Government agencies should learn this lesson and change their routine!

Subject to . . .

This clause starts that way and usually becomes "subject to seller's confirmation." That is one way of saying auction with reserve. A clause with that wording gives the seller a chance to back out, if he doesn't like the final auction price for the merchandise. So, even if you make the highest bid and think you won the prize, the subject to seller's confirmation could cancel the sale.

Such cancellations are not common, though. Sellers frequently have cold feet about selling their merchandise or property at auction. Auctioneers have a tough time trying to convince their client, the seller, to avoid having a reserve auction. The compromise is that clause: "subject to seller's confirmation." However, when the auction is over, the seller has to pay the auctioneer for having held that auction. Most sellers, faced with having to pay a large fee on something that wasn't sold, permit the sale to go through if the property sold for a fair price. In this perspective, you can see how the "subject to" clause doesn't carry that much weight.

Another "subject to" clause you might read in the conditions of sale is "subject to court confirmation." These may appear at bankruptcy or estate auctions where the judge sometimes has to approve the sale before it's valid. Again, if a fair price was received at auction, then this clause loses its teeth. Auctioneers specializing in bankruptcy tend to agree that this clause is rarely enforced, even when property or merchandise is sold for a ridiculously low price.

For your safety, prevent disappointment and ask the auctioneer (or one of his assistants) about the "subject to" clauses after you've read the conditions of sale. He has a better grasp on the seller's or trustee's intentions with the property or merchandise. And he'll let you know if it is just a routine inclusion or a serious concern. Then, you can determine your course of action based on the auctioneer's advice.

Absolute Auction

This is also called an auction without reserve. It has no price limitations. The highest bidder wins. When an auction is truly an absolute auction, there could conceivably be only one bidder who shows up and who then becomes the successful buyer by offering a single dollar bill for the merchandise or property. Rare, indeed, but such instances have happened. A true absolute auction is a no-holds-barred event.

Absolute auctions test the auctioneer's marketing and promotional skills to get a crowd of buyers there. His bid-calling can be average and he could have a successful auction if buyers show up. If they don't, then the auction will disappoint the seller. The winning bidders, on the other hand, will often be ecstatic.

Most auctions down through the ages were conducted using the absolute method. At one time, someone must have gotten an incredible deal. That brought in the reserve clause. Absolute public auctions are the purest form of auctions. If properly promoted, the buyer, the seller, and the auctioneer know exactly what the merchandise or property is really worth at that point in time. A well-conducted auction also acts as an instant appraisal on the value of those goods or real estate.

Phony Absolute Auctions

When is an absolute auction not really an absolute auction? Some auctioneers advertise their auctions on their fliers and in newspaper ads with big, screaming headlines that say ABSOLUTE AUCTION*. The asterisk means there's a note in fine print, often at the bottom of the page, that modifies the absolute auctions. This is a cheesy way of advertising. It's misleading to the consumer and makes him or her think that the auction is really absolute when it's not. For instance, instead of the 32 properties being offered at absolute, only three may be. Some auctioneers also call these modified absolute auctions and start with a high minimum bid, such as $10,000, $25,000, $50,000, or more.

An auctioneer who's doing this is trying to serve two masters: the client (the seller) and the prospective buyer. Every auctioneer understands that the words "Absolute Auction" are magic. Indeed they are. They usually draw big crowds and are what auctions are all about: a circuslike atmosphere, showdowns between bidders, and enough hype to carry away by the bushel. (I would recommend that anyone and everyone visit a real absolute auction. Even if you are not bidding, that auction is going to be exciting to watch. It's like a horse race.)

However, the problem one finds at the root of modified or minimum-bid absolute auctions is a first-time seller's fears that his properties will go for a song. Nightmares of someone buying a house or office building for $25 probably keep him awake at night, especially when the real estate market is soft. Thus, auctioneers sometimes bite the bullet and hold this type of dishonest absolute auction in an effort to draw the crowds and appease the seller.

Some auctioneers argue among themselves about the virtue of calling the entire auction absolute when only a handful of properties are sold

absolute. Many feel a tad guilty about this practice but don't have an honest solution. Some rationalize that because those few properties are being sold absolute, it is then acceptable to call the entire auction absolute. While auctioneers have so far avoided being called on the carpet for deceptive advertising, all but the most uninformed auction-goers have been reading between the lines and know that these are not absolute auctions.

In that same kettle of fish you will find another semi-deceptive advertising technique. The auctioneer advertises that he is holding an absolute auction. However, at the bottom of the auction flier your eye might wander across this special notice: "All bidders must bring a $50,000 cashier's check as a deposit."

If you don't show a cashier's check for $50,000 at registration, you don't get a bidder's number. So, you are automatically eliminated from buying at that auction. Auctioneers explain this away by insisting it qualifies the buyers and keeps the riffraff out. With luck, buyers will catch on to this auctioneer's trick and stay away.

Minimum Bids

Many government agencies are fond of having a minimum bid at their public auctions. The minimum bid is the lowest acceptable bid allowed by the auctioneer. It is usually the first bid recognized by the auctioneer. Bids go up from there. If no one makes the minimum bid, then the auction of that merchandise or property ends.

Sometimes it's a guessing game as to what the minimum will be. Some sealed-bid auctions even omit the minimum bid price. Your guess is as good as mine.

Smart auctioneers may work with a minimum bid but will accept one lower. They know full well that once the auction gets going, they will get their minimum bid or more. Once the auction is under way, bidders jump in and drive the price higher. The auctioneer will get much more than his minimum bid if he works the crowd.

Government agencies should listen to the experts in the auction field. Minimum bids at auction are not the way to go. Bidders get turned off by them and stay away. Auctions can get exciting without the minimum bid requirement.

Upset Price

This is the price that must be reached before the sale is valid. An auction with reserve will have an upset price. Legally, the merchandise or property cannot be sold below this price. It mainly applies to foreclosed properties with mortgages or trust deeds and other liens. When a buyer purchases such a property, most of his bid will be used to cover the outstanding debts owed.

Knockdown

This refers to the conclusion of the sale. The auctioneer has assigned the item to the highest bidder. He does this most often by knocking down the hammer, from which this term comes. At those auctions where a gavel or hammer isn't used, the auctioneer just points to the bidder and says "Sold."

The knockdown price is what the bidder agrees to pay for the auctioned item. It might also be called the strike price, which is the same thing. The item is struck from the auctioneer's list. So, terms like "knockdown" or "struck off" refer to the end of the sale on that item.

Opening Bid

This is the first bid that is made by a bidder to the auctioneer. It is an offer to buy the merchandise at that price. The opening bid may be less than the minimum bid. It may be higher than the minimum asked for by the auctioneer.

The auctioneer may ask a certain price for an item being auctioned. Bidders don't have to take him up on that offer. A bidder may counter with a lower price and often does. But what starts the auction going is the first offer placed by the bidder.

Increments

These are the spreads between bids. The increment first depends upon the size of the property or merchandise being sold and later the reluctance between two or more bidders to go higher. Each bid on a vehicle may increase by $100 (a $100 increment) or it may only increase by $25 (a $25 increment).

Increments are decided between bidders and auctioneer during the course of the action. An auctioneer may speed up the auction by demanding increments of $100 a bid. If bidders drop out, he may drop the bid increases to $50 to keep more bidders active. In the beginning, the pace may be set by the auctioneer, but that doesn't mean the bidders can't change the pace by backing off on the bidding, forcing him to slow down the increment increases or even decrease the increments.

Hand Signals

While not actually a term that is necessarily spoken at an auction, these are used. It can be as simple as pointing to your bidder's card or waving it in the air to the auctioneer to show him you're making a bid or as complex as a slice across the air. When you wave your hand horizontally, palm down or up, to or from your chest, that generally means you want to cut the increments in half. Example: If the auctioneer is asking for a jump from $600 to $700 on a car, and you wave your hand horizontally, that means you're offering $650. (I recommend you also shout $650 to the auctioneer so there's no confusion about your bid.)

Hand signals are frequently used to place bids at an auction. Simply raising your hand when the auctioneer calls out a bid shows that you are accepting his bid. (If you want to stretch during the auction, then turn your bidder's number toward you so the auctioneer can't see it and doesn't confuse your stretch for a bid.)

Little things like scratching your nose, tugging your ear, and wiping your face are not usually accepted hand signals at most government auctions. They may be common at art auctions but certainly not at car auctions. If you're worried about the slim possibility of confusion, just put your bidder's number in your pocket or purse. Auctioneers who can't see a bidder's number won't accept the bid.

Preparation

The best strategy one can take to an auction is preparation. Every opportunity is yours if you're prepared! Most amateurs go to an auction without ten minutes of preparation behind them. No professional quarterback would show up on the playing field without hundreds of hours preparing himself for that moment. A professional dancer, accountant, attorney, or salesman wouldn't either. Auctioneers are professionals and most have hundreds, if not thousands, of hours of auction experience backing them up.

To succeed at an auction you must put in some preparation. The actual time spent bidding on an item might only be a few minutes. In those few minutes you are the master of your fate. Amateurs who aren't prepared generally lose to the dealer. Either the bidder will pay too much for the item or will drop out too soon. The amount of preparatory time you invest will determine the results.

So, how do you make the most of those few minutes? You do your homework. There are a few shortcuts, which we'll discuss shortly, but don't count on them for your continued success. This homework can be relatively simple and may only take a few hours.

Wholesale Price Versus Retail Price

One of your toughest decisions is determining *how much* you should bid on something. Each type of merchandise or property has a wholesale and retail value attached to it. For instance a 1982 Volvo station wagon might have a retail value of $2,700 and a wholesale value of $1,500. That's a big spread. If you pay $2,500, you haven't saved much. However, should you bid $1,400 at auction and win, there's something to cheer about. The same goes for antiques, cellular telephones, computers, fax machines, boats, airplanes, scrap metal, and so on.

You should always aim to buy something in the neighborhood of the wholesale price or less. If you want to resell your auction purchase, there has to be a profit margin. Dealers understand this principle. You have to carry with you the "profit margin potential" in your head at the auction. Ask this question: how much can I make on this if I sell it to someone? That's your rule of thumb.

Even if you decide to keep the merchandise, such as a car, you should always leave room for error. There may be repairs needed on the car or the house. Figure that into your calculations. Your safe bet is to buy at or below wholesale. As a general rule of thumb, the retail price is approximately *double* what wholesalers will pay for something.

What Do You Want to Buy at the Auction?

There are a few routes you can take in getting a price tag for what you are going to bid on at the auction. Unfortunately, too many amateurs arrive at the auction site without an exact idea of what they want to buy. As a result, most of the bidders are just spectators. *Before* you pursue this research, you have to determine what it is you wish to buy at the auction. Name it. Do you want a new television? A computer? A car? Boat? Whatever it is, find that out first. That's exactly what a professional will do. In his mind he knows exactly what he wants to buy before he arrives.

In Sections Two and Three of this book you will find out how to receive auction notices for personal property (merchandise) and real estate in advance. Once you have this information, your first step is to study it and determine if there is something you wish to buy. Contact the government agency or auction house, find out if it is still scheduled, and ask if the item you desire will be auctioned. Don't show up at the auction without having done these simple steps.

A Little Homework Before the Auction

After you have determined the item or items on which you are willing to make a bid, then you do a little homework. It doesn't have to be complicated or time-consuming. Your research can simply be a few telephone calls. Here are a few ways you can determine the final price you may wish to pay on something at the auction.

1. Find a dealer or wholesaler in the Yellow Pages of your telephone book. Contact him and ask what a similar item costs.

2. Visit a large newsstand or bookstore. Find the appropriate book or specialty magazine that has to do with your desired item. There are price books and magazines for computers, antiques, boats, and cars. Some will even give the wholesale and retail value.

3. Visit the library and ask for reference books that carry price lists. Many libraries have these books and booklets even if they are not available at your local bookstore or newsstand.

4. Contact a liquidator or repossession company. These can also be found in the Yellow Pages of your telephone book. Ask what a similar item is going for.

These are the basic preparatory steps you must take before attending an auction. To find a great bargain does require a little homework. The next chapter covers further research actions that you can take to become even more of a professional.

Meet the Colonel

Some auctioneers still carry the honorary title of colonel, particularly in rural areas. Most auctioneers consider this an anachronism, dating back to the Civil War. It was the colonels who held the auctions after the Union Armies swept into the Deep South and confiscated Rebel property. The tag stuck after the Civil War and into most of the twentieth century. That's because colonels, after having left the Army, continued in the auction business. These guys were our first government auctioneers. While today's auctioneer may call himself a colonel, it's just a title. Rarely, if ever, will he be active in the armed services.

Most auctioneers at government auctions are not likely to be government bureaucrats. They are usually private auctioneers hired by the government agency to dispose of their property. Private auctioneers are professionals. Many government agency auctioneers have been trained at auction schools across the country while others receive basic bid-calling skills locally. Some are very professional while others aren't.

Professional auctioneers have sweet voices and are fast talkers. To compete against them you must understand their techniques. They have their skills down pat and use them freely throughout the auction. Unless you know them, you'll fall for their tricks nearly every time.

Bid-Calling Techniques

The focus of any auction is the bid-calling. An auctioneer calls out the bids to the crowd in order to get bidders to pay more. He's gone to auction school to learn all the techniques that will be used in an auction. He practices his bid-calling while driving down the road, in the shower, and maybe in his sleep. The auctioneer you will meet at an auction will use everything he knows to get you to go a little higher.

An auctioneer is going to practice when he's not auctioning. He'll do mouth exercises and lung exercises. Auctioneers practice calling out numbers. He's performing even when he's not in front of a crowd.

The way he calls out the bids is the secret to his success as an auctioneer. Knowing his secrets can help you succeed at an auction. Here are a few of the bid-calling techniques any professional auctioneer is going to have in his bag of tricks.

1. *Speed.* He will set the pace of the auction in the way he calls out bids. An auctioneer will speed up the bid-calling to get you involved. When an auction has just two bidders left, he may slow it down in order to get them jumping to make their next bid. Watch how the auctioneer uses speed and timing against you. His goal is not just to sell you, but to sell you *fast* and then move on to the next item for sale.

2. *Enthusiasm.* The auctioneer is *selling* you something. He will be excited and exciting. His purpose is to get you excited. If you fall for that, you'll bid more often and higher. He might act the showman, singing, joking, and laughing. All this is being done to get you to bid higher. Don't forget that. If he's good, his ringmen will be too. They'll be hopping around the crowd drumming up bidders, getting you to bid higher than you want.

3. *Varying.* If he's a real pro, the auctioneer will vary his routine. He won't come across as monotonous. He'll change his voice tone or the volume, raising it or lowering it to nail down your bid. He may adjust the sound system to raise or lower the volume. The auctioneer will even throw in a fast "Sold!" to catch you off guard. At larger auctions you might see auctioneers rotating. A fresh and relaxed auctioneer is a way of varying. Or he might just stop things and let the silence sink in. He'll even start with a low bid sometimes to get the crowd pumped up. You'd be amazed how quickly the bids skyrocket.

4. *Spotlight.* He may focus on you if you're an active bidder. At the same time, he might ignore you if you start the bidding too low, pretend you don't exist. Don't take this personally, either way. It's just another technique. An auctioneer uses his position on stage to get active bidders making higher offers. He may act like a stand-up comedian and heckle bidders who make low bids. Some might call you by name or ask your name to get on your friendly side.

"Hey Joe, this car has your name on it!" The auctioneer even uses his hands as a spotlight, waving among the crowd to bring in bidders, if he sees the last two bidders dying down. Don't get pulled into the bidding by this technique. He's counting on one last entry into the horse race.

5. *Playing off Bidders.* This is an easily detected technique unless you happen to be one of the last two bidders. Auctioneers will play sides, favoring one and then the other. Or just favoring one guy and forcing your fellow bidder to compete against you. The trick is to ignore this tactic altogether and concentrate on the item being auctioned.

6. *Feature Selling.* A salesman uses this technique. He'll run through the features of the merchandise and then start listing off the benefits you receive when you buy it. The trick is to get you hungry and panting for the item.

These are your basic techniques. They are designed to throw off your thinking, give you a false sense of security, and make you feel excited about something that you wouldn't ordinarily buy. Remember, the auctioneer is first and foremost a salesman. He may not be a bad guy, but the auctioneer is your opponent at the auction. The other bidders want a good deal too. Auctioneers know this and use the crowd to their advantage, which is selling the auction inventory.

Bidding Strategies

To compete with the professional auctioneer, you must have your own bag of tricks. After all, auctioneers study marketing techniques to draw a crowd, practice their bid-calling, and even resort to a few shady methods that we'll cover in Chapter 7. Auctioneers are commissioned salespeople and they are very good at what they do. They use the auction method of marketing to get sales. Their income depends on it.

You deserve to have some weapons in your arsenal. This also works with any salesperson, whether you are buying a car, boat, or a house. Auctioneers probably won't like your using these techniques. But, do you want to make a friend at the auction or buy something for a great price? You decide.

Countering the Auctioneer's Enthusiasm

As the auctioneer will be doing his best to draw you into the bidding, you've got to maintain your composure. This may be easier said than done. To remain unemotional and distant may be too much for most people.

Appearances are everything, though. Just as the auctioneer is smiling, laughing, and joking, you've got to come across deadpan, possibly even rigid-looking. Unless, of course, you can keep your usual facial expression and not get carried away.

One thing you might try is facial exercises. They're popular with people who want to take the sag out of their double-chin. Try staring into a mirror. Just stare into the mirror with a deadpan expression. Or shake your head from side to side. Make a slight scowl. Look a little negative. You'll be happy you practiced this if some overzealous ringman comes to your side and tries to get you bidding on a beat-up utility truck.

Remember, the auctioneer is doing his lung and mouth exercises, practicing his bidding chant, and boning up on his techniques. You should, at least, practice a few minutes' worth of facial exercises before going to the auction. I admit this is a rotten thing to do, but it works.

Low Bids

Auctioneers hate wise guys. They especially loathe bidders who start auctions with low bids. These are called joke bids. Mark Lewis made a joke bid of $15 on a $50,000 boat and won. So, don't tell me it doesn't work.

Low bids slow the auction down and throw off the auctioneer's pace. Use discretion with this technique. If you're the one continually starting each item off with a low bid, the auctioneer will turn the spotlight on you. Then, you'll be the joke.

Because of this possibility, make a low bid once or, at most, twice during the course of the auction. The best time to start things off with a low bid is at the very beginning of the auction. That usually catches people off guard. However, if junk is being sold as the first item at auction, which is often the case, then wait until the first desirable merchandise appears. Failing that, wait until the very end of the auction; by then, most people will have left and a low bid won't be so hard to digest.

Set Your Limit

Many bidders are doing this more often: setting a limit on how high they're willing to go to buy something. Let's say you want to buy that 1989 Cadillac. A few others might join in and have some say in the matter. However, if you've appraised it correctly, as described earlier, you probably won't pay more than $9,200, depending on its condition.

The way to prevent the auctioneer from getting you carried away is to *write it down*. Don't just make a mental note of it. That may or may not work depending on the ferocity of the bidding war on that car. If you've written it down, circled it, and put exclamation marks next to it, you still might go beyond that limit. Don't!

An auctioneer's success depends almost entirely on his stirring up the crowd and creating auction fever. (Remember the Dutch tulip bulbs and "Emperor" Pertinax!) Don't lose your head in the middle of bidding. The auctioneer is counting on your getting carried away. He may even joke about your set limit and say something like "too much for you?"

Whatever you do, accurately estimate your bidding limit, write the limit down, and don't go beyond it. Use the auction flier, the conditions of sale, the auction catalog, an index card, or just write it on the palm of your hand, but *do* write it down. Ignore the comments of other bidders, the auctioneer, the ringmen, or even your friends. Going past the set limit is probably just going to lead to trouble.

Shortcut Appraisals

OK, but what if my set limit is too low? More often than not, it's too high. But here's a preventive measure for you. This technique works in your favor and against the professionals in attendance.

At many car auctions, you're going to find a dealer or two buying up cars for his used car lot. He may send a buyer or some other representative. You will also see such professionals at other types of auctions, especially bankruptcy auctions. Look around the crowd. Spot the iron-jawed, reptilian-eyed gentleman with the cellular phone and the clipboard with a copy of the automobile blue book in his hip pocket. Alright, so he might not have a cellular phone and clipboard. That's the pro.

The same goes for the neatly dressed woman with the sharp pencil and auction catalog. She will be making notes beside each item or writing down knockdown prices. Watch out when no one is looking and she walks off with 15 typewriters at $25 each. This is a dealer and she's there to buy something for resale.

While you're doing the inspection rounds, talk it up. Make a few friends. Those who aren't talkative and fit the above description are probably professionals. Ask them what a particular item is worth. They'll offer an opinion.

Now, if you haven't done your homework, you may have to rely on that pro's opinion. It may be accurate or not. If you're not sure, ask another one who fits the bill. Compare the two. Ask what's wrong with the merchandise. He might say: "It's a diesel" or "Take a look at the tailpipe." That may be enough to give you a set limit. It's unreliable, but it's the best advice available for the lazy.

Piggybacking the Professional

Going head to head with a dealer can be fun. Or dangerous. For those who relish swan diving off cliffs or rock climbing, they will especially enjoy bidding against dealers. It's called piggybacking. You go along for the ride and then hop over your mount at the last moment to win the race.

You tag along next to the pro throughout the bidding and don't open your mouth. Usually, he may only have one competitor. As soon as the person drops out, wait until the auctioneer says "going once, going twice . . ." At that very moment, jump in and increase the bid by a small amount. It could be a few dollars or a hundred, depending on the size of that bid. The pro might raise your bid a bit. You tag along and increase his.

Auctioneers like it since they get more money. Professionals don't since they may have planned to resell the vehicle on their used car lot for a healthy profit margin. Watch out for the vengeful professional who catches onto this. You may be the one stuck with something you've overpaid for. Remember to stick to your set limit while doing the piggyback.

Messing Around with Increases

An auctioneer who's read this far is going to throw up his hands at this point and say something like: "You know, it's books like these that give me high blood pressure." This next technique is guaranteed to drive auctioneers absolutely up the wall.

During the auction the colonel is going to try to control the pace of the bidding. He'll do that by increasing bids at the bracket level he wants: $50 increments, $100 increments, or more. That doesn't mean *you* have to go along with this.

If he asks for $600, do a horizontal cutting motion with your hand. (Try it—place your palm down and horizontally against your breastbone, make a cutting motion outwardly in front of you.) While doing that say $550. Instead of going up the $100 he wants, make a $50 increase.

Do not make a smaller increase than half the auctioneer's expected increase. He might catch on to this and ignore your bid. Or refuse it. If you stay in the bidding, continue doing this. Should he accept the $50 incremental pace, cut that in half with your next bid. It slows down the auction pace. The auctioneer loses a little control.

Just as the bidding is winding down, you can start making even smaller increases, say $5 bids or $1 bids. This aggravates not only the auctioneer but the other bidder as well. It only works when there are only two bidders left. Otherwise, with more than two bidders, you risk being ignored. You could try it with more than two bidders as the bidding is reaching a peak, but don't count on getting acceptance of your bid. Wait until it's just you and another. Then try it. The other bidder catches on too and this really drives the auctioneers crazy.

Bid Abstracts

At least two government agencies will provide you with or sell you the results of the previous sealed-bid auction they held. This is incredible! Imagine how it must be to get the price list of what others paid on merchandise.

Where this is available, use it. You find out before you place your bid an approximate price you should offer, based on past auctions. Of course, the more thorough you are with these, compiling files as you go along, the more accurate your bids will be and the greater your chances of success.

Bid abstracts are generally only good for sealed-bid auctions. The only problem you may encounter is the diverse amount of merchandise and equipment offered at auctions. It varies frequently, so you have to stay on top of it. If you build up a good filing system and maintain accurate records, you'll soon have huge profits rolling in. Only in America!

Is It Worth Staying For?

Auctioneers use different methods in selling their inventory. Most will start with junk at the beginning and work up from there, either selling the luxury items in the middle or at the end of the auction. Some vary this and auction great things at the beginning and work down from there. Each auctioneer has his own pattern of operating.

Watch for what comes up at the beginning of the auction. Follow the trail the auctioneer is pursuing. He generally lines up his auction route with tags on the merchandise. The lower-numbered tags are usually the first ones up for auction. The higher ones are left for last.

See how the bidding goes and how many show up, leave early, arrive late, or stay because of the crowd's excitement. Judge accordingly whether or not you think there are going to be good prices found at this auction. Usually, there are a few auctions going on the same day in your area, particularly if you live in a big city. Prepare yourself for a bad auction by having a back-up in case the one you are attending was too well promoted and is rife with dealers and other professionals. The disadvantage is that the grass may not be greener on the other side.

If you do stay, and bidding is fast and furious, wait until the middle. There's a die-down period, usually before some spectacular merchandise is auctioned. That's when you might step in and find a very good deal. However, if it's not on your list and you haven't appraised it to your satisfaction, don't bid. If you find the bidding on that merchandise is slowing down, then step in at the very end of the bidding. Slow the auction down by making small incremental increases. That often works and could get you a surprise purchase.

Inspection

No matter how well your preappraisal on the price was done, if the merchandise isn't up to snuff, you could still buy a lemon. Professionals know the flaws in the merchandise or property. That sets them apart from the novices. Auctioneers may snidely smirk to themselves on how you're sticking to your set limit, only to later discover that you just bought a car without a radiator . . . or worse! Remember, at auction you are buying "as is, where is."

Your best counter to this is to bring along a professional. It may cost you a few dollars more, but it will save you a terrible headache if your purchase later smells like a skunk. There is recourse, as found in Chapter 7, but save the trouble in advance by being prepared.

A car mechanic might hire himself out for $50 or less to meet you at the auction and give you a hand on pricing and expected performance of your heart's desire. Other professionals do hire themselves out for appraisals and inspections. At a real estate auction it might be helpful to bring your attorney along. Of course, that costs more and he may spend half his time trying to talk you out of the property, but his knowledge, again, could save you from sleepless nights.

Compete with the professionals by hiring a professional to assist in the inspection and appraisal. If you're going to save $1,000 or more on a $5,000 car, why not invest up to $100 to make the right decision? Going alone to auctions where much is at stake is nuts. Bring along a professional, have him do the homework for you in advance, and really come prepared. You can and will do well at auctions. You'll find great bargains. Be sure you actually use the professional's advice.

An Auctioneer's Secret Code Words

One insider's tip that can also help you with appraisals is the code word. Most auctioneers use one kind or another. Merchandise is tagged by numbers. Above or below those numbers, or perhaps on the flip side of the tag, you will find three letters. Those three letters represent the auctioneer's estimate of what that merchandise or equipment will bring at auction. Auctioneers frequently wear the appraisal hat and judge well what an item should sell for. Those letters form a code that translates into dollar amounts. The auctioneer uses this code to instantly know where he expects his bidding to go. At the same time he keeps this a secret from the bidders.

Some of the cryptic codes that have been cracked so far are these: BLACKSMITH, BLACK HORSE, and GOLD BUYS IT. Here's what those letters represent:

```
B - L - A - C - K   S - M - I - T - H
1   2   3   4   5   6   7   8   9   0
```

```
B - L - A - C - K   H - O - R - S - E
1   2   3   4   5   6   7   8   9   0
```

```
G - O - L - D   B - U - Y - S   I - T
1   2   3   4   5   6   7   8   9   0
```

A tag might read BTT, which means that the auctioneer thinks the item should bring home $500. The problem, as you may have noticed, is *which* code word or phrase is the auctioneer using. BTT translates into $500 if he's using GOLD BUYS IT or it could be $199 if the auctioneer prefers BLACKSMITH.

The riddle to the puzzle is to find a number of these tags, jot down the code letters and do an instant appraisal yourself. You'll figure out which code he's using after a few wrong guesses. Armed with these three codes, see which tag has a letter missing from the other word or phrase. There are no G's in either BLACK HORSE or BLACKSMITH. Similarly, M won't appear in GOLD BUYS IT or BLACK HORSE. And the R is missing in both BLACKSMITH and GOLD BUYS IT.

Also, auctioneers will frequently round off the appraisal to the nearest hundred or with a zero digit, so a quick way is to look at the last letter. H means BLACKSMITH. E tells you it's BLACK HORSE. T is GOLD BUYS IT.

Of course, auctioneers may change their coding now that the secret is out. The way to crack the code is by knowing they will use a ten letter word that has no repeating letter. Let's see what they come up with next.

Auctioneer's Delight

What a pleasure it is for the auctioneer to see newcomers. He loves them. Not only does his crowd grow larger, but since you're new to the game, you stand a great chance of being an easy mark. After all, who'd ever think you carefully investigated the item you're going to bid on, let alone knew a great deal about it before coming to the auction. Heck! You're a sheep thrown to a hungry wolf when you show up at your first auction.

It's a great place. There are some interesting characters walking around. Plenty of excitement. A beautiful sunny day. And oh boy! There's that BMW you always wanted to buy. Well, why not? Let's just see if I can beat everybody else to it!

Don't! That's right, don't. Don't even think of buying at your first auction. Yes, there is such a thing as beginner's luck. And you have about as much chance of scoring the big kill at your very first auction as you do of hitting a home run in the World Series or throwing a winning touchdown in the Super Bowl.

Not only is the auctioneer counting on you to make a complete and utter fool of yourself at your very first auction, but the dealers and professionals see a good story to tell back at the office. It's written all over your face. The last thing you want to do is jump into the heat of bidding on your first time up. Now, if you happen to be only one of two or three bidders who show up, and there's a ton of available auction merchandise, sure go ahead . . . but only after the others have cleaned up and gone home.

I can't recommend highly enough that you go to a few auctions and just watch. Take a look. Restrain yourself. Be a spectator. If you want to get your feet wet, make a joke bid. Toss in a $100 offer on a $4,000 car. See if it gets accepted. But first make sure that the $4,000 car has an engine!

Your best course of action is to visit several different auctions, take notes, talk with professionals, and watch how various bidders find great bargains or overpay beyond belief. When you do get around to making your first buy at auction, you'll have learned from the mistakes and successes of others. It might still be an enervating experience, but you will have greatly improved your chances of success.

The next chapter will give you professional inside advice on how to become an expert auction participant. What you have just learned are the basics, and a few advanced skills, on how to succeed at an auction. The rules that follow are ironclad. If you do wish to succeed at an auction, whether it is a government auction or held for the government by a private auctioneer, follow the golden rules.

Golden Rules for Auction Participation

Any auction-goer who hopes to succeed will stick to these rules. They are brief reminders and a summary of what you have read in the first three chapters of this book. They weren't dreamt up in the middle of a sleepless night. These are based on interviews with hundreds of auctioneers and actual experience at auction. Stick to these rules and you should succeed. Ignore them and expect to overpay at auction.

1. *Never permit yourself to get auction fever.* This can be as simple as allowing yourself to get stuck on any one particular item and beating other bidders to death just so you can buy it. Inevitably, you will overpay. Go find a few tulips like the Dutch did. Look what it did to them.

2. *Always inspect the merchandise or property before making a bid.* You never know what it is you are buying until you've thoroughly inspected the auction item. An inspection is not a quick once-over, but a *full* investigation.

3. *Always appraise the merchandise or property before making a bid.* Find something of comparable value and use that as your price guide. Similarly, when trying to buy something, locate an equivalent piece of equipment, merchandise, or real estate.

4. *Always use a professional to assist you.* Until you, yourself, really become adept at quickly estimating the true resale value of an auction item, find someone who can. There are many different ways to do this. Some are covered in the next chapter, others were covered earlier.

5. *Never go beyond your set limit.* By strictly following the first four rules, you shouldn't

have a problem with this. Just in case, though, write your set limit down on a piece of paper. Use the conditions of sale, an auction flier, the auction catalog, scrap paper, or an index card. Just write it down before jumping into the bidding.

6. *Always read the conditions of sale before attending the auction.* You will find these in the auction flier or the catalog. If you don't find them there, call the auctioneer or government agency. Find out the required method of payment for your purchase, when payment in full is expected, and when you must remove or take possession of the property or merchandise.

7. *Always go to at least one auction before making your first purchase.* Preferably, you will visit several auctions as a spectator. Take notes and watch the bidders. Strike up conversations with the professionals and dealers. Pay attention to how they walk off with the bargains.

8. *Never make a bid at your first auction.* This is different from the previous rule. Making a bid and buying something are worlds apart. If you must make a bid, make one so low that you really don't intend to honor it. Place the bid at the very beginning of the auction and then drop out. It's not really making a bid, since you practically have no chance of actually buying the merchandise. Still I don't recommend it.

9. *Always ask questions if you are not sure about something.* Ask questions when you first receive an auction flier. Ask professionals at the auction. Ask the auctioneer. Ask your friends *only* IF they are well versed in the auction item and not just imagined experts. Find out what specialized words mean if you're not sure. Ask why that guy bought the copy machine for $2,500. Don't be shy.

10. *Never forget that the auctioneer is a salesman.* The auctioneer will use every trick he can to get bidders to pay more than the appraised value of something. That's his job. He uses professional techniques. He's not a bad guy, but his business is based entirely on commissions. The more you pay, the more he gets. Use every technique discussed thus far to save money.

11. *Never forget that you will need to take your shopping home with you.* After the auction, you have to take possession or move it. Read Chapter 8 for details.

4

Scoring the Big Hit

★★★

Being a professional means having the tools and mind-set of someone who is going to make a living at it. Professionals are not born into a career, but instead create one. They do this by hard work and acquiring specialized knowledge. Take a look at your current job. You succeed at it to the degree that you control these factors: hard work and specialized skills. The more you know and the better you apply it determines your success.

This chapter is designed to upgrade your skill when participating in an auction. In the previous chapters you tasted the flavor of auctions and saw that they require a little advance work. Most auction-goers will find that knowledge quite useful and should be capable of locating numerous bargains at many auctions. Good value is the name of the game. As auctioneers like to say, "You might not find a steal, but you ought to find a good deal at auction."

This chapter should give you the professional skills necessary to find more than just a good deal. At many auctions held around the United States, you can find a steal. It is possible, though not always likely. Finding the auction giveaway requires some hard work, good timing, and some luck. Even dealers and other professionals can get burned every now and then.

You won't need five to seven years of college, as you would to become a doctor or attorney. And you are not required to do killer double session exercise workouts daily as you would to play professional sports. You will need to prepare yourself in much the same way many professionals do when practicing their skills.

The following advice, tips, and references can be pursued to a greater or lesser degree, depending on whether you want to make a career of this, add a healthy spare-time income, or just plain find a succession of great bargains. Generally, it is the professional who finds repeat bargains. More often than not, it is the professional who "lucks" into an auction giveaway.

Dealers do their homework before going to an auction because their livelihood depends on it. How can a used car lot mark up vehicles for a profit if they don't first buy cars at bargain prices? The same holds true for army & navy stores, liquidators, and thousands of businesses across America. Professional auction-goers can be one-man shops or large, going concerns.

Practically anything you could buy in a department store is available at auction, including the real estate on which that department store stands. In fact, many of the goods you have already purchased brand-new, and at retail prices, passed through one or more auctions on their way to your home. Now, you can cut out the middleman on many of your purchases and buy at or below wholesale prices.

Leasing Companies

A repossession man, whose entire business consisted of picking up leased equipment on which companies had defaulted, once told me I should write a book on leasing companies. He told me it would be only two words long: don't lease!

Right now, as the economic picture continues to sour, and to the end of the twentieth century, businessmen should not have to lease. At auctions across America great deals can be found on previously used office equipment, making leasing unnecessary. This not only includes common equipment most businesses need, such as fax machines, computers, and photocopiers, but also specialized and unusual fixtures, furnishings, material, and gear.

If you want to get a pulse on the business climate, just call a few repo houses or liquidators, or attend an auction. They're a more reliable barometer than volumes of "expert studies" by ivory tower economists. Yesterday's successful business concern could be tomorrow's featured auction prize.

Dealers, Wholesalers, Professionals

Carpenters have their own tools. So do medical doctors. It is the same with plumbers and attorneys. Auto mechanics, dentists, chiropractors, hydrotherapists, and even accountants have specialized tools to achieve a result. Customers and clients go to them because they can deliver a specific result. Thus they get paid.

Amateurs don't get paid. They fiddle around, trying first this and then that. Put a group of amateurs in the same auction arena with a few professionals and look at who gets the bargains. And who overpays.

Professionals succeed because they have tools. Call them weapons if you like, since bidding at an auction is almost like going into battle if the bidding gets fierce. Their weapon is information. This is the information age. Those with the best information, the latest scoop, and the fastest, most

efficient utilization of that data are the big winners.

Reference Guides and Price Lists

Professionals refer to manuals, directories, reference guides, price lists, trade journals, and so forth before going to an auction. You should too. To compete on their level requires the use of specialty reference books. Each subject has its own definitive books, or pricing guides, on the subject. For example, because the automotive resale industry is enormous, there are many books quoting current wholesale and retail values of cars. Dealers and other buyers of numerous cars for resale keep the *National Automobile Dealer Association* (NADA) Blue Book closer to them than their wives.

In the next few pages, you will find examples of some definitive pricing guides and directories for many important specialties. Professionals use them. You should too. Many can be expensive investments. For those who are merely curious about these reference guides, visit your local library or call a professional on a specific price quote.

Vehicles

The most frequently used guide in appraising car values is the *National Automobile Dealer Association* (NADA) *Used Car Guide.* They have many editions; however, their most popular is the Yellow Book. Dealers get the Blue Book. Amazingly, the Yellow Book gives you price quotes on surveyed prices of dealerships around the country. The Blue Book does the same survey, but instead has wholesale price lists that are based on car auctions. It's amazing the way dealers trust auctions to set their prices!

The NADA books are used primarily by used car dealers, new car dealers (for trade-in values), banks and finance companies (to determine the amount to loan you), wholesalers (who buy fleets to resell), and other professionals involved in the secondary market. Annual subscriptions are about the cost of a few magazine subscriptions. However, many bookstores and newsstands around the country have begun carrying the Yellow Book. If you just want a single issue, pick one up at a major bookstore. It retails for about $9.95 and comes out monthly.

For a subscription, contact:

National Automobile Dealers Used Car
Guide Company
8400 Westpark Drive
McLean, Virginia 22102-9985
Telephone: (703) 821-7193
Fax: (703) 821-7269
Toll-Free: (800) 544-6232

Yellow Book: $43/ Monthly subscription
for 1 year
Blue Book: $44/ Weekly subscription for 1 year

These books give you late-model automobile prices. Regional editions are published through-out the country, so order the correct regional edition for your local area *or* the region where you will be doing your buying.

You may want the other NADA guides available for different types of vehicles. There are quite a few to choose from.

Older Car Guide (*for Model Years 1972–1981*)	$40 annual subscription with updates
Motorcycle Guide (includes ATVs, snowmobiles, and personal watercraft)	$45 annual subscription with updates
Recreational Guide	$85 annual subscription with updates
Small Boat Guide	$85 annual subscription with updates
Large Boat Guide	$60 annual subscription with updates
Mobile Home Guide	$85 annual subscription with updates

(NOTE: Subscription prices for these books are subject to change.)

Another recognized authority on automotive price lists is MacLean Hunter Market Reports, Inc. They have published since 1911 and are just as reliable. Their used car guide is the Automobile Red Book. It is also published in regional editions and comes out eight times per year.

For a subscription, contact:

MacLean Hunter Market Reports, Inc.
29 N. Wacker Drive
Chicago, Illinois 60606
Telephone: (312) 726-2802
Fax: (312) 726-4103
Toll Free: (800) 621-9907

They offer these publications for subscription:

Automobile Red Book	$49.50 annual subscription with updates
Older Car Red Book (*Model Years Prior to 1981*)	$68 annual subscription with updates
Motorcycle Red Book	$54.50 annual subscription with update
Recreational Vehicle Blue Book	$110 annual subscription with update
Farm Tractor Blue Book	$98 annual subscription with update
Van Conversion Blue Book	$60 annual subscription with updates
Truck Blue Book	$120 annual subscription with updates

(REMINDER: Subscription prices are subject to change.)

Cheaper and probably less reliably surveyed price lists are available at newsstands, bookstores, or by subscription. One magazine company has wholesale and retail price lists for different vehicles. They look like ordinary magazines and carry advertisements: Pace Buyer's Guides.

For subscription information, write to:

Pace Publications, Inc.
1020 North Broadway
Suite 111
Milwaukee, WI 53202

Their publications include:

Used Car Prices (includes trucks, vans, 4 × 4s)
New Car Prices (includes import cars)
New & Used Foreign Car Prices
Truck and Van Prices
Single copies can be purchased for $4.95, plus shipping and handling ($2.00)
Annual subscriptions are $21.95 (shipping free)
Annual subscriptions come out six or seven times per year depending on which publication you order.
(Remember, prices are subject to change.)

Computers

Computers are a popular item at auction. Unfortunately, there are so many different manufacturers, a variety of components from which to choose, and rapid technical developments. Computers are in a fast-changing world, apart from any other type of equipment.

With the advent of the computer's popularity has grown a cult of computer buffs. Those wishing to enter this world had better familiarize themselves with the basics of that language before participating at those auctions. Of course, if you don't do that, then bring along a computer whiz kid to advise you at the auction.

In any major bookstore or on any newsstand you will find a good-size rack of computer magazines. When flipping through those magazines make yourself conversant with the equipment: know its function and capabilities. Hundreds of computer retail stores have sprouted up around the country and carry books on the subject, as do office supply stores and even stationery stores. If you want to find out about computers, there are many books to choose from.

Price lists can be found in many computer magazines. Again, expect retail prices to be about double what wholesalers would pay. Computer devotees in some instances can lead you to accurate price estimates.

Professionals rely on a sourcebook of prices, just as car dealers do with NADA or MacLean Hunter. Another company has a similar subscription offer available to the trade and general public: Sybex Association of Computer Dealers. For a subscription, contact:

Sybex Association of Computer Dealers
15400 Knoll Trail
Suite 500
Dallas, Texas 75248
Telephone: (214) 233-5131
Fax: (214) 233-8269
Toll-Free: (800) 322-3241

They have a variety of subscription offers, depending on your demand for frequency and speed of delivery.

COMPUTER HOTLINES ANNUAL SUBSCRIPTION FEE

Weekly edition:	$119 sent First Class Mail
	$69 sent Third Class Mail
Monthly edition:	$39 sent First Class Mail
	$29 sent Third Class Mail

Also, because of the large demand for telephone equipment, they have available a telecommunications price list. It covers nearly everything in that field.

TELECOMMUNICATIONS GEAR (MONTHLY ONLY)
$49/annual subscription sent First Class Mail
$39/annual subscription sent Third Class Mail

Electronics

Many auctions have a variety of electronic gear available for sale. Some are inexpensive and may be worth a capricious fling, while others could cost a bundle and require research. It is not uncommon to find a good radio at police auctions for $1, but think again before going into a heated bidding war over a 32-track tape studio without first knowing what it's worth.

Electronics and related equipment each have specialized magazines where you can do some comparison shopping. Serious buyers of expensive equipment or any equipment in volume should first consult the trade directories.

One recommended research firm is Orion Research Corporation, located in Colorado. They also publish a computer price book, just as Sybex does.

For price guides, contact:

Orion Research Corporation
1315 Main Avenue
Suite 230
Durango, CO 81301
Telephone: (303) 247-8855
Fax: (303) 247-9783

These are the various publications they offer.

1. *Audio Blue Book.* Lists 33,000 products from over 144 manufacturers. Hardcover, 672 pages. Lists the following products: cassettes, compacts, 8-track and 4-track cartridges, digital audio discs, equalizers, integrated amplifiers, mixing boards, mobile citizen bands, pre-amplifiers, power amplifiers, raw speakers, receivers, reel-to-reels, scanners, signal processors, speakers, turntables, tuners, and walkie-talkies.
   Annual Edition: $149

2. *Camera Blue Book.* Lists 14,750 products from over 400 manufacturers. Hardcover, 290 pages. Lists nearly every item in the camera field including 35mm cameras, lenses, projectors, slide viewers, single 8 movie cameras, super 8 movie cameras, and 36mm movie cameras.
   Annual Edition: $129

3. *Car Stereo Blue Book.* Lists 9,000 products from over 200 manufacturers. Hardcover, 190 pages. Lists car cassettes, car digital audio disc players, car power amplifiers, car equalizers, and car speakers.
   Annual Edition: $79

4. *Guitar and Musical Instruments Blue Book.* Lists 26,000 products from over 500 manufacturers. Hardcover, 450 pages. Lists accordions, banjos, brass, winds, cellos, cymbals, drums, dulcimers, electric guitars, acoustic guitars, harps, keyboards, mandolins, marimbas, synthesizers, violins, woodwinds, and xylophones.
   Annual Edition: $129

5. *Professional Sound Blue Book.* Lists 12,000 products from over 500 manufacturers. Hardcover, 200 pages. Lists all professional sound equipment.
   Annual Edition: $99

6. *Video and Television Blue Book.* Lists 14,000 video products from over 450 manufacturers. Hardcover, 384 pages. Lists include over 8,000 televisions, broadcast cameras, professional recorders, VHS recorders, camcorders, large screen projectors, and more.
   Annual Edition: $129

7. *Office Equipment Blue Book.* Lists all manufacturers of cellular phones, fax machines, copiers, and typewriters.
   Annual Edition: $99

8. *Computer Blue Book.* Lists all computer manufacturers. Lists components including modems, disks, expansion ports, expansion memory, graphics, monitors, mouses, printers, scanners, terminals, work stations, and anything that has to do with a computer.
   Annual Edition: $120

This publishing company has various on-going specials of which you can take advantage. Prices are always subject to change. There is also a $3–$5 shipping and handling charge for each publication.

Antiques and Collectibles

Many people are fond of going to antique and collectible auctions. These are a throwback to the ancient Roman household auctions like the one conducted by Emperor Caligula. Many estate auctions sell antiques and other collectibles. Occasionally, you'll find such goods at bankruptcy auctions and U.S. Marshals Service auctions; businessmen and drug dealers alike have been found to be collectors.

There are several books sold in major bookstores that you may find useful in appraising collectibles. The definitive book on the subject is *Kovel's Antique and Collectible Price List* (Crown Publishers, New York), which is published annually, containing over 50,000 appraiser-approved prices. A comparable book is *Schroeder's Antique Price Guide* (Collector's Books, Kentucky), which also has annual editions.

Art

Art has been a mainstay at auctions for centuries, going back to Sotheby's and Christie's in 18th-century England and even earlier with the Roman household auctions, where art was a highly admired item. There are numerous books on art in any fine art bookstore or library.

Many collectors subscribe to *Art & Auction* magazine, which is published monthly. Its special edition, the annual International Directory, sells for $12 and is packed with art auction houses from around the world. The magazine is published monthly (11 issues) and the subscription price is $42.

For a subscription, contact:

Art & Auction
P.O. Box 11350
Des Moines, IA 50347-1350
Telephone: (800) 777-8718

Jewelry

Across the world, jewelry has always been a favorite among women, as well as men hoping to win over women. A large number of auctions throughout the country include jewelry. These include police auctions in major cities, private auction companies selling for the U.S. Marshals Service, and estate auctions.

Jewelry is difficult and complex to appraise. There isn't a single volume devoted to pricing the vast array of jewelry. Each jewelry designer creates his own style, which has a nebulous worth. The prestigious jewelers of New York City's Fifth Avenue and Beverly Hills' Rodeo Drive set prices based entirely on what they think customers will pay.

Jewelry, then, has an inherent value, depending on which stone, its size, clarity, color, etc. Gem prices are usually controlled first by cartels and then by large dealers. All this makes it extremely difficult to compete against dealers.

It is a subject that can be learned. You can get started with this book: *Gems and Jewelry Appraising: Techniques of Professional Practice* by Anna M. Miller, Van Nostrand Reinhold (New York).

As for resale value, if you plan on purchasing for investment, contact your local pawnshop (yes, the store with the three balls) and get the pawnbroker's opinion. His estimate is likely to be the worst return you can get for the item. So, if you buy the item for what he would pay, then you're probably doing alright. One drawback is he may want to see the item before he gives his opinion. Try showing him a picture of the piece from the auction catalog.

One word of advice on jewelry auctions: Don't compete against professionals at these sales unless you carefully use the piggybacking technique mentioned in the last chapter. Jewelry dealers are a closed society.

Coins

Estate sales, police auctions, Marshals Service auctions, and private auctions sell coins to collectors, dealers, and the curious. If you are an avid collector you should go to these auctions. Should you want to create a coin collection, try going to an auction.

There are numerous coin magazines in bookstores and newsstands that can be useful. Among them are:

Coinage Magazine
2660 E. Main Street
Ventura, CA 93003

Coin World
P.O. Box 150
Sidney, OH 45365

Coin Magazine
700 E. State Street
Iola, WI 54990

The Numismatist
818 N. Cascade Avenue
Colorado Springs, CO 80903
(This is published monthly by the American Numismatic Association.)

The definitive price guide used by many collectors and dealers is the *Handbook of United States Coins* (Western Publishing Company, Racine, Wisconsin). It is published annually in paperback. This book contains mint records and prices paid by dealers for all U.S. coins from 1616 to the present year. If unavailable from your local bookstore, order directly by writing to: Western Publishing Company, 1220 Mound Avenue, Racine, Wisconsin 53404. Do not confuse this book with another of their publications, which gives current retail prices: *A Guidebook of United States Coins.* You want the dealer edition (the Handbook).

Real Estate

Real estate auctions are growing faster than any other segment of the auction industry. They are popular for bidders, profitable for auctioneers, and speedy for sellers. Because of this you will see a boom in real estate auctions throughout the rest of this century. Better get prepared.

There are many ways to appraise real estate. Unfortunately, none of them have pinpoint accuracy when it comes to real estate auctions. Property that has sat unsold for several months is suddenly sold ... sometimes at a price buyers weren't biting on earlier. The auction itself determines the fair-market value of something. Fair-market value is nothing more mysterious then the price on which the buyer and seller agree to settle.

So, how *do* you estimate what you will bid at a real estate auction? The professional method is to do the following:

1. Contact the county property appraiser's office.

2. Find out what the selling price was of three comparable homes.

3. Evaluate when they were sold, the neighborhoods in which they sold, the size of the property, and its square footage. Deduct an appropriate percentage of cost using the above factors as a guideline. (For instance, you may wish to subtract 10% of the price if the property is 10% smaller, etc.)

4. Add up the three comparable sale prices. (Example: $100,000 + $124,000 + $97,000 equals $321,000.)

5. Divide this by three. (Using the above example: $321,000 divided by 3 equals $107,000.)

6. This will give you a set limit to work with at an auction. If you can pay less, great!

Of course, all this gets thrown out the window when an auction takes place. Others might not have appraised properly. Or, often, someone will "just die if they can't have that property" and start a ridiculous bidding war over it.

Another factor is that there may be liens on the property that require it be sold at a price above your set limit. Move on. There are tens of thousands of homes and other real estate across America begging to be bought.

Inspection

If you are going to succeed professionally at an auction, you must be extremely capable when inspecting the merchandise or property. Yes, you may occasionally get lucky and buy something decent inexpensively without a thorough inspection. But consistency is the key to being a professional. Just as you might throw a perfect spiral pass with a football to a friend once in a while, the professional will do it nearly every time.

Thorough and complete inspections give you that perfect spiral football throw 90% of the time. Even if you've appraised the equipment or property accurately, your auction purchase can still explode in your face when a poor inspection has been done. Inspections and appraisals go hand in hand. One can not be done without the other. They never are.

The two most common purchases at government auctions are vehicles and real estate. The government has a lifetime supply of both for every reader of this book. There are not likely to be shortages, either, in the distant future.

Experts in other fields abound. The Yellow Pages in your telephone book can lead you to excellent sources of inspection information. For example, do you want to buy an airplane at auction? Call a local executive airport and ask questions about airplanes. Find out what you should look for. The same holds true for jewelry, stereos, computers, boats, and other possible auction merchandise. Use the inspection checklists in the following sections as a guideline for other equipment and merchandise.

Automobiles

Dealers might have their mechanics go to the pre-auction vehicle inspections. You should too. Or you can hire one to come along with you only to the inspection if you want to save money or if you want to go alone to the auction.

Government agencies don't make it easy to do a proper inspection. Someday, they'll wise up and permit test drives. Automobile dealer auctions routinely use them and cars can be again put up for auction should the buyer find the vehicle unsatisfactory. Government auctions force bidders to buy as is, where is. Police auctions are worse. At those you can't even open the door to look inside—you have to hire a locksmith after you make the purchase to make you a key!

However, there is a checklist, as promised, which you can use to get an edge over the amateurs. This will tell you whether to even bother making an offer on the vehicle and, if you go ahead, how much to bid.

Your first inspection tour should be the exterior of the car. Here is a 5-point exterior checklist to use.

EXTERIOR

1. *Look at the paint job.* This tells you about the character of not only the car but the previous owner(s). Sloppy paint jobs mean a cheap, quick fixup of something more serious. It may be very bad, having air bubbles in different spots on the car. Paint on the chrome or around the moldings, different colors for the interior and exterior, and brushmarks can all spell other trouble. A new paint job on a car is probably covering rust or other damage.
   TIP: Bring a small magnet with you to vehicle auctions. Run the magnet along the side of the car. Metal will give the magnet a pull but body filler won't.
   ANOTHER TIP: Even without a magnet, you can still find body filler. Gently knock on the sides of the car. Hollow knocks mean metal. A solid sound usually means you've hit body filler.

2. *Look under the car.* You might see heavily rusted areas, a broken tailpipe, holes in the car, or other problem areas. Look for leaks. Puddles on the ground can mean serious problems, transmission leaks, oil pump, etc. If you see clear water, that's from the air conditioner.

TIP: Bring a penlight or small flashlight. Use it to look under the car.

3. *Look inside the tailpipe.* Without starting up the car you can detect major problems. Rub your finger on the inside of the tailpipe. Black and gummy slime shows the car may need a ring or valve job. Black and sooty means it needs a tune-up. Big difference in repair costs. TIP: Bring a handkerchief or two to the auction. After a few cars, you will either have a dirty shirt or won't be able to tell what's on your hands.

4. *Bounce the car.* Once it starts bouncing, it should only bounce one time after you stopped bouncing it. More than once means it needs new shocks.

5. *Look at the tires.* See if the tires are worn uniformly. Uneven tread wear can mean other more serious problems. An old clunker with new tires is on a par with a sloppy paint job. Something is going on.

INTERIOR

The interior of the car can give you further data with which to modify your bid. Here is a 5-point interior checklist to use.

1. *Look at the odometer.* An unrealistic odometer reading exists to deceive you. Multiply the age of the car by 12,000. If the car is six years old, the odometer should read in the neighborhood of 72,000. An odometer reading of something like 38,000 means it is at least 138,000. Or the odometer was turned back. Compare your analysis of the car's exterior with its odometer. Does it add up?

2. *Open the door on the driver's side.* Move it up and down. Is it weak? Does the door drop and fall? A weak driver's door can mean other hidden damage, as the owner abused the car.

3. *Look for decay on the inside of the car.* Look under the car mats and push on the floor-boards. Look for rust at the bottom of the doorframe. Look under the dashboard for loose or hanging wires. Push on the ceiling. Little things like this can affect resale value.

4. *Look in the radiator.* If the water is rusty, the radiator may need to be replaced. Engine oil may be leaking in the cooling system if you see a shiny, oily film; you'll have to make expensive repairs.

5. *Look at the dipstick.* Check the oil properly by wiping and dipping again. If it is gummy and gritty, the car has been poorly maintained. A milky brown or gray oil means expensive repairs. See if the oil is thick. Some owners will use a heavier oil weight to quiet valve lifters and cover up other engine problems. TIP: Bring a pocketful of paper towels or rags to the auction. This is dirty work.

ADDITIONAL HELP

An auctioneer's assistant will start up the car at many auctions. Pay attention when he does this. Stand behind the car as he is starting it up. Does it start up easily (battery problems, alternator, new starter)? What kind of smoke comes out of the car? (Blue smoke means serious engine problems.) Look under the hood after he's started the car. Is it shaking badly (new motor mounts)? Have him run it through the gears. Does it "clunk" (transmission problems)?

Vehicles are usually the second single largest purchase a person makes after a house. Figure the price of repairs into your bidding. What good is it to buy a car for half of Blue Book wholesale value only to discover you need to spend three or four times that amount to drive it?

Get the best book on the subject for buying a used car: *The Used Car Book* by Jack Gillis (Harper & Row, New York). Not only will you get useful tips on buying a used car, but you'll also find out which cars to avoid buying. Included is a section on repair ratings of cars.

Real Estate

Inspecting real estate is tougher than inspecting cars. Even professionals make mistakes. There are several points, though, which can make your decision easier to make. You should use the following checklist *before* hiring a certified property inspector. By using this real estate checklist, you will narrow down your selection of properties.

EXTERIOR

This check should be done first. Why look inside if the outside of the property doesn't meet your standards? Doing this inspection first will save you time.

1. Is the property located near a toxic waste dump, an abandoned mine or quarry, or a polluted lake, pond, or river?

2. What is the overall noise level of the property? Is the house behind an interstate highway or facing a main road? How much traffic passes by the front of the property?

3. What type of terrain is the property on? Does the land slope down to the house, potentially causing water damage?

4. How private is the property? What are the neighbors like?

5. What is the crime level of the neighborhood? Check with the local police department. Observe for yourself.

6. Is the property in a radon zone? Has it been tested for radon?

7. How close is the property to: a shopping center or mall? public transportation? a fire station? recreational or cultural facilities? religious institutions, schools, hospitals?

8. How does the roof look? Are the shingles warped? Check the gutters for needed maintenance.

9. What was your first impression of the property? Is this a place where you want to live? Could you easily find reliable tenants?

If one or more of the questions produce answers that seriously bother you about the property, then look elsewhere. Don't then look inside to see if the interior makes up for the outside. There are many real estate properties available.

INTERIOR

Should the property's exterior appeal to you, then do a thorough inspection of the interior, if this is possible. Usually, government agencies have hired real estate brokers to show the properties. Auction companies more frequently conduct tours of properties or will allow the opportunity for a property inspection. Take advantage of this.

1. *Look at the floors.* Are they level? Solid? Are they completely carpeted? Sellers may carpet the floor to cover defects, such as settling or a poor floor.

2. *Check for stains or peeling.* These may appear on the walls or ceiling. There may be water damage. This could mean a leaky roof. If so, check the attic more thoroughly. Also, look at the inside of the exterior doors. Check for rot or other damage.

3. *Check the basement.* Is it damp? Does it smell? Again, there may be water damage.

4. *Check the water pressure.* Turn on the shower and bathroom sink. Then, flush the toilet. Did water pressure come down to a trickle?

5. *Look for infestation.* Check darker areas to find mice droppings, dead insects, or other pests. Look in the attic, basement, under pipes, behind a refrigerator, and so forth, wherever you need a flashlight. Termite infestation can practically destroy a property's value.

6. *Look at the ceiling and walls.* Do you easily see the seams between the sheet rock panels? Is

the paint job sloppy? Feel the walls and ceiling. Are they lumpy? Loose?

7. *Make a list of needed repairs.* Calculate what these repairs will cost. For instance, if you are buying a HUD home and it has lead-based paint, you will have to remove it or pay to have it done. Find out from the real estate broker or the condition of sale what will be required of you when you purchase the property.

ADDITIONAL TIPS

There are many inspection actions that you may need to take. Some of the government properties are in a state of disrepair and may require a large investment to bring to speed. There may be rehab money available, as with HUD's Section 235 program. More often, the money comes out of your pocket. Remember that when determining what your set limit will be.

You should use a property inspector. There are many from whom to choose. Hiring one costs $100 or more, depending on your area. He or she should be a member of the American Society of Home Inspectors.

Failing that, hire a small general contractor who specializes in renovations. Let him know you are considering the purchase of a property and would like him to estimate the renovations. Have him inspect the property with you. He will point out defects that need repairs and give you a ballpark estimate.

There are many fine books on property inspections. One do-it-yourself manual is: *What's It Worth?: A Home Inspection and Appraisal Manual* by Joseph V. Scaduto, TAB Books, Summit, Pennsylvania.

Conclusion

One could summarize this chapter in a few simple words: appraise and inspect before you buy. Use the tools available to you for an accurate appraisal and a complete inspection. There are many. Professionals use them. So should you. If the tools for your area of interest haven't been covered here, contact a professional or a dealer to find out what tools he uses.

Such work doesn't take months or years to learn. It can take a few hours to get started and several days or weeks to understand well enough to succeed. Once you know the subject, your winning bids can pay handsome dividends.

5

Financing Your Auction Purchase

★★

Most newcomers fail to bring the proper method of payment. As a result they either forfeit their auction prize or scramble to make good on their bid. Professionals know exactly what their set limit is going to be. They carry that set limit in their pocket, usually in the form of cash, a cashier's check, or money orders.

Professionals scrutinize the conditions of sale. If in doubt, they will call the auction company or government agency and know what financial instrument is acceptable. You won't see them guessing at what the payment terms are, whether it's real estate or personal property.

You can simplify the matter just by bringing cash to an auction. This might make you uncomfortable, though. Professionals bring cashiers' checks or money orders to auction. Some will bring, where it is permissible, traveler's checks, certified checks, or business checks with letters from their banks guaranteeing payment.

Some government agencies have wised up and are accepting bank credit cards. Travel and entertainment charge cards have yet to become accepted forms of payment. Many auctioneers have permitted the use of bank credit cards to buy the merchandise. Unless you've got an unusually large line of credit, don't hope to purchase real estate this way.

One of the major reasons why many people are wary of purchasing merchandise at auction is the immediate payment factor. As Americans we've grown accustomed to the installment plan. Pay as you go. Buy something on credit, use it, and then pay later. This is not how you buy at auction. Dealers take advantage of the inexperienced in this way, but it doesn't have to be so. There are ways to finance your auction purchase using the methods professionals use.

Common Financing Methods

All financing techniques are based on using other people's money. It's been called OPM financing. All financing, if you carefully inspect it, is done with other people's money. Whether you are leasing, borrowing money from a relative or friend, charging on a credit card, or taking a bank loan, you are financing with someone else's money. The same methods of financing can be done at auction.

BANKS

The days of fast credit are gone, but banks still extend credit to good risks. You could apply for a car loan if you wish to buy at auction. Have the loan prepared well before you go to the auction.

The money can be waiting for you when you are successful. Of course, you may have to make special arrangements with auctioneers; this won't work at auctions held on a weekend (when banks are closed) and payment is due by the end of the day on which the auction was held.

In such cases, try taking a cash advance against your credit card(s), either for the entire auction purchase price or as a deposit. You may even wish to do a rollover. Purchase the item at auction using a cash advance. Then, borrow the money against the car purchase and pay back the credit card advance. Some loan officers may not approve this method. However, unless you are dealing with a human automatic teller machine, free and open communications with the bank officer may assist you in getting your loan approved.

Home equity loans (also known as secondary mortgages, 2nd and 3rd trust deeds) can also be arranged if your existing property has equity. You may already have a substantial and unused credit line against which to borrow. These can also be tapped for your auction purchase. They are cheaper than traditional car loans, credit card advances, and conventional bank financing because your house or property is the collateral. If your auction purchase is truly a bargain, then think about how much you are really saving—less interest, reduced purchase price. (Car dealerships are going to hate me for this!)

FRIENDS AND RELATIVES

This is relatively (pun) simple when making a small purchase, such as a used car. Many parents may even wish to buy their high school or college kids a car at auction. If you are missing wheels, auctions present terrific opportunities for vehicles. Should your savings be depleted and you are unable to find credit elsewhere, ask a friend or relative for a short-term personal loan.

However, if you plan on starting a part-time business or career reselling your auction bargains, friends and relatives may want to share in the profits. Most business start-ups are financed by relatives and friends. Others use business partners, where one guy does all the work while the other brings in finances to the relationship. Mr., Mrs., or Miss Gotbucks is the silent partner and the other guy or gal puts in what's called "sweat equity."

You can do this creatively and with grace, or not. Good manners help when you're trying to raise capital. Having a reputation for being hard-working and paying your bills won't hurt either. Going cap in hand to someone may sound disgraceful, but without it the wheels of commerce would stop turning overnight. The U.S. government does it when they sell treasury bills at auction. So do corporations when they sell bonds. All they're really doing is selling others IOUs. If you have confidence in them, you buy. Otherwise, you walk.

The same applies to you. If your friends and relations have confidence in your ability, they'll lend you money. Similarly, if they don't you will instead get a very good reason why they can't. No bucks means no confidence, unless they are in the same boat you are in, that is, they have no money.

Someone, though, always has money. There are various financing schemes you can concoct to have them "invest" in you. One of the more common is to borrow double what you actually need and then pay back some of it with a guaranteed investment. That usually settles down those who are hyper.

Most consider treasury bonds an extremely solid investment, although they have many disadvantages (low interest, long-term maturity date, etc.). You could borrow $5,000 from a relative and invest $2,500 in a treasury bond, which will eventually mature at the $5,000 level. Offer the relative a share in the profits if the scheme works as the incentive. The back-up of a treasury bond returning their original investment often puts them at ease.

If you did this with enough friends and relatives, you might raise enough dough to start an industry. Be sure you don't fritter it away on fast cars and exotic vacations or you'll never hear the end of it. Seriously, money is a touchy subject, enough to break up marriages, ruin partnerships, and defame one's good name. Raising capital after a debacle is harder the second time around.

GOVERNMENT FINANCING

This especially applies to real estate, but can also apply to starting a regular business. There are many federal and state government programs available to the eager and willing.

The Department of Housing and Urban Development and the Department of Veterans Affairs have specific loan and loan-guarantee programs for real estate purchases. State housing finance agencies also have lending programs under the supervision of HUD. Low-interest housing loans can be obtained from them. A directory of state housing finance agencies appears at the end of this chapter.

The Small Business Administration (SBA) has guaranteed over $3 billion annually in small business loans. Dealing with SBA paperwork can be frustrating, but funds are available from banks through the SBA's certified and preferred lender plans.

FHA loan guarantees are also available and can be arranged with a real estate broker when purchasing government real estate. The Resolution Trust Corporation, arguably the world's largest property owner and managed by government employees, also has financing programs available when you purchase their real estate.

The Farmer's Home Administration actively lends money to those families who wish to purchase agricultural or rural properties. There are offices in every state with generous lending programs.

While finding out about real estate or auctions, in Section Three, also ask the government agents at the above agencies about financing programs that are available and if you might qualify.

Unconventional Financing

Let's get one thing straight: unconventional financing does not mean meeting someone in a back alley and signing your life away for a bagful of cash. Finding a different method of financing does not mean breaking the law. Cynics may scoff at nontraditional methods of borrowing money. Yet new methods become traditional after they have been around for a while and gone through the customary modifications, in order to align or conform with their predecessors.

From the caveman to the investment banker, eager beavers will always find a new twist on how to raise money. Ways of raising money fall into three basic categories. Let's look into them.

PARTNERSHIPS

This can be as simple as borrowing money from a friend and splitting the profits after the original investment has been repaid or as complex as a formal limited partnership. Borrowing money from friends or relatives has already been discussed, but why not get ambitious?

ADVERTISE

When you've run out of friends or they are all broke like you, take out advertisements in local or national papers. You might try running a small advertisement that defines what you are going to do. For example, try running this or a similar advertisement in the business opportunities or finance section of the classifieds: FOUND A GREAT DEAL BUT LACK CASH! Call for details: (Your telephone number). You may wish to make the ad more specific to better qualify your responses (or get an answering machine to keep them from waking you up late at night!). Of course, you'd better have a great deal lined up at auction before going ahead with this. Otherwise you are lying.

Seriously, advertise for a partner. Someone may listen to your scheme and join you in your venture. Businesses do start that way. It's an aggressive sort of networking.

Your approach should be that you will exchange your hard work and growing expertise for a share of the profits. Some people get greedy at this point and demand a larger share than their partner is willing to give. Thus, another deal bites the dust.

Be practical and honest with your prospective partners in the early stages. Gain their trust. Later, when you're on equal ground, you can ask for an equal share.

Call this equity sharing or sweat equity or a silent partnership. The label is irrelevant. The principle is: "If you don't have the money, put in the time and effort." This is what happens each day when you go to work. You don't have the money so you work for someone else. With this concept, you are risking your time and effort for a greater return than a regular job.

LIMITED PARTNERSHIPS

If you are headed for the big time and don't wish to incorporate, you may consider a limited partnership. Your accountant, broker, financial planner, or attorney may be sold on your idea and may help you raise the financing. This requires salesmanship on your part and a good track record.

Consult an attorney before embarking on this idea. There are tax laws, fraud laws, and other investment laws to obey. Limited partnerships have raised enormous sums of money and purchased businesses. For example, George Steinbrenner purchased the New York Yankees from CBS using a limited partnership. That was sort of a foreclosure sale financed with OPM (as the Yankees were in the American League doghouse at the time and Steinbrenner temporarily appeared as their savior).

Movies, Broadway shows, real estate, equipment leasing, and technological R & D work has been brought to us frequently by limited partnerships. They were abused in the 1970s and 1980s because investors were guaranteed tax benefits, which the IRS later disallowed. But that doesn't mean you can't legitimately use them to honestly raise money for financing a business.

CLUBS

Throughout the 1980s real estate clubs flourished. Stock investing clubs still prosper. Investors pool their resources to purchase something they can't individually afford. Some join others in an investment so they can sleep well at night.

There is no reason why you can't purchase property or merchandise at auction by forming an investment club. If you want to start a small business buying and reselling merchandise at auction or amass a real estate portfolio by purchasing distressed government or bank properties, then consider an investment club.

A group of "once-a-week friends," poker buddies, or bowling teammates (you name it) could join forces and take advantage of some deals at government auction. You'd be surprised at how few people still do not know about these bargains. One investment banker, who was ready to purchase used construction equipment from dealers for export overseas, went into shock (and joy) when I showed him the prices he would pay in a negotiated sale. He was nearly hysterical when I explained that he could get even better prices by attending the auction!

In forming a club for such a purpose, you had better incorporate it. Incorporation attorneys usually advertise at the beginning of the classified section in your local papers. Costs are low, sometimes less than $300.

Clubs are fun, particularly when each of the investors are contributing an equal share. Involve them each with different tasks: someone gets the group on the government mailing list, another searches for buyers, another gets the merchandise accurately appraised, another does the inspections, and another makes the final decision on set limit. Of course, if you started the club, you should be the one who gets to buy at the auction!

CORPORATIONS

This can follow the pattern of the investment club, or you can do it alone or with a partner. Form the corporation and issue stock to friends and relatives. (Again, do consult an attorney!) As long as your promotions are among friends and contracts are signed, you can keep it simple.

Hire an investment banker to raise money for you *if* you have already proven yourself. This may not fly easily at first until you have more than an adequate track record. It may take years. There are SEC (Securities and Exchange Commission) filings that must be done—they can take months. If you love complexity in your life, go that route.

Starting with friends and relatives is the best route. After all, it's just a more sophisticated way of borrowing money. Wouldn't you rather sell them stock than ask for a loan? Take a tip from big business. They do it in the billions every business day on the stock exchanges.

Conclusion

Lack of finances is not a good reason for failure to participate in the auction experience. Business-men and corporations pay astounding fees to consultants, often resulting in nought. They hire such advisors for their skill, experience, and know-how.

You can rapidly build up expertise in auctions and offer this skill to those with money. Trade your know-how for their cash investment and share the profits. Laziness is an understandable excuse for not involving yourself at government auctions. But inability to raise the necessary cash to make an auction purchase won't hold water.

As with all financial advice, please consult with a local professional before implementing any recommendations. Clear your plans with a certified public accountant, attorney, tax attorney, real estate attorney, real estate broker, or an applicable professional. I do not recommend that you start any broad fundraising activities without having first consulted with a licensed professional in your area.

STATE HOUSING FINANCE AGENCIES

In this directory you will find state agencies that are responsible for administrating the State Homebuyers Program. Many states raise money for this program through the sale of mortgage revenue bonds.

Call your state's agency and request details about the program. Most programs allow a home-buyer to make a low downpayment and benefit from below-market interest rates. While part of the program is for first-time homebuyers, there is another section that is open to all interested borrowers, the Urban Target Area Program. There are income and housing price restrictions on both programs.

Your state agency will send you an information kit and/or brochure describing the program. Approved lenders are included in this information.

Alabama

Alabama Housing Finance
Authority
Ste. 408
2000 Interstate Park Dr.
Montgomery AL 36109
(205) 242-4310

Arizona

Arizona Department of
Commerce
3800 N. Central Ste 1400
Phoenix, AZ 85012
(602) 280-1300

Arkansas

Arkansas Housing
Development Agency
100 Main St.
P.O. Box 8023
Little Rock, AR 72203
(501) 682-5900

California

California Housing Finance
Agency
1121 L St., 7th Fl.
Sacramento, CA 95814
(916) 322-3992
5711 W. Slauson Ave
Ste 100
Culver City, CA 90230
(213) 736-2355

Colorado

Colorado Housing Finance
Authority
1981 Blake St.
Denver, CO 80202
(303) 297-2432

Connecticut

Connecticut Housing Finance
Authority
40 Cold Spring Rd.
Rocky Hill, CT 06067
(203) 721-9501

Delaware

Delaware State Housing
Authority
820 N. French St., 3rd Fl.
Wilmington, DE 19801
(302) 577-3720

District of Columbia

District of Columbia Housing
Finance Agency
1275 K St. N.W. Ste 600
Washington, D.C. 20005
(202) 408-0415

Florida

Florida Housing Finance
Office Agency
2574 Seagate Dr. Ste 101
Tallahassee, FL 32301-5026
(904) 488-4197

Georgia

Georgia Residential Finance
Authority
60 Executive Parkway South
Suite 250
Atlanta, GA 30329
(404) 679-4840

Hawaii

Housing Finance
7 Waterfront Plaza Suite 300
500 Alamonana Blvd.
Honolulu, HI 96813
(808) 587-0567

Idaho

Idaho Housing Authority
760 W. Myrtle
Boise, ID 83702
(208) 336-0161

Illinois

Illinois Housing Development
Authority
401 N. Michigan Ave.
Suite 900
Chicago, IL 60611
(312) 836-5362

Indiana

Indiana Housing Finance
Authority
1 N. Capital Ave.

Suite 515
Indianapolis, IN 46204
(317) 232-7777

Iowa

Iowa Finance Authority
100 E. Grand, Suite 250
Des Moines, IA 50309
(515) 281-4058

Kansas

Kansas Housing Finance
Authority
Office of City Administrator
701 North 7th St.
Kansas City, KS 66101
(913) 573-5030

Kentucky

Kentucky Housing Authority
1231 Louisville Rd.
Frankfort, KY 40601
(502) 564-7630

Louisiana

Louisiana Housing Finance
Agency
26445 Sherwood Forest Blvd.
Suite 200
Baton Rouge, LA 70816
(504) 295-8450

Maine

Maine State Housing Authority
353 Water St.
P.O. Box 2669
Augusta, ME 04338-2669
(207) 626-4600

Maryland

Maryland Community Housing
Authority
100 Community Place
Crownsville, MD 21032
(301) 514-7501

Massachusetts

Massachusetts Housing
Finance Agency
50 Milk St., 7th Fl.
Boston, MA 02109
(617) 451-3480

Michigan

Michigan State Housing
Development Authority
Plaza One Building
401 S. Washington
Lansing, MI 48909
(517) 373-8370

Minnesota

Minnesota Housing Finance
Corporation
400 Sibley St.
Suite 300
St. Paul, MN 55101
(612) 296-7613

Missouri

Missouri Housing
Development Commission
3770 Broadway
Kansas City, MO 64111
(816) 756-3790

Montana

Montana Board of Housing
2001 11th Ave.

Helena, MT 59620
(406) 444-3040

Nebraska

Nebraska Investment Finance
Authority
Gold's Galleria
1033 O St., Suite 218
Lincoln, NE 68508
(402) 434-3900

Nevada

Nevada Housing Division
Department of Commerce
1802 N. Carson
Suite 154
Carson City, NV 89701
(702) 687-4258

New Hampshire

New Hampshire Housing
Finance Authority
24 Constitution Dr.
Bedford, NH 03110
(603) 472-8623

New Jersey

New Jersey Housing and
Mortgage Finance Authority
CN 18550
3625 Quakerbridge Rd.
Trenton, NJ 08650-2085
(609) 890-1300
In New Jersey:
(800) 654-6873

New Mexico

New Mexico Mortgage Finance
Authority
P.O. Box 2047
Albuquerque, NM 87103

or
344 4th St. SW
Albuquerque, NM 87102
(505) 843-6880

New York

State of New York Mortgage
Agency
(Sunnie Mae)
260 Madison Ave., 9th Fl.
New York, NY 10016
(212) 696-9590

North Carolina

North Carolina Housing
Finance Agency
3300 Drake Circle
Suite 200
Raleigh, NC 27607
(919) 781-6115

North Dakota

North Dakota Housing Finance
Agency
1600 East Interstate Ave.
Bismarck, ND 58501
or
P.O. Box 1535
Bismarck, ND 58502
(701) 224-3434

Ohio

Ohio Housing Finance Agency
77th S. High St.
26th Floor
Columbus, OH 43215
(614) 466-7970
In Ohio: (800) 458-1700

Oklahoma

Oklahoma Housing Finance
Agency
1140 NW 63rd
Suite 200
Oklahoma City, OK 73116
or
P.O. Box 2670
Oklahoma City, OK
73126-0720
(405) 848-1144

Oregon

Oregon Housing Agency
1600 State St.
Suite 100
Salem, OR 97310
(503) 378-4343

Pennsylvania

Pennsylvania Housing
Finance Agency
P.O. Box 8029
2101 N. Front St.
Harrisburg, PA 17105-8029
(717) 780-3870

Rhode Island

Rhode Island Housing
and Mortgage Finance
Corporation
60 Eddy St.
Providence, RI 02903
(401) 751-5566
In R.I.: (800) 427-5560

South Carolina

South Carolina Housing
Authority

1710 Gervais St.
Columbia, SC 29201
(803) 734-8702

South Dakota

South Dakota Housing
Development Authority
221 S. Central
P.O. Box 1237
Pierre, SD 57501
(605) 773-3181

Tennessee

Tennessee Housing
Development Agency
401 Church St.
LNC Building Suite 700
Nashville, TN 37219-2202
(615) 741-4968
In TN: (800) 228-8423

Texas

Texas Housing Agency
811 Barton Springs Rd.
Suite 300
Austin, TX 78704
(512) 474-4663

Utah

Utah Finance Housing Agency
177 E. 100 South
Salt Lake City, UT 84111
(801) 521-6950

Vermont

Vermont Housing Finance
Agency
1 Burlington Square
P.O. Box 408
Burlington, VT 05402-0408
(802) 864-5743

Virginia

Virginia Housing Development
Authority
601 S. Belvedere St.
Richmond, VA 23220-6504
(804) 782-1986

Washington

Washington State Housing
Financing Commission
1111 3rd Ave.
Suite 2240
Seattle, WA 98101
(206) 464-7139

West Virginia

West Virginia Housing
Development Fund
814 Virginia St.E.
Charleston, WV 25301
(304) 345-6475
In WV: (800) 654-6652

Wisconsin

Wisconsin Housing &
Economic Development
Authority
1 S. Pickney, Suite 500
P.O. Box 1728
Madison, WI 53701-1728
(608) 266-7884
In WI: (800) 362-2767

Wyoming

Wyoming Community
Development Authority
123 S. Dublin
Casper, WY 82602
(307) 265-0603

6

Reselling for a Profit at Government Auctions

★★★

Winning a bid at the auction is just the beginning. If you want to succeed as a professional, you should know how to make a profit on your purchase. Buying at a low price does not always result in end-users immediately beating a path to your door. Especially if you keep it a secret.

Whether you are buying at auction to resell cars or millions of dollars' worth of equipment, you must market your prize. If you bought a HUD home for investment purposes, you'd want to find a tenant, right? Your first course of action might be to take out a small ad announcing that a rental is available. The same holds true with all merchandise.

The degree of your promotion is usually going to be proportionate to the dollar amount of the merchandise. A car bought from the General Services Administration for resale within your town may only merit a classified ad run for a week in the local paper. However, a large purchase, such as ten thousand leather belts bought at a U.S. Customs auction, would be another story.

Small Purchases

Buy a car at auction. Fix it up. Advertise it. Sell it. Your profit might be more than you make in a week. However, many will omit the second step:

fix it up. If you don't present the product in an appealing fashion, you limit your potential buyers and reduce its resale price.

Check with a mechanic. Find out what really needs to be replaced. Buy yourself a Chilton's guide from the local bookstore or check it out from the library. See if you can do it yourself. If not, invest a few dollars to make the purchase resellable for more.

Consumers are guilty of buying the sizzle, not the steak. Ask any sales manager or advertising man. He will tell you to hit the customer with pizzazz! Car buyers want a car that looks good and drives comfortably. Making it look good isn't necessarily expensive, but it is hard work.

The way to make any car look better is to do what detailers do. Wash it thoroughly. Wax the hell out of it. Shampoo and scrub the inside. Go over every nook and cranny with a toothbrush. Get the dirt out and make it shine.

If it needs body work, there are kits you can buy for small work. Touch-up paints are sold at car washes, auto stores, and dealerships. These are negligible investments, costing a few dollars.

Don't get caught up in restoring it to vintage condition unless that is your hobby. The idea is to fix it up for resale, not groom it for a trophy. Some individuals do operate in this fashion, though, and have been known to profit handsomely from it. Make sure you price your work into the profit so you're not working for free.

The preceding advice can apply to any small purchase, whether it's a stereo deck or jewelry. Your job is to make it presentable for resale. The more you put into it, the easier it will be resold. And this applies to larger merchandise as well as real estate.

Larger Purchases

When you buy more than a hundred of something or spend more than a few thousand dollars on a bulk purchase at auction, you become a dealer. The opportunity is there to make a bundle. Your risk is getting eaten alive and storing your auction prize in the garage for all eternity.

Make no mistake about it. Dealers buy at auction and profit from it. What's the secret to their success? It is really quite simple. The professional has already found a buyer(s) for the inventory or has one or more lined up who will buy it shortly.

Some are prepared to pay the cost of repairs or have employees to do this for them. Making it presentable for resale just means they double the price and increase their profit margin. That's the easy part.

Ah, but where do they find the buyers? Think for a moment what would happen to America if the entire country didn't have buyers. You wouldn't eat in the morning, for starters. Your car would never leave the driveway because there would be no gas. And worst of all, the shopping malls would close down. Heaven forbid!

Buyers are actively looking for bargains. Few attend auctions. That's beneath many of them. However, buyers will purchase container loads of jum-jum nuggets if that's their business. And, they will buy from you if they can get a good price. Auctions can provide you with the opportunity to sell to professional buyers.

Finding International Buyers

Where do you find the buyers? The best way is to advertise for them. Exporters, and others with overseas trading arrangements, read *The Journal of Commerce*. Consider advertising in *The Journal of Commerce* as rates are extremely low, less than $5.00 per line of advertising space. Subscribers take this newspaper seriously, as they pay over $200 annually to receive it daily.

Contact *The Journal of Commerce* to advertise or subscribe:

The Journal of Commerce
Two World Trade Center
New York City, New York 10048
Telephone: (212) 837-7000
Subscription: (800) 221-3777
Advertising: (800) 223-0243

You can also find buyers when advertising in *The Wall Street Journal*. The *Journal* is one of America's largest daily newspapers and is read throughout the world. It has regional and city editions throughout the United States. This national coverage can reduce your advertising cost. You can also advertise in Asia or Europe and reach international buyers.

For subscription or advertising information, contact:

The Wall Street Journal
Subscription: (800) 228-6262
Advertising: (800) 366-3975

Their 800 number routing system will direct you to the nearest office to answer your questions and assist you.

Those wishing to seriously pursue international contacts can use a media representative firm. You can advertise in the classified sections of their daily newspapers to attract buyers for your goods or to build a network of international buyers. There are several companies in the United States that represent overseas newspapers. The Dow Jones Company, which owns *The Wall Street Journal*, represents a few foreign magazines and newspapers wherein you could advertise for buyers.

For further information, contact:

Dow Jones International
120 Lexington Avenue

18th Floor
New York City, NY 10107
Telephone: (212) 808-6618
Fax: (212) 808-6652

By far the predominant international media firm representing European newspapers is:

Publicitas International
79 Fifth Avenue
12th Floor
New York City, NY 10003
Telephone: (212) 242-6600
Fax: (212) 924-8706

They represent dozens of newspapers worldwide and can assist you with classified advertising so you can export your auction purchase.

Another large media firm, representing newspapers in Mexico, Latin America, Europe, and Asia, is:

S. S. Koppe & Company
440 Ninth Avenue
11th Floor
New York City, NY 10001
Telephone: (212) 563-1900
Fax: (212) 563-1922

The true professional relies on one major source of information in conducting the resale end within the United States. They use *The Thomas Register*. Within this 25-volume set (over 47,000 pages) you will find tens of thousands of potential buyers. Your library probably has a set. Changes occur daily throughout the world of commerce, so you may wish to own your own set. About one million entry changes are made annually. The set costs about $240.

For a subscription, contact:

Thomas Publishing Company
Thomas Register of American
Manufacturers
One Penn Plaza
New York City, NY 10117-0138
Telephone: (800) 222-7900
Fax: (212) 290-7365

Develop a Network

Professionals appear at auctions with a pocketful of buyers or potential buyers for their would-be auction prizes. Using the methods described in the previous section, you should be able to develop a buyer's network.

However, networks of brokers also abound. You would be utterly astounded to discover how many one-man shops exist around the country. Many are aching for deals to export abroad or trade within the country. While you are at the library, look in the reference section for books and directories that will lead you to brokers. Read Sunday newspapers and find the liquidators who are advertising in the classified sections of large newspapers, such as *The New York Times, Washington Post, Los Angeles Times,* etc. Give them a call.

Believe me, once you get into a network it's hard to shake them off you. It is not that difficult to field dozens of new callers each week after you announce that you have a good deal on something. They talk. Soon they can be talking to you.

More Help

Caught in a jam and don't know where to get started in reselling your auction purchase? There are a few safety nets. You may try telephoning or writing the following organizations for assistance.

1. *The Chamber of Commerce of the United States.* Ask for the Small Business Programs Office for help. They may direct you to a local contact point. Telephone: (202) 659-6000

2. *The National Association of Manufacturers.* They represent over 10,000 manufacturers. Ask for their help. This group may refer you to others for assistance. Telephone: (202) 637-3000

3. *National Small Business United.* Ask for educational assistance. They may be able to help you network. Telephone: (202) 293-8830

4. *United States Hispanic Chamber of Commerce.* If you have a Hispanic heritage, they

may be able to match you with buyers. Telephone: (816) 531-6363

5. *National Business League.* They help in developing business for African-Americans. Again, you may be able to network through them. Telephone: (202) 829-5900

6. *Asian Pacific American Chamber of Commerce.* Provides assistance for Asian-Americans. Another networking opportunity. Telephone: (202) 659-4037

If you are going to concentrate on only exporting your auction purchase (not a bad idea), then you should contact this government agency for further assistance:

U.S. Small Business Administration
Office of International Trade, Room 501-A
1441 L Street, NW
Washington, DC 20416

Desperate for a Foreign Contact or Need One Right Now?

Having myself gone through the trauma of desperately trying to find a foreign contact within a few hours, I realized that foreign countries have "their soil" in the United States. Embassies are little outposts of their own country within ours. And they all have offices in Washington, D.C.

Should you ever get stuck with something or merely wish to develop an overseas contact, telephone directory assistance in Washington, D.C., and ask for the embassy of that country to which you would like to export. Request (humbly and politely) for a contact name or company that you may telephone or write in order to strike up a business relationship. Generally, they will assist you. Some may even send you their literature or refer you to traders.

The whole world can open up to you. Exporting your auction purchases overseas might bring you many times the profits you might expect by reselling them domestically. Don't be surprised to find some foreign nationals showing up at government auctions. Many have heard about the great deals found at these auctions. Foreign real estate buying syndicates have even been formed to purchase distressed properties at auctions. An aggressive entrepreneur could take advantage of this interest and profit handsomely.

Conclusion

These past three chapters have been designed to increase your skills so that you can become a professional auction-goer. Success at an auction does not stop with the winning bid. Your auction purchase just gives you a key to walk through a door. And the door you enter can either be one behind which lies a hefty reward, a staggering penalty, or a waste of time.

The direction you take depends on how professional you are after the auction is over. Some pros can turn the worst buys into a profit. Similarly, many inexperienced winners might take a good auction bargain and go nowhere with it.

Many will only wish to participate in one or two auctions. For these, auctions might only hold the attraction of buying a car for less than at a used car lot. Government sales might attract them toward a deeply discounted boat or airplane. These tips and advice can still benefit those individuals.

7

Fraud!

★★★

And What to Do About It!

When you buy at a department store or by telephone through catalog shopping, you have numerous safeguards to protect you from fraud. Until now, very few people knew the recourse they have in buying at auction. Yes, even the government makes mistakes, but we all know that anyway.

What do you do when the car you bought at auction was represented differently than what it actually turned out to be? Do you just drive it (or tow it) off and hang your head? You could. But that's not the smart thing to do.

For example, a while back I purchased several thousand dresses at a United States Customs auction. These were for export only and had to be shipped out of the country by a certain deadline or my company forfeited the prize. We had gotten an excellent deal on the dresses, but there was a problem. The United States Customs Service shortchanged us. In their auction brochure, they stated that there were a certain number of dresses. As it turned out, there were a few hundred missing.

I could have said: "Tough luck. That's the way the hand is dealt." I didn't. I had my secretary demand that U.S. Customs make good on my auction purchase. Amazingly, they complied. To soothe my discomfort, Customs sent us hundreds of handmade Irish cotton sweaters in beautiful colors. We would have broken even just on the bonus of the sweaters. We sold those sweaters directly to retailers and others for about $15 each. Later that same year those same sweaters were retailing in a catalog for more than $70.

By demanding that this government agency be responsible for its auction company's misrepresentation, my company profited handsomely from this transaction. Had we not acted in this way, I would have been stuck with a minor loss. You have recourse when you buy at auction, whether or not the auctioneer says the goods are "as is, where is." There are certain violations that void an auction contract and remedies that you can pursue to right the wrong.

Bid-Rigging and Rings

How would you like to find yourself bidding against seasoned professionals who would just as easily eat your heart with a dull spoon as look at you? As you go to some of the less well-promoted auctions, you might meet them. You had better keep your eyes open. Some of the bidding might not be aboveboard.

Dealers and wholesalers know they are breaking federal law. In a news report, a few ring members claimed that it was a privilege to have participated in these secretive rings. To them it showed that they had finally arrived in their profession. Unfortunately, law enforcement officials also arrived shortly thereafter at their door and arrested them.

HOW RINGS OPERATE

What's a ring? It is a loosely knit, but well-organized group of dealers in certain specialties who agree to fix the bidding. Just as crooks would buy an athlete for point shaving, or jockeys and trainers might throw a race, these dealers will appear at an auction with private agreements to rig the bidding. Ring members might be dealers or buyers of machinery, antiques, metals, fabric, cattle, or similar merchandise or equipment.

They may have only a few members go to the auction or many, depending on the size of the auction. Ring members will then agree not to bid competitively against one another. Each will decide to buy certain lots of items and be the sole bidder for that ring on different portions of the inventory. By doing this, prices are artificially depressed at the auction. Without competitive bidding the auctioneer may be forced to sell the merchandise or equipment for a song, and a poor tune at that.

Wait! It gets worse. The dealers then each bring a list of what they bought at auction. They pool together their auction bargains (now you know why they are sometimes called steals). And they hold another auction among one other. These dealers then pool together the auction proceeds and divvy it equitably among themselves. The auction winners can then buy the merchandise and get some of their purchase price back. That's called the knock-out, as the auction merchandise has been knocked out and sales are final. Because of the pooling, these rings are often called pools.

BID-RIGGING IS A FELONY

But whether these are called pools or rings, they are illegal. Bid-rigging is a felony. Agreements among buyers at auctions not to bid against one another for the purpose of purchasing goods at low and noncompetitive prices can be a criminal violation of the federal antitrust laws, punishable by fines and imprisonment. Section 1 of the Sherman Act (15 U.S.C. #1) prohibits bid-rigging agreements among competitors if they affect or restrain interstate commerce. Upon conviction, individuals are subject to a maximum fine of $250,000 and/or three years imprisonment. Corporations are subject to a maximum fine of at least $1 million.

Pools and rings can be difficult for the amateur to catch. Auctioneers should know better, though, especially if that auctioneer specializes in a particular area and sees the same dealers showing up at his auctions. At that point, the auctioneer is also guilty of this crime. If you do spot such activity at an auction or notice an irregularity that doesn't add up, let the auctioneer know about it immediately.

WHAT TO LOOK FOR

Things to watch for include: low turnout of auction-goers; winking, hand signals or other similar signs among the dealers when the auctioneer opens the bidding; a uniformity to the bidding, such as dealer #1 bids on a particular lot and buys it with little or no activity, then dealer #2 buys another lot, again with little or no competition; an auctioneer who is barely trying to get things going at the auction; a lot of handshaking or other signs of recognition to each other before or after the auction; an air of silence throughout the auction—auctions can get pretty noisy. Such illegal activity is most likely to occur at specialty auctions, such as those described earlier. Where there is a broad assortment of equipment or merchandise or a grab-bag sort of auction, these types of dealers aren't as likely to show up.

This practice is more widespread than the Justice Department or other government agencies are willing to admit. It closes you out of auctions. While there, you might feel you walked into somebody else's party or fraternity house. You did. It's rigged from the moment it starts. Bankruptcy auctions that are poorly promoted are most prone to this type of fraud. One manufacturer or wholesaler fails and the vultures jump in to wipe the bones clean.

Friends may go to an auction and each decide to bid separately and noncompetitively at auction. While this may be illegal because it is a restraint of trade, it is hardly what the law enforcement officials are most concerned about stamping out. One of the reasons that Dick Textor, a famous military surplus bargain finder, was barred temporarily from some government auctions was that he complained aloud about the low prices found at auctions. That is a loose interpretation of the law, but it was enforced in his case. Be careful about the way you make bids in the presence of friends!

RECOURSE

If you feel there has been an injustice done against you that involves bid-rigging, pools, or some similar conspiracy by professional dealers, then take immediate action. You might complain to the auctioneer. He may or may not act.

Many auctioneers who belong to professional organizations such as the National Auctioneers Association (NAA) or the Certified Auctioneers Institute (CAI) are honest and legitimate auctioneers. They don't want their trade or reputation damaged. Auctioneers depend on sales commissions for their livelihood. A series of bad auctions can severely hurt the auctioneer. Getting busted will ruin him. He has a vested interest in running an ethical auction.

Some auctioneers may do nothing about the ring or pool. Others may slough off your complaint. You should get full particulars of that auction, including the bidder numbers of those involved, the lot number of the merchandise sold, the day and time of the occurrence, and the name of the auction company. Write this all down. Immediately contact your state's attorney general or state attorney's office. You will find this in the Blue Pages at the beginning of your telephone book. The U.S. Justice Department's antitrust division has also been extremely active in their investigations of bid-rigging. File your complaint with them: U.S. Justice Department, Anti-Trust Division, (202) 514-2000. This can also be done in conjunction with your attorney if you have suffered a financial loss as a result of what occurred at the auction.

Shills

Since the beginning of auction history, bidders have been forced to compete against phony competition. This goes under many guises and names: shills, by-bidders, straws, sticks, puffing, etc. England was one of the first countries to strike back against puff bidding (that's what it is called there). Our auctions follow their precedent to outlaw this type of activity.

While arrests and penalties for using shills are not often heard of, it doesn't mean the practice has ceased. I personally witnessed a shill used against me a few years ago. Using the joke-bid strategy, I had bid $100 on a Jaguar. The auction stalled at around $400. Suddenly, a new bidder emerged, with the ringman's arm around my new competitor. He jumped in with a $1,000 bid and the bidding loosened up, driving the final price to over $4,000.

There are several actions that you can take against the auctioneer should that happen.

1. You can walk away from the auction and never go to that auctioneer's sales again.

2. If you get caught in a bidding war and find yourself the top bidder at an indigestible price, you can demand the sale be voided.

3. Should you be put at financial risk, you can and should contact your attorney to demand the sale be voided.

4. You can contact one of the associations to which the auctioneer belongs and demand he be censured, suspended, or terminated from that association.

5. You can contact your state's auctioneer licensing board, if your state has one, and file a formal complaint.

Of course, you may simultaneously pursue several courses of action. The use of shills and other forms of misrepresentation is one of the few major reasons why people do not attend auctions. Who wants to feel that they're fair game for a con artist? There aren't that many auctioneers who operate in this way, but those who do give auctions a bad name.

Misrepresentation

The "as is, where is" caveat will apply in most cases at auctions. However, there are circumstances where bidders have been lied to or defrauded in some way. Most will never know it. Some will shrug their shoulders. Others will make a fuss. At some auctions or with some auctioneers, you may be threatened with never being permitted to bid there again if you just walk away without paying for your auction purchase.

You will never see some of the tricks auctioneers use. Many never notice. Here's what some auctioneers do instead of using shills.

1. The auctioneer will make an air bid, also known as a puff bid. Let's say the auction is going slowly and he needs to pick things up. With one bidder left, he waves to some vague point in the auction crowd and raises the bid. No one raised the bidding. Yet, the bid went higher. He may even continue this to squeeze an extra few bucks out of the unsuspecting bidder. Or he may toss one of these in with two bidders left in order to make them think there is a third bidder interested. That gets things moving right along . . . upwards.
   NOTE: If this happens while you are bidding and you end up buying something for a high price, take the recommended action as mentioned later in this chapter.

2. During the auction he might, himself, bid. The auctioneer will use a house number. That's a little unfair since he may have no intention of purchasing the merchandise. He's really shilling without using a shill other than himself. This is a deliberate attempt to drive up the bidding. Don't expect him to do this frequently.

3. Using one of the above strategies, the auctioneer may trap you into buying something by backing out. For example, let's say the bidding is going between you and the phantom bidder. The auctioneer has just upped your bid through an air bid or the house number. At that point, you decide to back out or drop out of the bidding. He may go back to his invisible bidder and announce: "You want to drop out. OK, the winner is . . ." And he gives your bidder's number. Sound difficult? Not really. Often, and particularly at crowded auctions, bidders can't really see who is bidding against them. The auctioneer gambles on this margin and uses these methods.

4. Outright deception. The auctioneer may deceive you about the merchandise or equipment. Few do this, but watch out for it. He may make a misleading statement about the item and lead you into feeling comfortable with it. Those who haven't done a diligent inspection of the item are easy marks when this happens. A thorough inspection and appraisal will make this tactic useless.

5. Switching the merchandise. You bought item A but were given item B at the time you claimed your merchandise. It may have been a simple error or it might be a deliberate attempt to defraud you. Should this happen, under no circumstances should you ever pay for the merchandise.

So, you've been ripped off? Now what? Don't sit there like a wimp. Fight back. You have legal rights and recourse.

VOIDING THE SALE

There exists a legal contract between the auctioneer and the buyer when the auction hammer drops. Buyers are obligated to pay for their purchase. Auctioneers rarely pursue the deadbeats who stiff them. Auction-goers almost never complain about the auctioneer who cheats them, as long as they don't pay.

Should you ever get harassed by an auction company or make your payment and want a refund, you have full legal rights to do so, provided you have legitimately been conned by the auctioneer. Your best protection is a written report. Get the facts.

1. When did it happen? State the time and date.

2. Where did it happen? Give the location.

3. What exactly was done? State the deception used against you.

4. Who participated in the fraud? State the auctioneer's name and license number (if any). If possible, state his company's address and telephone number. State the bidding number used if it was a house number or fictitious number. Give names, if possible, of ringmen or shills used by the auctioneer.

5. State the bidding increments: at what point you started your bidding, and at what point the deception started. If the merchandise was defective and misrepresented, report the statements made about the item.

Your next action, if you paid money, should be to hire an attorney. In the section that follows, you will find out where else to file your report. NOTE: When filing your report, be sure to send the auctioneer a copy. Give him every opportunity to make good on his "error." Many will.

Licensing Auctioneers

The best way to keep auctions fair and auctioneers honest is to license them. King Henry the VII of 15th-century England was the first to license auctioneers in the modern age. Answering complaints from local merchants who were losing business to the auctioneers, King Henry made it the law of the land for auctioneers to be licensed. He did this to tax them. Henry was no dummy. His reign was marked by England's rapid recognition as a world power, and there was lots of cash left over when he died. Henry was on a licensing binge and auctioneers became somewhat regulated because of his actions.

Since then, England has had strict licensing laws about auctioneers. America hasn't. The National Auctioneers Association has been on a major crusade for a number of years to get auctioneers across America licensed. Your state may or may not license auctioneers.

Licensing auctioneers keeps them honest and ethical. Just as nearly all members of the health and financial professions are licensed, so should auctioneers be. Licensed and certified auctioneers are likely to be more fair in their dealings with the general public. For example, many in-house government auctioneers are not licensed. Some of them have never gone to auction school. Many make mistakes or annoy auction-goers with their impertinence or sloppiness. Government agencies, to increase their gross sales, should rely on private, licensed, and certified auctioneers to do their work. Bidders will get more out of their auctions and attendance will probably skyrocket.

WHERE TO COMPLAIN

It's sad that some auctioneers will run a dishonest auction. However, if those bad apples were eliminated, then there would be a lot more fun at auctions. Do your part in reporting those who are in any way deceptive or those who have damaged your pocketbook.

You should file complaints about NAA member auctioneers directly to:

The National Auctioneers Association
8880 Ballentine
Overland Park, KS 66214

If your state requires that auctioneers be licensed, you should file a complaint directly with your state's government agency. If your state does not have a licensing board, then contact your state's consumer protection agency and file a formal complaint, using the procedures found in Voiding the Sale on page 77.

STATES THAT LICENSE AUCTIONEERS

In those states that license auctioneers, you should file your report with the state where the fraud occurred and, if applicable, with the state where the auctioneer is based. Their license to practice may be revoked. While some states do not license auctioneers, many towns and cities within those states issue licenses and permits. File a complaint with those local government agencies.

Alabama

Alabama State Board of Auctioneers
109 Downtown Plaza
Cullman, AL 35055
(205) 739-0548

Arkansas

Arkansas Auctioneers Licensing Board
221 W. Second, Suite 228
Little Rock, AR 77201
(501) 375-3858

California

California Auctioneer Commission
1130 K Street, Suite 1120
Sacramento, CA 95814
(916) 324-5894

District of Columbia

Department of Consumer and Regulatory Affairs
614 H Street, NW
Washington, DC 20001
(202) 727-7100

Florida

Department of Professional Regulation
1940 N. Monroe Street
Tallahassee, FL 32399-0762
(904) 488-5189

Georgia

Georgia Auctioneers Commission
166 Pryor Street, SW
Atlanta, GA 30303
(404) 656-2282

Hawaii

Business License Division
1455 S. Beretania Street
Honolulu, HI 96814
(808) 973-2810

Idaho

Office of the Governor
State Capitol,
Boise, ID 83720

Indiana

Professional Licensing Agency
State Office Building, Room 1021
100 N. Senate Avenue
Indianapolis, IN 46204

Kansas

Office of the Attorney General
Second Floor
Kansas Judicial Center
Topeka, KS 66612-1597
(913) 296-2215

Kentucky

Kentucky Board of Auctioneers
400 Sherburn Lane, Suite 343
Louisville, KY 40207
(502) 588-4453

Louisiana

Louisiana Auctioneers
Licensing Board
8017 Jefferson Highway, Suite
B-3
Baton Rouge, LA 70809
(504) 925-3921

Maine

Board of Licensing of
Auctioneers
State House Station #35
Ausgusta, ME 04333
(207) 582-8723

Maryland

Department of Licensing and
Regulation
501 St. Paul Place, 15th Floor
Baltimore, MD 21202
(301) 333-6200

Massachusetts

Division of Standards
One Ashburton Place
Boston, MA 02108
(617) 727-3480

Minnesota

Contact your county auditor's
office to file a complaint.

Mississippi

Department of Agriculture and
Commerce
Weights and Measures Division
P.O. Box 1609
Jackson, MS 39215-1609
(601) 354-7077

Missouri

Executive Office
P.O. Box 720
Jefferson City, MO 65102

Nebraska

Nebraska Real Estate
Commission
P.O. Box 94667
Lincoln, NE 68509
(402) 471-2004

New Hampshire

New Hampshire Board of
Auctioneers
Secretary of State
Capitol Building, Room 204
Concord, NH 03301
(603) 271-3242

North Carolina

North Carolina Auctioneers
Licensing Board
3509 Haworth Drive, Suite 306
Raleigh, NC 27609
(919) 733-2182

North Dakota

Public Service Commission
Grain Elevator Division
State Capitol
Bismarck, ND 58505

Ohio

Division of Licensing
77 S. High Street
Columbus, OH 43266-0546
(614) 466-4130

Oklahoma

Contact your county treasurer

Pennsylvania

Department of State
Bureau of Professional and
Occupational Affairs
P.O. Box 2649
Harrisburg, PA 17105
(717) 783-1253

Rhode Island

Department of Business
Regulations
Division of Licensing and
Consumer Protection
Auctioneers Licensing Section
233 Richmond Street, Suite 230
Providence, RI 02903-4230
(401) 277-3857

South Carolina

South Carolina Auctioneers
Commission
915 S. Main Street, Suite 221
Columbia, SC 29201
(803) 734-3193

South Dakota

South Dakota Real Estate
Commission
P.O. Box 490
Pierre, SD 57501
(605) 773-3600

Tennessee

Tennessee Auctioneer
Commission
500 James Robertson Parkway
Volunteer Plaza Building
Nashville, TN 37043-1152
(615) 741-3236

Texas

Department of Licensing and
Regulation
P.O. Box 12157
Austin, TX 78711
(512) 463-7331

Vermont

Secretary of State
109 State Street
Montpelier, VT 05602
(802) 828-2363

Virginia

Department of Commerce
3600 W. Broad Street
Richmond, VA 23230-4917
(804) 367-8519

Washington

Professional Licensing
Services,
Auctioneer Section
P.O. Box 9649
Olympia, WA 98504
(206) 586-4575

West Virginia

Commissioner of
Agriculture,
Marketing and Development
Division
State Capitol
Charleston, WV 25305
(304) 348-2210

Licensing Real Estate Auctioneers

There are a number of states which require that auctioneers selling real estate have real estate licenses. As real estate auctions are growing by leaps and bounds, more auctioneers will come under scrutiny, particularly from real estate brokers who are losing their commissions to them.

Should you be defrauded at a real estate auction, contact the applicable government agency in the previous section. If that state only requires that auctioneers be licensed to hold real estate auctions, file your complaint to the appropriate office from the list that follows:

Alaska

Real Estate Commission
P.O. Box D
Juneau, AK 99811
(907) 465-2542

Arizona

Arizona Department of
Revenue
1600 W. Monroe
Phoenix, AZ 85035
(602) 542-2076

Colorado

Colorado Real Estate
Commission
1776 Logan Street
Denver, CO 80203
(303) 894-2166

Nevada

Real Estate Division
1665 Hot Springs Road
Las Vegas, NV 89710
(702) 687-4280

New Mexico

Regulation and Licensing
Department
725 St. Michael's Drive
Santa Fe, NM 87501
(505) 827-7000

New York

New York State Office of
Business Permits and
Regulatory Assistance
Gov. Alfred E. Smith State
Office Building
17th Floor
P.O. Box 7027
Albany, NY 12225
(518) 474-8275

Oklahoma

Real Estate Commission
4040 N. Lincoln Boulevard
Suite 100
Oklahoma City, OK 73105
(405) 521-3387

Oregon

Real Estate Agency
158 - 12th Street, NE
Salem, OR 97310-0240
(503) 378-4170

Wyoming

Office of the Attorney
General
State Capitol
Cheyenne, WY 82002
(307) 777-7841

8

Tying Up Loose Ends

★★★

Before we wrap up this entire section on getting you ready for government auctions, we shall tie up all the loose ends on auction preparation. There are still a few tips to go over. And, of course, what do you *do* with your auction prize right after you've won?

Government agencies and private auctioneers do not run a delivery service. Not only will you not get credit when you buy at auction, but you also have to remove the merchandise yourself. Claiming your auction award or prize should be simple. Sometimes, it's not.

Time Limit

Many auctions impose an immediate deadline on merchandise removal. Private auctioneers may give you until the end of the auction day, or a few days, to take your new possessions away. Most government agencies are more lenient, particularly with seized bid sales, where you may have 30 days to move the merchandise out. The conditions of sale gives the specific deadline date and time.

Failure to remove by the due date and time can mean either forfeiture of the auction award or storage fees. For example, when U.S. Customs says "remove within 36 hours of auction date," they don't mean 37 hours. Better not tangle on this point. Some government agencies will charge you storage fees, which can amount to a few dol-lars per day to hundreds of dollars, depending on the quantity of the purchase.

"Pack 'Em Up, Ship 'Em Out"

The great thing about going to a public auction is that you can take what you buy home with you. Of course, this also depends on what you buy. Bringing along a compact car is hardly any use if you're buying office furniture, a motorcycle, or a bedroom set. So, your preparation for an auction must include plans to remove and transport your prize from the auction site.

Somewhere between discovering what you desire to buy at the auction and after you've gotten a rough appraisal figure, you should make advance arrangements for carting away your item. Auctioneers prefer, or sometimes demand, that you remove your prize upon full payment. Most government agencies have strict removal requirements and heavily penalize you for failure to transfer your item by the deadline. Check your conditions of sale before making your purchase. You might not be prepared to satisfy the requirement at that particular auction.

Removal and transporting your auction bargain is a matter of logistics. Just as you would diligently research to determine what you plan to buy all the way through to the inspection, you should also research what methods of transport are needed to remove the item. For instance, if you buy a few office desks at auction, you might need a pickup truck or a large van to take them away.

Renting a U-Haul van for the day is not inappropriate if you plan on larger purchases. Bringing the family station wagon is adequate for smaller items, and it can be convenient should you buy a few bicycles, a computer, or small copy machine. However, if the item is large and removal must be immediate, your only option may be to hire a moving company. Look in the Yellow Pages of your telephone book for reliable rental firms and moving companies. Here are a few national firms renting trucks:

Budget Car and Truck Rental
Ford Rent-A-Truck Leasing
Hertz/Penske Truck Rental
Ryder Truck Rental
Thrifty Truck Rental
U-Haul Company

These are national moving companies you may find in your Yellow Pages.

Allied Van Lines
Bekins Moving and Storage
Global WorldWide Moving
Mayflower Transit
North American Van Lines
Terminal Van Lines
United Van Lines

For smaller purchases and/or short hauls, it may pay to rent a van or truck yourself. For bulk quantity merchandise/equipment or long-distance shipping, hiring a professional moving company could be more economical in the long run.

Driving It Away

One mistake some make is forgetting to bring a friend (or make other arrangements) to help them drive away their newly purchased vehicle. Unless the auction is being held within walking distance, you're probably going to be driving there, right?

So, make some arrangements to have a friend or someone drive your new purchase home.

I know this sounds too simple and stupid to include here, but many get caught up in the excitement of going to an auction that no provisions are made if one wins at it. Successes *do* happen at auction, you know.

Towing It Away

If you don't bring a friend or your new vehicle needs repair work, you have two choices. At some of the sloppier government auctions, cars are sold with deflated tires. Cars sitting around for a few weeks or months can "get ill" (tires are just one symptom). Other repair problems might include a missing engine, no transmission, etc. Get the picture? You may want to buy cars like this for the parts or to fill in the missing puzzle pieces. Great deals are often found with problem cars. The cost of fixing them up is not that major.

Hire a towing company to bring it home to you. Charges can be steep, however: a few dollars per mile towed and a minimum charge of $40. Forget about transporting it long-distance. That would cost an arm and a leg. U.S. Customs allowed this to happen with some of their auction vehicles. They were paying $700 or more to have $500 cars towed across parts of Texas! And they couldn't figure out how come they were losing money by holding auctions.

The do-it-yourselfer will have already figured out another solution. Rent a tow bar. Some of you already own one. Just hook up the tow bar to the car and drive it away. If you don't have one, rent one from companies that rent trucks, trailers, and large vans, such as U-Haul or the others mentioned previously. Should you be new to using a tow bar, your major precaution is remembering to turn the ignition key to "on." That allows the towed car mobility. Otherwise you'll have trouble behind you for the entire trip.

In a Pinch

You bought something bigger than will fit inside your car. How about putting it on the roof? For a small investment you can buy a rooftop carrier. Failing that, get a few blankets and some rope. (Depending on how fragile it is you might want to be cautious about the preceding advice and consider another method.) Securely tie the merchandise atop your roof with the rope and drive off.

If you expect rain, buy some plastic paint drop sheets from a hardware store. Bundle up your merchandise in this. Remember to tie it all down.

Problems with Sealed Bids

(AND HOW TO SOLVE THEM)

Government auctions plentifully offer sealed bids. They have fantastic bargains available at them. Many public auctions also permit the telegraph, mailed-in, or faxed bids. Placing those bids is easy. Getting the stuff back home is the hard part, not to mention finding out if it's worth buying or not. Both of those problems can be solved. Department of Defense Military Surplus auctions have people they can recommend to you. These are often retired personnel who will inspect the merchandise you wish to bid on, give you an idea of what you might bid, and then package/ship it off to you or another destination after you've made your purchase. Check in Section Two for telephone contact numbers for assistance.

Private auctioneers can be contacted for referral assistance in transportation of merchandise. Some may have helpers looking for a few extra dollars. Try asking them. For appraisal, you may just ask the auctioneer for the appraised value of the merchandise and place your sealed bid that way. It's not the best method, but it gives you a range. You can adjust your bid accordingly. Placing a bid that is 80% of appraised value is generally a safe bet.

Other government agencies are less helpful. The General Services Administration has a custodian with a telephone number. He may be of some aid, but you will have to handle the shipment yourself.

Hiring someone to pick it up is the safest ap-

proach. All but the dumbest auctioneers, and virtually every government agency, will demand that you supply that person with a letter authorizing the removal of your auction prize. It can be a simple letter that states: "John Doe has my authorization to remove Lot #4453 from your premises. My bidder number was #817. To confirm this, please telephone (or fax) me at this number _____." Then, sign it, date it, and give it to your mover. It need not be more complex than that.

NO HELP FROM THE GOVERNMENT WHEN REMOVING SEALED-BID AUCTION AWARDS

Government agencies will lend a hand, barely, when you wish to package up and transport your auction prize. Usually, one of the employees may help you move it off the premises. As for loading, you are on your own. Bring a friend to lend a hand if you expect it to be heavy or bulky.

MORE ON SHIPPING

If your purchase is in sizable quantity, have it shipped in pieces. Just package everything into cardboard boxes, wrap securely, and send with a trucking or parcel company. This can work with large numbers of items or smaller ones when they are a considerable distance from where you live.

At auctions where you expect to buy smaller quantities, just bring some cardboard boxes along in your car and packaging material, in case you buy something fragile. Old newspapers are used widely to prevent breakage, but you should also use Styrofoam bubbles for added protection.

Complaining at the Removal Site

This can happen at either public oral auctions or sealed bid sales. The merchandise isn't up to snuff. Something could be wrong with it. If there is a problem, ask for help. At one General Services Administration (GSA) auction a bidder discovered there was a serious problem with the car he just bought. He moaned aloud and pleaded with one of the GSA mechanics for assistance. That employee took the matter into his own hands and exchanged the defective car for a different car, which wasn't already sold at auction. (No, I won't give out my sources!) The bidder drove away in a better car than he had purchased.

I would not recommend using this as a standard practice to upgrade your auction purchase. However, if the merchandise or equipment really is defective, or has been in some way misrepresented by the auctioneer, make a complaint. Procedures for handling such complaints have already been discussed in the previous chapter. But sometimes you can get immediate satisfaction—not always, but every now and then.

Exporting Your Auction Purchase

More bidders of large purchases at auction are finding export to their liking. There are many countries sorely in need of heavy construction machinery, office equipment, and other merchandise found at auction. Since the government doesn't really want to be in either the auction or real estate business, they're not likely to be dragged into exporting auctionable merchandise.

It's up to auction-goers. Exporting can be profitable. At U.S. Customs auctions it could be mandatory. When you buy "export only" equipment or merchandise at U.S. Customs auctions, you have a short deadline of not only removing your purchase from the auction site, but also getting it the heck out of the country. For this you need a freight-forwarding firm. They are located near international airports in major cities. Many U.S. Customs auctions are located in such metropolitan areas, so that's convenient. Find these freight-forwarding firms in the Yellow Pages of your telephone book.

Freight forwarders usually offer a complete service: they will pick up the merchandise, pack it professionally for shipping (U.S. Customs scores low points on this), and store it in a bonded warehouse for you until it is ready to leave the country. Once your merchandise is in a bonded warehouse

it is officially "out of the country." Pretty easy, huh?

There are many freight-forwarding companies available for hire. One I have used, Amerford International, is reliable and moderately priced. They have offices across the United States and ship internationally. At the end of this chapter is a complete list of Amerford International locations throughout the United States.

Evidence of Title

When purchasing mobile merchandise, like a car, boat, airplane, or motorcycle, you must obtain some evidence of title from the auctioneer or government agency. Generally, the auction bill of sale is valid for ordinary equipment or merchandise. When buying from the GSA, they will give you a standard form 97 that is evidence of your purchase. But, for an automobile and other vehicles you need to register with your state's Department of Motor Vehicles (DMV).

When financing your vehicle using the evidence of title or bill of sale, the bank may assist you in obtaining title to it. After all, they will be the first lienholder on that title. Inquire about this assistance from your loan officer. You will have to pay the government agency or auctioneer in full before going to your bank for a loan. Some loan officers should work with you in providing financing for your auction purchase.

You are required to properly register your new vehicle after the auction. Some auctions companies have established a line to the DMV to assist their winning bidders with temporary registrations. The responsibility, though, lies with you to adhere to your state's laws.

Insurance Card

Some states may require that you present a valid insurance card on your present vehicle before allowing you to drive, sail, or fly off with your new purchase. Bidders should bring to the auction their current and valid insurance card along with their driver's license.

Dealing with Clunkers

Your best bargains are found with the dirtiest vehicles. With these the battery is probably dead, tires could be flat, and the exterior a nightmare. If you're handy with tools or are devoted to making things clean, then buy junkers. Not only is competition lacking on these, but even the auctioneer won't try hard to jack up the prices on them.

When purchased, these will have to be towed behind you, using a tow bar, or by hiring a towing service. If you are serious about doing this for a living, invest in an air compressor and other small equipment. Inflate the tires at the auction site. Many compressors can be hooked right into the cigarette lighter of the car. Bring along a replacement battery for your new car.

Bidding on these clunkers should not be at full wholesale value, as listed in your Blue Book. Cars priced at those wholesale levels are in good, clean condition. That may or may not apply at many government auctions. Wholesale Blue Book prices are determined at dealer auto auctions, where cars are often "prepped" before the sale. Many private auctioneers will clean up the merchandise and equipment before sale, but the government hasn't taken that cue yet. Police auctions and IRS sales will offer the vehicle or merchandise in unkempt condition.

When making bids on such merchandise, figure in the cost of restoring or cleaning it up. Someone has to do it, either a mechanic or yourself. Bid accordingly.

When It's Not There

Let's say you did all of your research and preparation for a specific item or items to be offered at auction. But when you get there, all ready to bid and buy, it's not there. What happened? Somebody already bought it before the auction took place.

At an increasing number of auctions creative techniques are being used. Auctioneers do try to hustle the auction merchandise and get the best prices fast for their sellers or the government agency. Missing items are due to one of these factors, which all add up to the same thing: it is not being sold at the auction you were planning to attend.

1. The auctioneer got offered a top-bid price from someone or a number of people, concluding a negotiated sale before the scheduled auction.

2. The auctioneer offered or accepted sealed bids on the merchandise/property before the scheduled auction.

3. The auctioneer took sealed bids and then held a separate public oral auction with the three highest bidders before the scheduled auction.

4. One final possibility is the seller withdrew the merchanise/property before the auction. That happens occasionally when sellers get cold feet.

A precaution you can take to avoid complete and utter disappointment is to check with the auction company the day before going to the auction. When calling the government agency holding the sale, telephone the contact name listed on the auction catalog. Why show up and find it missing? Be prepared for this possibility.

Mailing Lists

In the remainder of this book you will find ways to have your name placed on numerous government and private mailing lists. There are tremendous advantages to doing this. You find out in advance what is going to be held at public auction. Many times you will receive auction notices that aren't well publicized. Sealed-bid sales are promoted in a low-key way since these are geared to dealers—who usually get the best prices because they are on top of things. You can be playing the same game as they are, if you get your name on mailing lists.

With the growth of catalog shopping, getting on specialized mailing lists is a sort of honor. Don't abuse this. Professional auction-goers appreciate the surplus of free mailings from government agencies. When I am eager to find out about a certain type of equipment, I will have my name or another's placed on several mailing lists. The flurry of catalogs, auction notices, fliers, and brochures hitting the mailbox is overwhelming. These rarely cost more than the telephone call made to receive them.

Some auctioneers and government agencies have started charging to be placed on their mailing lists. The large number of inquiries to them created by my previous book and others who copied it has brought this about. Hopefully, economic stress will force auctioneers and government agencies to realize that the *more* bidders attending, the higher the final sales prices. If not, and if this trend continues of getting on "everyone's mailing list," then expect private auctioneers and government agencies to charge you nominal fees to be placed on their mailing list.

For the Lazy

Although you can be placed on many, many mailing lists for absolutely nothing more than the telephone call to the agency or auctioneer, some will still not take advantage of this. There's hope for the lazy.

One private firm compiles many of the government auction announcements from around the country into a bi-weekly newsletter. Now, you can simply subscribe to their newsletter and avoid making more than a telephone call to them. The disadvantage is that you limit yourself to the number of auctions. They will cover most of the main auctions: General Services Administration and Department of Defense auctions, some of the Marshals Service auctions, a few police and sheriff auctions, and some U.S. Customs auctions. However, there are thousands of auctions that won't fit into their eight-page newsletter.

On the other hand, it is worth the six-month trial subscription fee ($29) as an entry point. Later, when you see how eye-popping the bargains can be, you might want to refer to Sections Two and Three of this book. There are a lot of auctions going on!

For a subscription, contact:

National Auction Bulletin, Inc.
4419 West Tradewinds Avenue
Fort Lauderdale, FL 33308
Telephone: (305) 491-1799
Fax: (305) 772-7944
Toll-Free: (800) 327-2049

AMERFORD DIRECTORY
USA Offices

Atlanta (D.E.I.O.)

430 Plaza Drive
College Park, GA 30349
TEL: (404) 767-5478
FAX: (404) 767-5487
Manager: Doug Travis

Baltimore (O.P.)

2500 A. Broening Highway
Suite 202
Baltimore, MD 21224
TEL: (301) 633-3870
FAX: (301) 633-3878
Manager: Welsey Koerbier

Boston (D.E.I.O.)

135 Bremen Street
E. Boston, MA 02128
TEL: (617) 569-5830
TLX: 4430183
FAX: (617) 569-0261)

Charlotte (D.E.I.O.)

1912 Cross Beam Drive
Charlotte, NC 28217
TEL: (704) 357-0922
TLX: 4613045
FAX: (704) 357-0748
Manager: Mike Alger

Chicago (D.E.I.O.)

2707 Coyle Avenue
Elk Grove Village, IL 60007
TEL: (708) 593-3377
TLX: 4330168
FAX: (707) 593-6695
Manager: Anthony Fiacchino

Cleveland (D.E.I.O.)

17991 Englewood Drive,
Suite A
Middleburg Heights, OH
44130
TEL: (216) 243-0900
TLX: 4332121
FAX: (216) 243-8270
Manager: Joseph Elliott

Dallas (D.E.I.O.)

751 Portamerica Place,
Suite 700
Grapevine, TX 76051
TEL: (817) 481-2801
TLX: 4630064
FAX: (817) 488-4120
Manager: Berniece Eaken

*Dayton

P.O. Box 753
Vandalia, OH 45377
TEL: (513) 235-1120
FAX: (513) 339-6660
Manager: John Zaenglein

Denver (D.E.I.O.)

3251 Revere Street
Building 2, Suite 200
Aurora, CO 80010
TEL: (303) 367-8680
TLX: 4323048
FAX: (303) 367-9176
Manager: Diana Bomar

Detroit (D.E.I.O.)

11677 Wayne Road, Suite 111
Romulus, MI 48174
TEL: (313) 941-7800
TLX: 4320017
FAX: (313) 941-0030

Hartford (D.E.I.O.)

Bradley International Airport
Windsor Locks, CT 06096
TEL: (203) 522-6114
TLX: 4436039
FAX: (203) 627-3276
Manager: Peter Brinkmann

Houston (D.E.I.O.)

16550 Air Central Boulevard
Houston, TX 77032
TEL: (713) 443-1177
TLX: 4620311
FAX: (713) 443-2642
Manager: Debbie Forrester

Indianapolis (D.E.I.O.)

5601 Fortune Circle S. Ste. M
Indianapolis, IN 46241
TEL: (317) 244-9501
TLX: 4336-18
FAX: (317) 244-9505
Manager: Wanda Ray

Jersey City (O.P.)

66 York Street
Jersey City, NJ 07302
TEL: (201) 333-0220
TLX: 139227
FAX: (201) 333-5508
Manager: Michael Renz

Kansas City (D.E.)

10302 NW Prairie View Road
Kansas City, MO 64153
TEL: (816) 891-7660
TLX: 6875088
FAX: (816) 891-7614
Manager: Lesha Davis

Los Angeles (B.D.E.I.O.P.)

431–441 N. Oak Street
Inglewood, CA 90302
TEL: (213) 673-1611
TLX: 4720516
FAX: (213) 673-8644
Manager: Scott Herron

Memphis

3378 One Place
Memphis, TN 38116
TEL: (901) 346-0935
FAX: (901) 332-6400

Miami (D.E.I.O.)

7879–85 NW 21st Street
Miami, FL 33122
TEL: (305) 592-7740
TLX: 441512
FAX: (305) 592-4317
Manager: Toney Ciero

Milwaukee (D.E.)

2200 East College Avenue
Cudahy, WI 53110
TEL: (414) 764-2553
TLX: 49600061
FAX: (414) 764-2623
Manager: Jerline Royal

Minneapolis (D.E.I.O.)

1355 Mendota Heights Rd.
Suite 200
Mendota Heights, MN 55120
TEL: (612) 688-8606
TLX: 4310116
FAX: (612) 688-8612
Manager: Daniel Young

Nashville (D.E.)

141 Space Park Road
Nashville, TN 37211
TEL: (615) 331-8590
FAX: (615) 834-9929
Manager: Royce Dugan

Newark (D.E.I.)

15 Fenwick Street
Newark, NJ 07114
TEL: (201) 242-5800
TLX: 4754195
FAX: (201) 824-4552
Manager: Mike DeBartolome

New York (B.D.E.I.O.)

218–01 Merrick Blvd.
Jamaica NY 11413
TEL: (718) 528-0800
TLX: 420695
FAX: (718) 656-7393
Manager: Andrew Walters

Orlando (D.E.I.O.)

6300 Hazeltine National Dr.
Suite 118
Orlando, FL 32822
TEL: (407) 856-1887
TLX: 441257
FAX: (407) 856-1354
Manager: Eric Burhans

Philadelphia (D.E.I.O.)

8/9 Park Square Bldg. S.
777 Henderson Blvd.
Felcroft, PA 19032
TEL: (215) 461-2336
TLX: 4761028
FAX: (215) 461-1919
Manager: Nancy Dotsicas

Phoenix (D.E.I.)

2810 S. 24th St., Suite 106
Phoenix, AZ 85034
TEL: (602) 273-4870
TLX: 4725045
FAX: (602) 275-6841
Manager: Judy Svechovsky

*Providence

37 Cypress Street
Warwick, RI 02888
TEL: (401) 461-8678
FAX: (617) 569-0261
Manager: James Hughes

*Rochester

455 Perinton Hills Office Park
Fairport, NY 14450
TEL: (716) 425-4910
FAX: (716) 425-7929
Manager: Peter Laiosa

Salt Lake City (D.E.I.)

5080 Amelia Earhart Dr.
Salt Lake City, UT 84116
TEL: (801) 537-7111
TLX: 4979658
FAX: (801) 537-7825

San Diego (D.E.I.)

2719 Kurtz St.
San Diego, CA 92110
TEL: (619) 298-6671
TLX: 4723025
FAX: (619) 298-0425
Manager: Cheri Carpenter

San Francisco (B.D.E.I.O.)

1336–42 Marsten Road
Burlingame, CA 94010
TEL: (415) 877-6866
TLX: 470597
FAX: (415) 579-0209
Manager: Frank McMenomy

San Juan (D.E.)

Cargo Area
San Juan International Airport
San Juan, PR 00913
TEL: (809) 791-2435
TLX: 3252882
FAX: (809) 791-4009

Seattle (D.E.I.O.)

Cascade Commerce Park
7003 S. 216th Street
Kent, WA 98032
TEL: (206) 872-7311
TLX: 4971202
FAX: (206) 872-7913
Manager: Greg Harrison

St. Louis (D.E.)

4520 Woodson Road
St. Louis, MO 63134
TEL: (314) 429-2940
TLX: 4312076
FAX: (314) 429-2818
Manager: Linda Dolgin

*Syracuse

The Pickard Building
Suit 118

5858 East Molloy Road
Syracuse, NY 13211
TEL: (315) 455-5733
FAX: (315) 455-5735
Manager: Steven Smith

Tampa (D.E.I.)

5410-C Pioneer Park Blvd.
Tampa, FL 33623
TEL: (813) 881-1887
FAX: (813) 886-8135

Tucson

4211 South Santa Rita
Tucson, AZ 85714
TEL: (602) 741-9980
FAX: (602) 573-3754

Corporate Offices

CORPORATE WORLD HEADQUARTERS
INCLUDING ACCOUNTING

One Cross Island Plaza
Rosedale, NY 11422
TEL: (718) 481-4200
TLX: 420695
FAX: (718) 481-4290

FASHION AIR DIVISION

1336–42 Marsten Road
Burlingame, CA 94010
TEL: (415) 877-6888
TLX: 470597
FAX: (415) 348-5723

Reference Marks & Service Keys

B-Brokerage Service
D-Domestic Air Freight
Service
E-Export Air Freight Services
*-Amerford Sales Office

I-Import/Breakbulk Freight
O-Ocean Export/Import Breakbulk
P-Project Cargoes

Conclusion

★★★

This concludes Section One. Because a great deal has been covered, let's do a quick summary.

1. Study and understand the golden rules of auction participation before going to an auction. You may need to refer to them periodically. Try reading them before and after each auction until you get the hang of the rules. These are at the end of Chapter 3.

2. To be a professional requires preparation. Auctions and auctioneers have gotten sophisticated. This trend will continue. Make every effort to become professional in attitude at auction.

3. Decide what you want to buy before going to an auction. There is often so much to choose from that you should contact the auction house or government agency prior to making that decision. Most will be happy to help you and answer your questions.

4. Get price comparisons from the applicable sources mentioned in Chapter 4. Appraise before you establish a set limit.

5. Inspect before you make your first bid. Precaution inspections are mandatory. You may have an hour or a week or more to properly inspect the merchandise, equipment, or property. Use that preview period to do a thorough inspection.

6. Use a professional for your inspection until you can comfortably and rapidly do one yourself.

7. If you are buying for resale, try to have buyers lined up even before you attend. Chapter 6 discusses the various methods of doing this.

8. Know the method of acceptable payment at the auction and prepare accordingly. Many will only accept cash, cashiers' checks, or money orders. Others can be more lenient. Make arrangements to get cash quickly if that is required.

9. Be prepared to remove the merchandise or equipment by the deadline date. It may be at the end of the auction day or 30 days later. Make all necessary arrangements before attending the auction. You may need to bring a friend or equipment. Hiring an individual or a moving firm to ship the auction prize may be required.

10. Restudy this summary before attending an auction to ensure that you are fully prepared for winning.

A FINAL NOTE. If you are going to an auction, arrive there prepared. Once you are fully prepared, as any professional would be, the only thing stopping you from success is a winning attitude. If the winning attitude is missing or you are nervous, then review the summary steps. You may need to review the golden rules for auction participation. Preparation for the auction is the key to your success. Luck is great when it happens but don't count on it. If you are really prepared, Lady Luck has a better chance of visiting your doorstep.

Section Two

★★★

Mini-Glossary

★★

Below are some of the important words you should understand before reading Section Two. This book contains several specialized words, which when not completely understood in their context, could prevent you from becoming skilled in this subject.

These are only a few of the basic terms. A full glossary of specialized words and terms appears at the end of this book. Please use this glossary when coming across unfamiliar terms in this subject. Use a regular dictionary for other words that you do not understand.

Surplus   Something that is no longer needed. It could be an excess of something, out-of-date, unusable, or just no longer needed.

Personal Property   In this use it refers to something that is not real estate. It could be equip-ment, machinery, merchandise, or even cloth-ing. This term distinguishes something being sold at auction from real estate.

Seized Property   Personal property or real es-tate that has been seized by a local, state, or government agency as a result of a criminal act having been committed by its owner.

Foreclosed Property   Real estate that has been taken over by a lender or other creditor because the debtor did not meet his/her financial obliga-tions in a timely fashion.

Abandoned Property   Personal property or real estate that has been left behind. It could be a vehicle left in the streets with the intention to desert it, or real estate that the owner has va-cated with no intention of returning.

Introduction

★★

Ability is of little account without opportunity.
—NAPOLEON BONAPARTE

Opportunity and bargains are more than amply provided at government auctions. You will be amazed at the great deals some have found at auction. Frequently, these people are just like you, normal auction-goers. Sure, professionals and dealers come to auctions and are regular buyers. Their livelihood depends on finding great bargains. Now you have the chance to take advantage of the great auction boom in America. The following chapters will show you who has merchandise for auction, how to contact them, and how you can participate in their auctions. You'll also find evaluations of each government agency's performance record at the end of the chapter followed by a telephone and/or address directory.

This section explains the government agencies handling personal property, merchandise, and equipment auctions. Included are federal, state, and local government agencies. Most of what you will find when contacting them will be personal property, not real estate. Personal property is defined as vehicles, boats, airplanes, office equipment, jewelry, and other tangible, portable merchandise and equipment. At some auctions you might find oddball equipment and merchandise. Many individuals do attend auctions simply for that purpose—to find the unusual. This is also

considered personal property, even if it is equipment or food waste. It's the way government agencies classify these auctions and refer to the merchandise.

Throughout this section there are a few government agencies that hold real estate auctions as well as personal property auctions. The main subject of this section is, however, personal property, merchandise, and equipment, not real estate. For example, although the Internal Revenue Service holds both personal property and real estate auctions, I have included the IRS in this section, Section Two, and not Section Three because IRS bargains in personal property are less complex than those you may find at their real estate auctions.

The Resolution Trust Corporation holds personal property auctions to dispose of fixtures and equipment from failed savings and loan institutions. Their largest assets are foreclosed real estate holdings that run into the tens of billions of dollars. Thus, the major discussion of the RTC rightfully belongs in Section Three.

For a different reason, the General Services Administration has been included in both Sections Two and Three. Each branch of the GSA has two distinct and separate regional offices: one sells personal property and the other, real estate. The two regional offices' procedures and mailing lists are different. As a result it is easier to distinguish between the two; they are almost different government agencies.

Different Categories

Section Two is laid out with a specific pattern in mind. Chapters 9, 10, and 11 contain the government agencies that specialize in selling government surplus. Chapters 12, 13, and 14 cover those agencies that sell seized assets (property, merchandise, equipment) at their auctions. Chapters 15, 16, and 17 are about agencies that hold auctions for repossessed personal property. Finally, Chapters 18 and 19 include those government agencies selling abandoned or unclaimed vehicles and merchandise.

A ratings system and brief agency summary has been provided at the end of this section to assist you in deciding which government agency auctions you should attend. The ratings are determined mainly by the value found at those agency's auctions.

Throughout most of the section, chapters about federal agencies are given precedence over the state or local government agency. Chapter 15 is the exception to the rule. That's because the County Sheriffs could be in either the seizure or the repossession business.

Mailing Lists

One of the major benefits of this book is to provide you with directory information so that you can readily contact one or more government agencies and ask to be placed on their mailing lists. Getting on the government mailing lists has not always been an easy task. There is no single, centralized government agency that provides you with up-to-date, accurate information about government auctions. The General Services Administration (GSA) probably has the most efficient system, but it is far from effective or accurate. None of their information is complete. After you contact the GSA for the first time, you may sympathize with the ordeals this book's researchers have undergone.

Having your name placed on many of these government mailing lists is free. Auction notices will be sent to you at no cost for a period of time. That period of time is determined by whether or not you respond and participate in their auctions. Some government agencies have cut-off times; if you don't send in a bid after three to five mailings, the agency will cease mailing you auction catalogues, brochures, or notices. This is done purely for economical reasons.

Some government agencies will charge you a fee. These are noted in the applicable chapters. The fee is usually small, affordable. A few private auctioneers have also started charging to send fliers. As postal rates continue to increase, many firms have to charge for these mailings.

Fair-Market Value

Perhaps the most misunderstood term having to do with auctions and virtually *all* sales of property and real estate is fair-market value. A government agency may state that it always gets fair-market value for something or that buyers will pay "about fair-market value." The General Services Administration and the U.S. Marshals Service, for instance, ride this hobbyhorse.

The definition of fair-market value is nothing more than the agreed-upon price between a buyer and a seller. It is more completely defined in *Black's Law Dictionary* (Sixth Edition) as: "The amount at which property would change hands between a willing buyer and a willing seller, neither being under any compulsion to buy or sell and both having reasonable knowledge of the relevant facts."

It is, further, the agreed-upon observation and rule that an auction *determines* the fair-market value of property or real estate. The final bid price is what a buyer was willing to pay and what a seller was willing to accept. The auctioneer's gavel determines the fair-market value.

This information is being provided to you because you will hear and read this term in government auction notices. The intention is not really to mislead or deceive you. Basically, Washington politics dictate to each government agency that you "cover your backside."

When any agency makes the claim that "we only sell at fair-market value," it is as superfluous as your saying aloud: "I am talking." Of course you are. And when something is sold at auction, it is being sold at fair-market value—whether the government agency lost its shirt on the item or not.

Appraisals

Government agencies also boast about having done accurate appraisals on merchandise, property, and real estate before it goes to auction. Any informed reader would know that this is not always possible. Just read old newspaper clippings about how the government "misestimated" one thing or another. For example, the Resolution Trust Corporation incorrectly appraised their real estate values, based on earlier savings and loan appraisals. Errors could be as high as in the *billions* of dollars. Some appraisal, huh?

Another great appraisal was the $50,000 boat that sold for $10. That had been appraised by federal officials at about $50–55,000. The going price at auction was $10. Even if other bidders jumped in, I seriously doubt it would have sold for more than $5,000–$10,000. So even though it was a great deal, the fair-market value was not likely to have been more than $10,000. On that day, though, the fair-market value of that specific boat *was* $10.

Appraising in an uncertain economic climate is more art than science. It's sophisticated guesswork that is a logical attempt to predict what a buyer *might* pay for a house or car. Throughout the research of this book it was common to hear from auctioneers and others that if you were to ask 100 different appraisers for the worth of something you would be given 100 different prices for

the same item. Blue Book wholesale prices, as you discovered from the previous section, are derived from automobile dealer auctions held around the country. Even those are updated weekly to reflect changing market conditions.

Each government agency uses similar auction methods, with some slight variations. Nearly all claim to hold auctions with reserve. But reserve prices can be manipulated and may not even represent the accurate fair-market value of the auction item. In some cases a government agency may be trying solely to demonstrate to congress or the media that it always gets top price at its auctions. This only happens on occasion. For the most part, auctions are where you find bargains.

Methods

You will be warned to avoid those government agency auctions where bargains are not to be found. Of course, all readers will be encouraged to participate in those auctions where great deals, or even steals, can be found. Don't be disappointed if every auction you attend doesn't have the "steal of the century." Where professional, nongovernment auctioneers hold the sale and are given complete control by the government agency, there will be good deals, but few, if any, steals.

One major warning is this: if you do register for a federal government auction, become the winning bidder, and walk away from the auction without paying for and claiming your prize, you risk being banned from future government auctions, not only by that agency but also potentially from other federal government agency auctions. Be careful when you buy. If you do win, pay. Those who don't pay aren't likely to be welcome at future auctions.

Good luck at the auction and may the best man or woman win!

9

The General Services Administration

★★

This federal agency plays a very large role in government merchandise auctions. Auctions, though, play a small part in their overall duties as a government agency. The GSA was originally created to manage government property and records, sort of like a civilian quartermaster. This is the agency that supervises the construction and operation of government buildings. They procure and distribute the supplies for the federal government. Aside from that, they are also responsible for civilian traffic and communications facilities, managing the computer facilities of the government, and stockpiling strategic materials and equipment.

What we're interested in is how the GSA disposes of all surplus civilian merchandise, equipment, and nonforeclosed government real estate. The GSA sells merchandise and equipment through their auction program, managed by the Property Management Division, which oversees federal bureaus in eleven regions around the United States.

The GSA is best known for their automobile auctions. Many individuals look for good-to-average bargains at these auctions. In fiscal year 1990, the GSA sold 46,000 vehicles for a total of $120 million, at an average of about $2,600 per vehicle. During this same period, though, the

GSA also sold $26 million in personal property and merchandise.

While the GSA often boasts it is the main disposition arm of the federal government, their holdings and sales are overshadowed by the vast number of real estate properties held by the Resolution Trust Corporation (RTC) and the Federal Deposit Insurance Corporation (FDIC). Many individuals, and even some media people, are often confused in thinking that the GSA is the primary, or only, government agency holding auctions.

This isn't true. There are a large number of state surplus auctions held around the country, not to mention sheriff sales, police auctions, bankruptcy auctions, tax sales, postal auctions, military surplus sales, and others. The GSA's role in auctions is not as dominant as it once was, but it still holds a large share of the government surplus auction market.

Background

The GSA is involved in two distinct areas of auctions: personal property/merchandise/equipment/vehicles *and* real estate. Personal property auctions are held through the Federal Service Supply Bureaus of the GSA. Real estate sales are done by the GSA's Federal Property

Resource Service. Section Three contains information about these real estate sales.

Surplus merchandise for GSA auctions comes from many other branches of government. Some of the agencies include:

Department of the Interior
U.S. Fish and Wildlife Services
Bureau of Land Management
Federal Communications Commission
Immigration and Naturalization Service
U.S. Border Patrol
U.S. Department of Labor
The Federal Bureau of Investigation
The Internal Revenue Service
Department of Energy

As you can imagine, there could be tens of thousands of items available at auction, with a variety that would range from soup to nuts. As a special note, please understand that merchandise sold by the GSA at their auctions, which comes from the above (and other) government agencies, is just their *surplus* equipment, not properties that an enforcement agency (such as IRS or FBI) has confiscated from criminals or tax offenders. In some areas, the Marshals Service will turn over vehicles and other property to the GSA to sell on their behalf.

There are two types of GSA merchandise auctions, public auctions and sealed-bid sales. The predominant merchandise sold by GSA at public auctions is surplus cars. These are typically three-

---

SALE DATE: SEPTEMBER 25, 1991 - 1:00PM   SALE NUMBER: 92FBPS-91-241   PAGE NUMBER: 8

LOT	DESCRIPTION	QUANTITY	LOT	DESCRIPTION	QUANTITY
069	TRUCK: 1985 DODGE, W/UTILITY BODY, 8 CYL, AT, PS, PB, AC, RADIO, DUAL WHEELS. EST MI: 51,483. VIN NO:1B7MD34W8FS661682, TAG:G43-22498, (4793131155#5626) (R3)	1 EA	081	TRUCK: 1988 CHEVROLET BLAZER, 4X4, 8 CYL, 4SPD MT, PS, PB, AC, W/MANUAL LOCKING HUBS. ODOMETER 50073 S/N:1GNEV18KXJF150240, TAG:G62-15616, RA, (4793131163#5765) (R3)	1 EA
070	PICKUP: 1986 DODGE, W250, 4X4, 8 CYL, 4SPD MT, PS, PB, AC,RA,ODOMETER:53,977, S/N 1B7KW24W1GS066492, TAG NO:G63-11175, (4793131155#5628) (R3)	1 EA	082	VAN: 1988 CHEVROLET ASTRO, 7-PASS., AT, AC, PS, PB, 6 CYL, RADIO, EST MI:60,304, TAG:G44-75985, VIN:1GNDM15ZXJB187375, (4793131211#6649)(R2)	1 EA.
071	TRUCK: 1985 DODGE, W/UTILITY BODY, 8 CYL, 4X4, AT, PS, PB, AC. EST MI:59,697. VIN NO: 1B7KW34W1FS627553, TAG:G63-11178, (4793131155#5635) (R3)	1 EA	083	CARRYALL: 1986 CHEVROLET SUBURBAN, 4WD, 8 CYL, 4SPD MT, AC, PS, PB, RADIO,ODOMETER 58,870, TAG:G63-11169, S/N:1G8GK26M1GF176099, (4793131211#6642) HAS LOCKING HUBS ***********	1 EA
072	UTILITY: 1987 CHEVROLET BLAZER, 4X4, 8 CYL, RA, 4SPD MT, PS, PB, AC. ODOMETER:61,794, S/N 1GNEV18H4HF150491, (G62-13794;4793131155#5636)	1 EA	084	VAN: 1990 DODGE, B350 VAN, 12-PASS, 8 CYL, AT, PS, PB, AC, RADIO, EST MI: 62,301, TAG: G43-43474, VIN:2B5WB35Y7LK771443, (4793131144#6644)	1 EA
073	CREWCAB: 1987 CHEVROLET, 8 CYL, 4X4, 4SPD MT, PS, PB, RADIO, DUEL TANKS, AC, W/MANUAL LOCKING HUBS. EST MI:62,850, TAG NO:G63-12284, VIN NO: 1GCHV33K6HS149726, (4793131155#5645) (R3)	1 EA	085	VAN: 1985 PANEL, CARGO VAN, 8 CYL, 4X4, AT, PS, PB, AC, RADIO. EST MI:49,544, TAG:G63-14296, VIN:1GCGG35MOF7173332, (4793131211#6646)(R2) *** HAS LOCKING HUBS ***	1 EA
074	PICKUP: 1988 CHEVROLET, C10, 8 CYL, AT, PS, PB, AC, RADIO. EST MI:68,253, TAG NO:G41-78686, VIN:1GCDC14H6JZ227205, (4793131155#5649) (R3)	1 EA	086	VAN: 1985 DODGE 15-PASS, 8 CYL, AT, PS, PB, AC, RA ODOMETER: 59357, S/N 2B5WB31W1FK313390, (TAG #G43-35519; 479313 1232#6897)	1 EA
075	CARGO VAN: 1985 DODGE, B250, 6 CLYL, AT, PS, PB, REPAIRS REQUIRED. EST MI:50,071, VIN NO: 2B7HB23H7FK275169, TAG NO:G42-49459, (4793131155#5650) (R3)	1 EA	087	VAN: 1985 FORD ECONOLINE VAN, EXTENSIVE REPAIRS RE QUIRED, PLEASE INSPECT & BID ACCORDINGLY, ODOMETER READING UNAVAILABLE, (1531AA1192#0248) ***********	1 EA
076	TRUCK: 1987 DODGE W/UTILITY BODY, 8 CYL, 4SPD MT, PS, PB, AC, RADIO, EST MI:69,303, VIN NO: 1B7KD2452HS512986, TAG NO:G43-35523, (4793131155#5651) (R3)	1 EA	088	VAN: 1986 DODGE MAXIVAN, 8 CYL, AT, AC, POOR CONDI TION, BODY DAMAGE, ENGINE OVERHAUL REQUIRED ***** S/N 2B5WB33WXGK591638, ODOMETER: 196,962 (FLEET #P6338: 1531AA 0355#00129)	1 EA
077	TRUCK: 1988 CHEVROLET BLAZER, 4X4, 8 CYL, 4SPD MT, PS, PB, AC, W/MANUAL LOCKING HUBS,ODOMETER 54,838, VIN NO:1GNEV18K7JF153659,(TAG NO:G62-14688, RA, (4793131155#5654)	1 EA	089	VAN: 1986 DODGE MAXIVAN, EXTENSIVE REPAIRS RE- QUIRED, PLEASE INSPECT & BID ACCORDINGLY (1531AA 0355#0027)	1 EA
078	VAN: 1990 DODGE, B350, 12 PASS., 8 CYL, AT, PS, PB, AC, RA, ODOMETER:60,768, TAG:G43-43473, S/N:2B5WB35Y5KL771442, (4793131155#5671) (R3)	1 EA	090	SEDAN: 1979 BUICK LE SABRE, 4 DR, 8 CYL, AC, S/N 4N69X9H626068, ODOMETER: 93,699, REPAIRS RE- QUIRED (2093040184#0011) ** INOPERABLE **	1 EA
079	PICKUP: 1985 CHEVROLET, W10, 4X4, 8 CYL, AT, PS, PB, W/MANUAL LOCKING HUBS. EST MI:56,099, VIN NO: 1GCEK14H9FJ182693, TAG NO:G62-14531, (4793131155#5686) (R3)	1 EA	091	SEDAN: 1982 TOYOTA CRESSIDA, 4-DR, 6 CYL, EXTEN- SIVE REPAIRS REQUIRED, S/N JT2MX62E3C0D40465, ODOMETER: 77,634 (209304 0184#0008)	1 EA
080	PICKUP: 1985 CHEVROLET, C10, 4X4, 6 CLY, 4SPD MT, PS, PB, EST MI:49,096, VIN:1GCEK14N9FJ158223, TAG:G62-14532, (4793131155#5687) (R3)	1 EA	092	RAMCHARGER: 1985 DODGE RAMCHARGER, 3 DR, 8 CYL, AC S/N 1B4GW12T9ES341562, ODOMETER: 101,827, (2093040184#0012) ** EXTENSIVE REPAIRS REQUIRED **	1 EA
			093	SEDAN: 1981 CHRYSLER LEBARON, 4 DR, 8 CYL, AC, S/N 2C38M46LXBR158655, ODOMETER: 68,201,	1 EA

THE GENERAL SERVICES ADMINISTRATION   101

year-old compact cars: Escorts, Tempos, etc. The average mileage is about 36,000, often less. So, their cars are usually well maintenanced.

In recent years, the GSA has taken over several of the U.S. Marshals Service's seized-merchandise disposal responsibilities. The Marshals Service, which appears to relish the glory of being on the fringes of drug busts, seems more inclined to have the GSA or others handle the mop-up operations, i.e., disposing of the seized merchandise. The Marshals Service's contribution of confiscated personal property, usually luxury items, accounts for some dazzle at the GSA public auctions.

At GSA sealed-bid sales you will see a vast array of merchandise available. Here are some of the common and specialized types of equipment that were recently sold at some of their sealed-bid auctions.

acoustical cabinets
ADP equipment
amplifiers
bicycle trainers
calculators
carbon dioxide extractors
chairs
computers
dental laboratories
dictating/transcription equipment
dosimeter chargers
ergometers
filing cabinets
fitness equipment
FM signal generators
fuel pumps
hydraulic press microfiche
kitchen equipment
mass spectrometer
medical equipment
mobile radios
motors
partitions
photocopiers
pumps
safes
scrap copper wire
tables
telephone encoders
telephone systems
typewriters
whirlpool tubs

As you can see, the GSA really is a soup-to-nuts operation. While professionals may shun their vehicle auctions, many dealers, wholesalers, medical doctors, photographers, computer buffs, and others will participate in these auctions.

Procedures

The General Services Administration relies heavily on hotline tape-recorded messages to inform would-be bidders about the date, time, and location of their auctions. Their messages usually give callers a minimum of information: date, time, location, and a vague description of the merchandise up for auction. Some of these recordings refer you to other phone numbers or locations where auctions are held.

Interested bidders are invited to show up at the auction site if they wish to participate. For economical reasons, the GSA will not aggressively pursue your inquiry. If you wish to obtain more information about the auction, then you have to demand an auction catalog, brochure, or flier.

Recently the GSA has been attempting to energize their auctions with more spot-bid auctions. This is just a sham on the auction-going public. It's a guessing game of who's bidding what. The GSA auctioneer hopes to reel in an overzealous amateur making a high bid. Even if the bidders wise up and don't get carried away, the auctioneer can then withdraw the merchandise or equipment. A pretty silly way to hold an auction, huh? Spot bids follow the procedure described in Chapter 2.

Those persons wishing to participate in a sealed-bid sale, should contact the regional office in their state and request an application form. You will be sent GSA form 2170, which is the surplus personal property mailing list application. Fill it out as follows:

1. Enter your name and full address in the spaces provided.

2. Mark the geographic area of bidding interest. There are usually several states to choose from. Select one or two, but not more than four.

3. Beneath that you will find two categories: usable personal property and recyclable. Most will pick "usable." Mark that one unless you are a scrap dealer.

4. Affix a stamp and mail it in.

5. You should start getting mailings in about two to six weeks. These are called invitations for bid (IFB). Instructions are enclosed on how to participate and whether or not deposits are required with your bid.

Special Characteristics

GSA public auctions are uniformly auctions with reserve. Their auctioneers may or may not state a minimum bid. If the merchandise does not meet their selling price, it is withdrawn from auction. Bidders can get frustrated by the GSA's failure to let them know just what their reserve price is. Dealers and other professionals have stopped going to their vehicle auctions because they won't save more than 30% off the market value of the car, usually less.

GSA auctions are conducted by in-house staff. They are trained auctioneers, but some lack incentive or good manners. The head of one auction school criticized their auctioneers' lack of motivation; he rated them about 40% good and the rest bad. Another professional auctioneer rated the Atlanta GSA office as having the most competent auctioneers.

The General Services Administration has a very limited advertising budget. For years they have relied mostly on fast-buck mail order firms, which promote "get rich books" in the classified sections of newspapers, to provide them with interested auction-goers. Of course, the GSA, in their typically bureaucratic fashion, condemns those companies for promoting great auction bargains or

steals. Do not be surprised to find some to be rude or unhelpful. Persistence is the key to getting on their mailing list for sealed-bid sales.

GSA sealed-bid sales generally offer pretty decent bargains. Typewriters sell for about $25, unless there is an overzealous bid placed. The GSA appraisers aren't as meticulous in estimating the true market value of surplus office equipment, so take advantage of sealed-bid sales before they tighten up the rules.

Tips

If you call their hotline number and listen to their tape-recorded message, it is advisable that you also contact the regional office for an auction flier. Information is scanty (giving location, date, time, preview period, etc.), so you should write down the public sale number. This tells you which auction it is. Then, you can ask for the flier promoting that auction. Getting the auction flier takes some work. Keep trying if you are rejected or put off on the first attempt.

If you do attend a GSA public auction sale, look for something other than vehicles. Sometimes, they will have merchandise seized from drug dealers and turned over to GSA for resale by the U.S. Marshals Service. At one auction, held near Washington, D.C., the GSA sold fur coats, signed Salvador Dali prints, Rolex watches, oriental rugs, a large-screen Mitsubishi television, and other collectibles. One Valentino fur sold for $550, the Dali prints for $350, and other items sold for $40 to $185. Pretty good bargains!

Their sealed-bid sales offer better bargains. One bidder wrote me a letter a few years ago and included his bill of sale from the GSA—he had paid only $90 for about $2,500 in computer equipment. In September 1991, at a sealed-bid auction, one woman bought several computer monitors, keyboards, two disk drives, and two printers, all for $310. As you can see, the GSA hardly did a thorough job appraising that purchase!

To find out comparison prices, courtesy of the GSA, try this method. Simply make a joke bid on your first try and enclose a self-addressed stamped envelope with your bid form. Make a written request for the bid abstract. The GSA will send it to you. From that you can compile a file system of what typical merchandise sells for. By doing so, your next bid doesn't have to be a joke, except on the GSA! You'll get a good deal that way.

A faster way is just to call the custodians listed in the auction catalog. There are usually several per sealed-bid sale, as GSA sealed-bid auctions are located in various states within one region. Ask the custodian about the last auction and find out what "things" went for. There's a good chance he will tell you. That can immediately help you in making an intelligent, possibly successful, bid on the current sealed-bid sale. Also, if the merchandise didn't get reasonable bids, or any bids at all, the custodian can tell you that it will be offered at the next auction. You'll have a head start on other bidders!

As all merchandise is previously owned by the government, the successful bidder gets clear title to it. Usually, he will have a deadline (30 days or less) to remove the merchandise or equipment from storage and pay for it. Transportation and shipping arrangements are up to the new owner.

Once you've won, be sure you get a receipt for your purchase. For vehicle auctions, you are given standard form 97. On other property ask for a certificate of release with the bill of sale. These give you title to the purchase.

Paying with cash, cashiers' checks, money orders, or certified checks is usually acceptable. Some offices have started taking bank credit cards. Check your conditions of sale in the auction catalog.

As with all federal government agency auctions, pay for your purchase. Do *not* walk away at the end of the auction if you have made a successful bid. When you buy the property, you must pay for it. Otherwise, you may be banned from future bidding at all federal government auctions.

Evaluation

Vehicle auctions are okay. They're not the best place to find a great bargain, but the vehicle stands a good chance of being clean and running well. The GSA takes good care of their property. If seized merchandise is sold at auction, it may be in poor or damaged condition.

Public auctions are held in different cities within each region, other than the home-based city. Figure that wherever there is a federal building, and a GSA outpost, you will find a public oral auction there occasionally. Most GSA regions hold monthly public auctions. Again, your best bet is to attend a vehicle auction, which is the main reason why many bidders show up, and make your bids on the "out-of-context" equipment being sold. You won't have as much competition.

In the recent past, it was not unusual to drive away in a nice car for about $600 or so. Those days are gone. Some bidders have been found purchasing cars for more than appraised value. Don't let that happen to you. Come armed with your Blue Book!

Sealed-bid auctions usually draw a professional crowd. Medical doctors, dentists, and photographers participate as well as dealers. Hard-to-find, unusual, or specialized equipment can be sold quite inexpensively. With some of that equipment repairs may be needed, and this may be stated in the auction catalog next to the item.

The main disadvantage of sealed bid sales is that they could be distant from where you live. This makes an accurate appraisal difficult or expensive. Merchandise and equipment for these sales are scattered around the United States.

The GSA is eager to jump into bed with other government agencies and handle their auctions as well. One GSA staff member confided that they are hoping to enter other areas, such as Veterans Affairs and HUD properties, as well as Small Business Administration liquidations. The GSA has been successful in establishing a national auction program and kept the bad press to a minimum. So, you may be seeing more of them in the future in other areas.

Don't think this bureaucratic machine doesn't make mistakes. A few years ago they sold valuable computer parts to one bidder through a sealed-bid auction for less than $100. On the computer's hard drives were Justice Department legal records and strategies. Estimated value: $1 million. Hopefully, the bidder didn't sell out to a drug lord.

If you wish to find out more about General Services Administration auctions or want to participate, you are invited to telephone or write to the office in your region found in the directory that follows. For further information about GSA real estate, see Section Three.

FEDERAL SUPPLY SERVICE BUREAU DIRECTORY
Office of Sales General Information: 1 (800) GSA-1313

REGION ADDRESS & PHONE NUMBER	AREAS SERVED

National Capitol Region

National Surplus & Sales Center Federal Supply Service Bureau 6808 Loisdale Rd. Springfield, VA 22150 (703) 557-0384 Hotline: (703) 557-7796 HQ Personal Property (703) 557-0814	D.C. Metropolitan area, Montgomery & Prince Georges Counties, MD, Fairfax, Arlington, Loudon, Prince William Counties, and the cities of Alexandria & Falls Church, VA.

Region One

Federal Supply Service Bureau 10 Causeway St. 4#2FBP-1 Boston, MA 02222 (617) 565-7322 Hotline: (617) 565-7326	Connecticut, Maine, Massachusetts, New Hampshire, Rhode Island, Vermont Auctions every other week. Sealed bids monthly.

Region Two

Federal Supply Service Bureau 26 Federal Plaza #2FBB-2 New York, NY 10278 (212) 264-3592 Hotline: (212) 264-4824 Toll free: (800) 488-SALE	New Jersey, New York, Puerto Rico, Virgin Islands

REGION ADDRESS & PHONE NUMBER	AREAS SERVED

Region Three

Federal Supply Service Bureau
Personal Property Sales Section
841 Chestnut St.
Suite 540
Philadelphia, PA 19107
(215) 597-6574
Hotline: (215) 597-7253

Delaware, Maryland, Pennsylvania, Virginia, (except D.C. metro area), West Virginia. Send postcard to: GSA Sales, 900 Market Street, Philadelphia, PA 19107 to get on mailing list.

Region Four

General Services Administration
404 West Beach St., #4FBB
Atlanta, GA 30365
(404) 331-3064
Hotline: (404) 331-5177
(407) 876-7637 Florida

Alabama, Florida, Georgia, Kentucky, Mississippi, North Carolina, South Carolina, Tennessee

Region Five

General Services Administration
Federal Supply Service Bureau
Sales Services, Mail Staff 34-5
230 S. Dearborn St.
Chicago, IL 60604
(312) 353-5504
(312) 353-6064
Hotline: (312) 353-0246

Illinois, Indiana, Michigan, Minnesota, Ohio, Wisconsin

To get on mailing list, send postcard to: GSA Sales, 230 S. Dearborn St., Chicago, IL 60604

Region Six

Excess Property Sales
GSA Federal Supply Bureau
#6FP-P
4400 College Blvd.
Suite 175
Overland Park, KS 66211
(913) 236-2500
(913) 236-2525

Iowa, Kansas, Missouri, Nebraska

No hotline number. Surplus sealed-bid/vehicle auctions.

Region Seven

General Services Administration
819 Taylor Street
Fort Worth, TX 76102
(817) 334-2352

Arkansas, Louisiana, New Mexico, Oklahoma, Texas

Only sends catalogs by mail. Auctions scheduled as needed. No hotline number.

Region Eight

General Services Administration
Federal Supply Service Bureau
Building 41
Denver Federal Center
Denver, CO 80226
(303) 236-7698
Hotline: (303) 236-7705

Colorado, Montana, North Dakota, Utah, Wyoming

No hotline number. About 50 auctions/year, minimum bids only. Prefers to keep mailing list within the region only.

Region Nine

525 Market Street, 29th Floor
San Francisco, CA 94105
(415) 774-5240, San Francisco
(415) 744-5120 Personal Property
(415) 744-5952 Real Estate
(415) 744-6067 Fleet Mgmt. Center

For Southern California:
5600 Rickenbacker Rd.
Building 5 E
Bell, CA 90201
(213) 894-5323
Hotline: (213) 894-5162
(213) 894-5158—Bid abstracts

Serves: Arizona, N. California, Guam, Hawaii, Nevada

Real estate prices are competitive, 80–90% or retail. They auction for RTC and FDIC. These can be absolute auctions.

Region Ten

General Services Administration
Excess Personal Property Sales
400 15th Street SW
Auburn, WA 98001
(206) 931-7566
Hotline: (206) 931-7763
(206) 931-7950—vehicles, every 3rd Thursday.

Idaho, Oregon, Washington

10

Department of Defense

★★★

Inside the vast caverns of the Pentagon resides the little-known Defense Logistics Agency, which is a department within the Department of Defense. From Washington, D.C., this agency rules the world of military surplus auctions. Auctions are conducted on military bases throughout the United States and in over a dozen countries around the world. The Department of Defense is an important player in the government auction business and potentially one of the most lucrative for auction-goers.

Its auction arm is the Defense Reutilization and Marketing Service (DRMS), with three main regional centers in the continental United States, one regional center in Hawaii that services Far Eastern military auctions, and a regional center in West Germany that services England, Europe, and Turkey. National headquarters for DRMS is in Memphis, Tennessee. The field offices are called DRMOs, short for Defense Reutilization Marketing Offices, and are located on U.S. military bases in nearly all states and in 20 countries.

As America spends billions on defense, a good deal of that is deemed surplus. The Defense Reutilization Marketing Service sells personal property, merchandise, equipment, and scrap previously owned by the Defense Logistics Agency, Army, Navy, Air Force, Marine Corps, and other departments within the Department of Defense.

GATE PASS

DRMO AUCTION

BLDG 89 AREA C   TIME:0730 - 1500
GOOD JULY 8 THRU 11

DISPLAY THIS PASS ON THE LEFT SIDE OF THE DASHBOARD

AUTHORIZED *2729 513*
Wright Patterson AFB, Ohio
Richard L. Oake

Background

Department of Defense auctions have a reputation for being the laughingstock of the surplus world. While the Pentagon spends $145,000 on a new fax machine, their DRMOs might sell an old fax machine for about $10–$20. While defense contractors milk taxpayers for billions, DRMOs might be found selling a Secret Service safe (with the blueprints to the White House grounds in it) for a few dollars. VCRs might sell for as low as $20, computers could go for $60–$500. One Congressman has called them the "biggest discounter since K-Mart."

Unfortunately, we taxpayers are subsidizing these bargains. Rip-offs can be caught coming and going; coming from the defense contractors and

IFB   27-1079   OMB No. 22-R0200

INVITATION NO.

END—USE CERTIFICATE

(STATEMENT REGARDING DISPOSITION AND USE OF PROPERTY)

RETURN WITH BID

NAME & ADDRESS OF BIDDER AS SHOWN IN BID & AWARD PAGE

NAME _____

ADDRESS _____

_____

1. INSTRUCTIONS. This form must be submitted to the Sales Contracting Officer of the United States prior to the acceptance by the United States of America of the bid submitted by the above named bidder pursuant to the above-numbered invitation.

2. COMMODITIES. This statement applies to the commodities on which we have submitted our bid pursuant to the above-numbered invitation.

3. NATURE OF BUSINESS. (Use separate sheet if needed.)

    a. We are a _____
                                  (Sole proprietorship, partnership, corporation, other)

    b. Our address is (P.O. box address of itself is not acceptable): _____

    _____

    c. The names and addresses of our branch offices are: _____

    _____

    d. The names and addresses of our partners or corporate officers and directors are: _____

    _____

    e. If a bidder is acting as an agent the names and addresses of all principals are: _____

    _____

    f. The nature of our (and our principal's) business is _____

    _____

4. DISPOSITION OF COMMODITIES: Check and complete appropriate entry or entries. (Entry c or d must be checked.)

    a. ☐ The commodities if sold to us, will not be sold or otherwise disposed of by us for use outside of: _____
                                                  (Name of country or countries)

    _____

    b. ☐ May be re-exported in the form received to the following country or countries: _____
                                            (Name of country or countries)

    _____

    c. ☐ If sold by us, our buyer(s) may be: _____
                                           (Names and addresses)

    d. ☐ Our customers are unknown at the present time.   Written approval for the resale of any property covered by this contract will be required from the Defense Reutilization and Marketing Sales Contracting Officer prior to sale when indicated on DRMS Form 1427, Notice of Award, Statement and Release Document, unless they are named in paragraph 4c above.

5. SPECIFIC END-USE. (Check and complete appropriate entry or entries.)

    a. We will use the commodities referred to in paragraph 2 for:

        (1) ☐ Resale in the form received.

        (2) ☐ Production or manufacture of _____
                                      (Name of final product)

    in _____
                              (Name of country or countries)

    and distribution in _____
                            (Name of country or countries)

DRMS Form 2   (Previous edition is obsolete)
Mar 90
NSN 7540-00-000-002

PAGE NO.   25

```
              DEPARTMENT OF DEFENSE

         GOVERNMENT
          SURPLUS
           SALE
                              CONDUCTED BY
                                 DRMO

                                 T A M P A

OFFERING:  AUDIO/VISUAL EQUIPMENT    DESKS      REFRIGERATION EQUIPMENT
                      ELECTRONICS    TYPEWRITERS

           OFFICE MACHINES      CLEANING EQUIPMENT     BICYCLES

           MEDICAL EQUIPMENT         CHAIRS       AUTOMOTIVE EQUIPMENT/PARTS

           BOOKS/CASSETTE          GAME TABLE      DATA PROCESSING EQUIPMENT

           ****************************************************************

             ********************************************************

               **************************************************

                 **********************************************

                   ****************************************

DATE AND TIME:  25 APRIL 1991        SALE NUMBER:    31-1566
                9:00 A.M.

REGISTRATION:   25 APRIL 1991        SALE SITE: MACDILL AFB, FL
                7:30 A.M.                       BLDG. 1110

CONTACT:    JERRY HALL              METHOD:  AUCTION
            813/830-2871

INSPECTION:  22, 23, 24 APRIL 1991
             8:00 A.M. THRU 3:00 P.M.
(Excluding week-ends and Holidays)

IMS Form 1927
Jul '90
N 754600L001927
```

going with the DRMO auctions. In dozens of interviews, I have talked with bidders who have found eye-popping deals involving a wide array of merchandise. When one man questioned a representative from a regional center as to why several thousand brand-new nurses' uniforms sold for less than $1 each (retail $15 or more), he was told someone ordered the wrong color. The military wanted green, not blue!

Other surplus dealers even buy spare parts at these auctions, storing their auction prizes in warehouses. Inevitably, Uncle Sam buys them back at many times the price sold to the dealer. Ouch!

Congressman John Kasich, in a 1989 press release, complained that the Defense Department auctioned off a $3,500 device for just $700, an unused electric coil-winder sold for $65 when a similar model retails for $8,000, and that the Air Force was selling spare parts, only to later buy them back at higher costs. Honorable congressman, it still goes on!

Their security is even worse. A note in auction catalogs says that military equipment classified for battle use has been "demilitarized." (That means made into scrap.) One Pennsylvania electronics dealer bought and exported military scramblers, periscopes, and M-60 tank antennas, which eventually reached Iran. Another frequent attendee purchased a confidential tank scope, worth hundreds of thousands, for a few hundred dollars.

Their catalog also requires that you file an end-user certificate on some of their military equipment to prevent it from being resold to unfriendly nations, such as Iraq, Ethiopia, and others. However, the running joke in the surplus business is that you leave the end-user certificate blank, to be filled in at a later date. No one keeps track of these. I asked about it myself and was instructed to "let them know when I finally resold my merchandise to someone."

The public relations people for the Department of Defense have traditionally responded to media inquiries with the pat line: "These are just garage sales." One nationally syndicated columnist wrote of such nonsense, "Monte Hall never dished out better deals."

Special Characteristics

There are three tiers in the Defense Reutilization and Marketing Service hierarchy. At the top is the headquarters of the DRMS located in Memphis, Tennessee. Under them are five regional offices called Defense Reutilization and Marketing Regions (DRMRs), located in Ogden (Utah), Columbus (Ohio), Memphis (Tennessee), Hawaii, and West Germany. Finally, at the low end of the totem pole are more than a hundred Defense Reutilization and Marketing Offices (DRMOs) located in all but six states and throughout the world.

Public auctions occur at the DRMO and DRMR level. Sealed bids are managed through the National Sales Office in Memphis, Tennessee, which maintains the national bidders list and assists regional centers in sending you auction catalogs.

```
Sale Number    27-2728
Sale Site      DRMO COLUMBUS, 3990 E. Broad St., Bldg. 14-1, Columbus OH 43216
Sale Date      3 October 1991
Sale Time      9:00 A.M.
Property Inspection Begins   30 Sep 91 thru 2 Oct 91
                             7:30 til 3:00
                             3 Oct 91 from 7:00 A.M. til 9:00 A.M. ONLY


IMPORTANT NOTICES:


1. Sales catalogs will not be mailed prior to this sale.  Catalogs will be available for
customer pickup on the first day of inspection.

2. Items may be withdrawn during continuation of required screening.  If you would like
information on withdrawn items prior to inspection, please contact the DRMO.

3. Additional items may be added to this sale.  Identification of any items added will be
available at the DRMO during the inspection period.
```

```
*** LOCATION : 89, DRMO WRIGHT PATTERSON
*****************************************************************
*** LOCATION : BLDG 89
*****************************************************************
 1. GOLF CLUBS, LEFT HANDED:  Power Belt,          1     LT
    Grand Slam, Irons 4 sets (incomplete)

 2. EXXON MEMORY TYPEWRITER:                        1     EA

 3. VIDEO DISK PLAYER:  Pioneer                     1     EA

 4. HARDWARE:  Est. wt. 80 Lbs.                     1     LT
    *FOLLOWING ARTICLE(S) APPLY:
    13 MILITARY MUNITIONS LIST ITEMS (MLI)
    17 MUNITIONS LIST AND STRATEGIC LIST ITEMS (MLI/SLI)

 5. VEHICULAR COMPONENTS:  Est. Wt. 280 Lbs.        1     LT

    *FOLLOWING ARTICLE(S) APPLY:
    13 MILITARY MUNITIONS LIST ITEMS (MLI)
    17 MUNITIONS LIST AND STRATEGIC LIST ITEMS (MLI/SLI)

 6. INSTRUMENTS AND LABORATORY EQUIPMENT:           1     LT
    Est. Wt. 120 Lbs.

 7. TAPE DECKS:  International Tapetronics          1     LT
    Corp., Model WP.  6 ea.

 8. READER/PRINTERS:  Consisting of:               1     LT
    1 ea. - Bell & Howell, Spacemaster
    1 ea. - Micron Corp., RP 700
```

The National Sales Office conducts national sales by sealed bid of Department of Defense surplus property. Sealed-bids usually require a 20% deposit against your bid. Merchandise is awarded to the successful bidder.

DRMOs and DRMRs conduct local public auctions of a large variety of items in small quantities. Sometimes, they will hold a local spot-bid auction instead of the public-outcry auction. They will provide bid forms. The local offices will even have retail sales of merchandise and equipment at fixed prices.

You will find a wide variety of merchandise at both the sealed-bid sales, spot-bid, and public-outcry auctions. Vehicles, furniture, and office equipment are what often brings the nonprofessionals. Dealers show up for the items suitable for recovery of parts and recyclable materials (for example, ferrous and nonferrous metals, plastics, paper, textiles, rubber, chemicals, and other such items).

In the United States, each of the three DRMRs also has specialty equipment or property. Aircraft will only be sold by DRMR Ogden, Utah. Ships are sold only by DRMR Columbus, Ohio. Items such as explosives will only be auctioned by DRMR Memphis, Tennessee.

Local auctions usually have vehicles, pup tents, office equipment, household items, electronics, tires, bicycles, data-processing equipment, hardware, and many things you might never find elsewhere. (Real estate is rarely, if ever, sold by the DRMRs or DRMOs. The GSA real estate offices usually sell the property when military bases close down.) Categories of merchandise likely to be available at auction are found on pages 123 to 135.

Hawaii may handle all Pacific Rim sealed-bid sales, but it is suggested you contact the DRMO sales offices in Japan, Korea, and the Philippines. Europe is handled through the DRMR in Wiesbaden, Germany, but scheduled auctions and information can be obtained through several European and British DRMOs. Remember, the U.S. Military has bases throughout the world and prefers to dispose of equipment and materials there rather than shipping it stateside.

Procedures

Each DRMO and DRMR maintains a local bidders list for their local sales. Contact the office nearest you to get on their mailing list. If you are

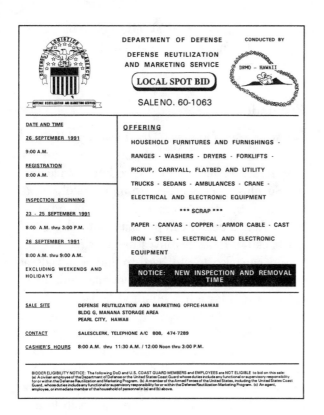

in Europe or the Far East, contact the DRMR sales office in the applicable region. If you don't send in a bid after three auction mailings, your name may be removed from the mailing list.

If you wish to participate in the larger auctions, you should call or write to the National Sales Office in Memphis, Tennessee, and ask for the Surplus Property Bidders Application:

National Sales Office
P.O. Box 5275 DDRC
2163 Airways Boulevard
Memphis, TN 38114-5210
(901) 775-4974

You will be sent a catalog explaining the procedures for having your name placed on the national auction mailing list and the mailing list application. There is no fee charged to have auction catalogs sent you. However, should you fail to participate after five mailings, your name may be removed from this list. You will have to reapply to receive more mailings or send in bids.

Until recently, local auctions were scheduled on an irregular or regular basis, depending on the military base's available surplus merchandise or its personnel. However, orders have been issued to schedule auctions on a 4-week, 6-week, or 8-week rotation.

Preview periods for local auctions are usually three days prior to the sale. You may inspect from 8 AM to 3 PM. Registration is normally at 7:30 AM and auctions start between 8 AM and 9 AM, depending on the location. Check with the local office for their auction schedule, available merchandise, and other particulars.

Payment at Department of Defense local auctions can be made within five business days of the sale date, but only in cash or a cashier's check. Pay in the exact amount, as no change is given. Some bidders have money wired from their banks to the Defense Office, which saves on carrying cash or getting a cashier's check in the exact amount, since you never know how much merchandise you may buy.

If you successfully bid on something and then walk off, never to return, don't go back. More than likely you will be banned from not only DRMO auctions, but also from many other government agency auctions. Stiff price to pay if you want to take advantage of these bargains.

Tips

To get on these mailing lists, I recommend you make the long-distance telephone call to Memphis. Writing them has usually led to no result. Sometimes it may take more than one telephone call to receive the catalog.

Use a bank credit card to secure your bid. The bid deposit is normally 20% of the amount you wish to offer on the merchandise. Here's a secret: when you charge your bid deposit on a bank credit card, *unless* you win the bid, the DRMR won't debit your card! (I guess now that this secret is out, the government might clamp down.)

Contact the National Sales Office and ask for assistance in previewing the merchandise or equipment. They may be able to refer someone to

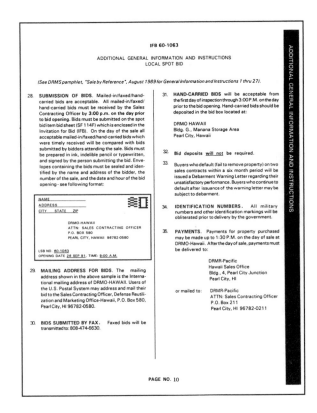

terrific profit. Often, if all else fails, you can at least use this method to come ahead or break even on your bid.

Evaluation

Go to these auctions. The local DRMO and DRMR auctions sell lots of junk: valves, pumps, motors, scrap, and the like. Who buys it? Dealers do. Surplus dealers expect to immediately *triple* their investment on average. That's right, on average. Often, a dealer can purchase something and get back *ten times* his investment or more.

You can also locate hard-to-find materials at these auctions. Equipment generally sells for a song. Trucks for a few hundred dollars, more or less. Scrap can be bought and resold almost immediately.

The DRMRs usually underestimate the resale value of the merchandise and equipment. Appraisals are often inaccurate. Something could be called in "fair" condition and be practically brand-new.

These auctions are a great way to make healthy profits. Occasionally, you may buy something you can't resell, but in the long run, bidders frequently come out ahead. Refer to Chapter 6 for exporting and reselling your purchase. It helps to have a list of potential buyers before you attend.

Vehicles at these auctions are pretty old or have high odometer readings. But the prices are incredible. At worst, you could resell the spare parts for a profit! Here's a sampling of prices one magazine reporter found at DRMO auctions held at four military bases in the southeastern United States:

ITEM	PRICE
1971 Chrysler New Yorker	$10
1977 Pontiac	$15
Dodge Sedan	$17.50
Oldsmobile Sedan	$20
1973 Honda	$20
Honda Sedan	$27.50
1976 Buick Skylark	$30

you, usually a retired employee, who can inspect on your behalf and report back to you. Inspection periods on DRMR sealed bid sales are 14 days so you have enough time to get this done. Removal times are now 20 days and you can also hire this same person to package and ship your purchase home or to your end-buyer.

For a $5 fee the National Sales Office will send you the bid abstract for the previous sealed bid sales. Just participate in one sealed bid sale—send in a joke bid if you wish—and include a $5 cashier's check. The DRMR will mail you the bid abstract. Then you can compare successful bids on similar merchandise and equipment for the future. You may be shocked by the prices at which the Defense Department is selling merchandise. Don't say I didn't warn you.

Using the bid abstract not only gives you a basis for price comparisons but also a network of buyers! Yes, you can contact other bidders, failed or successful, and try to sell them your purchase. This can work in a pinch and you might not make a

Item	Price
Toyota Sedan	$32.50
1971 Fiat Spider Convertible	$35
1968 Buick Skylark	$50
1979 Chevrolet Chevette	$55
1976 VW Rabbit	$55
1972 Buick Sportswagon	$60
1977 VW Sirrocco	$60
1978 Toyota Celica	$60
1978 Chevrolet Citation	$80
1979 Ford Granada	$85
1979 Ford Fiesta	$85
1980 Ford Pinto	$95
1981 Datsun 310	$100
1980 Toyota Tercel	$110
1976 Dodge Sports Van	$150
1979 Ford Fiesta	$175

What about other merchandise? Here's a few sample prices from those same auctions. These were actual sales prices!

Item	Price
15 Metal Desks	$2.50
27 Pair Window Drapes	$10
2 Refrigerators	$10
IBM Selectric Typewriter	$12.50
25 Lawnmowers	$15
15 Telephones	$17.50
170 Library Books	$20
Canon Copier	$20
AMF Sailboat	$20
3 Window Air Conditioners	$25
Litton Fax Machine	$25
Microwave Oven	$35
6 Color Television Sets	$35
Camper Trailer	$50
Tractor Mower	$55
10 Wood Desks	$65
House Trailer	$115
2 Johnson Outboard Motors	$235
1976 McKee Craft Boat	$285

DEFENSE CONTRACT ADMINISTRATIVE SERVICES (DRMS, DRMR, AND DRMO) REGIONS DIRECTORY

Defense Reutilization and Marketing Service

National Bidders List
Defense Reutilization
and Marketing Service
P.O. Box 1370
Battle Creek, MI 49016-1370
(616) 961-7331

Defense Reutilization and Marketing Regional Sales Offices

COLUMBUS, OH

926 Taylor Station Rd.
Blacklick, OH 43215-9615
(614) 238-2281

MEMPHIS, TN

2163 Airways Blvd.
Memphis, TN 38114-5052
(901) 775-6858

OGDEN, UT

Bldg. 2A-1
500 W. 12th St.
Defense Depot Ogden
Ogden, UT 84407-5001
(801) 399-6662

EUROPE

Lindsey AS
APO NY 09633
06121-82-3505

PACIFIC

Building 12
Camp H.M. Smith,
HI 96861-5010
(808) 474-0491

Defense Reutilization and Marketing Offices United States

Alabama

DRMO-ANNISTON

Anniston Army Depot
Anniston, AL 36201-5090
(205) 235-7733/7133
Auction every 2 mos.

DMRO-FORT MCCLELLAN

(ZWSE)
Bldg. T342
Anniston, AL 36205-5000
(205) 235-7133
Auction every 2 mos.

DRMO-HUNTSVILLE

Bldg. 7408
Redstone Arsenal, AL
35898-7230
(205) 876-9634
Auction every 6 wks.

DRMO-MONGTOMERY

Bldg. 900/Gunter AFS
Mongtomery, AL 36114-5000
(205) 279-4194
Auction every 2 mos.

DRMO-RUCKER

Bldg. 1313
Fort Rucker, AL 36362-5286
(205) 255-2275/5263
Auctions irregular.

Alaska

DRMO-ANCHORAGE

P.O. Box 866
Bldg. 34-600
Elmendorf AFB AK
99506-0866
(907) 552-3911
Auction once/mo.

DRMO-FAIRBANKS

P.O. Box 35028
Fort Wainwright, AK
99703-0028
(907) 353-7334/6318
Auction once/mo.

Arizona

DRMO-HUACHUCA

P.O. Box 104
Fort Huachuca, AZ
85613-0104
(602) 533-2074
Auction twice/mo.

DRMO-SZT

Luke AFB
Glendale, AZ 85309-5000
(602) 856-7144
Auction once/mo.,
except in summer.

DRMO-TUCSON

P.O. Box 15011
Tucson, AZ 85708-0011
(602) 750-5041
Auction once/mo.

DRMO-YUMA

MCAS P.O. Box 12397
Yuma, AZ
85364-5000
(602) 726-2748
Auction twice/mo.

Arkansas

DRMO-EAKER AFB

Bldg. 427
Eaker AFB AR 72317
(501) 762-7479
Auction twice/mo.

DRMO-FORT CHAFFEE

(ZMFC)
Bldg. 339
Fort Chaffee, AR
72905-5000
(501) 484-2862
Auction twice/mo.

DRMO-LITTLE ROCK

Little Rock AFB
Jacksonville, AR
72099-5000
(501) 988-6782
Auction 3X/mo.

California

DRMO-ALAMEDA

Warehouse 5
2155 Mariner Square Loop
Alameda, CA
94501-1022
(415) 869-8309
Auction once/mo.

DRMO-BARSTOW

Marine Corps Logistics Base
Bldg. 226
Barstow, CA 92311-5145
(619) 577-6561
Auction once/mo.

DRMO-EDWARDS

P.O. Box 308
Edwards AFB, CA
93523-5000
(805) 277-2209
Auction once/mo.

DRMO EL TORO

P.O. Box 21
E. Irvine, CA 92650-0021
(714) 726-2335/3846
Auction once/mo.

DRMO-MARE ISLAND

Code 1005
Bldg. 655, Door 18
Vallejo, CA
94592-5021
(707) 646-3235
Auction twice/mo.

DRMO-MCCLELLAN

Bldg. 700
McClellan AFB, CA
95652-6448
(916) 643-3830
Auction once/mo.

DRMO-MOFFETT

Bldg. 127
Naval Air Station
Moffett Field, CA
94035-5127
(415) 404-4375
Auction once/mo.

DRMO-NORTH ISLAND

P.O. Box 337
Imperial Beach, CA
92032-0337
(619) 545-8055
Auction once/mo.

DRMO-NORTON

Bldg. 948
Norton AFB, CA
92409-6488
(714) 382-6164
Auction once/mo.

DRMO-ORD

P.O. Box 810
Marina, CA 93933-0810
(408) 242-7189
Auction every other month.

DRMO-PENDLETON

SZ3139-P.O. Box 1608
Oceanside, CA
92051-1608
Auction-no set time.

DRMO-PORT HUENEME

NCBC Bldg. 513
Port Hueneme, CA
93043-5025
(805) 982-5636/5637/5638
Auction once/mo.

DRMO-SAN DIEGO

P.O. Box 337
Imperial Beach, CA
92032-0337
(619) 437-9456/9439/9440
Auction 3X/mo.

DRMO-STOCKTON

Rough & Ready Island
Stockton, CA 95203-4999
(209) 944-0267/0268/0260
Auction once/mo.

DRMO-TRAVIS

Bldg. 724
Travis AFB, CA
94535-7100
(707) 424-3137
Auction twice/mo.

DRMO-VANDENBURG

Box 5127
Vandenburg AFB, CA
93437-6100
(805) 866-9852
Auction every other month.

Colorado

DRMO-COLORADO SPRINGS

Fort Carson Bldg. 318
Colorado Springs, CO
80913-5044
(719) 579-4355
Auction once/mo.

DRMO-DENVER

Bldg. 621
Rocky Mountain Arsenal
Commerce City, CO
80022-2180
(303) 289-0378
Auction every 6 wks.

PUEBLO DEPOT ACTIVITY

Bldg. 163
Pueblo, CO
81001-5000
(719) 549-4111

Connecticut

DRMO-GROTON

Naval Submarine Base
New London Box 12
Groton, CT
06349-0012
(203) 449-3523/3524

Delaware

DRMO-DOVER

Bldg. 114
Dover AFB, DE
19902-6468
(302) 678-6165/6166
Auction every 4 to 6 wks.

Florida

DRMO-EGLIN

Bldg. 525
Eglin AFB, FL
32542-5280
(904) 882-2822/2823/2824
Auction once/mo.

DRMO-HOMESTEAD

Bldg. 607
Homestead AFB, FL
33039-5000
(305) 257-7425/7426
Auction every 4 mos.

DRMO-JACKSONVILLE

P.O. Box 82
Jacksonville, FL
32212-0082
(904) 772-9248/9249
Auction once/mo.

DRMO-KEY WEST

NAS Harry S. Truman
Annex Bldg. 795
Key West, FL 33040-0006
(305) 292-5271/5272
Auction every 4 to 5 mos.

DRMO-PATRICK

Bldg. 1391
Patrick AFB, FL
32925-7469
(407) 494-6507/7912
Auction every 6 wks.

DRMO-PENSACOLA

US Naval Air Station
Bldg. 685N
Pensacola, FL 32508-7404
(904) 452-2451
Auction once/mo.

DRMO-TAMPA

Bldg. 1110
P.O. Box 6838
MacDill AFB, FL
33608-0838
(813) 830-2871/2872/2873
Auction every 2 mos.

Georgia

DRMO-ALBANY

Marine Corps. Logistics Base
Albany, GA 31704-5045
(912) 439-5966/5967/
5969/5970
Auctions every 4 mos.

DRMO-BENNING

P.O. Box 3760
Columbus, GA
31903-0760
(404) 545-7206/3497/7214
Auctions once/mo.

DRMO-FOREST PARK (ZWAF)

Fort Gillem Bldg. 310-B
Forest Park, GA
30050-5000
(404) 363-5117/5118
Auction once/mo.

DRMO-GORDON

Bldg. 10601
Fort Gordon, GA 30905-5667
(404) 791-3749/2487
Auctions once/mo.

DRMO-STEWART

P.O. Box 10
Hinesville, GA
31313-0010
(912) 767-8863/8878/
8893/8899
Auctions once/mo.

DRMO-VALDOSTA (ZWAE)

Bldg. 997
Moody AFB, GA
31699-5260
(912) 333-3349/4667
Auctions every 3 to 4 wks.

DRMO-WARNER ROBINS (ZWA)

Bldg. 1602
Robins AFB, GA
310998-5000
(912) 926-2164/3159/4541
Auctions twice/mo.

Idaho

DRMO-MOUNTAIN HOME

P.O. Box 4068
Mountain Home AFB, ID
83648-4068
(208) 828-2306
Auction once/year.

Illinois

DRMO-CHANUTE

Bldg. 734
Chanute AFB, IL
61868-5000
(217) 495-2701/3131
Auction twice/mo.

DRMO-GREAT LAKES

Naval Training Center
Bldg. 3212A
Great Lakes, IL
60088-5798
(708) 688-3655/3656
Auctions once/mo.

DRMO-ROCK ISLAND

Rock Island Arsenal
Bldg. 154
Rock Island, IL
61299-7030
(309) 782-1617/1618/1619
Auctions every 4 wks.

DRMO-SCOTT

Bldg. 4141
Scott AFB, IL
62225-5000
(618) 256-3105/4497/5964
Auction every 6 wks.

Indiana

DRMO-CRANE

Naval Weapons Support
System
Bldg. 2034
Crane, IN 47522-5091
(812) 854-3442/1554/1728
Auction once/mo.

DRMO-INDIANAPOLIS

Bldg. 124
Fort Benjamin Harrison,
IN 46216-7400
(317) 543-6615/6616
Auctions once/mo.

Kansas

DRMO-LEAVENWORTH

Bldg. 269
Fort Leavenworth,
KS 66027-6500
(913) 684-2878/2383
Auctions twice/mo.

DRMO-MCCONNELL

Bldg. 1349
McConnell AFB
KS 67221-6100
(316) 652-4098/4099/4101
Auctions twice/mo.

DRMO-RILEY

P.O. Box 2490
Fort Riley, KS
66442-2490
(913) 239-6202/6203/
6204/6205
Auctions once/mo

Kentucky

DRMO-CAMPBELL (ZMJ)

P.O. Box 2555
Fort Campbell
KY 42223-5000
(502) 798-4762
Auctions every 4 to 6 wks.

DRMO-KNOX

Bldg. 2962 Frazier Rd.
Fort Knox, KY 40121-5640
(502) 624-5755/1328
Auctions once/mo.

DRMO-LEXINGTON

Lexington-Blue Grass Depot
Lexington, KY 40511-5108
(606) 293-3436/3543/
3405/4125
Auctions once/mo.

Louisiana

DRMO-BARSDALE (ZWS)

Bldg. 4964
Barsdale AFB, LA
71110-6100
(318) 456-4898/3216/3309
Auctions once/mo.

DRMO-POLK

P.O. Box 901
Fort Polk, LA
71459-0901
(318) 535-4068/4609/2401
Auctions once/mo.

Maine

DRMO-BRUNSWICK

Naval Air Station
Bldg. 584
Brunswick, ME
04011-5000
(207) 921-2627/2452
Auctions every 2 mos.

DRMO-LIMESTONE

P.O. Box 1021
Loring AFB, ME 04751-6100
(207) 999-6193/2464/7134
Auction every 6 wks.

Maryland

DRMO-ABERDEEN

Aberdeen Proving Grounds
Aberdeen, MD
20755-5001
(301) 278-2235/4785/2435
Auctions once/mo.

DRMO-MEADE

P.O. Box 388
Fort Meade, MD
20755-0388
(301) 677-6366
Auctions once/mo.

DRMO-PATUXENT

Bldg. 604
Naval Air Station
Patuxent River, MD 20670
(301) 863-3316
Auction every 6 wks.

Massachusetts

DRMO-DEVENS

P.O. Box 69
Fort Devens, MA 01433-5690
(508) 796-2418
Auctions every 6 wks.

Michigan

DRMO-SAWYER

Bldg. 417
K.I. Sawyer AFB, MI
49843-6100
(906) 346-2254/2432
Auction every 6 wks.

DRMO-SELFRIDGE

Bldg. 590
Selfridge ANG Base, MI
480454-5003
(313) 466-5191
Auctions every 2 mos.

DRMO-WURTSMITH

P.O. Box 3001
Wurtsmith AFB, MI
48753-6100
(517) 747-6332/6357
Auction every 6 wks.

Minnesota

DRMO-DULUTH

148FIG
Minnesota Air National Guard
Duluth International Airport
Duluth, MN 55811-5000
(218) 723-7441/7452/7453
Auction every 6 wks.

Mississippi

DRMO-COLUMBUS (CMAF)

Bldg. 152
Columbus AFB, MS
39701-5000
(601) 434-7463/7464/7465
Auction every 3 to 4 mos.

DRMO-KEESLER

Bldg. 4422
Keesler AFB, MS 39534-5000
(601) 377-2505/2393
Auction 2nd Tuesday every mo.

Missouri

DRMO-LEONARD WOOD

Gas St. Bldg. 2391
Fort Leonard, MO
65473-5820
(314) 596-7101
Auction every 6 wks.

DRMO-WHITEMAN

P.O. Box 6010
Whiteman AFB, MO
65305-6100
(816) 687-3308/3521

Montana

DRMO-GREAT FALLS

Bldg. 1531
Malstrom AFB, MT
59402-6100
(406) 731-6346/6347
Auction every 2 mos.

Nebraska

DRMO-OFFCUTT

Bldg. 559
Omaha, NE 68113-3200
(402) 294-2425
Auction every 2 mos.

Nevada

DRMO-NELLIS

Bldg. 1035 Area III
Nellis AFB, NV 89191-5000
(702) 652-2002
Auction every 2 mos.

New Hampshire

DRMO-PORTSMOUTH

Portsmouth Naval Shipyard
P.O. Box 2028
Portsmouth, NH
03801-2028
(207) 438-2282
Auction every 2 mos.

New Jersey

DRMO-BAYONNE

Military Ocean Terminal
Bldg. 63
Bayonne, NJ 07002-5301
(201) 823-7541/7209/
5996/5997
Auction once/mo.

DRMO-LAKEHURST

Naval Air Engineering Center
Bldg. 75
Lakehurst, NJ 08733-5010

(201) 323-2661/2669/
7373/7374
Auction every 3 wks.

DRMO-XPOS

US ARDEC
Bldg. 314
Pickatinny Arsenal, NJ
07806-5000
(201) 724-4219/4747

New Mexico

DRMO-CANNON

Bldg. 215
Cannon AFB, NM 88103-2606
(505) 784-2436
Auction every 4 mos.

DRMO-HOLLOMAN

Bldg. 112
Holloman AFB, NM
87117-6001
(505) 479-3747/2213
Auction every 6 wks.

DRMO-KIRTLAND

Bldg. 1025
Kirtland AFB, NM 87117-6100
(505) 846-6959
Auction every 2 mos.

New York

DRMO-PLATTSBURGH

Plattsburgh AFB
P.O. Box 864
Plattsburgh, NY 12901-0864
(518) 565-5778/5779/5431
Auction every 2 mos.

DRMO-ROME

Bldg. T-8
Griffin AFB, NY
13441-6100
(315) 330-3400/4822
Auction once/mo.

DRMO-ROMULUS

Seneca Army Depot
Romulus, NY 14541-5011
(607) 869-1236
Auction once/mo.

DRMO-WATERVLIET

Watervliet Arsenal
Bldg. 145
Watervliet, NY
12189-4050
(518) 266-4112/5126
Auctions every 2 mos.

North Carolina

DRMO-BRAGG

Bldg. J, 1334 Knox St.
Fort Bragg, NC 28307-5000
(919) 396-5222
Auction once/mo.

DRMO-CHERRY POINT

PSC 4298
MCAS Cherry Point, NC
28533-4298
(919) 466-2743/5905/3338
Auction every 4 wks.

DRMO-LEJEUNE

Louis Rd. Bldg. 906
Camp Lejeune, NC
28542-5000
(919) 451-5613/5652/2302
Auction every 2 mos.

North Dakota

DRMO-GRAND FORKS

Grand Forks AFB
Bldg. 432
Grand Forks, ND
58206-6100
(701) 747-3780/3781/3782/
3783/3784
Auctions every 6 wks.

DRMO-MINOT

401 Bomber Blvd.
Minot AFB, ND
58705-5010
(701) 723-6120
Auctions 60 to 90 days.

Ohio

DRMO-COLUMBUS

3990 E. Broad St.
P.O. Box 13297
Columbus, OH
43213-5000
(614) 238-3244
Auctions once/mo.

DRMO-WRIGHT PATTERSON

Bldg. 89 Area C
Wright Patterson AFB, OH
45433-5000
(513) 257-4291/4203/7823
Auctions every 6 wks.

Oklahoma

DRMO-MCALESTER

US Army Ammunition Plant
McAlester, OK 74501-5000
(918) 421-2248/2249
Auctions 4 to 6 mos.

DRMO-OKLAHOMA CITY (ZOA)

Tinker AFB/L-11
Oklahoma City, OK
73145-5000
(405) 739-7135
Auction once/mo.

DRMO-SILL (ZOB)

Bldg. 3373 Naylor Rd.
Fort Sill, OK 73503-6900
(405) 351-4703/3415/3295
Auctions once/mo.

Oregon

DRMO-HERMISTON

Umatella Army Depot
Hermiston, OR 97838-9544
(503) 564-8632, Ext. 5273
Auction once/yr.

Pennsylvania

DRMO-CHAMBERSBURG

Letterkenny Army Depot
P.O. Box 229
Chambersburg, PA
17201-0229
(717) 267-5425/8852
Auction once/mo.

DRMO-MECHANICSBERG

5450 Carlisle Pike
P.O. Box 2020
Mechanicsberg, PA
17055-0788
(717) 790-3325/3135
Auction once/mo.

DRMO-PHILADELPHIA

2800 S. 20th St.
Bldg. 26-C
Philadelphia, PA 19101-8419
(215) 952-5914
Auction once/mo.

DRMO-TOBYHANNA

P.O. Box 366
Tobyhanna, PA 18466-0366
(717) 894-7455
Auction once/mo.

Rhode Island

DRMO-DAVISVILLE

P.O. Box 985
Davisville, RI 02854-0985
(401) 267-2294/2213
Auction-no set time.

South Carolina

DRMO-CHARLESTON

P.O. Box 5716
N. Charleston, SC
29406-0715
(803) 743-5176/5177
Auction once/mo.

DRMO-JACKSON

Bldg. 1902
Fort Jackson, SC
29207-6050
(803) 751-7716/3271
Auction once/mo.

DRMO-SHAW

Bldg. 26
Shaw AFB, SC 29152-0890
(803) 668-3556
Auction once/mo.

South Dakota

DRMO-ELLSWORTH

Ellsworth AFB
Bldg. 1801
Rapid City, SD 57706-6100
(605) 385-1021
Auction every 4 mos.

Tennessee

DRMO-MEMPHIS

2163 Airways Blvd.
Memphis, TN 38114-5297
(901) 775-6155/4987
Auction every 2 mos.

DRMO-NAVAL AIR STATION (ZMAE)

Bldg. S.6
Millington, TN 38054-5027
(901) 873-5670
Auction every 5 to 6 wks.

Texas

DRMO-BLISS

P.O. Box 8029
El Paso, TX 79908-9991
(915) 568-8503
Auction every 2 mos.

DRMO-CARSWELL

Bldg. 1360
Carswell AFB, TX
76127-6100
(817) 782-5321/5748
Auction no set time.

DRMO-CORPUS CHRISTI

Bldg. 22
Naval Air Station
Corpus Christi, TX
78419-5600
(512) 939-2936/2933/3359
Auction every 6 to 8 wks.

DRMO-HOOD

Bldg. 4289 (80th) St.
P.O. Drawer 6
Fort Hood, TX 76544-0210
(817) 287-4770/8824/
8822/3315
Auction every 4 wks.

DRMO-SHEPPARD

DRMO 37, Bldg. 2135
Sheppard AFB, TX
76311-5000
(817) 676-2712/4933
Auction every 8 wks

DRMO-SAN ANTONIO

Bldg. 3050 E. Kelly
Kelly AFB, TX 78241-5000
(512) 925-7766/6167/
6168/6169
Auction once/wk.

DRMO-TEXARCANA

P.O. Box 1330
Hooks, TX 75561-1330
(903) 334-3177/3178
Auction once/mo.

Utah

DRMO-HILL

Bldg. 890
Hill AFB, UT 84056-5000
(801) 777-6557
Auction once/mo.

DEFENSE DEPOT OGDEN

500 W. 12th St.
Ogden, UT 81001
(801) 399-7281
Auction once/mo.

DRMO-TOOELE

Tooele Army Depot
Bldg. 2010
Tooele, UT 84074-5019
(801) 833-3571
Auction once/mo.

Virginia

DRMO-BELVOIR

Stop 566/SX 151 W
Bldg. 2517
Fort Belvoir, VA
22060-0566
(703) 664-6551/6553/6554
Auction once/mo.

DRMO-CAMP ALLEN

Salvage Yard
Bldg. CAO 429 Annex
Norfolk, VA 23511-0060
(804) 444-5689/5366
Auction every 2 wks.

DRMO-NORFOLK

Norfolk Naval Station
P.O. Box 15068
Norfolk, VA 23511-0068
(804) 444-5366/5472
Auction every 2 wks.

DRMO-RICHMOND

DGSC 8000
Jefferson Davis Highway
Richmond, VA
23297-5000
(804) 275-4407/4943
Auction once/mo.

DRMO-WILLIAMSBURG

Cheatham Annex Bldg. 16
Naval Supply Center
Williamsburg, VA
23187-8792
(804) 887-7289/7164
Auction once/mo.

Washington

DRMO-FAIRCHILD

P.O. Box 1321
Fairchild AFB, WA
99011-1321
(509) 247-2350
Auctions quarterly

DRMO-LEWIS

P.O. Box 56
Tillicum, WA 98492-0056

(206) 967-4890
Auction once/wk.

DRMO-WHIDBEY ISLAND

NAS Whidbey Island
Oak Harbor, WA
98278-5100
(206) 257-2501
Auction every 3 mos.

Wisconsin

DRMO-SPARTA

Fort McCoy, Bldg. 2184
Sparta, WI 54656-6002
(608) 388-3718
Auction every 6 wks.

Wyoming

DRMO-WARREN

Bldg. 808
Francis E. Warren AFB
WY 82005-6100
(307) 775-3959/3970
Auction twice/mo.

Defense Reutilization and Marketing Offices Outside the USA

Pacific Region

KOREA

DRMR Pacific
Sales Field Office Korea
APO San Francisco 96483-0120
Telex: 787 22 88 6 DPDRKS

DRMO Pusan
APO San Francisco 96259-0269
051 801 3404
051 801 3413

DRMO Dupyong
APO San Francisco 96483-0120
0325 24 4629

PHILIPPINES

DRMR Pacific
Sales Field Office
Philippines
Box 46
FPO San Francisco 96651-1523
Subic Bay 047 382 6110
Clark 049 394 7240

HAWAII

DRMO Hawaii
Box 580
Pearl City, HI 96782-0580
(808) 474-6872

JAPAN

DRMO Okinawa
Box 4497
APO San Francisco 96331-3008
0989 381 111
Telex: 695 526

DRMO Sagami
APO San Francisco 96343-0063
0462 51 1520 Ext. 228 4242
0427 59 4148 FAX

DRMO Yokota
APO San Francisco 96328-5000
Handled by DRMO Sagami

DRMO Yokosuka
(Navy Scrap Yard)
P.O. Box 161
FPO Seattle 98762-2980
0468 26 2911
Ext. 234 5806/4422

DRMO Misawa
APO San Francisco 96519-5000
0176 53 5181
Ext. 226 3448/4052

DRMO Iwakuni
FBO Seattle 98764-5017
0827 21 4171
APO NY 09019
586-943272

Europe

ENGLAND

DRMO Huntingdon
APO NY 09238
480-432117

TURKEY

DRMO Ankara
APO NY 09254
90-41-255100

DRMO Incirlik
APO NY 09289
009071-14228, Ext. 3155/6037

GREECE

DRMO Athens
APO NY 09223
003001-9815-830

ITALY

DRMO Aviano
APO NY 09293
39-434-31393

DRMO Naples
APO NY 09520
539-81-724 Ext. 5218/5282

DRMO Vicenza
APO NY 09221
39-444-517651/517275

BELGIUM

DRMO Chievres
APO NY 09088
0682 75484
0682 75146 FAX

SPAIN

DRMO Torrejon
APO NY 09283
01 665-3387 5311

DRMO Rota
FPO NY 09540
0568 23000
Ext. 2091

DRMO Zaragoza
APO NY 09286
0763 26711
Ext. 2166

CLASSES OF PROPERTY SOLD

Recyclable Materials

CLASS NO.	DESCRIPTION
8305A	Textiles including Synthetic Fabric
9450A	Paper (e.g., newsprint, manila cards)
9450B	Rubber (e.g., tires and tubes)
9450C	Miscellaneous (e.g., leather, plastic, fiberglass, etc.)
9450D	Exposed Film/Spent Hypo Solution
9450E	Waste Oil, Jet Fuels, Paints, Chemicals, Waxes, and Lubricants
9450F	Food Waste
9450G	Industrial Diamond Containing Materials

CLASS NO.	DESCRIPTION
9660A	Precious Metals, All Types
9660B	Gold and Silver Plated or Brazed on Base Metal
9670C	Cast Iron
9670D	Prepared Heavy Melting Steel
9670E	Unprepared Heavy Melting Steel
9670F	Prepared Light Steel (black and/or galvanized)
9670G	Unprepared Light Steel (black and/or galvanized)

CLASS NO.	DESCRIPTION
9670H	Unprepared Mixed Heavy and Light Steel
9670J	Turnings and Borings (steel and/or wrought iron)
9670K	Stainless Steel Alloys, Magnetic and Nonmagnetic (e.g., 300 and 400 series types except types 310 and 446 of the American Iron and Steel Institute)
9670L	High Temperature Alloys: Nickel and Cobalt Base which are Copper Free
9680B	Copper, Copper-Base Alloys and Copper Containing Materials (includes spent bullets, casings, and shells)
9680C	Copper-Bearing Materials (e.g., motors, armatures, generators, etc., but excludes electrical and electronic materials)
9680D	Miscellaneous Electrical and Electronic Materials (includes steel or aluminum armored cable, etc., but excludes copper-bearing materials)
9680E	Aluminum and Aluminum Alloys (excludes material in Class 9680F)
9680F	Aircraft sold for recovery of basic metal content, parts and components
9680G	Magnesium Alloys
9680H	Lead, Lead-Base Alloys, Antimony, Zinc and Zinc Alloys (includes lead-acid-type storage batteries)
9680J	Bullet and Projectile Metals (to be recovered from target, artillery and bombing ranges)
9680K	Storage Batteries (nickel-iron-alkaline types)
9680L	Storage Batteries (silver-zinc, nickel-cadmium and mercury types)
9680M	Tin and Alloys (includes tin-base babitt metal and block tin pipe, but excludes tin cans and terneplate)

Usable Property

Weapons (Accessories)

CLASS NO.	DESCRIPTION
1005	Holsters, slings, small arms accessories

Nuclear Ordnance Equipment

CLASS NO.	DESCRIPTION
1190	Specialized Test and Handling Equipment, Nuclear Ordnance (e.g., specially designed trucks and trailers, slings and hoists, etc.)*

Fire Control Equipment

1220	Fire Control Computing Sights and Devices*
1240	Optical Sighting and Ranging Equipment*
1260	Fire Control Designating and Indicating Equipment*
1265	Fire Control Transmitting and Receiving Equipment, except Airborne*
1270	Aircraft Gunnery Fire Control Components*
1280	Aircraft Bombing Fire Control Components*
1285	Fire Control Radar Equipment, except Airborne*
1290	Miscellaneous Fire Control Equipment (e.g., Control Directors and Systems, Stabilizing Mechanisms, and Sonar Equipment)*

Guided Missile Equipment

| 1440 | Launchers, Guided Missile* |
| 1450 | Guided Missile Handling and Servicing Equipment (e.g., specially designed trucks and trailers, slings, hoists, jacks, etc.)* |

Aircraft; and Airframe Structural Components

1510A	Single Engine Aircraft
1510B	Twin Engine Aircraft
1510C	Multi-Engine Aircraft
1520	Aircraft, Rotary Wing (e.g., helicopters)

Class No.	Description
1550	Drones (e.g., complete drones used for targets, training, surveillance, etc.)
1560A	Airframe Structural Components, etc., peculiar to Single Engine Aircraft
1560B	Airframe Structural Components, etc., peculiar to Multi-Engine Aircraft
1560C	Airframe Structural Components, etc., peculiar to Helicopters

Aircraft Components and Accessories

Class No.	Description
1610	Aircraft Propellers and Component Parts
1615	Helicopter Rotor Blades, Drive Mechanisms and Components (e.g., rotors, yokes, blades, blade sets, clutches, transmissions, etc.)
1620	Aircraft Landing Gear Components
1630	Aircraft Wheel and Brake Systems
1650	Aircraft Hydraulic, Vacuum, and Deicing System Components
1660	Aircraft Air Conditioning, Heating, and Pressurizing Equipment
1670	Parachutes and Aerial Pick Up, Delivery, and Cargo Tie Down Equipment*
1680	Miscellaneous Aircraft Accessories and Components

Aircraft Launching, Landing, and Ground Handling Equipment

Class No.	Description
1710	Aircraft Arresting, Barrier, and Barricade Equipment
1720	Aircraft Launching Equipment*
1730	Aircraft and Space Vehicle Ground Handling and Servicing Equipment
1740	Airfield Specialized Trucks and Trailers

Ships, Small Craft, Pontoons, and Floating Docks

Class No.	Description
1905A	Aircraft Carriers (for scrapping only)
1905B	Battleships, Cruisers, Destroyers (for scrapping only)
1905C	Landing Ships (e.g., LSM, LSMR, LSSL, LST, etc.)
1905D	Minehunters, Minesweepers, Minelayers
1905E	Submarines (for scrapping only)
1905F	Landing Craft (e.g., LCVP, LCPL, LCM, etc.)
1910	Transport Vessels, Passenger and Troop
1915	Cargo and Tanker Vessels
1925A	Ferry
1925B	Harbor Utility Craft
1925C	Repair Ships
1925D	Tugs (e.g., YTB, YTL, ATA, etc.)
1930A	Fuel Barge, Gasoline Barge, Water Barge
1930B	Lighters (open and covered)
1935	Barges and Lighters, Special Purpose (e.g., derrick, piledriver, torpedo testing barges, barge-mounted cranes, etc.)
1940B	Patrol Craft (e.g., PC, PCS, SC, YP, PCE, etc.)
1940C	Seaplane Tenders
1940D	Small Craft under 40 feet in length powered and non-powered
1945	Pontoons and Floating Docks (e.g., pontoon ramps, etc.)
1950	Floating Dry Docks
1990	Miscellaneous (all other vessels and service craft not included in property category numbers 1905A through 1950)

Ship and Marine Equipment

Class No.	Description
2010	Ship and Boat Propulsion Components (excludes engines and turbines)
2020	Rigging and Rigging Gear
2030	Deck Machinery
2040	Marine Hardware and Hull Items (e.g., anchors, hatches, rudders, oars, etc.)
2050	Buoys

CLASS NO.	DESCRIPTION
2090	Miscellaneous Ship, Marine, and Commercial Fishing Equipment (includes sails, marine furniture, ladders, etc.)

Railway Equipment

CLASS NO.	DESCRIPTION
2210	Locomotives
2220	Rail Cars
2230	Right-of-Way Construction and Maintenance Equipment, Railroad
2240	Locomotive and Rail Car Accessories and Components
2250	Track Materials, Railroad (e.g., rails, frogs, fish plates, etc.)

Motor Vehicles, Trailers, and Cycles

CLASS NO.	DESCRIPTION
2310A	Passenger sedans/station wagons
2310B	Ambulances and Hearses
2310C	Buses
2320A	Trucks and Truck Tractors one ton and heavier capacity
2320B	Amphibian Vehicles
2320C	Jeeps and all four-wheel drive vehicles of less than one ton capacity
2320D	Trucks with two-wheel drive of less than one ton capacity
2330	Trailers (e.g., semitrailers, house trailers, semitrailer dollies, etc.)
2340	Motorcycles, Motor Scooters, and Bicycles

Tractors

CLASS NO.	DESCRIPTION
2410	Tractors, Full Track, Low Speed (e.g., caterpillar and crawler, etc.)
2420	Tractors, Wheeled (e.g., agricultural and industrial wheeled tractors, etc.)
2430	Tractors, Track Laying, High Speed

Vehicular Equipment Components

CLASS NO.	DESCRIPTION
2510	Vehicular Cab, Body, and Frame Structural Components

CLASS NO.	DESCRIPTION
2520	Vehicular Power Transmission Components
2530	Vehicular Brake, Steering, Axle, Wheel, and Track Components
2540	Vehicular Furniture and Accessories
2590	Miscellaneous Vehicular Components (e.g., A-frames, bulldozer blades, crane booms, etc.)

Tires and Tubes

CLASS NO.	DESCRIPTION
2610	Tires and Tubes, Pneumatic, except Aircraft
2620	Tires and Tubes, Pneumatic, Aircraft
2630	Tires, Solid and Cushion (includes rubber track laying treads)
2640	Tire Rebuilding and Tire and Tube Repair Materials/Machinery

Engines, Turbines, and Components

CLASS NO.	DESCRIPTION
2805	Gasoline Reciprocating Engines, except Aircraft; and Components
2810	Gasoline Reciprocating Engines, Aircraft; and Components (e.g., only aircraft prime mover types)
2815	Diesel Engines and Components
2820	Steam Engines, Reciprocating and Components
2825	Steam Turbines and Components
2835	Gas Turbines and Jet Engines, except Aircraft; and Components (e.g., airborne auxiliary and ground gas turbine power units for aircraft engine starting, etc.)
2840	Gas Turbines and Jet Engines, Aircraft and Components°
2845	Rocket Engines and Components°
2895	Miscellaneous Compressed Air and Wind Engines; Water Turbines and Wheels; and Components

Engine Accessories

CLASS NO.	DESCRIPTION
2910	Engine Fuel System Components, Nonaircraft

CLASS NO.	DESCRIPTION
2915	Engine Fuel System Components, Aircraft
2920	Engine Electrical System Components, Nonaircraft
2925	Engine Electrical System Components, Aircraft
2930	Engine Cooling System Components, Nonaircraft
2935	Engine Cooling System Components, Aircraft
2940	Engine Air and Oil Filters, Strainers, and Cleaners, Nonaircraft
2945	Engine Air and Oil Filters, Strainers, and Cleaners, Aircraft
2950	Turbosuperchargers
2990	Miscellaneous Engine Accessories, Nonaircraft
2995	Miscellaneous Engine Accessories, Aircraft

Mechanical Power Transmission Equipment

3010	Torque Converters and Speed Changers
3020	Gears, Pulleys, Sprockets, and Transmission Chain
3030	Belting, Drive Belts, Fan Belts, and Accessories
3040	Miscellaneous Power Transmission Equipment

Bearings

3110	Bearings, Antifriction, Unmounted
3120	Bearings, Plain, Unmounted
3130	Bearings, Mounted

Woodworking Machinery and Equipment

3210	Sawmill and Planing Mill Machinery
3220	Woodworking Machines (excludes hand-held power-driven tools)
3230	Tools and Attachments for Woodworking Machinery

CLASS NO.	DESCRIPTION

Metalworking Machinery

3411	Boring Machines
3412	Broaching Machines
3413	Drilling and Tapping Machines
3414	Gear Cutting and Finishing Machines
3415	Grinding Machines
3416	Lathes (excludes speed lathes)
3417	Milling Machines
3418	Planers and Shapers
3419	Miscellaneous Machine Tools (e.g., gun rifling machines, speed lathes, etc.)
3422	Rolling Mills and Drawing Machines
3424	Metal Heat Treating and Nonthermal Treating Equipment
3426	Metal Finishing Equipment
3431	Electric Arc Welding Equipment (excludes welding supplies and associated equipment)
3432	Electric Resistance Welding Equipment
3433	Gas Welding, Heat Cutting, and Metalizing Equipment
3436	Welding Positioners and Manipulators
3438	Miscellaneous Welding Equipment
3439	Miscellaneous Welding, Soldering, and Brazing Supplies and Accessories
3441	Bending and Forming Machines
3442	Hydraulic and Pneumatic Presses, Power Driven
3443	Mechanical Presses, Power Driven (includes forging presses)
3444	Manual Presses
3445	Punching and Shearing Machines
3446	Forging Machinery and Hammers (excludes forging presses)
3447	Wire and Metal Ribbon Forming Machines (excludes roll forming machines)
3448	Riveting Machines (excludes power-driven hand-riveting machines)
3449	Miscellaneous Secondary Metal-Forming and Cutting Machines

CLASS NO.	DESCRIPTION
3450	Machine Tools, Portable
3455	Cutting Tools for Machine Tools (excludes flame cutting tools)
3456	Cutting and Forming Tools for Secondary Metalworking Machinery
3460	Machine Tool Accessories
3465	Production Jigs, Fixtures, and Templates
3470	Machine Shop Sets, Kits, and Outfits

Service and Trade Equipment

3510	Laundry and Dry Cleaning Equipment
3520	Shoe Repairing Equipment
3530	Industrial Sewing Machines and Mobile Textile Repair Shops (excludes shoe sewing machines)
3540	Wrapping and Packaging Machinery
3550	Vending and Coin-Operated Machines
3590	Miscellaneous Service and Trade Equipment (includes barber chairs, kits, hair clippers and shears, etc.)

Special Industry Machinery

3605	Food Products Machinery and Equipment (excludes kitchen and galley equipment)
3610	Printing, Duplicating, and Bookbinding Equipment
3615	Pulp and Paper Industries Machinery
3620	Rubber and Plastics Working Machinery
3625	Textile Industries Machinery
3635	Crystal and Glass Industries Machinery
3645	Leather Tanning and Leather Working Industries Machinery
3650	Chemical and Pharmaceutical Products Manufacturing Machinery
3655	Gas Generating Equipment (excludes meteorological equipment)

CLASS NO.	DESCRIPTION
3680	Foundry Machinery, Related Equipment and Supplies (e.g., molding machines, tumbling mills, foundry dextrine, core paste, etc.)
3685	Specialized Metal Container Manufacturing Machinery and Related Equipment
3690	Specialized Ammunition and Ordnance Machinery and Related Equipment*
3695	Miscellaneous Special Industry Machinery

Agricultural Machinery and Equipment

3710	Soil Preparation Equipment
3720	Harvesting Equipment
3740	Pest, Disease, and Frost Control Equipment
3750	Gardening Implements and Tools

Construction, Mining, Excavating, and Highway Maintenance Equipment

3805	Earth Moving and Excavating Equipment
3810	Cranes and Crane-Shovels (excludes barge-mounted cranes)
3815	Crane and Crane-Shovel Attachments
3820	Mining, Rock Drilling, Earth Boring, and Related Equipment
3825	Road Clearing and Cleaning Equipment
3830	Truck and Tractor Attachments (e.g., augers, blades, sweepers, etc.)
3835	Petroleum Production and Distribution Equipment (includes wellheads, pumping equipment, and gas distribution equipment)
3895	Miscellaneous Construction Equipment (e.g., asphalt heaters and kettles, concrete mixers, pile drivers, cable laying, lashing, spinning, and reeling equipment, etc.)

CLASS NO.	DESCRIPTION

Materials Handling Equipment

3910 Conveyers

3920 Material Handling Equipment, Nonself-Propelled (e.g., hand trucks, and material handling trailers)

3930 Warehouse Trucks and Tractors, Self-Propelled

3940 Blocks, Tackle, Rigging, and Slings

3950 Winches, Hoists, Cranes, and Derricks

3960 Elevators and Escalators

3990 Miscellaneous Materials Handling Equipment (e.g., skids/pallets)

Rope, Cable, Chain, and Fittings

4010 Chain and Wire Rope

4020 Fiber Rope, Cordage, and Twine

4030 Fittings for Rope, Cable, and Chain

Refrigeration and Air Conditioning Equipment

4110 Self-Contained Refrigeration Units and Accessories

4120 Self-Contained Air Conditioning Units and Accessories

4130 Refrigeration and Air Conditioning Plants and Components

4140 Fans and Air Circulators, Nonindustrial

Fire Fighting, Rescue, and Safety Equipment

4210 Fire Fighting Equipment (including Fire Trucks)

4220 Marine Lifesaving and Diving Equipment (excludes lifesaving boats)

4230 Decontaminating and Impregnating Equipment

4240 Safety and Rescue Equipment

Pumps and Compressors

4310 Compressors and Vacuum Pumps

4320 Power and Hand Pumps

4330 Centrifugals Separators, and Pressure and Vacuum Filters

Furnace, Steam Plant, and Drying Equipment

4410 Industrial Boilers

4420 Heat Exchangers and Steam Condensers

4430 Industrial Furnaces, Kilns, Lehrs, and Ovens (excludes food industry ovens, metal heat treating and laboratory-type furnaces)

4440 Driers, Dehydrators, and Anhydrators

4450 Industrial Fan and Blower Equipment

4460 Air Purification Equipment

Plumbing, Heating, and Sanitation Equipment

4510 Plumbing Fixtures and Accessories

4520 Space Heating Equipment and Domestic Water Heaters

4530 Fuel Burning Equipment Units

4540 Miscellaneous Plumbing, Heating, and Sanitation Equipment

Water Purification and Sewage Treatment Equipment

4610 Water Purification Equipment**

4620 Water Distillation Equipment, Marine and Industrial**

4630 Sewage Treatment Equipment

Pipe, Tubing, Hose, and Fittings

4710 Pipe and Tube (for other than underground, electrical, or laboratory use)

4720 Hose and Tubing, Flexible (e.g., hose and tubing, hydraulic, air, chemical, fuel and oil hose assemblies)

4730 Fittings, and Specialities

CLASS NO.	DESCRIPTION

Valves

| 4810 | Valves, Powered |
| 4820 | Valves, Nonpowered |

Maintenance and Repair Shop Equipment

4910	Motor Vehicle Maintenance and Repair Shop Specialized Equipment (excludes hand tools)
4920	Aircraft Maintenance and Repair Shop Specialized Equipment
4925	Ammunition Maintenance and Repair Shop Specialized Equipment*
4930	Lubrication and Fuel-Dispensing Equipment
4931	Fire Control Maintenance and Repair Shop Specialized Equipment*
4933	Weapons Maintenance and Repair Shop Specialized Equipment*
4935	Guided Missile Maintenance, Repair, and Checkout Specialized Equipment*
4940	Miscellaneous Maintenance and Repair Shop Specialized Equipment (includes paint spraying equipment)
4960	Space Vehicle Maintenance, Repair, and Checkout Specialized Equipment*

Hand Tools

5110	Hand Tools, Edged, Nonpowered
5120	Hand Tools, Nonedged, Nonpowered
5130	Hand Tools, Power Driven
5133	Drill Bits, Counterbores, and Countersinks: Hand and Machine
5136	Taps, Dies, and Collets: Hand and Machine (excludes punching, stamping, and marking dies)
5140	Tool and Hardware Boxes
5180	Sets, Kits, and Outfits of Hand Tools

Measuring Tools

| 5210 | Measuring Tools, Craftsmen's |

CLASS NO.	DESCRIPTION
5220	Inspection Gages and Precision Layout Tools
5280	Sets, Kits, and Outfits of Measuring Tools

Hardware and Abrasives

5305	Screws
5306	Bolts
5307	Studs
5310	Nuts and Washers
5315	Nails, Keys, and Pins
5320	Rivets
5325	Fastening Devices
5330	Packing and Gasket Materials
5340	Miscellaneous Hardware and Metal Screening
5345	Disks and Stones, Abrasive
5350	Abrasive Materials
5355	Knobs and Pointers

Prefabricated Structures and Scaffolding

5410	Prefabricated and Portable Buildings
5420	Bridges, Fixed and Floating (excludes pontoons and floating docks)
5430	Storage Tanks
5440	Scaffolding Equipment and Concrete Forms
5445	Prefabricated Tower Structures
5450	Miscellaneous Prefabricated Structures (e.g., bleachers)

Lumber, Millwork, Plywood, and Veneer

| 5510 | Lumber and Related Basic Wood Materials (e.g., plywood) |

Construction and Building Materials

5610	Mineral Construction Materials, Bulk
5640	Wallboard, Building Paper, and Thermal Insulation Materials
5650	Roofing and Siding Materials
5660	Fencing, Fences, and Gates

CLASS NO.	DESCRIPTION
5670	Architectural and Related Metal Products (e.g., door frames, fixed fire escapes, grating, staircases, window sash, etc.)
5680	Miscellaneous Construction Materials (e.g., metal lath, airplane landing mats, traction mats, tile, brick, nonmetallic pipe and conduit)

Communication Equipment

CLASS NO.	DESCRIPTION
5805	Telephone and Telegraph Equipment
5815	Teletype and Facsimile Equipment
5820	Radio and Television Communication Equipment, except Airborne (excludes home-type radio and television equipment)
5821	Radio and Television Communication Equipment, Airborne
5825	Radio Navigation Equipment, except Airborne
5826	Radio Navigation Equipment, Airborne
5830	Intercommunication and Public Address System, except Airborne
5831	Intercommunication and Public Address Systems, Airborne
5835	Sound Recording and Reproducing Equipment (excludes phonographs, home-type, and dictation machines)
5840	Radar Equipment, except Airborne*
5841	Radar Equipment, Airborne*
5845	Underwater Sound Equipment (includes only communication types of infrared equipment)*
5895	Miscellaneous Communication Equipment

Electrical and Electronic Equipment Components

CLASS NO.	DESCRIPTION
5905	Resistors
5910	Capacitors
5915	Filters and Networks
5920	Fuses and Lightning Arresters
5925	Circuit Breakers
5930	Switches

CLASS NO.	DESCRIPTION
5935	Connectors, Electrical
5940	Lugs, Terminals, and Terminal Strips
5945	Relays, Contactors, and Solenoids
5950	Coils and Transformers
5955	Piezoelectric Crystals*
5960	Electron Tubes
5961	Semi-Conductor Devices and Associated Hardware
5965	Headsets, Handsets, Microphones, and Speakers
5970	Electrical Insulators and Insulating Materials
5975	Electrical Hardware and Supplies
5977	Electrical Contact Brushes and Electrodes
5985	Antennas, Waveguides, and Related Equipment
5990	Synchros and Resolvers (includes autosyn motors, selsyn generators, synchro receivers, torque amplifiers, etc.)
5995	Cable, Cord, and Wire Assemblies: Communication Equipment
5999	Miscellaneous Electrical and Electronic Components

Electric Wire, and Power and Distribution Equipment

CLASS NO.	DESCRIPTION
6105	Motors, Electrical
6110	Electrical Control Equipment
6115	Generators and Generator Sets, Electrical
6120	Transformers: Distribution and Power Station
6125	Converters, Electrical
6130	Power Conversion Equipment, Electrical
6135	Batteries, Primary
6140	Batteries, Secondary
6145	Wire and Cable, Electrical
6150	Miscellaneous Electric Power and Distribution Equipment

CLASS NO.	DESCRIPTION

Lighting Fixtures and Lamps

6210	Indoor and Outdoor Electric Lighting Fixtures
6220	Electric Vehicular Lights and Fixtures (includes railroad and aircraft fixtures)
6230	Electric Portable and Hand Lighting Equipment
6240	Electric Lamps
6250	Ballasts, Lampholders, and Starters

Alarm and Signal Systems

6320	Shipboard Alarm and Signal Systems
6340	Aircraft Alarm and Signal System
6350	Miscellaneous Alarm and Signal Systems

Medical, Dental, and Veterinary Equipment and Supplies

6505	Drugs, Biologicals, and Official Reagents***
6510	Surgical Dressing Materials
6515	Medical and Surgical Instruments, Equipment, and Supplies
6520	Dental Instruments, Equipment, and Supplies
6525	X-Ray Equipment and Supplies
6530	Hospital Furniture, Equipment, Utensils, and Supplies
6540	Opticians' Instruments, Equipment, and Supplies
6545	Medical Sets, Kits, and Outfits

Instruments and Laboratory Equipment

6605	Navigational Instruments
6610	Flight Instruments
6615	Automatic Pilot Mechanisms and Airborne Gyro Components

CLASS NO.	DESCRIPTION
6620	Engine Instruments (includes all aircraft, marine, and vehicular engine instruments)
6625	Electrical and Electronic Properties Measuring and Testing Instruments
6630	Chemical Analysis Instruments (e.g., gas analyzers, hydrometers, etc.)
6635	Physical Properties Testing Equipment (e.g., balancing machines, industrial X-ray machines, torque bearing testers, etc.)
6636	Environmental Chambers and Related Equipment
6640	Laboratory Equipment and Supplies
6645	Time-Measuring Instruments
6650	Optical Instruments
6655	Geophysical and Astronomical Instruments
6660	Meterological Instruments and Apparatus
6665	Hazard-Detecting Instruments and Apparatus
6670	Scales and Balances
6675	Drafting, Surveying, and Mapping Instruments
6680	Liquid and Gas Flow, Liquid Level, and Mechanical Motion Measuring Instruments
6685	Pressure, Temperature, and Humidity Measuring and Controlling Instruments
6695	Combination and Miscellaneous Instruments (e.g., lie detectors, meter registers, etc.)

Photographic Equipment

6710	Cameras, Motion Picture
6720	Cameras, Still Picture
6730	Photographic Projection Equipment
6740	Photographic Developing and Finishing Equipment
6750	Photographic Supplies
6760	Photographic Equipment and Accessories

CLASS No.	DESCRIPTION
6770	Film, Processed
6780	Photographic Sets, Kits, and Outfits

Chemicals and Chemical Products

6810	Chemicals (includes nonmedicinal chemical elements and compounds, such as naphtha solvents, acetone, etc.)
6830	Gases: Compressed and Liquefied
6840	Pest Control Agents and Disinfectants
6850	Miscellaneous Chemical Specialties (e.g., antifogging compound, antifreeze, deicing fluid, etc.)

Training Aids and Devices

6910	Training Aids (e.g., cutaway models, vehicle training aids, etc.)
6920	Armament Training Devices (e.g., silhouette targets, etc.)*
6930	Operational Training Devices (e.g., flight simulators, etc.)*
6940	Communication Training Devices*

Furniture

7105	Household Furniture
7110	Office Furniture
7125	Cabinets, Lockers, Bins, and Shelving
7195	Miscellaneous Furniture and Fixtures

Household and Commercial Furnishings and Appliances

7210	Household Furnishings (e.g., bed blankets, mattresses, and pillows, etc.)
7240	Household and Commercial Utility Containers
7290	Miscellaneous Household and Commercial Furnishings and Appliances (e.g., carpets, tile, draperies, awnings, etc.)

CLASS No.	DESCRIPTION

Food Preparation and Serving Equipment

7310	Food Cooking, Baking, and Warming Equipment
7320	Kitchen Equipment and Appliances
7330	Kitchen Hand Tools and Utensils
7350	Tableware
7360	Sets, Kits, and Outfits: Food Preparation and Serving

Office Machines and Data Processing Equipment

7410	Punched Card System Machines
7420	Accounting and Calculating Machines
7430	Typewriters and Office Type Composing Machines
7440	Automatic Data Processing Systems: Industrial, Scientific, and Office Types
7450	Office-Type Sound Recording and Reproducing Machines
7460	Visible Record Equipment (e.g., rotary files, etc.)
7490	Miscellaneous Office Machines (e.g., cash registers, check machines, label printing machines, etc.)

Office Supplies and Devices

7510	Office Supplies
7520	Office Devices and Accessories
7530	Stationery and Record Forms (excludes standard forms approved for Government-wide use)

Books and Other Publications

7610	Books and Pamphlets

Musical Instruments, Phonographs, and Home-Type Radios

7710	Musical Instruments and Accessories

CLASS NO.	DESCRIPTION
7730	Phonographs, Radios, and Television Sets: Home-Type

Recreational and Athletic Equipment

7810	Athletic and Sporting Equipment
7830	Recreational and Gymnastic Equipment

Cleaning Equipment and Supplies

7910	Floor Polishers and Vacuum Cleaners
7930	Cleaning and Polishing Compounds and Preparations

Brushes, Paints, Sealers, and Adhesives

8010	Paints, Dopes, Varnishes, and Related Products
8030	Preservative and Sealing Compounds
8040	Adhesives

Containers, Packaging, and Packing Supplies

8105	Bags and Sacks
8110	Drums and Cans
8115	Boxes, Cartons, and Crates
8120	Gas Cylinders
8125	Bottles and Jars
8130	Reels and Spools
8135	Packaging and Packing Bulk Materials (e.g., baling wire, waterproof barriers, corrugated and wrapping paper, etc.)
8140	Ammunition and Nuclear Ordnance Boxes, Packages, and Special Containers
8145	Shipping and Storage Containers

Textiles, Leather, Furs, Apparel and Shoe Findings, Tents and Flags

8305B	Textile Fabrics
8340	Tents and Tarpaulins

Clothing and Individual Equipment

CLASS NO.	DESCRIPTION
8405	Outerwear, Men's
8410	Outerwear, Women's
8415	Clothing, Special Purpose, Safety, Protective, and Athletic
8420	Underwear and Nightwear, Men's
8430	Footwear, Men's
8435	Footwear, Women's
8440	Hosiery, Handwear, and Clothing Accessories: Men's
8445	Hosiery, Handwear, and Clothing Accessories: Women's
8460	Luggage
8465	Individual Equipment (e.g., ammunition belts, intrenching tool carriers, sleeping and duffel bags, flying goggles, sun glasses, etc.)
8475	Specialized Flight Clothing and Accessories*

Agricultural Supplies

8710	Forage and Feed

Live Animals

8820	Live Animals

Fuels, Lubricants, Oils, and Waxes

9110	Fuels, Solid
9130	Liquid Propellants and Fuels, Petroleum Base
9135	Liquid Propellant Fuels and Oxidizers, Chemical Base
9140	Fuel Oils
9150	Oils and Greases: Cutting, Lubricating, and Hydraulic
9160	Miscellaneous Waxes, Oils, and Fats

Nonmetallic Fabricated Materials

9310	Paper and Paperboard

CLASS NO.	DESCRIPTION
9320	Rubber Fabricated Materials
9330	Plastics Fabricated Materials
9340	Glass Fabricated Materials
9350	Refractories and Fire Surfacing Materials
9390	Miscellaneous Fabricated Nonmetallic Materials (e.g., asbestos fabricated materials, cork and fibre sheets, etc.)

Metal Bars, Sheets, and Shapes

CLASS NO.	DESCRIPTION
9505	Wire, Nonelectrical, Iron and Steel
9510	Bars and Rods, Iron and Steel
9515	Plate, Sheet, and Strip: Iron and Steel
9520	Structural Shapes, Iron and Steel
9525	Wire, Nonelectrical, Nonferrous Base Metal
9530	Bars and Rods, Nonferrous Base Metal

CLASS NO.	DESCRIPTION
9535	Plate, Sheet, Strip, and Foil: Nonferrous Base Metal
9540	Structural Shapes, Nonferrous Base Metal
9545	Plate, Sheet, Strip, Foil, and Wire: Precious Metal

Primary Metal Products

CLASS NO.	DESCRIPTION
9630	Additive Metal Materials and Master Alloys
9640	Iron and Steel Primary and Semifinished Products (e.g., ingots, pigs, billets, blooms, muck bar, skelp, rods for wire, sheet bar, etc.)
9650	Nonferrous Base Metal Refinery and Intermediate Forms (e.g., ingots, slabs, mercury, etc.)

* Certain items in this property category number are required to be demilitarized. Specific information will be given in the invitation for bid when issued.

** The purchaser must certify on certain stills and distilling apparatus in this property category that he will comply with the provisions of the Internal Revenue Code and with regulations issued thereunder. Specific information will be given in the invitation for bid when issued.

*** Certain items in this property category number are sold only to registered manufacturers of narcotic drugs.

DEFENSE REUTILIZATION AND MARKETING SERVICE
DEPARTMENT OF DEFENSE
SURPLUS PROPERTY BIDDERS APPLICATION

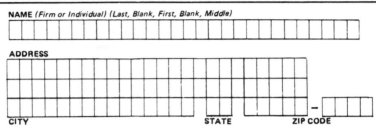

NAME *(Firm or Individual) (Last, Blank, First, Blank, Middle)*

ADDRESS

CITY   STATE   ZIP CODE

COMPLETION INSTRUCTIONS:

1. Fill in the blanks provided for your name, address, city, state and zip code.
2. Circle the class number of surplus property in which you are interested and circle the geographical area(s) desired. This will assure that you receive Invitations for Bids only when they contain the property you desire in the specific area you have designated.

(Circle numbers of classes of surplus property desired)

RECYCLABLE MATERIALS *(See pages 21 and 22)*

RSC	A	B	C	D	E	F	G	H	I	J	K	L	M	N	Z
01	8305A	9450A	9450B	9450C	9450D	9450E	9450F	9450G	9660A	9660B	9670C	9670D	9670E	9670F	
02	9670G	9670H	9670J	9670K	9670L	9680B	9680C	9680D	9680E	9680F	9680G	9680H	9680J	9680K	
03	9680L	9680M													

USABLE PROPERTY *(See pages 22 to 48)*

RSC	A	B	C	D	E	F	G	H	I	J	K	L	M	N	Z
04	1005	1190	1220	1240	1260	1265	1270	1280	1285	1290			1440	1450	
	A	B	C	D	E	F	G	H	I	J	K	L	M	N	Z
05	1510A	1510B	1510C	1520	1550	1560A	1560B	1560C	1610	1615	1620	1630	1650	1660	
06	1670	1680	1710	1720	1730	1740	1940D	2010	2020	2030	2040	2050	2090	2210	
07	2220	2230	2240	2250	2310A	2310B	2310C	2320A	2320B	2320C	2320D	2330	2340	2410	
08	2420	2430	2510	2520	2530	2540	2590	2610	2620	2630	2640	2805	2810	2815	
	A	B	C	D	E	F	G	H	I	J	K	L	M	N	Z
09	2820	2825	2835	2840	2845	2895	2910	2915	2920	2925	2930	2935	2940	2945	
10	2950	2990	2995	3010	3020	3030	3040	3110	3120	3130	3210	3220	3230	3411	
11	3412	3413	3414	3415	3416	3417	3418	3419	3422	3424	3426	3431	3432	3433	
12	3436	3438	3439	3441	3442	3443	3444	3445	3446	3447	3448	3449	3450	3455	
	A	B	C	D	E	F	G	H	I	J	K	L	M	N	Z
13	3456	3460	3465	3470	3510	3520	3530	3540	3550	3590	3605	3610	3615	3620	
14	3625	3635	3645	3650	3655	3680	3685	3690	3695	3710	3720	3740	3750	3805	
15	3810	3815	3820	3825	3830	3835	3895	3910	3920	3930	3940	3950	3960	3990	
16	4010	4020	4030	4110	4120	4130	4140	4210	4220	4230	4240	4310	4320	4330	

HQ DRMS Form 340 Jun 89 *(Previous edition to be used until exhausted)*

CONTINUED ON REVERSE

Defense Contract Administration Services Regions (DCASR)

From time to time, some of a contractor's inventory is left over after completing a contract. This is U.S. government-owned property, although it may now be in the possession of the contractor. It is considered surplus and sold by another branch of the Department of Defense Logistics Agency.

To find out how to purchase at these sales, write to these sales contacts:

Boston

Commander
Defense Contract Administration Services
Region, Boston
495 Summer Street
Boston, MA 02210-2184

New York

Commander
Defense Contract Administration Services
Region, New York
201 Varick Street
New York, NY 10014-4811

Philadelphia

Commander
Defense Contract Administration Services
Region, Philadelphia
2800 South 20th Street
Philadelphia, PA 19101-7478

Atlanta

Commander
Defense Contract Administration Services
Region, Atlanta
805 Walker Street
Marietta, GA 30060-2789

Cleveland

Commander
Defense Contract Administration Services
Region, Cleveland
Federal Office Building
1240 E. Ninth Street
Cleveland, OH 44199-2036

Chicago

Commander
Defense Contract Administration Services
Region, Chicago
O'Hare International Airport
P.O. Box 66475
Chicago, IL 60666-0475

St. Louis

Commander
Defense Contract Administration Services
Region, St. Louis
1136 Washington Avenue
St. Louis, MO 63101-1194

Dallas

Commander
Defense Contract Administration Services
Region, Dallas
1200 Main Street
Dallas, TX 75202-4399

Los Angeles

Commander
Defense Contract Administration Services
Region, Los Angeles
11099 South La Cienega Boulevard
Los Angeles, CA 90045-6197

11

State Surplus Auctions

★★

Your state probably has a surplus auction. Like the two federal agencies in Chapters 9 and 10, which sell surplus, your state is likely to be in the equipment auction business. State governments, collectively, have an enormous amount of personal property and equipment for sale. Selling used equipment helps raise much-needed cash for state treasuries.

State governments have their own kind of "General Services Administration" auctions. Those holding the auctions go by different names in each state. Sometimes they're called The Department of Management and Budget or simply The Department of Administration. Other times it might be The Department of Motor Vehicles auctions. As a result, some old auction hands call these DMV auctions.

All but a few states have merchandise/personal property/equipment auctions. Most, but not all, of what you find at these auctions are cars and trucks. From time to time, you might see food service equipment, shop equipment (welders, saws, generators, etc.), furniture, printing equipment, and the like. Remember, state governments run each state sort of like a corporation. They have administrators, state police, revenue collections, and other functions. When something gets worn out, they sell it.

With many states experiencing budget problems, expect this area to grow in the coming years.

States will be quick to sell their used vehicles to buy new ones, especially if they can get a good price at auction.

Background

Taking the cue from the federal government, state agencies started selling their used cars at auctions. As this caught on, additional merchandise and equipment got added to the auction list. With the increase and popularity of auctions, more bidders show up at these surplus sales.

Some states have a sophisticated network of state surplus auctions. In Tampa, Florida, one can go to a monthly private auction company's yard and find state vehicles, county vehicles, and private vehicles. Others have irregular or once-a-year surplus auctions.

County and city governments also have annual auctions for surplus equipment across America. Keeping track of them is nearly impossible. Interested bidders should contact their county seat, city manager, or mayor's office and find out when the next auction will be held. Usually, these are held at the beginning or end of the school year.

Procedures

For state surplus auctions, use the directory that follows and request to be placed on their mailing list. They don't have hotline tape-recorded messages. Many of these auctions are held in your state's capital. Some auctions are held in the state's major cities or wherever there is a state government presence.

Only a few of the states charge to be on their mailing lists. Most will gladly invite you to their auctions and send you auction fliers free of charge. Nearly all are friendly and helpful, welcoming you to their auctions.

Their fliers are usually 8½ inches by 11 inches, sheets folded, and many have just recently started using colored ink and paper with their auction notices. That shouldn't put you off to their auctions, though. It's the merchandise that counts.

Special Characteristics

Virtually all state surplus (and county or city government auctions) are held by public outcry. Here and there you might find a sealed-bid sale, but they are rare. The number of vehicles fluctuates from state to state. Some may have as little as four vehicles being sold, others 200 or more.

The average frequency of state surplus auctions is about once every three months. Some states will hold as many as two per month. Check with your state for details.

Prices vary with the number of auctions, number of vehicles per auction, and timing. In a survey of average prices at state surplus auctions, cars appear to fall into the $1,000 category. Many sell for $500 or less while some go over the $3,000 mark.

With surplus police cars, you often have to agree to repaint the vehicle within a certain time limit. Other modifications may be required. You may need to tow your vehicle from the auction site until the changes are made.

Tips

Go to state surplus auctions. You have a better-than-average chance of buying a very good car at a great price. Some states, like New Jersey, have sold highway patrol cars in the past for as little as

$75. One frequent auction-goer raved that he bought a couple of cars at those auctions for his nephews' Christmas presents.

Not all states have great deals or great vehicles available. Many do. On a flier promoting Michigan's vehicle auctions, more than half the cars were less than four years old. State policemen aren't the only state government employees who drive cars!

Added Bonus

State surplus agencies sometimes sell state university property at their auctions. They provide this service on a consignment basis, for a commission. Minnesota has the best program of all states. According to one auctioneer, Kurt Kiefer, state university auctions provide the best deals anywhere in the auction business. Kurt, you see, not only auctions for government agencies, but also buys at auctions that he does not run. His best deal ever was four van loads of audio-visual equipment for only $17. He said he made his money back on that deal before he even left the auction. At another state university auction, one individual bought equipment worth $2,000 for only $1.

State universities are beneficiaries of major corporations who donate research equipment, computer equipment, printing equipment, and so forth. Corporations do this for a tax write-off. State universities use the equipment for two to three years and then sell it off. A new supply keeps coming in.

Planning for these auctions is atrocious. Auctioneers are usually called in a week before the auction to sell the equipment. No appraisals are done. Very little advertising is done. It's almost like an "insider" auction. If you don't already know about them, you never find out about them.

How do you find out about state university auctions? Very difficult. Minnesota plans their state university auction calendar in advance. Many states don't. In fact many state universities hold their own auctions. Below are states that handle these university auctions. If your state is not listed, then contact your state university's purchasing division or, at the larger ones, the property disposition division. Ask the person in charge when their next state university auction is being held. I would think these have better deals available than even the state surplus agencies, since they are less-well promoted.

For those states that only sell vehicles and furniture, or just vehicles, contact one or more state universities as well and ask about their auction program. Leave no stone unturned, as these programs offer incredible steals.

State Surplus Departments That Handle University Auctions

Alabama	
Arkansas	(Vehicles and furniture only)
California	(Sacramento area only)
Connecticut	
Colorado	(Some, but not all)
Delaware	(Delaware State College only)
Florida	(Vehicles and furniture only)
Georgia	
Iowa	(Vehicles only)
Illinois	
Kentucky	(University of Kentucky has its own auction)
Louisiana	
Maine	(Some do, some don't)
Maryland	(Some auctions are held on school premises)
Massachusetts	(Some universities hold their own auctions)
Michigan	(Vehicles only)
Minnesota	(Mostly held at the college site)
Missouri	(Smaller colleges only)
Montana	
Mississippi	
New Hampshire	
Nevada	(Some do, some don't)
New York	(Properties sold on site by sealed bids)
North Carolina	(Sealed bids are used)
Ohio	(Vehicles only)
Pennsylvania	(Vehicles only)
South Carolina	(State surplus may or may not auction their merchandise)
Tennessee	
Vermont	(Vehicles only)
Virginia	(Property sold on site by sealed bids)
Washington	(Some community colleges only)
West Virginia	(Small colleges and community colleges only)
Wisconsin	(Sometimes)

Evaluation

If you are looking for a second car, a truck or van, state surplus auctions probably offer you a consistently better chance than federal government auctions. Your chances of finding car bargains are better at your state's surplus sales than at a General Services Administration vehicle auction. States are not as finicky about reserve prices as the GSA.

Many state surplus auctions are conducted by private auctioneers, who are more pleasant to deal with than GSA in-house auctioneers. Very few of the state surplus heads were rude or unpleasant to interview. Many were extremely helpful.

Do not expect to easily buy and sell vehicles for large profits or make a career from it. Most of what sells at state surplus is older, poor quality merchandise. Some of it is trash. Yet, when you look past the negative aspect of state surplus, enough good vehicles and merchandise are offered to make it worth your time and effort. Start attending their auctions. Overall, you should find good deals there.

Go to state university auctions whenever you can. These may not have vehicles, as many will be sent to their state's surplus division for separate auction. But, if you want different types of equipment and machinery, including computers, printing facilities, audio-visual equipment, and other similar items, university sales may offer you the best quality bargains anywhere in the auction business.

STATE GOVERNMENT AGENCIES DIRECTORY

State Surplus Auctions

There are various state surplus auctions one can go to for vehicles, equipment, merchandise, and assorted items. Each area may have a different department to contact. Those to be contacted, with information about them, are as follows:

Alabama

State Agency for Surplus Properties
4401 North Blvd.
Montgomery, AL 36121
(205) 277-5866
Contact: Charles Bush
No set day for auctions—when they have enough to sell.

Alaska

Dept. of Administration
Division of General Services and Supply
2400 Viking Dr.
Anchorage, AK 99501
(907) 279-0596
Contact: Roy Stevens or Mark Ford
Auctions held once a year no specific date. Phone
907-465-2172. Mailing list available.

Arkansas

D. F. & A.
Marketing and Redistribution
6620 Young Road SW
Little Rock, AR 72209
(501) 565-8645
Contact: Carol Ann Eichelmann

Do not have auctions. Open store on Wednesday from 7:30 am until 3:00 pm for priced purchasing. Large items such as vehicles, machinery and lawn equipment sold through sealed bids, must be registered in advance for sealed bids.

Arizona

State of Arizona
Surplus Property
Management Office
1537 W. Jackson St.
Phoenix, AZ 85007
(602) 542-5701
Contact: Jan Pixley
Three times a year—January, May & Sept. Mailing list available.

California

Dept. of General Services
State Garage
1416 Tenth St. S.
Sacramento, CA 95814
(916) 445-4851
Contact: Norma Wood
Sacramento—Held the second Sat. of the month at 1421 Richards Blvd. 10:00 am. Mailing list available. L.A.—

Not on regular date, whenever needed. 122 S. Hill St. Mailing list available.

Colorado

State Fleet Management
1001 W. 62nd Ave.
Denver, CO 80216
(303) 287-7940
Contact: Paul Jensen

Connecticut

Surplus Center
60 State St. Rear
Wethersfield, CT 06109
(203) 566-7018
Contact: Jacqueline Dion
General store open daily from 12:00 pm to 3:45 pm. Prices marked on articles.

Delaware

Dept. of Administrative Services
Division of Purchasing
P.O. Box 299
Delaware City, DE 19706
(302) 834-7081
Contact: Yvonne Gregg
Auctions held twice a year,

no set date. Held on the grounds of Governor Bacon Health Center. Mailing list available.

Washington, D.C.

Dept. of Administrative Services
2000 Adams Place N.E.
Washington, DC 20018
(202) 576-7850
Contact: Raymond Terry
Auctions held the third Thursday of the month at 2000 Adams Place, N.E. No mailouts.

Florida

Dept. of General Services
Bureau of Motor Vehicles and Watercraft
Rm. B-69, Larson Bldg.
Tallahassee, FL 32399-0950
(904) 488-4290
Contact: Ed Underwood

Auctions held four times a month. Held at various locations. Auctions held by First Cast Auctions 904-772-0110. Mailing list available.

Georgia

Dept. of Administrative Services
Surplus Properties
1050 Murphey Ave., Bldg. 1A
Atlanta, GA 30310
(404) 756-4800

Three or four auctions held at different locations. Mailing list available.

Hawaii

Call Only
(808) 523-4871 or 4874
Auctions for City and County of Honolulu ONLY. Auctions held when enough surplus is available. No mailing list available. Auction line 808-527-6789.

Idaho

Dept. of Transportation
3311 W. State St.
Boise, ID 83703
(208) 334-3630
Contact: Buz Shelton
Dept. of Law Enforcement auction held once a year. No set date; mailing list available. Dept. of Transportation sells to other agencies.

Illinois

Dept. of Central Management Services
Property Control Division
3550 Great Northern Ave.
Springfield, IL 62707
(217) 793-1813
Contact: Dolores Walden
Three personal property and three vehicle auctions are held each year at the Illinois State Fairgrounds, Springfield. Mailing list cost, $20 per year.

Indiana

State Surplus Property
545 W. McCarty St.
Indianapolis, IN 46225
(317) 232-1365
Contact: Patty Bauguess

Iowa

State Vehicle Dispatcher Division
301 E. Seventh
Des Moines, IA 50319
(515) 281-5121
Contact: Deb Bales

Kentucky

Dept. of Finance
Division of Personal Property
501 Holmes St.
Frankfort, KY 40601
(502) 564-2213
Contact: Doug Lathram
Approximately 30 auctions are held each year throughout different locations in the state. Mailing list are available.

Louisiana

Louisiana Division of Administration
Property Assistance Agency
P.O. Box 94095
Baton Rouge, LA 70804
(504) 342-6861
Contact: Clinton Thompson
Auctions are held the second Sat. of each month at 1502 N. 17th St. in Baton Rouge. Mailing list available.

Maine

Surplus Properties
Station 95
Augusta, Maine 04333
(207) 289-5750
Contact: David Patterson
Auctions are held four or five

times a year at the AMHI Complex, Hospital St. (Rt. 9W). Fliers are sent to the people who registered at the previous auctions.

Maryland

Call Only
(301) 799-0440
Contact: Al Jackson
General Store open daily from 8:00 am to 6:00 pm in Jessup, MD, on Brock Bridge Road. No auctions are held and no mailings.

Massachusetts

State Surplus Properties Office
1 Ashburton Place, Rm. 1009
Boston, MA 02108
(617) 727-2920
Contact: Peter Ray or Frank Kelly
Auctions held twice a month every other Sat. on the grounds of Cushing Hospital in Framingham; vehicles only. Notices placed in the *Boston Globe.*

Michigan

State of Michigan Department of Management and Budget
Office Services Division
3353 N. Logan
Lansing, MI 48913
(519) 373-1837
Contact: Doug Dodge
Variety of auctions held throughout the state. Send for a card to get the calendar of auctions. Mailing list also available.

Minnesota

Materials Management Division
Materials Service and Distribution,
Surplus Operation
5420 Hwy. 8 Arden Hills
New Brighton, MN 55112
(612) 296-5177
Contact: Gene Glaeser
Special Hotline: (612) 296-1056
Auctions are held twice a month at various locations. Mailing list available at $30 a year. Gene Glaeser in charge of Hot Line; 612-296-1056.

Missouri

State Surplus Properties
P.O. Box 1310
Jefferson City, MO 65102
(314) 751-3415
Contact: Ed Goff
Auctions are held approximately every two months, some out of Jefferson City. Also have sealed bid materials. Mailing list available.

Montana

Property Supply Bureau
Capitol Station
930 Lyndale
Helena, MT 59620
(406) 444-4514
Contact: Terrie Howell
Auctions held once a year in the fall. Heavy equipment at the Highway Dept. and vehicles at the Lewis & Clark Center. Mailing list available.

Mississippi

Dept. of Public Safety
P.O. Box 958
Jackson, MS 39205
(601) 987-1212 or
987-1453(direct)
Contact: James W. Bennett

Governor's Office of General Services
Bureau of Surplus Properties
P.O. Box 5778
Jackson, MS 39208
(601) 939-2050
Contact: Tracy Byas

Mississippi Wildlife Conservation Dept.
P.O. Box 451
Jackson, MS 39205
(601) 362-9212 or (601) 364-2092

Public Safety Vehicles to Mid-South auctions (601) 956-2700. Auctions held the first Tuesday of the month. Surplus properties auctioned every six months on Highway 468 in Jackson.

Nebraska

Materials Division
Mall Level—State Office Bldg.
301 Centennial Mall S.
P.O. Box 94901
Lincoln, NE 68509
(402) 479-4890
Vehicles auctioned three times a year by Talor and Martin. Fliers available. Other surplus 3-5 times a year at 5001 S. 24th St. No fliers available.

Nevada

State Purchasing Division
Capitol Complex
505 E. King, Rm. 400
Carson City, NV 89701
(702) 687-4070
Contact: Betty Shewlett
Call or write for sealed bid
forms and information. Open
bid is held in Reno annually.
Auctions for general
merchandise held once a year
on the second Sat. in August.
Vehicles in Oct. sealed bids
held at the Reno Warehouse.
Mailing list available.

New Hampshire

State Surplus Property
78 Regional Dr., Bldg. 3
Concord, NH 03301
(603) 271-2126
Contact: Armand Verville
Auctions held twice a year on
Quinton St. No set date.
Mailing list available.

New Jersey

State of New Jersey
Distribution Center
1620 Stuyvesant Ave.
Trenton, NJ 08628
(609) 530-3300
Contact: Frank Rich
Auctions held on vehicles as
needed, from the Distribution
Center. Information sheets
available the day before.

New Mexico

New Mexico Hwy. and
Transportation Dept.
Equipment Section, SB-2

P.O. Box 1149
Santa Fe, NM 87504
(505) 827-5580
Contact: Mike Maes
Vehicles and general
merchandise auctions held
once a year in Sept. Held at
the District Five yard next to
the State Police. Mailing list
available.

New York

Surplus
Albany, NY 12226
(518) 457-6335
Contact: Harry Feisthamel
Calendar available in March,
vehicles once a week at various
locations throughout the state.
Information posted in
newspapers.

North Carolina

State Surplus Property
P.O. Box 33900
Raleigh, NC 27636
(919) 733-3889
Contact: Jessie Murphy
$15 fee to be on the mailing
list for residents.
$25 for nonresidents.
Sealed bids. Pick up
information at the Surplus
Office in Raleigh.

North Dakota

Highway Department
Airport Rd.
Bismarck, ND
No mailing list
Call Only
(701) 224-2543
General auction held once a

year in May at the Bismark
location. No mailing list.
Notice of auctions placed in 10
area newspapers.

Ohio

State & Federal Supplies
Administrative Services
226 N. Fifth St.
Columbus, OH 43266-0584
(614) 466-5052
Auctions held every four
months. General auction at 226
N. Fifth St. Vehicles at 650
Harwood Ave. Auctions are
also held throughout the state.
Mailing list available.

Oklahoma

Central Purchasing
State Capitol Bldg., Rm. B4
Oklahoma City, OK 73105
(405) 521-4951
Contact: Steve Dwyer
To get on the mailing
list by mail, address letters to
Mr. Bob Liste.
Occasional general auction,
mostly sealed bids. Write for
registration form. Must be
registered for bids. Mailing list
available.

Oregon

Surplus Properties
1655 Salem Industrial Dr., NE
Salem, OR 97310
(503) 378-4714
Contact: Cheryl Winn
If writing to be put on the
mailing list, send a business-
sized envelope, SASE. General
Store open every Friday from

9 am to 2 pm. Occasional auction for vehicles and heavy equipment. Mailing list available.

Pennsylvania

Dept. of General Services
Bureau of Vehicle Management
2221 Foster St.
Harrisburg, PA 17125
(717) 783-3132 or 787-3162
Contact: Frank Belty
Once a month on a Thursday (not set) at 2221 Foster St. State used cars. Mailing list available.

Rhode Island

No Auctions

South Carolina

Dept. of Hwys. and Public Transportation
Procurement Office
191 Park St.
Columbia, SC 29202
(803) 737-6635
Contact: G. C. Cross
Motor Pool Vehicles

South Carolina
Surplus Properties
1441 Austin Ave.
West Columbia, SC 29169
(803) 822-5490
Contact: Tom Rayfield

Auctions for public transportation held on a Wednesday at the Equipment Division, 1500 Shop Road, 10 am. Mailing list available. Surplus properties, General Store daily 8 am to 4:30 pm. 1441 Austin Ave. Auctions 6-8 weeks as needed, no mailouts.

South Dakota

State Property Management
701 E. Sioux
Pierre, SD 57501
(605) 773-4935
Contact: Rick Boorhes
Auctions are held twice a year at four locations throughout the state. Mailing list available.

Tennessee

No mailing list (Nashville Only)
Call Only
(615) 741-4896
Contact: Brenda Grant
Auctions are held every 4-5 weeks, vehicles only at 6620 Centennial Blvd. Mailing list available at $35 a year.

Texas

State Purchasing and General Services Commission
P.O. Box 13047, Capitol Station
Austin, TX 78711-3047
(512) 463-3381
Contact: Marilyn Grimes
Auctions are held every two months at different locations in Austin. Must send in application for mailing list to address in book.

Utah

Utah State Surplus
522 S. 700th Street W
Salt Lake City, UT 84101
(801) 533-4616
Contact: Troy Manwaring
Auctions every three months. No set date. Everything sold from 522 S. 700th St. W. Mailing list available.

Vermont

Central Surplus
Properties Agency
RR 2, Box 350
Montpelier, VT 05602
(802) 828-3394
Contact: Lee Wallace
Auctions held twice a year in May & Sept. from Rt. 302 Transportation Garage, Auctioneer Thomas Hershak 1 (800) 634-7653.

Virginia

Division of Purchases and Supply
P.O. Box 1199
Richmond, VA 23209
(804) 786-3876
Contact: Marquis Bolton
Auctions are held several times a month at different locations in the state. Fliers available by mail.

Washington

Dept. of General Administration
State Office of Commodities Redistribution
2805 'C' St., S.W., Door 49, Bldg. 5
Auburn, WA 98001
(206) 931-3944
Contact: Darrel Green
Auctions for vehicles are held five times a year. General merchandise once a month at Auburn location. Mailing list available.

West Virginia

West Virginia State Agency for
Surplus Property
2700 Charles Avenue
Dunbar, WV 25064
(304) 768-7303
Contact: George Agglerback or
Ken Frye
Auctions for everything once a
month at 2700 Charles Ave.
Mailing list available also
published in newspapers.

Wisconsin

State Property Program
P.O. Box 7867
Madison, WI 53707
(608) 266-8024
Contact: Rex Owens
Auctions for vehicles are held
once a month throughout the
state. Each Department
disposes of general
merchandise as it sees fit.

Wyoming

State Motor Vehicle
Management Services
723 W. 19th St.
Cheyenne, WY 82002
(307) 777-6855
Contact: George Tsuda
Auctions for vehicles are held
2-3 times a year at 19th St.
Mailing list available. General
merchandise is held in state
surplus for its own use.

12

United States Marshals Service

★★

The U.S. Marshals Service is a branch of the U.S. Justice Department. Until recently, personnel in the Marshals Service were considered by their peers in the FBI or Justice Department to be working in dead-end jobs. Years ago, this service was only entrusted with either providing security in federal courtrooms or transporting criminals across state lines.

In the mid-1970s, because of the National Asset Seizure and Forfeiture Program, the U.S. Marshals Service was assigned to manage and sell the seized assets of administrative or judicial forfeiture. It wasn't much at first, but not much was expected of the Marshals. After all, they were not highly regarded by other law enforcement agencies. But, as the drug trade flourished, the DEA and FBI started busting these crooks and seizing their assets. Suddenly, the Marshals Service found itself foursquare in the auction business and the media spotlight.

Imagine the Marshals Service's embarrassment and humiliation to have been publicized as the government agency that sold a $50,000 boat for a mere $10 to a fisherman from Maine! Marshals' spokesmen argued among themselves and in the media for up to two years, giving a variety of excuses as to why this came about. Some explanations included that the normal auctioneer (a fe-

male employee) was off having a baby that day, that the boat didn't actually float (despite film footage showing it in the water), and that the boat wasn't really worth $50,000 (even though appraisers gave it that value). Government bureaucrats were so embarrassed by this giveaway that the U.S. Marshals Service even tried to bill (unsuccessfully) the buyer for docking fees and storage costs in addition to his $15 purchase price.

Because of this auction bargain the Marshals Service has since aggressively pursued a public relations campaign promoting the way in which buyers at their auctions overpay. You will often find Marshals spokesmen insisting that merchandise, equipment, and property auctioned at their auctions is sold at higher than appraised value. Get the message?

Background

The National Asset Seizure and Forfeiture (NASAF) Program gave Marshals Service officials a whole new sense of power. With the popularity of *Miami Vice*, the television series, drug dealers' vehicles, boats, airplanes, and other luxury trappings electrified viewers. When assets like those could be found at a local Marshals Service auction, customers flocked like lemmings. The media ate it up. Drug auctions had all the elements of a good feature: big money, violence, sex, fame, controversy. Fueled by news stories, auctions started getting packed. All that drove up final sales prices, making good bargains hard to find at a Marshals Service auction.

Then attorneys for drug dealers got smart and started manufacturing liens on the crooks' property. With real estate it was easy, but what to do about the Porsches, computers, and high-speed motorboats? Easy. They formed shell leasing companies from which drug dealers "leased" their personal property.

To add time to the auction process, attorneys would keep their clients' cases in appeals courts. Some of these cases might go on for two to five years. Great! So, a beautiful vehicle seized in 1985 might not hit the auction until 1990! Imagine the condition of a vehicle kept in storage, perhaps with inadequate maintenance, for five years. Not exactly a great cruising machine.

Some drug dealers are not taking their forfeited property lightly. In the past many have been content to have their spouses, relatives, mistresses, and friends repurchase their properties for them at auction. When that fails, however, revenge might be the only recourse. For example, one drug dealer's home, which was expected to fetch up to $300,000 at auction, was torched just before the sale was held. The property brought back only $50,000 to government coffers.

Complicating further the holding of Marshals Service auctions has been the decentralized manner in which the auctions might be held. Each office operates their program individually from 49 separate districts, with little established policy. Unfortunately, the Marshals Service is a throwback to the Wild West, where many district offices operated autonomously. No one has dragged them into the 20th century.

In many cases, you might not know who is conducting the auction. Some districts will hand over their seized assets to the GSA and have them run the auction. Others hire private auctioneers. And still other districts sell the property themselves.

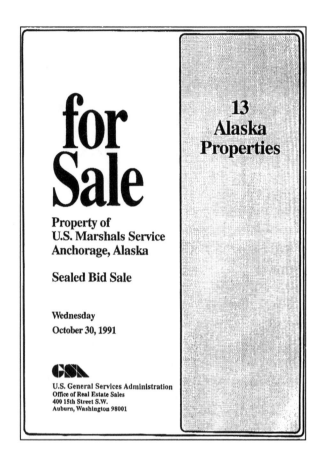

for Sale

13 Alaska Properties

Property of
U.S. Marshals Service
Anchorage, Alaska

Sealed Bid Sale

Wednesday
October 30, 1991

GSA

U.S. General Services Administration
Office of Real Estate Sales
400 15th Street S.W.
Auburn, Washington 98001

Special Characteristics

Goods and merchandise at Marshals Service auctions come primarily from drug busts, although quite a bit has come from white-collar crime activities. Usually, the DEA and FBI contribute the largest shares of the overall take. The Marshals try to manage the business or property and eventually pass it on to auction.

Marshals Service auctions have a reserve price. They are not professional appraisers, though, and can make mistakes. For example, if something is really worth $10,000 and the Marshals Service appraiser prices it at $7,500, then the Marshals can claim they sold it for above appraisal price when the item sells for $8,200 at auction. Efforts are being made to hire professional companies so mistakes like these aren't made.

Finding out about these auctions poses another problem. As mentioned earlier, there is no fixed pattern or logic to who will be selling the seized merchandise. You might receive a private auctioneer's flier advertising U.S. Marshals Service seized assets for sale at their next auction. However, these auctioneers will often include other merchandise and equipment with the seized assets. So, you never know which is what. Suckers will be lured to these auctions, hoping to buy some drug dealers' luxuries.

To make matters more difficult, the Marshals maintain no centralized mailing list. They do not encourage telephone calls and actually resent inquiries about their auctions. Most potential bidders will be directed to read their local newspaper classifieds. This is great for newspaper sales, but a waste of time for many auction amateurs.

Marshals Service auctions also suffer from a multiple personality disorder. Some are public oral auctions. Others may be sealed-bid. A scattering are done by negotiated sale or with spot-bid sales. With real estate, you are never certain whether the property will be listed with a broker or sold at auction.

When a government agency depends almost entirely on media hype, their auction hat is being worn by others. Some reports have it that the Marshals Service doesn't really want to be in the auction business. This information comes directly from U.S. Marshals Service sources. But, as any popular entertainer knows, it's tough to be out of the spotlight.

Procedures

There are two types of assets managed by the Marshals Service: criminal and civil. Both come to auction, eventually. Civil assets are so described because they are the profits of a criminal activity. Drug crooks have been found to be laundering their cash through restaurants, lumber mills, leasing companies, retail stores, and yes, laundromats. It's up to the Marshals to keep those businesses running so they can be profitably sold. Sometimes they don't do such a great job, so there's the possibility of picking up one of the businesses inexpensively.

Criminal assets are those confiscated in the commission of a crime: cash, fast boats, expensive cars, computers, or airplanes. These take longer to release because of the judicial process. Assets must be available to be used as evidence for the duration of the trial.

Because of certain lessons learned, their public auctions will have minimum bids and reserve prices. Private auctioneers will be forced to insert this clause: "Subject to confirmation by the seller." The Marshals Service will make that stick and you might not know until days later whether or not your final bid won.

Their confiscated property appears regularly in *USA Today*, usually on Wednesday. (Apparently, the Marshals Service hasn't caught on that the best day to advertise in *USA Today* is Friday.) The advertisement of property and merchandise doesn't mean it will be auctioned immediately, but you'll get a good idea of what's up for sale. A good deal of what is advertised is "seized cash." You can't buy that at auction. Perhaps if you could, then the Marshals might claim they got back more than it was worth!

Payment and removal of merchandise depends entirely on the conditions of sale. It conforms with other government agency auctions and private auctioneer terms. If you attend, bring cash or a cashier's check. Expect to ship it out quickly, as there will be a deadline.

Tips

Talking to anyone from the U.S. Marshals Service about getting a good bargain at their auctions is like poking a monkey in a small cage with a sharp stick. The fear of losing the spotlight and their new toy, the auction business, has made for bad manners. Reporters will parade four-color photographs and canned news stories of how a $300,000 classic car was sold for $1.6 million. Or other such nonsense.

If you want to buy into the hype, go to their auctions. The Marshals Service is running a media circus and the admission is overpriced. Such auctions are ripe for auction fever. Don't go to Marshals Service auctions. You won't find good deals. And, if you do go, don't tell them I sent you.

Success at an auction is based on being where the bidders aren't or buying something that the professionals and most auction-goers aren't looking for. If you want a good deal on U.S. Marshals Service seized assets, try a GSA public auction that is featuring vehicles but also selling other property. At those you stand a chance of saving 30%–50%, perhaps a bit more.

Don't be caught dead buying a vehicle from the U.S. Marshals Service. During the bidding, you will either keep your cool and drop out of the sale, or lose your senses and overpay. There are many other places to find good deals on vehicles.

Evaluation

All the ballyhoo about luxury vehicles and other fancy struttin' stuff just keeps the professionals away. Dealers and wholesalers know that a lot of publicity is going to bring in the local yokels—and that they're going to pay through the nose for a piece of that glamour.

Let the Marshals Service sit in their media spotlight for a while longer. Just don't go to their auctions. The press and television crews will get bored. They'll come back to earth eventually. Pendulums swing both ways. Just wait it out.

As one U.S. Marshals Service official told a British reporter a few years ago: "We've got four horses doing nothin' but eat hay. There's a goin' restaurant without a chef . . . We also got boats rotting in Florida and planes freezing to pieces in Alaska. As for cars . . . we could go into business against Chrysler."

Finally, for those who still insist on attending these auctions, the U.S. Marshals Service recently instituted an offensive practice at one of their sealed-bid sales. All bidders were required to sign a certification consenting to a background investigation check on themselves before their bid would be acknowledged by the Marshals Service.

UNITED STATES MARSHALS SERVICE DIRECTORY
District Offices

KEY: N = NORTH   OWN = Hold their own auctions.
     S = SOUTH   PRIVATE = Turned over to private auctioneer.
     E = EAST   GSA = Turned over to GSA.
     W = WEST
     C = CENTRAL
     D = DISTRICT OFFICE
     M = MIDDLE

Name District	Address Phone	Who Holds Auctions	Other Info
N/Alabama	1729 5th Ave. N. Rm 240 Birmingham, AL 35203 (205) 731-1712	Own	Ad in *Birmingham Knees,* under legal in classified.

Name District	Address Phone	Who Holds Auctions	Other Info
M/Alabama	Court, Lee & Moulton Sts. Rm 224, Federal Building Montgomery, AL 36104 P.O. Drawer 4249-36104 (205) 223-7401	Own	Few auctions. Ad in paper 3 weeks prior.
S/Alabama	113 St. Joseph St. Rm. 413, US Courthouse Mobile, AL 36601 P.O. Box 343 (205) 690-2841	Own	
D/Alaska	222 W. 7th Ave. #28 Rm A135, US Courthouse Anchorage, AK 99513 (907) 271-5154	Own	
D/Arizona	230 N. 1st Ave. Rm 8204, US Courthouse Phoenix, AZ 85025 (602) 379-3621	Private	*Vehicles:* Tucson-Gary's Towing, (602) 574-9161. Yuma-Thompson Towing, (602) 726-5561. *Real Estate:* Any broker in phone book.
E/Arkansas	5th & Gaines St. Rm 445, US Courthouse Little Rock, AR 72203 P.O. Box 8-72203 (501) 324-6256	Own	
W/Arkansas	6th St. & Rogers Ave. Rm 315, US Post Office Ft. Smith, AR 72902 P.O. Box 2626-72902 (501) 783-5215	Own	

Name District	Address Phone	Who Holds Auctions	Other Info
N/California	450 Golden Gate Ave. Rm 20005, US Courthouse San Francisco, CA 94102 P.O. Box 36056 (415) 556-3930	GSA	GSA Phone No.: (800) 472- 1313 (menu)
E/California	650 Capitol Mall Rm 1020, US Courthouse Sacramento, CA 95814 (916) 551-2861	GSA	*Info:* (916) 551- 2779 (menu) *Real Estate:* Prudential of California: (707) 528-7751
C/California	312 N. Spring St. Rm G-23, US Courthouse LA, CA 90012	GSA	GSA Phone No.: (213) 894-5162, includes Real Estate, Vehicles & Personal Property
S/California	940 Front St. Rm LL B-71 US Courthouse San Diego, CA 92189 (619) 557-6620	Private	*Vehicles*-AAA Galleries: (619) 338-8429 *Real Estate:* Any broker.
D/Colorado	1929 Stout St. Rm C-324, US Courthouse Denver, CO 80294 P.O. Drawer 3599 (303) 844-2801 (303) 844-2806 (Auction info)	Own	

Name District	Address Phone	Who Holds Auctions	Other Info
D/Connecticut	141 Church St. Rm 323, US Courthouse New Haven, CT 06510 P.O. Box 904-06504 (203) 773-2107	Private	*Vehicles:* S. Auto Auctions, Windsor Locks, CT (203) 623-2617 *Personal Property:* very little. *Real Estate:* Invite 10 brokers to open house, choose 1 for 6 months. Sale at fair market price.
District of Columbia	3rd & Constitution Ave. NW Rm 1103, US Courthouse Washington, DC 20001 (202) 633-1750	Own	
Associate Marshall, DC Superior Court	500 Indiana Ave. NW US Superior Court Bldg. Rm C-250 Washington, DC 20001 (202) 879-1118	Own	Advertise in *Washington Post* and *Law Reporter*
D/Delaware	844 King St. Rm 4311 US Courthouse Wilmington, DE 19801 (302) 573-6176	Private	*Vehicles:* Bellaire & Ironhill Auctions (302) 453-9138 *Real Estate:* Listed in newspaper. *Personal property:* In newspaper. If not sold, taken to larger auction in Phila.
N/Florida	110 E. Park Ave. Rm 100, US Courthouse Tallahassee, FL 32302 P.O. Box 2907 (904) 681-7676	Own	

Name District	Address Phone	Who Holds Auctions	Other Info
M/Florida	611 Florida Ave. Rm 200, US Courthouse Tampa, FL 33601 (813) 228-2146	Own & Private	*Vehicles:* To Cape GSA: (407) 867-7637 *Real Estate:* Listed in newspaper. *Personal property:* very little, listed in *Tampa Tribune*, and auctioned locally.
S/Florida	301 N. Miami Ave. Rm 205 Federal Courthouse Square Miami, FL 33128-7785 (305) 536-5346	GSA	GSA Phone: (407) 867-2874
N/Georgia	75 Spring St. SW Rm 1669, Federal Bldg. Atlanta, GA 30303 (404) 331-6833	Private	*Vehicles:* Hot line (404) 523-1548 *Real estate:* Prudential Real Estate: 1 (800) 688-8767
M/Georgia	3rd & Mulberry Sts. Rm 101 US Courthouse Macon, GA 31202 P.O. Box 7 (912) 752-8280	Own & Private	*Vehicles:* Storage T. Lynn Davis: (912) 788-4091 *Personal property:* auctioned monthly by Marshals. *Real estate:* very little.
S/Georgia	125 Bull St. Rm 333, US Courthouse Savannah, GA 31412 P.O. Box 9765 (912) 944-4212	Own	
D/Guam	238 Archbishop Flores St. 507 Pacific News Bldg. Agana, Guam 96910 P.O. Box 4496 011-671-472-7351	Never had an auction. If so, ad in newspaper.	

Name District	Address Phone	Who Holds Auctions	Other Info
D/Hawaii	300 Ala Moana Blvd., Rm C103 US Courthouse Honolulu, HI 96850 P.O. Box 50184 (808) 541-3000	Vehicles-Own Other-Private	*Hot line #:* (808) 541-3610 *Vehicles:* GSA-(808) 541-1972 *Real Estate:* Multi-listed thru rotation. *Personal property:* listed in Legal Notices for 1 wk. before local auction.
D/Idaho	550 W. Fort St. Rm 741 US Courthouse Boise, ID 83724 P.O. Box 010 (208) 334-1298	Private	
N/Illinois	219 S. Dearborn St. Rm 2444 Chicago, IL 60604 (312) 353-0101 (hotline)	Private	
C/Illinois	6th & Monroe Sts. Rm 333 US Courthouse Springfield, IL 62701 P.O. Box 156-62705 (217) 492-4430	Own	
S/Illinois	750 Missouri Ave. Rm 027, US Courthouse E. St. Louis, IL 62201 (618) 482-9336	Own	
N/Indiana	204 S. Main St. Rm 233 Federal Bldg. South Bend, IN 46624 P.O. Box 477 (219) 236-8291	Private	Very few auctions

Name District	Address Phone	Who Holds Auctions	Other Info
S/Indiana	46 E. Ohio St. Rm 227 US Courthouse Indianapolis, IN 46204 P.O. Box 44803-46244 (317) 226-6566	Private	Hot line #: (317) 226-6566
N/Iowa	101 First St. SE Cedar Rapids, IA 52401 (319) 362-4411	Ads in paper.	
S/Iowa	E. 1st & Walnut Sts. Rm 208, US Courthouse Des Moines, IA 50309 (515) 284-6240	Private	*Vehicles:* GSA: (515) 284-4450 *Real Estate:* Brokers chosen from approved list.
D/Kansas	444 SE Quincy Rm 456 Federal Bldg. Topeka, KS 66683 (913) 295-2775	GSA-Kansas	
E/Kentucky	Barr & Limestone Sts. Rm 162 Federal Bldg. Lexington, KY 40507 P.O. Box 30-40501 (606) 233-2513	Own & Private	*Vehicles:* Auto Dealer Exchange of Lexington: (606) 263-5163. *Real Estate:* Ads in counties where seizure occurred.
W/Kentucky	601 W. Broadway Rm 114 US Courthouse Louisville, KY 40202 (502) 582-5141	Private	*Vehicles:* Parker Storage: (502) 636-5817 *Real Estate:* Listed with area brokers.
E/Louisiana	500 Camp St. Rm C-600 US Courthouse New Orleans, LA 70130 (504) 589-6079	Own	

Name District	Address Phone	Who Holds Auctions	Other Info
M/Louisiana	707 Florida St. Rm 204 US Courthouse Baton Rouge, LA 70801 (504) 389-0364	Own	
W/Louisiana	500 Fannin St. Rm 2A10 Federal Bldg. Shreveport, LA 71161-3022 P.O. Box 53 (318) 226-5255	Own & Private	*GSA:* (817) 334-3281 *Auctioneer:* Mike Pederson, (318) 494-1333
D/Maine	P.O. Box 349 Portland, ME 04112 (207) 780-3355	Own & Private	Ad in *Portland Press Herald,* auction with Police Dept. Few held.
D/Northern Mariana Islands	P.O. Box 570 Susupe, Saipan 011-671-472-7351	Sub-station of Guam	
D/Maryland	101 W. Lombard St. Rm 605 US Courthouse Baltimore, MD 21201 (301) 962-2220	Own & Private	*Vehicles:* auctioned thru Parkville Auto, (301) 668-6600. *Real Estate:* listed in *Baltimore Sun,* if not sold, auctioned by U.S. Marshals. Listings also in *USA Today,* 3rd Wed. of each month.
D/Massachusetts	Congress & Water Sts. Rm 1616 US Courthouse Boston, MA 02101 P.O. Box 352 (617) 223-9721	Own & Private	*Hot line:* (617) 223-9651 *GSA:* (617) 565-1955
E/Michigan	231 W. Lafayetter St. Rm 120 Federal Bldg. Detroit, MI 48226 (313) 226-7755	Private	

Name District	Address Phone	Who Holds Auctions	Other Info
W/Michigan	110 Michigan Ave. Rm 544 Federal Bldg. Grand Rapids, MI 49503 (616) 456-2438	Private	*Vehicles:* Midwest Auto Auction (313) 538-2100
D/Minnesota	110 S. 4th St. Rm 574 US Courthouse Minneapolis, MN 55401 (612) 348-1935	Own & Private	*Hot line:* (612) 348-1955
N/Mississippi	911 Jackson Ave. Rm 348 Federal Bldg. Oxford, MS 38655 P.O. Box 887 (601) 234-6661	Own	*Vehicles:* Very few. *Real Estate:* listed in county where seizure occurred.
S/Mississippi	235 E. Capitol St. Rm 404 US Post Office Jackson, MS 39205 P.O. Box 959 (601) 965-4444	Own	
E/Missouri	1114 Market St. Rm 108 US Courthouse St. Louis, MO 63101 (314) 539-2212	Own	
W/Missouri	811 Grand Ave. Rm 509 US Courthouse Kansas City, MO 64106 (816) 426-3521	GSA	*GSA:* (314) 236-2500
D/Montana	316 N. 26th St. Rm 5110 Federal Bldg. Billings, MT 59101-1362 P.O. Box 2179-59103 (406) 657-6284	Own & Private	*GSA:* (406) 657-6279 Some auctioned by Marshals Office.
D/Nebraska	215 N. 17th St. Omaha, NE 68102 P.O. Box 1477-68101 (402) 221-4781	Private	*GSA:* (402) 822-6152 *Real Estate:* Handled locally.

Name District	Address Phone	Who Holds Auctions	Other Info
D/Nevada	300 Las Vegas Blvd. S. Rm 424 US Courthouse Las Vegas, NV P.O. Box 16039 (702) 388-6052 (702) 388-6163	Private	Legal ads in *Review Journal* for everything. Auctioneer chosen at time of auction.
D/ New Hampshire	55 Pleasant St. Rm 409 Federal Bldg. Concord, NH 03302 P.O. Box 1435 (603) 225-1632	GSA & Private	*GSA: Vehicles* (603) 225-1537 *Real Estate:* Open house, choose local agency—fair market price.
D/New Jersey	500 US Courthouse & Post Office Newark, NJ 07101 P.O. Box 186 (201) 645-2404	Own & Private	*GSA:* (800) 488-7253 5-minute tape.
D/New Mexico	500 Gold Ave. SW Rm 12403 US Courthouse Albuquerque, NM 87103 P.O. Box 444-87103 (505) 766-2933	Private	Auctioneer: Ron Patton, (505) 867-4389—everything.
N/New York	10 Broad St. Rm 213 Federal Bldg. Utica, NY 13501 (315) 732-2123	Private	*Vehicles & Personal property:* Martin & Sons, Plattsburgh, NY (518) 561-0491 *Real Estate:* From vendors list, must get 90% of value.
E/New York	225 Cadman Plaza E. Rm 172 US Courthouse Brooklyn, NY 11201 (718) 330-7493	Own & Private	Do own auctions, or in conjunction with NY City.

Name District	Address Phone	Who Holds Auctions	Other Info
S/New York	1 St. Andrews Plaza 114 US Courthouse Annex NY, NY 10007 (212) 791-1100	Own	Legal ads in the *New York Times*
W/New York	68 Court St. Rm 129 US Courthouse Buffalo, NY 14202 (716) 846-4851	Private	*Vehicles:* To a sub-contractor. *Real Estate:* To approved list of vendors—list market value.
E/North Carolina	310 New Bern Ave. Rm 744 Federal Bldg. Raleigh, NC 26540 (919) 856-4153	Private	Legal ads in *Raleigh News & Observer*—everything
M/North Carolina	324 W. Market St. Rm 234 US Courthouse Greensboro, NC 27402 P.O. Box 1528 (919) 333-5354	Private	*Vehicles:* Crews Auc-tion (919) 993-2762 *Real Estate:* Local agency, must get fair market value.
W/North Carolina	Otis St. Rm 315 US Post Office Ashville, NC 28802 P.O. Box 710 (704) 259-0651	Own	
D/North Dakota	655 1st Ave., N. Rm 115 Old Federal Bldg. Fargo, ND 58102 P.O. Box 2425-58108 (701) 235-3050	Own	

Name District	Address Phone	Who Holds Auctions	Other Info
N/Ohio	201 Superior Ave. B-1 US Courthouse Cleveland, OH 44114 (216) 522-2150	Own	*Vehicles:* Baker Motor Vehicles: (216) 676-5920 *Real Estate:* Broker, Selected list. *Personal property:* to local auction house small quantity.
S/Ohio	110 E. 5th St. Rm 815 US Post Office & Courthouse Cincinnati, OH 45202 P.O. Box 688-45201 (513) 684-3594	Private	*Vehicles:* Ron's Pre-Owned Auto—(513) 891-8692 (auctioned) *Real Estate:* Legal section—*Cincinnati Enquirer*
N/Oklahoma	333 W. 4th St. Rm 4557 US Courthouse Tulsa, OK 74102 P.O. Box 1097-74101 (918) 581-7738	GSA-Vehicles Private	*GSA:* (918) 581-7628 *Real Estate:* Williams & Williams, (918) 250-2012
E/Oklahoma	P.O. Box 738 Muskogee, OK 74402 (918) 687-2523	Own & Private	*Vehicles:* Any auctioneer available. *Real Estate:* Accept bids from local agencies & choose 1.
W/Oklahoma	200 NW 4th St. Rm 2418 New Federal Bldg Oklahoma City, OK 73102 P.O. Box 886-73101 (405) 231-4206	Private	
D/Oregon	620 SW Main St. Rm 420 US Courthouse Portland, OR 97205-3087 (503) 326-2209	Own	

Name District	Address Phone	Who Holds Auctions	Other Info
E/Pennsylvania	601 Market St. Rm 2110 US Courthouse Philadelphia, PA 19106 (215) 597-7272	GSA & Private	*Vehicles:* Vile Meier, (215) 628-2303 *Real Estate:* Barry Sloshberg—(215) 925-8020
M/Pennsylvania	Washington Ave. & Linden St. Rm 411, Federal Bldg. Scranton, PA 18501 P.O. Box 310 (717) 346-7277	Private	*Real Estate, Seized:* Jeff Harlick, Specialized Properties (412) 261-0740
W/Pennsylvania	7th & Grant St. Rm 539 US Courthouse Pittsburgh, PA 15219 (412) 644-3351	Private	*Vehicles:* Investment Auto—(412) 452-2277 *Real Estate:* Prudential Property (412) 261-6500 *Personal Property:* Ad in *Pittsburgh Press*
D/Puerto Rico	Rm 400 US Courthouse & Post Office Bldg San Juan, PR 00902 P.O. Box 3748 (809) 766-5929	GSA	GSA: (212) 788-4636
D/Rhode Island	Kennedy Plaza Rm 303 US Courthouse Providence, RI 02901 P.O. Box 1524 (401) 528-5300	Private	*USA Today Providence Journal* ads show how to proceed.
D/South Carolina	1845 Assembly St. Rm B31 US Courthouse Columbia, SC 29201 P.O. Box 1774 (803) 765-5821	Property-GSA Vehicles-Own	*Vehicles:* few, done locally. *GSA:* (800) 473-7836

Name District	Address Phone	Who Holds Auctions	Other Info
D/South Dakota	400 S. Phillips Ave. Rm 216 Federal Bldg. Sioux Falls, SD 57102 P.O. Box 1193-57101 (605) 330-4351	Property-GSA Vehicles-Own	
E/Tennessee	Main & Walnut Sts. Rm 212 Federal Bldg. Knoxville, TN 37901 P.O. Box 551 (615) 673-4577	Private & Own	Very little. Ad in local paper, legal notices.
M/Tennessee	801 Broadway Rm 866 US Courthouse Nashville, TN 37203 (615) 736-5417	Private	Recording.
W/Tennessee	167 N. Main St. Rm 1029 Federal Bldg. Memphis, TN 38103 (901) 544-3304	Private	Few vehicles, handle locally. *Real Estate:* Per court order, or thru agency.
N/Texas	1100 Commerce St. 16F47 Federal Bldg. Dallas, TX 75242 (214) 767-0836	Private	Information: (214) 767-2058
E/Texas	211 W. Ferguson St. Rm 305 Federal Bldg. Tyler, TX 75702 P.O. Box 299-75710 (903) 592-8216	Own & GSA	*Vehicles:* Used as official cars for government or police. No real estate.
S/Texas	515 Rusk Ave. Rm 10130 US Courthouse Houston, TX 77002 P.O. Box 61608-77208 (713) 229-2800	Private	*Hotline:* (713) 229-2806
W/Texas	655 E. Durango Blvd. Rm 235 US Courthouse San Antonio, TX 78206 (512) 229-6540	Private	*Vehicles:* Auction- eers chosen at time of auction. *Real Estate:* To Urban Systems: (512) 227-9435

Name District	Address Phone	Who Holds Auctions	Other Info
D/Utah	350 S. Main St. B20 US Post Office & Courthouse Salt Lake City, UT 84110 P.O. Box 1234 (801) 524-5693	Own	
D/Vermont	Elmwood Ave. & Pearl St. Rm 621 Federal Bldg. Burlington, VT 05402 (802) 951-6271	Private	Thomas Hurchak, Co. (802) 985-9195, for everything.
D/Virgin Islands	Veterans Drive Rm 371 US Courthouse St. Thomas, VI 00801 P.O. Box 9018-00901 (809) 774-2743	Private	Very little.
E/Virginia	200 S. Washington St. Rm 104 Federal Bldg. Alexandria, VA 22313 P.O. Box 20227 (703) 235-2713	GSA	*GSA:* (703) 557-7785, for everything.
W/Virginia	210 Franklin Rd. SW Rm 247 Federal Bldg. Roanoke, VA 24009 P.O. Box 2280 (703) 982-6230	Private	*Real Estate:* Listed in local paper.
E/Washington	W. 920 Riverside Ave. Rm 888 US Courthouse Spokane, WA 99210 (509) 353-2781	Private	*Vehicles:* Thru different auction companies. *Real Estate:* Ads in paper where property was seized. *Personal property:* Auctioned by Marshals at courthouse where seized.

Name District	Address Phone	Who Holds Auctions	Other Info
W/Washington	1010 5th Ave. Rm 300 US Courthouse Seattle, WA 98104-1188 (206) 442-5500	Private	*Vehicles:* James J. Murphy Co. (206) 486-1246 *Real Estate:* Listed in *Daily Commerce Journal* *Personal Property:* In *USA Today*, 3rd Wed. of month.
W/West Virginia	300 3rd St. Rm 317 Federal Bldg. Elkins, WV 26241 P.O. Box 1454 (304) 636-0332	Own, Ad in paper	
S/West Virginia	500 Quarrier St. Rm 4302 Federal Bldg. Charleston, WV 25330 P.O. Box 2667 (304) 347-5136	Own	
E/Wisconsin	517 E. Wisconsin Ave. Rm 310 Federal Bldg. Milwaukee, WI 53202 (414) 297-3707	Own & Private	*Information:* (414) 297-1919
W/Wisconsin	120 N. Henry St. Rm 440 Federal Courthouse Madison, WI 53703 (608) 264-5161	Own	*Information:* (608) 264-5198
D/Wyoming	2120 Capitol Ave. Rm 2124, Joseph C. O'Mahoney Federal Ctr. Cheyenne, WY 82001 P.O. Box 768-82003 (307) 772-2196	Own & Private	See Cheyenne & Casper newspapers. *Denver Post, USA Today* (3rd Wed. every month, in Life Section)

13

The Internal Revenue Service

★★★

Here's one agency that needs no introduction. If you haven't ever heard of the IRS, then they probably want to meet you. As you know, the Internal Revenue Service collects taxes. Individuals and corporations who don't pay on time, don't pay enough, disagree with IRS procedures, or make a lot of noise about IRS collection tactics are prime targets for having their personal property and real estate seized. Nearly all celebrities are at risk with the IRS.

This agency relies exclusively on fear tactics to get voluntary compliance, which means getting you to file your income taxes. Methods used are not dissimilar to those of the KGB or Gestapo in the old regimes. This spills over into their auctions.

IRS auctions have been a quiet joke in the auction industry. Bargains abound. These are not well publicized unless you happen to be a celebrity or an activist. Ordinary people just lose their property with hardly a notice in the back pages of the local gazette.

On the U.S. Government Organizational Chart, you'll find the IRS in the Executive Branch, under the Department of the U.S. Treasury. Interestingly, the United States Tax Court, where officially authorized decisions to seize property are made, is under the jurisdiction of the legislative branch, congress. Of course, most IRS auctions are held with just local and internal authorization. They play by their own rules. Authority is given to them by their own manuals and codes. Seizure comes about from Internal Revenue Code section 6331.

Background

IRS auctions have traditionally offered some of the better deals of all government auctions. That's because the IRS just wants its back taxes and could care less about appraised value. When a $5,000 car gets sold for $500 and the IRS is still owed $4,500, then the taxpayer gets billed the deficiency. Tough luck. Woody Herman, the jazz great, had his mansion seized and then sold at auction; he spent the rest of his life failing to fully pay off the deficiency judgment against him.

In the past, houses have gone for a song. One report shows a two-story house with a minimum bid of only $320. Rental income on the same property was $300/month! Fortunately, taxpayers are given up to 180 days to redeem their properties. Which, of course, can make it sticky for the buyer when buying real estate. On the other hand, someone who's out back taxes also gets slapped with interest and penalties, so recovering the property is difficult.

Nowdays, the IRS is trying to upgrade its auction image. Their solution has been to offer properties at 80% of appraised value. This is called the forced sale price. Appraisals are not always done professionally. What happens if they don't get the minimum bid? It's lets-make-a-deal time.

Worse yet, many taxpayers are now taking the IRS to court on those deficiency balances. Motions are being filed that claim the IRS did not act as a neutral party in disposing of the taxpayer's personal property or real estate. Claims also state that the IRS didn't get a fair-market value price because their agents failed to act in the same way a professional auctioneer would. You see, IRS collection agents are often the auctioneers as well. Is that a stacked deck or what?

What does all this mean for the future of IRS auctions? To quote a senior IRS official who spoke at a governmental affairs seminar sponsored by the National Auctioneers Association and held in Washington, D.C., in early, 1991: "The IRS is in a shake-out phase concerning auctions." The use of private auctioneers is being considered to help prevent a major IRS meltdown. I don't think a lot of tears will be shed if that happens.

Special Characteristics

The IRS auction system is decentralized. Secretive, too. Try getting a hold of a local IRS auction telephone number. You won't find it, unless the number appears on an auction notice. For the most part you are required to write to the IRS or telephone their 800 number. Remember that the IRS doesn't hire the most competent employees. Racism, internal politics, and other chaos also pervade this agency, so you must be patient with them.

If the IRS operator claims there are no auctions, ask for the collections division. Once you've reached that office, ask for notices of any public or sealed-bid auctions. These are announced on form 2434 so you might need to jog their memory by asking if any form 2434s are available.

IRS auctions are not well planned or heavily promoted unless a celebrity, such as Willie Nelson or Redd Foxx, gets slammed. (Even this strategy doesn't always work in favor of the IRS—Redd Foxx's home was withdrawn from auction.) Do not expect an auction calendar or a monthly schedule from the IRS. They hold them sporadically, after tax seizures.

Occasionally, the IRS will advertise in larger newspapers. I found one notice in *USA Today*. That is rare. To track IRS auctions might require spending your mornings reading the public or legal notice section of your newspaper. Their classified ads are tiny, in fine print, and loaded with a lot of useless data. You are likely to find them wedged between government contracts for bidding and storage auctions. And they won't tell you much. Try calling the 800 number in your area and get an auction flier.

When you finally get the auction notice, it won't look like any other invitations for bids or private auctioneer fliers. Receiving a form 2434, notice of public auction sale, could make your tummy queasy. After all, it does look like *your* property is being auctioned. Hopefully, it's not.

Details are explained on this form. If you have questions, a telephone contact name and number appears at the bottom of the form. That's usually the chief of the collections division. As he may be busy (pulling the wings off flies), his secretary or assistant should be able to answer your questions.

Most of what you need to know is located on the form, including a brief description of the items. You should confirm its accuracy and inquire about the condition of the property. While you're on the phone, ask whether or not the auction is still scheduled. Section 6337 of the IRS code does provide for redemption of property, so the auction can be cancelled before the sale.

Because many people fear the IRS, sealed-bid sales are popular. Even at their public auctions, bidders are often given the opportunity of mailing in a bid rather than appearing in person. The only way a sealed bid will be accepted by the IRS is by

Form **2222** (Rev. 10-80)	Department of the Treasury - Internal Revenue Service **Sealed Bid for Purchase of Seized Property** *(See instructions on back)*	Please type or print plainly

NOTE: Terms and conditions of sealed bid sales are provided in regulations under section 6335 of the Internal Revenue Code and are summarized in the instructions on the back of this form.

Name and Address of Bidder	Bid Made by: *(Check appropriate box)*
	☐ Individual ☐ Partnership ☐ Corporation

Item or Group Number	**Description of Property** *(Description must conform to that in the public notice of sale without qualification or reservation. Attach separate sheets if necessary.)*	**Amount Bid**
		$
	Total Amount of Bid	$

Remittance enclosed in the amount of $ _____

If you submitted remittance with alternative bid or agreement to bid, enter amount here: $ _____
(See instructions 4 and 5)

Signature of Authorized Person	Name and Title	Date

(This Space Reserved for Use of District Director)

Award	Return of Remittance to Unsuccessful Bidder
Accepted as to Items or Groups Numbered	I acknowledge receipt of the remittance submitted with this bid.
Total Amount of Accepted Bid $	
Remittance Applied to Bid	
Balance Due on *(Date)* $	Signature, Title, and Date
Signature and Title	
Address	Remittance Returned by Mail on *(Date)*
Certificate of Sale Issued on *(Date)*	Signature of Revenue Officer

Form **2222** (Rev. 10-80)

using form 2222. Obtain one from the IRS branch holding the sale. In a rush, the IRS will fax you this form.

A handful of cities have IRS hotline telephone numbers. Without speaking to an IRS agent, you can listen to a tape-recorded message describing upcoming auctions. Additional information can be requested by calling the contact name and number given on the taped message.

Procedures

Probably the biggest drawback to IRS auctions is the fear people might have of attending them. The IRS has brought this bad publicity upon itself. Who else would think of harassing the black community by jotting down the license plate numbers on luxury cars owned by Muhammed Ali fans at his boxing matches? And then having his supporters audited by IRS agents!

That doesn't stop some people from attending their auctions. As mentioned earlier, great deals can be found. A friend of mine purchased practically the entire inventory of an IRS-seized nightclub. For less than $2,000 he bought about '$50,000 worth of restaurant equipment. Items that were worth about $1,200 were sold to him for about $20. What's that, two cents on the dollar?

Which begs the question: "Why are they selling for so low?" That's easy. The IRS isn't monitored by congress, as is the GSA, or humiliated in the press, as is the Marshals Service. All they want to gain from the auction proceeds is the back taxes owed. *Period.* A truck could be appraised for $1,500, the IRS might give it a forced sale value of $1,200, but it might only bring $400. If the taxes due were $800, then the taxpayer is billed for the deficiency of $400 and is out a truck!

Yes, the IRS will claim to demand a minimum bid or have a reserve price. Reality makes for a different story. Let's say only two bidders show up (or just one) and the highest bid is $400. The IRS may withdraw the item from the auction. Occasionally they will. More often, they will take the money, selling it to the highest bidder, regardless of minimum bid and reserve price. They have taxes to collect, not auctions to run.

Am I making this up? Hardly. One acquaintance had his food manufacturing plant seized by the IRS for back taxes. It was a corporation, so he wasn't ruined. At the IRS auction, he sent in an employee who was only one of two bidders attending. The equipment he wanted repurchased was bought at eye-popping deals by his employee. He personally repurchased that equipment, bankrupted his corporation, and thumbed his nose at the IRS.

So, don't feel too sorry about going to an IRS auction. Many are held for corporations that are no longer in business. And you can find great deals at the auctions, whether it is a public or sealed-bid auction.

Now, the final drawback to the IRS auction: they don't finance or wait around for their bucks. Full payment is required immediately upon acceptance of your winning bid. They do auction a lot of real estate and you can work out terms—often 30 to 45 days—after dropping a downpayment of about 20%. The method of payment is cash, certified check, cashier's check, or money order. Of course, you do make the check out to the IRS.

Tips

Go to their auctions wearing sunglasses, pay in cash, and don't give your name. Ha! Only joking. Your biggest concerns for attending an IRS auction are in this order:

1. Confirm that the auction hasn't been cancelled.

2. Inspect the merchandise as you would any other auction before bidding.

3. Watch out for other liens on the equipment, merchandise, or property. These may or may not be mentioned in the auction notice. The IRS does not guarantee title!

4. Bring cash or a cashier's check, as you must pay in full immediately following the auction.

Of course, it doesn't hurt to avoid addiction to IRS auctions. Paranoid as their collections agents are, you will probably end up on some audit list if you are the successful bidder at many of their auctions. Especially, if you report a low annual salary, such as under $25,000 a year.

As with all auctions, merchandise, equipment, and property are sold "as is, where is." Participating at their auctions forfeits any rights you have to recourse against the U.S. government. They may even be wrong in their appraisal, the qualtity of the merchandise, or something else, and you have no remedies.

A Private Auctioneer's Comment about IRS Auctions

G. Robert Diero, an auctioneer used by the IRS, makes a few important comments about their auctions and procedures. The IRS is a very monolithic organization and very difficult to deal with. Washington sets no overall policy.

In the past ten years, the only change he has seen in their auctions is that they send their agents for two-day training seminars. IRS has also set up auction teams that run around the U.S. holding auctions that are a waste of taxpayer money. He criticized their practices in this way:

The IRS lacks any auctioneering technology.

Auctions are conducted in uncomfortable surroundings.

Auctions are both poorly advertised and organized.

The IRS demands payment in full on the spot.

The IRS doesn't guarantee title on your purchase.

According to Mr. Diero's observations, IRS auctioneers are inexperienced and, as a result, get a lower value on the property being sold. As long as private auctioneers are not used, auction-goers can find good bargains at IRS auctions while taxpayers pay the penalty.

Evaluation

IRS auctions are still worth attending despite all the caveats. You stand an excellent opportunity of finding a great deal at their auctions. The merchandise available can include anything under the sun. After all, if you can see it, it can be seized by the IRS. Look around your house and at your neighbor's property. All that you see could be up for auction some day.

Your main difficulties are not knowing what will be sold and pricing it under these limitations. So much variety is available, though. Some professionals have caught on to the great deals at these auctions and will show up. (Remember to wait until the professional drops out before you start bidding.) If they don't show up, enjoy the auction. Be sure to bring cash or cashiers' checks, as payment in full is demanded immediately after the sale.

As taxpayers are reading this book, I would be remiss not to mention some effective recourse one has with the IRS, should your property ever come up for tax seizure. Many taxpayers don't know they have rights when dealing with the IRS. The IRS may even state that you have no rights. That's not true. The Taxpayer's Bill of Rights, passed by congress a few years ago, gives taxpayers many rights they didn't previously have. For a copy of your Taxpayer Bill of Rights, call 1-800-IRS-1913 (also 213-957-7746).

The IRS has clearly demonstrated over the past few decades that it has become increasingly an agency out of control. Recently, there has been tremendous congressional interest in IRS abuses, especially when agents have driven taxpayers to suicide. One sad tale came from a mother of two small children who turned to prostitution so she could raise enough money to pay her tax bill and prevent her home from being sold at auction. It's time that taxpayers collectively blow the whistle on the IRS and congress takes a serious look at an alternative tax system.

IRS DIRECTORY

Internal Revenue Service

ALL STATES:

Call this number, or the hotline numbers below, and request to be put on the mailing list. Or, write to the appropriate address below.

ALL STATES:

(800) 829-1040

HOTLINE PHONE NUMBERS:

San Francisco:
(415) 556-5021

Seattle:
(206) 553-0703

Los Angeles:
(213) 894-5777

Sacramento:
(916) 978-5520

New York City:
(718) 780-4020

Internal Revenue Service Offices Addresses

ALABAMA

500 22nd Street S.
Room 300
Birmingham, AL 35233

ALASKA

P.O. Box 101500
Anchorage, AK 99510

ARIZONA

2120 N. Central Avenue
Phoenix, AZ 85004

ARKANSAS

P.O. Box 3778
Little Rock, AR 72203

CALIFORNIA

450 Golden Gate Ave.
Stop 4313
San Francisco, CA 94102

55 Market Street
San Jose, CA 95113

4330 Watt Avenue
North Highlands, CA 95660

P.O. Box C-11
Laguna Niguel, CA 92677

P.O. Box 1431
300 N. L.A. St.
Los Angeles, CA 90053

COLORADO

Dominion Plaza
600 17th Street
Denver, CO 80202

CONNECTICUT

135 High Street
Stop 160
Hartford, CT 06103

DELAWARE

P.O. Box 28
Wilmington, DE 19899

DISTRICT OF COLUMBIA

Assistant Commissioner
(International)
950 L'Enfant Plaza SW
Washington, DC 20024

FLORIDA

P.O. Box 35045
Stop 5700
Jacksonville, FL 32202

1 University Drive
Building B
Ft. Lauderdale, FL 33324

GEORGIA

P.O. Box 1005
Room 525
Atlanta, GA 30370

HAWAII

P.O. Box 50089
Honolulu, HI 96850

IDAHO

550 W. Fort Street
Box 041
Boise, ID 83724

ILLINOIS

230 S. Dearborn Street
DP #28-5
Chicago, IL 60804

P.O. Box 19204
Springfield, IL 62794

INDIANA

P.O. Box 44211
Indianapolis, IN 46244

IOWA

P.O. Box 313
Des Moines, IA 50302

KANSAS

P.O. Box 2278
Stop 5000-WIC
Wichita, KS 67202

KENTUCKY

P.O. Box 1735
Stop 500
Louisville, KY 40201

LOUISIANA

500 Camp Street
Stop 4
New Orleans, LA 70130

MAINE

P.O. Box 1020
Augusta, ME 04330

MARYLAND

P.O. Box 538
Baltimore, MD 21203

MASSACHUSETTS

P.O. Box 9112
JFK Post Office
Boston, MA 02203

MICHIGAN

P.O. Box 330500
Stop 22
Detroit, MI 48232

MINNESOTA

P.O. Box 64450
St. Paul, MN 55164

MISSISSIPPI

100 W. Capital Street
Suite 504,. Stop 4
Jackson, MS 39269

MISSOURI

P.O. Box 1457
St. Louis, MO 63188

MONTANA

Federal Building
2nd Floor
Drawer 10016
Helena, MT 59626

NEBRASKA

106 S. 15th St.
Stop 33
Omaha, NE 68102

NEVADA

300 Las Vegas Blvd., So.
Las Vegas, NV 89101

NEW HAMPSHIRE

P.O. Box 720
Portsmouth, NH
03801

NEW JERSEY

425 Raritan Center Pkwy.
Edison, NJ 08818

NEW MEXICO

P.O. Box 1967
Albuquerque, NM 87103

NEW YORK

P.O. Box 60
General Post Office
Brooklyn, NY 11202

P.O. Box 3000
Church Street Station
NY, NY 10008

L.W. O'Brien Federal Building
Clinton Ave. & N. Pearl St.
Albany, NY 12207

P.O. Box 266
Niagara Square Station
Buffalo, NY 14201

NORTH CAROLINA

320 Federal Place
Greensboro, NC 27401

NORTH DAKOTA

P.O. Box 8
Fargo, ND 58107

OHIO

P.O. Box 1579
Cincinnati, OH 45201

P.O. Box 99183
Cleveland OH 44199

OKLAHOMA

P.O. Box 66
Oklahoma City, OK 73101

OREGON

P.O. Box 3341
Portland, OR 97208

PENNSYLVANIA

P.O. Box 12050
Room 741
Philadelphia, PA 19105

P.O. Box 2488
Pittsburgh, PA 15230

RHODE ISLAND

P.O. Box 6867
Providence, RI 02940

SOUTH CAROLINA

1835 Assembly Street
Room 466
Columbia, SC 29201

SOUTH DAKOTA

P.O. Box 370
Aberdeen, SD 57402

TENNESSEE

801 Broadway
Nashville, TN 37203

TEXAS

P.O. Box 250
Austin, TX 78767

1100 Commerce Street
6000 DAL
Dallas, TX 75242

3223 Briar Park
Houston, TX 77042

UTAH

P.O. Box 2069
Salt Lake City, UT 84110

VERMONT

199 Main Street
Burlington, VT 05401

VIRGINIA

P.O. Box 10107
Richmond, VA 23240

WASHINGTON

915 2nd Avenue
Stop 200
Seattle, WA 98174

WEST VIRGINIA

P.O. Box 1138
Parkersburg, WV 26102

WISCONSIN

P.O. Box 493
Milwaukee, WI 53201

WYOMING

308 W. 21st Street
Cheyenne, WY 82001

14

United States Customs Auctions

★★

International travelers are familiar with U.S. Customs agents who greet them upon entering the country. However, Customs has quite a few more duties than that. They're responsible for collecting revenues from imports and administering the tariff laws, especially with regard to quotas. Customs is empowered with seizing contraband and narcotics coming into the United States (or leaving it for that matter).

They have many other duties related to protecting American business from fraudulent practices, particularly from foreign countries. Customs enters the auction picture mainly as a result of quota dumping, narcotics seizures, or confiscating contraband. Most of what you will find at their auctions come from those three areas.

Background

U.S. Customs does not hold its own auctions. So don't call a U.S. Customs office for auction dates and locations. They've contracted out this end of the business to a private auction house. Previously, auctions conducted by U.S. Customs were a bargain hunter's paradise! A spectrophotometer, new at $30,000, sold for $38. One bidder walked away with a Waterford crystal candelabrum, valued at $300, for only $40. Ski vests, retailing at

$56, sold for $8. There were thousands of bargains!

After some bad press on these great bargains, Customs wised up and hired a private company to do their auctions, Northrop World-Wide Aircraft. Northrop wasn't in the auction business, so they, in turn, hired a private auctioneer who ran an auction school. Things went well for a few years. Dealers stopped coming to these auctions because the deals had died.

Then Northrop put in their own auctioneers. Business picked up again for dealers. Bargains, though not as good as before, were still to be found. Northrop ran into some grand jury problems, more bad press, and a lot of noise from congress. Customs had them replaced.

Now, E. G. & G. Dynatrend, a private auction company, handles the U.S. Customs auctions. Same type of goods, different auction house. Customs can blame them if you find great bargains at these auctions.

You'll find a motley assortment of auction goods. At one auction in Miami, Florida, the sales flier listed vehicles, bulk quantities of merchandise, a television set and VCR, camera equipment, Krugerrands (for export only), T-shirts, electronic equipment, silk fabric, motorcycles, and a few boats.

Customs auctions are held regularly at these ten different auction sites around the country on a cyclic basis. More locations may be added in the future.

Eastern United States: Jersey City, New Jersey
Miami, Florida
San Juan, Puerto Rico
Central United States: El Paso, Texas
Edinburg, Texas
Laredo, Texas
Western United States: Los Angeles, California
San Diego, California
Nogales, Arizona
Yuma, Arizona

Dynatrend appears to be following in their predecessor's footsteps, occasionally having specialty auctions in different cities. Auctions in those areas have usually been preceded by a short newspaper advertising campaign. You can also find out about them by calling E. G. & G. Dynatrend.

Procedures

E. G. & G. Dynatrend has a public auction line, which they affectionately call PAL. You can call (703) 351-7887 anytime—they run tape-recorded messages—and listen to information about upcoming Customs auctions being held around the United States. The taped messages will tell you the auction location, date, and time of the auction, as well as a brief and general description of the auction merchandise.

Should you wish further details, you can hold (rotary phone) or press 0 on your touchtone phone to speak to a public information officer (available only Monday through Friday, 8 AM–5 PM eastern time). When speaking to him or her, ask for a sample auction flier for a specific upcoming auction. Dynatrend has sent these sample copies free of charge to callers.

You can also get regular auction notices sent to you by subscription. Annual subscription fees run from $25–$50, depending on whether you want regional or national coverage.

In the past, Customs has had sealed-bid sales for vehicles and large, unusual items. Most are held public auction–style, open, increasing, and by outcry.

Special Characteristics

Auction merchandise is sold by lot, in its entirety. Sales of the merchandise are done, usually, in the sequence listed in the auction catalog. During the auction, announcements will often be made to spell out the export status of the merchandise, clear up descriptions of the merchandise, or regarding withdrawn merchandise.

The terms of sale at Customs auctions are the same as the conditions of sale at other auctions (see Chapter 2, page 27). The terms of sale describe the auction procedures and regulations for that auction.

At some of their public auctions you may be permitted to submit a sealed bid by registered mail with a cashier's check. If your bid is unsuccessful, they will return your bid and check by certified mail.

After you make a successful bid, head over to the cashier to get your notice of award (NOA). This is your paid receipt and allows you to pick up the merchandise. Full payment is expected in either cash or cashier's check. You can either have the cashier's check made out to yourself and then signed over to E. G. & G. Dynatrend or have it made out directly to U.S. Customs Service/E. G. & G. Dynatrend Agent. Some locations will make it easier and accept bank credit cards.

You must remove your auction prize by the date specified in the terms of sale or you will be billed for storage. Failure to do so will result in forfeiture of the merchandise. If the export-only merchandise was seized, it usually must be shipped out of the United States within 30 days. On general merchandise that is export only, you have 60 days from the auction sale to get it out of the country.

Tips

U.S. Customs vehicles are generally in poor condition. When they are in good condition, bidders will probably not find good deals. Export-only merchandise is great, but you have a deadline to remove it from the country. You should have foreign buyers or brokers solidly lined up before buying, or you risk spending a hectic three to four weeks reselling your purchase profitably.

When you are buying, bring a few smaller cashiers' checks made out to yourself, rather than one large check made out to Dynatrend. If you don't buy, just deposit them back in the bank. Also, Dynatrend does not normally give change back on those checks for more than 10% of the cashier's check.

Evaluation

U.S. Customs auctions are probably in professional hands with E. G. & G. Dynatrend. We'll see what the future brings. They are certainly friendlier than Northrop was and less generous than Customs was when they did their own auctions. These auctions still rely on the mystique of seizing a drug dealer's luxury item, rather than on the general, ordinary merchandise that is the bulk of the available auction property.

Most aircraft dealers stopped going to Customs auctions several years ago because people were paying retail. This is one of the disadvantages of these sales. Agents or attorneys of drug dealers have gone to these auctions with briefcases, suitcases, and even grocery bags filled with hundred-dollar bills to buy back their property. Of course, this drives up the price.

With luck, the way Customs handled seized assets has improved. One boat they let sit in the water for seven straight years (no maintenance) at a cost to taxpayers of $100 per day. Finally, it was sold for scrap, bringing in only $12,000—a loss of almost $250,000!

You are not likely to find great deals, as these auctions are well promoted and have amateur appeal, as do the U.S. Marshals Service auctions.

As an exporter you can do well. Watch out for the 30-day or 60-day deadline on export-only merchandise.

Some good deals are available from time to time, but they are inconsistent. Most bidders go once and then never return. Great bargains may come again. You'll know it when the dealers return in droves!

Subscription Application

For general information about U.S. Customs auctions write to:

E. G. & G. Dynatrend
U.S. Customs Service Support Division
2300 Clarendon Boulevard
Suite 705
Arlington, Virginia 22201

or telephone the public auction line (PAL) at (703) 351-7887. If you have a rotary phone, please wait for the public information officer to come on the line and answer your questions. If you have a touch-tone phone, here are the current listings on their menu. Push one of the numbers below on your keypad when the taped message begins.

Subscription Information	Push 1
General Program Information	Push 2
Eastern U.S. Sales	Push 3
Wait and then	
for Miami	Push 8
for Jersey City	Push 9
for Specialty Sales	Push 10
Central U.S. Sales	Push 4
Wait and then	
for El Paso, TX	Push 11
for Edinburg, TX	Push 12
for Laredo, TX	Push 13
for Specialty Sales	Push 14
Western U.S. Sales	Push 5
Wait and then	
for Los Angeles	Push 15
for San Diego	Push 16
for Nogales, AZ	Push 17
for Specialty Sales	Push 18

Should you wish to subscribe to their auction mailings, you will be charged an annual fee. Subscription applications should be mailed to:

E. G. & G. Dynatrend
U.S. Customs Service Support Division
P.O. Box 75847
Chicago, IL 60675-5847

15

County Sheriff Sales and County/City Marshals Auctions

★★

The sheriff is like the chief executive officer of a corporation. His job is to run the county government. Usually, this amounts to a bit more than having his deputies act as process servers and check out county crime. They are usually too busy to think about auctions. But the onus falls on them either to act as the auctioneer or hire one, when feasible, which it usually is not.

Sheriff auctions go back to medieval England and Europe, where the sheriff was the guy who foreclosed on the peasant for not paying his taxes. Then he sold the peasant's merchandise at auction. Back then, the sheriff had someone else call the bids while he described the merchandise. Nowadays, he wears both hats.

In cities such as New York and Los Angeles, this job is done by a city or county marshal, which is different from the U.S. Marshals Service. These officers are part of the local government and have nothing to do with the federal government. They repossess the property or, usually, a vehicle and then hold the auction themselves.

Procedures

These auctions are advertised in local papers. You can try to find out about upcoming auctions by calling your county sheriff, or city or county marshal. Most won't welcome your call because they have other duties. Much of their telephone traffic is from upset people whose assets have been seized.

One suggestion is to send a self-addressed and stamped envelope with a letter requesting to be sent a flier announcing the next auction. If you're a gambler, send a package of such SASEs. Pray they won't peel off your stamps and trash your envelopes. Some are "good ole guys" and may help you. As there are thousands of counties across the United States, you may have to check the Blue Pages in your telephone book to find their address and telephone number. Major counties across the United States have been listed in the directory at the end of this chapter.

Special Characteristics

Merchandise which comes up for auction by the county sheriff or local government marshal is usually repossessed. Occasionally, there will be merchandise from a small drug bust. That doesn't mean the property is poor quality or ordinary. Some of it may be office equipment seized from businesses unable to satisfy judgments against them. It can be cars or other vehicles.

Frequently you will find lower-class real estate at these sales. In New York City, for example, most city marshal real estate sales are held in minority-concentrated neighborhoods. Great, if your goal in life is to be a slum lord, or are just starting out and want to buy a starter home. Bidders do attend them and they are sold.

In some larger cities, personal property will be sold by a private auctioneer or auction company. Sheriff-seized property will be thrown in with other surplus merchandise. Often, you won't know which is which.

Tips

Watch out for liens on property. You may find a great deal on something only to discover that you now own a lien. This is not an asset. When the buyer purchases property with a lien, he is responsible for paying the previous owner's debt. To avoid this, take a trip to your county courthouse for some title research. Ask your county clerk, or her assistants, for help in doing one. They are not complicated. Title companies generally charge $150–$350 to do one for you; the main reason for this fee is they insure that the title is clean. Do it yourself. It won't take more than a few hours, at most.

Sheriff sales are fantastic places to find good bargains. The man who bought a $100,000 house for $15 purchased it at a sheriff sale. Remember, the sheriff is not a professional auctioneer. So, he's not likely to be affable, heavy into marketing techniques, or a professional appraiser. He just wants to hold the auction, get it over with, and return to his line of duty: serving summonses.

Make sure you have clear title to what you buy. Find out in advance how payment is to be made and terms for removal of the merchandise. Customs vary greatly around the country. Your safest bet is to bring cash, a cashier's check, or money orders.

Contact your local sheriff or city/county marshal about their personal property or merchandise/equipment auctions. Look in Section Three, Chapter 29, for Tax Sales, as many sheriffs handle these as well.

Evaluation

The quality of the merchandise available at these auctions will differ from county to county. Deals are generally good to better-than-average, depending on the bid-calling, appraisal skill, and marketing know-how of the local sheriff. Money usually goes to pay creditors, not to fill the county government coffers, so the interest level is often low.

Because there is no centralized clearinghouse of auction information, as found with some federal government agencies, finding out about these auctions takes work. Check your local newspaper's classifieds, call your county sheriff, or try sending those self-addressed, stamped envelopes for upcoming auction information. Auction notices can also be posted in the county courthouse.

COUNTY SHERIFFS SALES DIRECTORY

Alabama

Mobile County Commissioners
P.O. Box 1443
Mobile, AL 36633
(205) 937-0264

609-8655 for vehicles and property under court order. 609-4782 other vehicles. Ads in *Mobile Press Register*.

Arizona

Sheriff of Maricopa
102 W. Madison
Phoenix, AZ 85003
(602) 256-1000

(602) 234-0517 for vehicles. Miscellaneous posted at Sheriff's Office. Posted in *Arizona Business Gazette*.

Pima County Sheriff's Dept.
Civil Processing Unit
P.O. Box 910
Tucson, AZ
(602) 740-5510

Personal property & vehicles posted in *Morning Star Weekend*. Foreclosures—Green Valley and in Superior Court Bldg.

California

Orange County Sheriff's Dept.
Orange County Register
1141 E. Chestnut
Santa Ana, CA 92705
(714) 568-4359
or
Orange County Sheriff
P.O. Box 449
Santa Ana, CA 92702
(714) 647-7000

Vehicles to United Auction (714) 946-3386 Merchandise—two auctions a year. Mailing list available. Call (714) 568-4359.

Kern County Sheriff's Dept.
Civil Division
P.O. Box 2208
Bakersfield, CA 93303
(805) 861-7653

All vehicles and merchandise sold through: Ed Rogers Enterprises, 3737 Gilmore, Bakersfield, CA 93308 (805) 322-2192.

Fresno County Sheriff's Dept.
Fresno County Bldg.
2200 Fresno Street
Fresno, CA 93724
(209) 488-3939

All auctions posted in the windows of the Courthouse.

Los Angeles County
Vehicle Auction
2500 S. Garfield
City of Commerce, CA 90040
(213) 720-6952 or 720-6951

Hot Line (213) 720-6951.

Riverside County Garage
4293 Orange St.
Riverside, CA 92501
(714) 275-6890

United Auctions (714) 946-3386.

Sacramento County
6670 Elvas Avenue
Sacramento, CA 95819
(916) 732-3841
or
Roger Ernst Associates
Auctioneer
P.O. Box 3251
Modesto, CA 95353
(209) 527-7399

Vehicles & merchandise, whatever the county sends them.

San Diego Public Administrators Office
5201-A Ruffin Road
San Diego, CA 92123
(619) 694-3500
or
U.S. Marshall Civil
940 Front St., LLB-71
San Diego, CA 92189
(619) 694-2920

Auctions 3rd Wednesday of the month.

Every four months for vehicles and office equipment. (619) 560-1677—Auctioneers.

San Francisco Sheriff's Dept.
Civil Division, 333 City Hall
Federal Bldg., Hall of Justice
(Adjacent, Room 101)
San Francisco, CA 94102
(415) 554-7230

Santa Clara County
San Jose Sheriff's Dept.
Purchasing Dept.
1608 Las Plumas
San Jose, CA 91533-1695

Vehicles—Nationwide (707) 255-1766. Mailing list available for others.

Colorado

Denver Sheriff's Dept.
Civil Division
City & County Bldg.
Denver, CO 80202
(303) 640-5192

Will not give information over the phone. See the *Daily Journal;* or they are posted in the City and County Bldg.

Connecticut

Hartford County Sheriff's Dept.
P.O. Box 6302
Hartford, CT 06106
(203) 566-4930

Check the legal section of the *Hartford Courant.* Very seldom have anything, taken to the state surplus in Weathersfield.

Delaware

New Castle County Sheriff's Dept.
11th & Kingn St.
Wilmington, DE 19801
(302) 571-7568

Real estate—2nd Tues. of month in Public Bldg. List cost $5. Also published in *Wilmington Journal.*

Florida

Duval County
Office of Sheriff
(Jacksonville Police)
501 E. Bay St.
Jacksonville, FL 32202

Vehicles; two auctions a year. General merchandise every three months.

Dade County
Metro Dade Police Dept.
Sheriff's Services
Civil Process Bureau, 13th Fl.
Dade County Courthouse
Miami, FL 33130

Auction every Wednesday.

Orange County Sheriff's Dept.
P.O. Box 1440
Orlando, FL 32802
(407) 657-2500

Ads in the *Orlando Centennial* Legal Section only.

Sarasota County Sheriff's Dept.
P.O. Box 4115
Sarasota, FL 34237-34230
(813) 951-5800

No auctions. Have sales to pay cost. Ads in *Herald Tribune.*

Hillsborough County
Sheriff's Dept.
Fiscal Division
P.O. Box 3371
Tampa, FL 33601
(813) 247-8031 or 247-8033

Vehicles to Tampa Machinery and Auction.
Merchandise—ads in the *Tampa Tribune*. Tampa
Machinery & Auction, P.O. Box 16000-B Tampa,
FL 33687 (813) 986-2485

Palm Beach County
Sheriff's Dept.
3228 Gun Club Road
Palm Beach, FL 33406
(407) 471-2000

Vehicles two a year—spring and fall. Mailing list
week before (407) 332-3200. Merchandise
donated to charity.

Georgia

Fulton County Sheriff
136 Pryor St., Room 108
Atlanta, GA 30303
(404) 730-5100

Orders from Superior Court on what is to be
auctioned. October 1st—land. Nov. 2—airplanes.
Ads—*Fulton County Daily Report.*

Hawaii

Honolulu County
Sheriff's Dept.
2nd Fl., 111 Alaska Street
Honolulu, HI 96813
(808) 548-4222

Auctions at random, no mailing list, ads in the
morning and evening newspaper.

Illinois

Cook County Sheriff's Office
Real Estate Division
50 W. Washington, Room 701-A
Chicago, IL 60602
Personal Property:
(312) 443-3345
Real Estate:
(301) 443-3341
or
Sheriff Dept. Auto Pound
3146 S. Archer Avenue
Chicago, IL 60608
(312) 890-3355

Personal property twice a month, posted on the
board in City Hall. Real estate—each Tuesday,
Wednesday and Thursday. Sheriff's deed only.
Vehicles, whenever enough, title clear.

Indiana

Allen County Sheriff's Dept.
Civil Division
Courthouse, Room 100
Fort Wayne, IN 46802
(219) 428-7632

Foreclosure sales only. Auction if more than one bidder. Monday through Thursday. Occasional RV. Ads in *Journal Gazette*.

Marion County Sheriff's Dept.
822 City-County Bldg.
Indianapolis, IN 46204
(317) 231-8415
or
Property Room
40 S. Alabama
Indianapolis, IN 46204
(317) 231-8294

Mortgage foreclosures. Ads in *Indianapolis Commercial*. Vehicles and personal property. Premiere Auctions (317) 636-7536. Ads in *Star News*.

Kentucky

Jefferson County Police Garage
3528 Newburg Road
Louisville, KY 40218
(502) 452-2671

No auctions. Vehicles sent to Louisville Auto Auction in Indiana. (812) 283-0734.

Louisiana

E. Baton Rouge Parish
(County) Sheriff's Dept.
Foreclosure Dept. Room 229
P.O. Box 3277
Baton Rouge, LA 70821
(504) 389-4818

Foreclosures and moveables every Wednesday.

Orleans Parish (County)
Civic Sheriff's Dept.
Moveable/Real Estate
421 Loyola Ave.
New Orleans, LA 70112
(504) 523-6143

Real estate every Thursday. Moveables every Wednesday.

Maryland

Baltimore City Sheriff's Office
104 Courthouse
Baltimore, MD 21201
(301) 396-5826

Everything listed in the Legal Section (back page) of the *Baltimore Sun*.

Massachusetts

Suffolk County Sheriff's Office
Civil Process Division
11 Beacon St., Suite 1300
Boston, MA 02108
(617) 227-2541

Listed in the *Boston Herald*. Auctions on Friday. Call before going as most settled before auction.

Michigan

Washtenaw County
Sheriff's Dept.
2201 Hogback Road
Ann Arbor, MI 48107
(313) 971-3911

Auctions held twice a year.

Stanton Real Estate & Auctioneers
144 S. Main
Vermontville, MI 49096
(517) 726-0181

Holds auctions for the Sheriff's Dept. and also state.

Wayne County Sheriff's Dept.
1231 St. Antoine
Detroit, MI 48226
(313) 494-3060

Personal property with city once a month. Vehicles—Auto Salvage (313) 479-2500.

Kent County Purchasing Dept.
Comptrollers Office
300 Monroe, NW
Grand Rapids, MI 49503
(616) 774-3500

Personal property once a year. Ad in the *Grand Rapids Press*.

Minnesota

Ramsey County Sheriff's Dept.
Civil 14 W. Kellog Blvd.
St. Paul, MN 55102
(612) 292-6030

Personal property—3 a week. Real estate—3 a day. Vehicles—when needed. Posted in *St. Paul Legal Ledger* (612) 222-0059.

Missouri

St. Louis County Sheriff's Dept.
7900 Carondelet
Clayton, MO 63105
(314) 949-0809 or 949-3010

Ads placed in the *St. Louis Post* and in public buildings.

Jackson County
Purchasing & Supply Division
City Hall Building
414 E. 12th, 3rd Floor
Kansas City, MO 64106
(816) 881-3978

No auctions.

Sheriff's Dept.
City of St. Louis, Civic Court Bldg.
11 N. 11th St., 1st Floor N.
St. Louis, MO 63101
(314) 622-4851

Real estate ads, *Post Dispatch.*

Nebraska

Douglas County
Purchasing Dept., Room 902
Civic Center
Omaha, NE 68183
(402) 444-7158

Vehicles through city auctions. Personal property one a year. Mailing list available. Real estate—none.

Nevada

Clark County
Sheriff's Civic Bureau
309 S. 3rd St., Suite 230
Las Vegas, NV 89155
(702) 455-4237

Posted in Court House and Sheriff's office. Ads in *Las Vegas Review Journal* and *Nevada Legal News.*

New Jersey

Mercer County Sheriff's Dept.
209 S. Broad St.
Trenton, NJ 08650
(609) 989-6100

Real estate every Wednesday. Ads in *Trenton Times* and *Princeton Packet.* Vehicles posted—Municipal Bldg.

New Mexico

Bernalillo County Sheriff's Dept.
Court Services Division
P.O. Box 1829
Albuquerque, NM 87103
(505) 768-4140

Real Estate ads in *Albuquerque Journal* on Fridays. Personal property and vehicles when needed.

Ohio

Summit County Sheriff's Dept.
209 S. High St.
Akron, OH 44308
(216) 379-2278 or 379-2150

Vehicles 1 to 2 a year. Ad in *Akron Beacon Journal,* Real estate Friday. Personal property— Ad in *Akron Legal News.*

Hamilton County
Sheriff's Dept.
11021 Hamilton Avenue
Cincinnati, OH 45239
(513) 825-1500

Personal property and vehicles twice a year. Legal notice in *Post* and *Inquirer.* Real estate every Thursday. Ad in *Cincinnati Index.*

Cuyahoga County Sheriff's Dept.
1215 W. Third Street
Cleveland, OH 44113
(216) 443-6000

Every Monday Ad in *Daily Legal News* (Real estate).

Franklin County Sheriff's Dept.
369 S. High Street
Columbus, OH 43215
(614) 462-3360

Real estate every Friday—Hall of Justice, other sales in *Columbus Dispatch.*

Montgomery County
Purchasing Dept.
41 N. Perry St.
Dayton, OH 45422
(513) 225-6464 or 225-4357

Lucas County Courthouse
Civil Division
700 Adams & Erie St.
Toledo, OH 43624
(419) 245-4000 or 245-4480

Real estate Tuesday and Friday. Vehicles every 3 years. No personal property.

Mahoning County Sheriff's Dept.
Court Services Office
21 W. Boardman Street
Youngstown, OH 44503
(216) 740-2388

Vehicles & personal property on demand. Real estate every other Tuesday. Ads in *Daily Legal News.*

Oklahoma

Oklahoma County Sheriff's Dept.
321 Park Avenue
Oklahoma City, OK 73102
(405) 236-1717

Foreclosed property every Tuesday. Ads in local papers.

Tulsa County Sheriff's Dept.
500 S. Denver
Tulsa, OK 74103
(918) 596-5601

Foreclosed property Tuesday and Thursday. Room 119. Vehicles twice a year.

Oregon

Multnomah County Sheriff's Dept.
2505 SE 11th Avenue
Portland, OR 97202

Call (503) 255-3600 ext. 500 for hot line news.

Pennsylvania

Lehigh County Sheriff's Dept.
P.O. Box 1548
Allentown, PA 18105
(215) 820-3175

Foreclosure sale once a month. Ad in the *Morning Call*, vehicle and personal property at the convenience of lawyer.

Philadelphia County
Procedure Surplus Property
Disposal Room 1330
15th & JFK Blvd.
Philadelphia, PA 19102-1685
(215) 686-4765

Foreclosure sales first Monday of the month (215) 683-3535. Ads rotate in different papers.

Allegheny County Sheriff's Dept.
111 Courthouse
Pittsburgh, PA 15219
(412) 355-4704 or 355-4700

Luzern County Courthouse
North River Street
Wilkes Barre, PA 18711
(717) 825-1651

Real estate 1st Monday of month. Listed in *Wilkes Barre Citizens Voice* and *Hazelton Speaker.*

Rhode Island

Sheriff's Office of Providence County
250 Benefit St.
Providence, RI 02903
(401) 277-3510

One or two a year. Listed in *Providence Journal*, usually settled before auction.

South Carolina

Charles County Sheriff's Office
2 Courthouse Square
Charleston, SC 29401
(803) 723-6710

Watch for listing in *Charleston News & Courier*.

Pitt County Sheriff's Dept.
Main County Office Bldg.
1717 W. Fifth Street
Greenville, SC 27834
(919) 830-6302 or 830-6306

One general auction a year. Listed in *Greenville Daily Reflector*.

Tennessee

Knox County Sheriff's Dept.
400 Main Street
Knoxville, TN 37902
(615) 521-2432

Personal property 1 to 2 a year.

Shelby County
Memphis Police Dept.
Property & Evidence Division
201 Poplar
Memphis, TN 38103
Property: (901) 576-2550
Vehicles: (901) 353-8200

Personal property 2 to 3 times a year. Vehicles, every Tuesday.

Davidson County
Madison Sheriff's Dept.
506 Second Avenue N.
Nashville, TN 37201

Auctions for everything posted on the first and third floor at the Courthouse.

Texas

Travis County Sheriff's Dept.
P.O. Box 1748
Austin, TX 78767
(512) 322-4610 or 322-4615

Real estate first Tuesday of month, on the Courthouse steps. Vehicles once a month. Listed in the *Travis American Statesman*.

Dallas County Sheriff's Dept.
Civil Section
600 Commerce
Dallas, TX 75202
(214) 653-3500

Real estate, first Tuesday of month, Courthouse steps. Personal property posted in public buildings. Ads in *Daily Commercial Record.*

El Paso County Sheriff's Dept.
800 E. Overland Street
El Paso, TX 79901
(915) 546-2217

Vehicles (915) 858-3903. Real Estate (915) 544-3910.

Harris County
Sheriff Purchasing
1001 Preston
Show Room 670
Houston, TX 77002

Hot Line (713) 755-5036.

Bexar County Courthouse
Purchasing Dept.
San Antonio, TX 78207
(512) 270-6020
or
Bexar County Sheriff's Dept.
200 N. Comal
San Antonio, TX 78207
(512) 270-6020

Real estate first Tuesday of the month. List published monthly. Personal property and vehicles listed in *San Antonio Light.*

Utah

Salt Lake County Sheriff's Office
Civil Division
437 S. 200 East
Salt Lake City, UT 84111
(801) 535-5441 or 468-2556
or 535-5425

Court-ordered real estate sold every Tuesday. Ad in *Intermountain Commercial Record.*

Virginia

Richmond Sheriff's Dept.
808 E. Marshall St.
Richmond, VA 23219
(804) 780-6600

Vehicles and property 3 to 4 times a year. Real estate—front of courthouse daily. Ad in *Richmond News Leader.*

Norfolk Sheriff's Dept.
P.O. Box 3908
Norfolk, VA 23514
(804) 441-2341

Notices in the courthouse. Auctioneer—Calvin Zed.

Washington

Dept. of Public Safety
King County Police
513 Third Avenue, Room W 150
Seattle, WA 98104
(206) 293-3800
or
King County Sheriff's Dept.
516 Third Avenue
Seattle, WA 98104
(206) 296-4078

Personal property two or three a year.

Wisconsin

Milwaukee County Sheriff's Dept.
821 W. State Street
Milwaukee, WI 53233
(414) 278-4907

Vehicles three times a year. Personal property every two weeks. Real estate every Monday— Courthouse annex.

COUNTY/CITY MARSHALS AUCTIONS DIRECTORY

California

Los Angeles County
Marshall
110 N. Grant, Rm. 525
L.A., CA 90012
(213) 974-6311

Vehicles, when available.

San Diego County Marshall
220 W. Broadway
San Diego, CA 92101
(619) 531-3995

Court-ordered sales only.

Orange County Marshall
909 N. Main St., Ste. 2
Santa Ana, CA 92701
(714) 569-3700

Auctions posted in the courthouse.

Georgia

City Marshall
55 Trinity Ave., Ste. 1350
Atlanta, GA 30335
(404) 330-6270

Ads in the "Auction Block" section of *The Sun Atlantic Constitution*. Auctioneer: Wayne Evans Auction Co. (800) 282-8460.

New York

City Marshalls Office
City Hall, Rm. 215
Albany, NY 12207
(518) 434-5106

Vehicles, very few, posted in public buildings.

New York Dept. of
Investigations
City of New York
Marshall's Bureau
(212) 825-5953

Ads in *The New York Times*.

City Marshalls Office
Public Safety Bldg. Rm. 508
511 State St.
Syracuse, NY 13202
(315) 473-6703

Very few auctions, notice posted in courthouse. No real estate.

Texas

City Marshall's Office
715 E. 8th St.
Austin, TX 78701
(512) 482-5393

Auctions every 2 mos. by: Gaston & Sheehan Auctioneers, P.O. Box 856, Pflugerville, TX 78660 (512) 251-3002. Personal goods and real estate. Autos (city & confiscated): Rene Bates Auctioneers, Rte. 4, McKinney, TX 75070 (214) 548-9363

16

United States Trustees Bankruptcy Auctions

★★★

The United States Trustee program started as an experiment many years ago. Basically, they appoint and oversee bankruptcy trustees in regional districts around the country. Bankruptcy trustees report to the U.S. Trustee's Office on case progress and completions. The real action is at the auctioneer level. Bankruptcy trustees are so overloaded that they usually leave a large part of their work to the auctioneer.

Bankruptcy trustees are often attorneys. Lawyers normally leave the tough work up to someone else to do. In this case, that's the auctioneer. Aside from the paperwork, the auctioneer is often given the task of handling the property transfer from start to finish.

Background

There are several U.S. Trustee offices around the country. They are busy with caseloads. With bankruptcies setting new records each year around the world (pretty soon we may all be bankrupt), the number of auctions has risen. For instance, in the first half of 1991, one in every 50 companies in England went into liquidation. The Japanese, who spent much of the 1980s on a roll, left their creditors back home screaming with over $29 billion in unpaid debts in the first seven months of 1991.

Americans fared far worse. Between March 31, 1990, and March 31, 1991, 65,768 companies filed for bankruptcy. Overall, about 1 million individuals and companies accepted protection under U.S. Bankruptcy laws. And these figures don't include those who walked away from their businesses or simply disappeared—a good deal of those possessions were probably sold at a county sheriff's auction, warehouse sale, or landlord sale.

Because of the growing economic crisis, bankruptcy attorneys, trustees, and judges are busier than ever. And so are auctioneers. Bankruptcy auctions are held so often that many are not widely promoted. Sometimes the bankrupt's property is too small to warrant an auction. As the economic situation worsens throughout the 1990s, the only problem one might expect with bankruptcy auctions could be lack of attendance.

Procedures

There are two main ways to find out about bankruptcy auctions, and two minor methods. You can read the classified advertising section of your local newspaper to find out about these auctions. That's a proven method. I use it from time to time. Or you could look up auctioneers in your Yellow

Pages and call them. That's unpredictable. Besides, there are other ways.

The following method is slow and takes many phone calls, but it does work. Contact the U.S. Trustee in your area and ask for a list of bankruptcy trustees near home. You may have to visit their offices and copy the list by hand. Many will send it to you.

After you get this list, telephone the bankruptcy trustees in your area and ask for the names of the auctioneers they use. Finally, you can contact those names and ask to be placed on their mailing lists. While you're on the phone with them, find out if they have anything for sale. Many will jump at that bite. This is how you get a negotiated sale started!

You could also contact the bankruptcy auctioneers located in Section Four of this book. The list is far from complete as limited by space and does not include every auctioneer under the sun who could hold a bankruptcy auction. This book

could have been either about government auctions or simply an auctioneer's directory. There are thousands of auctioneers across America. The National Auctioneers Association boasts over 5,000 members, many who specialize in liquidations. If you wish their free directory, send $5 to cover shipping and handling to:

National Auctioneers Association
8880 Ballentine
Overland Park, Kansas 66214
Attn: Director of Publications

Special Characteristics

Most of what goes on behind the scenes at bankruptcy auctions is neither useful nor necessary. It's all legal finagling, reams of paperwork, and Section 341 meetings. (A Section 341 meeting is the first meeting between the creditors and the debtor; they usually get to vent their spleen on him.)

The main attraction of bankruptcies is the auction itself. More often than not, these auctions are held by public outcry. Negotiated sales are frequent, as auctioneers will call their steady buyers or vice versa. There are sometimes sealed-bid sales to the trustees office via the auctioneer. Or just directly to the auctioneer.

The merchandise at bankruptcy auctions, of course, varies depending on who went bankrupt. Business failures could turn up a load of office equipment, vehicles, and real estate. Personal bankruptcies differ with the amount of the individual's former wealth. When Texas governor John Connally went bankrupt, the auction sold Chippendale and Louis Quatorze furniture, more than 200 paintings (albeit fake copies), elephant tusks, silver sets, china, and Winchester rifles, among hundreds of other valuable pieces; it took a 93-page catalog to describe his auction.

Are there steals at bankruptcy auctions? You bet! A tapestry formerly owned by the stock brokerage house Drexel Burnham (of Michael Milliken fame) and valued at $6,000 sold for a mere $180 at one bankruptcy auction. Leon Spinks (the boxer who downed Muhammed Ali) had his giant screen projection TV sell for $575, about a quarter of its value. A farmer had his farm sold out from under him for 18 cents on the dollar. Anecdotes about famous auction steals gush from auctioneers specializing in these liquidations. One of my favorites is about how all the contents and fixtures in a pet store sold for just $3 because only one bidder showed up.

One leading New Hampshire auctioneer has been holding an average of five auctions a day. Buyers are finding steals. A $250,000 apartment building in downtown Manchester sold for $500 plus back taxes. One auction brought only $6,500 for a home valued at $28,000.

Tips

One worry newcomers express is that bankruptcy auctions are "subject to court confirmation." Auctioneers handling these auctions say that that's a lot of bunk. Most federal bankruptcy judges are so backlogged that they rarely require proof of fair-market value and trust their trustee's affidavit implicitly.

Please understand that a flock of bankruptcy attorneys have told me that the biggest losers in either Chapter Seven (straight liquidation) or Chapter Eleven (reorganization) bankruptcies are the creditors, who are now indirectly the new owners. Bankruptcy auctions are notorious for not bringing a good price to the seller. That means tremendous opportunities for buyers.

Many of these auctions, though, can be specialized. This means that you might show up for an auction and only find rolls of fabric or a warehouse of stationery or truckloads of plumbing supplies. Such discoveries should be followed by the realization that your competition will be hardcore professionals.

Such auctions are potential breeding grounds for rings, bid-rigging, and pools. Many types of businesses are closed societies. All the dealers know each other since they compete against each other daily. When one fails, like vultures they swoop to pick their friend's bones dry. You might show up at one and feel left out. That's okay. Bid against them. They'll drop out at a price you can live with.

One of the best tips you can use in attending such an auction is to find the "out of context" merchandise. Find something that is being sold but doesn't really belong there. That's how you beat the professionals, since they won't bid against you. The pro is there to buy something cheap and make three to ten times his money back. He's not looking for a car at an auction that is mainly featuring copiers or telephone equipment. And that car can be yours!

Evaluation

Bankruptcy auctions are consistently the *best* auctions you can attend. In today's economic climate, and probably through the end of the century, we are going to see new records set for bankruptcies. This means tremendous opportunity for those who buy at bankruptcy auctions.

One can either buy merchandise or equipment at a deep discount or buy a set of something, reselling the excess to friends at a profit. Many start careers or part-time jobs by going to auctions. Reselling isn't difficult if your purchase price is below wholesale. That can mean steady profits for those so inclined.

Not every auction is going to appeal to the average bidder. Some specialized auctions will have little or nothing that may interest you. Finding the exact item you might want to buy can take a little research. While buying it in a department store is certainly easier, getting that item at auction will cost you a small fraction of what you'd normally pay. And besides, when you pay cash for it, there's no credit card statements to worry about either.

Whatever you do wish to buy is available at bankruptcy auctions. It could be a vehicle, a boat, airplane, office equipment, a computer, a bedroom set, or other furniture. Somewhere, someplace, a bankruptcy auctioneer is selling what you want.

UNITED STATES TRUSTEES DIRECTORY

Bankruptcy Sales

United States Trustee
Old Custom House
1 Bowling Green
Room 534
New York, NY 10004
(212) 480-3804

United States Trustee
Boston Federal Building
10 Causeway St.
Boston, MA 02222
(617) 565-6360

United States Trustee
60 Park Place
Suite 210
Newark, NJ 07102

United States Trustee
Strom Thurmond Federal Bldg.
1835 Assembly St.
Room 1108
Columbia, SC 29201
(803) 765-5886

United States Trustee
115 S. Union St,
Suite 210
Alexandria, VA 22314
(703) 557-7176

United States Trustee
1418 Richard Russell Bldg.
75 Spring St. S.W.
Atlanta, GA 30303
(404) 331-4437

United States Trustee
113 Saint Claire Ave. N.E.
Suite 200
Cleveland, OH 44114
(216) 522-7176

United States Trustee
U.S. Courthouse
46 E. Ohio St.
Room 258
Indianapolis, IN 46204
(317) 226-6101

United States Trustee
331 Second Ave. S.
Suite 540
Midland Square Bldg
Minneapolis, MN 55401
(612) 373-1200

United States Trustee
Columbine Bldg.
Room 300
1845 Sherman St.
Denver, CO 80203
(303) 844-5188

United States Trustee
Custom House
701 Broadway
Room 313
Nashville, TN 37203
(615) 736-5584

United States Trustee
175 W. Jackson St.
Room A-1335
Chicago, IL 60604
(312) 886-5785

United States Trustee
Federal Office Building
911 Walnut St.
Room 806
Kansas City, MO 64106
(816) 426-7959

United States Trustee
Transportation Center
425 Second St. S.E.
Room 675
Cedar Rapids, IA 52401
(319) 364-2211

United States Trustee
Texaco Center
400 Poydraf St.
Suite 1820
New Orleans, LA 70130
(504) 589-4018

United States Trustee
4400 Louisiana St.
Suite 2500
Houston, TX 77002
(713) 653-3000

United States Trustee
U.S. Courthouse
Room 9C60
1100 Commerce St.
Dallas, TX 75242
(214) 767-8967

United States Trustee
320 N. Central Ave.
Suite 100
Phoenix, AZ 85004
(602) 379-3092

United States Trustee
601 Van Ness Ave.
Suite 2008
San Francisco, CA 94102
(415) 556-7900

United States Trustee
Federal Building
Room 3101
200 N. Los Angeles St.
Los Angeles, CA 90012-4790
(213) 894-6387

United States Trustee
Wells Fargo Bank B
101 W. Broadway
Suite 440
San Diego, CA 92101
(206) 624-5124

United States Trustee
Park Place Bldg.
1200 Sixth Ave.
Room 600
Seattle, WA 98101
(206) 553-2000

17

Small Business Administration Auctions

★★★

Congress created the Small Business Administration (SBA) in 1953 to help small businesses in America get a leg up. For the most part, the SBA guarantees bank loans for small businessmen. Generally, when a business is unable to obtain conventional bank financing, the owner goes to the SBA for assistance.

Through the SBA's Certified or Preferred Lending Plan, designated banks are able to expedite loan requests for small businesses. Direct SBA loans are extremely hard to get and usually are given to the physically disadvantaged. The SBA's primary source of auction activity is their loan guarantee program. Auctions come about when the business fails. That's because businesses are forced to pledge collateral against these guaranteed loans. The collateral is then auctioned off by the bank that lent the money.

Background

The Small Business Administration does not want to be in the auction business. That's the sour end of their job. The entire purpose of this agency is to help businesses get started or expand. Who wants to hear the bad news about business failures? Not the SBA. Their field offices will try to put as much distance between the failure and themselves as

they can. The banks that lent the money don't mind a whit. The SBA guaranteed most of the loan—as much as 90%. They just write the bank a check to cover their loss.

This brings us, of course, back to the SBA auction program. When an SBA-backed company fails, their inventory, equipment and/or real estate is repossessed by the bank. This can, and often does, include office equipment, inventory, restaurant equipment, printing equipment, and other business-type hard assets that can be quickly resold.

Special Characteristics

When the business fails and the bank cancels their loan, a little finger pointing goes on between the bank and the SBA. Often, the SBA tells the bank, "Hey guys, it's your problem. Just sell it." The bank discreetly hires an auctioneer and quietly auctions off the inventory or equipment. The SBA really doesn't want to know from Adam about that failure. The bank is quite content to have the property auctioned and get their money back. The SBA just writes a check to cover the loan guarantee.

Often, banks may just buy the property at the

auction, if it is a house or building, and include it in their real estate owned department as a non-performing asset. This entails a mere paper transfer and no cash is exchanged. Buyers get a second chance to purchase the property, frequently for less than the bank paid at the auction for it, by contacting the bank's real estate owned department and making an offer.

In some cases, the bank tells the SBA to handle the auction themselves, at which point, the SBA field office will either recruit an auctioneer or conduct the auction itself. Recently, SBA headquarters advised the field offices that they should hire a private auctioneer. We'll see what develops.

If the SBA field office hires a private auctioneer, their general policy is to rotate the business among local auctioneers and play no favorites. Finding out who they're using is not the easiest task. You may reach just an answering machine when you call some SBA offices.

When auctions are held by either the bank or the SBA, they are public auctions. This shouldn't stop you from attempting a negotiated sale, either with the SBA, the bank, or the private auctioneer. Consider SBA auctions in the same way you would a bankruptcy auction, as described in Chapter 16.

SBA auctions are sporadic. There is no set monthly schedule. They do not hold them on any regular basis. These auctions could be going on all around us and we might never know. Occasionally, you might see an auction flier or classified advertisement that says: "SBA Liquidation" or "SBA Auction." That's about the only way you would find out that such auctions existed at all.

The type of merchandise or equipment found at these auctions would be the same found at a bankruptcy auction: anything and everything. Soup to nuts. Just like a GSA public auction, but without the GSA's strict organization and firm policy on reserve prices.

You will also find real estate at SBA auctions because that collateral may have been pledged. I've seen developers' subdivisions sold through an SBA-appointed auctioneer. Be on the lookout for real estate as well as personal property at these auctions.

Procedures

You may contact an SBA field office for information about their auctions. The rote statement given out to callers is: "We don't handle the auctions. We rotate auctioneers." It varies from office to office but that is the net result.

Request the list of auctioneers that the SBA field office uses. Persist on this point. You may be told that no auctions are going on in their area. Remember that there is no fixed auction schedule. Sales are held when property/merchandise has been repossessed.

There is a backdoor. I had to find one. No one else ever did before. The SBA has been so useless in promoting their auctions. So, this is the first time you are reading this anywhere.

The Backdoor

1. Contact the SBA field office for a list of their certified or preferred lending institutions. These are the banks that lend money to SBA applicants. The SBA guarantees the loan with these banks. They have a system set up to quickly expedite the loan request and loan guarantee.

2. Get the list of banks from the SBA. You may get their entire list for the whole country. At last count there were 681 certified lenders and 162 preferred lenders. It doesn't matter which you contact as they both lend money that the SBA guarantees.

3. Contact each of those banks in your area or state. Ask them *when* the auction is being held or which auctioneer is being, or has been, hired to conduct the SBA-repossessed or foreclosed auction.

That gets you through the backdoor to find out about SBA auctions. Go directly to the bank, as they are the prime candidate to be supervising the property disposal. You may be referred to an auctioneer.

However, since you have gone to such trouble to "help out" the government, why not take it a step further? Deal directly with the bank and do a negotiated sale. The loan officer or the head of the bank's property disposition division may have the same lethargy about the property that has stricken the SBA. It could be your lucky day!

Evaluation

Guess what? If SBA auctions are comparable to bankruptcy auctions, then why not go to those as well? There are reasons why.

A primary reason why you might not find an outrageous steal at an SBA auction is that all sales are subject to seller confirmation. Depending on the integrity and competence of the local field office, there may be a demand that the property sells for "fair-market value." That doesn't eliminate the possibility of saving 20%–40%, though. Beyond that, don't count on much.

Another reason is the bank. Banks are not charitable institutions. Some bank presidents and other officers have been caught stealing for their benefit or that of friends, but that's not charity. It's greed. The bank definitely wants to recover its 10%–25% share of the loot. There may be interest and penalties atop that. Understand that the bank will try to recover every penny. So, while you may find a good bargain, you won't be stealing the pants off the bank.

Try calling the SBA field offices. If they won't help you, go through the backdoor.

SMALL BUSINESS ADMINISTRATION DIRECTORY

Regional Offices

California

71 Stevenson Street
20th Floor
San Francisco, CA
94105-2939
(415) 744-6429
Regional Office

Colorado

999 18th Street
Suite 701
Denver, CO 80202
(303) 294-7186
Regional Office

Georgia

1375 Peachtree Street, NE
5th Floor
Atlanta, GA 30367-8102
(404) 347-2797
Regional Office

Illinois

300 S. Riverside Plaza
Suite 1975 South
Chicago, IL 60606
(312) 353-0359
Regional Office

Massachusetts

155 Federal Street
9th Floor
Boston, MA 02110-1744
(617) 451-2023
Regional Office

Missouri

911 Walnut Street
13th Floor
Kansas City, MO 64106
(816) 426-3608
Regional Office

New York

26 Federal Plaza
Room 3100
New York, NY 10278
(212) 264-7772
Regional Office

Texas

1100 Commerce Street
Room 3C36
Dallas, TX 75242
(214) 767-7643
Regional Office

Washington

2615 4th Avenue
Room 440
Seattle, WA 98121
(206) 553-8544
Regional Office

District Offices

Alabama

2121 8th Avenue N.
Suite 200
Birmingham, AL
35203-2398
(205) 731-1344
District Office

Alaska

222 W. 8th Avenue
#67
Anchorage, AK 99513-7559
(907) 271-4022
District Office

Arizona

2005 N. Central Avenue
5th Floor
Phoenix, AZ 85004
(602) 379-3732
District Office

Arkansas

320 W. Capitol Avenue
Room 601
Little Rock, AR 72201
(501) 324-5871
District Office

California

2719 N. Air Fresno Drive
Fresno, CA 93727-1547
(209) 487-5189
District Office

330 N. Grand Boulevard
Suite 1200
Glendale, CA 91203-2304
(213) 894-2956
District Office

880 Front Street
Suite 4-B-29
San Diego, CA 92188-0270
(619) 557-5440
District Office

211 Main Street
4th Floor
San Francisco, CA
94105-1988
(415) 744-6804
District Office

901 W. Civic Center Drive
Suite 160
Santa Ana, CA 92703-2352
(714) 836-2494
District Office

Colorado

721 19th Street
Room 407
Denver, CO 80201-0660
(303) 844-6540
District Office

Connecticut

330 Main Street, 2nd Floor
Hartford, CT 06106
(203) 240-4700
District Office

Delaware

1 Rodney Square
Suite 412
Wilmington, DE 19801
(302) 573-6295
District Office

District of Columbia

1111 18th Street NW
6th Floor
Washington, D.C. 20036
(202) 634-1500
District Office

Florida

1320 S. Dixie Highway
Suite 501
Coral Gables, FL 33146-2911
(305) 536-5521
District Office

7825 Baymeadows Way
Suite 100-B
Jacksonville, FL
32256-7504
(904) 443-1900
District Office

Georgia

1720 Peachtree Road NW
6th Floor
Atlanta, GA 30309
(404) 347-4749
District Office

Hawaii

300 Ala Moana Boulevard
Room 2213, Box 50207
Honolulu, HI 96850
(808) 541-2990
District Office

Idaho

1020 Main Street
Suite 290
Boise, ID 83702
(208) 334-1696
District Office

Illinois

500 W. Madison
Ste. 1250
Chicago, IL 60661
(312) 353-4528
District Office

Indiana

429 N. Pennsylvania Street
Suite 100
Indianapolis, IN
46204-1873
(317) 226-7272
District Office

Iowa

373 Collins Road NE
Room 100
Cedar Rapids, IA
52402-3147
(319) 393-8630
District Office

210 Walnut Street
Room 749 Federal Building
Des Moines, IA 50309
(515) 284-4762
District Office

Kansas

110 E. Waterman Street
Wichita, KS 67202
(316) 269-6616
District Office

Kentucky

600 Dr. Martin Luther
King Place, Rm. 188
Louisville, KY 40202
(502) 582-5976
District Office

Louisiana

1661 Canal Street
Suite 2000
New Orleans, LA 70112
(504) 589-6685
District Office

Maine

40 Western Avenue
Room 512
Augusta, ME 04330
(207) 622-8378
District Office

Maryland

Equitable Building
10 N. Calvert Street
Third Floor
Baltimore, MD 21202
(301) 962-4392
District Office

Massachusetts

10 Causeway Street
Room 265
Boston, MA 02222-1093
(617) 565-5590
District Office

Michigan

477 Michigan Avenue
Room 515
Detroit, MI 48226
(313) 226-6075
District Office

Minnesota

100 North 6th Street
Suite 610-C Butler Square
Minneapolis, MN

55403-1563
(612) 370-2324
District Office

Mississippi

101 W. Capitol Street
Suite 400
Jackson, MS 39201
(601) 965-4327
District Office

Missouri

323 West 8th Street
Suite 501
Kansas City, MO 64105
(816) 374-6762
District Office

815 Olive Street
Room 242
St. Louis, MO 63101
(314) 539-6600
District Office

Montana

Federal Building
301 S. Park
Room 528, Drawer 10054
Helena, MT
59626
(406) 449-5381
District Office

Nebraska

11145 Mill Valley Road
Omaha, NE 68154-3949
(402) 221-3604
District Office

Nevada

301 East Stewart Street
Room 301
P.O. Box 7527
Las Vegas, NV 89125-7527
(702) 388-6611
District Office

New Hampshire

143 N. Main Street
P.O. Box 1257
Concord, NH 03302-1257
(603) 225-1400
District Office

New Jersey

60 Park Place
4th Floor
Newark, NJ 07102
(201) 645-2434
District Office

New Mexico

625 Silver Avenue SW
Suite 320
Albuquerque, NM 87102
(505) 766-1870
District Office

New York

26 Federal Plaza
Room 3100, 31st Floor
New York, NY 10278
(212) 264-4355
District Office

P.O. Box 7317
100 S. Clinton Street
Room 1071
Syracuse, NY 13261-7317
(315) 423-5383
District Office

North Carolina

200 N. College Street
Room A-2015
Charlotte, NC 28202-2173
(704) 344-6563
District Office

North Dakota

657 Second Avenue North
Room 218
Fargo, ND 58108
(701) 239-5131
District Office

Ohio

1240 E. 9th Street
Room 317
Cleveland, OH 44199
(216) 522-4180
District Office

85 Marconi Boulevard
Room 512
Columbus, OH 43215
(614) 469-6860
District Office

Oklahoma

200 NW 5th Street
Suite 670
Oklahoma City, OK 73102
(405) 231-4301
District Office

Oregon

222 S.W. Columbia Street
Suite 500
Portland, OR 97201-6605
(503) 326-2682
District Office

Pennsylvania

475 Allendale Road
Suite 201
King of Prussia, PA 19406
(215) 962-3846
District Office
960 Penn Avenue
5th Floor
Pittsburgh, PA 15222
(412) 644-2780
District Office

Puerto Rico

Carlos Chardon Avenue
Room 691
Hato Rey, PR 00918
(809) 766-4002
District Office

Rhode Island

380 Westminster Street
5th Floor, Room 511
Providence, RI 02903
(401) 528-4561
District Office

South Carolina

1835 Assembly Street
Room 358, Strom Thurmond
Bldg.
Columbia, SC 29201
(803) 765-5376
District Office

South Dakota

101 S. Main Avenue
Suite 101
Sioux Falls, SD 57102-0527
(605) 330-4231
District Office

Tennessee

50 Vantage Way
Suite 201
Nashville, TN 37228-1500
(615) 736-7176
District Office

Texas

1100 Commerce Street
Room 3C-36
Dallas, TX 75242
(214) 767-0608
District Office

10737 Gateway West Blvd.
Suite 320
El Paso, TX 79912
(915) 540-5586
District Office

222 E. Van Buren Street
Suite 500
Harlingen, TX 78550
(512) 427-8533
District Office

2525 Murworth
Suite 112
Houston, TX 77054
(713) 660-4409
District Office

1611 Tenth Street
Suite 200
Lubbock, TX 79401
(806) 743-7462
District Office

7400 Blanco Road
Suite 200
San Antonio, TX 78216
(512) 229-4535
District Office

Utah

125 S. State Street
Room 2237
Salt Lake City, UT
84138-1195
(801) 524-5800
District Office

Vermont

87 State Street
Room 205
Montpelier, VT 05601-0605
(802) 828-4474
District Office

Virginia

400 N. 8th Street
Room 3015
Richmond, VA 23240
(804) 771-2617
District Office

Washington

915 Second Avenue
Room 1792
Seattle, WA 981174-1088
(206) 553-5534
District Office

Farm Credit Building
W. 601 First Avenue
10th Floor E.
Spokane, WA 99204-0317
(509) 353-2807
District Office

West Virginia

168 West Main Street
5th Floor
Clarksburg, WV 26301
(304) 623-5631
District Office

Wisconsin

212 E. Washington Avenue
Room 213
Madison, WI 53703
(608) 264-5261
District Office

Wyoming

100 East B Street
Room 4001
Casper, WY 82601
(307) 261-5761
District Office

Branch Offices

California

660 J Street, Rm. 215
Sacramento, CA
95814
(916) 551-1426
Branch Office

Guam

Pacific Daily News Building
Room 508
Agana, Guam 96910
(671) 472-7277
Branch Office

Illinois

511 W. Capitol Street
Suite 302
Springfield, IL 62704
(217) 492-4416
Branch Office

Massachusetts

1550 Main Street
Room 212
Springfield, MA 01103
(413) 785-0268
Branch Office

Michigan

300 S. Front Street
Marquette, MI 49885
(906) 225-1108
Branch Office

Mississippi

One Hancock Plaza
Suite 1001
Gulfport, MS 39501
(601) 863-4449
Branch Office

Missouri

620 S. Glenstone Street
Suite 110
Springfield, MO 65802
(417) 864-7670
Branch Office

New York

111 W. Huron Street
Room 1311
Buffalo, NY 14202
(716) 846-4301
Branch Office

333 East Water Street
4th Floor
Elmira, NY 14901
(607) 734-8130
Branch Office

35 Pinelawn Road
Room 102E
Melville, NY 11747
(516) 454-0750
Branch Office

100 State Street
Room 410
Rochester, NY 14614
(716) 263-6700
Branch Office

Ohio

525 Vine Street
Room 5028
Cincinnati, OH 45202
(513) 684-2814
Branch Office

Pennsylvania

301 Chestnut Street
500 B, City Towers Bldg.
Harrisburg, PA 17101-2742
(717) 783-2525
Branch Office

20 N. Pennsylvania Avenue
Room 2327
Wilkes-Barre, PA 18701-3589
(717) 826-6497
Branch Office

Texas

606 N. Carancahua
12th Floor, Suite 1200
Corpus Christi, TX 78476
(512) 888-3331
Branch Office

819 Taylor Street
Room 8A-27, 8th Floor
Fort Worth, TX 76102
(817) 334-3777
Branch Office

West Virginia

550 Eagan Street
Room 309
Charleston, WV 25301
(304) 347-5220
Branch Office

Wisconsin

310 W. Wisconsin Avenue
Suite 400
Milwaukee, WI 53203
(414) 297-3941
Branch Office

Posts of Duty

Arizona

Federal Building
300 W. Congress Street
Box FB-33
7th Floor
Tucson, AZ 85701
(602) 670-6715
Post of Duty

California

6477 Telephone Road
Suite 10
Ventura, CA 93003
(805) 642-1866
Post of Duty

Florida

501 E. Polk Street
Suite 104
Tampa, FL 33602-3945
(813) 228-2594
Post of Duty

5601 Corporate Way
Suite 402
W. Palm Beach, FL
33407-2044
(407) 689-3922
Post of Duty

Georgia

52 North Main Street
Room 225

Statesboro, GA 30458
(912) 489-8719
Post of Duty

Louisiana

500 Fannin Street
Room 8A-08, Federal Building
Shreveport, LA 71101
(318) 226-5196
Post of Duty

Nevada

50 S. Virginia Street
Room 238
Reno, NV 89505-3216
(702) 784-5268
Post of Duty

New Jersey

2600 Mt. Ephraim Avenue
Camden, NJ 08104
(609) 757-5183
Post of Duty

New York

445 Broadway, Room 222
Albany, NY 12207
(518) 472-6300
Post of Duty

Texas

300 East 8th Street
Room 520
Austin, TX 78701
(512) 482-5288
Post of Duty

505 E. Travis
Room 103
Marshall, TX 75670
(903) 935-5257
Post of Duty

Virgin Islands

4C & 4D Este Sion Frm.
Room 7
St. Croix, VI 00820
(809) 778-5380
Post of Duty

Veterans Drive
Room 283
St. Thomas, VI 00801
(809) 774-8530
Post of Duty

Wisconsin

500 South Barstow Road
Room 17
Eau Claire, WI 54701
(715) 834-1573
Post of Duty

Disaster Area Offices

360 Rainbow Boulevard South
3rd Floor
Niagara Falls, NY 14303
(716) 282-4612

One Baltimore Place
Suite 300
Atlanta, GA 30308
(404) 347-3771

4400 Amon Carter Road
Suite 102
Ft. Worth, TX 76155
(817) 267-1888

1825 Bell Street
Suite 208
Sacramento, CA 95825
(916) 978-4578

18

United States Postal Service Auctions

★★

In 1971 the U.S. Postal Service replaced the Post Office Department with the intention of running this government agency more like a business. The president of the United States appoints a governing board to supervise this organization. And the postmaster general takes the heat each time something goes wrong.

One's most common thought about the Postal Service is: "Why does the mail take so long?" Keeping the agency profitable and bringing us occasional price increases is the main business of the postmaster general. Auctions are treated more like an afterthought. The merchandise that is available for postal auctions is really a byproduct of the system.

Background

Labels fall off packages. Sometimes, people move without leaving forwarding addresses. Or packages are given an incomplete or incorrect address. Parcels end up in the dead parcel branch of the postal service. On a regular basis they are gathered together for auction at five regional centers where auctions are held.

U.S. Postal auctions are only good for those living in the five cities where auctions are held—unless you happen to be visiting. In major cities

there's another way to buy from the U.S. Postal Service. Many post offices have surplus vehicles for sale or auction.

Surplus vehicles have been sold for years: jeeps, vans, and trucks. The sales were operated like used car lots sales, often held inside wire fences, with the vehicles having fixed prices. Now, the trend has been, in some areas, to hold auctions for these postal vehicles. Perhaps they're trying to stimulate demand or catch a few people off guard so that they pay higher prices for the vehicles.

Special Characteristics

Since there are two distinct areas here, let's cover Postal auctions first. U.S. Postal auctions are conducted in five cities throughout the country: New York City, Philadelphia, Atlanta, St. Paul (Minnesota), and San Francisco. Auctions are held on a fairly regular schedule in most of these areas. Notices or catalogs are sent to prospective bidders. Mailing lists are kept by the Postal Services, although you may have to pay a small fee to receive these mailings.

The type of merchandise available at these auctions is usually retail-store category items. Most popular are books, compact discs, videos, sporting goods, and clothing. Gifts lost in the mail. You can

Prices are not at the giveaway level. They are not bad prices, but you won't find steals. You might save a few bucks. If you have a delivery business or small retail shop, the investment might be worth it. You just go there, shop around, and buy if you like what you see.

Procedures

Postal Service auctions generally start about 10AM and end usually not later than 3:30PM. Inspection periods are held on the day of the auction, about one to two hours before it starts. Auction dates vary, but are fairly regular.

Only San Francisco has a catalog or mailing list compiled for their Postal auctions, but you are charged $4 if you wish it sent to you. Philadelphia and St. Paul, Minnesota, will send a free flier ten days before the auction. Atlanta has a free catalog that you can pick up at their main post office. New York has a free catalog that you receive when you attend the inspection period or the auction.

Upon registering, you are given a bidding paddle, which serves as your bidder identification number. Auctions are held in this way:

1. All those interested in bidding hold their paddles up.

2. The auctioneer starts at the minimum bid and makes steady but rapid increases in small increments.

3. You drop your paddle down when the price is more than you want to pay.

4. The winning bidder is the one whose paddle remains in the air.

The auctioneer proceeds through the auction very quickly as there is a lot of merchandise to be auctioned. Bid increases might only be $2, and there is no hype at these auctions.

The auctioneer is a postal employee. He or she acts as an auctioneer on a regular basis. During

---

Sale of Used Postal Vehicles, 06-91

The Postal Service will offer at fixed-prices 35 used vehicles in varying states of roadworthiness from deteriorated to drive-away, and in age from 1973 to 1981.

23 Right-hand drive 1/4-ton Jeeps 73-81, $200-$600

2 Right-hand drive 1/2-ton Stepvans 73-74, $300-$350

5 Left-hand drive 1/4-ton Jeeps 73-74, $300-$400

4 K-car station wagons 81, $50-$425

1 Pinto 80, $50

Because of our agreement with the National Rural Letter Carriers Association, rural letter carriers of the area will have an exclusive ten-day presale opportunity to purchase the right hand drive vehicles before they are offered to the general public.

January 28-February 6, Rural Letter Carriers exclusively; February 7-16, General Public may also buy; February 17-27, Other postal employees, except those ineligible as explained below, may also buy.

Vehicles will be available for sale from 8 AM to 4 PM, Monday through Friday at:

1801 Broadway Avenue, Gate K*
Cleveland OH 44101-9721

*Enter at Gate G, turn left to access road, pass gate J.

Call (216) 443 - 4040.   See over for details.

---

find unusual items there. It's not a bad place to go Christmas shopping. Someone already did, and now you bid just one price for all of it.

All of this is sold in tubs, bins, or lots. You bid on a potpourri of merchandise at one shot. The Postal Service is kind enough to frequently bunch together the same kind of merchandise in tubs or bins. Dozens or hundreds of books might be in one bin.

Auction locations for the merchandise are right in the Postal Office center. These are not always brightly lit, air-conditioned spaces. And there's so much merchandise to inspect in a short period of time, that these auctions are more of a grab bag than anything else.

At the vehicle sales, you're buying fairly well-used equipment. One-quarter-ton jeeps, vans, and trucks are their main items up for sale. You might find "none available at present." That's not uncommon. The Postal Service sells when there are surplus vehicles. "When" is *the* problem, as even the postal branches aren't sure when they'll have vehicles for sale.

the holiday periods, someone may substitute for the regular auctioneer. Keep in mind that the Postal Service is just trying to get rid of surplus merchandise that they've unwillingly accumulated.

There are minimum bids at these auctions. Often they are ridiculously low: $20 or $30 for a bin of merchandise. The San Francisco Postal auctions draw quite a crowd, often 200 to 300 bidders. Tubs of books start with a minimum bid of $300 while other merchandise may begin as low as $30. Higher-valued items are likely to start with higher minimum bids. While there has been mention that there are reserve prices, this rarely happens. Too many bidders have come to buy something.

Dealer competition may occur on items like books, tapes, and CDs. Usually it's a free-for-all. Many are looking for unusual bargains at good prices. These indeed can be found. At one postal auction, Rolex watches were sold while at another, someone purchased a rare violin bow.

Evaluation

The U.S. Postal Service is not exactly the place to look for a vehicle. But household items, leisure items, and other unusual merchandise turn up. Good bargains can be found. There are limitations. The auctions are held in only five cities, with the largest held in New York and San Francisco. This makes it difficult for most bidders to attend. These are not necessarily bargains worth going out of your way for. If you live in those cities or visit them when there is an auction, go see for yourself.

Auctions generally last from about 10AM until noon or 2:30PM at the latest. These are quickie auctions, with high-speed bidding. Cash is preferred, although some accept money orders and cashiers' checks. Merchandise should be removed by 3:30PM the day of the auction.

POSTAL AUCTIONS DIRECTORY

Atlanta

U.S. Postal Service
Undeliverable Mails Branch
Dead Parcels Branch
730 Great SW Parkway
Atlanta, GA 30336
Superintendent: S. C. Batchelor
(404) 344-1625

Monthly Auctions
Viewing at 8AM
Free Catalog
About 200 lots available
Minimum Bids of $30

New York

U.S. Postal Service
380 West 33rd Street
New York City, NY 10199
(212) 330-3800

Auctions every 5–6 weeks
Viewing at 8AM
Free Catalog
About 200 lots available
New York sends no notices
Call for next auction date
Minimum Bids of $30

Philadelphia

U.S. Postal Service
2970 Market Street
Room 531-A
Philadelphia, PA 19104-9886
(215) 895-8140

Auctions every few months
Viewing at 8AM
About 100 lots available
Sends free auction flier on request

San Francisco

U.S. Postal Service
390 Main Street
San Francisco, CA 94105-9502
(415) 543-1826

Monthly Auctions
Viewing at 8AM
200–300 attendees
Over 200 tubs or bins
Charges $4 per catalog
Minimum bids of $30 & up

St. Paul, Minnesota

U.S. Postal Service
443 Fillmore Street
St. Paul, MN 55107
(612) 293-3082

Auctions every few months
Viewing at 8AM
Sends free flier on request
Minimum Bids of $20

POSTAL VEHICLES AUCTIONS DIRECTORY

U.S. Postal Service— Vehicles

All purchased cash, money order, or bank check.

Alabama

U.S. Postal Service
708 E. South Blvd.
Montgomery, AL 36119
(205) 244-7500

Alaska

Postal Service Supply Office
Vehicle Maintenance
8221 Petersburg
Anchorage, AK 99507-3132
(907) 349-8900

Arizona

U.S. Postal Service
Vehicle Maintenance Facility
4949 E. Van Buren
Phoenix, AZ 85026
(602) 225-3341
(602) 225-3367 Vehicle info.

Arkansas

General Mail Facility Fleet
4700 E. McCain Blvd.
N. Little Rock, AR 72231
(501) 945-6710

California

Fleet Maintenance Division
1300 Evans Ave.
San Francisco, CA 94105-9603
(415) 550-5212

Colorado

U.S. Postal Service
915 S. Logan
Denver, CO 80209
(303) 297-6730

Connecticut

U.S. Post Office
Vehicle Maintenance Service
85 Weston St.
Hartford, CT 06101
(203) 524-6240

Delaware

U.S. Post Office
Vehicle Maintenance
147 Quigley Blvd.
Wilmington, DE 19850
(302) 323-2237

Sales of Used Postal Tractors, Vans, & Pickups - 91-01, 04-91, 05-91

6600151 - 1976 White Single-Axle Tractor Model RX2-42T-06
Engine: Cummins NTC230PT   Trans: Spicer SST-1062-A, 6-speed
Clutch: Spicer AS1402   Mileage: 145,888
Rear Axle Capacity: 23,000 lbs.   **Price: $2,750.00**

8601004, 8601077 - 1979 Mack Single-Axle Tractors Model MC611P
Engine: 6-cylinder diesel ET673   Trans: Fuller RT 910, 10-speed
Clutch: 14" Spicer self-adjusting   Mileages: 320,195; 241,070 respectively
Rear Axle Capacity: 23,000 lbs.   **Price: $6,500.00 EACH**

8601241 - 1979 Mack Tandem Tractor Model MC612S
Engine: 6-cylinder diesel ETAZ 673   Trans: Fuller RT 1110 10-speed
Clutch: 14" Spicer self-adjusting   Mileage: 254,480
Rear Axle Capacity: 34,000 lbs.   **Price: $10,000.00**

0920078, 0920079 - 1981 Dodge Ram 1/2 Ton Fender Pickups
Model: D150 Utiline Pickup   Mileages: 117,298; 128,419 respectively
Trans: Automatic   Power Steering   **Price: $2,225.00; $2,025.00**

1930046, 1930047 - 1981 Ford Panel Vans with passenger seat
Model: F100   Mileages: 118,988; 123,025 respectively
Trans: Automatic   Steering: Power   **Price: $2,125.00; $2,050.00**

* **8902002** - 1978 Ford 2-Ton 4x4 Stake Body with Waltco Liftgate
Model: F600   Trans: Manual   Mileage: 75,287   **Price: $3,275.00**

* **0941055** - 1980 Chevrolet 3/4 Ton 4x4 Stake Body with Tommy Gate
Model: C-20   Trans: Manual   Mileage: 166,018   **Price: $4,550.00**

* These vehicles may not be available on January 28; call (216) 443-4040 before visiting to inspect.

Conditions of Sale

1. Sale begins on Monday, January 28, 1991, at 8 AM.

2. Sale will be on a first-come, first-served basis.

3. Ten percent down holds a vehicle for five days; failure to complete payment within that time irrevocably forfeits the deposit and withdraws the offer.   *(Over)*

Florida

U.S. Post Office
2800 S. Adams
Tallahassee, FL 32301-9998
(904) 878-7268

Georgia

U.S. Post Office
Vehicle Maintenance Facility
3900 Crown Rd.
Atlanta, GA 30304-9721
(404) 765-7735

Hawaii

U.S. Postmaster
c/o Manager, Fleet
Maintenance
89 Sand Island Rd.
Honolulu, HI 96819
(808) 845-1026

Idaho

U.S. Post Office Garage
770 S. 13th
Boise, ID 83707
(208) 383-4225

Illinois

Main Post Office Garage
2105 E. Cook
Springfield, IL 62703
(217) 788-7241

Indiana

U.S. Post Office Garage
615 S. Capitol Ave.
Indianapolis, IN 46225-9721
(317) 464-6081

Iowa

U.S. Post Office
1165 Second Ave.
Des Moines, IA 50318-9121
(515) 283-7720

Kansas

U.S. Post Office Garage
424 S. Kansas Ave.
Topeka, KS 66603
(913) 295-9167

Kentucky

U.S. Postal Service
1420 Gardiner Lane
P.O. Box 3111
Louisville, KY 40232-9111
(502) 454-1891

Louisiana

Main Post Office Garage
Vehicle Maintenance Dept.
750 Florida Blvd.
Baton Rouge, LA 70021
(504) 381-0388

Maine

Main Post Office
171 Kennebec Street
Portland, ME 04101
(207) 871-8467

Maryland

U.S. Postal Service
6 Waelchli Ave.
Baltimore, MD 21227
(301) 625-8931
(301) 242-1487

Massachusetts

U.S. Postal Service
135 A Street
Boston, MA 02210
(617) 654-5771 or 654-5292

Michigan

U.S. Post Office
4800 Collins Rd.
Lansing, MI 48924
(517) 337-8736

Minnesota

U.S. Postal Service
314 Eva Street
St. Paul, MN 55107
(612) 349-3082

Mississippi

U.S. Post Office
350 E. Silas Brown St.
Jackson, MS 39301-5201
(601) 968-5784

Missouri

U.S. Postal Service
Vehicle Maintenance Facility
3535 Katherine Rd.
Quincy, IL 62301-9998
(217) 224-4950

Montana

No auctions—see San
Francisco
& Salt Lake City

Nebraska

U.S. Postal Building
Maintenance
700 R. St.
Lincoln, NE 68501
(402) 473-1630

Nevada

U.S. Post Office
2000 Vassar St.
Reno, NV 89510-9997
(702) 788-0626

New Hampshire

U.S. Post Office
Vehicle Maintenance Facility
955 Goffs Falls Rd.
Manchester, NH 03100-7221
(603) 644-4022

New Jersey

Main Post Office
Vehicle Maintenance Facility
680 State Hwy. 130
Trenton, NJ 08650
(609) 581-3089

New Mexico

U.S. Post Office
1135 Broadway, NE
Albuquerque, NM 87101
(505) 848-3887

New York

U.S. Postal Garage
201 11th Ave.
New York City, NY 10199-9721
(212) 330-4904

North Carolina

U.S. Postal Office
310 Newborne Ave.
Raleigh, NC 27611
(919) 831-3702

North Dakota

U.S. Post Office
220 E. Rosser Ave.
Bismarck, ND 58501
(701) 221-6517

Ohio

U.S. Postal Service
850 Twin River Dr.
Columbus, OH 43216
(614) 469-4255

Oklahoma

Main Post Office
Vehicle Services
320 S.W. Fifth St.
Oklahoma City, OK
73125-9105
(405) 278-6159 or 278-6154

Oregon

U.S. Post Office
Vehicle Maintenance Facility
918 NW Park Ave.
Portland, Oregon 97208
(503) 294-2444

U.S. Post Office
1050 25th SE
Salem, OR 97301
(503) 370-4700

Pennsylvania

Philadelphia Post Office
Garage
30th and Chestnut
Philadelphia, PA 19104
(215) 895-9297

Rhode Island

U.S. Postal Service
Vehicle Maintenance
55 Corliss Street
Providence, RI 02904
(401) 276-6800

South Carolina

U.S. Post Office
1601 Assembly St.
Columbia, SC 29201-9122
(803) 733-4692

South Dakota

U.S. Postal Service
Vehicle Maintenance Facility
500 E. Boulevard
Rapid City, SD 57701-5709
(605) 394-8648

Tennessee

U.S. Post Office Garage
707 Chestnut St.
Nashville, TN 37229-9721
(615) 885-9275

Texas

U.S. Postal Service
10410 Perrin Beitel
San Antonio, TX 78284
(512) 657-8528

Utah

U.S. Post Office
Vehicle Maintenance Dept.
1760 W. 2100 S.
Salt Lake City, UT 84199-9721
(801) 974-2350

Vermont

U.S. Postal Service
Vehicle Maintenance Facility
1800 Page Blvd.
Springfield, MA 01152-9721
(413) 785-6383

Virginia

U.S. Post Office Garage
1001 School St.
Richmond, VA 23232
(804) 775-6155

Washington, D.C.

U.S. Postal Service
Fleet Operations
980 V. St., NE
Washington, D.C. 20018-9601
(202) 832-0158

Washington

U.S. Postal Service
3825 S. Warren
Tacoma, WA 98409
(206) 756-6140

West Virginia

U.S. Post Office
Vehicle Maintenance Facility
602 Donnelly St.
Charleston, WV 25301-9721
(304) 357-4158

Wisconsin

U.S. Postal Service
Vehicle Maintenance
Madison, WI 53703
(608) 246-1300

19

City Police Auctions

★★★

Police are part of the local government. Their main jobs are to preserve order and prevent, detect, and stop crime. In today's inner city, drugs have made that chore far more dangerous than ever. It is practically an impossible task in the larger metropolitan areas.

Auction merchandise comes to police auctions often as a result of a minor crime, whether it was a heisted television its owner wrote off to receive the insurance, an abandoned car loaded with traffic tickets, or an unregistered bicycle. Glamorous merchandise is only occasionally found at these auctions. Most bidders showing up at police auctions are looking for dirt-cheap cars.

Background

Except for in the larger cities, police auctions will be held infrequently. In some areas where crime is not rampant, they might only be held annually, often in the summer. Major metropolitan areas, though, hold auctions on a regular basis to clear out their warehouses.

Much merchandise is available because of insurance claims on unrecovered property, failure by victims to file police reports, and stiff fines for parking violations. Larger cities have to empty out their storage areas to make room for new acquisitions. Monthly auctions are not uncommon in such places.

In smaller towns across America, merchandise is so scarce that it might get thrown in with the city government surplus sales held annually. City governments clean house by holding auctions; some will include all the seized bicycles for the year at their auctions. Some police departments have huge storage areas overflowing with bicycles. And great deals can be found on those.

Procedures

Many larger police departments contract on a spot or long-term basis with auctioneers to sell off this abandoned property. Those auctioneers are usually given the prime meat of the police auctions—the vehicles. Some police officers still auction vehicles in many smaller cities, where it is warranted.

Other abandoned merchandise is normally sold by the police department. This might include jewelry, TVs, VCRs, radios, and other similar items. Burglars, often crack or other drug addicts, pick up things they can easily carry and quickly resell. So you won't find a dining room set or a living room loveseat at police auctions.

In coastal cities, it is possible to find boats auctioned. These, like cars, have either been abandoned or have some violation against them. Don't expect these to be brand-new boats in top condition.

Many police departments have set up auction hotline tape-recordings for interested buyers. Where this service is not available, police departments will have a special direct telephone number to call about their auctions. This is separate from their direct line that callers normally use to report crimes. Remember, when calling the police, their main job is to fight crime, not sell off its by-product.

Don't expect an auction flier. Some police departments do have them, while others just tell you where to show up and how many vehicles are being auctioned. Most of what is available is trash. It is inexpensive and you can find outrageous bargains, but most auction merchandise found here is junk.

Bidders have purchased bicycles for $1 or really expensive ones for about $50. Radios go for about $1. Television sets can sell for $30. Cars might be sold for $300 and up. At one auction, a friend reported one late-model Volvo selling for $600. Not a bad deal.

Special Characteristics

Usually, there are no minimum bids and no reserve prices. After all, this is abandoned property and local governments are not bound, like the GSA, to get fair-market value. Police departments, or their auctioneers, will get whatever the market will bear.

Prices on vehicles vary by condition of the vehicle and the city where the auction is held. In Dallas, for example, the quoted average price was $340. A 1988 Ford in good condition might sell for 15% below the Blue Book wholesale price. Not a bad deal!

There is a catch to buying at police auctions. Vehicles are really sold "as is, where is." You can't start them up. You can't open the hood. Heck, you can't even open the door to look inside. After you've made your successful bid, it will be necessary to hire a locksmith to make a key so you can open up the vehicle and drive it off.

Vehicles are not likely to be cream puffs or dreamboats. These are abandoned vehicles. But some have thousands of dollars in parking violations, making it impractical for the car owner to pay them. So, when the car is finally towed away, it's abandoned at the city pound. While you will find many ugly cars, some ain't bad and you can get good deals on those.

Title to the car is *not* guaranteed. At least not completely guaranteed. Just like an IRS auction, your purchase may not completely stick. Some buyers experience complications in getting title to the vehicle back from the Department of Motor Vehicles (DMV). Again, this varies from city to city. In Los Angeles, title problems happen daily. Out of 1,200 cars sold annually in Dallas, this may only occur once or twice each year.

Buying merchandise other than vehicles at police auctions can be a lot of fun. Prices are at the giveaway level. Merchandise can include jewelry, televisions, VCRs, and whatever else a burglar can steal. Bicycles sell for spare change, as do most other things. Dealers usually show up just to buy bicycles. Bid accordingly.

Tips

When buying a pig in a poke, pay less. You never know what repairs are needed on the vehicle. Blind buying is risky, so never pay more than you could recover by selling the parts. Around 80%–90% of what sells at these auctions is junk. Problems with title to the vehicle could turn out to be a nightmare, especially if the DMV refuses to give you title. Usually, you're stuck with it. Then what? Sell it for parts. It's dangerous ground to walk on.

Police departments in major cities try to do a title search. However, because they're in a rush or busy with other matters, something could be missed or an error made. It's your lemon at that point. The city doesn't want it back. In fact the old owner could file a legal claim against the city.

The best tip you could follow is this. Call your state's Department of Motor Vehicles. Find out what that police department's track record has been with vehicle titles and complaints at police auctions. They can give you a rundown. Then make your own decision.

Evaluation

Aside from the title problem and the high ratio of junk compared to good vehicles, police auctions are a good bet, even if you can't start up the car or do a proper inspection. Remember the police car Dan Aykroyd drove around in with John Belushi in the movie *The Blues Brothers?* He bragged about how he bought that car at a police auction. It looked ugly, but it had a lot of power under the hood.

You *can* find good deals at police auctions if you are willing to take the risks. Inspections are pure guesswork. This keeps bidding low, since few are starry-eyed enough to get carried away. Auction fever isn't likely to hit you at a police auction. So police auctions might be a good training ground for the novice auction-goer. If you haven't been to an auction, try these first.

At merchandise auctions held by the police, you are dealing with a nonprofessional auctioneer, in many cases, so you can do well. As noted earlier, expect a few bicycle shop owners to show up at these auctions and walk off with deals. Just jump in and get a good bicycle for yourself.

CITY POLICE AUCTIONS DIRECTORY

City	Phone	Type of Merchandise
Albany, NY	(518) 434-5135	Vehicles
Albuquerque, NM	(505) 857-8670	Vehicles & Merchandise
Allentown, PA	(215) 437-7753	Vehicles & Merchandise
Atlanta, GA	(404) 658-6876	Merchandise
	(404) 624-4208	Vehicles
Austin, TX	(512) 280-5121	Vehicles
	(512) 445-6964	Merchandise
Baltimore, MD	(201) 366-8300	Vehicles & Merchandise
Birmingham, AL	(205) 254-2000	Vehicles & Merchandise
Boston, MA	(617) 247-4579	Auction Hotline
Buffalo, NY	(716) 851-4569	Vehicles & Merchandise
Charlotte, NC	(704) 336-3190	Vehicles
Charlotte, SC	(803) 577-7434	Merchandise
Chicago, IL	(312) 747-6224	Merchandise
Cincinnati, OH	(513) 352-6480	Merchandise
	(513) 352-6371	Vehicles
Cleveland, OH	(216) 623-5366	Vehicles

City	Phone	Type of Merchandise
Columbus, OH	(614) 645-4620	Vehicles
	(614) 645-4736	Merchandise
Dallas, TX	(214) 670-3350	Merchandise & Vehicles
Dayton, OH	(513) 449-1007	Merchandise
Denver, CO	(303) 295-4361	Vehicles
Detroit, MI	(313) 596-2092	Merchandise
	(313) 267-7174	Vehicles
Fort Worth, TX	(817) 335-8247	Vehicles
	(817) 877-8247	Merchandise
Greensboro, NC	(919) 373-2192	Vehicles & Merchandise
Honolulu, HI	(808) 527-6789	Vehicles
	(808) 943-3283	Merchandise
Houston, TX	(713) 222-8371	Merchandise & Vehicles
Indianapolis, IN	(317) 236-3474	Merchandise & Vehicles
Jacksonville, FL	(904) 630-2215	Vehicles & Merchandise
Kansas City, MO	(816) 234-5000	Vehicles
Las Vegas, NV	(702) 229-3550	Vehicles
	(702) 229-3473	Merchandise
Little Rock, AR	(501) 490-1360	Vehicles
	(501) 371-4643	Merchandise
Los Angeles, CA	(213) 485-9515	Hot Line—Gives phone numbers for:
	(818) 337-9529 (Nationwide Commercial Auctions)	Personal property, narcotics property, bicycles, tools, office machines, etc.
	(213) 894-2495	Real Estate—This is the U.S. Marshal's hot line.
	(213) 485-2256	Surplus Vehicles—This is the GSA number.
Louisville, KY	(502) 588-2578	Vehicles
	(502) 588-2410	Merchandise
Memphis, TN	(901) 576-6683	Vehicles & Merchandise
Miami, FL	(305) 575-5174	Merchandise & Vehicles
Minneapolis, MN	(612) 348-2991	Vehicles
Nashville, TN	(615) 862-7800	Vehicles & Merchandise

City	Phone	Type of Merchandise
Newark, NJ	(201) 733-6260	Vehicles & Merchandise
New Orleans, LA	(504) 565-7450	Vehicles
Newport News, VA	(804) 247-8625	Merchandise
New York, NY	(212) 406-1369	Hot line number
Norfolk, VA	(804) 441-2215	Vehicles
Omaha, NE	(402) 444-5784	Vehicles & Merchandise
Orlando, FL	(407) 246-2414	Vehicles & Merchandise
Philadelphia, PA	(215) 686-4765	Vehicles
Phoenix, AZ	(602) 262-7626 (602) 261-8731	Vehicles Merchandise
Pittsburgh, PA	(412) 355-5683	Vehicles
Portland, OR	(503) 823-1800	Hot line number
Raleigh, NC	(919) 890-3240 (919) 890-3395	Vehicles Merchandise
Richmond, VA	(804) 780-4660 (804) 780-6726	Vehicles Merchandise
Rochester, NY	(716) 428-7210 (716) 428-7434	Vehicles Merchandise
Sacramento, CA	(916) 449-5316	Merchandise & Vehicles (They will put you on their mailing list.)
St. Louis, MO	(314) 444-5540 (314) 622-4000	Merchandise Vehicles
St. Paul, MN	(612) 292-3642 (612) 292-3637 (612) 292-3769	Vehicles Merchandise Hot line number
St. Petersburg, FL	(813) 893-7521	Bicycles
Salt Lake City, UT	(801) 799-3101 (801) 799-3041	Vehicles Merchandise
San Antonio, TX	(512) 299-7455 (512) 299-7570	Vehicles Merchandise
San Diego, CA	(619) 531-2767	Hot line number
San Francisco, CA	(415) 553-9751	Hot line number, gives the following numbers:

City	Phone	Type of Merchandise
	(415) 621-8605	Vehicles—City towing
	(415) 923-6352	Vehicles—City central warehouse
	(415) 744-5240	Narcotics property
	(415) 744-5120	For brochure.
San Jose, CA	(707) 255-5850	Vehicles
	(408) 277-4000	Merchandise
Seattle, WA	(206) 684-8187	Vehicles & Merchandise
Syracuse, NY	(315) 448-8444	Vehicles & Merchandise
Tacoma, WA	(206) 847-9161	Vehicles & Merchandise Auctioneer—Harold Mather
Tampa, FL	(813) 893-7560	Merchandise
	(813) 225-5880	Vehicles
Toledo, OH	(419) 245-3233	Vehicles & Merchandise
Tulsa, OK	(918) 596-7552	Vehicles & Merchandise
Virginia Beach, VA	(804) 427-5616	Vehicles
Washington D.C.	(202) 767-7586	Merchandise
	(202) 404-1068	Vehicles
West Palm Beach, FL	(407) 659-8036	Vehicles & Merchandise
Wichita, KS	(316) 268-4111	Vehicles & Merchandise
Wilmington, DE	(302) 654-5151	Vehicles & Merchandise

Conclusion

★★★

Which government agencies are the worst? Which have the best deals? What follows is a rating system of who's got the best bargains. Unfortunately, I did not rate the government agencies by incompetence or arrogance. Some are officially arrogant and obstreperous, such as the IRS and the U.S. Marshals Service. Others are conservative, such as the General Services Administration and U.S. Customs. Subjective decisions based on general attitude are left to you.

The Best

The best auctions will be found at government agencies in the following order. The number of stars (*) given shows the degree of bargain you might expect to get.

1. *The U.S. Trustees.* Bankruptcy auctions offer repeated steals and good bargains. Lackadaisical bankruptcy trustees, an overworked federal court system, and frequently poor promotions make bankruptcy auctions the place to be. Don't be surprised to find dealers and wholesalers there. For those who worry about a federal bankruptcy judge approving your theft at these auctions, I answer with "what court confirmation." These are rubber stamp approvals.

※※※※※

2. *Department of Defense.* Thank God their auction staff is not guarding our nation. There are more holes in their sealed-bid sales and DRMO auctions than you could count with a Cray computer. They do sell a lot of junk or Defense would be #1 in this rating. Outrageous bargains abound. Taxpayers foot the Pentagon's caprices *and* auction incompetence. Many have built businesses on what this government agency gives away. Anyone who says there are no bargains here hasn't been to one of their auctions. Even Pentagon spokesmen don't claim to get fair-market value. That tells you something, doesn't it?

※※※※※

3. *Internal Revenue Service.* IRS auctions are a form of bankruptcy sale. Taxpayers lose, bidders win. The IRS has been universally condemned and congress should consider an alternative tax system or a national sales tax. What IRS auction system? No set policy means great deals for those willing to put up with arrogance and incompetence. They lose one star for not guaranteeing title and not having a regular auction program.

※※※※

4. *General Services Administration Sealed-Bid Sales.* Do not confuse these with their public

auctions. Repeated deals are found by those who bid. While the GSA trumpets getting fair-market value, bidders continue to steal them blind.

****

5. *State Surplus Auctions.* Bargains vary from state to state. Most of what is sold can really be trash. Find a state university auction and you can really score big. Some states don't have them. Cheap place to buy vehicles. Some are well used.

****

6. *Small Business Administration.* Once you go to the auctioneer, you'll be fine. They would have scored higher on this list. You will find bargains and near-steals. The hard part is finding out about them.

**

7. *County Sheriffs/City and County Marshals Sales.* These would score higher except City and County Marshals sales aren't great. Sheriff sales have offered, and still do offer, steals. Sheriffs are not auctioneers. They try their best but have other things to worry about. Merchandise is unpredictable. There is no co-ordinated auction program. Promotions are poor. Liens must be researched. They do not guarantee title.

*

8. *City Police Auctions.* They don't permit inspections. You might not get title to the car. It may be an ugly boat. A lot of "ifs" here. If inspections were permitted and titles were guaranteed, then these would be at the top of the list. Of course, if that happened, everyone would go to them and prices would shoot up. A lot of trash to sift through if you're looking for a car. Prices are great. Their merchandise auctions are often giveaways.

*

9. *U.S. Postal Service.* These can be high-speed auctions and confusing (the bidding paddles and auction procedure). Their turnouts show that people do get bargains. Great for books and CDs, videos, and oddities. Their jeep/vehicle sales offer average deals. Scarcity of locations is a problem for most auction-goers.

*

The Worst

These have the worst bargains available at their auctions. The number of thumbs down (👎👎 is two thumbs down, for instance) shows how bad the bargains are. There are only three government agencies that offer terrible bargains. In many cases you'll overpay.

1. *United States Customs.* Unless you are an exporter or nuts, stay away from these auctions. Bidders overpay. E. G. & G. Dynatrend is now running a professional auction service. Drug bust hype will air on television and appear in the press. That will keep bringing bidders to auctions. They had great bargains while Northrop was running the program, especially in 1989 and early 1990. Wait until things settle down and people stop coming to their auctions. If you export or want to export, disregard this rating. 👎

2. *General Services Administration Public Auctions.* You will save 10%–30% on a vehicle, maybe, at a GSA auction. If you just have to go, buy something that isn't featured. Luxury vehicles are heavily promoted, so buy those elsewhere. Surplus vehicles offer OK bargains. Stay away from the U.S. Marshals Service contributions. 👎👎

3. *United States Marshals Service.* These auctions are the worst places to go to buy anything. Imagine going to a department store and offering to pay *more* than the price tag. Once the media stops sucking up to these guys, the yokels will cease attending and driving prices through the roof. Deals do slip through but only occasionally. 👎👎👎

Section Three

★★★

Mini-Glossary

★★★

Below are some of the important words that you should understand before reading Section Three. This book contains several specialized words, which when not completely understood in their context, could prevent you from becoming skilled in this subject.

These are only a few basic terms. A full glossary of specialized words and terms appears at the end of this book. Please use it when coming across unfamiliar terms in this subject. Use a regular dictionary for other words that you do not understand.

REOs   This is a made-up word from the letters of *real estate owned*. It refers to real estate that the banks have repossessed from their debtors. The real estate was pledged as collateral against the loan; the borrower failed to make timely payments. This property is also called a nonperforming asset because the bank no longer makes money on the property, from interest payments, as it normally would. An REO department in a bank or government agency has employees who specialize in reselling this property. Otherwise, it is deadwood to them.

Lien   A legal claim against a property, placed there to satisfy a debt. A lien is put on a property to ensure that the creditor eventually gets paid, if the property is sold. The proceeds from the sale could go to satisfy that debt.

Loan Guarantee   The government guarantees that a loan will be paid. If the debtor fails to meet his/her timely financial obligations, and the property is foreclosed, then the government will pay this debt on behalf of the debtor. A variation of this is a government-insured loan, which means the same thing.

Title   This means ownership of something.

Clear Title   Ownership of something without a lien or other limitation. Something with clear title is marketable to others without difficulties.

Introduction

★★★

Fortune is like the market, where many times,
if you can stay a little, the price will fall.
— FRANCIS BACON

The state of American real estate is rapidly approaching conditions that would bring tears of joy to the eyes of the late Lord Nathan Rothschild. Rothschild was most famous for capitalizing on Napoleon's defeat at Waterloo. Trading on inside information that Wellington had won the battle, he first sold stock shares to deceive his fellow London Stock Exchange traders. They panicked and dumped their shares. He bought all they had to offer. Later in the same day, when news of the battle's outcome hit the trading floor, those stock shares skyrocketed. From this strategy came the term: "Buy when blood is running in the streets."

This closely describes the direction in which real estate, and thus the economy, may be heading during the 1990s. The United States government is the country's largest holder or guarantor of real estate property. Estimates have these guarantees or outstanding loans in excess of *one trillion dollars.* As any stockbroker could tell you, that's one heck of a market maker. To paraphrase an old cliché about Wall Street: these days whenever congress coughs, the real estate world panics.

That's because the federal government, through its subsidiaries and beneficiaries, directly or indirectly controls the largest amount of foreclosed property ever amassed in the history of the world. And its asset base is growing, not shrinking. In one fell swoop, the U.S. government could determine the fate of real estate prices for the next 100 years by instantly dumping these foreclosed properties on the open market. The dollar amount of government-held foreclosed property can only be roughly estimated. Analysts have valued these holdings at anywhere from $100 *billion* to *one-half trillion dollars.*

At the same time, increasing numbers of homeless are wandering the streets of major inner cities, young couples rent because they cannot afford the sizable down payment on a home of their own, and government officials announce depressing real estate sales figures. The one undisputed fact is this: there is a lot of available real estate in the United States. Government agencies are holding these properties almost in the same way that a cartel would lower its daily production to keep oil prices firm.

Ignorance is a major factor. Not enough prospective homebuyers know of the vast number of available real estate properties and the opportunities the federal government and others are trying to provide these families. One need only flip through the pages of this section to discover that REO (real estate owned) departments have been established and government employees are in place to *sell* these properties.

In many parts of the United States the housing arena is a buyer's market. The U.S. government is a seller and is overloaded with properties. Now is the time for many prospective homebuyers to cross the threshold and benefit from the many available real estate properties the government is stockpiling. Bargains and discounts depend on the savvy of the buyer. That finesse is based upon knowledge. The keys to that door can be found in Section Three of this book. Contact the various government agencies and others with foreclosed property and start negotiating.

20

The Resolution Trust Corporation

★★

Before the end of this century, the Resolution Trust Corporation (RTC) could well become America's real estate version of the Ford Motor Company's Edsel. Their primary mission is to dispose of failed savings and loan institutions' assets, much of which includes foreclosed real estate.

In May 1989, one reporter wrote: "The federal government is creating a monster." After weeks of haggling and cane-thumping, congress finally presented President Bush with legislation that only the most starry-eyed optimists believed would permanently handle the savings and loan crisis.

The S & L bailout plan was contingent upon a few Pollyanna economic forecasts. Among these were that:

1. There would be no recession through the entire decade of the 1990s.

2. At the same time inflation would come to a halt.

3. Deposits at savings and loans would grow 7% annually (at that time depositors were emptying out their bank account at S & Ls to the tune of several billion dollars monthly).

When President Bush signed into law the Financial Institutions Reform, Recovery, and Enforcement Act (FIRREA) on August 9, 1989, the Resolution Trust Corporation (RTC) was born. It was the richest baby ever to step into this world. The RTC had the western hemisphere's largest pool of liquidated private property. Its asset base dwarfed any corporation's on the Fortune 500 list. For starters, congress gave the RTC $35 *billion* to cover immediate savings and loan institution losses. The RTC needed $15 *billion* more to cover those immediate losses.

In its first two years of operation the RTC drained $80 *billion* from the budget in order to sell $5.4 billion in properties. Cap in hand, it asked for $80 *billion* more! In two of my earlier books I had naively predicted that the S & L bailout would cost taxpayers more than $250 *billion*. Some people questioned me about such a high forecast. Well, friends, the bailout bill (after interest) might cruise past the *one trillion dollar* mark before the dust settles!

The savings and loan bailout could well do what no war has yet done: bankrupt the United States of America. In fact, the government is torn in two directions. On the one hand, dumping such a vast amount of real estate onto the open market in one fell swoop could depress property prices well into the next century. But, if the government keeps pouring bad money after good into this black hole, taxes could get so high that no one would be able to afford a home anyway!

Background

The Resolution Trust Corporation cut its teeth using the same marketing methods that failed savings and loans and the now defunct Federal Asset Disposition Association used. As an anxious congress waited for something (anything) to happen, the RTC began compiling lists of properties it would offer for sale. Rep. Charles Schumer (D-NY), one of the Congressmen who helped create the RTC, loudly complained to the press: "You have the most major financial crisis since World War II and it's hardly on their radar screen."

Five months after its creation in January 1990, the RTC published its inventory, a four-volume set of real estate listings. Many of these listings were incomplete, out of date, or incorrectly priced. Some properties had already been sold. Thousands were not yet included. Although this set created a publishing phenomenon, even with a $50 price tag, property didn't move.

Professional investors knew that congressional politics had tied the RTC's hands with the 95% rule. That mandate specified the RTC would only sell property at not less than 95% of appraised value. Few would realize until later, during the summer of 1990, that RTC prices were based on the old, inflated S & L appraisals—the same exaggerated numbers game that had originally bankrupted those financial institutions.

Of course, property was slow in moving. The largest RTC sale was of a swank Palm Spring resort hotel, for $66 million, to a Japanese real estate company, Maruko California, Inc. Ironically, this was the subsidiary of a Tokyo-based real estate company that got its start in the 1970s by introducing closet-sized apartments to the Japanese. Sales throughout 1990 weren't even keeping up with fresh inventory from new bank failures. RTC was taking giant steps backward.

The Problem

The RTC came about as the right idea at the wrong time using the wrong solutions. Bad timing started the RTC on the wrong foot. The Tax Reform Act of 1986 punctured the speculative real estate boom that spread throughout the country. No longer were real estate investors able to enjoy hefty tax write-offs in this area. That helped bring about the full impact of the S & L crash.

The cost of putting order into the catastrophe and just patching up the damage that had already been done was grossly underestimated. For instance, the great S & L giveaway by the Federal Home Loan Bank Board at the end of 1988, where banks were given away like Christmas presents, cost the taxpayers billions.

The RTC was expected not just to dispose of the real estate inventory, some of which was tied up in the courts, and some rotting away or partly constructed, but it also had to dispose of the loans to an already shaky banking community. The Federal Asset Disposition Association (FADA) that preceded the RTC was an industry-wide joke. One might call on a particular asset and ask about it. FADA's comeback was often: "Gimme a price." Lowball offers were sometimes accepted. Employees who left FADA when it died found their way to the RTC's doorstep.

Just as ex-Nazis came to work for the CIA after World War II, senior managers and executives from failed savings and loans, some whose decisions ruined their banks, also started new careers at the RTC. The pinstriped men who created the problem were now in positions to "solve" it.

Record keeping has been a joke. Congress wrote a $24 million check to the RTC for a computerized tracking system that could track the billions of dollars in seized thrift properties. What happened? Garbage in, garbage out. S & L records were missing, data was confusing, and the system was pronounced virtually useless by the General Accounting Office in September 1991.

Further, the Resolution Trust Corporation relied entirely on real estate brokers to sell properties. Yes, in a booming economy, real estate brokers do alright. So do order takers on late-night infomercials. All one does is sit back and wait for the phone to ring. The RTC's phones weren't ringing with buyers. So real estate brokers didn't move properties.

One could write a book about the RTC, pointing out its flaws and predicting each step of the impending catastrophe. However, that won't solve the problem. Before suggestions are made on how you can cash in on the seized thrift fiasco for your own real estate portfolio, let me make a few modest suggestions as to what steps can be taken to solve the S & L bailout crisis.

The Solution

Congress and the RTC must cross two major thresholds. Both have failed to quickly change tactics that have failed.

Congress should immediately repeal the Tax Reform Act of 1986. By not offering any incentive to invest in real estate, the U.S. government is discouraging this vital area of the economy. For example, eliminating tax deductions for consumer installment debt, when such debt takes on record annual highs, is a direct slap in the face to an already pulverized wage earner. Tax reform has failed miserably. Look at the economy.

The RTC could probably dispose of properties in an orderly fashion, and do so quickly, by implementing real estate auctions. The auction method of marketing real estate was given a hearty endorsement in a recent study (June 1991) prepared by Kenneth Leventhal and Company for the RTC.

The one hang-up in the study was that many brokers feel that auctions won't effectively sell real estate. American real estate brokers are living in the 1960s. They are thirty years behind the times. In Australia, real estate is sold almost exclusively by auctions. Property there can be listed and sold within the month.

The U.S. attitude toward real estate auctions is "there must be something wrong with the property if it's being sold at auction." In Australia the attitude is "if it's not being sold at auction, then there really is something wrong with the property."

The RTC needs speed to sell properties. Their one botched attempt to hold the largest real estate auction ever (next to Didius Julianus's purchase of the Roman Empire) failed because the auction company was forced to pay most of the advertising freight (about $2 million) out of pocket. The auctioneer was out of his league, the RTC hung him out to dry, and the satellite mega-auction never took place in November 1990 as scheduled.

Yet, thousands of foreign investors and even more American investors had been waiting eagerly to jump on what was up for sale. Invitations never went out. The RTC took another giant step backward.

Earlier in May 1990 the RTC came to its senses and began increasing discounts. This was like putting a Band-Aid on a nuclear blast victim. Sellers across many parts of the U.S. were frantically trying to unload their homes and buyers weren't buying those. The RTC had to compete against better, more attractive properties. More giant steps back.

By relying on real estate brokers alone, the RTC has been bleeding the government budget. Since the fourth quarter of 1991, it has begun a series of real estate and FFE (furniture, fixtures, and equipment) auctions to move property. The RTC could create an auction enthusiasm never before seen in America by not only increasing its reliance upon auctions to sell property but also by holding absolute auctions. That would really drive homebuyers to their doorsteps!

Kurt Kiefer, an auctioneer, held a series of personal property auctions for the RTC in North Dakota during September 1991. He drew several thousand bidders to a town of only 40,000. Many were dealers and professionals. Kurt confided to me that through his intense advertising effort, he sold merchandise and equipment at the auction for higher than appraised value. He even found some dealers overpaying!

The RTC can move property at auctions. Auctions have already been proven to work in selling real estate. Now it just has to have more of them and faster. And then everybody wins. Except, of course, the traditional real estate broker . . . but he could spend a few weeks at the Missouri Auction School and then join the fray.

Procedure

There are two types of status for a seized savings and loan: conservatorship and receivership. A conservator is legalese for the individual appointed by a court to liquidate a business. When the savings and loan has been placed under a conservatorship, then it is often managed by an FDIC employee prior to being turned over to the Resolution Trust Corporation (FDIC is covered in the next chapter).

This process takes approximately 12 to 18 months. The actual condition of that bank is not dissimilar to a bankrupt corporation. It is in liquidation. The conservator's goal is to sell property and raise cash. Refresh your memory by reviewing Chapter 16 (U.S. Trustees and Bankruptcy auctions). See tips below.

Once the conservator has cleaned up his predecessor's mess, the property is turned over to the RTC, which now holds its assets in receivership. Receivership is legalese used when a court has appointed someone, acting on behalf of the creditors, to protect, sell, and distribute the assets of the failed company. This is similar to a Chapter Seven bankruptcy, where one closes the doors and sells off the assets. The trustee gets the best price possible, and the judge legally ends the ballgame.

When properties arrive at receivership, they are officially turned over to real estate brokers or put up for auction. Any legal problems connected with those assets have been solved.

Special Characteristics

There are three categories of RTC disposals. Personal property is sold, frequently by public auction. These are called FF&E auctions, abbreviated for fixtures, furniture, and equipment auctions. At these auctions you will find cars, computers, artwork, and furniture.

Real estate is occasionally sold at auction, but more frequently it is offered through real estate brokers. Less important to the average person are the sales of loans. That's right. Individuals' debts are auctioned to the highest bidder, who then retains the right to collect them.

RTC uses three main ways to dispose of assets by special event: auctions, sealed bids, and portfolio sales. The latter includes several assets packaged into one and auctioned off to the highest bidder. This can also be done via negotiated sale. You can receive their monthly Special Sales Event Calendar by calling: 1 (800) 348-1484.

The RTC has beefed up its promotional departments. With a single toll-free call, you can receive quite a few educational brochures, including a booklet on how to buy real estate from the RTC. Call 1 (800) 431-0600 (or 1 (202) 416-4200) or write to:

RTC National Sales Center
Suite 710
1133 21st Street NW
Washington, DC 20036

You can also call the RTC and get a specific asset report for a small fee ($5.00) or free. Just tell the operator the type of property you wish to buy and limit the geographic area. The RTC does charge per listing, so the larger the area and the greater the types of properties, the more this service will cost.

When I called the RTC, I limited the number of properties to less than 50 by naming the type of property (single family house) and by pinpointing the geographic location to the first three numbers of a zip code. The RTC would normally have charged me $5.00, but they had a temporary suspension on this fee. It cost nothing to use this service.

If they do charge you, the fee can be billed on a bank credit card. To use this service, call: 1 (800) RTC-3006.

The RTC will also explain its general financing guidelines to you. If you are unable to obtain conventional financing, the RTC will assist you. For residential property (including condominiums) the RTC will accept a down payment for as little as 3% of the sales price when it is within the dollar limits of the Affordable Housing Disposition Program (AHDP). These AHDP limits are as follows:

One unit dwelling	$67,500
Two unit dwelling	$76,000
Three unit dwelling	$93,000
Four unit dwelling	$107,000

Loan terms are for 30 years. The interest rate is determined by the Federal National Mortgage Association's 30-day mandatory delivery rate as published in the previous Wednesday's *Wall Street Journal*, which is about the same as conventional mortgages. The RTC may also pay a portion of the closing costs.

For further information and to find out if you may qualify, call toll-free: 1 (800) 533-8951.

Programs are also available for those wishing to purchase commercial real estate or land from the RTC. Again, if you fail to qualify for conventional financing, the RTC will finance. The RTC prefers you make a 20%–25% down payment but will consider down payments as low as 15%. The minimum sale price for which they will finance on commercial properties is $500,000. Loan terms are normally for three, five, or seven years.

For details on commercial financing programs, call the same toll-free telephone number: 1 (800) 533-8951.

RTC Real Estate Auctions

There are two types of property sold at an RTC real estate auction: general and affordable. General means available to anyone with no restrictions as to property use, whether it is to be owner occupied or rented out. Affordable means for your occupancy only; the procedure, deposit, pricing, financing, etc., are geared to attract a lower-income prospective homebuyer.

When you attend an RTC auction, you will have to show a cashier's check (written to yourself) at the entrance in order to receive a bidder's card. The amount should be for $1,000 if you are bid-

ding under the general category and $500 for the affordable category. Should your bid win, deposits are 10% for the general category and 3% for the affordable category.

Your cashier's check is applied to the deposit and the balance can be paid by a personal or business check. Closing is within 60 days. The sale is not contingent upon financing. Additionally, within ten days of the auction, you must show proof to the RTC that you applied for financing within five days of the auction.

As soon as your bid wins, the RTC auctioneer will have you sign a bid confirmation form, confirming your bid. It will list the property sold and the amount you bid on that property. At that time you will also execute the purchase and sale agreement. If you are eligible for RTC financing, you should file the loan application at that time.

Financing is available for affordable housing. If you fall into the general category you might consider a 203K rehab loan through a loan broker, a Section 203(b) home mortgage insurance loan, or financing from your state's housing finance authority.

There are a number of real estate auctioneers who may be able to assist you with RTC auctions. The two below have performed successfully with the RTC. Please contact them for assistance in buying at RTC auctions: Dietch National Auctioneers at 1 (800) 257-2800 and/or Latham Auctioneers at 1 (800) 552-8426.

Special Tip about RTC Auctions

Financing can be a problem for some bidders. If the deal falls through, you could be first in line. Simply fill in a backup buyer's card and turn it in when the auction ends. You might still get that property if the highest bidder defaults. At least it will come on the market again, and the RTC may contact you about purchasing it.

Tips on Buying from the RTC

This is a case of the early bird gets the worm. If you are willing to roll up your sleeves and work a bit, you can wiggle through an RTC backdoor. Remember when we discussed conservatorship earlier in this chapter? (Review it quickly if you don't remember.)

Instead of waiting the 12 months to 18 months for a property to go into receivership, jump at the first bite. Find out what properties are currently in conservatorship. Contact the conservator directly. Find out what properties are available on which you could make an offer.

There may be furniture, fixtures, and equipment that the conservator might want to sell, or real estate. It behooves this new manager to rid himself of nonperforming assets as early as possible. This brings cash into the bank and removes dirty laundry from his cleaning list. Banks don't like having a large inventory of real estate–owned property. Seized thrifts had more than they could digest and that is why they failed.

Find out from the RTC or by reading the papers which thrifts were recently seized—they've gone down at the pace of a few hundred per year. Savings and loans are actually waiting in line to be bailed out. So, when the business pages announce the headline story, find out the details regarding who will take over the thrift and when. Then, you be the first in line to make a deal.

Before the RTC there were a number of conservators who held auctions and great deals were found. My wife bought a few excellent collectibles and Persian rugs for very little money at their auctions. In July 1989 *Time* magazine reported that a mint-condition Bentley sold for $10,050 at one of these auctions.

Get to the RTC property while it's still with the conservators. That's Kurt Kiefer's advice, and he auctions for the RTC.

Evaluation

The Resolution Trust Corporation offers great opportunities to a wide range of buyers. This leap into the auction system is encouraging and it will spice up the depressed American real estate picture. It will benefit both the taxpayers and auction-goers.

Don't expect the giveaways that occurred when the RTC first opened up shop. Some investors were snapping up real estate for ten or twenty cents on the dollar. One couple claimed to have bought nearly 800 properties from the RTC, many for under $10,000 and some for a little more than $1,000. These were not the down payments but the final sales prices!

Bargains like these, while never widely promoted, might still be found, not at RTC auctions but by dealing directly with the bank's conservator. It behooves the wise investor to search out recently failed banks and contact the new bank manager.

The RTC offers a large amount of distressed property and is under tremendous stress to sell. Many first-time homebuyers may qualify for the Affordable Housing auctions. Their low down payment feature should attract many renters to buy homes. Others may find government financing appealing.

The 1990s may later be remembered as the era of incredible government real estate giveaways. The RTC has been at the forefront of these real estate bargains. And you will find those bargains still available by the end of this decade.

For additional RTC telephone numbers, use the directory that follows.

RESOLUTION TRUST CORPORATION DIRECTORY

Main Operator	(202) 416-6900
General Information	(202) 416-6940
Assets for Sale	(800) 431-0600
S&L for Sale—Marketing Division	(202) 416-7119
Announcements on Scheduled Meetings	(202) 416-6985
Scheduled Meetings	(202) 416-6985
Consumers Affairs	(800) 424-5488
Becoming a Contractor or Broker for the RTC	(202) 416-7261
Press Office	(202) 416-7557
Inquiries about Assets for Sale	(800) 431-0600
Information on Rules and Policies (Reading Room)	(202) 416-7115
	(800) 842-2970
Freedom of Information Act Inquiries	(202) 416-7451
Announcements on Scheduled Meetings	(202) 416-6985
Inquiries about Becoming a Contractor or Broker for Agency	(800) 872-4033
Public Affairs Office	(800) 424-5488
Other General Information	(202) 416-6940

East Region

Baton Rouge Consolidated
Office
100 St. James Depot Building
Baton Rouge, LA 70802
(504) 339-1375
(800) 447-8790

Northeast Consolidated Office
1000 Adams Avenue
Valley Forge Corporate Center
Norristown, PA 19403
(215) 650-8500
(800) 782-6326

Southeast Consolidated Office
4200 West Cypress Street
Suite 101
Tampa, FL 33607
(813) 870-7000
(800) 283-1241

Mid-Atlantic Consolidated
Office
100 Colony Square
Suite 2300
Atlanta, GA 30361
(404) 881-4840
(800) 628-4362

Central Region

Mid-Central Consolidated
Office
Board of Trade Building II
4900 Main Street
Kansas City, MO 64112
(816) 531-2212
(800) 365-3342

Lake Central Consolidated
Office
25 N W Point Blvd.
Elk Grove, IL 60007
(708) 806-7750
(800) 284-6197

North Central Consolidated
Office
3400 Yankee Drive
Egan, MN 55122
(612) 683-0036
(800) 873-5815

Southwest Region

Metroplex Consolidated Office
3500 Maple Avenue
Dallas, TX 75219
(214) 443-2300
(800) 782-4674

Gulf Coast Consolidated Office
2223 West Loop South
Houston, TX 77027
(713) 888-2700
(800) 833-5937

Southern Consolidated Office
8961 Tesoro Drive, Suite 200
San Antonio, TX 78217
(512) 525-6500
(800) 531-4455

Northern Consolidated Office
321 South Boston
Tulsa, OK 74101
(918) 587-7600
(800) 456-5382

West Region

Central Western Consolidated
Office
2910 North 44th Street
Phoenix, AZ 85018
(602) 224-1776
(800) 937-7782

Coastal Consolidated Office
1901 Newport Blvd., 3rd Floor
East Wing
Costa Mesa, CA 92628
(714) 631-8600
(800) 283-9288

Intermountain Consolidated
Office
1515 Arapahoe St., Tower 3
Suite 800
Denver, CO 80202
(303) 556-6500
(800) 542-6135

21

The Federal Deposit Insurance Corporation

★★

Ever notice the initials FDIC when you visit a bank? These letters should be visible in a few different places at your bank, even on your bank statement. Why? Because it stands for the Federal Deposit Insurance Corporation, which insures that if that bank fails, you will get your money. Those letters are telling you that your money is safe because the FDIC is protecting it.

There's a big kitty that banks contribute to as a safeguard for your money. This kitty is like a big backstop on a baseball field, and it exists to prevent the bank run horrors of the 1930s—a time when over 4,000 banks failed! That's the theory at least. Reality will, over the next decade or two, probably test that conviction for all it's worth.

As a preview to what might happen to your money in the bank during the next few years, let's look at a few facts and figures.

1. From 1950 through 1980 only 151 FDIC-insured banks failed.

2. In 1988, the number of failed banks soared to 200, more than in the previous thirty years.

3. In 1989, 206 banks failed.

4. In 1988, the FDIC insurance fund lost over *four billion* dollars, its first-ever annual loss.

5. In 1989, the insurance fund lost $800 million more.

6. The original guidelines demanded that $1.25 be set aside for every $100 of insured deposits. This was the safe point and created that backstop.

7. In 1990, the fund plummeted to 70 cents for every $100 of insured deposits.

8. In 1991, banks started charging customers a fee that would be used to make up the difference.

At the end of November 1991 congress passed a bill increasing the FDIC's borrowing authority by $70 billion to cover the costs of bank failures. About $45 billion of these funds are expected to be loaned to the FDIC for working capital. They will repay this, plus interest, to the U.S. Treasury from the asset sale of failed banks.

Ten years ago, hardly anyone thought it possible that the FDIC would ever need a congressional bailout bill to prevent bank runs. That day has come. As we move through this decade, it is not unlikely that Americans will experience bank runs similar to those in the 1930s. That's how shaky the banking system really is.

```
Federal Deposit Insurance Corporation
P.O. Box 7549
Newport Beach, CA 92658-7549


Attn:  Real Estate Marketing


If you would like to continue to receive the marketing packet or have a
change in mailing address,  please complete the information requested below.
The Western Regional Property, list is mailed every two months
upon your request.


PLEASE PRINT CLEARLY TO GUARANTEE MAILING.


( )  Check here if change of address


Name_____

Firm_____

Address_____

City_____

Telephone # (    ) _____


If we can be of further assistance,  feel free to contact the Marketing
Department at (800) 234-0867 or (714) 263-7700.


Thank you for your interest.
```

toward an economic apocalypse and will continue heading in that direction until the Tax Reform Act is repealed.

The main culprits in the banking–real estate mess were not only the banks for panting after marginal borrowers and throwing money in their faces, but also the federal regulators. The feds didn't play hardball soon enough. Regulations were relaxed. In some areas, guidelines were about as loose as the morals at a Nevada brothel (one of which sold at auction a few years ago).

What does all this mean to you? It means that there are properties in the marketplace which the FDIC and others are under stress to sell. You only need make a few telephone calls to the FDIC sales offices and find yourself bombarded with available properties. The FDIC is eager to promote its REOs.

Background

The banking industry and real estate are so thoroughly entwined that one can no longer survive without the other. Both seem to be going down the tubes. The number of foreclosed properties that beg to be sold is astonishingly large, and the number of failed banks is just as large.

How was this real estate mess created? Charles Peabody, Senior Analyst for Kidder, Peabody, a large New York brokerage house, offered me a logical explanation: "During the 1980s there was a change of structure. The bookable pool of quality assets was exhausted. Banks then attempted to qualify marginal borrowers in order to put volume on their balance sheets. They changed their rules about real estate loans." Translation: Banks ran out of credit-worthy customers and started cutting corners.

What else happened? Tax reform. The Tax Reform Act of 1986 killed real estate investment in this country. It was no longer possible to buy real estate for tax deductible advantages. As the impact of this "reform" started rippling throughout the economy, businesses began falling flat on their faces. Since then, the U.S. has been limping along

FDIC Auctions

Until December 1991 FDIC property was only occasionally sold at auction. Most of those auctioned were undesirable properties—junk that real estate brokers couldn't unload. During 1990, the FDIC held only 40 auctions, many throughout Texas.

However, on December 6 and 12, 1991, the FDIC held two very large real estate auctions and promoted them very heavily, selling more undeveloped land and real estate on those dates than they had perhaps sold in the previous two years. The December 12 auction was held at the Fairmount Hotel in Dallas, Texas, and was broadcast via satellite to auction sites at Marriott Hotels in Boston, Orlando, Denver, and Los Angeles. Tens of thousands of people responded to advertisements for this auction, which claimed that $500 million of the FDIC real estate assets were being sold in one day. Several hundred hopeful bidders turned up and paid a $50,000 registration fee for the right to place a bid on those properties.

About 20% of these bidders were attending an auction for the first time. Virtually all bidders were veteran real estate investors. Everyone but the most cynical expected to find great bargains at what was being promoted as the largest real estate auction ever to be held.

Good bargains were found. One appealing draw to the auction was the fact that the FDIC offered nonconventional financing options to investors with down payments as low as 25%. Some properties sold for as much as 50% below the highest estimated price range listed in the catalog. Many sold at 30% discounts, while more than a few sold at or above the estimated price.

All were commercial properties, which consisted of hotels, motels, office buildings, multi-family apartment complexes, retail store buildings, strip centers, and industrial real estate. While there were many bargains, it was clearly an auction for the upper classes. The least expensive properties sold for $300,000 to $900,000, the most expensive for $3 million and up. The ten-story Triad Building in Dallas topped the auction list, selling at $10.6 million. Overall, sales prices averaged around $1.5 million.

While the auction was exciting during a few moments of its six-hour length, hardly enough property was sold to place a solid dent in the FDIC's inventory: about 120 properties were sold—subject to confirmation—of the 180 offered for sale. Approximately $250 million of the expected $500 million was raised. While even the highest FDIC officials are not completely certain of the count and value of their inventory, educated guesses place it around 4,000 properties worth more than $2 billion.

As predicted by numerous professional auctioneers before December 12, this auction was doomed to failure. Many wondered if large televised ballroom auctions were the answer as opposed to smaller regional auctions. Others criticized the government, not just the FDIC, for taking so long to sell their properties at auction. Properties depreciate, require maintenance, and are expensive to carry for long periods. The sane solution continually offered to government agencies is to auction off the property within a few weeks of the repossession. This rarely happens, and taxpayers foot the bill for that incompetence.

According to Alan S. McCall, Assistant Director (Credit) of the FDIC's Division of Liquidation, it took the FDIC several months during 1991 to determine whether or not to have an auction. Once decided, they gave the auction company, Ross-Dove, and the real estate brokerage firm, Grubb & Ellis, a few short months to prepare for such a sale. On the footsteps of the much ballyhooed and later cancelled November 1990 RTC auction, most media barely covered this event. It was a credit to the auction company that this real estate sale did as well as it did.

Perhaps after this the FDIC will have learned its lesson and will continue with more and smaller real estate auctions of its inventory. After all, it's the taxpayers who really suffer when their properties stagnate on the books instead of passing quickly into the hands of investors.

Special Characteristics

Unless the FDIC adopts the auction method of marketing real estate, most of what you would hope to purchase from them will be offered to you from real estate brokers, either from their in-house staff or from contracted brokerage firms in the area where the property is held. Because there are thousands of properties and on the average only a few hundred sold by auction each year you should expect to make your offers directly to real estate brokers.

Some FDIC offices inherit also the properties of defunct S & Ls. The RTC is supposed to take over and market those properties, but the FDIC takes over some. Understand that the banking community is a closed society. Former S & L managers could be FDIC employees today. William Seidman, for example, was head of the FDIC before running the RTC.

There is no scarcity of FDIC properties. In the FDIC's spring (1991) catalog you will find more than 200 pages of properties worth in excess of $250,000. That's about 2,600 listings to choose from, with a combined asking price of more than $1 billion!

Properties fall into these categories:

1. Residential Properties
     Single-Family Homes
     Apartments
     Condominiums
     Duplexes

2. Commercial Properties
     Office Buildings
     Retail Shops
     Mixed Use Properties
     Hotels
     Motels
     Resorts

3. Multifamily Properties
     Mobile Home Parks
     Apartment Projects
     Condominium Projects

4. Land
     Developed
     Undeveloped

Procedures

The FDIC has catalogs of real estate listings they will send you. Contact the FDIC sales office in your area or the area where you wish to purchase property. There are two types of offices: regional sales offices and consolidated sales offices. Contact the office that covers the area where you wish to buy. Ask to speak to the liquidation division. FDIC employees are generally friendly and very helpful in sending you the property listings.

There are two basic types of categories of interest to the average buyer:

1. Residential property listings for that FDIC region. Each region can cover several states.

2. Investment property listings for the Eastern or Western United States. For example, when contacting the Atlanta Regional Office, you might be sent investment property listings for Michigan, Pennsylvania, or even Nevada.

Additionally, there is a quarterly catalog listing high-end properties. Real estate offered starts at $250,000, but many of the properties list above the $1 million mark.

When you contact the FDIC office, specify which type of property interests you. Try to be as exact as possible, giving the region, category of property (residential, commercial, land, multi-family), and price range. Information will be sent to you within a week.

For your free catalog, contact the nearest FDIC office from the directory that appears at the end of this chapter.

Understanding the Property Listing

In the listings you receive are three columns of information. One might look like this:

PROPERTY REFERENCE	ASSET DESCRIPTION	PRICE ASSET NUMBER

DISTRICT OF COLUMBIA

Washington 110 Morse Street NE	One-story former bank building with basement. 8,900 Sq. Ft.	$800,000 60373

Contact Atlanta real estate office: (404) 880-3120

The address is Washington, D.C. It is a commercial property, formerly a bank. The asking price is $800,000. The asset number is 60373. To inquire about that specific property, you would contact the Atlanta sales office at the telephone number shown.

There are variations on this, depending on the regional office. Some are very clear, such as the listings from Texas. On those pages, you will find a line for each property, listing this information:

1. Property number

2. Type of property

3. Description of the property

4. Address, including city, county, state

5. Asking price for the property

6. The real estate agent's name

7. Telephone number to contact him or her

As these are separate from the high-end quarterly catalog listings ($250,000 and up), you will find additional types of properties listed in the consolidated office pamphlets, such as farms, ranches, and industrial properties.

Either next to the listing or the listing sheet is your contact phone number. It may be a real estate broker or the FDIC regional or consolidated office. That is the telephone number you call to find out more about the property.

Please note that the FDIC's listings may not be completely reliable. Some are out of date, a few properties have been sold, and still other information may be incorrect. The FDIC does not guarantee accuracy.

Making the Bid

The FDIC sells its properties primarily through real estate brokers or in-house staff, depending entirely on whether the FDIC or the broker is managing the property.

Once you have reviewed the listings and decided which might interest you, contact the FDIC office or the real estate broker listed on the price sheet. Make your bid.

It does not have to be the asking price. The FDIC may accept less, as is their prerogative. Some reports show that the FDIC will often accept 10%–15% less than the asking price. As with all sellers and government agencies, you will be told that properties sell for fair-market value. Market conditions, as you know, dictate fair market value, not someone's say so.

The FDIC claims to work faster than the RTC in getting your offer accepted. That remains to be seen. They place the blame on the broker if it takes too long. You are dealing with a federal bank agency, so you might expect lags of 30–60 days in finding out whether your bid has been accepted.

FDIC properties are often in better condition than Resolution Trust Corporation properties and bring a higher sales price. Most real estate buyers won't qualify to purchase many FDIC properties because they cost too much, bargain or no bargain. But an aggressive investor should be on the lookout for repossessed savings and loan properties marketed through the FDIC. (For example, much of the December 6 sealed bid sale on undeveloped land that occurred through the Dallas FDIC Regional Office was originally held by two defunct government agencies: Federal Savings and Loan Insurance Corporation [FSLIC] and Federal Asset Disposition Association [FADA].)

As a rule, do not attend FDIC auctions unless you wish to buy large, unwanted properties. Remember, until their December 1991 auction, the FDIC mainly sold at auction what their brokers considered junk. Even before that auction, both FDIC and Grubb & Ellis officials confided that several of those properties could never be sold and would not sell at the auction, even with heavily discounted price tags. Perhaps the FDIC will change its modus operandi and superannuate my advice.

Your best bet in buying FDIC properties is to review their regional catalogs and purchase directly from their brokers. Because real estate is depressed throughout many parts of the country and because their late 1991 auction forced their liquidation department to revalue their inventory, you might do well to make initial offers of 30% below the listing price. After all, this is foreclosed property you are hoping to purchase, so your offer should be well below the asking price.

The FDIC is now an agency-on-the-run. Having been forced to seek funds from congress, living in a decade where banks are in a consolidation state and facing the reality of a depressed real estate market, the FDIC should be in the position to make deals. While not quite as desperate as the RTC to unload property, the large amount of expected bank failures in 1992 and 1993 should keep their inventory at near bursting levels throughout this decade.

Contact the applicable regional office in the directory that follows for your free FDIC catalog(s).

FEDERAL DEPOSIT INSURANCE CORPORATION (FDIC) DIRECTORY

Regional Offices

Atlanta

(404) 525-0308
Regional Director-Liquidation
FDIC
Marquis One Building
Suite 1400
245 Peachtree Center Ave. N
Atlanta, GA 30303

Chicago

(312) 207-0200
Regional Director-Liquidation
FDIC
30 S. Wacker Drive
32nd Floor
Chicago, IL 60606

Dallas

(214) 754-0098
Regional Director-Liquidation
FDIC
1910 Pacific Avenue
Suite 1600
Dallas, TX 75201

Kansas City

(816) 234-8000
Regional Director-Liquidation
FDIC
2345 Grand Avenue
Kansas City, MO 64108

New York

(212) 704-1200
Regional Director-Liquidation
FDIC
452 Fifth Avenue, 21st Floor
New York, NY 10018

San Francisco

(415) 546-1810
Regional Director-Liquidation
FDIC
25 Ecker Street, Suite 1900
San Francisco, CA 94105

FDIC Division of Liquidation Offices

FDIC
Division of Liquidation
8th Floor Liquidation
1776 F Street NW
Washington, D.C. 20429
(800) 842-2970

Atlantic Region

Marquis One Building
Suite 1400
245 Peachtree Center Ave. N
Atlanta, GA 30303
(404) 522-1145

6001 Financial Plaza
Shreveport, LA 71129
(318) 686-6700

5778 S. Semoran Blvd.
Orlando, FL 32822
(407) 273-2230

Chicago Region

9525 W. Bryn Mawr
Rosemont, IL 60018
(708) 671-8808 or 8800

Dallas Region

14651 Dallas Parkway
Suite 200
Addison, TX 75240
(214) 239-3317

7324 Southwest Freeway
Suite 1600, Arena Tower #2
Houston, TX 77074
(713) 270-6565

303 Air Park Drive
Midland, TX 79705
(915) 685-6400

999 NW Grand Blvd.
Oklahoma City, OK 73118
(405) 842-7441

321 S. Boston
Tulsa, OK 74103
(918) 587-7600

Kansas City Region

Board of Trade Building II
4900 Main Street
Kansas City, MO 64112
(816) 531-2212

7570 West 21st St.
Bldg. 1046, Suite A
Wichita, KS 67212
(316) 729-0301

New York Region

425 Fifth Avenue, 21st Floor
New York, NY 10010
(212) 704-1200

San Francisco Region

4 Park Plaza
Irvine, CA 92714
(714) 263-7100

707 17th St., Suite 300
Denver, CO 80202
(303) 296-4703

2870 Zanker Road
San Jose, CA 95134
(408) 434-0640

22

Fannie and Freddie

★★

Fannie Mae

During the Great Depression of the 1930s, congress concocted a scheme to "create" money so that people could buy homes. Thus, in 1938 was born a new government agency, the Federal National Mortgage Association. Signed by President Roosevelt as part of the National Housing Act, it originally operated as a subsidiary of the Reconstruction Finance Corporation. By 1954, this agency took on semiprivate status, being owned jointly by private stockholders and the federal government. Like a stock split, the agency, in 1968, spun off the Government National Mortgage Association (GNMA), which became part of the Department of Housing and Urban Development (HUD). What happened to that agency? It was sold to private stockholders for a mere $216 million! In terms of assets it is now the *third* largest corporation in America!

Fannie Mae, as it is known in the banking business, had one mission: to rescue the American housing market from the depression and bring liquidity to the banking system. Judging by the condition of the housing market and the current state of our banks, it looks like it failed. Banks had two problems in 1938: they were faced with mounting foreclosures, and savings accounts were running dry. Sound familiar? The economic climate over 50 years ago is just about the same as it

is today. Can Fannie Mae bail out the housing market again? Hardly. In fact, Fannie Mae may need to be bailed out itself.

Few people know these facts about Fannie Mae:

1. By the end of 1988 Fannie Mae had only $2.3 billion in equity against mortgage lending of over $278 billion.

2. Investors who purchase Fannie Mae's common stock invariably believe that the corporation has "implicit guarantees" by the federal government to protect it.

3. Some may even still believe that it is part of the federal government. Proponents claim that Fannie Mae is backed by the full faith and credit of the U.S. government.

4. It is not. The treasury secretary has the authority to purchase obligations up to $2.25 billion at any time, at his discretion. That's Fannie Mae's backstop. What happens to the other $272 *billion* in commitments? That authority was established in 1957 when $2.25 billion represented about 60% of Fannie Mae's debt. That backstop now stands at about 2% of its obligations.

At one time the Federal National Mortgage Association was congressionally chartered. The federal government sold its last shares in 1970 to private investors when its final obligations to HUD were fulfilled. Here is a quote from the budget of the United States government (special analyses) regarding Fannie Mae's current relationship with the federal government: "In 1968 it became a privately owned corporation, and its stock is now fully transferable and is listed on major stock exchanges."

Here is a profile of types of investors who now own Fannie Mae by percentage of ownership:

Commercial banks	34%
Individuals	33.5%
State and local governments	12%
Pension funds, trusts, estates	7%
Corporations	7%
Insurance companies	3.5%
Savings institutions	3%

Further, if you flip through Fannie Mae's brochures, you may never see the Federal National Mortgage Association. It really isn't part of the federal government.

Ah, but therein lies the rub! Fannie Mae is still a government sponsored enterprise under the auspices of the Department of Housing and Urban Development. Because of this it enjoys enormous tax breaks and has an implicit federal guarantee on its debt. For instance, taxpayers, through such benefits, are actually subsidizing Fannie Mae and Freddie Mac to the tune of nearly $4 billion annually. These corporations can have their cake and eat it, too.

Background

Fannie Mae does provide money to the housing market. Since 1938 it has raised over $450 *billion*. Although homebuyers don't simply get money directly from Fannie Mae, the actual procedure sounds more convoluted than it really is. This is how Fannie Mae helps people buy homes:

1. The bank or mortgage lender agrees to lend the prospective homebuyer money for the purchase of property.

2. The bank or mortgage lender then sells that "loan" to Fannie Mae.

3. Fannie Mae may keep that loan in its portfolio for investment purposes *or*

4. Fannie Mae groups that loan together with other loans into a package, "guarantees" it, and then resells it to investors.

How does Fannie Mae raise this money? The corporation, like any other, issues its own debt—through bond financing, for the purchase of the mortgages. Its department of international financing beats bushes in the world financial markets to raise capital.

For example, a wealthy Japanese widow might indirectly be your lender, not your local bank. It could even be a British insurance firm, an Italian automobile firm, a Kuwaiti oil sheik, or the sultan of Brunei. Because of the Fannie Mae mystique, investors cough up bucks. And those funds pass from Fannie Mae through banks into the housing market. If that money ever dried up, housing loans in America would come to an abrupt halt! Of course, the U.S. government has a vested interest in keeping Fannie Mae above water. Just don't count on it when push comes to shove.

Congress has reached its bursting point on further banking subsidies. And both Fannie Mae and Freddie Mac have less capital backing each investment than privately owned banks, about half what federal regulators demand of these banks. In the recent past, these agencies have bankrolled such scandals as the General Development Corporation and Freedlander Mortgage Company. Even frivolous Citicorp mortgage lenders benefited from Fannie Mae and Freddie Mac laxity. Should senators and representatives ever confront a bailout of either agency, those implicit federal guarantees might soon vanish. It's a dilemma that congress and taxpayers will soon face.

Special Characteristics

Fannie Mae keeps some of those loan packages in its own investment portfolio, as mentioned earlier. Because of this practice, or because they can't find buyers for their loan packages, Fannie Mae gets stuck with foreclosed properties. These aren't bank real estate–owned properties. That's because Fannie Mae put up the money. When a mortgage or trust deed goes into default, Fannie Mae has to recover the repossessed property.

Fannie Mae has been burned a few times. When the homeowner fails to make timely mortgage or trust deed payments, the property goes through the foreclosure procedure, ending up back in Fannie Mae's nest as a repo. It holds around 7,000 real estate properties that are being marketed primarily through real estate brokers.

The number of repos or REO (real estate–owned) properties varies among the regions of the country. While the Philadelphia and Dallas areas are loaded with Fannie Mae REOs, the Western Regional Office includes only about 200 properties, many of them in Alaska.

Fannie Mae specializes in single family residences, not commercial property, land speculation, or multidwelling units. Properties are likely to be in the $130,000 to $150,000 loan range, many much less. These are higher-class properties than many RTC residences, and certainly better quality than Veterans Affairs or HUD properties.

Procedures

The country is broken up into five Fannie Mae regions. You can contact those regions for further information and literature. When you do receive their brochures, please realize that they are probably out of date and some of the information is misleading. For example, Fannie Mae states they have auctions. In each of the regional offices, no one in the REO department knew of any upcoming auctions or had heard of one in the recent past. The Atlanta regional office had properties coming up for auction in North Carolina in the near fu-

Dear Home Buyer:

Thank you for your recent inquiry about Fannie Mae. We are pleased to be able to serve you by enclosing the information you requested.

Fannie Mae does not lend money to consumers, but buys mortgages from a national network of 4,000 approved lenders who do originate mortgage loans, including mortgage bankers, savings and loan institutions, and commercial banks.

Fannie Mae's position as the nation's largest single investor in conventional home mortgages enables it to offer a broad range of mortgage products to local lenders. Any Fannie Mae lender may offer any product; however, all lenders do not offer all products.

A partial list of Fannie Mae approved lenders in your state is enclosed. For additional information, please contact the lender of your choice.

Sincerely,

Bonnie O'Dell

Bonnie J. O'Dell
Manager, Public Information Office

ture. That was only two properties compared to the other 1,000 that are being shown by real estate brokers.

When you contact one of the regions, your first request should be to speak to someone in the REO department. Their main business is not reselling repossessed properties, but providing capital for new homes to be bought. Don't waste your time talking to anyone other than an employee in the REO department.

As soon as you've gotten past the greetings, ask for the name or names of real estate brokers in *your* area who handle Fannie Mae repossessed homes. You may be interested in other areas, so ask for the real estate broker(s) who show those properties. Those are your contacts. Once you've gotten this information, forget about having any further dealings with Fannie Mae. You don't need to.

Contact the real estate brokers and have them mail or fax you information about their Fannie Mae properties. Some of these brokers may handle other bank or government agency repossessions. Have them send you several listings.

SERO Community Home Buyers Program and 3/2 Option Participating Lenders

	Lender Name	Home Office	State	Contact	Phone	3/2	Area Offered
1	UPDATED 8-23-91	-	-	-	-	-	-
2	AmSouth Mortgage Company	Birmingham, AL	AL	Woody Woodfin	205-581-4620	no	Birmingham area
3	Carl I. Brown Mortgage	St. Louis, MO	AL	Loan Officer	816-931-8988	yes	Nationwide EXCEPT ND,SD,HI,AK,LA
4	SouthTrust Mortgage	Birmingham, AL	AL	Shirley Hill	205-254-8392	no	Birmingham only
5	American Home Funding	Rockville, MD	DC	Russell Rothstein	301-984-6300	yes	DC and MD
6	Arbor National Mortgage	Westbury, NY	DC	Loan Officer	301-468-2244	yes	Metro DC area
7	Arbor National Mortgage	Westbury, NY	DC	Randall Boykin	804-359-4411	yes	DC area
8	Crestar Mortgage	Richmond, VA	DC	Contact Local Branch	804-254-1741	yes	DC, MD, VA
9	Dominion Bankshares Mortgage Corp.	Fairfax, VA	DC	Mindy Clayton	703-827-2050	yes	All VA, DC, MD
10	First Advantage Mortgage Corporation	Columbia, MD	DC	Gwen Riley	202-637-6235	yes	DC area
11	First Commonwealth Savings Bank	Alexandria, VA	DC	Patti Thompson	703-739-5757	yes	Northern VA, DC Metro Area
12	First Town Mortgage Co.	Secaucus, NJ	DC	Mark Schaefer	301-681-0600	yes	DC, MD, VA
13	First Washington Mortgage	Annandale, VA	DC	Kevin Connelly	703-642-2400	yes	All VA, DC, MD
14	Guaranty/Shelter Mortgage	Silver Spring, MD	DC	Chuck Sandine	301-439-2100	yes	Metro DC & surrounding MD counties
15	Maryland National Mortgage Corp.	Baltimore, MD	DC	Contact Local Branch		yes	MD,VA,DC,DE,PA,NJ
16	Vista Federal Savings Bank	Fairfax, VA	DC	Theresa Ballard	703-934-2121	yes	No. VA, MD, DC
17	American Bank of Bradenton	Bradenton, FL	FL	John Nash	813-795-3050	yes	Manatee County
18	American Home Funding	Tampa, FL	FL	Sally Harmon	813-289-8430	yes	Miami,Jacksonville,Tampa,Orlando,
19	American Home Funding		FL				St. Petersburg, Ft. Lauderdale
20	American S & L of FL	Miami, FL	FL	Bob Greenwald	305-770-2094	yes	Palm Beach, Dade, Broward Counties
21	BancNewEngland Mortgage Co.	E. Providence, RI	FL	Mort. Info. Line	800-426-3684x7580	no	All of FL
22	Bank of Bradenton	Bradenton, FL	FL	Lloyd Geiger	813-755-1212	yes	Manatee County
23	Barnett Bank of Manatee County	Bradenton, FL	FL	Deborah Escalante	813-753-0708	yes	Manatee County
24	C & S National Bank	Sarasota, FL	FL	Park Fugate	813-954-2500	yes	Manatee County
25	Carteret	Del Ray, FL	FL	Judy Warner	407-243-2023	yes	All of FL
26	Citizens Federal Bank	Ft. Lauderdale, FL	FL	Ann Clark	305-599-6600	yes	FL,CA,IL,OH,VA
27	Commonwealth United/USAS	Houston, TX	FL	Buck Bibb	713-963-6500	yes	PA,NJ,DE,FL,GA,IL,OK,KS,MO,NC,OR,
28	First Commercial Bank of Manatee	Bradenton, FL	FL	Wayne Turner	813-756-0611	yes	Manatee County
29	First Federal of Florida	Bradenton, FL	FL	Carolyn Keller	813-758-1483	yes	Manatee County
30	First Federal S & L of Palm Beach	West Palm Beach, FL	FL	Eddie Nussbaum	407-844-3786	yes	Palm Beach Area
31	First Florida Bank	Tampa, FL	FL	Harry Hedges	813-224-1111	no	All of FL
32	First National Bank of Manatee	Bradenton, FL	FL	Eric Seibert	813-794-6969	yes	Manatee County
33	First Union National Bank	Bradenton, FL	FL	Susan Scott	813-798-2649	yes	Manatee County
34	Florida Home Loan Corporation	Jacksonville, FL	FL	David Ginn	800-343-2111	yes	All of FL
35	GMAC	Orlando, FL	FL	John Lindsay	407-660-8191	yes	Orlando area
36	Goldome Federal Savings	Palmetto, FL	FL	Mason Pruner	813-723-1671	yes	Manatee County
37	Huntington Mortgage Company	Naples, FL	FL	Carol Kirchdorler	813-263-5912	yes	All of FL
38	ICM Mortgage Corporation	Tampa, FL	FL	Mike Fernandez	813-971-7940	yes	Tampa area
39	ICM Mortgage Corporation	Orlando, FL	FL	Danielle Smith	407-295-0082	yes	Orlando area

At this point, proceed with the real estate brokers as you normally would in buying a home. Each region of the country, depending on its housing market, may or may not have bargains. Figure on a savings of 15% below appraised value being a bargain. With Fannie Mae, if you can save more than that, you've done well.

Special Zip Code Service

Fannie Mae provides a free and interesting service for prospective homebuyers. Simply call this toll-free number (1 [800] 553-4636) and ask for a computer printout of Fannie Mae repossessed homes in your area. Give the operator your name, address, and the zip code where you wish to purchase property. You'll receive a printout of the available properties in the mail. Fannie Mae has been using a voice-mail system, so you may not reach a human operator. Give your name and address so you can be sent information.

You can also write Fannie Mae and ask for this service. Just request the zip code(s) of your choice by dropping a note to:

Fannie Mae Properties
P.O. Box 13165
Baltimore, MD 20203

Tip

One of the advantages of buying Fannie Mae repossessed homes is that some of their offices provide direct financing. Ask for financing details when you call one of the regional offices about repossessed property. They will send you a complete loan information package.

Evaluation

Fannie Mae sells repossessed residential properties. They are under no stress to sell properties,

Dear Home Buyer:

Thank you for your interest in Fannie Mae properties. We are pleased to provide you with the most recent listing to aid you in your search. For additional information about individual properties, please contact the real estate broker of your choice or the broker whose phone number appears with the property.

We cannot guarantee the accuracy of prices and other information related to the properties as stated in the list. Because of recent sales activity, some properties may not be available at the time you receive the list. Also, since we regularly add new properties, the broker may have additional Fannie Mae listings that do not appear on the list.

We are pleased to be of service to you.

Sincerely,

Patrick O'Neill

Patrick F. O'Neill
Senior Vice President For Real Estate Sales

PROPERTY ADDRESS CITY	ZIP	BR/BA LIST	BROKER NAME AGENT	PHONE NUMBER
STATE: FL CITY/COUNTY: PINELLAS				
3196 WHISPERING DR S	33541	2/3	C-21 OMNIMARK GROUP	(813)393-2121
LARGO		$71,900	J.R. SAUNDERS	
8720 9TH ST. N	33702	/	C-21 OMNIMARK GROUP	(813)393-2121
ST. PETERSBURG		$59,900	J.R. SAUNDERS	
6875 80 AVE NORTH	34665	/	C-21 OMNIMARK GROUP	(813)393-2121
PINELLAS PARK		$49,900	J.R. SAUNDERS	

nor under congressional mandate to get fair-market value. Your offers should be in line with other similar bank repossessed property. As the property is placed with a real estate broker, competition is as strong as your local housing market and the broker handling the residence.

Some Fannie Mae officials have claimed to have had these foreclosed properties repaired to make them appealing to homebuyers. This practice may vary from city to city. Bank repossessions usually move fast because buyers would rather pay less now and fix up later. You should be able to find good deals when buying from Fannie Mae. But there is not enough profit margin if you wish to buy for investment purposes.

Contact the nearest regional office from the directory that follows for Fannie Mae property listings.

FEDERAL NATIONAL MORTGAGE ASSOCIATION DIRECTORY

Fannie Mae Properties
P.O. Box 13165
Baltimore, MD 20203
1 (800) 553-4636

Home Office

3900 Wisconsin Avenue NW
Washington, D.C. 20016-2890
(202) 752-7000

Northeastern Region

510 Walnut Street
16th Floor
Philadelphia, PA 19016-3697
(215) 575-1400

Serves These States:
Maine, Vermont, New Hampshire, Connecticut,
Massachusetts, New Jersey, New York, Delaware,
District of Columbia, Virginia, Pennsylvania, West
Virginia

Southeastern Region

950 Pace Ferry Road
Suite 1800
Atlanta, GA 30326-1161
(404) 365-6000
(404) 365-6093

Serves These States:
Alabama, Florida, Georgia, Kentucky, Mississippi,
North Carolina, Tennessee, South Carolina

Midwestern Region

One South Wacker Drive
Suite 3100
Chicago, IL 60606-4667
(312) 368-6200

Serves These States:
Illinois, Indiana, Iowa, Michigan, Minnesota,
Ohio, Nebraska, North Dakota, South Dakota,
Wisconsin

Southwestern Region

Two Galleria Tower
13455 Noel Road
Suite 600
Dallas, TX 75240-5003
—or—
P.O. Box 650043
Dallas, TX 75265
(214) 991-7771

Serves These States:
Arkansas, Colorado, Kansas, Louisiana, Missouri,
New Mexico, Oklahoma, Texas

Western Region

135 N. Los Robles
Suite 300
Pasadena, CA 91101
(818) 568-5000

Serves These States:
Alaska, Arizona, California, Guam, Hawaii, Idaho,
Montana, Nevada, Oregon, Utah, Washington

Freddie Mac

Freddie Mac is the pet name of the Federal Home Loan Mortgage Corporation. It was created by congress in 1970 to do the same thing Fannie Mae was supposed to do. Since Fannie Mae became a private corporation about that time, someone in the government saw a need for a bastard twin. Apparently, the Government National Mortgage Association, Fannie Mae's spin-off, was not enough.

To reassure you of its solvency, Freddie Mac is owned by banks, specifically savings institutions . . . some who have been bailed out by the RTC. By the end of 1988 their equity was $1.6 billion against $243.2 billion in outstanding mortgage commitments. Their purpose has mainly been to provide financing to savings and loans. Many of those loans are now being packaged for resale by the RTC.

Because of its association with many failed S & Ls, Freddie Mac instituted a self-protective measure: It began repurchasing mortgage obligations from commercial banks, mortgage banks, and other private lenders. Just like Fannie Mae,

Freddie Mac does not lend funds directly to the prospective homebuyer; it buys packages of mortgage obligations, guarantees them, and resells them to private investors.

Background

Just like Fannie Mae, Freddie Mac's properties also go into foreclosure. Freddie Mac just doesn't promote the fact that its properties sometimes foreclose. Unless you follow the procedures below you might walk away thinking that Freddie never has any properties for sale.

Well, it does have only about 5,000 foreclosed properties. Freddie gets these properties back after the foreclosure process has been completed. Properties are quietly turned over to real estate brokers, probably with instructions not to mention where they came from. Like they fell from the sky.

Real estate brokers know a few marketing "come-ons," so they headline their listing sheets with BANK REPOS. Or something like that. Makes for a few raised eyebrows.

Freddie Mac doesn't sell real estate–owned

properties in the same way that the Colombian drug lord isn't the guy hanging out on your street-corner pushing the crack. Of course, the money finds its way back to Bogota or Medellin in the same way your purchase amount scoots back to Freddie Mac when you buy their properties. They really *do* sell real estate. Getting them to admit it is another thing.

Procedure

So if Freddie Mac is such a pain, why bother? Well, it only takes two phone calls with Freddie Mac. A lot less hassle. It took me about five minutes of phone work from start to finish to speak to a Freddie Mac real estate specialist, get the name of his mainstay real estate broker in a desired California county, and persuade that broker's secretary to fax Freddie's available offerings to my home. That's a lot less work than you might have to do with some other government agencies.

Here's what you do:

1. Call one of the Freddie Mac regional offices nearest you.

2. Ask for the REO (real estate–owned) department that handles your state, even the county where you wish to find property.

3. When you speak to this person, ask for the name of the real estate broker who handles Freddie Mac properties in the state (and county) where you wish to buy.

4. Call the real estate broker. Let him or her know that you spoke to Freddie Mac's REO department (use that person's name) and you wish to find out about any available Freddie Mac properties.

That's the long and short of it. Shouldn't take more than a few minutes. Work with the real estate broker at that point. No need to call back Freddie Mac unless you want another broker's name.

Evaluation

Freddie Mac specializes in single-family homes. Their properties are at the higher end, more so than Fannie Mae homes. That's because Freddie's loan limits are higher, just under $200,000, versus Fannie Mae, who lends in the $130,000 range.

They don't hold auctions, so nearly all of your contact work will be with a real estate broker. Depending on the market conditions, you should be able to save about 5%–10% on the appraised price, perhaps more.

FEDERAL HOME LOAN MORTGAGE ASSOCIATION DIRECTORY

Northeastern Region:

Connecticut, Delaware, District of Columbia, Maine, Maryland, Massachusetts, New Hampshire, New Jersey, New York, Pennsylvania, Puerto Rico, Rhode Island, Vermont, Virginia, and West Virginia

Office:
2231 Crystal Drive
Suite 900
Arlington, VA 22202
(703) 685-4500

Customer Assistance:
(800) 373-3343

Southeastern Region:

Alabama, Florida, Georgia, Kentucky, Mississippi, North Carolina, South Carolina, and Tennessee

Office:
2839 Pace Ferry Road
Suite 700
Atlanta, GA 30339-3718
(404) 438-3800

North Central Region:

Illinois, Indiana, Iowa,
Michigan, Minnesota,
Nebraska, North Dakota, Ohio,
South Dakota, and Wisconsin

Office:
333 W. Wacker Drive
Suite 3100
Chicago, IL 60606-1287
(312) 407-7400

Southwestern Region:

Arkansas, Colorado, Kansas,
Louisiana, Missouri, New
Mexico, Oklahoma, and Texas

Office:
Four Forest Plaza
Suite 700
12222 Merit Drive
Dallas, TX 75251
(214) 702-2000

Western Region:

Alaska, Arizona, California,
Guam, Hawaii, Idaho,
Montana, Nevada, Oregon,
Utah, and Washington

Office:
15303 Ventura Blvd.
Suite 200
Sherman Oaks, CA 91403
(818) 905-0070

23

The Department of Housing and Urban Development

★★★

Established in 1965, The Department of Housing and Urban Development (HUD) replaced the Housing and Home Finance Agency, whose powers, functions, and duties HUD inherited. The main function of HUD is to administer the U.S. government's housing programs and supervise or regulate financing programs that would assist homeownership.

Because HUD oversees the government financing of housing, separate from bank financing of real estate, it comes into the real estate–auction picture when a foreclosure occurs. Its mainstay is providing lower-income housing, predominantly for minority neighborhoods and especially in inner cities. A good deal of it has been subsidized in one form or another.

Background

HUD is involved in auctioning government real estate because a homeowner defaulted on an FHA-insured mortgage. First the property is foreclosed, then it reverts back to the federal government after completion of the foreclosure process. HUD pays the lending institution, as part of the government-insured loan, the mortgage, or loan balance.

HUD then places the property again on the market to recoup its investment. On the average, this procedure brings the Department of Housing and Urban Development a loss of about $20,000 per home. Guess who really foots that bill? That's right, you do.

Low down payments (5% or less and often as little as $100 down), marginally qualified homebuyers, and economic downturns are the major reasons why HUD properties are readily foreclosed. HUD is caught between the demand to provide affordable housing and the reality of economic uncertainties. It's a tough path to walk.

HUD has recently been aggressive in marketing its properties. Radio commercials have aired to select markets asserting the recurrent theme of "affordable housing." This basically means cheap houses for less money. At a time when housing prices are soft, rents are high, and money is scarce, a HUD home doesn't look so bad, does it?

The number of properties HUD has held at any given time is usually in excess of 50,000. That's a lot of properties!

Special Characteristics

There are a number of HUD properties that you never hear about. Most locally advertised proper-

Uncle Sam *WANTS YOU* to Buy a HUD House!

BIDS RECEIVED: 4:30 P.M. WEDNESDAY, JULY 26, 1989
BIDS OPENED: 9:00 A.M. THURSDAY, JULY 27, 1989
INITIAL LISTING DATE: JULY 16, 1989

IMPORTANT INFORMATION

- HUD PROPERTIES ARE OFFERED FOR SALE TO QUALIFIED PURCHASERS WITHOUT REGARD TO THE PROSPECTIVE PURCHASER'S RACE, COLOR, RELIGION, SEX OR NATIONAL ORIGIN.
- PLEASE CONTACT A BROKER OF YOUR CHOICE TO INSPECT OR BID ON ANY OF THE PROPERTIES LISTED.
- NO STRUCTURAL OR SYSTEM WARRANTIES.
- THESE PROPERTIES MAY CONTAIN CODE VIOLATIONS.
- PURCHASERS MUST OBTAIN THEIR OWN FINANCING.
- FOR PROPERTIES CHECKED LBP (LEAD BASED PAINT) — ANY STANDARD RETAIL SALES CONTRACT SUBMITTED BY AN OWNER-OCCUPANT MUST BE SUBMITTED WITH A COMPLETED ADDENDUM TO SALES CONTRACT — LEAD BASE PAINT HEALTH CERTIFICATE.
- HUD RESERVES THE RIGHT TO REJECT ANY OR ALL OFFERS OR TO WITHDRAW A PROPERTY PRIOR TO BID OPENING.
- ALL SALES MUST CLOSE WITHIN 60 DAYS OF CONTRACT ACCEPTANCE, UNLESS OTHERWISE SPECIFIED.
- AN EARNEST MONEY DEPOSIT EQUAL TO 5% OF THE SALES OFFER, NOT TO EXCEED $2,000, BUT NO LESS THAN $500 IS REQUIRED WITH EACH OFFER TO PURCHASE. ATTENTION: CONTACT YOUR BROKER FOR DETAILS ON HUD'S EARNEST MONEY FORFEITURE POLICY.
- BROKERS SHOULD PRE-QUALIFY THEIR BUYERS AND NOT SUBMIT OFFERS FROM PURCHASERS WITH INSUFFICIENT INCOME OR SERIOUS CREDIT PROBLEMS.
- BROKERS SHOULD HOLD THE EARNEST MONEY IN A NON-INTEREST BEARING ACCOUNT AND SUBMIT A PERSONALLY SIGNED CERTIFICATION WITH THE BID.
- ALL BIDS MUST BE SUBMITTED ON THE NEW SALES CONTRACT DATED 8/88, PROPERLY COMPLETED AND SIGNED, FRONT AND BACK.

A POCKETFUL OF MIRACLES FROM HUD

The following properties are offered with no listing price. HUD will accept the highest competitive bid on any property where the bid price provides a net return to HUD which is 80 percent of the unlisted price. HUD's predetermined unlisted price will be announced at the bid opening.

AS-IS PROPERTIES

FHA CASE #	ADDRESS	BDRMS	BTHS
INDIANAPOLIS			
151-151256-203	918 W. 32nd St.	2	1
151-141258-203	929 N. Ketcham St.	4	1
151-134986-203	1053 N. Tremont Ave.	2	1

EQUAL HOUSING OPPORTUNITY

DEPARTMENT OF HOUSING AND URBAN DEVELOPMENT

151 N. Delaware St., Room 350   Indianapolis, IN 46204-2526
INFORMATION: 226-7043, (8:00 A.M.-4:45 P.M.)
BID RESULTS: 226-6811—(AFTER 5:00 P.M.)

AS-IS PROPERTIES

FHA CASE #	ADDRESS	BDRMS	BTHS	LISTING PRICE
CICERO				
151-277818-703	929 Shoreline Dr.	3	2	$74,500
GASTON				
151-232227-203	RR 2 Box 140A	3	1	$25,100
BARGERSVILLE				
151-241338-203	1540 North Road 450 West	3	1	$33,900 LBP
BLOOMINGTON				
151-201255-265	3521 Tilson Pl.	3	1½	$38,500 LBP
DANVILLE				
151-216286-203	51 S. Tennessee St.	3	1	$25,150 LBP
GREEENCASTLE				
151-265655-703	7 S. Arlington	3	1	$33,750 LBP
HARTFORD CITY				
151-117444-235	1015 W. Cleveland Ave.	3	1	$19,950 LBP
KOKOMO				
151-234907-203	1020 S. Delphos	2	1½	$24,700 LBP
LAFAYETTE				
151-237235-203	1012 S. 30th St.	3	1½	$33,200 LBP
MARION				
151-226596-203	1014 E. 32nd St.	3	1	$19,000 LBP
MODOC				
151-246750-203	200 S. Main St.	4	2	$21,100
INDIANAPOLIS				
151-270735-748 (***FIRE DAMAGE)	3510 E. 25th St.***	3	1	$500
151-242020-203	3652 Birchwood Ave.	3	1	$22,500 LBP
151-075401-203	3825 Boulevard Pl.	2	1	$12,000 LBP
151-279737-221	3502 N. Brouse Ave.	2	1½	$22,500 LBP
151-099141-203	4516 Calhoun St.	4	1	$21,500 LBP
151-258040-203	2415 N. Centennial St.	2	1	$24,000 LBP
151-242420-221	4912 Crittenden	2	1	$28,000 LBP
151-221130-703	3558 Decamp Dr.	3	1	$33,900
151-219416-203	3602 N. Grant Ave.	2	1	$26,000 LBP
151-294381-221	2237 Goodlet Ave.	2	1	$26,500 LBP
151-221119-252	1638 N. Goodlet Ave.	3	1	$29,600 LBP
151-278777-234	4470 Abbey Creek Ln.	2	1	$27,500 LBP
151-159087-203	2635 N. Guilford	3	1	$8,000 LBP
151-228250-203	2430 & 2432 N. Lasalle St.	2	2	$17,500 LBP
151-212965-203	1440 N. Milburn	2	1	$16,000 LBP
151-205817-235	9525 Meadowlark Dr.	3	1	$39,500
151-087838-303	1223 S. Pershing Ave.	2	2	$13,500 LBP
151-219417-221	4428 Priscilla Ave.	3	1½	$36,500 LBP
151-236828-503	4006 Rookwood	3	1½	$34,000 LBP
151-269064-303	2830 W. St. Clair	3	1	$20,900 LBP
151-280343-221	922 N. Tacoma Ave.	3	1	$21,500 LBP
151-284326-748	757 N. Wallace Ave.	3	1	$41,500 LBP
151-230075-221	2028 N. Warman Ave.	3	1	$25,700 LBP
151-231047-203	1711 N. Winfield Ave.	2	1	$25,000 LBP
151-226937-203 (**STRUCTURAL DAMAGE)	3227 Park Ave.**	5	1	$12,000 LBP

FHA INSURED FINANCING AVAILABLE

FHA CASE #	ADDRESS	BDRMS	BTHS	LISTING PRICE
INDIANAPOLIS				
151-236117-203	3628 Breen Dr.	3	2	$49,900

IMPORTANT INFORMATION/

Now's your chance to take advantage of excellent real estate values offered by HUD.

SALES CONTRACT FORM

ALL OFFERS MUST BE SUBMITTED ON THE SALES CONTRACT form HUD-9548 (8/88). Previous editions are obsolete and will not be accepted. (THE CORRECT FORM IS DATED (8/88) IN THE BOTTOM RIGHT HAND CORNER OF THE FORM). PLEASE NOTE THAT THE BUYER MUST INITIAL ON THE REVERSE SIDE OF ALL COPIES OF THE FORM.

PROPERTY AVAILABILITY — (813) 228-2602

You may obtain the status of properties offered for sale by calling (813)228-2602. The information will be provided utilizing the STATUS I.D. NUMBER as shown in this advertisement. Be sure to use the most current ad since the status I.D. numbers change in each ad.

NEW LISTING

LISTING DATE: December 30, 1988
★★Code I, "As-Is" - FHA Insured Sales★★
No Warranty with Mortgage Insurance
($100 downpayment to owner/occupants)

Status I.D.	Address	Asking Price	BR/Bath	FHA Case No.
	CLEARWATER			
1	505 Madison Ave	55,000	3/2	093-258292
	NEW PORT RICHEY			
2	4509 Westmoreland Ct	30,000	2/2	093-195470
	TAMPA			
3	7715 Citronella Ct	29,000	1/1	093-239584
4	4717 Stonepoint Pl	35,000	3/2	093-206434
5	14010 Village View Dr	35,000	2/2.5	093-215243

★★Code III, "All Cash, As-Is"★★

	CLEARWATER			
6	2074 Madrid Ct N	34,000	2/2	093-179851
	ST PETERSBURG			
7	2811 Boca Ciega Dr N	32,000 (LBP)	1/1	093-178524
8	2350 - 1st Ave S	18,000 (LBP)	2/1 (FI)	093-217345
9	4018 - 32nd Ave N	34,000 (LBP)	2/1	093-218723
	TAMPA			
10	2208 Hanna Ave E	26,000	3/1	093-249620
11	2518 St John St	24,000 (LBP)	3/1	093-224837
12	125 Thomas St W	24,000 (LBP)	2/1	093-260116
13	4109 - 9th St N	19,000 (LBP)	3/1	093-226222
14	9406 - 13th St N	33,500	4/2	093-238677

All sealed and identifiable bids on above properties must be date stamped in the Tampa HUD office by 4:15 pm, January 9, 1989. The Bid Opening date at the Tampa HUD office on this offering is 9:00 am, January 10, 1989 except for full-price or higher offers which will be opened under the "Express Bid" Procedure.

LISTING DATE: December 23, 1988
★★Code I, "As-Is" - FHA Insured Sales★★
No Warranty with Mortgage Insurance
($100 downpayment to owner/occupants)

Status I.D.	Address	Asking Price	BR/Bath	FHA Case No.
	SEBRING			
15	728 Garland Ave	52,500	3/2	093-208760

★★ Code III, "All Cash, As-Is" ★★

	LAKELAND			
16	703 Alamo Dr	28,000 (LBP)	3/2	093-147631
17	1027 Lime St W	25,000 (LBP)	2/2	093-239603
	SEBRING			
18	304 Vanwall Terrace	43,000	3/2	093-196964
	ST PETERSBURG			
19	1411 Fargo St. S	15,000 (LBP)	4/1	093-237672
20	2962.5 - 2nd Ave. S	14,500 (LBP)	2/1	093-237186
21	750 - 15th Ave S	4,500 (LBP)	2/1	093-239798
23	3801 - 17th Ave S	7,500 (LBP)	2/1	093-214369
24	1026, 1026 .5 1036, 1036.5 19th St. S	39,000 (LBP)	9/4	093-233043
25	1825 - 19th St S	14,000 (LBP)	3/1	093-237130
26	1740 - 34th Ave N	26,000 (LBP)	3/1	093-265696
27	601 - 49th St. S	39,000 (LBP)	3/1	093-235064
	TAMPA			
28	106 Euclid Ave W	16,500 (LBP)	2/2	093-257837
29	2917 Lake Ave E	15,000 (LBP)	3/1	093-240602
30	2906 - 23rd Ave E	12,000 (LBP)	3/1	093-246705
31	5906 - 48th St	24,000 (LBP)	3/1	093-205239

All sealed and identifiable bids on above properties must be date stamped in the Tampa HUD office by 4:15 pm, January 3, 1989. The Bid Opening date at the Tampa HUD office on this offering is 9:00 am, January 4, 1989 except for full-price or higher offers which will be opened under the "Express Bid" Procedure.

EXTENDED LISTING

Properties listed below are available until sold or relisted under 10 day sealed bid period:

★★ Code I, "As-Is" - FHA Insured Sales ★★
No Warranty With Mortgage Insurance
($100 downpayment to owner/occupants)

Status I.D.	Address	Asking Price	BR/Bath	FHA Case No.
	LUTZ			
32	15107 Morning Dr	38,000	2/1 (FI)	093-196378
	NEW PORT RICHEY			
33	2812 Royal Stewart Dr	67,000	3/2	093-228024
	ORLANDO			
34	6829 Magnolia Pointe Ct	50,000	2/2	094-141786
	TAMPA			
35	4325 Aegean Dr, #234B	33,000 (LBP)	2/1 (FI)	093-248282
36	16633 Brigadoon Dr	33,000 (Row)	2/1.5	093-210708
38	6446 Reef Cir	49,000	2/1	093-239576
39	5013 Terrace Village	36,500 (Row)	2/1.5	093-213680

★★ Code III, "All Cash, As-Is" ★★

	AUBURNDALE			
41	1985 Hobbs Rd	20,000 (LBP)	3/1	093-222127
	BARTOW			
42	7205 Thomas Jefferson Cir	42,000	3/2	093-199768
	CLEARWATER			
43	13867 - 61st St	27,000 (LBP)	1/1	093-273472
	OLDSMAR			
44	200 Corkwood Ln	39,000	2/2	093-215484
	OVIEDO			
45	3420 Harrow Ln	49,000	2/2 **	094-151114
	SANFORD			
46	204 Yaie Dr	34,000	3/1	094-124901
47	208 Yale Dr	35,000	3/1.5	094-116601
	ST PETERSBURG			
48	4410 Fairfield Ave S	20,000 (LBP)	2/1	093-192616
49	805 Preston Ave S	12,500 (LBP)	3/1	093-272050
50	2463 - 2nd Ave N	39,000 (LBP)	4/2	093-245746
51	4437 - 9th Ave S	17,000 (LBP)	1/1	093-217524
52	1944 - 12th Ave S	19,000 (LBP)	2/1	093-247946
53	3242 - 16th Ave S	23,500 (LBP)	2/1	093-247809
54	3468 - 17th Ave S	10,000 (LBP)	1/1.5	093-244391
55	5713 - 17th Ave S	12,000	Vacant lot	093-129697
56	1120 - 26th Ave S	7,500	Vacant lot	093-127089
57	1702 - 43rd St S	5,000	Vacant lot	093-201581
58	1734 - 45th St S	15,000 (LBP)	2/1	093-225891
	TAMPA			
59	2314 Arch W	24,000 (LBP)	3/1	093-237155

LEAD-BASED PAINT WARNING

(LBP) - Indicates house was constructed prior to 1978 and may contain lead-based paint. The following addendum to the contract is required for owner/occupant bidders: ADDENDUM TO SALES CONTRACT, "Lead-Based Paint Health Hazard - Property Constructed Prior to 1978", (Tampa Form 178OP), Must be submitted with offers identified with (LBP) if the bidder is an owner/occupant. THIS ADDENDUM DOES NOT APPLY TO INVESTOR BIDDERS.

FLOOD INSURANCE — FLOOD HAZARD AREAS

Properties identified with (FI) or ** indicate the following:
(FI) Flood Insurance Required on Code I Sales

** This property is located in a designated "Special Flood Hazard Area"

EARNEST MONEY DEPOSITS

EARNEST MONEY DEPOSIT CHECKS FROM THE BIDDER MUST BE IN THE FORM OF A CERTIFIED CHECK OR MONEY ORDER. PERSONAL CHECKS ARE NOT TO BE ACCEPTED. BROKERS WHO ACCEPT PERSONAL CHECKS AND CANNOT PRODUCE THE EARNEST MONEY DEPOSIT UPON REQUEST WILL BE REPORTED TO FREC AND REMOVED FROM HUD'S LIST OF APPROVED BROKERS.

"EXPRESS BID - FULL PRICE OFFER"*

"EXPRESS BIDS" FOR TODAY'S "NEW LISTING" WILL BE OPENED DAILY STARTING NEXT TUESDAY AT 2:30pm. ALL BIDS MUST BE RECEIVED BY 2:00 pm & BE IDENTIFIED AS AN "EXPRESS BID - FULL PRICE OFFER"*. THE RESULTS OF THE DAILY EXPRESS BID OPENING WILL BE AVAILABLE AFTER 12:00pm THE FOLLOWING DAY.

* A MINIMUM "FULL PRICE OFFER" MUST PROVIDE A BID PRICE OF AT LEAST THE ASKING PRICE AND A "NET TO HUD" OF AT LEAST 91% OF THE ASKING PRICE WITH A BROKER'S SALES COMMISSION NOT TO EXCEED 6%. OFFERS NOT MEETING THESE REQUIREMENTS WILL NOT BE CONSIDERED UNDER THE "EXPRESS BID" PROCEDURE.

- Purchasers must obtain their own financing for sale.
- Please contact a Real Estate Broker of your choice to see or bid on any of the properties listed.
- THESE PROPERTIES MAY CONTAIN CODE AND/OR ZONING VIOLATIONS. BIDDER IS RESPONSIBLE FOR VERIFYING STATUS WITH PROPER AUTHORITIES.
- HUD reserves the right to reject any or all bids and to waive any informality or irregularity in any bids.

SALES PROGRAMS AVAILABLE

- Code I, "As-Is" - FHA Insured sales. No repairs.
- Code III, "All Cash, As-Is."

☖ U.S. Dept. of HUD

PROPERTY DISPOSITION BRANCH

Mailing Address
P.O. Box 172265
Tampa, FL 33672-0265

Street Address
700 East Twiggs St.
Room 527
Tampa, FL 33602-4029

ties are single-family residences. Others are for sale. For those, contact your nearest local or regional office.

You can also telephone the regional office nearest you for information and auction dates (for sealed-bid sales) on these type of properties:

Hospitals
Apartment complexes
Planned-unit developments
Duplexes, triplexes, or four-unit buildings
Vacant lots

All properties will be sold on an as-is basis. You are responsible for repairs or improvements. Applications can be filed with HUD to receive rehab loan money. There are still active loan programs. Call your local or regional office (found in the directory at the end of this chapter) for the free booklet: *Programs of HUD*. Or if you wish, write a letter requesting the current booklet to:

Department of Housing and Urban
Development
Washington, DC 20410-4000

Properties may carry HUD mortgage insurance. You may seek an FHA-insured loan from a conventional lender, such as a bank or mortgage company, and use the funds to buy the HUD home. The newspaper advertisement describing the HUD property will state: FHA INSURED FINANCING AVAILABLE. It may also be called a CODE I listing. This gives you the advantage of making a lower down payment and/or getting a better interest rate.

More frequently, properties will be on all-cash terms. This doesn't mean you pay the entire sum yourself. It does mean HUD won't finance the property. Finding a lender to finance the property is up to you. The newspaper advertisement describing the HUD property will state: AS-IS PROPERTIES. It may also be called a CODE III listing. You will have 30–60 days to obtain conventional financing. Extensions can be purchased with a nonrefundable extension fee.

Procedure

Buying a HUD home could be simplified. For some reason (bureaucratic insanity?) HUD uses a sealed-bid program to market its properties. Was it dreamt up late one night by a former real estate broker who was being ordered by his superiors to dump these properties faster? Probably something along those lines.

The program works like this (really, it does!):

1. HUD lists their properties in a newspaper, often the major paper, usually on a Friday or weekend. More than likely you will see their ads in the classifieds.

2. There will be two types of listings: new listings and extended listings. Homes being offered under new listings generally appear for the first time. These are the ones HUD has recently acquired through the foreclosure process and is eager to sell. Their asking price is the minimum bid. Extended listings were once new listings and didn't get sold.

3. With the appearance of that advertisement, you can now make a bid on the property of your choice. However, you can't just call HUD and say: "Hey, I'll pay that much." You are required to mail a bid to HUD. But . . . you can't just mail the bid yourself.

4. Your next step is to contact HUD and find out which real estate brokers are handling these properties or leaf through your Yellow Pages and figure out which real estate brokers handle HUD properties.

5. You then meet with the HUD-approved real estate broker so he can show you the property and help you complete the HUD-approved bidding form (HUD form-9548). This is your application to bid on the property.

6. For the bid to be considered you must include an earnest money deposit. This varies with the property and the type of listing. Prior to November 1991 HUD homes in depressed areas

were offered with down payments as low as $100. This practice has been eliminated. Currently, properties eligible for an FHA-insured loan will be offered with 3% down for owner-occupant purchases. Earnest money varies from region to region; it could be as low as $500 and can reach as high as $2000 in some areas. Please have your broker clearly identify how much earnest money you will have to put down before proceeding further with your bid.

7. The bid has a deadline, often ten days, when it must be received by HUD. Make sure your broker gets the bid to HUD before the deadline date and time.

Tips

In making a sealed bid, you can send in an offer for less than the asking price, especially with an extended listing. When the local HUD office does not receive bids on a property or only sees unacceptable bids, they reevaluate their asking price. Sometimes, a broker or bidder may point out that certain improvements will be needed to bring it to the "fair-market value" price.

HUD has been known to lower their asking price based on this. The most they are likely to reduce the price is 10% in most areas, rarely, if ever, lower. Some mail order firms have promoted "HUD homes for $1." If you see such an advertisement, you should first realize that its promoter is (and thus the materials are) not current with the times. There are Urban Homesteading Programs, which once were run by HUD, that do offer lotteries where you could buy a home for $1. See Urban Homesteading Programs on page 258 for further information about these.

Homes often do sell below market value despite what HUD may claim in sanitized press releases or in media interviews. In one survey a few years ago, HUD's inspector general found that over half of this agency's homes were being offered at 10%–40% below market value. Figure that into your bid when evaluating HUD's asking price.

Another way to have your bid accepted is to persuade the broker to reduce his/her commission on the deal. Bringing the broker's commissions down a bit could make the difference in getting your bid approved or rejected. This may require negotiations with your broker. Remember, he or she is a commissioned salesperson and may budge if it is the difference between winning or losing the deal.

Finally, HUD has the right to accept or reject any bid. If a property has remained on the market for an unreasonably long period, persistence can get your bid accepted. You must show HUD how it benefits by taking your bid, how repairs may be needed that require a certain amount of investment. It is to your benefit to document such claims with professional estimates.

You might consider the extended listings if you are skilled with tools and willing to work on your property. These are sold far below market value. Bargains are available but they do require renovation. Other individuals and investors didn't buy at the asking price. Perhaps you will.

One way to check up on HUD's success with their sealed-bid auction is to call the regional or local office about 30 minutes after the recently advertised deadline. Ask the office what prices the homes sold for. If this data is not forthcoming, ask *if* the house sold at the asking price. Sometimes the agent will drop a hint about the selling price.

This gives you an idea as to whether or not the property is still available and the range of acceptable offers on the property. If a number of properties are selling for more than the asking price, then you might look elsewhere. Should few bids be accepted, then stepping in at that point might land you an attractive deal.

Additional Information

There are a few further useful points of information you should know about HUD homes.

Lead-Based Paint Warnings

Some HUD homes are advertised with lead-based paint (LBP) warnings. Prior to 1978 some

Questions and Answers About HUD Homes

The information in this Guide applies to any type of home you may consider. But now we want to give you some specific advice about buying HUD Homes and a brief summary of their advantages.

What are HUD Homes?

When mortgage lenders foreclose on an FHA insured mortgage home, they can file a claim with FHA to have HUD pay the balance due on the mortgage and assume ownership of the foreclosed property. These properties, which include single-family homes, townhomes, and condominiums, are then put up for sale as HUD Homes.

Why Look Into a HUD Home?

Because HUD can open the door to the home you want at the price you can afford. Here's how:

You can get into a HUD Home with less cash than you'd need for most others because HUD may pay your closing costs.

Many HUD Homes require only a 3% down payment instead of the usual 10-20%. And you can buy some HUD Homes for as little as $100 down!

HUD will pay your real estate broker's commission — up to the standard of 6% of sales price.

HUD Homes are priced at fair market value.

Most HUD Homes are ready for you to move in immediately.

Who Can Buy a HUD Home?

Any qualified buyer can purchase a HUD Home, regardless of race, color, religion, sex, national origin, handicap, or familial status.

What If the HUD Home Needs Repairs?

Not every HUD Home needs fixing up, but, when one does, it can be a real home bargain. For example, HUD may lower the price on the home to reflect the fact that the buyer will have to invest money to make improvements. You then might be able to buy a bigger house than you thought you could afford. Or, HUD might offer a special program that includes money for improvements as part of an FHA-insured financing program. Your broker will have details.

HUD makes no warranties on its homes. If any problem is discovered after you buy the home, it's your responsibility to fix it. For this reason, you may wish to have a professional inspect the home before making an offer on it.

homes were painted with lead-based paint. If such a home is offered, you will be required to post an escrow until it is removed. Escrow amounts vary upon the size of the house and region; they range from about $600 to $1,500. The money is returned after proof that the paint has been removed.

Express Bids

If you don't wish to quibble over HUD's asking price, file an express bid. This means you are bidding the asking price or more. Have your real estate broker write EXPRESS BID—FULL PRICE OFFER on the outside of the envelope so that your bid receives priority. It will be opened before the deadline, usually between 12:00 and 2:30 PM the day after it is received.

In hot real estate markets, HUD homes may have several bidders eager to buy the same ones. If you intend to buy that house, quickly (but thoroughly) do your homework. Comparison shop with HUD's previous sealed-bid sales as suggested in the Tips section (page 256). Then make an express bid.

Express bids are opened in the order in which they are received. If yours gets to HUD first and is comparable to another's bid, then you win. Should it arrive after someone's offer at the same price, then they win.

Don't forget to enclose a certified or cashier's check as your earnest-money deposit. Some other bidders might forget. The broker may be new to the process. That might make a difference in the express-bid winner.

Finding a HUD-Approved Real Estate Broker

When you telephone your local or regional HUD office, you may not be given a HUD-approved real estate broker. Some may say: "We don't make it a practice of referring brokers." Uh-huh. There are two ways to get around this. Otherwise, your next step is to look through your Yellow Pages and start calling real estate brokers to see if they handle HUD homes.

OPTION #1. Ask the local or regional HUD office for the names of real estate brokers who have filed HUD form-9556. This could produce names of local brokers. Real estate brokers wishing to represent bidders in the sale of HUD properties must file this form. On it they must agree to comply with Federal Fair Housing Laws and Affirmative Marketing Regulations. If you use a broker who hasn't filed this form, then your bid will not be accepted by HUD. (Ask your broker if he or she has filed HUD-9556 to be on the safe side.)

OPTION #2. Ask the local or regional HUD office for the names of FHA-approved lenders. You will be given a list of banks, mortgage companies, and other lending institutions. Call or visit those banks and ask for the names of real estate brokers who are HUD-approved. It takes a little more work but gets the job done if previous attempts fail.

Urban Homesteading Programs

Funds are provided for this program under Section 810 of The Housing and Community Development Act of 1974. In fiscal year 1988, $14,400,000 was appropriated. Since the program's inception over $128 million has been allocated to this program.

You can really buy a home for $1. Usually, it's more like $11. But your bid is dependent on the luck of the draw. The program is run like a lottery. You pay $10 (or more) to file an application fee. The application drawn from the "hat" is the winner. And he pays a buck for the house.

What HUD does is buy back the foreclosed property and then turn it over to the local community to resell. The purpose is to provide a low- or moderate-income family with a first-time home.

There are restrictions:

1. The homeowner must agree to live there for five years.

2. You must be at least 18 years of age.

3. The applicant must have an annual income of at least $12,000 but not more than $18,950 if single; not more than $21,650 (if married without children); and not more than $24,350 if there are three or more in the family.

4. Within three years the property must be brought up to local code standards.

Rehabilitation money may be provided by the city through a 3% federal loan program payable over 20 years.

How Much Home Can You Afford?

You can save yourself a lot of wheel-spinning in your home search if you take a minute to figure out in just what price range you should be looking.

First, decide how much you can afford in a monthly mortgage payment. Lenders have guidelines they use to decide whether to lend you the mortgage money you need to buy your home. Your real estate broker will discuss these financial qualifications with you. Generally, a lender will want your monthly mortgage payment to total no more than 29% of your monthly gross income (that's your monthly income before taxes and other paycheck deductions are taken out.) These are FHA guidelines; you'll want to check with your mortgage lender for their specific requirements.

To make it simple, the chart on the left lists some examples of annual gross income, monthly gross income and the amount of this monthly income available for your mortgage payment (figured at 29%). Find your annual and monthly gross income and look across to locate the corresponding amount you have for your monthly mortgage.

Once you know how much you can spend on your monthly mortgage payment, you're on your way to finding out how much home you can afford. Your loan interest rate will make a big difference, too. You'll be able to buy a higher-priced home if you pay 9% interest than if you pay 11% interest. Ask your real estate broker to help you estimate your interest rate and then figure a realistic home price range.

Annual Gross Income	Monthly Gross Income	29% of Gross Income*
$15,000	$1,250	$ 363
20,000	1,667	483
25,000	2,083	604
30,000	2,500	725
35,000	2,917	846
40,000	3,333	967
45,000	3,750	1,088
50,000	4,167	1,208

*Average housing expense as a percent of gross income.

Evaluation

Many HUD properties are called handyman's specials or fixer-uppers. These are not going to be the first-class quality mansion you fantasize about. They are foreclosed properties, financed by a government agency specializing in providing affordable housing.

A HUD home can be an ideal starter home for young newlyweds. This may be a chance to enter the homeowner's market. But not all HUD properties go to first-time homebuyers.

Aggressive real estate investors buy HUD properties in beat-up neighborhoods, fix them up (often with government money), and then profitably resell them. One investor in the Tampa Bay area has been profiting by thousands of dollars just buying up HUD's deadwood, rehabilitating them, and profitably reselling them. This is not easy street; he works very hard for those profits.

Most consider HUD as a first leg-up on buying a home because of the price range. Generally expect to buy one for under $100,000, perhaps as low as $15,000, depending on the region and the condition of the property. But, as FHA limits were increased a few years ago to as high as $124,875, some properties may soon be selling in that range.

There is also nothing wrong with finding an FHA-approved lender and applying for a Section 203(b) when buying a HUD home for all cash. Anyone meeting the cash investment on the property, the mortgage payments, and credit requirements should get approved. It's been in effect since 1934 when it was passed as a section within the National Housing Act. Through fiscal year 1988, over $374 billion has been guaranteed by Section 203.

From time to time, HUD offers large multifamily properties for sale. Such properties consist of generally more than 80 units: large apartment buildings, nursing homes, and even hospitals. To receive these notices, write or telephone the contractor below to have your name placed on their mailing list.

HUD Multifamily Project Sales
P.O. Box 779
Adelphi, MD 20783
Telephone (Answering Machine):
(301) 434-3212

Once on this mailing list you will receive notices of multifamily properties up for sale, either a "Prospectus and Invitation to Bid for HUD-owned Property" or "Foreclosure Sale" notices. Because this form of offering differs from HUD single-family homes and smaller multifamily homes offered through newspaper advertisements, you may have questions about this bidding process. Telephone or write this office to have your specific questions answered on the auction, once you have received your prospectus on the desired property:

HUD Multifamily Property Sales Branch
Washington DC 20410-8000
Telephone (202) 708-1220

Contact your local HUD office to find out about available properties, upcoming advertisements, or general assistance. HUD has many loan programs available. These are described in *Programs of HUD*. Remember to call your local or regional office for the most recent copy.

HOUSING AND URBAN DEVELOPMENT (HUD) DIRECTORY
Field Office Addresses and Telephone Numbers

Region 1 Boston

BOSTON REGIONAL OFFICE

Room 375
Thomas P. O'Neill Jr. Federal
Building
10 Causeway St.
Boston, MA 02222-1092
(617) 565-5234
Boston Globe Sunday, Sundays
only

Field Offices

BANGOR OFFICE

First Floor
Casco Northern Bank Building
23 Main St.
Bangor, ME 04401-6394
(207) 945-0467
Bangor Daily News, Friday
only

BURLINGTON OFFICE

Room B-2B, Federal Building
11 Elmwood Ave.
P.O. Box 879
Burlington, VT 05402-0879
(802) 951-6290
Times Augusta, Sunday only,
World Vermont, Wednesday
only

HARTFORD OFFICE

First Floor, 330 Main St.
Hartford, CT 06106-1860
(203) 240-4523
*Hartford Enquirer, Bridgeport
Post, New London
Daily, Norwich Bulletin*—
Once/month, last Sunday of
month

MANCHESTER OFFICE

Norris Cotton Building
275 Chestnut St.
Manchester, NH 03101-2487
(603) 666-7458
Union Leader, Sunday only

PROVIDENCE OFFICE

330 John O. Pastore Federal
Building
U.S. Post Office-Kennedy Plaza
Providence, RI 02903-1785
(401) 528-5351
Providence Sunday Journal,
Sunday only

Region 2 New York

NEW YORK REGIONAL OFFICE

26 Federal Plaza
New York, NY 10278-0068
(212) 264-8053
Daily News, Sunday only

Field Offices

ALBANY OFFICE

Leo W. O'Brien Federal
Building
North Pearl St. & Clinton Ave.
Albany, NY 12207-2395
(518) 472-3567
Must contact R.E. brokers for
listings.

BUFFALO OFFICE

Fifth Floor, Lafayette Court
465 Main St.
Buffalo, NY 14203-1780
(716) 846-5755
*Buffalo News, Rochester
Democrat & Chronicle*,
Saturday only.

CAMDEN OFFICE

The Parkade Building
519 Federal St.
Camden, NJ 08103-9998
(609) 757-5081

NEWARK OFFICE

Military Park Building
60 Park Place
Newark, NJ 07102-5504
(201) 877-1686
Call or write for current listing
to be mailed to you.

Region 3 Philadelphia

PHILADELPHIA REGIONAL OFFICE

Liberty Square Building
105 South 7th St.
Philadelphia, PA 19016-3392
(215) 597-2560
Philadelphia Enquirer, Sunday only

Field Offices

BALTIMORE OFFICE

Third Floor, The Equitable Building
10 North Calvert St.
Baltimore, MD 21202
(410) 962-2520
Sunday Sun, on Sunday, *Baltimore Times* and *Afro-American News*, on Friday

CHARLESTON OFFICE

Suite 708, 405 Capitol St.
Charleston, WV 25301-1795
(304) 347-7036
W. Virginia Beacon Digest, *Charleston Sunday Gazette*, *Herald Despatch*, twice/month on Sunday

PITTSBURGH OFFICE

412 Old Post Office Courthouse
7th Avenue and Grant St.
Pittsburgh, PA 15219-1939
(412) 644-6388
Saturday Post, *Saturday Courier*, *Sunday Pittsburgh Press*

RICHMOND OFFICE

First Floor, The Federal Building
400 North 8th St.
P.O. Box 10170
Richmond, VA 23240-0170
(804) 771-2575
Richmond Times Despatch, *Virginia Pollite Daily Press*, Friday

WASHINGTON, D.C. OFFICE

820 First St. NE
Washington, DC 20002-4205
(202) 275-8185

WILMINGTON OFFICE

Suite 850, 824 Market St.
Wilmington, DE 19801-3016
(302) 573-6300
Properties handled by Regional Office. Contact a broker for listings.

Region 4 Atlanta

ATLANTA REGIONAL OFFICE

Richard B. Russell Federal Building
75 Spring St.
Atlanta, GA 30303-3388
(404) 331-4739
Atlanta Journal, Sunday

Field Offices

BIRMINGHAM OFFICE

Suite 300, Beacon Ridge Tower
600 Beacon Parkway West
Birmingham, AL 35209-3144
(201) 290-7617
Check Sunday papers for: Birmingham, Mobile, Montgomery—Sunday only.

CARIBBEAN OFFICE

New San Juan Office Building
159 Carlos Chardon Avenue
San Juan, PR 00918-1804
(809) 766-6121
Call and request listings be mailed to you, or contact local real estate broker.

COLUMBIA OFFICE

Strom Thurmond Federal Building
1835-45 Assembly St.
Columbia, SC 29201-2480
(803) 765-5592
State Newspaper, Friday and Saturday

CORAL GABLES OFFICE

Gables 1 Tower
1320 South Dixie Highway
Coral Gables, FL 33146-2911
(305) 662-4500
Coral Gables News, Friday only

GREENSBORO OFFICE

415 North Edgeworth St.
Greensboro, NC 27401-2107
(919) 333-5363
Contact brokers for listings.

JACKSON OFFICE

Suite 910, Dr. A.H. McCoy Federal Building
100 West Capitol St.
Jackson, MS 39269-1096
(601) 965-4738

JACKSONVILLE OFFICE

325 West Adams St.
Jacksonville, FL 32202-4303
(904) 791-2626
Times Union, Friday only

KNOXVILLE OFFICE

Third Floor,
John J. Duncan Federal
Building
710 Locust St.
Knoxville, TN 37902-2526
(615) 549-9384
Chattanooga and Knoxville
papers, Sundays

LOUISVILLE OFFICE

601 West Broadway
P.O. Box 1044
Louisville, KY 40201-1044
(502) 582-6255
*Sunday Courier Journal,
Lexington Herald,
Kentucky Post*—Saturdays

MEMPHIS OFFICE

Suite 1200
One Memphis Place
200 Jefferson Ave.
Memphis, TN 38103-2335
(901) 544-3367
Commercial Appeal—Saturday
and Sunday, *Memphis*—
Tuesday and Thursday, *Tri-
State Defender*—Friday

NASHVILLE OFFICE

Suite 200
251 Cumberland Bend Drive
Nashville, TN 37228-1803
(615) 736-5213
Tennessee—Sunday,
Metropolitan Times—Monday,

Nashville Pride—Friday,
Courier—Monday

ORLANDO OFFICE

Suite 270, Langley Building
3751 Maguire Boulevard
Orlando, FL 32803-3032
(407) 648-6441
Orlando Sentinel, on Friday

TAMPA OFFICE

Suite 700,
Timberlake Federal Building
Annex
501 East Polk St.
Tampa, FL 33602-3945
(813) 228-2501
Tampa Tribune on Friday

Region 5 Chicago

CHICAGO REGIONAL OFFICE

547 West Jackson Boulevard
Seventh Floor
Chicago, IL 60661
Attn: Property Disposition
(312) 353-5680
Chicago Sunday Times—Home
Section

Field Offices

CINCINNATI OFFICE

Room 9002, Federal Office
Building
550 Main St.
Cincinnati, OH 45202-3253
(513) 684-2884
Enquirer, Post, Daily News—
Thursdays only

CLEVELAND OFFICE

Room 420
One Playhouse Square
1375 Euclid Avenue
Cleveland, OH 44114-1670
(216) 522-4065
*Cleveland Plain Dealer, Akron
Beacon Journal*, every other
Sunday

COLUMBUS OFFICE

200 North High St.
Columbus, OH 43215-2499
(614) 469-7345
Call and Post—Thursday,
Columbus Despatch—Sunday

DETROIT OFFICE

Patrick V. McNamara Federal
Building
477 Michigan Avenue
Detroit, MI 48226-2592
(313) 226-6280/226-7144
Detroit News—every other
Friday

FLINT OFFICE

Room 200
605 North Saginaw St.
Flint, MI 48502-2043
(313) 766-5109
Flint Journal, Saginaw News—
Sunday

GRAND RAPIDS OFFICE

2922 Fuller Ave. NE
Grand Rapids, MI 49505-3499
(616) 456-2137
See largest local papers—
Monday

INDIANAPOLIS OFFICE

151 North Delaware St.
Indianapolis, IN 46204-2526
(317) 226-7043
Write or call to receive listings,
or contact a broker.

MILWAUKEE OFFICE

Suite 1380
Henry S. Reuss Federal Plaza
310 West Wisconsin Avenue
Milwaukee, WI 53203-2289
(414) 297-3214
Milwaukee Journal—Sunday

MINNEAPOLIS-ST. PAUL OFFICE

220 Second St. South
Minneapolis, MN 55401-2195
(612) 370-3000
*Minneapolis Star Tribune, St.
Paul Express*—Sunday

SPRINGFIELD OFFICE

Suite 206, 509 West Capital St.
Springfield, IL 62704-1906
(217) 492-4085
Properties are handled from
Chicago office, or contact any
broker that handles HUD
listings.

Region 6 Fort Worth

FORT WORTH REGIONAL OFFICE

1600 Throckmorton
P.O. Box 2905
Fort Worth, TX 76113-2905
(817) 885-5505

*Dallas Morning News, Times
Herald*, and *Daily Telegraph*—
Friday

Field Offices

ALBUQUERQUE OFFICE

625 Truman St. NE
Albuquerque, NM 87110-6472
(505) 262-6472
Albuquerque Journal—Friday

DALLAS OFFICE

Room 860, 525 Griffin St.
Dallas, TX 75202-5007
(214) 767-8359
Dallas Times—Friday

HOUSTON OFFICE

Suite 200, Norfolk Tower
2211 Norfolk
Houston, TX 77098-4096
(713) 653-3274
Eastern Chronicle—Friday

LITTLE ROCK OFFICE

Suite 200, Lafayette Building
523 Louisiana St.
Little Rock, AR 72201-3707
(501) 378-5931

LUBBOCK OFFICE

Federal Office Building
1205 Texas Avenue
Lubbock, TX 79401-4093
(806) 743-7276
*El Paso, Avalanche Journal,
Odessa Reporter*, and *Midland
Reporter*—Sunday

NEW ORLEANS OFFICE

Fisk Federal Building
1661 Canal St., #3100
New Orleans, LA 70112-2887
(504) 589-7246
Times—every other Sunday

OKLAHOMA CITY OFFICE

Murrah Federal Building
200 NW 5th St.
Oklahoma City, OK
73102-3202
(405) 231-5464
*Black Chronicle, Daily
Oklahoma*—Saturday

SAN ANTONIO OFFICE

Washington Square
800 Dolorosa
San Antonio, TX 78207-4563
(512) 229-6758
*Daily Star, San Antonio Light,
Statesman, Corpus Christi
Caller*—Friday

SHREVEPORT OFFICE

Joe D. Waggoner Federal
Building
500 Fannin St.
Shreveport, LA 71101-3077
(318) 226-5402
Shreveport Thrifty Nickle—
Thursday

TULSA OFFICE

Suite 110, Boston Place
1516 South Boston St.
Tulsa, OK 74119-40432
(918) 581-7451
Thrifty Nickle—Thursday

Region 7 Kansas City

KANSAS REGIONAL OFFICE

Room 200, Gateway Tower II
400 State Ave.
Kansas City, KS 66101-2406
(913) 236-2162
Information Number: (913) 236-2100

Field Offices

DES MOINES OFFICE

Room 259, Federal Building
210 Walnut St.
Des Moines, IA 50309-2155
(515) 284-4215
Des Moines Register—Sunday

OMAHA OFFICE

Braiker/Brandeis Building
210 South 16th St.
Omaha, NE 68102-1622
(402) 221-3879
Omaha World Herald—Sunday

ST. LOUIS OFFICE

Third Floor, Robert A. Young
Federal Building
1222 Spruce St.
St. Louis, MO 63103-2836
(314) 539-6560
Post Despatch—Sunday

Region 8 Denver

DENVER REGIONAL OFFICE

Executive Tower Building
1405 Curtis St.
Denver, CO 80202-2349
(303) 844-6518
Denver Post, Rocky Mountain News—Friday

Field Offices

CASPER OFFICE

(Note: Property handled by
Denver Regional Office,
above.)
4225 Federal Office Building
100 East B St.
P.O. Box 580
Casper, WY 82602-1918
(307) 261-5252

FARGO OFFICE

Federal Building
653 2nd Ave. North
P.O. Box 2483
Fargo, ND 58108-2483
(701) 239-5666
All major papers in ND—
Sunday

HELENA OFFICE

Room 340, Federal Office
Building
301 South Park
Drawer 10095
Helena, MT 59626-0095
(406) 449-5283

SALT LAKE CITY OFFICE

Suite 220, 324 S. State St.
Salt Lake City, UT 84111-2321
(801) 524-5216
Tribune, Ogden Examiner, any
major locals—Friday

SIOUX FALLS OFFICE

(Note: Property handled by
Denver Regional Office,
above.)
Suite 116, "300" Building
300 N. Dakota Ave.
Sioux Falls, SD 57102-4223

Region 9 San Francisco

SAN FRANCISCO REGIONAL OFFICE

Phillip Burton Federal
Building and U.S. Courthouse
450 Golden Gate Ave.
P.O. Box 36003
San Francisco, CA 94102-3448
(415) 556-5900
(This number gives currently
available property, updated
weekly on Friday.)

INDIAN PROGRAMS OFFICE REGION IX

Suite 1650, 2 Arizona Center
400 North 5th St.
Phoenix, AZ 85004-2361
(602) 379-4156
(For Indian housing on
reservations. Property
is run by the tribes.)

Field Offices

FRESNO OFFICE

Suite 138, 1630 Shaw Ave.
Fresno, CA 93710-8193
(209) 487-5033
Fresno Bee—Sunday
You can go into V.A. office and
pick up current listings.

HONOLULU OFFICE

Prince Jonah Federal Building
300 Ala Moana Boulevard
P.O. Box 50007
Honolulu, HI 96850-4991
(808) 541-1343
Contact real estate brokers for
property. Office will only give
lists to brokers.

LAS VEGAS OFFICE

Suite 205
1500 E. Tropicana Ave.
Las Vegas, NV 89119-6516
(702) 388-6500
Review Journal, Centinel, El Mondo — every other Sunday

LOS ANGELES OFFICE

1615 West Olympic Boulevard
Los Angeles, CA 90015-3801
(213) 251-7136
L.A. Sunday Times

PHOENIX OFFICE

Suite 1600, 2 Arizona Center
400 North 5th St.
P.O. Box 13468
Phoenix, AZ 85004-2361
(602) 379-4434
Tribune—Saturday
Republic—Wednesday

RENO OFFICE

1050 Bible Way
P.O. Box 4700
Reno, NV 89505-4700
(702) 784-5356
Recorded message of
properties, call:
(702) 784-5383

SACRAMENTO OFFICE

Suite 200, 777 12th St.
Sacramento, CA 95814-1997
(916) 551-1351
Sacramento Bee, Stockton Record, Search Light—every other Friday

SAN DIEGO OFFICE

Room 5-S-3, Federal Office
Building
880 Front St.
San Diego, CA 92188-0100
(619) 557-5310
Call local broker for listing.

SANTA ANA OFFICE

Box 12850
34 Civic Center Plaza
Santa Ana, CA 92712-2850
(714) 836-2446
Major local papers—Thursday

TUCSON OFFICE

Suite 410
100 North Stone Ave.
Tucson, AZ 85701-1467
(602) 670-5223
Call or write for property
description.

Region 10 Seattle

SEATTLE REGIONAL OFFICE

Arcade Plaza Building
1321 Second Ave.
Seattle, WA 98101-2058
(206) 553-1700
Tacoma P.I. and *Times*—
Sunday

Field Offices

ANCHORAGE OFFICE

Federal Building—U.S.
Courthouse
222 West 8th Ave. #64
Anchorage, AK 99513-7537
(907) 271-4170
Incrude, Daily News—Friday

BOISE OFFICE

Federal Building—U.S.
Courthouse
550 West Fort St.
P.O. Box 042
Boise, ID 83724-0420
(503) 326-2671
Statesman, Idaho State Journal, Caroline Coeur D'Aline—every other Friday

PORTLAND OFFICE

520 Southwest Sixth Ave.
Portland, OR 97204-1596
(503) 326-2671
Sunday Oregonian

SPOKANE OFFICE

8th Floor East
Farm Credit Bank Building
West 601 First Ave.
Spokane, WA 99204-0317
(509) 353-2510
Spokane Review—every other Sunday

24

Department of Veterans Affairs

★★

Formerly known as the Veterans Administration (VA), this government agency is primarily in the business of providing financial and health-related services to U.S. military veterans. One of these services provided is housing guarantees for the veteran. Because a veteran may often be ineligible for conventional financing, the government will guarantee his mortgage or loan.

Just like others, veterans are capable of defaulting on home loans and mortgages. In the same way HUD steps in to repurchase the property from the bank that lent the money, the Department of Veterans Affairs (DVA) may buy the property at auction to recoup its guarantee. By doing so, the DVA will lose money. In fiscal year 1988, for example, it posted an average loss per property of $18,600.

Background

Many prospective homebuyers may avoid VA-repossessed properties on the assumption that, having no military experience, they are not eligible. Anyone can buy VA-repossessed properties. You don't even have to be a U.S. citizen! The VA has so many properties that they may never re-

duce their holdings to zero. Generally, the DVA has about 25,000 properties on the market at any given time. They reached a low, recently, of approximately 18,000 properties. However, the number of repossessed properties has sometimes gone past the 30,000 mark.

As the U.S. economy destabilizes further into the twenty-first century, the number of VA properties should rise accordingly. Veterans are victims of the VA's low- or no-down payment benefit. On paper, the maximum guarantee the VA is supposed to lend is 60% of the loan amount or $27,500, whichever is less. That's what it should be.

However, many lenders have lent up to *four times* the $27,500 guarantee with *no down payment* required! Guarantees don't usually require a down payment until after the loan amount exceeds $110,000. Then, a 25% down payment is demanded. Sometimes, loan amounts go as high as $135,000 with the 25% down payment.

Take a veteran with few valuable civilian skills and put him in a nonmilitary environment. Many, for instance, are marginally educated. Spin the economic picture a bit as has been done over the past ten years. What you get is a breeding ground for VA foreclosures!

Procedures

Veterans Affairs has a less sophisticated bidding process compared to HUD's. Unfortunately, they don't make it an aggressive practice to sell their homes. Rarely is there an urgency to attract buyers, as with HUD's ten-day sealed-bid deadline. The sole attraction of a VA-repossessed home is the possibility of buying it with little or no down payment. What got the VA into hot water is the same procedure that will keep them there.

Buying a VA repo requires that you visit your local real estate broker. He may or may not have all the available VA properties in his portfolio. You can short-cut the look-and-see process by first contacting your local VA office (see the directory that follows this chapter). Ask for a copy of their current property listings.

There are two types of listings that the VA will send you. They are defined as follows:

1. *Regular (or New) Listing.* Offers must be made at the listed price if you wish to obtain VA financing. When you get conventional financing, you should be able to deduct 10% of the asking price. Offers below the list price will not be considered unless you bring in your own financing.

2. *Special Listing.* Such properties have often been reduced for quick sale. They were promoted as regular listings and failed to move. Now, the VA is willing to take less. Reasonable offers below the list price will be considered. Depending on the market, that offer could be 10% or more below the list price.

The real estate broker will show you the properties. Inspect them with a fine-tooth comb. These are repos. The VA is not always on top of things in the inspection and maintenance department. Renovations are nonexistent. All properties are sold as-is.

Making a Bid on the Property

To make the VA an offer fill out VA Form 26-6705, which the real estate broker will provide you. This is also called "the offer to purchase" and acts as a contract of sale. If you are obtaining conventional financing, there will be no further forms to submit. You will be required to deposit an earnest money deposit of $100 into your broker's escrow account, whether you are making an all-cash offer or asking for VA financing.

If you want the VA to finance this property, include a $5.00 money order with Form 26-6705 so that the VA can access your credit report. At that time, you will have three other forms to complete. They are:

1. *VA Form 26-6705b:* Credit Statement for Prospective Purchaser. This is a credit application showing your credit history and bank accounts.

2. *VA Form 26-8497:* Request for Employment Verification. You will be asked to submit one form for each place of employment for the prior five years.

3. *VA Form 26-8497a.* Request for Deposit Verification. You will be asked to submit a form for each bank account where you have a deposit or outstanding loan account.

Your real estate broker should have these forms on file and ready for you to complete. They are no different from the regular bank forms needed to obtain conventional financing. In either event you will have to complete one or another set of forms to purchase the VA property.

If the VA accepts your offer, your broker will be notified and then pass on the good news to you.

Priorities

If multiple bids are submitted within a specific period of time, the VA will determine the winning bid using the criteria below, in order of priority. (This is more likely to happen with regular [new] listings than special listings.)

1. All cash offers (when not below 10% of the listing price).

2. Amount of the purchase. Highest bid wins.

3. The amount of the down payment. For example, if bids received are the same, someone offering to make a larger down payment will get the property, when that down payment exceeds the required down payment by more than 3% of the list price.

4. How acceptable the bidder's credit risk is compared to another. Those with better credit will get the property.

5. Whether or not the bidder will occupy the property. Owner-occupants receive a higher priority.

6. Veterans are preferable to nonveterans if all else is equal.

7. Should the previous criteria not break the tie, the first bid received wins over later offers.

More Information

If you wish to invest in the property, not as an owner-occupant, then you may be asked to make a 5% down payment. Your priority is below others who may wish to purchase the property. Investors competing against owner-occupants could be forced to make a higher offer to ensure they get the property.

The VA will pay closing costs up to a certain limit when they finance the property, but you will have to pay a 1% funding fee. As in buying other property, it's your job to obtain the necessary insurance, prepay interest for the rest of the month, prepay a tax deposit into escrow, etc.

Real Estate Auctions

Veterans Affairs has not been actively selling their properties at public auction. However, a series of auctions held for more than 1,700 VA properties located in the Greater Houston area and throughout Oklahoma substantially reduced their inventory in a few short weeks. These auctions attracted thousands of registered bidders looking for great deals.

Nothing of this order has occurred since. The VA has been lackadaisical in moving property by auction. It is one solution that worked but was not repeated. The VA should review and reinstate this successful action. Doing so might reduce their inventory again.

Evaluation

VA properties are often the bottom rung of the housing ladder. Some properties, in the past, have even been listed for a few thousand dollars. Few properties ever reach the $100,000 price range. Most average in the $40,000 to $65,000 price bracket. These are affordable homes in less fortunate neighborhoods, good for the lower-income family that would like to stop renting.

Some purchase these properties for investment, though not with the interest level demonstrated for HUD homes. They can be below-average rental properties for investors. Resale value depends on the amount of renovations done on property and how well that area improves. It's a risky gamble.

VA properties are generally lower class than HUD homes. Less down payment is required, sometimes none. The VA will occasionally finance, depending on market conditions. They will try to discourage it. But, when properties just sit there, someone willing to take one or more off their hands might look pretty good to them.

Contact your local VA office in the directory that follows and ask to speak with someone in the property management division. Ask for a copy of their recent listings. Although these are reserved exclusively for VA-approved real estate brokers, you will usually be allowed to receive one mailing from that office.

DEPARTMENT OF VETERANS AFFAIRS OFFICE DIRECTORY

Alabama

474 S. Court Street
Montgomery, AL 36104
(205) 223-7025
Will send out list to public one
time, must see broker for
additional lists.

Alaska

235 E. Eighth Avenue
Anchorage, AK 99501
(907) 271-2215
May pick up list at V.A. or
contact broker.

Arizona

3225 N. Central Avenue
Phoenix, AZ 85012
(602) 263-5411
Tucson Star, Arizona Republic,
Phoenix Gazette, every other
Friday

Arkansas

P.O. Box 1280
North Little Rock, AR 72115
(501) 370-3800
Democrat and *Gazette*, on
Sunday

California

Federal Building
11000 Wilshire Blvd.
Los Angeles, CA 90024
(213) 575-7175

Los Angeles Times, on Sunday.
Also responsible for Southern
Nevada.

211 Main Street
San Francisco, CA 94105
(415) 495-8900
Get listings from broker.
San Francisco also covers
Northern Nevada.

Colorado

44 Union Blvd.
Box 25126
Denver, CO 80225
(303) 980-1300
Rocky Mountain News, every
other Wednesday

Connecticut

450 Main Street
Hartford, CT 06103
(203) 278-3230
Currently do not advertise in
papers. You can contact them
and receive listings in the mail.
All approved brokers will have
listings available.

Delaware

1601 Kirkwood Hwy.
Wilmington, DE 19805
(302) 998-0191
Must contact broker; they do
not send out list.

District of Columbia

941 N. Capitol Street, NE
Room 90-1-12
Washington, D.C. 20421
(202) 208-1325
Washington Post, on Wednesday

Florida

144 First Avenue S.
St. Petersburg, FL 33731
(813) 898-2121
St. Pete Times, Tampa Tribune
on Fridays

Georgia

730 Peachtree Street, NE
Atlanta, GA 30365
(404) 881-1776 or in GA you
can dial 1 (800) 827-2039
Atlanta Constitution, Tuesday
once a month

Hawaii

PJKK Federal Building
300 Ala Moana Blvd.
Honolulu, HI 96813
(808) 541-1476

Idaho

550 W. Fort Street
Box 044
Boise, ID 83724
(208) 334-1900
Will send current listings if you
call or write, or check your
real estate brokers.

Illinois

536 South Clark Street
P.O. Box 8136
Chicago, IL 60680
(312) 353-2049
Chicago Sunday Times (Home
Life section), every other
Friday

Iowa

210 Walnut Street, Room 985
Des Moines, IA 50309
(515) 284-4675
Des Moines Register, bi-weekly
on Monday. Look in the major
local papers for area you want.

Kentucky

600 Martin Luther King Jr.
Place
Louisville, KY 40202
(502) 584-2231
Within state of Kentucky call
1 (800) 827-2050. Will mail
current listings if you call or
write.

Louisiana

701 Loyola Avenue
New Orleans, LA 70113
(504) 589-7191
Call or write for property
listings or check your
real estate broker.

Maine

Maine is now being run by the
New Hampshire office.
Contact NH for property
listings at (603) 666-7654.

Maryland

31 Hopkins Plaza
Baltimore, MD 21202
(301) 962-4466
Must contact office for listings
or go to your broker.

Massachusetts

Closed. Call New Hampshire
office at (603) 666-7654.
They will send the listings
available for MA.

Michigan

Patrick V. McNamara
Federal Bldg.
477 Michigan Avenue
(313) 226-4200
Call and they will mail current
listings.

Minnesota

Federal Bldg., Room 124 East
Fort Snelling
St. Paul., MN 55111
(612) 725-3870
Pioneer Press and *Star Tribune*,
every three weeks. Call
Minnesota office for
information on North and
South Dakota.

Mississippi

100 West Capitol Street
Jackson, MS 39269-0199
(601) 965-4873
Clarion Ledger, Tuesday and
Wednesday

Missouri

Federal Bldg., Room 4705
1520 Market Street
St. Louis, MO 63103
(314) 539-3144

Montana

Property Management
Ft. Harrison, MT 59636
(406) 442-6410 ext. 344/345
Billings Gazette, on Sundays.
Will also send brochure if you
call or write.

Nebraska

5631 S. 48th Street
Lincoln, NE 68516
(402) 437-5031
Must go to real estate broker
for list of properties.

Nevada

Call California number to get
information on Nevada
properties.

New Hampshire

Federal Bldg.
275 Chestnut Street
Manchester, NH 03101
(603) 666-7654
All New England states are
now handled out of New
Hampshire. Please call them
and they will send all listings.

New Jersey

20 Washington Place
Newark, NJ 07012
(201) 645-2150
Call or write and they will
send their listings.

New Mexico

Dennis Chavez Federal Bldg.
U.S. Courthouse
500 Gold Avenue SW
Albuquerque, NM 87102
(505) 766-3361
They put out a list the first
Monday of every month. See
your broker and they will send
the listing.

New York

111 W. Huron Street
Buffalo, NY 14202
(716) 846-5191

North Carolina

Federal Bldg.
251 N. Main Street
Winston-Salem, NC 27155
(919) 748-1800
Will mail listings to you.

North Dakota

See St. Paul, Minnesota, for
information.

Ohio

Federal Bldg.
240 E. Ninth Street
Cleveland, OH 44199
(216) 522-3583
Write or call. They will send
current list.

Oklahoma

125 S. Main Street
Muskogee, OK 74401
(918) 687-2161
*Oklahoma City Times, Tucson
World*, every other Thursday.

Oregon

1220 SW Third Avenue
Office 1420
Portland, OR 97204
(503) 326-2484
Must contact broker for
listings.

Pennsylvania

P.O. Box 8079
5000 Wissahickon Avenue
Philadelphia, PA 19101
(215) 438-5225
Philadelphia Enquirer, Friday

Rhode Island

Call New Hampshire office for
information.

South Carolina

101 Assembly Street
Columbia, SC 29201
(803) 765-5154
State newspaper, every Sunday

South Dakota

Call St. Paul, MN office for
information.

Tennessee

110 Ninth Avenue South
Nashville, TN 37203
(615) 736-5241
Clocksville Leaf, Sunday; *Tri-
State Defender*, Friday

Texas

2515 Murworth Drive
Houston, TX 77054
(713) 664-4664
Houston Chronicle, Thursday.
Call for other property listings.

Utah

Federal Bldg.
125 S. State Street
Salt Lake City, UT 84111
Tribune, every other week

Vermont

Call New Hampshire office for
information.

Virginia

210 Franklin Road SW
Roanoke, VA 24011
(703) 982-6141
Call or write to receive list for
properties.

Washington

915 Second Avenue
12th Floor Federal Bldg.
Seattle, WA 98174
(206) 624-7200
Call or write and they will
send a brochure of current
listings.

West Virginia

640 Fourth Avenue
Huntington, WV 25701
(304) 529-5046
Write or call and listings will
be sent to you.

Wisconsin

5000 West National Ave.
Bldg. 6
Milwaukee, WI 53295
(414) 384-2000 or 383-8680
Send a self-addressed stamped
envelope and they will send
you current listings.

Wyoming

2360 E. Pershing Blvd.
Cheyenne, WY 82001
(307) 778-7330
Listings are in major local
papers and come out every
other Wednesday.

25

The General Services Administration

★★★

The GSA has two distinct branches of property disposal. Chapter 9 covered the personal property, merchandise, and equipment side of the General Services Administration, whose auctions are marketed and overseen by their Federal Service Supply Bureaus. This chapter will deal exclusively with their real estate branch, known as the Federal Property Resources Service.

Many auction newcomers confuse these two distinct branches of the GSA. Some who wish mailing information about property fail to specify real estate or personal property. One may reach the wrong office and get the wrong mailing. This branch has offices in many, but not all, of the regions where personal property is sold.

Both have auctions. The Federal Property Resources Service (FPRS) only sells real estate. They have fewer auctions than their buddies in Federal Service Supply. FPRS also has less frequent mailings and a more complicated procedure for participating in these auctions.

Special Characteristics

As mentioned in Chapter 9, the GSA manages the government's civilian property as one of their major duties. That includes the buildings. When cut-

backs or obsolesence bring about the necessity to sell the buildings, the GSA is handed the baton. It could be a military base, postal facility, vacant land, or a single-family residence.

Because the General Services Administration is well known for having government auctions—remember, some think the GSA is the *only* player in the government auction game—they don't have a hard time attracting bidders. Also, they're under no pressure from congress to sell, sell, sell, as is the RTC. In fact, the FPRS branch is a quiet little bureau that hardly anyone ever hears about.

They don't have many auctions, nor have they many properties to sell. During a three-month period of 1991 only 55 properties were offered for auction, many by sealed bid. In that time period the GSA advertised the following:

19 residential properties (single-family homes, condominiums, estates)

A 1,440-acre ranch

Three apartment complexes

A housing complex with 37 acres and 77 buildings

Two farms

16 miles of railroad tracks (!)

Ten strip shopping centers in one package

13 commercial properties, including restaurants and a donut shop

Five former postal office buildings

13 parcels of land (one as large as 983 acres)

Two schools

A few warehouses

As you can see, the federal government has been busy spending taxpayer money. It's up to the GSA to get back every penny it can.

The GSA properties that finally do arrive at a public auction sale are first required to be offered to a host of other not-for-profit buyers, such as other federal agencies, state and local governments, and even public health and educational institutions. (Those wishing to participate in these programs should contact regional representatives of the Departments of Education and Health and Human Services.) Attempts will even be made to lease property until it is released for sale. Ordinary buyers are then offered properties that aren't snapped up by other government agencies or non-profit organizations.

According to a senior GSA spokesman, they aggressively demand fair-market value. Under the Federal Land Policy and Management Act of 1976, the GSA is required to retain federal lands or sell them at fair-market value. Being under no pressure to sell, it is simple to just say no when they don't get the desired price.

Procedures

To participate in a GSA public auction or sealed-bid sale for real estate, your first step is to obtain the quarterly catalog from the Federal Property Resources Service found in the directory. Telephone your nearest sales office. There are four regional offices and two field offices.

After you receive their quarterly catalog, locate any of the properties that may interest you. Telephone the sales office in which the property is located. For instance, you may currently reside in Ohio, but the desired property is located in Alaska. You would then telephone the San Francisco sales office, unless another telephone number is provided in the listing.

By making this second telephone call, you can receive a brochure, prospectus, or other details about the property. You will then have the date of the auction or deadline for sealed-bid submissions, as well as other necessary steps to follow.

One of the requirements of attending a GSA real estate auction or making a sealed bid is the deposit requirement. No bidder will be registered unless he or she arrives with a cashier's check made out for the minimum bid amount. This could be $50,000 or $500,000, depending on the property and the GSA's requirements. Sealed bids must be accompanied by a 10% deposit. So if you don't show up with a check, forget about placing a bid. You'll be lucky to be allowed admittance to the auction.

When purchase has been made you must come up with the balance of the funds by the deadline date, usually 30 days. The GSA will provide financing for you, depending on the price paid at auction. Of all sales, 90% are financed conventionally, while the GSA will carry the mortgage about 10% of the time. Mortgages held by the GSA have a ten-year maximum on them. And they expect you to pay a good price, even above fair-market value, before extending the financing.

While the GSA sells most of their properties at public or sealed-bid auctions, some real estate is occasionally sold through real estate brokers or by a negotiated sale. Complex industrial properties and other special-purpose properties require the services of qualified regional real estate broker organizations to find bona fide purchasers. Negotiated sales come about with properties that have a low fair-market value and make it impractical to advertise for competitive bids. In either event, the fastest way to find out about these properties would be to contact the regional GSA office nearest you, just as you would for upcoming auction sales.

Tips

For convenience sake, complete the application for one future real estate mailing that comes with the quarterly catalog. This GSA branch does not maintain a mailing list. If you wish to continue receiving the catalog, you must reapply each time.

On the application, specify the locations where you are interested in purchasing property. Each state has a four digit code you must fill in (example: Arizona–0004; Vermont–0050). You can choose up to three locations per application.

Also, there are four different types of property you can choose from:

1. Agriculture, timber, grazing, minerals
2. Commercial
3. Industrial
4. Residential

Just check the box(es) where your interest falls.
The application should be mailed to:

U.S. General Services Administration
(9KS)
525 Market Street
San Francisco, CA 94105

(Please note: There has been discussion and one report that the GSA will move to Oakland, California, in 1993, so there may soon be an address change.)

Evaluation

Don't even think of sneaking in a lowball bid with the GSA's Federal Property Resource Service. They have too many restrictions, allowing only buyers with a proven deposit to register and selling without stress. For years, many people haven't even heard of this division within the GSA. Few probably know how to buy from them.

At many GSA property auctions, only a handful of bidders show up. These are not the highly publicized Resolution Trust Corporation auctions or the United States Customs auctions. This agency is quiet and conservative and would like to keep it that way.

You may find a reasonable deal, but don't hope to score big if you're the only one who shows up. The GSA auctioneer will just stick to the reserve price and withdraw the property if your offer doesn't match or exceed it.

Property up for sale is not often glamorous. In some catalogs you might find some beachfront property, a few ranches, and larger estates. Mainly, the GSA offers old buildings, warehouses, unimproved land, and other forms of commercial property.

There is hope! During the rest of the 1990s, military bases are scheduled for closure. Large tracts of this land are expected to be sold in the coming years. Already developers are scheming to cash in. There may be some politics over which agency will sell off these military bases. If you're hoping to get an incredible bargain at these future land sales, pray that the Department of Defense, not the GSA, gets the nod to auction them.

GENERAL SERVICES ADMINISTRATION DIRECTORY

Regional Offices

BOSTON REAL ESTATE OFFICE

Office of Real Estate Sales
(2DR-1)
U.S. General Services
Administration
10 Causeway Street
Room 1079
Boston, MA 02222
(617) 565-5700

Oversees sales for these states:
Maine, New Hampshire,
Vermont, Massachusetts,
Rhode Island, Connecticut,
New York, New Jersey, Ohio,
Indiana, Michigan, Illinois,
Wisconsin, Minnesota, Puerto
Rico, and the Virgin Islands.

ATLANTA REAL ESTATE OFFICE

Office of Real Estate Sales
(4DR)
U.S. General Services
Administration
Peachtree Summit Building
401 West Peachtree Street
Atlanta, GA 30365-2550
(404) 331-5133

Oversees sales for these states:
Pennsylvania, Delaware,
Maryland, District of
Columbia, West Virginia,
Virginia, Kentucky, Tennessee,
North Carolina, South
Carolina, Georgia, Alabama,
Mississippi, and Florida.

FORT WORTH REAL ESTATE OFFICE

Office of Real Estate Sales
(7DR)
U.S. General Services
Administration
819 Taylor Street
Ft. Worth, TX 76102
(817) 334-2331

Oversees sales for these states:
Colorado, Montana, North
Dakota, South Dakota, Utah,
Wyoming, Kansas, Nebraska,
Arkansas, Louisiana,
Oklahoma, New Mexico, and
Texas

SAN FRANCISCO REAL ESTATE SALES OFFICE

Office of Real Estate Sales
(9DR)
525 Market Street
San Francisco, CA 94105
(415) 744-5952

Oversees sales for these states:
Alaska, Arizona, California,
Idaho, Nevada, Oregon,
Washington, Guam, and
Hawaii.

Field Offices

CHICAGO FIELD OFFICE

Office of Real Estate Sales
(2DRF-5)
U.S. General Services
Administration
230 South Dearborn Street
Room 3864, Mailstop 38-1
Chicago, IL 60604
(312) 353-6045

WASHINGTON FIELD OFFICE

Office of Real Estate Sales
(9DR-F)
U.S. General Services
Administration
GSA Center
Room 2422
Auburn, WA 98001
(206) 931-7547

26

Farmers Home Administration

★★★

The Farmers Home Administration (FmHA) was established in 1946 and is within the U.S. Department of Agriculture. As anyone in their state offices will tell you, it is in the business of lending money. It was designed to support and act as a lender to rural America, to get its feet back on the ground after World War II and not let that part of the economy revert to the Depression years.

Unfortunately, there are foreclosures. Few FmHA officials will wish to discuss their real estate auction program or their foreclosed properties. Telephone calls to these government agents could make you think Farmer Jones is waiting outside his door to blast the agent's brains out for repossessing his farm. It could eventually come to that.

Background

Right now, there are nearly 7,000 foreclosed properties in FmHA hands. If you are expecting to visit an FmHA-sponsored auction, don't make airplane reservations yet. In 1990, they sold only 15 properties through auctions. Currently, FmHA has about 1,000 properties that they have difficulty in selling.

Additionally, FmHA has lent farmers and others money against the collateral of farm machin-ery. Some of that has been repossessed during the foreclosure process and could be sold at auction. However, farm auctions have created ugly press for the FmHA, such as magazine photographs of a farmer crying over the loss of his land while a Snidely-Whiplash type smirks over having picked it up for 18 cents on the dollar.

The FmHA guidelines call for every backstop and assistance to prevent farmers and rural Americans from losing their properties. Before foreclosures occur, the debtor is given many chances to catch up on the back debt and to forestall the calling in of the loan. Moratoriums are issued. Loans are extended. But, sadly, foreclosures still happen. The economy and other obstacles don't allow pleasantries in the pastoral life. Foreclosures are a fact of life.

Washington has relegated farm properties onto a distant backburner where they are slowly reaching a boiling point. Someday soon, news from the heartland will again make headlines. Farmers will probably never forget the 1988 elections, where their early support for George Bush was crucial, and how foreclosure notices were delayed in being mailed to them until a few days after the November elections.

There is thought toward again holding farm foreclosed-property auctions. It may create more trouble than it is worth for the FmHA. However, having 7,000 properties sitting around ain't a pretty picture either.

Procedure

Practically the only way to buy an FmHA-foreclosed property is through a real estate broker. Just call one of the FmHA offices and ask for their list of real estate brokers.

State offices of the Farmers Home Administration are located in the directory at the end of this chapter. Call your local state office and give the agent the city or county where you wish to purchase property. The agent will refer you to the real estate broker showing that property.

Some offices may explain that the FmHA doesn't sell properties, they lend money. That's fine, just ask for the name of the real estate broker handling it. Some offices may put you on their mailing list and send you a flier about upcoming sales.

Other offices will advertise in the local papers. For example, the Arkansas FmHA office takes out, through their real estate broker, a series of three ads to sell the properties. Thirty days after the first ad has run, they will drop the price by 5% if it has not sold. Then, the price falls another 5% after 60 days if it remains on the market. After 90 days it drops another 5% to get it sold. Some properties just don't get sold.

The amount of available property varies greatly from state to state. Alaska, for example, has very few farms, so you won't find many repossessions. The Alabama office, when interviewed, said they had a moratorium on repossessing farms (as of September 1991), but did sell homes. They use the sealed-bid method as well as advertise in local papers.

"We Just Lend Money"

That's the refrain from the FmHA. Since this is what you will hear when you call, why not ask them to lend you some? You might try buying one of their foreclosed properties using the FmHA's money. There's plenty floating around, according to the heads of the FmHA state offices. If it is property with a house on the land, the loan procedure can be rushed through within 30 days.

Financing is available for lower, middle, and high income buyers. Interest rates are often about 1% below conventional mortgage rates. There are plans to start a guaranteed housing program, where a bank lends the money and the FmHA guarantees the loan (similar to loan guarantees by the Small Business Administration, FHA, and VA).

Evaluation

Life on the farm ain't sitting around chewing on hay. Farmers put in long days and work hard. On the other hand, this may be exactly what you're looking for.

Before jumping into this, there are a few basics you should know. Farm auctions are usually attended by long-established farmers who have made it a practice of absorbing retiring farmers. Fewer farmers have been starting up, which makes agribusiness a rather closed society. Most farm auctions are held absolute. Properties are often sold at auction to neighbors and friends; most farmland is purchased by those living within 25 miles of the auction site. Investors who do buy farmland at auction usually buy in depressed areas, where neighboring farmers are also hurting for cash and can't participate.

Buying from the FmHA requires going through a broker. The way to liven up those state agents is to let them know you want to borrow money to buy one of their foreclosed properties. That wakes them up.

Most of their properties are either farm or rural residential. The only problem with small towns or out-of-the-way places is finding work. Getting out of the country is what many there yearn for. These might be ideal places for the retired to purchase, especially if they are living on a pension.

Contact the state offices listed in the directory for further details.

FARMERS HOME ADMINISTRATION DIRECTORY
State Director List

Alabama

Dale N. Richey
Aronov Building, Room 717
Montgomery, AL 36104
(205) 832-7077

Alaska

Roger E. Willian
634 S. Bailey, Suite 103
Palmer, AK 99645
(907) 745-2176

Arizona

Clark R. Dierks
210 East Indianola
Suite 275
Phoenix, AZ 85012
(602) 640-5086

Arkansas

Robert L. Hankins
700 W. Capitol, P.O. Box 2778
Little Rock, AR 72203
(501) 324-6281

California—(Nevada)

Richard E. Mallory
194 West Main Street, Suite F
Woodland, CA 95695
(916) 666-3382

Colorado

Judy A. Jaklich
655 Parfet Street
Room E-100
Lakewood, CO 80219
(302) 697-0308

Connecticut

See Massachussets

Delaware—Maryland

G. Wallace Caulk
4611 S. Dupont Highway
P.O. Box 400
Camden, DE 19934
(302) 697-0308

Florida

L. James Cherry, Jr.
4440 NW 25th Place
P.O. Box 147010
Gainesville, FL 32614-7010
(904) 338-3400

Georgia

Thomas M. Harris
Stephens Federal Building
355 E. Hancock Avenue
Athens, GA 30610
(404) 546-2162

Hawaii

Daniel K.J. Lee
Federal Building, Room 311
154 Waianuenue Avenue
Hilo, HI 96720
(808) 961-4781

Idaho

Michael A. Field
3232 Elder Street
Boise, ID 83705
(208) 554-1301

Illinois

Jack L. Young
Illini Plaza, Suite 103
1817 S. Neil Street
Champaign, IL 61820
(217) 398-5235

Indiana

George Morton
5975 Lakeside Boulevard
Indianapolis, IN 46278
(317) 290-3100

Iowa

Robert R. Pim
Federal Building, Room 873
210 Walnut Street
Des Moines, IA 50309
(515) 284-4663

Kansas

John R. Price
1201 SW Summit
Executive Court
P.O. Box 4653
Topeka, KS 66683
(913) 295-2870

Kentucky

Mary Ann Baron
333 Waller Avenue
Lexington, KY 40504
(606) 233-2733

Louisiana

John C. McCarthy
3727 Government Street
Alexandria, LA 71302
(318) 473-7920

Maine

Nathaniel A. Churchill
444 Stillwater Avenue
Suite 2
P.O. Box 405
Bangor, ME 04402-0405
(207) 947-6160

Maryland

See Delaware

Massachusetts—Rhode Island—Connecticut

Theodore Fusaro
451 West Street
Amherst, MA 01002
(413) 253-3471

Michigan

Calvin C. Lutz
1405 South Harrison Road
Room 209
East Lansing, MI 48823
(517) 337-6631

Minnesota

Russ Bjorhus
Farm Credit Building
Room 410
375 Jackson Street
St. Paul, MN 55101
(612) 290-3842

Mississippi

James B. Huff, Sr.
Federal Building, Room 831
100 W. Capitol Street
Jackson, MS 39269
(601) 965-4316

Missouri

Douglas A. Elliott
601 Business Loop 70 West
Parkade Center, Suite 235
Columbia, MO 65203
(314) 876-0976

Montana

Eugene E. Coombs
900 Technology Boulevard
Suite B
P.O. Box 850
Boseman, MT 59771
(406) 585-9416

Nebraska

James L. Howe
Federal Building, Room 308
100 Centennial Mall N.
Lincoln, NE 685084
(402) 437-5551

Nevada

See California

(See Nevada Sub-State Office on last page of directory.)

New Hampshire

See Vermont

New Jersey

Takashi Moriuchi
Tarnsfield &
Woodlane Roads
Tarnsfield Plaza, Suite 22
Mt. Holly, NJ 08060
(609) 267-3090

New Mexico

Vivian G. Cordova
Federal Building, Room 3414
517 Gold Avenue SW
Albuquerque, NM 87102
(505) 766-2462

New York

Pierre L. Labourdette
James M. Hanley
Federal Building, Room 871
100 S. Clinton St.
P.O. Box 7318
Syracuse, NY 13261-7318
(315) 423-5290

North Carolina

Larry W. Godwin, Sr.
4402 Bland Road, Suite 260
Raleigh, NC 27607
(919) 790-2731

North Dakota

Marshall W. Moore
Federal Building, Room 208
Third & Rosser, P.O. Box 1737
Bismark, ND 58502
(701) 250-4781

Ohio

Allen L. Turnbull
Federal Building, Room 507
200 North High Street
Columbus, OH 43215
(614) 469-5606

Oklahoma

Ernest Hellwege
USDA Agricultural Center
Stillwater, OK 74074
(405) 624-4250

Oregon

Don Thompson
Federal Building, Room 1590
1220 SW 3rd Avenue
Portland, OR 97204
(503) 326-2731

Pennsylvania

D. Eugene Gayman
1 Credit Union Place
Suite 330
Harrisburg, PA 17108-2996
(503) 326-2731

Rhode Island

See Massachusetts

South Carolina

Nicholas P. Anagnost
Strom Thurmond Federal
Building
1835 Assembly Street
Columbia, SC 29201
(803) 765-5163

South Dakota

Marvis T. Hogen
Federal Building, Room 308
200 Fourth Street SW
Huron, SD 57350
(605) 353-1430

Tennessee

Randle Richardson
Federal Building
U.S. Courthouse, Room 538
Nashville, TN 37203
(615) 736-7341

Texas

Neal Sox Johnson
Federal Building, Suite 102
101 South Main
Temple, TX 76501
(817) 774-1301

Utah

E. Lee Hawkes
Federal Building, Room 5438
125 S. State Street
Salt Lake City, UT 84138

Vermont—
New Hampshire—V.I.

Bernice R. Murray
141 Main Street
Montpelier, VT 05602
(802) 223-2371

Virginia

Lloyd A. Jones
400 N. 8th Street
Richmond, VA 23240
(804) 771-2451

Washington

Earl F. Tilley
Federal Building, 319
P.O. Box 2427
Wenatchee, WA 98807
(509) 662-4352

West Virginia

John C. Musgrave
P.O. Box 678
75 High Street
Morgantown, WV 26505
(304) 291-4791

Wisconsin

Donald W. Caldwell
1257 Main Street
Stevens Point, WI 54481
(715) 341-5900

Wyoming

Michael F. Ormsby
Federal Building, Room 1005
P.O. Box 820
100 East B Street
Casper, WY 82602
(307) 261-5271

Nevada Sub-State Office

Sub-State Director

Roger Van Valkenburg
1179 Fairview Drive, Suite C
Carson City, WV 89701
(702) 887-1222

27

Bureau of Land Management

★★

Under the U.S. Department of the Interior is the Bureau of Land Management (BLM). One of the BLM's functions is to dispose of public lands that, as a result of planning, either are no longer needed for the purpose they were acquired for in the first place or are no longer economical to manage. Their official position for selling such land is that "it would serve an important public objective." Like what? Well, again, their position is: "such as expansion of communities and economic development." For whom? Developers who can buy U.S. government land for a good price?

One can get thoroughly confused in dealing with the BLM. Much of the information you will receive is out-of-date. Some of their "current" literature I checked had disconnected telephone numbers. Unless you ask about one particular aspect of what this bureau handles, you might draw a blank on the other end of the line.

Background

BLM sales are rarely publicized, are hard to find out about, and leave one with nagging questions about how closely their practices follow their procedures. A few telephone calls to the BLM state offices will tell you that there is no coordinated Bureau of Land Management. At best it is disjointed. When calling state offices of the BLM, you may be told that the BLM no longer sells land.

Another may inform you that there are no auctions.

However, in 1990 more than 8,212 acres of public land were sold for about $7.6 million. That is a little more than $900 an acre. How were they sold? Who bought them? Finding answers might take lengthy investigations, since many of the BLM state officials can't recall ever having sold land. One BLM official from Alaska informed me that they hadn't sold land since 1983; BLM donates it to the state.

Other research proved equally futile. Trying to pry ordinary data from the BLM is about as frustrating as interrogating a parrot. This information is being provided to you as a warning about what you may come against when you telephone this government agency.

Procedures

The Bureau of Land Management does sell land. In 1990, the Arizona state office sold six acres. California's state office sold 2,892 acres. Most of the land in the next few years will probably be sold in Nevada because the Department of the Interior has ordered land sold. Nevada was chosen, probably, because of its growing economy and because housing prices have surged there recently.

The BLM does hold land auctions. Prices are attractive and auctions are generally attended by local property owners who want to increase their landholdings. Auctions are advertised in the local papers. If a property is very attractive, then it may also be advertised in a nearby larger-circulation newspaper.

Normally, sealed bids are accepted by the local BLM office on the advertised land. It may go to auction *after* sealed bids have been received (a tactic to get a better price by having several high sealed bids compete against each other). No real estate brokers are used by BLM. If your bid wins, you pay 20% down and have 180 days to raise the balance.

Oil and Gas Leases

Oil and gas leases are available through some BLM offices. The Montana, New Mexico, and California BLM offices offer oil and gas leases. Some others may also offer leases during 1992 and 1993. These are sold by auction. There are fees to participate:

1. Pay a $10.00 fee to get on the mailing list. You will be mailed a flier that announces upcoming auctions.

2. There is a $75 administrative fee if your bid wins.

3. There is a $2 bonus bid per acre.

4. If your bid wins, you pay a $1.50/acre rental fee in advance.

Your minimum bid would then be at least $3.50/acre. It takes about one week to finish the transaction and get the papers for your lease. The lease duration is for five years.

Mining Act of 1872

Would-be prospectors may enjoy getting the opportunity to file a mining claim offered by the Bureau of Land Management. (Remember Charlie Chaplin's classic movie, *Gold Rush?*) Passed by congress in 1872, this law is still in effect. Americans have the right to mine public land.

In early 1989, the U.S. General Accounting Office released a report showing that some individuals and companies had taken advantage of this law. Despite loud barking in the media and congressional furor over the giveaways, no changes ever came about. Here are a few of the many deals some found through the Bureau of Land Management's 1872 Mining Law Program:

1. 160 acres near a world-class Colorado ski resort, purchased for $400 in 1983 and now worth $1.6 million

2. 19 acres inside the Phoenix city limits sold by the BLM for $47 in 1987 are now worth more than $300,000

3. 34 acres near Yosemite National Park bought for $170 in 1985 and now valued at over $500,000

4. 319 acres bought near mountain resorts outside Las Vegas for only $775 are now worth over $1 million.

In a study of 20 transactions made over a ten-year period, it was found that over $48 million in public land was sold for about $4,500! Congress found out about it when the BLM was ready to sell another $47 million worth of land for $16,000! No wonder the BLM doesn't like to give many details on the telephone!

Using the Mining Act of 1872

To utilize this law you have to apply for a mineral patent, which gives you the exclusive title to the locatable minerals beneath the land. In most cases, you also get title to the surface and other resources. The one bug on buying the land, as poetically described by one BLM official, is this: "No livin', no lovin', just minin'." You cannot build on this land and you must sign an affidavit that mining is all you will do on it.

The Mining Law does not apply to government-owned land in these three states: Texas, Oklahoma, and Kansas.

There are also a number of procedures that must first be followed before you can patent the claim (get exclusive rights to the land):

1. You must discover a valuable mineral deposit that meets certain criteria. Gravel, clay, sand, and such don't qualify. Lead and asbestos do! So does gold, silver, and copper.

2. The claim must be surveyed by a BLM-approved mineral surveyor.

3. You must post a "notice of intent to patent" on the claim site and publish this notice in a local newspaper for a 60-day period.

4. You must pay the BLM a nonrefundable $250 filing fee per application and an additional $50 filing fee per additional claim/site in the application.

5. You must show the BLM evidence of a right of title to the claim or site and prove that no one else got there first or is living on it.

6. You are required to show the BLM proof of discovery of a valuable mineral deposit.

7. You must show the BLM proof that not less than $500 worth of development work has been done to benefit each claim or site.

Then, upon completion of all that, you can buy acreage. Lode claims (on a proven mineral vein) are sold at $5/acre; placer claims (near a mineral vein) at $2.50/acre. Annually, you must pay $100 to BLM and a $5.00 administrative fee. A federal mineral inspector will examine your application and the claim or site to verify your claim. Expect an annual inspection to demonstrate that you are actively working the claim.

To intelligently participate in patenting a claim, you will have to familiarize yourself with topographic maps, which are available from the Department of the Interior's U.S. Geological Survey (USGS). The central source of these maps and other related materials is:

Earth Science Information Center
U.S. Geological Survey
National Center
Reston, Virginia 22092

Maps and reports are available for purchase from:

U.S. Geological Survey
Branch of Distribution
Box 25286
Federal Center
Denver, CO 80225

You should also familiarize yourself with specific mineral commodities, as well as mining and milling techniques. Contact this government agency for important information:

U.S. Bureau of Mines
Office of Public Information
Washington, DC 20241

There is further information available from a Geological Survey and Bureau of Mines cooperative effort. Write to this office for technical assistance about mineral deposits, mining, and prospecting:

Minerals Information Office
Department of the Interior
18th and C Streets, NW
Washington, DC 20240

You can also contact the Commissioner of Public Lands in the state where you wish to patent a mining claim. Write to the commissioner care of that state in its state capital about state geological surveys and state mining laws and regulations.

Evaluation

The BLM does have auctions. It does sell land. And it does lease oil and gas lands. If you run into problems contacting the state offices in the directory that follows, tell them I told you the above is true. It may not be true at every office at every moment in the future. But, it is true now at some offices. Don't say I didn't warn you about their confusion(s). Give them a hoot using the directory that follows.

BUREAU OF LAND MANAGEMENT DIRECTORY

Alaska

Anchorage Federal Bldg.
22 W. 7th Avenue #3
Anchorage, AK 99513-7599
(907) 271-5555

California

Federal Office Bldg.
2800 Cottage Way,
Rm. E 2841
Sacramento, CA 95825
(916) 978-4754

Colorado

2850 Youngfield Street
Lakewood, CO 80215
(303) 239-3600

Idaho

3380 Americana Terrace
Boise, ID 83706
(208) 334-3000

Montana, North Dakota & South Dakota

Granite Tower
222 N. 32nd Street
P.O. Box 36800
Billings, MT 59107
(406) 255-2913

Nevada

850 Harvard Way
P.O. Box 12000
Reno, NV 89520-0006
(702) 785-6400

New Mexico, Oklahoma, Texas & Kansas

Joseph M. Montoya Federal Bldg.
South Federal Place
P.O. Box 1449
Santa Fe, NM 87504-1449
(505) 988-6000

Oregon & Washington

1300 N.E. 44th Street
P.O. Box 2965
Portland, OR 97208
(503) 280-7002

Utah

Consolidated Financial Center
Suite 301
324 South State Street
Salt Lake City, UT 84111-2303
(801) 539-4001

Wyoming & Nebraska

2515 Warren Avenue (82001)
P.O. Box 1828
Cheyenne, WY 82003
(307) 775-6256

Eastern States Office (All other states)

350 S. Pickett Street
Alexandria, VA 22304
(703) 461-1400

28

Probate and Estate Auctions

★★★

When someone dies, a judge must decide whether or not the deceased's last will and testament is valid. The court procedure to determine such validity, and subsequently the disposal of the estate, takes place in the state's probate court. Some states call it by another name. For example, New York has a surrogate's court that carries out this function. Maryland and Pennsylvania have orphan's courts instead of a probate court.

The probate court reviews the entire estate and the judge frequently has a "subject to court confirmation" duty to perform in approving sales. An executor (executrix if a woman) is named in the will to carry out the instructions of the will. He or she would dispose of the deceased's property in an orderly fashion, pay inheritance taxes, and settle the debts of the deceased.

At some point the executor will hire an auctioneer, usually through the advice or assistance of the estate's attorney, and dispose of the property. Such an auction will be known as an estate sale. Auctioneers compete for these types of auctions. They are extremely profitable for the auctioneer and broadly pursued by many.

Other types of estate sales do not fall under government jurisdiction. They might come about because of a divorce, retirement, or relocation. Relocation auctions were popular in colonial America and well into the 19th century as pio-neers headed westward. Waves of immigrants were able to buy property at bargain prices and get a fresh start in the New World. The same holds true today.

Background

Estate auctions contain a mixture of real estate and other personal property. The centerpiece of the estate sale is usually the real estate, unless a buyer was found prior to the auction. You will often find one or more automobiles, a house, furniture, collectibles, and small equipment.

Of course, where the decedent left a large property inheritance, you will find an abundance of fine art, one of a kind catches, antiques, luxury property, coin collections, and other evidences of prosperity. The size and contents of an estate sale are entirely dependent on the wealth of the deceased.

Auctioneers may combine several properties to get a bigger turnout. Doing this can mean more advertising dollars for promotions and a greater selection to choose from. Some of these composite estate sales might occur as personal property (fine art, collectibles, antiques) is presented at local auction storefronts. Property is turned over to the auction company on a consignment basis. Some offer good deals.

Special Characteristics

Estate sales, while offering an assortment of personal property, count on the real estate to bring in the lion's share of the auction take. The feature may be the house or some other important collection: coins, antiques, or art. It depends on how the auctioneer markets that auction.

Real estate will bring a fair price, and going directly to the auction might not bring you the best bargain. Usually, the property sale requires a court confirmation. The judge will ask for appraisals and often demand that property is sold within 10% of fair-market value. Since real estate comprises the bulk of the estate sale, it will be more closely scrutinized.

Your best bet at an estate auction is to buy the real estate *before* the sale date. Use the negotiated-sale method in dealing with the auctioneer or the estate's attorney.

Tips

Contact the auctioneers found in your area in the directory that follows. Get your name on their mailing lists for upcoming estate sales. They'll be happy to have you aboard.

When you receive their auctions fliers, look carefully at the auction flier for out-of-context items. While the feature may be the house or some collection, search for the items that appear as also-rans. You won't find photographs of these.

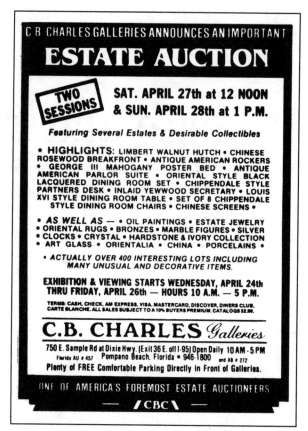
These auction items are afterthoughts, included by the auctioneer just to show you the large inventory available at the auction.

Most bidders will show up for the sizzle. Auctioneers will count on the centerpiece to bring home the bacon. That's where the high bidding will occur. Such features often get bidders into a frenzy and that means the winning price will be too high.

If you locate something in the auction flier that appeals to you, then call the auctioneer and find out more about the out-of-context item. Is it in good condition? Is this merchandise the kind or model type you want? Squeeze him for details before wasting your time at the auction. You might have to jog his memory. Remember, this isn't the big item at the auction so he may not recall much about it.

Those are the items you should buy at estate sales. Stay away from the featured items. You'll get good prices by looking for the out-of-context merchandise.

Another Strategy

Some will consider this too gross to bother with. Those who use this method make out like bandits. In the movie, *War of the Roses,* starring Michael Douglas and Kathleen Turner, Mrs. Rose bought her dream house by accidentally visiting a relative of the recently departed. The next-of-kin sold it for a song.

Other people use a variation of that type of visit. They read the obituaries. This strategy calls for visiting or telephoning the surviving spouse and offering to purchase their property. (I warned you that this sounds gross.) It's a form of negotiated sale prior to the execution of the will.

One budding taxi-cab entrepreneur buys his cars this way. Especially when purchasing from the elderly, you really are buying from "that little old lady who only drove her car on Sunday." Often, the person will want to sell to extinguish the memory of the deceased. Few will be tough negotiators, so you can find a good deal this way.

More Tips

Waiting until the estate sale is promoted by the auctioneer may not bring the best bargain. If using the previous strategy does not appeal to you, do what auctioneers do. They contact probate (or surrogate) court judges, court staff, estate attorneys, law office employees, and court clerks to find out about upcoming property dispositions. You can also do this.

It requires telephone work, leg work, and time. However, contacting these people can lead you to the auctioneer before the auction takes place. Or it can get you in the front door before the auctioneer.

After you've gotten this far, make a negotiated sale offer. Name your price directly to the estate's attorney or the auctioneer. They may take it immediately. If the offer is refused, come back to them before the auction. Stagefright jitters hits everyone, including auctioneers. If the marketing hasn't been done well, or should the auctioneer perceive a "thin market" (where few bidders will attend), he may jump on your offer.

If the property hasn't been accurately appraised or there is demand by the seller to quickly raise cash, you can purchase property at a large discount. Savings can go as high as 40% below market value. If you can buy it for 15%–20% below the area's going price, then consider you've done well.

You can use this method up to the day before the auction. How many auctions have a poor turnout? That depends on geography and market conditions. Sometimes, you can make a negotiated sale right off the auction flier.

Again, you may not be permitted to purchase the real estate using this method. There may be complications. That should not stop you from trying to purchase the other personal property. It may just be fodder, and the auctioneer could be willing to dispose of it cheaply. Make him an offer to take it off his hands.

Evaluation

Usually, when someone dies, the survivor is caught in a scramble to raise cash for the estate taxes. This creates a forced-sale atmosphere. And that is when you can find a great bargain, whether it is real estate or a vehicle. Often, potential inheritors have been found to be waiting for Aunt Sally to depart this world. When she finally does, they are just as frustrated by the long, arduous probate procedure. Add to this a soft economy in many parts of the country, and you can find a good real estate deal, or bargains in merchandise and collectibles.

Selling the deceased's house is common. Often the widow will want a smaller property or condo in a retirement area. Tax problems increase the incentive to sell quickly. Negotiated sales are highly recommended, either directly with the survivor, with the estate's attorney, or the auctioneer. Of the three, I would avoid the estate's attorney. Most are stuffed shirts and take too long to make a decision.

Contact the auctioneers in the directory that follows. If you wish, use the other methods described in this chapter.

PROBATE AND ESTATE AUCTIONS DIRECTORY

In this directory you will find auctioneers who have been found to frequently hold estate auctions. Attorneys and executors of estates hire them. They may specialize in other areas of auctioneering.

There may be additional auctioneers in your area who have been omitted. Every effort has been made to provide you with adequate auctioneer contacts to get you started.

NOTE: "CAI" after an auctioneer's name indicates that he/she is certified by the Certified Auctioneers Institute.

Probate-Estate/ Household Auctioneers

Alabama

Behel, Don, CAI
Don Behel Realty &
Auctions, Inc.
Rt. 4, Box 505
Killen, AL 35645
(205) 757-4100
FAX (205) 757-4087

Brown, Richard
7595 Hwy. 72 W.
Madison, AL 35758
(205) 837-6229
FAX (205) 830-9653

Farmer, David
Farmco Auctioneers &
Liquidators
P.O. Box 1725
Albertville, AL 35950
(800) 445-4608

Faulkner, William F.
2222 E. Arbor Dr.
Huntsville, AL 35811

Holland, Daniel R., CAI
Holland Realty & Auctions
Rt. 3, Box 416
Rogersville, AL 35652

Knotts, Edward V., CAI
Knotts R.E. & Auction Co.
411 E. 2nd St.
Sheffield, AL 35660
(205) 386-7048
FAX (205) 386-0110

Montgomery, John H.
613 Memorial Dr. SW
Decatur, AL 35601
(205) 350-6959

Perrin, Joyce L.
Vintage Auctions
Rt. 1, Box 388C
Guntersville, AL 35976
(205) 586-5784

Alaska

Kingston, Kathleen A.
Kingston's Auction Co.
P.O. Box 101614
Anchorage, AK 99510-1614
(907) 345-6413
FAX (907) 276-8357

Arizona

Hatcher, Dayle F.
Auction Realty USA
6201 E. Justine Rd.
Scottsdale, AZ 85254-1946
(602) 483-1467
FAX (602) 948-1403

Hiple, Timothy
American West Auction, Inc.
HCR Box 4640
Benson, AZ 85602
(602) 586-2859
FAX (602) 325-2608

Kane, C.R. Kip
SW R.E. Auctioneers
1121 E. Missouri, #100
Phoenix, AZ 85014-2723
(602) 263-0050
FAX (602) 263-0085

Knuth, Dan
41656 Rattlesnake Rd.
Queen Creek, AZ 85242
(602) 987-9083

Arkansas

Adams, Wayne
P.O. Box 130
Bradley, AR 71826
(501) 894-6300

Grady, Sr., Kenneth G.
P.O. Box 59
Tuckerman, AR 72473
(501) 349-5106
FAX (501) 349-5150

Guthery, Donnie
20th Century Collectibles
Rt. 8, Box 236
Fayetteville, AR 72701
(501) 839-3274

Herrmann, Clay
Rt. 7, P.O. Box 233
Hot Springs, AR 71901
(501) 623-0107

Looper, Jimmy L.
RR #1, Box 298A
Greenwood, AR 72936
(501) 996-4401

Shepard, James
RR #1, Box 301
Corning, AR 72422
(501) 276-5351

Shoe, Alvin
Box 97
Delaplaine, AR 72425
(501) 249-3207

Stafford, David K.
Rt. 1, P.O. Box 1317
Donaldson, AR 71941
(501) 384-5352

Sullivan, Connie P.
Connie Sullivan Auction Co.
15610 Viney Woods Rd.
Mabelvale, AR 72103
(501) 847-8545

Wilson, Lonnie C.
P.O. Box 2507
Alma, AR 72921
(501) 474-9100

Wooley, Brad H., CAI
Brad H. Wooley Auction Inc.
9 Lombardy Lane
Little Rock, AR 72207
(501) 664-3826
FAX (501) 664-3826

California

Brockman, Morris
545 E. Main St.
Stockton, CA 95202
(209) 465-3182

Cardoza, John A., CAI
1288 W. 11th St. Ste. 286
Tracy, CA 95376
(209) 832-0260

Chezan, Emanuel J.
J. M. & B. Antiques
Auction Sales
545 E. Main
Stockton, CA 95202
(709) 465-3182

Cooper, Jan
Box 18
North Highlands, CA 95660
(916) 331-0904

Dorfman, Joseph
1730 Bodega Ave.
Petaluma, CA 94952
(707) 765-1944

Fendley, John
410 El Noka La.
Santa Rosa, CA 95409
(707) 538-5424

Fern, Don
1718 N. McClelland
Santa Maria, CA 93454
(805) 922-2522

Hitchcock, Greg
5151 Robin Wood Rd. #21
Bonita, CA 92002
(619) 472-5278

Horton Jr., Bobby A.
All American Auction
7546 Meadowair Way
Sacramento, CA 95822
(916) 455-3741
FAX (916) 455-7457

Johnston, Bob
3830 E. Sussex Way
Fresno, CA 93726
(209) 226-6549

Root, Evan
P.O. Box 504
Woodbridge, CA 95258
(209) 369-2521

Speight, Carl
P.O. Box 62974
Los Angeles, CA 90062
(213) 281-8456

Williams, Frank J.
United Auction Services
P.O. Box 107
Crescent Mills, CA 95934
(916) 284-6176
FAX (916) 284-6178

Colorado

Johnson, Robert L.
2535 E. Hwy. 34
Greeley, CO 80631
(303) 356-2998

Kleinsteiber, Robert E.
903 Platte Drive
Ft. Lupton, CO 80621
(303) 857-6093

Van Berg, E.S.
P.O. Box 647
Sterling, CO 80751
(303) 522-1950

Connecticut

Kaoud, Isam F.
27 Danbury Rd. Rt. 7
Wilton, CT 06897
(203) 762-0376

Schafer, David J.
82 Bradley Rd.
Madison, CT 06443
(203) 245-4173

Zetomer, Arthur
Park City Auction Service
P.O. Box 6314
Bridgeport, CT 06604
(203) 333-5251

Delaware

Kring, Jeffry C.
Jeffry C. Kring Auctioneer
P.O. Box 5602
Newark, DE 19714-5602
(302) 738-6968

Perialas Jr., James P.
29 Tiverton
Newark, DE 19702
(302) 454-1699

Pope, James C.
P.O. Box 81
Lewes, DE 19958
(302) 645-7722
FAX (302) 645-7718

District of Columbia

Evans, W. Ronald, CAI
Capitol City Enterprises Ltd.
407 H St. NE

Washington, D.C. 20002
(202) 543-2828
FAX (202) 547-2545

Florida

Arey, Chester M., CAI
Arey's Auction Team, Inc.
P.O. Box 1953
Deland, FL 32721-1953
(904) 738-0050

Banks, William S.
Banks Auction
2577 SE Madison St.
Stuart, FL 34997
(407) 287-5334
FAX (407) 287-1570

Bateman, F.F. (Ted)
Bateman & Associates
P.O. Box 427
Valrico, FL 33594
(800) 676-0987

Blecha, Wayne H.
P.O. Box 999
Paisley, FL 32767-0999
(407) 889-0842

Brandendurger, Paul W.
2959 Mercury Rd.
Jacksonville, FL
32207-7912
(904) 730-2911
FAX (904) 730-2911

Cappella, Joseph A.
404 W. Lantana Rd.
Lantana, FL 33462
(407) 585-5512
FAX (407) 585-6888

Chana, Kurt E.
413 Willow Brook
Longwood, FL 32779
(407) 869-8519

Clifford, Donna C.
Auctions & Sales by Donna
751 Baldwin Rd.
Palm Harbor, FL 34683
(813) 786-3858

Coakley, John W.
540 E. Compton Court
Deland, FL 32724
(904) 738-7974

Coburn, Joe E.
7545 N. Palm Oak Dr.
Hernando, FL 32642
(904) 344-5818

Criswell, Bob
5616 Sailfish Drive
Lutz, FL 33549
(813) 265-3811

Dell, Lewis C.
Dell's Auction Service
204 Old Monroe Rd.
Sanford, FL 32771
(407) 323-5620

Eggleston, Bernie
Eggleston Auctioneers
4601 W. Kennedy Blvd.
Ste 214
Tampa, FL 33609
(813) 282-0057

Elting, Robert W.
Action Auctioneers
11023 Desota Rd.
Riverview, FL 33569

Fullom, Cliff K.
Land & Sea Auctions, Inc.
P.O. Box 1062
Marathon, FL 33050
(800) 654-1889

Gould, David M.
6600 SW 122 St.
Miami, FL 33156
(305) 284-8129

Haworth, Richard L.
Venice Auction
601 Spur St.
Venice, FL 34292
(813) 485-4964

Hennessee, Rob
6835 Maple Lane
Tampa, FL 33610
(813) 626-2341
FAX (813) 626-2341

Higgenbotham, Martin, CAI
Higgenbotham Realty, Inc.
1666 Williamsburg Square
Lakeland, FL 33803
(813) 644-6681

Janacek, Rod
Janacek Auctioneers
P.O. Box 475
Fort White, FL 32038
(904) 497-1509

Johnson, Ray
701 S. Bumbey Ave.
Orlando, FL 32806
(407) 896-1399

Kelsey, Thomas C.
530 Timber Ridge Dr.
Pensacola, FL 32534
(904) 968-5185

King, Hellen B.
AAPT Realty Inc.
7800 N. Carl G. Rose Hwy.
Hernando, FL 32642-2102
(904) 726-0275
FAX (904) 726-0235

Knieriem, James B.
1414 60th St. S
Gulf Port, FL 33707
(813) 341-0006

Kratschman, Joseph C.
26 Lone Oak Rd.
Spring Hill, FL 34610
(904) 799-7102

Marcovitch, Allen J.
Anaheim Realty & Auctions
1155 SW 25th Ave.
Boynton Beach, FL 33426
(407) 734-8029

Melburg, Charles D.
4306 Devonshire Lane
Orlando, FL 32812
(407) 898-3975

Messer, Ed
AAPT Realty, Inc.
7800 N. Carl G. Rose Hwy.
Hernando, FL
32642-2102
(904) 726-0275
FAX (904) 726-0235

Myers, Lenny A.
Myers, Richard L., CAI
Myers Real Estate
Auction Service
P.O. Box 2062
Winter Park, FL 32790-2062
(407) 644-7295
FAX (407) 644-7380

Neiswander, John, CAI
5115 N. Socrum Loop Rd.
#43
Lakeland, FL 33809-4213
(813) 859-7633

New, Gary C.
Auction Associates Inc.
4823 Silver Star Rd., Ste. 160
Orlando, FL 32808
(407) 297-7695
FAX (407) 297-7695

Parfitt, Patricia S.
7611 S. Orange Blossom
Terr. #315
Orlando, FL 32809
(813) 644-6681
FAX (813) 644-6686

Regenhold, Rick H.
Regenhold Auctions
611 S. Myrtle Ave, Ste B
Clearwater, FL 34616
(813) 461-1666

Smith, Charles
The Place For Real
Estate, Inc.
2 E. Camino Real
Boca Raton, FL 33432
(407) 383-6570

Speal, Jr., Frank
Frank's Antiques
P.O. Box 516
Hilliard, FL 32046
(904) 845-2870

Strait, Harold
4159 Hidden Branch Dr. N.
Jacksonville, FL 32257
(904) 260-0516

Watts, Alley D.
Pioneer Antique Gallery &
Auction
10909-13A Atlantic Blvd.
Jacksonville, FL 32211
(904) 641-6000
FAX (904) 641-6116

Williams, Dixie L.
8329 Allen Drive
Brooksville, FL 34613
(904) 596-4801

Williams, Phyllis
Phyllis Williams
Auction Co.
15361 Thornton Rd.
Fort Myers, FL 33908
(813) 481-5003

Williams, Richard M.
1556 Highway 97 S.
Cantonment, FL 32533
(904) 623-0141

Georgia

Ansley, Hershel P.
Ansley Realty
323-B E. Jackson St.
Thomasville, GA 31792
(912) 228-4456

Barfield, Maurice, CAI
Southeastern Auction Inc.
Rt. 2, P.O. Box 323
Doerun, GA 31744
(812) 985-5700

Childs, Billy J., CAI
Hudson & Marshall, Inc.
717 North Avenue
Macon, GA 31298
(800) 841-9400
FAX (912) 743-6110

Hudson Jr., B.G.
Hudson & Marshall Inc.
717 North Avenue
Macon, GA 31298
(800) 841-9400
FAX (912) 743-6110

Kibler, Rodney
Kibler Auctions
9020 Vanns Tavern Rd.
Gainesville, GA 30506
(404) 781-8369

Lanes, Larry
Brent Lane & Associates Inc.
717 North Avenue
Macon, GA 31298
(912) 743-8120
FAX (912) 742-3877

Marshall III, Asa M., CAI
Hudson & Marshall Inc.
717 North Avenue
Macon, GA 31298
(912) 743-1511

Marshall IV, Asa M.
Hudson & Marshall Inc.
717 North Avenue
Macon, GA 31298
(912) 743-1511

Rich, Ed
6538 Heardsville Rd.
Cumming, GA 30130
(404) 887-4141

Strickland, John S., CAI
Strickland Realty & Auction
P.O. Box 429
Moultrie, GA 31776
(912) 985-7730

Suarez, John
Barbara & John Suarez
Auctioneers & Appraisers
1980 S. Walkers Mill Rd.
Orchard Hill, GA 30266-0349
(800) 446-7874
FAX (404) 227-0873

Sutton, William F., CAI
717 North Avenue
Macon, GA 31298
(912) 743-1511
FAX (912) 743-6110

Toles, Bobby J.
Atlas Auction Co.
617 Shorter Avenue
Rome, GA 30161
(800) 992-2155
FAX (404) 235-5571

Hawaii

Adolfi, Jr., Frank J.
1427 Akamai Place
Kailua, HI 96734
(808) 262-7730

Idaho

Kuhnen, William
11269 Lake Hazel Rd
Boise, ID 83709
(208) 362-0871

Lockhert, Bob
1407 Powers
Lewiston, ID 83510
(208) 743-7886

Ralls, Ronald R.
11985 S. Cloverdale
Kuna, ID 83634
(208) 362-5132

Illinois

Beck, William B.
RR #2, Box 259
Edinburg, IL 62531
(217) 325-3351
FAX (217) 325-3313

Bickers, Michael W.
Auction Liquidators
420 W. State
Charleston, IL 61920
(217) 348-0288

Boyd, Rondel L.
P.O. Box 160
Oblong, IL 62449
(618) 592-4233

Burke, Don S.
RR 2, Box 191
McLeansboro, IL 62859
(618) 643-4527

Clingan, Jim
P.O. Box 52
Royal, IL 61871
(217) 582-2868
FAX (217) 582-2861

Croisant, Darwin L.
3727 Rt. 251 S.
Mendota, IL 61342
(815) 539-7903

Decker, William, CAI
Decker Realtor Auctioneer
Rt. 2, Box 29
Milford, IL 60953
(815) 889-4213
FAX (815) 889-4113

Draper, Robert D.
#1 Draper Lane
Ohio, IL 61349
(815) 376-2001

Gaule, William L., CAI
114 E. Walnut
Chatham, IL 62629
(217) 483-2484
FAX (217) 483-2485

Geer, Roberta L.
55 White Oak Circle
St. Charles, IL 60174
(708) 377-4625
FAX (708) 377-4680

Gregory, Stan
Alexis Realty
RR 1
Alexis, IL 61412
(309) 482-5575

Hannam, Rolland R.
805 E. 2nd St.
Galesburg, IL 61401-6115
(309) 342-5494

Hayunga, Phil
4482 Lamm Rd.
Freeport, IL 61032
(815) 235-2323

Holley, Otis D.
Barliant Auction Co.
4701 W. Augusta Blvd.
Chicago, IL 60651
(312) 378-7171
FAX (312) 378-5285

Honnold, Carl E.
14 N. Central
P.O. Box 44
Casey, IL 62420
(217) 932-4015

Housh, Chuck Jr.
Route 1, Box 265
Monee, IL 60449
(312) 534-5090

Jeffries, Timothy J.
2642 Vermont St.
Quincy, IL 62301
(217) 223-0017

Kaestner, Edgar A.
404 W. Main St.
Valmeyer, IL 62295
(618) 935-2234

Lane, Leon
316 E. Harrison
Sullivan, IL 61951
(217) 728-7132

Lenhart, Doyne, CAI
Rt. 2, Box 12
Georgetown, IL 61846
(217) 662-8644
FAX (217) 662-2484

Lenzen, Frederick W.
Rt. 1, Box 23
Grays Lake, IL 60030
(708) 546-0077

Luke, Joy
Joy Luke Fine Arts
Broker & Auctions
300 E. Grove St.
Bloomington, IL 61701
(309) 828-5533

McAnly, Howard
P.O. Box 602
Rochelle, IL 61068
(815) 562-6957

Newton, John L.
P.O. Box 1412, Hwy 45N
Vienna, IL 62995
(618) 658-3141

Ollis, Joe D.
Joe Ollis Auction Service
Rt. 4, Box 293
Marion, IL 62959
(618) 964-1431

Parker, Gregory O., CAI
Dunnings Auction Service
755 Church Rd.
Elgin, IL 60123-9302
(708) 741-3483
FAX (708) 741-3589

Plocar, Joseph M.
Antique Enterprises Inc.
203 N. Water St.
Wilmington, IL 60481
(815) 476-9020

Reid, Keith
Box 99
Albion, IL 62806
(618) 445-2233

Rossen, Jerry
Jerry Rossen Auction Service
1013 Mildred
University Park, IL 60466
(708) 534-1510

Roth, Jim, CAI
Rt. 5, E
Peoria, IL 61611
(309) 266-6784

Swanson, Swanie, CAI
144 E. Church St.
Sandwich, IL 60548
(815) 786-2363

Swing Jr., Paul L.
RR #1, Box 362
Lawrenceville, IL 62439
(618) 943-2794

Indiana

Abernathy, Terry C., CAI
Abernathy Auction &
Real Estate
21 W. Union St.
Liberty, IN 47353
(317) 458-5826

Baber, Steven J.
SJB Associates Inc.
P.O. Box 599
New Palestine, IN 46163
(317) 861-4495

Bayman, James D.
P.O. Box 497
South Whitley, IN 46787
(219) 723-4055

Butts, Virgil W., CAI
600 W. National Ave.
Brazil, IN 47834
(812) 446-2322
FAX (812) 446-2322

Campbell, Harold L.
57105 Country Rd. 21
Goshen, IN 46526
(219) 294-1328

Crum, Lincoln
Crum's Auction & Realty
4909 Hamburg Pike
Jeffersonville, IN 47130
(812) 282-6043

Curtis, Terry W., CAI
6218 Conservation Dr.
Jeffersonville, IN 47130
(812) 283-8586

Ellenberger, Robert, CAI
130½ W. Market St.
Bluffton, IN 46714
(219) 824-2426
FAX (219) 824-1728

Evans, Larry
Rt. 1, Box 223
Mentone, IN 46539
(219) 353-7121

Frantz, R. D.
Frantz & Associates,
Auction Realty
P.O. Box 511
Warren, IN 46792-0511
(219) 375-2056

Hamilton, Frances
Rt. 1, P.O. Box 191
Rossville, IN 46065
(317) 379-2284

Lacy, Phillip H.
Lacy Auction & Realty Co.
329 E. Division Rd.
Valparaiso, IN 46383
(219) 462-1402

Lambright, Harvey C., CAI
112 N. Detroit St.
LaGrange, IN 46761
(219) 463-2013

Lawson, Jack
Lawson Bros. Auctioneers
P.O. Box 327
Danville, IN 46122
(317) 745-6405
FAX (317) 745-6406

Liechty, William G.
Phil's Auction Co.
1105 W. Park St.
Berne, IN 46711
(219) 589-2648

Marshall Jr., John W., CAI
J. Marshall Assoc.
623 Westchester Dr.
Evansville, IN 47710

Michael, Greg M., CAI
P.O. Box 7
Camden, IN 46917
(219) 686-2400

Ness, Kurt J.
Ness Brothers
18 W. Washington St.
Huntington, IN 46750
(219) 356-3911

Ott, Robert V., CAI
Ott Auctioneer
c/o 1st National Bank
800 Lincolnway Rm. 311
LaPorte, IN 46350
(219) 362-3365

Ratts, Noble
2223A Rome Drive
Indianapolis, IN 46208
(317) 431-0606

Schulze, Curtis D., CAI
Farmcraft Service, Inc.
Route 1, Box 157
Oxford, IN 47971
(317) 385-2266
FAX (317) 385-2670

Stevens, Donald R., CAI
3105 E. 10th St.
Anderson, IN 46012
(317) 778-8091
FAX (317) 778-7294

Strakis, Herman D., CAI
3333 W. Troy
Indianapolis, IN 46241
(317) 244-8063
FAX (317) 244-3767

Vogel, Phillip L., CAI
909 U.S. 24 East
Monticello, IN 47960

Iowa

Arnold, Jay
Arnold Auction Service
RR 1, Box 18
Mallard, IA 50562
(712) 425-3538

Bousselot, Norman
Route 1, Box 18
Calamus, IA 52729
(319) 246-2628

Buckles, Howard W.
Buckles Auctioneering
Service
1002 6th St.
Keosauqua, IA 52565
(319) 293-3012

Claussen, Leroy
3611 Parkdale Dr.
Bettendorf, IA 52722
(319) 332-9341

Collins, Warren
1155 6th St.
Jessup, IA 50648
(319) 827-1066

Cone, Kevin
RR 1, Box 137
Alta, IA 51002
(712) 284-2726

DeWitt, Jr., George G.
DeWitt Auction Service
Rt. 3, Box 174E
Council Bluffs, IA 51501
(402) 221-3507

Forristal, Pat
McGuire Auction Company
126 N. Main
Holstein, IA 51025
(712) 368-2635
FAX (712) 368-2784

Hamilton, William W., CAI
Hamilton Auctions
2216 N. 3rd St.
Clinton, IA 52732
(319) 243-5828
FAX (800) 222-8450

Hattermann, Todd J.
P.O. Box 162
Paulina, IA 51046
(712) 448-3602

Helgerson, Martin R.
Route 3, Box 151
Ottumwa, IA 52501
(515) 683-1915

Johnson, Roy B., CAI
P.O. Box 405
Buffalo Center, IA 50424
(515) 562-2032

Langstraat, Jerry
Northside Sales Company
725 11th Avenue
Sibley, IA 51249
(712) 754-3213

Law, Donald G.
300 5th Ave. SW
LeMars, IA 51031-2163
(712) 546-8188

Morehead, Gregory P., CAI
Morehead Auction Co.
25 S. Clinton St.
Albia, IA 52531
(515) 932-7129

Rogers, Jerry A.
Box 89
Union, IA 50258
(515) 486-2475

Ryan, Dale J.
RR #1, Box 197
Decorah, IA 52101
(319) 382-9533
FAX (319) 382-8785

Sears, Larry
Rt. 1, Box 85
Malcolm, IA 50157
(515) 528-4974

Skretta, Julian A.
206 N. Pine
West Union, IA 52175
(319) 422-3182

Smith, Dale E.
801 3rd Ave. NW
Pocahontas, IA 50574
(712) 335-4114
FAX (712) 335-3111

Starling, Dennis G.
RR 1, Box 101
Lost Nation, IA 52254

Stewart, Bill
3808 72nd St.
Urbandale, IA 50322
(515) 279-4434
FAX (515) 244-1171

Stewart, Wayne, CAI
P.O. Box 265
417 S. Park Pl.
Audubon, IA 50025
(712) 563-4288
FAX (712) 563-2111

Sweeney, John J.
612 Rossville Road
Waukon, IA 52172
(319) 568-4170

Thies, Earl
Box 309
Ames, IA 50010
(515) 232-3322

Wears, Brent, CAI
RR 1, Box 360
Solon, IA 52333
(319) 644-3779

Kansas

Berning, Russell
Berning Auction
Box 113
Marienthal, KS 67863
(316) 379-4446

Boesker, Leland W.
RR 2, Box 28
Moundridge, KS 67107
(316) 345-2603

Brown, Earl
Showcase Auctions
130 E. Main St.
Garder, KS 66030
(913) 884-6900

Carlin, Wayne E., CAI
Carlin's Auction/Real Estate
Box 310
Osborne, KS 67473
(913) 346-5778

Ediger, Richard W.
119½ N. Main
P.O. Box 488
Buhler, KS 67522
(316) 543-6633

Frederick, J.D.
JD Frederick & Associate
P.O. Box 3531
Wichita, KS 67201
(316) 267-1191

Gehrer, Kory J.
Rt. 1, Box 123
Newton, KS 67114
(316) 283-5309

Horigan, Dan D.
P.O. Box 56
Frankfort, KS 66427
(913) 292-4977

Hunt, Myron B.
1002-B E. 23rd St.
Hutchinson, KS 67502-5652
(316) 663-7428

Kobbeman, Shawn
RR 3, Box 68
Lincoln, KS 67455
(913) 524-3041

Koch, Vern E.
Koch Auction Service
1822 Cow Palace Rd.
Newton, KS 67114
(316) 283-6700

Olmsted, Timothy
Box 207
Beattle, KS 66406
(913) 353-2487

Olson, Galen D.
Olson Realty & Auction
1109 Easter
Wakeeney, KS 67672
(913) 743-2774

Shivers, Ronald L.
300 Summit Dr.
Abilene, KS 67410
(913) 263-7488

Stricker, Jerry L.
Rt. 1, Box 137B
Gardner, KS 66030
(913) 884-7074

Veal, Stan R.
Box 56, Rt. 4
Abilene, KS 67410
(913) 263-7787

Willis, Charles
4308 Troup
Kansas City, KS 66102

Kentucky

Birdwhistell, E. Glenn
154 S. Main St.
Lawrenceburg, KY 40342
(502) 839-3456

Blackford, Glen
Rt. 3, Box 29
Russellville, KY 42276
(502) 726-9238

Brewer, John C.
P.O. Box 579
105 N. Main St.
Stanton, KY 40380
(606) 663-4663
FAX (606) 663-4588

Bush, J. Randall, CAI
2689 Red Mill Rd.
Elizabethtown, KY 42701
(502) 765-2298
FAX (502) 737-7787

Butler, Dwight
Box 194
Harned, KY 40144
(502) 756-5859

Conder, Jim
P.O. Box 368
Leitchfield, KY 42755
(502) 259-3114

Conners, Jr., Andy J.
302 Tincher Dr.
Versailles, KY 40383
(606) 873-8429

Darlin, John R., CAI
Main Auction Inc.
3540 Winding Dr.
Lexington, KY 40517
(606) 273-3133
FAX (606) 273-3133

Deane, Silas
5785 Hwy. 144
Owensboro, KY 42303
(502) 926-8553
FAX (502) 926-8574

Durham III, John L., CAI
Durham & Durham, Realty
& Auction
135 N. 3rd St.
Denville, KY 40422
(606) 236-2770

Erler, Donald R.
Century 21, Hall Powell &
Associates
1850 S. Hwy. 53
LaGrange, KY 40031
(502) 222-1114
FAX (502) 222-3470

Freeman, S.D.
110 Hospital St.
Cediz, KY 42211
(502) 522-3101

Fries, Richard D.
Butcher Auction & Realty
RR 2, Box 392
Butler, KY 41006
(606) 635-3197

Gibson, William S., CAI
1708 N. Mayo
Pikeville, KY 41501
(606) 432-8181
FAX (606) 478-9838

Gribbins, Jr., Aleck, CAI
Gribbins Auction House
2712 Crums La.
Louisville, KY 40216
(502) 447-9572

Helm II, Harold H., CAI
River Realty & Auction Co.
215 Breckenridge La
Louisville, KY 40207
(502) 893-6611
FAX (502) 893-2181

Hungerford, Dennis L.
Col. D's Auction Service
P.O. Box 59
Eddyville, KY 42038
(502) 388-2985

Hunt, Thomas R., CAI
Hunt Realty & Auction Co.
66131 W. Bypass Ave. W, #A
Bowling Green, KY
42101-4968
(502) 782-2200
FAX (502) 843-8780

Jones, Harvey M.
Wilkerson Realty & Auction
1224 E. Bryant St.
Corbin, KY 40701
(606) 528-1157

Kessler, John M.
P.O. Box 271
Campbellsville, KY 42718
(502) 465-7051

Kessler, Wayne
Box 271
Campbellsville, KY
42719-0271
(502) 465-7051

Kurtz, William B., CAI
Kurtz Auction Co.
305 Fredericka St.
Owensboro, KY 42301
(502) 926-8553

Levy, Stuart G.
5602 Harrods Cove
Louisville, KY 40059
(502) 228-5254

Lewis, Stephen D.
129 E. Main St.
Morehead, KY 40351
(606) 784-4168
FAX (606) 784-4160

Maddox, Alan
501 School St.
Beaver Dam, KY 42320
(502) 274-9672
FAX (502) 274-5610

Maglinger, Gary L.
Maglinger Auction & Realty
1331 W. 5th St.
Owensboro, KY 42301
(502) 683-5923
FAX (502) 683-5923

Mills, Larry
P.O. Box 143
Greensburg, KY 42743
(502) 932-4998

Price, Jim, CAI
Price Realty & Auction Co.
12211 Old Shelbyville Rd.
Suite D
Louisville, KY 40243
(502) 244-1509

Riden, Billy F.
Riden Auction & Realty
114 W. Main St.
Providence, KY 42450
(502) 667-2570
FAX (502) 667-2097

Roy, Ralph D.
Box 578
W. Cumberland Ave.
Jamestown, KY 42629-0578
(502) 343-3334
FAX (502) 343-3033

Sexton, James C.
200 S. Main
Harrodsburg, KY 40330
(606) 734-7585
FAX (606) 734-9923

Thomason, David B., CAI
216 Buckman St.
P.O. Box 722
Shepherdsville,
KY 40165
(502) 955-7342
FAX (502) 543-5414

White, Dwain C., CAI
Thomas White & Sons,
Auction & Real Estate
Box 355
Kuttawa, KY 42055
(502) 388-2420

Willett, Roscoe
Real Estate & Auction Sales
6720 Contest Rd.
Paducah, KY 42001
(502) 554-0065

Louisiana

Brown, Lyn B.
Sencore Auction Service
20391 Chef Menteur Hwy.
New Orleans, LA 70129
(504) 254-1601
FAX (504) 254-4861

Maine

Blair, Robert R.
Blair's Auction Service
P.O. Box 3908
Wells, ME 04090
(207) 646-7475
FAX (207) 646-4144

Caprara, Victor A.
RFD #3, Box 3530
Winthrop, ME 04364
(207) 377-2080

Keating III, James J.
JJ Keating Inc.
Rt. 1 North
Kennebunk, ME 04043
(207) 985-2097

McMorrow, Joseph, CAI
McMorrow Auction Co.
Rt. 1, Box 825
Mechanic Falls, ME 04256
(207) 345-9477

Maryland

Bradstreet, Mark E.
Middletown Valley Auction
Service
P.O. Box 1
Tuscarora, MD 21790
(301) 874-2303

Cox, Jimmy
9409 Old Marlboro Pike
Upper Marlboro, MD 20772
(301) 599-6285

Griffin, Jim
EG's Auction Sales
202 West A St.
Berlin, MD 21811
(301) 641-4448

Isennock Sr., Robert L.
Isennock Auction
Services Inc.
4203 Norrisville Rd.
White Hall, MD 21161
(301) 557-8052

Martin, Clair L.
P.O. Box 499
Margansville, MD
21767-0499
(301) 797-4428

Nelson, Edward N., CAI
U.S. Rt. 50
P.O. Box 95
Trappe, MD 21673
(301) 476-3140

Reedy, Jack
1631 N. Main St.
Hampstead, MD 21074-3006
(301) 239-8110
FAX (301) 239-4551

Rigdon, H.B., CAI
Rigdon Auctioneers
P.O. Box 625
Forest Hill,
MD 21050
(301) 836-2787
FAX (301) 836-2738

Smith, Joseph D.
JD Smith & Co.
1722 Denton Court
Crofton, MD 21114
(301) 721-5446

Thomas, Robert P., CAI
Arbor Realty & Auction Co.
Rt. 925N, Box 278
Waldorf, MD 20601
(301) 449-4444
FAX (301) 843-0513

Massachusetts

Castelnovo, Edward J.
219 Front St.
Weymouth, MA 02188
(617) 335-7597

Devlin, Paul L.
Devlin Auctioneers
6 Columbus Rd.
Peabody, MA 01960
(508) 532-2228

Durant, Susan
1133 West St.
Attleboro, MA 02703
(617) 226-1196

Healey, Garrett D.
Garrett Auctioneers
76 High Street
Danvers, MA 01923
(617) 233-7227

Kaminski, Frank C.
Frank Kaminski Co., Inc.
193 Franklin St.
Stoneham, MA 02180
(617) 438-7595
FAX (617) 665-7418

Paine, Stanley J.
1198 Boylston St.
Chestnut Hill, MA 02167
(617) 731-4455
FAX (617) 566-0840

Potvin, Robert L., CAI
Potvin Auction & Realty
Box 808
Blair House
West Brookfield, MA 01585
(508) 867-3346

Santos, Michael
Bristol Auctioneers
568 Washington St.
Wellesley, MA 02181
(617) 235-9035

Torteson, James R., CAI
10 Hope Avenue
Oxford, MA 01540
(508) 987-2277

Valyou, Leroy N., Jr.
12 Hilltop Circle
West Newbury, MA 01985
(508) 363-2946

Michigan

Albrecht, Herbert, CAI
Herb Albrecht, CAI & Assoc.
3884 Saginaw Rd.
Vassar, MI 48768
(517) 823-8835

Ballor, R. William, CAI
Bill Ballor Auction Service
201 North 1st St.
P.O. Box 249
Linwood, MI 48634
(517) 697-4212

Boyk, John S., CAI
Boyk's Auction Service
7878 Cathro Rd.
Alpena, MI 49707
(517) 356-9589

Egnash, Ray
P.O. Box 184
Howell, MI 48843
(517) 546-7496

Freund, Ken
Auction Way Sales, Inc.
P.O. Box 3096
2443 S. Old 27
Gaylord, MI 49735
(517) 732-7808

Hecht, Gerald W., CAI
9849 Bradley Rd.
Frankenmuth, MI 48734
(517) 652-2242

Hinsdale, Larry D.
394 Copeland Rd.
Coldwater, MI 49036
(517) 238-2619

Krol, Bernedia
K & K Auction Services
2020 Hunter Rd.
Brighton, MI 48116
(313) 227-8040
FAX (616) 229-2204

Matsel, Richard J.
162 Ottawa Dr.
Pontiac, MI 48053
(313) 288-3522

Reeser, Steve, CAI
1465 N. Cedar
Mason, MI 48854
(517) 699-2210
FAX (517) 699-3064

Ringel, Ronald W.
11444 Big 4 Rd.
Bear Lake, MI 49614

Stanton, Steven E.
Stanton's Auctioneers &
Realtors
144 S. Main
Vermontville, MI 49096
(517) 726-0181
FAX (517) 726-0060

Strye, Joye R.
315 W. Grant St.
Caro, MI 48723-1519
(517) 673-4649

Whalen, John M., CAI
5844 Gotfredson Rd.
Plymouth, MI 48170-5075
(313) 459-5144

Minnesota

Baker, John E.
Rt. 3, Box 171
Appleton, MN 56208
(612) 394-2489

Braastad, Steven
Steve's Auction Service
2761 229th Ave. NW
St. Francis, MN 55070
(612) 753-2572

Christian, Gregory J., CAI
Quicky Auction House
19150 Territorial Rd.
Osseo, MN 55369
(612) 428-2271
FAX (612) 428-8355

Imholte, Frank B.
8160 Country Rd. 138
St. Cloud, MN 56301
(612) 255-9398

Kiffmeyer, Barney
Rt. 1, Box 70A
Kimball, MN 55353
(612) 253-1477

Marguth, Terry
1500 E. Bridge St.
Redwood Falls, MN 56283
(507) 644-8433
FAX (507) 644-2425

Mitchell, Cliff
Mitchell Auction Service
P.O. Box 390

Albany, MN 56307-0390
(612) 845-2244
FAX (612) 845-2187

Nord, Ronald D.
Box 3451
215 Ruby St.
Mankato, MN 56002
(507) 625-7653

Norling, Lefty
Norling Auction Service
Box 141
Kandiiyohi, MN 56251
(612) 382-6566

Pinske, Bill
325 West Main St.
Arlington, MN 55307
(612) 964-2250

Scheffler, Richard
Scheffler Auctioneering
Rt. 1, P.O. Box 67
Morton, MN 56270
(507) 697-6257

Schroeder, Orville M.
106 W. Adams St.
Caledonia, MN 55921
(507) 724-2874

Spanier, David E.
Spanier Auction Service
5128 Julien St.
St. Peter, MN 56082
(507) 931-4259

Swenson, Rand, CAI
Swenson Auction Service
1963 29th St.
Circle South
Moorhead, MN 56560
(218) 233-7410

Wiedemoth, E.H.
564 Clark St.
Hutchinson, MN 55350
(612) 587-2210

Mississippi

Ingram, Charles H.
870 Green Acres Dr.
Hernando, MS 38632
(601) 429-7546

Johnson, Lannie E.
Rt. 3, Box 297A
Fulton, MS 38843
(601) 862-2835

Johnson, Merry K.
Rt. 3, Box 297A
Fulton, MS 38843
(601) 862-2835

Ozborn, Kline Jr.
Box 651
Canton, MS 39046
(601) 859-3845
FAX (601) 859-7828

Thompson, Holly
Rt. 1, Box 85B
Madison, MS 39110
(601) 853-1145

Missouri

Arnaman, H. Willard
1312 E. Main St.
P.O. Box 123
Unionville, MO 63565
(816) 947-2883

Atterberry, Larry P., CAI
Atterberry & Associates
Auction Co.
79121-70th Drive SE
Columbia, MO 65201
(314) 474-9295

Bayless, Alan
Box 14068
Parkville, MO 64152
(816) 587-7575

Burger, Ron
Ron Burger Auction Service
Rt. 1, Box 1085
Scott City, MO 63780
(314) 264-2501

Hall, Clarence
P.O. Box 113
Pleasant Hill, MO 64080
(816) 987-3246

Hamilton, Robert F.
P.O. Box 231
Kimberling City, MO 65686
(417) 739-2047

Lambert, Mike
Mike Lambert Enterprises
Inc.
Rt. 3, Box 181
Kirksville, MO 63501
(816) 665-7889
FAX (816) 665-1139

Long, Billy, CAI
Billy Long Auction & Realty
1950-L S. Glenstone
Springfield, MO 65804
(417) 882-5664
FAX (417) 882-7653

McFadden, Leslie J.
Leslie McFadden Auction
Service
8025 Rt. W
Jefferson City, MO 65101
(314) 635-6003

Montgomery, Richard
716 Beardsley Court
Ferguson, MO 63135
(314) 521-0768

Pickett, Eddie
Rt. 1, Box 162
Stewartsville, MO 64490
(816) 669-3433

Wells, Jim
Ace Auction Service
104 Friendship Lane
Clinton, MO 64735
(816) 885-3725

Nebraska

Garey, Marsden, CAI
1610 Parkview Dr.
Grand Island, NE 68801
(308) 384-9011

Hoffschneider, Mike
RR 1, Box 184
Beaver Crossing, NE 68313
(402) 532-7425

Maly, John L.
Maly Auction Service
1636 N. Garfield St.
Fremont, NE 68025
(402) 721-8879

Marshall, Robin
Rt. 1, Box 26
Elm Creek NE 68836
(308) 856-4102

Miller, Gerald E.
402 W. Main St.
Hartington, NE 68739
(402) 254-3908

Sanders, Harry
1107 N. Broad St.
Fremont, NE 68025
(402) 721-0860
FAX (402) 727-7818

Stander, Earl E.
E & E Auction Service
RR 1, Box 180
Weeping Water, NE 68463
(402) 267-5435

Rudolph, Harry
15719 S. 99th
Papillion, NE 68128
(402) 339-8129

Thomsen, Charles, CAI
RR 2,
Hooper, NE 68031
(402) 654-2464
FAX (402) 721-0109

Nevada

Chadwick, George H.
1325 S. Maryland Pkwy
Las Vegas, NV 81904
(702) 387-8980
FAX (702) 384-3552

White, Burton J.
Select Service/Burton White
5319 W. Tara Ave.
Las Vegas, NV 89102
(702) 566-9200
FAX (702) 564-3589

New Hampshire

Martin, Douglas C.
Martin Associates
P.O. Box 505
Wakefield La.
Hampstead, NH 03841
(603) 329-6758

Reidy, Daniel F.
Daniel F. Reidy, Auctioneer
44 High St.
Golfstown, NH 03045
(603) 497-4812

New Jersey

Glaubman, Alan J.
Burman's Auction Gallery
33 W. Blackwell St.
Dover, NH 07801
(201) 361-3110

Howell, Donald F.
369 Beech St.
Teaneck, NJ 07666

Koty, Robert, CAI
Bob Koty, Professional
Auctioneer & Appraiser
P.O. Box 625
Freehold, NJ 07728
(908) 780-1265

Krawitz, Jerry
74 Godwin Ave.
Ridgewood, NJ 07450
(201) 652-6424

Williams, Arthur A.
252 Oneida Place
North Plainfield, NJ 07060
(201) 756-6297

New York

Alestra, Dennis
Divine Wood
9724 3rd Ave.
Brooklyn, NY 11209
(718) 748-1345

Bergerson, Carl H.
80 Howard St.
Wellsville, NY 14895
(716) 593-3434

Bontrager, Alfred, CAI
Alfred Bontrager Realtor
13238 Broadway
Alden, NY 14004
(716) 937-3323
FAX (716) 937-9393

Castellano, Art J.
Auction by Eastlake
2115 Hillside Ave.
New Hyde Park, NY 11040
(516) 746-5544

Cummins, Dean D.
RD Box 67
Cato, NY 13033
(315) 626-2248
FAX (315) 626-2666

Deuble, Carl G., Sr.
4030 E. River Rd.
Grand Island, NY 14072
(716) 773-1692

Doyle, Robert A., CAI
Doyle Auction & Appraisers
137 Osborne Hill Rd
Fishkill, NY 12524
(800) 243-0061
FAX (914) 896-5874

Dumas, Paul E.
RD 2
P.O. Box 273
Plattsburg, NY 12901
(518) 562-0561

Gansz, Duane E., CAI
Gansz Auction & Realty
14 William St.
Lyons, NY 14489
(315) 946-6241
FAX (315) 946-6747

Hagan, Thomas J.
T.J.'s Auctions
41-71 249th Street
Little Neck, NY 11363
(718) 225-1224
FAX (718) 224-3390

Haroff, Edward T.
Haroff's Auction Service
P.O. Box 71, Pine Lane
Schroon Lake, NY 12870
(518) 532-9600

Howard, Peter S., CAI
Howard & Reimold
P.O. Box 496
Findley Lake, NY 14736-0496
(716) 769-7447
FAX (716) 769-7447

Joki, Robert, CAI
674 Lake Avenue
Saratoga Springs, NY 12866
(518) 584-5548

Knapp, Dorothy, CAI
158 Germonds Rd.
West Nyack, NY 10994
(914) 623-5710

Knapp, Michael W.
Auction by Knapp
RD 1, Box 62
Utica, NY 13502
(315) 732-2042

Lambrecht, Dale A., CAI
RD 3, Box 307
Walton, NY 13856

Manasse, Melvin J.
P.O. Box 738
Whitney Point, NY 13862
(800) 626-2773

Moyer, Randall B.
12354 Broadway #3
Alden, NY 14004
(716) 937-7493

O'Sullivan, Jack
Jack O'Sullivan
Professional Auctioneer
2626 Kings Hwy.
Brooklyn, NY 11229
(718) 252-5167
FAX (718) 951-0340

Pepper, Ray
401 W. State St.
Olean, NY 14760
(716) 372-7100
FAX (716) 372-7126

Scherrer, Russ
206 Brinkman St.
Buffalo, NY 14211
(716) 894-5731

Seipp, Frank E.
9 Park Lane
Rockville Center, NY 11570
(516) 764-7459
FAX (516) 764-7460

Visscher, Howard W.
Rd. 1, Box 507
Nichols, NY 13812
(607) 699-7250

Vlasto, Lou
L & L Liquidators
166 Botsford St.
Hempstead, NY 11550
(516) 292-6770

Wheeler, Ronald L.
Family Auction Center
RD 5, Rt. 57, P.O. Box 327
Fulton, NY 13069
(315) 695-2059
FAX (315) 695-4745

Zientek, Anthony H.
Zientek Realty & Auction
4759 Rt. 98
North Java, NY 14113
(716) 457-3497

North Carolina

Burch, Thomas R.
Burch & Co.
P.O. Box 867
Roanoke Rapids, NC 27870
(919) 537-7126

Byers, Donald W., CAI
407 Sterling Rd.
Jacksonville, NC 28546
(919) 455-5640

Curlee, Ernest J., CAI
American Auction
Associates, Inc.
9327-B Albemarle Rd.
Charlotte, NC 28227
(704) 535-1724

Deal, Robert W.
403 Highway 10 East
Newton, NC 28658
(704) 464-3635
FAX (704) 465-6263

Glenn, Samuel D.
P.O. Box 787
Monroe, NC 28111
(704) 289-6704

Hawley, George T.
Auctions by George
P.O. Box 1299
Greenville, NC 27835
(800) 443-3654

Johnson III, James W.
Johnson Properties
120 E. Depot St.
Angier, NC 27501
(919) 639-2231
FAX (919) 639-2232

Keeter, James T.
Keeter Auction Company,
International
Rt. 5, Box 291
Forest City, NC 28043
(704) 245-5020
FAX (704) 245-5020

King, John D., CAI
J.D. King Realty & Auction
529-A S. Church St.
Asheboro, NC 27203
(919) 626-4400

Lawing, W. Craig, CAI
Lawing Auction Company
5521 Brookshire Rd.
Charlotte, NC 28216
(800) 632-3043

Lawson, Dilmon B.
P.O. Box 411
Pilot Mountain, NC 27041
(919) 368-4412

Mendenhall, Wayne, CAI
Mendenhall Auction Co.
P.O. Box 7344
High Point, NC 27264
(919) 887-1165

Miller, Jack W.
Jack Miller Auction Co.
9 W. 5th St.
Tabor City, NC 28463
(919) 653-5252

Pierce, Keith J., CAI
P.O. Box 5215
5500 S. Main St.
Winston-Salem, NC
27113-5215
(919) 764-5338
FAX (919) 764-8642

Propst, Clyde
P.O. Box 563
Concord, NC 28026-0563

Rogers, R. Bracky, CAI
Business Center, P.O. Box 729
Mt. Airy, NC 27030
(919) 789-2926
FAX (919) 789-2310

Rowe, Gordon E.
216 Canterbury Rd.
Mooresville, NC 28115

Tate, Harvey L., CAI
Rt. 2, Box 208
Burlington, NC 27217
(919) 421-3282

Troutman, Jr., Lonnie
J., CAI
150 E. Water St.
Statesville, NC 28677
(704) 873-5233

Whitt, Marshall A.
2310 S. Broad St.
Winston-Salem, NC 27127
(919) 748-9364

North Dakota

Penfield, Bob
P.O. Box 111
Bowman, ND 58623
(701) 523-3652

Vogel, Steve
SRV Auction Co.
P.O. Box 417
Casselton, ND 58012
(701) 347-5485

Ohio

Andrews, Stephen E.
51-7 S. Jefferson Rd.
Wooster, OH 44691
(216) 262-9186

Baier, Thomas A., CAI
2719 Fulton Dr. NW, Ste C.
Canton, OH 44718
(216) 455-1911
FAX (216) 455-1859

Bambeck, Herb, CAI
Rt. 1, Box 392
Dover, OH 44622
(216) 343-1437
FAX (216) 343-1437

Basinger, J. Paul, CAI
7039 Bishop Rd.
Poland, OH 44514
(216) 757-1169
FAX (216) 757-1292

Bates, Don L.
7010 Ragland Rd.
Cincinnati, OH 45244
(513) 421-4525
FAX (513) 561-8880

Bayman, Anthony M.
1200 Nicklin Ave.
Piqua, OH 45356
(513) 778-8017

Beitzel, Herbert L.
RFD 2, P.O. Box 2228
New Philadelphia, OH 44663
(216) 339-5197

Brough, Chad W.
3653 S. Harris-Salem Rd.
Oak Harbor, OH 43449
(419) 898-0290

Burgess, Walter R.
17708 Woodbury Ave.
Cleveland, OH 44135
(216) 251-4540

Canterbury, Gerald R., CAI
5999 Avon-Belden Rd.
North Ridgeville, OH 44039
(216) 327-9394
FAX (216) 327-9394

Deatley, Herbert
413 Jefferson St.
Greenfield, OH 45123
(513) 981-4560

Duvall, Donald D.
7450 Linnville Rd. SE,
Newark, OH 43055
(614) 323-1436

Farnsworth, Harold R., CAI
8003 River Styx Rd.
Wadsworth, OH 44281
(216) 336-6057

Garner, Sr., Larry W., CAI
L.W. Garner
Realty/Auctioneers

332 S. Lisbon St., Box 323
Carrollton, OH 44614
(800) 452-8452
FAX (216) 627-3788

Hayes, Evelyn, CAI
Prosperity Productions
920 Beverly Road
Cleveland Heights, OH
44121
(216) 381-3878

Hoyle, William L.
7068 Dunstans Lane
Toledo, OH 43617
(419) 841-9892
FAX (419) 385-6834

Jay, Kenneth
Mickelson Real Estate
U.S. Rt. 127 N.
Paulding, OH 45879
(419) 399-5359

Kaspar, Robert J.
5718 Little Portage Road
Port Clinton, OH 43452
(419) 734-2930

Kearns, Clair E.
Box 277
Belmont, OH 43718

Kessler, Dave
P.O. Box 100
New Paris, OH 45347
(513) 437-7071

Kiko, James R., CAI
811 Fox Avenue
Paris, OH 44669
(216) 445-9357
FAX (216) 453-1765

Kiko, John D., CAI
Russ Kiko Assoc., Inc.
2805 Fulton Dr. NW
Canton, OH 44718
(216) 455-9357
FAX (216) 453-1765

Kramer, Horace J.
108 W. Main Street
Eaton, OH 45320-1906
(513) 456-1101

Lentz, Jeffrey M.
Lentz Auction Service
P.O. Box 28
Botkins, OH 45306
(513) 693-3100

Polakovic, John F.
40 Applewood Dr.
Oregon, OH 43616
(419) 691-5862

Retcher, Sr., William H.
11693 Rd. 1
Montpelier, OH 43543
(419) 485-8141

Robinson, Jerry D.
Robinson Auction Service
523 Adrien Street
Delta, OH 43515
(419) 822-3555

Sheridan, Keith
3644 Wilberforce-
Clifton Road
Cedarville, OH 45314
(513) 766-2021

Straley, William C., CAI
Straley Realtors &
Auctioneers
323 E. Main St.
Van Wert, OH 45891
(419) 238-9733
FAX (419) 238-3506

Ux, Dan B.
137 First St.
New London, OH 44851
(419) 929-1148

Wagner, Robert J., CAI
B. Wagner & Assoc., Inc.
1444 N. Main St.

N. Canton, OH 44720
(216) 499-9922
FAX (216) 499-5864

Wallick, Don R.
81 E. Iron Avenue
Dover, OH 44622
(216) 343-6734
FAX (216) 343-3655

Oklahoma

Bridges, Billy
Bridges Auction & Sales Co.
P.O. Box 398
Elgin, OK 73538
(405) 492-4260
FAX (405) 492-5244

Brink, Terry H., CAI
Kent & Brink
422 N. 14th
Frederick, OK 73542
(405) 335-5732

Bruce, Joe D.
Bruce Auction
RR 2, Box 470
Welch, OK 74369
(918) 233-7074

Dulaney, Sue, CAI
Rt. 4, Box 273
Claremore, OK 74017
(918) 342-5176
FAX (918) 342-5187

Godfrey, Donald D.
5105 NW 19th St.
Oklahoma City, OK 73127

Hines, Les
C & H Auctions
P.O. Box 521
Temple Hill, OK 73568
(405) 342-5133
FAX (405) 353-6109

Spitler, Paul D.
Spitler Auction, Inc.
P.O. Box 685
Prague, OK 74864
(405) 567-3523

Stallings, Joey G.
502 N. Sheridan Rd.
Lawton, OK 73505
(405) 355-8302
FAX (405) 355-3550

Wiggins, C. Perry, CAI
4720A W. Owen K.
Garriott Road
Enid, OK 73701
(405) 233-3066
FAX (405) 237-4915

Wilkinson, W.W. Buck
923 S. 85th E. Avenue
Tulsa, OK 74112
(918) 838-3279

Wolfe, Michael E.
200 W. 12th Street
Ada, OK 74820
(405) 436-1281
FAX (405) 436-1578

Oregon

O'Keefe, Arthur J.
11733 Hwy 62
Eagle Point, OR 97524
(503) 826-2192

Pennsylvania

Alderfer, Sanford L., CAI
P.O. Box 1
Harleysville, PA 19438
(215) 368-5477
FAX (216) 368-9055

Beamesderfer, Calvin E.
471 Weavertown Road
Myerstown, PA 17067
(717) 866-2998

Blum, George F., CAI
Blum's Inc.
2500 West End Ave.
Pottsville, PA 17901
(717) 622-3089

Boswell, James M., CAI
P.O. Box 3073
West Chester, PA 19381
(215) 692-2226
FAX (215) 692-2042

Brown, Jeffie L.
1 Graystone Lane
Levittown, PA 19055
(215) 336-8800
FAX (215) 336-8804

Cox, Alan D.
18551 Elgin Road
Corry, PA 16407
(814) 664-7526

Deibert, George N., CAI
P.O. Box 72
Klingerstown, PA 17941
(717) 425-3313

Dobozynski, Joe, CAI
AAA Auction Service Inc.
RD 1, Box 420
Mifflintown, PA 17059
(717) 436-9594

Finkel, Arnold
3425 Iron Bridge Rd.
Allentown, PA 18104
(215) 395-0808

Gilbert, Jacob A.
Rt. #1
Wrightsville, PA 17368
(717) 252-3591

Hahn, Wil, CAI
Wil Hahn Auction Company
102 West Main Street
Bath, PA 18014
(215) 837-7140
FAX (215) 837-9451

Hock, Donald E.
205 Dutch Hill Road
Bloomsburg, PA 17815

Hostetter, Lee W., CAI
Lee Hostetter Real Estate
124 Blackhawk Road
Beaver Falls, PA 15010
(412) 847-1880
FAX (412) 847-3415

Hostetter, Jr., Sherman, CAI
Hostetter Auctioneers/Real
Estate
124 Blackhawk Rd.
Beaver Falls, PA 15010
(412) 847-1880
FAX (412) 847-1881

Keller, Mark K.
RD #1, Box 64
Landisburg, PA 17040
(717) 789-3616

Koser, Paris E.
RD #2, Box 492
Everett, PA 15537
(814) 735-3300

Krall, Peter H., CAI
Willow Brook Farms
Catasauqua, PA 18032
(215) 264-1088

McKeown, Michael J.
956 North 9th St.
Stroudsburg, PA 18360
(717) 424-2762

Moyer, Charles L.
5444 Vera Cruz Rd.
Center Valley, PA 18034
(215) 967-2727

Nicolls, W. Bruce
733 Terrace St.
Meadville, PA 16335
(814) 333-1989
FAX (814) 333-1988

Niebauer, Joseph P.
Rd. 1, Box 130
Irvona, PA 16656
(814) 672-5541

Randazzo, Salvatore A.
1030 Linden Ave.
Erie, PA 16505
(814) 838-2437

Rentzel, Blaine N.
Box 222
Emigsville, PA 17318
(717) 764-6412
FAX (717) 764-5492

Wakeley, Thomas J.
1969 Oakford Ave.
Oakford, PA 19053
(215) 355-2152

Young, James C.
P.O. Box 186
Dewart, PA 17730
(717) 538-1620

Rhode Island

Phillips, Edward F.
1049 Greenwich Ave.
Warwick, RI 02886
(401) 737-9060

South Carolina

Leonardi II, Robert J.
P.O. Box 1417
Easley, SC 29641-1417
(803) 233-3615

Meares, Larry J., CAI
P.O. Box 57, Pelzer, SC 29669
(803) 277-0504
FAX (803) 277-3255

Smith, Frank O., Jr.
524 Clinkscales Rd.
Anderson, SC 29624
(803) 832-6655

South Dakota

Olesen, Charles A.
1620 Dana Dr.
Sioux Falls, SD 57105
(605) 339-0365

Tennessee

Alexander, Marvin E., CAI
239 University St.
P.O. Box 129
Martin, TN 38237-0129
(901) 587-4244
FAX (901) 587-2698

Ayers, Haskel, CAI
2201 Jackson Pike
P.O. Box 1467
LaFollette, TN 37766
(615) 562-4941
FAX (615) 562-8148

Blackford, Robert L.
3937 Gallatin Rd.
Nashville, TN 37216
(615) 228-2541
FAX (615) 227-6106

Carman Jr., Harold G.
Rt. 1, Box 635
Castalian Springs,
TN 37031
(615) 374-9326
FAX (615) 255-4939

Cayce, Clinton R.
Beck & Beck
Realty & Auction
1450 Janie Ave.
Nashville, TN 37216
(615) 226-6915
FAX (615) 227-7053

Cole, David L.
Blue Ridge Properties Inc.
1337 Magnolia Ave.
Kingsport, TN 37664
(615) 378-4411

Edwards, Dr. Hugh F.
Rt. 12, Box 438
Greeneville, TN 37743
(615) 639-6781
FAX (615) 639-0851

Elder, Thomas E.
Gene Elder Auction
3449 Summer Avenue
Memphis, TN 38112
(901) 324-4382

Hamilton, Jr., George, CAI
P.O. Box 536
Dunlap, TN 37327
(615) 554-3999

Hobbs, Fred R.
P.O. Box 126
131 N. Main St.
Eagleville, TN 37060
(615) 274-6826

Johns, Royce G., CAI
Royce Johns
Realty/Auctions
236 3rd Ave. North
Franklin, TN 37064
(625) 790-0414

Lynch, Tom P.
Carlton Lynch
Realty & Auction
1215 Dinah Shore Blvd.
Winchester, TN 37398
(615) 967-0678
FAX (615) 967-0694

Murphy, James R.
2304 Memorial Blvd.
Springfield, TN 37172
(615) 384-7919
FAX (615) 384-7884

Orr, George C., CAI
Lewis-Orr Realty
Auction Sales
123 S. Jackson St.
Tullahoma, TN 37388
(615) 455-3447

Orr, John W.
610 Stone Blvd.
Tullahoma, TN 37388-3001
(615) 455-3447

Redenbaugh, Richard G.
Redenbaugh Auction
RR 3, Box 286, T
Tellico Plains, TN 37385
(615) 253-2666

Shepard, Tom
Nashville Auction &
Realty Co., Inc.
1407 Lebanon Rd.
Nashville, TN 37210
(615) 255-4933
FAX (615) 255-8052

Texas

Alley, Lesley, R.
P.O. Box 1092
Del Rio, TX 78841
(512) 774-4255
FAX (512) 774-1222

Burnett, B. Randall, CAI
4009 Piping Rock
Houston, TX 77027
(713) 961-5557
FAX (713) 626-7832

Cleghorn, Michael L.
Cleghorn & Assoc.
P.O. Box 90065
Austin, TX 78709
(512) 892-0109

Cutberth, Dale
#9 Manchester
Amarillo, TX 79106
(806) 376-9607
FAX (806) 374-7474

DeVore, Russell
DeVore Marketing
Auction/Realtors
P.O. Box 61872
San Angelo, TX 76906-1872
(915) 942-6666

Dickson, David J.
Dickson Diversified Services
16402 Mill Dr.
P.O. Box 280
Rosharon, TX 77583
(713) 595-2337

Espensen, K.L., CAI
Espensen Co., Realtor-
Auctions
2212 Primrose St. #C
McAllen, TX 78504
(512) 687-5117
FAX (512) 687-7967

Henson, Roy P.
Alph Int'l Mktg Services, Inc.
Rt. 3, Box 3786
Chandler, TX 75758
(903) 849-2221
FAX (903) 849-2883

Kaddatz, Alvin
Kaddatz Auctioneering
Box 972, Hillsboro, TX 76645
(817) 582-3071

Lawless, Ed
RR 2, Box 52
Linden, TX 75563
(214) 756-5733

Moses, Dwayne
Moses & Zuber Auctioneers
Rt. 1, Box 311
Ralls, TX 79357
(806) 253-2945

Ogle, Jack V., CAI
Ogle Auction & Realty
Rt. 2, Box 66A
Greenville, TX 75401
(903) 454-1091

Rudd, Charles D.
13214 Holly Park
Houston, TX 77015
(713) 453-2912

Segars, Ralph
10925 Estate Lane #105
Dallas, TX 75238
(214) 343-4055
FAX (214) 343-8252

Stall, Dorothy
1202 Saxony Lane
Houston, TX 77058
(713) 333-1000
FAX (713) 333-3020

Storey, Henry R.
Rt. 4, Box 182
Brownwood, TX 76801
(915) 646-3956

Thomas, Brett R.
Rt. 6, Box 420
Mt. Pleasant, TX 75455
(903) 572-4517

Van Hauen, Jack W.
17 Rancho Dr.
Keller, TX 76248-5002
(817) 431-1712
FAX (817) 831-4465

Vermont

Stevenson, Frederick A.
Fred's Auction Service
HCR 30, Box 56
Barnet, VT 05821
(802) 592-3202

Virginia

Boone, John D
J.D. Boone Auction & Realty
Rt. 2, Box 10
Speedwell, VA 24374
(703) 621-4811

Bowman, George M.
P.O. Box 212
Clifton Forge, VA 24422
(703) 362-4411

Cole, A. Barry, CAI
Rt. #1, Box 182
Callaway, VA 24067
(703) 483-4539

Counts, Ted, CAI
Realty & Auction Co.
8314 Timberlake Rd.
Lynchburg, VA 24502
(804) 237-2991
FAX (804) 239-1333

De Loach, Greg, CAI
P.O. Box 165
Stephens City, VA 22655
(800) 274-6020
FAX (703) 869-6020

Des Roches, Jim
5100 Hingham Dr.
New Kent, VA 23124
(804) 932-3717

Green, Donnie G.
Green Auction & Realty
Rt. 1, Box 636
S. Boston, VA 24592
(804) 575-7924
FAX (804) 575-7926

Hines, Larry N.
Hines Real Estate & Auction
P.O. Box 302
Jonesville, VA 24263
(703) 346-3657
FAX (703) 346-0151

Sellars, Douglas V.
6174 Pattie Court
Haymarket, VA 22069
(703) 754-0328

Sheets, Stephen G., CAI
15 S. Jefferson St.
Roanoake, VA 24011
(703) 345-8885

Smeltzer, Don P., CAI
Smeltzer's Auction & Realty
1316 E. Main St.
Luray, VA 22835
(703) 743-4747
FAX (703) 743-9380

Smith, Grayson L.
Rt. 2, Box 255A
Warsaw, VA 22572
(804) 333-4894

Staples Jr., Philip D.
4100 Stuart Avenue
Richmond, VA 23221
(804) 358-0500

Summs, William J.
Atlantic Auctions, Ltd.
1195 Lance Rd.
Norfolk, VA 23502
(804) 461-6867
FAX (804) 461-2147

Tull, Ronald I., CAI
Tull Realty & Auction Co.
3912 Woodburn Rd.
Annandale, VA 22003
(703) 280-5555

Updike, Buddy
P.O. Box 330
King George, VA 22485
(703) 371-5965

Williams, Frederick J.
F.J. Williams Realty &
Auction Company
P.O. Box 201
Winchester, VA 22601
(703) 662-3539

Washington

Burnham, Elmer L.
658 Road L NE
Moses Lake, WA 98837
(509) 766-9100
FAX (509) 766-9925

Ehli, Randall L.
Ehli Auctions Inc.
2042-112th St.
South Tacoma, WA 98444
(206) 537-7255
FAX (206) 537-7302

Hill, I. Andrew
Andy's Auction Service
2312 174th St. E.
Tacoma, WA 98445
(206) 531-7398

Honey, Jr., George P.
Northwest Auction Service
P.O. Box 397, 2003 Mac Place
Entlat, WA 98822
(509) 784-1938

Paasch, Norman E.
17811 Fifth Ave. SW
Seattle, WA 98166
(206) 246-8262

Stalheim, David L.
7117 44th Ave. E.
Tacoma, WA 98443-1925
(206) 531-9404

West Virginia

Belmont, Gary R.
Belmont Auction Co.
1252 Dorsey Ave.
Morgantown, WV 26505
(304) 292-4314

Cooper, Jerry L.
1008 Summers St.
Hinton, WV 25951
(304) 466-3760

Felosa, Joseph A., CAI
Felosa Auction/Realty, Inc.
Box 179
77 Felosa Drive
Haywood, WV 26366-0179
(304) 592-0738
FAX (304) 592-0738

Meadows, Monroe B.
Meadows Auction & Realty
P.O. Box 23
Meadow Bridge, WV 25976
(304) 484-7043

Wisconsin

Berkshire, Gerald & Rita
Colonel's Auction Service
1117 Bushnell St.
Beloit, WI 53511
(608) 365-5089

Donahoe, Joseph
627 Harriett St.
Box 133
Darlington, WI 53530
(608) 776-2156

Gillen, Melville
Gillen Auction Service
P.O. Box 45
Pound, WI 54161

Goodman, Alex M.
2214 Sunrise Drive
La Crosse, WI 54601
(608) 781-3900

Hazlewood, William J., CAI
935 Model Railroad
Rice Lake, WI 54868
(800) 345-2040

Lust, Richard O., CAI
Lust Auction Services
P.O. Box 4421
Madison, WI 53711
(608) 833-2001
FAX (608) 833-9593

Mantz, C. A.
Archie Mantz Auctioneer
7085 Winnebago
Fond Du Lac, WI 54935
(414) 921-1528

Murdoch, Donna C.
Murdoch Auction Service
636 Sheldon St.
Madison, WI 53711
(608) 238-0530

Murray, Lee A., CAI
Dells Auction Service
P.O. Box 212
Wisconsin Dells, WI 53965
(608) 254-8696

Otto, Earl A.
10815 Co. Trk. A.
Kiel, WI 53042
(414) 773-2469

Schmit, Gene W.
1211 12th Ave.
Grafton, WI 53024
(414) 377-4668
FAX (414) 377-1114

Schomisch, Arthur
Schomisch Auction Service
1817 S. Jefferson St.
Appleton, WI 54915
(414) 734-9382

Schuster, Jon S.
708 2nd Ave.
Onalaska, WI 54650
(608) 783-7653
FAX (608) 783-6079

Spies, John R.
184 S. Washington St.
Waterloo, WI 53594
(414) 478-3365

Stewart, Laverne L.
5902 Michier Rd.
Eau Claire, WI 54701
(715) 834-6664

Wagner, Jim
American Auction
Rt. 4, Box 217
Wantoma, WI 54982
(414) 787-2680

Walla, Willia, L.
Walla's Auction &
Real Estate
1723 County J
Little Suamico, WI 54141
(414) 826-5472

Weisensel, Taylor W.
3016 Vercauteren Dr.
Green Bay, WI 54313-5896
(414) 336-3050

Wyoming

Brown, Kenneth R.
Kenneth Brown Enterprises
P.O. Box 133
Riverton, WY 82501
(307) 347-3408

Olson, Lavar D.
347 Broadacres
Riverton, WY 82501
(309) 856-9347

29

Tax Sales

★★★

Tax sales are held at the local government level. These should not be confused with IRS tax sales. There is good reason to think both are the same. The IRS collects federal income taxes. Local county government collects ad valorem, or property, taxes. Just as the IRS rounds up our income taxes so that congress can disburse them to run the federal government, counties charge property owners a percentage fee of the assessed value of that property. Collected funds are disbursed to run the county.

Some property owners are unable to pay these taxes. Unlike IRS tax protestors who refuse to pay, property owners generally can't pay their ad valorem taxes. Some county taxes are low, amounting annually to a few hundred dollars, on an average property. An expensive property in a highly taxed county might be tagged with a $10,000 (or more) annual assessment.

Background

When home or property owners fail to pay these local taxes, they are sent delinquent notices by the county assessor's office. (Titles of this office vary from state to state.) After the deadline for paying these taxes has elapsed, many states will hold a "tax certificate sale" on those taxes.

What occurs at this sale is that the county will hold an auction to sell the right to collect those taxes. Bidders pay the property owner's taxes and receive a tax certificate in return. That certificate entitles the bidder to a high interest rate return on the investment, often as high as 18%.

The county gets its taxes. The property owner eventually redeems the certificate by paying his taxes plus interest and penalties or the property ends up at a county tax sale. It will be sold, usually on the courthouse steps, in the county lobby, or wherever the county decides. The sheriff or a county clerk assistant will auction the property to the highest bidder.

Procedure

Property with delinquent back taxes is sold very slowly. It often takes many years to sell such property. Usually, it will be foreclosed for failure to pay the mortgage or trust deed before it is sold for back taxes. Additionally, many states have redemption periods of several months, during which the property owner can repay the back taxes (plus interest and penalties) and recover the property. So do not be disappointed if there are no regularly scheduled tax auctions in your area.

To find out about tax auctions, simply call the county offices located in the directory. (If yours has not been included, please locate your county tax collection or tax assessor's office in the Blue

Pages of your telephone book. This office will be located in the county seat.)

During your call, ask the clerk about upcoming auctions. There may be none. If so, ask how you would find out about these auctions when they do occur. He or she may be able to tell you in which newspapers they will be advertised or where in the courthouse a notice would be posted.

On occasion, and depending on the county office, notices of upcoming auctions could be mailed to you. Find out what the fee for such a service would be. It might only cost a few dollars. Follow up your telephone call with a request in writing. Send a stamped, self-addressed envelope with your written request for auction notices.

As an added precaution, make it a habit of calling once a month to find out if any auctions are scheduled. The value of these tax auctions cannot be underestimated. Doing this can keep you up to date. It saves time compared to visiting your courthouse. Auction notices are not always sent or not mailed regularly, jeopardizing your chance to participate.

Special Characteristics

Tax sales are poorly attended. Most who show up are the property owners, to buy back their homes, or the mortgage company, bank or other lender with a vested interest in buying back the property. Occasionally, professional investors will show up. These are your competition.

Typically, the bulk of property sold at a tax sale consists of undeveloped land. Parcels of raw land are prime candidates for the tax sale. Speculators whose investment didn't pan out and developers who never built upon their land often pay their property taxes last, if ever. Such property, at a tax sale, can often sell for far below market value, or occasionally at giveaway prices.

Sometimes, and this is what makes them worthwhile, no one will show up. You may be the only bidder, should the mortgage holder or lender fail to attend. By their absence, they waive the right to the property, due to their failure to ensure that the

taxes were paid. As I said, it is rare. The property might also not be worth bidding on.

In early 1991, a Florida man bought a parcel of land, valued in excess of $100,000, through a tax sale. His winning bid: $120! The judge upheld the ruling when the opposing party's attorney disputed the tax-sale's validity. Good bargain for that tax-sale bidder.

Evaluation

Tax sales are not regularly scheduled in most areas of the country. Lenders show up at them to buy back their investment. Professionals appear occasionally to jump on opportunities presented when any mistakes are made in the process. Your chances of finding an outrageous bargain at one of these sales is about as good as winning the lottery.

Staying on top of them takes a lot of work. Showing up for tax auctions can bring you a string of disappointments. Their offerings are slim and such homes can be in extremely bad condition. However, some people do win lotteries, probably more often than those buying property at tax auctions for outrageous bargains.

You could outbid the lender for the property, at which point he would receive his investment back and you would buy the property free and clear.

Bidding against the lender requires a lot of cash, though, since you must pay for the purchase then and there, without financing. There will be a certain set limit the lender will not pass. That gives you the opportunity of buying the property at a safe resale level.

Contact the county offices listed in the directory and find out about tax auctions.

TAX SALES DIRECTORY

Alabama

Jefferson County Tax Sales
Tax Collectors Office
16 North 21st St.
Birmingham, AL 35263-0010
(205) 325-5500
O.Z. Hall

Arizona

Pima County Tax Sales
Treasurer's Office
Attn: Delinquent Taxes Dept.
115 N. Church Ave
Tuscon, AZ 85701
(602) 740-8341
James Kirk

California

Kern County Tax Sales
Real Estate
Tax Collectors Office
Redemption Division
1415 Truxton Ave.
Bakersfield, CA 93301
(805) 861-2357
Phil Franey

Los Angeles County Tax Sales
Tax Collector
225 North Hill
Los Angeles, CA 90012
(213) 974-2045
Sandra Davis

San Diego County Tax Sales
1600 Pacific Hwy Rm 162
San Diego, CA 92101-2474
(619) 236-3121
Paul Boland

El Paso County Tax Sales
Treasurer's Office
27 E. Vermijo Ave.
Colorado Springs, CO 80903
(719) 520-6666
Sharon Shipley

Colorado

Denver County Tax Sales
Delinquent Real & Personal
Property
Treasury Division
144 West Colfax Ave.
Denver, CO 80202
(303) 575-3458
Steve Hutt

Connecticut

Hartford Tax Sales
Tax Collectors Office
550 Main St.
Hartford, CT 06103
(203) 722-6096
Donald LeFevere

New Haven Tax Sales
200 Orange St.
New Haven CT 06510
(203) 787-8051
Salvador Calderero

Fairfield Tax Sales
Tax Collector
888 Washington Blvd.
Stamford, CT 06901
(203) 977-4089
John Mello

Waterbury Tax Sales
Tax Collectors Office
235 Grand St.
Waterbury, CT 06702
(203) 574-6811
Consilia Maiorano

Delaware

New Castle County Tax Sales
Sheriff's Office
11th & King Sts.
Wilmington, DE 19899
(302) 571-7564
Ann Elder

District of Columbia

Washington D.C. Tax Sales
Real Property Tax Office
300 Indiana Ave. NW
Washington, D.C. 20001
(202) 727-6441
Mr. Mersha

Florida

Broward County Tax Sale
Revenue Director
Delinquent Real Estate
Governmental Center Annex
1155 Andrews Ave.
Fort Lauderdale, FL 33301
(305) 468-3425
Joseph Rosenhagen

Duval County Tax Sale
Circuit Court Clerks Office
330 East Bay St.
Jacksonville, FL 32202
(904) 630-2059
Bob Fergerson

Dade County Tax Sales
Tax Collection Division
Delinquent Real Estate Tax
140 West Flagler Street
Miami, FL 33130
(305) 375-5455
Fred Ganz

Florida Department of
Revenue
Collection Division
541 S. Orlando Ave.
Suite 301
Maitland, FL 32751
(407) 623-1141
Deborah McGowan

Pinellas County Tax Sales
Tax Collectors Office
315 Court St.
Courthouse 3rd Floor
Clearwater, FL 34616
(813) 462-3383
O. Sanford Jasper

Hillsborough County Tax Sales
Tax Collector—Real Estate
Hillsborough County
Courthouse
Tampa, FL 33602
(813) 272-6070
Melvin Smith

Georgia

DeKalb County Tax Sales
Tax Commissioners Office
Delinquent Tax Office
120 West Trinity Place
Rm 110
Decatur, GA 30030
(404) 371-2107
Eugene Adams

Hawaii

Honolulu County Tax Sales
Department of Taxation
530 Punchbowl Street
Honolulu, HI 96813
(808) 523-4972
Grace Makamura

Illinois

Cook County Tax Sales
Cook County Collectors Office
118 N. Clark St., Rm 112
Chicago, IL 60602
(312) 443-6234
Edward Rosewell

Peoria County Tax Sales
Peoria County Clerk
Peoria County Courthouse
324 Main St., Rm 101
Peoria, IL 61602-1368
(309) 672-6059
Edward O'Connor

Winnebago County Tax Sales
Winnebago County Treasurer
400 West State St.
Courthouse, Rm 122
Rockford, IL 61105
(815) 987-3010
Douglas Aurard

Indiana

Vanderburgh County Tax Sales
Vanderburgh County Treasurer
One NW M.L. King Blvd
Rm 212
Evansville, IN 47708-1882
(812) 426-5248
Pat Tuley

Lake County Tax Sales
Lake County Treasurers Office
2293 N. Main St.
Crown Point, IN 46307
(219) 775-3760
Irene Holonga

Marion County Tax Sales
Marion County Treasurer's
Office
200 E. Washington Rm 1060
Indianapolis, IN 46204
(317) 236-4040
Mary Buckler

St. Joseph County Tax Sales
County/City Building
227 W. Jefferson
South Bend, IN 46601
(219) 284-9531
Cindy Boble

Iowa

Cedar Rapids City Tax Sales
City Treasurer's Office
930 1st St. SW
Cedar Rapids, IA 52404
(319) 398-3464
Michael Stevenson

Scott County Tax Sales
County Treasurer's
Department
416 W. 4th St.
Davenport, IA 52801
(319) 326-8670
William Cusack

Polk County Tax Sales
Polk County Treasurer's Office
111 Court Ave.
Des Moines, IA 50309
(515) 286-3060
Mary Malone

Kansas

Shawnee County Tax Sales
County Counselor
200 East 7th St., Room 203
Topeka, KS 66603
(913) 291-4042
Linda Jeffrey

Sedgwick County Tax Sales
Foreclosure Department
Sedgwick County Courthouse
525 North Main Street
Wichita, KS 67203
(316) 383-7595
Jerry McCoy

Kentucky

Fayette County Tax Sales
Master Commissioner's Office
Fayette County Court Clerk
910 1st National Building
167 W. Main St., Suite 910
Lexington, KY 40507
(606) 254-1637
Clyde Stapleton

Jefferson County Tax Sale
Jefferson County
Commissioners
600 W. Jefferson
Louisville, KY 40202
(502) 625-5934
J.R. Bartholomew

Louisiana

Baton Rouge Parish Tax Sale
Baton Rouge Sheriff's Dept.
Civil Division Property Tax
Office
P.O. Box 70
Baton Rouge, LA 70821
(504) 389-4810
Elmer Litchfield

Jefferson Parish Tax Sale
Jefferson Parish Sheriff's Office
Tax Department
P.O. Box 130
Gretna, LA 70054
(504) 363-5714
Harry Lee

Cado Parish Tax Sale
Sheriffs Office Tax Dept.
501 Texas St., Rm 101
Shreveport, LA 71101-5410
(319) 226-6538
Don Hathaway

Maryland

Baltimore City Tax Sale
Tax Sales Division
200 North Holiday St, Rm 1
Baltimore, MD 21202
(302) 396-3981
Ottavio Grande

Massachusetts

Boston City Tax Sales
Department of Revenue
100 Cambridge St.
Boston, MA 02204
(617) 727-4201
Bob Crist

Springfield City Tax Sales
Redevelopment Authority
73 State St.
Springfield, MA 01103
(413) 787-6538
George Vaselacopolis

Worcester City Tax Sales
Bureau of Land Use Control
City Hall, Room 209
455 Main St.
Worcester, MA 01608
(508) 799-1146
Timothy Cronin

Michigan

Washtenaw County Tax Sales
County Treasurers Office
101 East Huron
Ann Arbor, MI 48107
(313) 994-2520
Michael Stimpson

Wayne County Tax Sales
Department of Treasury
400 Monroe, Suite 520
Detroit, MI 48226
(313) 224-5990
Raymond Wojtowicz

Genesee County Tax Sales
County Treasurers Office
1101 Beach Street
Flint, MI 48502
(313) 257-3054
William Barkley

Kent County Tax Sales
County Treasurers Office
P.O. Box Y
Grand Rapids, MI 49501
(616) 774-3641
John Boerma

Ingram County Tax Sales
Treasurers Office, Courthouse
P.O. Box 215
Mason, MI 48854
(517) 676-7220
Donald Moore

Minnesota

Hennepin County Tax Sales
Forfeited Property Dept.
300 South 6th St., Rm 603A
Minneapolis, MN 55487
(612) 348-3734
Gordon Ramm

Mississippi

Hinds County Tax Sales
County Tax Collector
P.O. Box 1727
Jackson, MS 39215
(601) 968-6587
Glynn Pepper

Missouri

Jackson County Tax Sales
County Manager of Revenue
Property Tax Division
415 E. 12th St., Rm 100
Kansas City, MO 64106
(816) 881-3232
Mike Pendergrast

Greene County Tax Sales
Tax Collector
940 Boonville
Springfield, MO 65802
(417) 868-4036
Scott Payne

Clayton County Tax Sales
Tax Collectors Office
41 South Central
St Louis, MO 63105
(314) 889-2208
Robert Peterson

Montana

Lewis & Clark County Tax
Sale
Department of Treasury
City County Building
316 N. Park
Helena, MT 59624
(406) 443-1010
Joyce Saisbury

Nebraska

Lancaster County Tax Sale
County Treasurers Office
City-County Building
555 S. 10th St.
Lincoln, NE 68508
(402) 471-7425
R.J. Nurenberger

Douglas County Tax Sales
County Treasurers Office
Real Estate Division
Civic Center
1819 Farnam
Omaha, NE 68183
(402) 444-7081
Sam Howell

Nevada

Clark County Tax Sales
Treasurers Office
225 Bridger E. 1st Floor
Las Vegas, NV 89155
(702) 455-4323
Clark Astin

Washoe County Tax Sale
Washoe County Treasurers
Office
P.O. Box 11130
Reno, NV 89520
(702) 328-2510
Gary Simpson

New Jersey

Union County Tax Sales
Tax Collectors Office
50 Winfield Scott Plaza
Elizabeth, NJ 07201
(908) 820-4115
Mr. Chiodo

Hudson County Tax Sales
County Tax Lien Dept.
280 Grove St.
Jersey City, NJ 07302
(201) 547-5125
Denise Zambardino

Essex County Tax Sales
Property Management Div.
32 Green St. 4th Fl.
Newark, NJ 07102
(201) 733-8060
Marshall Cooper

Passaic County Tax Sales
Tax Assessors Office
City Hall
155 Market St.
Paterson, NJ 47505
(201) 881-4795
George Sokalski

New Mexico

Bernallo County Tax Sales
Taxation and Revenue Dept.
Property Tax
First National Bank Bldg. East
5301 Central Ave. NW
Albuquerque, NM 87108
(505) 827-0881
Pat Padilla

New York

Albany County Tax Sales
Real Property Tax Service
Agency
112 State St., Room 820
Albany, NY 12207
(518) 447-7050
John Lynch

Erie County Tax Sales
Real Property Taxation
95 Franklin St.
Buffalo, NY 14202
(716) 858-8333
Mr. Kowaleski

New York City Tax Sales
Department of Real Property
25 Elm Place
Brooklyn, NY 11201
(718) 935-9500
Mimi Shu

Monroe County Tax Sales
City Hall, Room 28B
30 Church St.
Rochester, NY 14614
(716) 428-6951
Allen Fitzpatrick

Onondaga County Tax Sales
Finance Department, 15th Fl
421 Montgomery St.
Syracuse, NY 13202
(315) 435-2426
Raymond Banach

Westchester County Tax Sales
Real Property Tax Commission
110 Grove Street L-222
White Plains, NY 10601
(914) 285-4325
Margaret Cimarra

North Carolina

Mecklenburg County Tax Sales
Tax Collector
P.O. Box 31457
Charlotte, NC 28231-6077
(704) 336-4600
John Petroskey

Guilford County Tax Sales
County Attorneys Office
Delinquent Tax Dept.
301 W. Market Street
Greensboro, NC 27401
(919) 373-3852
Jerry Weston

Forsyth County Tax Sales
County Attorneys Office
704 Hall of Justice
Winston-Salem, NC 27101
(919) 727-2216
Gene Price

North Dakota

Burleigh County Tax Sales
Auditors Office
221 North 5th St.
Bismark, ND 58501
(701) 222-6713
Kevin Glatt

Ohio

Hamilton County Tax Sales
Delinquent Taxes, Real Estate
138 East Court St.
Room 402
Cincinnati, OH 45202
(513) 632-8570
Robert Goering

Cuyahoga Falls
Sheriffs Department
Land Sale
1215 W. 3rd St.
Cleveland, OH 44113
(216) 443-6038
Robin Krause

Lucas County Tax Sales
Treasurers Office
Foreclosure Dept., 6th Fl.
One Government Center
Toledo, OH 43604
(419) 245-4057
Ray Kast

Oklahoma

Oklahoma County Tax Sales
County Treasurers Office
320 Robert S. Kerr
Oklahoma City, OK 73102
(405) 278-1300
Joe Barnes

Tulsa County Tax Sales
Treasurers Office
Delinquent Tax Dept.
Tulsa County Admin. Bldg.
500 South Denver
Tulsa, OK 74103
(918) 596-5070
John Cantrall

Oregon

Lane County Tax Sales
Foreclosure Department
Property Tax Division
125 E. 8th Ave,
Eugene, OR 97401
(503) 687-4174
Jeff Faw

Clakamas County Property
Management
902 Abernethy
Oregon City, OR 97045
(503) 650-3335
Cheryl Vannier

Pennsylvania

Lehigh County Tax Sales
Tax Claims B
Delinquent Tax Office
455 Hamilton
Allentown, PA 18101
(215) 820-3119
Franklin Baer

Rhode Island

Providence County Tax Sale
Tax Collector, City Hall
25 Dorrance St.
Providence, RI 02903
(401) 331-5252
Caroline Brazzil

South Carolina

Richland County Tax Sales
County Treasurers Office
2020 Hampton St.
P.O. Box 11947
Columbia, SC 29211
(803) 748-4900
Cordelia Pasky

South Dakota

Hughes County Tax Sales
Treasurers Office
104 E. Capitol
Pierre, SD 57501
(605) 224-9231
Maggie Oliva

Tennessee

Davidson County Tax Sales
Chancery Court
Metro Courthouse, Room 2
Nashville, TN 37201
(615) 259-5526
Judy Carnegie

Texas

Randall County Tax Sales
Tax Office
P.O. Box 997
Canyon, TX 79015-0997
(806) 655-7001
Sue Lambert

Travis County Tax Sales
Tax Assessor & Collector
P.O. Box 1748
Austin, TX 78767
(512) 473-9473
Nelda Wells Spears

Harris County Tax Sales
1001 Preston St.
Houston, TX 77002
(713) 224-1919
Jack Abercia

Utah

Salt Lake County Tax Sales
Auditors Office
Office N-2200
2001 South State St.
Salt Lake City, UT 84111
(801) 468-3381
Arthur Monson

Vermont

Waterbury County Tax Sales
Property Evaluation
43 Randall St.
Waterbury, VT 05676
(802) 241-3500
Sandra Brodeau

Virginia

Richmond County Tax Sales
Treasurers Office
P.O. Box 400
Warsaw, VA 22572
(804) 333-3555
John Hutt

Washington

Thurston County Tax Sales
Treasurers Office
2000 Lakeridge Dr.
Olympia, WA 98502
(206) 786-5550
Michael Murphy

West Virginia

Kanawha County Tax Sales
State Auditors Office
Land Development Dept.
State Capitol Building
Room 212
Charleston, WV 25305
(304) 348-2262
Glenn Gainer Jr.

Wisconsin

Dane County Tax Sales
County Treasurers Office
210 Martin Luther King Jr.
Blvd., Room 114
Madison, WI 53709
(608) 266-4151
James Amumbson

Conclusion

★★

Which government agencies have the best bargains? Which ones have the worst? The ratings system provided in this section has to be far different from what was done in Section Two. Real estate comparisons fall into the apples-versus-oranges dilemma.

There are several federal sources of excellent real estate bargains: the Resolution Trust Corporation, HUD, and the Veterans Administration. However, the properties these agencies are selling may not appeal to a large sector of prospective homeowners. In the same light, not everyone will head west to stake a mining claim with the Bureau of Land Management or buy a farm from the Farmers Home Administration.

Only one government agency has no desire to play ball when it comes to selling real estate: The General Services Administration's Federal Property Resources Service. While many agencies have good deals available and count on books like this to refer buyers to them, the GSA has little energy or desire to make their offerings exciting. This is just as well, because the GSA annual offerings are few and far between.

So, to conclude this section with anything more than a summary of the government agency's offerings would be misleading and useless to prospective homebuyers or real estate investors. Here is a summary of the real estate sources found in Section Three, with the types of property that one might find with them.

1. *The Resolution Trust Corporation.* The RTC holds a broad array of properties, from single-family homes to vacant land to apartment buildings, hotels, resorts, industrial parks, and so forth. They are in a negotiating phase because earlier efforts failed. A trend toward holding local real estate auctions has just started. GOOD BUYS are available with many of their properties. Expect this to continue for several years. OVERALL GREAT DEALS AVAILABLE.

2. *The Federal Deposit Insurance Corporation.* While fundamentally in the same lifeboat as the RTC, yet not with as much attendant publicity, the FDIC has future troubles. They have large commercial real estate holdings and many residential properties. In some cases, the FDIC has taken over savings and loan properties that should have gone to the RTC. They hold few auctions. Their brochures are a wonder to behold, but their sales staff is lethargic. SOME GOOD DEALS AVAILABLE IF YOU PERSIST.

3. *Fannie Mae and Freddie Mac.* They hold mainly single-family homes that are sold indi-

rectly through real estate brokers. They are not under the same stress as the RTC to sell, but troubles could loom for both if the housing market heads lower. SOME GOOD DEALS.

4. *Department of Housing and Urban Development*. Lower-class housing properties is their specialty. Affordable housing for marginally qualified borrowers who wish to make low down payments. Investors buy their extended listings to fix up and resell. Homebuyers bid on regular listings. VERY GOOD DEALS AVAILABLE for both these groups.

5. *Department of Veterans Affairs*. A notch below HUD properties. Same types of buyers. Their special listings often need extensive renovation. GOOD DEALS AVAILABLE but be prepared to invest in renovations.

6. *General Services Administration*. A hodgepodge of properties. Few deals, if any. Has no reason to sell. Will finance if you overpay. FIND ANOTHER PLACE TO BUY YOUR REAL ESTATE.

7. *Farmers Home Administration*. Holds many properties with real estate brokers through their state offices. Will more readily talk about lending you money than selling you property. Get them to talk about both. GOOD DEALS AVAILABLE AND LOW-COST FINANCING TO BOOT. Move to the country.

8. *Bureau of Land Management*. For the rugged investor who will live on pork and beans heated over an open campfire. This agency is strictly for the adventurous who want to capitalize on the federal government's urge to give land away at $5 an acre or less. GOOD IF THIS IS YOUR BAG.

9. *Probate and Estate Auctions*. Go to local auctioneers, scout through courthouses, and find very good deals. Negotiated sales work best with these properties. Past surveys show that buyers can save as much as 40% below market value in purchasing these properties. Hard to find out about and research work needed. Roll up your sleeves. Get on a lot of private auctioneer mailing lists. VERY GOOD DEALS AVAILABLE.

10. *Tax Sales*. Unpredictable at best. Frustrating and a waste of time for many who try this. Some good deals can be found. Occasional steals go to either the very lucky or the very patient. Mostly those blessed with luck. Competition is often the professionals and lending institutions. SLIM PICKINGS. GOOD DEALS ON A LUCKY DAY.

Section Four

★★

Introduction

★★

This section is entirely composed of private auctioneers, their names and telephone numbers (and in some cases, their fax numbers). Budget cuts and other concerns have forced government agencies to use private auctioneers. Some are on spot contracts, lasting one or a few auctions. Others are on annual or long-term contracts.

Auctioneers have been part and parcel of bankruptcy auctions since Roman times. Aside from local sheriffs, who have traditionally inherited the job of repossessing or foreclosing debtor property, the government keeps an arm's distance from these auctions.

The RTC has not mobilized its employees to become part of the auction process. Wisely, they have hired private auctioneers to hold auctions. If enough are held, this should act as a model for government agencies to emulate. Not that government agencies should involve themselves further in the auction process. Instead, the agencies should realize that auctions belong in professional and private hands, which will benefit the public and government alike.

As the decade progresses, private auctioneers will hold an increasing share of government auctions. Many professional auction-goers appreciate dealing with private auctioneers, as evidenced by their attendance at many private auctions and their absence from many government-held auctions.

This section is comprised of six separate chapters, listing different auction specialties. There exist many more specialized categories, but these six are the ones likely to interest the greatest number of auction participants.

Please do not frivolously contact these auctioneers. They are businessmen and have only so many hours in each day. Additionally, being placed on their mailing lists should be considered a privilege, not a birthright. Postage and printing for auction notices costs money.

Do not ask to be placed on their mailing lists just to fill your mailbox or for lack of something else to do. It hurts not only the auctioneer, but the seller and the rest of us auction-goers. Some auction companies have started charging a small fee to be placed on their mailing list. This is the result of many irresponsible callers who never intended to show up at an auction. Please do not be one of them. *Do* call for auction fliers when you are researching or seriously interested in attending an auction. That's what auctioneers are there for.

You will find auctioneers to be some of the friendliest people alive. Remember that they are salesmen and very good ones at that. Auctioneers have a vested interest in having you attend their auctions. Usually, the more bidders attending, the higher the average price paid per item.

Many will find the private auctioneer to be a refreshing change from the government bureaucrat, hunched in his cubicle, all the while resenting your phone call. Relax and enjoy dealing with private auctioneers. Many will even give you free advice on how you can improve your bidding skills. Ask them and see what happens.

ONE LAST TIP: Frequently it is difficult to reach an auctioneer. Here's an inside secret: Call them on Monday. That is normally their off-day. On most other days, you are likely to find the auctioneer away from his office . . . holding an auction, of course!

30

Private Auctioneers Used by the Government

★★

Government agencies increasingly rely on private auctioneers to conduct their sales. The directory that follows lists many private auctioneers who have been used by the government. This is not a complete list and cannot be: government agencies sometimes hire auctioneers on a one-time basis and at other times on an annual basis.

These auctioneers also hold private auctions.

You should look into those auctions. Good deals can be found at many auctions on vehicles, boats, airplanes, computers, and other merchandise or equipment.

Contact auctioneers in your area or in those areas where you wish to participate in government or private auctions.

PRIVATE AUCTIONEERS DIRECTORY

Atlanta

Arwood Auction Company
P.O. Box 250085
Atlanta, GA 30325
(404) 423-0110

The Dobbins Company
P.O. Box 2001 Station N
Atlanta, GA 30325
(404) 352-2638

Hudson & Marshall
4751 Best Road
Suite 300
Atlanta, GA 30337
(404) 763-0211

Boston

Jerome J. Manning, Inc.
313 Congress Street
Boston, MA 02210
(800) 521-0111

Garrett Auctioneers
76 High Street
Danburst, MA 01923
(508) 535-3271

Barton K. Hyte Company
15 Court Square
Boston, MA 02108
(617) 720-0939

Chicago

Hanzell Galleries
1120 S. Michigan
Chicago, IL 60605
(312) 922-6234

Michael Natchbar
4040 N. Kedzie
Chicago, IL 61068
(312) 539-7460

Marcie Rath
38 W. 196th—Route 20
Elgin, IL 60120
(708) 696-0375

Auction Services, Inc.
5338 North Lotus Avenue
Chicago, IL 60120
(312) 631-2255

Sheldon F. Good & Co.
333 W. Wacker Drive
Suite 450
Chicago, IL 60606
(312) 630-0915

Cincinnati

Delbert Cox &
Arthur Auctions
4674 Cincinnati-Brookville
Road
Cincinnati, OH 45013
(513) 738-3475

Semple & Associates
Box 44006
Cincinnati, OH 45244
(513) 724-1133

Cleveland

Bankers Motor Vehicle
4985 W. 150th Street
Cleveland, OH 44135
(216) 676-5920

Donn & Associates
21437 North Park Drive
Cleveland, OH 44126
(216) 331-5505

Rosen and Company
319 The Arcade
Cleveland, OH 44114
(216) 621-1860

Grossman Inc.
3749 Grosvenor Road
S. Euclid, OH 44118
(216) 932-0777

Bambeck Auctioneers Inc.
Route 4, Box 405
Dover, OH 44622
(216) 343-1437

Dallas

Keith Carey
2850 N. Main
Mansfield, TX 76063
(817) 265-1852

Pollack, Southwest
12750 Merit Drive
Suite 830
Dallas, TX 75251
(214) 239-9788

Rosen Systems
2520 W. Mockingbird Lane
Dallas, TX 75235
(214) 350-2381

Miller & Miller Auctioneers
2525 Ridgemar Blvd.
Suite 100
Fort Worth, TX 76116
(817) 732-4888

Rene Bates Auctioneers, Inc.
Route 4
McKinney, TX 75070
(214) 542-1604

Jim Short-Nelson Inc.
11811 Preston Road
Suite 100
Dallas, TX 75230
(214) 980-7539

Denver

Olde Cumberlin Auctions
1215 Edison Street
Box 248
Brush, CO 80723
(303) 842-2822

McCrea & Company
Auctioneers
5895 East 72nd Avenue
Commerce City, CO 80022
(303) 289-4437

Detroit

Mr. Bill Stanton
144 S. Main
Vermontville, MI 49096
(517) 726-0181

P.H.C. of Michigan
1844 Morang Street
Detroit, MI 48205
(313) 371-5100

Midwest Auto
14666 Telegraph Road
Detroit, MI 48239
(313) 538-2100

Farris Brothers
6665 W. Vernor
Detroit, MI 48209
(313) 843-5720

Robert Williams & Co.
17376 W. 12 Mile Road
Southfield, MI 48076
(313) 646-7090

L. M. Koploy & Co.
23100 Providence Drive
Suite 192
Detroit, MI 48075
(313) 559-0660

Houston

Windsor Auctions
911 Brenda Street
Houston, TX 77076
(713) 680-8001

Hart Galleries
2311 Westheimer
Houston, TX 77098
(713) 524-2979

R. E. Laird
510 Berring Drive
Suite 300
Houston, TX 77057
(713) 787-0330

Indianapolis

Allied Auctioneers
P.O. Box 167
Fountaintown, IN 46130
(317) 897-5268

Herman Strakis
3333 W. Tory
Indianapolis, IN 46202
(317) 244-8063

Marsh Auction Gallery
1205 E. New York Street
Indianapolis, IN 46202
(317) 636-3374

Kansas City

Cable Car Auction & Realty
1036 W. Ironwood
Olathe, KS 66061
(913) 782-8009

Alpyne Auctioneers
732 F. Sunnyside School Rd.
Blue Spring, MO 64015
(816) 461-0042

A-1 Auctions
3026 S. 37th
Kansas City, MO 66061
(914) 384-2775

Los Angeles

Butterfield & Butterfield
7602 Sunset Blvd.
Los Angeles, CA 90046
(213) 850-7500

Van Cleves & Company
1010 Kaiser Road
Napa, CA 94558
(707) 255-5850

Kennedy Wilson
3110 Main Street
Suite 200
Santa Monica, CA 90405
(213) 452-6664

Miami

Auction Company of Florida
911 N.E. 199th Street
Suite 105
N. Miami Beach, FL 33179
(305) 651-0500

Sugarman Auction Co.
18500 N.E. 5th Avenue
N. Miami Beach, FL 33179
(305) 651-0101

Harry P. Stamples
7875 N.W. 77th Avenue
Miami, FL 33166
(305) 761-8744

Minneapolis

Quickie Auctions
22895 141st Avenue R
Rogers, MN 55374
(612) 428-4217

Wayne Pike Auctions
P.O. Box 387
Princeton, MN 55371
(612) 389-2700

Kurt Kiefer Auctions
P.O. Box 745
Fergus Falls, MN 56538
(800) 435-2726

New York City

Jackson Hecht Assoc.
10 East 21st Street
Suite 1608
New York City, NY 10010
(212) 505-0880

Stuart L. Medow & Assoc.
2935 West 5th Street
Brooklyn, NY 11224
(718) 996-2405

Philadelphia

John Hirsh Auctioneers
3330 S. 20th Street
Philadelphia, PA 19415
(215) 336-8800

Freeman Fine Arts
1808 Chestnut Street
Philadelphia, PA 19103
(215) 562-9275

Quaker City Auctioneers
2860 Memphis Street
Philadelphia, PA 19134
(215) 426-5300

William F. Comly
1825 East Boston
Philadelphia, PA 19125
(215) 634-2500

Pittsburgh

Anderson Auctioneers
Box 2824A
Georgetown, PA 15043
(412) 734-4244

Hostetter Auctioneers
124 Black Hawk Road
Beaver Falls, PA 15010
(412) 847-1880

Johnson Auction Service
147 Flaugherty Road
Coraopolis, PA 15108
(412) 457-1100

Portland

Harvey Berlant
Beaverton, OR 97005
(503) 641-8989

American Auctioneering
85322 Jasper Park Road
Pleasant Hill, OR 97455
(503) 266-1551

Steve Van Gordon Auctions
P.O. Box 520
Canby, OR 97013
(503) 266-1551

Sacramento

Huisman Auctioneers
7923 Stockton Blvd.
Sacramento, CA 95823
(916) 682-3338

Roger Ernst & Assoc.
824 Kiernan Avenue
Modesto, CA 95356
(209) 527-7399

Shuffield Auctions
712 Garden Highway
Yuba City, CA 95911
(916) 673-5189

San Diego

H & M Goodies Auction
130 E. 8th Street
National City, CA 92050
(619) 474-8296

Mark Gorin & Assoc.
18837 Brookhurst Street
Suite 210
Fountain Valley, CA 92708
(619) 560-1677

McCormick Auction Co.
743 El Cajon
San Diego, CA 92020
(619) 447-1196

San Francisco

A. R. S. Auctioneers
1755 10th Avenue
San Francisco, CA 94122
(415) 566-6464

Ashman Co. & Auctioneers
1415 Oakland Blvd.
Walnut Creek, CA 94596
(415) 682-8100

Rabin Brothers
660 3rd Street
San Francisco, CA 94107
(916) 441-2405

Ross-Dove Company
330 Hatch Drive
Foster City, CA 94404
(415) 571-7400

Van Cleves & Co.
1010 Kaiser Road
Napa, CA 94558
(707) 255-5850

Seattle

Auctions Inc.
19520 66th Avenue W.
Lynwood, WA 98036
(206) 771-4232

James G. Murphy
P.O. Box 82160
Kenmore, WA 98028
(206) 486-1246

St. Louis

Robert Merry Auctions
5501 Milburn Road
St. Louis, MO 63129
(314) 487-3992

Midwest Auction Service
566 1st Capitol
St. Charles, MO 63301
(314) 946-0392

Tampa/St. Petersburg

Action Auctioneers
8955 Palm River Road
Tampa, FL 33619
(813) 677-4677

Tampa Machinery Auction
11720 Highway 301
Thonotasassa, FL 33592
(813) 986-2485

Washington D.C./Baltimore

Adam A. Weschler & Son, Inc.
905 E Street, NW
Washington, DC 20004
(202) 628-1281

Adams & Winer Auctioneers
330 West 23rd Street
Baltimore, MD 21211
(301) 366-8300

Car & Truck Auction
1370 West North Avenue
Baltimore, MD 21217
(301) 669-1666

Douglas K. Goldsten
Auctioneers, Inc.
3408 Wisconsin Ave, NW
Washington, DC 20016
(202) 966-0100

R. L. Rasmus Auctioneers
6060 Tower Court
Suite LL-1
Alexandria, VA 22304
(703) 370-2338

31

Bankruptcy Auctioneers

★★

Many auctioneers hold bankruptcy auctions. Some specialize in commercial liquidations; others in farm liquidations.

There are a number of ways to close a business and never go into bankruptcy. Some companies might shut down their operations, hire an auctioneer to sell off their property (machinery, equipment, inventory, fixtures, etc.) and settle with creditors outside of the court process. Many creditors will jump at such settlements, as their attorneys understand what meager funds may remain after the company's assets pass through the federal bankruptcy system.

The list of auctioneers that follows includes the main types of liquidations. This directory can be used as a supplement to Chapter 16, United States Trustees, for commercial bankruptcy auctioneers, and as a supplement to Chapter 26, Farmers Home Administration, for farm liquidations.

After having attended enough auctions, you will discover that there are greater bargains, and more of them, at auctions that don't pass through the court system. Search these auctions out. They are not officially "government" auctions, but can, nonetheless, be great finds.

Please contact the auctioneers near you or where you expect to participate, from the directory that follows. These auctions come highly recommended by the professionals. Don't worry, there's enough to go around.

BANKRUPTCY AUCTIONEERS DIRECTORY

Alabama

Acton, Mike F.
Acton & Associates
P.O. Box 43028
Birmingham, AL 35243
(205) 823-2330

Behel, Don, CAI
Don Behel Realty &
Auction, Inc.
Rt. 4, Box 505
Killen, AL 35645
(205) 757-4100
FAX (205) 757-4087

Brown, Richard
7595 Highway 72 West
Madison, AL 35758
(205) 837-6229
FAX (205) 830-9653

Farmer, David
Farmco Auctioneers
& Liquidations
P.O. Box 1725
Albertville, AL 35950
(800) 445-4608

Faulkner, William F.
2222 E. Arbor Dr.
Huntsville, AL 35811

Hancock, Greg
11 Red Fox Dr.
Pelham, AL 35124
(205) 663-7611

Knotts, Edward V., CAI
Knotts RE & Auction Co.
411 E. 2nd St.
Sheffield, AL 35660
(205) 386-7048
FAX (205) 386-0110

Montgomery, John H.
613 Memorial Dr., SW
Decatur, AL 35601
(205) 350-6959

Alaska

Joyner, Donald L.
Joyner-Bolts Quality
Auction
P.O. Box 211145
Anchorage, AK 99521-1145
(907) 276-6804

Kingston, Kathleen A.
Kingston's Auction Co.
P.O. Box 101614
Anchorage, AK 99510-1614
(907) 345-6413
FAX (907) 276-8357

Mulready, Jane
8618 Gail Ave.
Juneau, AK 99801
(907) 789-2821

Arizona

Bradley, Rex V.
Valley Auctioneers
8560 E. Cortez St.
Scottsdale, AZ 85260
(602) 948-2323
FAX (602) 274-2069

Centabar, Richard
43344 N. Murphy Ave.
Queen Creek, AZ 85242
(602) 987-3717

Kundert, Stanley D.
1309 E. Benson Hwy.
Tucson, AZ 85714
(602) 294-0823

McDaniel, Doak W.
Box 686, Sonoita, AZ 85637
(602) 455-5660

Poulsen, Gary L., CAI
15220 N. 51st Place
Scottsdale, AZ 85254-2281
(602) 996-6201
FAX (602) 971-6144

Vieu, Theodore R.
3350 E. Wetstones
Vail, AZ 85641
(602) 762-5091

Arkansas

Guthery, Donnie
20th Century Collectables
Rt. 8, Box 236
Fayetteville, AR 72701
(501) 839-3274

Hightower, Ray A.
308 Rock St., P.O. Box 388
Little Rock, AR 72203
(501) 376-2361
FAX (501) 376-3776

Knight, William H.
Route 1
Manila, AR 72442
(501) 562-2405
FAX (501) 562-6552

Looper, Jimmy L.
RR #1, Box 298A
Greenwood, AR 72936
(501) 996-4401

Magee, Gary N.
Rt. 3, Box 16
Piggott, AR 72454

Stafford, David K.
Route 1, P.O. Box 1317
Donaldson, AR 71941
(501) 384-5352

Sullivan, Connie P.
Connie Sullivan Auction Co.
15610 Viney Woods Rd.
Mabelvale, AR 72103
(501) 847-8545

Vanover, Tommy
Vanover & Tucker
P.O. Box 1762
Springdale, AR 727665
(501) 756-6785

Wilson, Lonnie
P.O. Box 2507
Alma, AR 72921
(501) 474-9100

Wooley, Brad H., CAI
Brad H. Wooley Auction Inc.
9 Lombardy La.
Little Rock, AR 72207
(501) 664-3826
FAX (501) 664-3826

California

Albino, Ali
Albino Auction Co.
8921 San Leandro St.

San Leandro, CA 94621
(415) 635-9654
Fax (415) 635-9656

Brewer, Allen
Allen Brewer
8301-5 Mission Gorge Rd.
Santee, CA 920711
(619) 448-8866

Burtzlaff, Jr., Paul G., CAI
1229-690 Vienna Dr.
Sunnyvale, CA 94089
(408) 745-7070

Daly, Jr., James, CAI
International Auction
Service & Antiques
6320 Monterey St.
Gilroy, CA 95020
(408) 847-4038

Dorfman, Joseph
1730 Bodega Ave.
Petaluma, CA 94952
(707) 765-1944

Fern, Don
1718 N. McClelland
Santa Maria, CA 93454
(805) 922-2522

Hansen, Maurice N.
P.O. Box 3610
San Clemente, CA 92674
(714) 661-8020
FAX (714) 661-8083

Hitchcock, Greg
5151 Robin Wood Rd. #21
Bonita, CA 92002
(619) 472-5278

Hoch, Mike
10728 50th St.
Mira Loma, CA 91752

Hochman, Jr., S. M.
P.O. Box 429
Templeton, CA 93465

(805) 434-3400
FAX (805) 434-3389

Isett, Greg
Pacific Coast Auction Service
6001-88th St., Ste D
Sacramento, CA 95828
(916) 381-6088
FAX (916) 381-3548

Macon, Mike, CAI
Macon Brothers Auctioneers
558 S. Washington St.
Sonora, CA 95370
(209) 532-0112
FAX (209) 532-1594

Main, Robert W.
7640 Benbow Dr.
Garberville, CA 95440
(707) 923-2311
FAX (707) 923-2767

McCormack, James K., CAI
McCormack Auction Co.
743 El Cajon Blvd.
El Cajon, CA 92020-4905
(619) 447-1196

McEnerney, Gary A.
13331 Alabama Rd.
Galt, CA 95632
(916) 685-6500
FAX (916) 686-8504

Mulrooney, Jim
Mulrooney Auction Co.
P.O. Box 748
Galt, CA 95632
(209) 745-4542

Nestel, Stephen
210 Porto St.
Manhattan Beach, CA 90266
(213) 545-3743
FAX (213) 546-7105

Owens, Dale
Owens Auction Co.
P.O. Box 1056
Newcastle, CA 95659
(916) 663-1911

Reinders, Wm. R. Bill
Van Tassell Realty & Auction
735 W. Middle Ave.
Morgan Hill, CA 95037
(408) 779-5868
FAX (408) 444-2981

Root, Evan
P.O. Box 504
Woodbridge, CA 95258
(209) 369-2521

Sarlak, Khosrow
Grand USA Auction Co.
1442 E. Lincoln Ave. #154
Orange, CA 92665
(714) 289-0123

Sass, Robert, CAI
Abe's Auctions
5531 Fulton Ave.
Van Nuys, CA 91401
(818) 909-9408

Sloan, Todd
Sloan Auction Co.
12016 Waxwing Court
Penn Valley, CA 95946
(800) 367-5335
FAX (916) 632-1603

Speight, Carl
P.O. Box 62974
Los Angeles, CA 90062
(213) 281-8456

Tichenor, Richard E.
3951 Mt. Brundage
San Diego, CA 92111
(619) 292-4168

Vantassell, Vance J.
917 G St.
Sacramento, CA 95814
(916) 444-8633

Williams, Frank J.
United Auction Services
P.O. Box 107
Crescent Mills, CA 95934
(916) 284-6176
FAX (916) 284-6178

Colorado

Dickensheet, W. J.
Dickensheet & Assoc.
2021 S. Platte River Dr.
Denver, CO 80223
(303) 934-8322

Kleinsteiber, Robert E.
903 Platte Dr.
Ft. Lupton, CO 80621
(303) 857-6093

Rosvall, Charles R.
1238 S. Broadway
Denver, CO 80210
(303) 722-4028
FAX (303) 777-2032

Rundell, E. W.
1521 E. Hwy. 50
P.O. Box 237
Salida, CO 81201
(719) 539-3262

Smith, Randell N., CAI
0151 Mel Rey Rd.
Glenwood Springs, CO 81601
(303) 945-9723

Ven Berg, E. S.
P.O. Box 647
Sterling, CO 80751
(303) 522-1950

Connecticut

Gagliardi, Thomas
Thomas Industries
74 Forbes Ave., 2nd Fl.
New Haven, CT 06512-1610

Manheimer, Seymour
P.O. Box 421
New London, CT 06320
(203) 443-5942
FAX (203) 444-0759

Zetomer, Arthur
Park City Auction Service
P.O. Box 6314
Bridgeport, CT 06604
(203) 333-5251

Delaware

Conley, Larry W.
RD 3, Box 215-D
Bridgeville, DE 19933
(302) 337-8601

Green, John G.
1104 Middletown/Warrick Rd.
Middletown, DE 19709
(302) 378-4722

Hechter, Charles
19 Indian Rd.
Newark, DE 19711
(302) 738-9918
FAX (302) 994-3567

Kring, Jeffry C.
Jeffry Kring, Auctioneer
P.O. Box 5602
Newark, DE 19714-5602
(302) 738-6968

District of Columbia

Evans, W. Ronald, CAI
Capital City Enterprise, Ltd.
407 H Street NE
Washington, D.C. 20002
(202) 543-2828
FAX (202) 547-2545

Gross, Ames
1155 Connecticut Ave. NW
Washington, D.C. 20036
(202) 429-6554

Florida

Albritton, Kale
1023 Euclid Ave.
Lakeland, FL 33801
(813) 687-3938
FAX (813) 687-0610

Arey, Chester M., CAI
Arey's Auction Team, Inc.
P.O. Box 1953
Deland, FL 32721-1953
(904) 738-0050

Banks, William S.
Banks Auction
2577 SE Madison St.
Stuart, FL 34996
(407) 287-5334
FAX (407) 287-1570

Blecha, Wayne H.
P.O. Box 999
Paisley, FL 32767-0999
(407) 889-0842

Brandenburger, Paul W.
2959 Mercury Rd.
Jacksonville, FL 32207-7912
(904) 730-2911
FAX (904) 730-2911

Campbell, David
Campbell Auctioneers
1047 Bayshore Dr.
Englewood, FL 34223-2302
(813) 475-7166

Campen, Ben, CAI
Ben Campen Auctioneers
P.O. Drawer 1209
Gainesville, FL 32602
(904) 375-6600
FAX (904) 371-1990

Chana, Kurt E.
413 Willow Brook
Longwood, FL 32779
(407) 869-8519

Coakley, John W.
540 E. Compton Ct.
Deland, FL 32724
(904) 738-7974

Criswell, Bob
5616 Sailfish Dr.
Lutz, FL 33549
(813) 265-3811

Croom, Dan R.
P.O. Box 3262
Longwood, FL 32779
(407) 788-3040

Deller, Ronald J.
Deller's Auction Center
112 S. Lunar Terr.
Inverness, FL 32650
(904) 344-8121

Dietrich, George T.
2156 Seminole Trail
Orlando, FL 32833
(407) 568-2351

Driggers III, Walter J.
AAPT Realty Inc.
7800 N. Carl G. Rose Hwy.
Hernando, FL 32642-2102
(904) 726-0275
FAX (904) 726-0235

Eggleston, Bernie
Eggleston Auctioneers
4601 W. Kennedy Blvd.
Suite 214
Tampa, FL 33609
(813) 282-0057

Ellis, Ronald L.
Ron Ellis
Realtor & Auctioneer
3600 S. Atlantic Ave.
New Smyrna Beach
FL 32169
(904) 423-8866

Elting, Robert W.
Action Auctioneers
11023 Desota Rd.
Riverview, FL 33569

Fisher, Lamar P. and Louis
B. Jr. & III, CAI
Fisher Auction
Company, Inc.
431 NE First St.
Pompano Beach, FL 33060
(305) 942-0917

Frazier, Jerry R.
408 N. 5th St.
Lake City, FL 32055
(904) 755-2816

Fullom, Cliff K.
Land & Sea Auctions, Inc.
P.O. Box 1062
Marathon, FL 33050
(800) 654-1889

Gould, David M.
6600 SW 122nd St.
Miami, FL 33156
(305) 284-8129

Graham, Jim, CAI
Jim Graham Inc.
Auctioneers-Realtors
204 US 1
N. Palm Beach, FL 33408
(407) 842-7605
FAX (407) 844-2100

Harwig, Anton H.
P.O. Box 282
Flagler Beach, FL 32126
(904) 439-2765

Haworth, Richard L.
Venice Auction
601 Spur St.
Venice, FL 34292
(813) 485-4964

Janacek, Rod
Janacek Auctioneers
P.O. Box 475
Fort White, FL 32038
(904) 497-1509

Johnson, Edward
9920 Steven Dr.
Polk City, FL 33868
(813) 984-3228

Johnson, Ray
701 S. Bumby Ave.
Orlando, FL 32806
(407) 896-1399

Kazaleh, Freddie S.
Professional Auctioneers, Inc.
P.O. Box 24465
Jacksonville, FL 32241-4465
(904) 733-9260

Kelsey, Thomas C.
530 Timber Ridge Dr.
Pensacola, FL 32534
(904) 968-5185

King, Hellen B.
AAPT Realty Inc.
7800 N. Carl G. Rose Hwy.
Hernando, FL 32642-2102
(904) 726-0275
FAX (904) 726-0235

Kirkland, Carol J.
Kirkland Auction Gallery
1907 Wahalaw Court
Tallahassee, FL 32301
(904) 877-6180

Knieriem, James B.
1414 60th Street So.
Gulfport, FL 33707
(813) 341-0006

Marcovitch, Allen J.
Anaheim Realty & Auctions
1155 SW 25th Avenue
Boynton Beach, FL 33426
(407) 734-8029

McGerity, Francis C.
5386 Countryfield Circle
Ft. Myers, FL 33905
(813) 694-0510

Mesmer, Jack
Auction USA Inc.
1554 Thornhill Circle
Ovledo, FL 32765-6538
(407) 366-1700

Messer, Ed
AAPT Realty Inc.
7800 N. Carl G. Rose Hwy.
Hernando, FL 32642-2102
(904) 726-0275
FAX (904) 726-0235

Moates, Robert C.
4082 Belair La. #20
Naples, FL 33940
(813) 262-4921

Montambault, Leon
4406 Cobia Dr.
Tampa, FL 33617
(813) 985-5453
FAX (813) 935-0716

Myers, Lenny A.
Richard Myers
Auction & Realty
P.O. Box 2062
Winter Park, FL 32790-2062
(407) 644-7295
FAX (407) 644-7380

Myers, Richard L., CAI
Myers Real Estate
Auction Service
P.O. Box 2062
Winter Park, FL 32790-2062
(407) 644-7295
FAX (407) 644-7380

Neiswander, John, CAI
5115 N. Socrum Loop Rd.,
#43
Lakeland, FL 33809-4213
(813) 859-7633

New, Gary C.
Auction Associates, Inc.
4823 Silver Star Rd.
Suite 160
Orlando, FL 32808
(407) 297-7695
FAX (407) 297-7695

Passonno, Ralph F.
6141 Bay Isles Dr.
Boynton Beach, FL 33437
(407) 738-9055

Pravda, Don
16345 W. Dixie Hwy.
N. Miami Beach, FL 33160
(305) 944-4030
FAX (305) 949-1689

Regenhold, Rick H.
Regenhold Auctions
611 S. Myrtle
Clearwater, FL 34616
(813) 461-1666

Sanders, Virgil
P.O. Box 5517
Ocala, FL 32678-5517

Selby, Brent L.
1013 W. Camino Real
Boca Raton, FL 33486
(407) 391-9145
FAX (407) 391-0139

Shuler, Cliff
422 Julia St.
Titusville, FL 32780
(407) 267-8563
FAX (407) 383-3147

Sklarey, Seth, CAI
Box K, Coconut Grove
Miami, FL 33233-0140
(305) 374-1166
FAX (305) 379-0653

Smith, Donald J.
4925 University Dr.
Leesburg, FL 34748
(904) 787-5486

Strait, Harold
4159 Hidden Branch Dr. N
Jacksonville, FL 32257
(904) 260-0516

Thompson, Judy
411 NE 25th Ave.
Ocala, FL 32670
(904) 732-7101
FAX (904) 732-8525

Weise, Timothy J.
525 SW Buswell Ave.
Port St. Lucie, FL 34983-8736
(407) 878-6217
FAX (407) 878-6394

Williams, Richard M.
1556 Hwy. 97 S
Cantonment, FL 32533
(904) 623-0141

Worcester, Eugene A.
3323 Meadow Run Circle
Venice, FL 34293
(813) 497-4060
FAX (813) 921-7103

Georgia

Ansley, Hershel P.
Ansley Realty
323-B East Jackson St.
Thomasville, GA 31792
(912) 228-4456

Arwood, David G., CAI
Arwood Auction Co., Inc.
P.O. Box 4485
Marietta (Atlanta), GA 30061
(404) 423-0110
FAX (404) 424-5200

Barfield, Maurice, CAI
Southeastern Auctions, Inc.
Route 2, P.O. Box 323
Doerun, GA 31744
(812) 985-5700

Childs, Billy J., CAI
Hudson & Marshall, Inc.
717 North Ave.
Macon, GA 31211
(800) 841-9400
FAX (912) 743-6110

Dobbins, Walter
The Dobbins Co.
Box 20001 STA.
N. Atlanta, GA 30325
(404) 352-2638

Grant III, P. T., CAI
Hudson & Marshall, Inc.
717 North Ave.
Macon, GA 31211
(800) 841-9400
FAX (912) 743-6110

Hudson, Jr., B. G.
Hudson & Marshall, Inc.
717 North Ave.
Macon, GA 31211
(800) 841-9400
FAX (912) 743-6110

Kibler, Rodney
Kibler Auctions
9020 Vanns Tavern Rd.
Gainesville, GA 30506
(404) 781-8369

Lane, Larry
Brent Lane & Assoc., Inc.
717 North Ave.
Macon, GA 31211
(912) 743-8120
FAX (912) 742-3877

Ledbetter, Gary B.
315 15th Street SE
Georgetown, Apt. G-6
Moultrie, GA 31768
(912) 890-2550

Marshall III and IV, Asa M.
Hudson & Marshall Inc.
717 North Ave.
Macon, GA 31211
(912) 743-1511

Register, Jr., L. E.
Auctions Unlimited
Watkinsville, GA 30677
(404) 769-5561

Stoutenburg, Karen
Abel Auctions &
Liquidations
6460 Warren Dr.
Norcross, GA 30093
(404) 263-0438
FAX (404) 447-6567

Strickland, John S., CAI
Strickland Realty & Auction
P.O. Box 429
Moultrie, GA 31776
(912) 985-7730

Suarez, John
Barbara & John Suarez
Auctioneers & Appraisers
1980 S. Walkers Mill Rd.
Orchard Hill, GA 30266-0349
(800) 446-7874
FAX (404) 227-0873

Sutton, William F., CAI
717 North Ave.
Macon, GA 31211
(912) 743-1511
FAX (912) 743-6110

Toles, Bobby J.
Atlas Auction Company
617 Shorter Ave.
Rome, GA 30161
(800) 992-2155
FAX (404) 235-5571

Whitney, Chuck, CAI
Hudson & Marshall, Inc.
4751 Best Rd., Suite 240
Atlanta, GA 30337
(404) 763-0211
FAX (404) 763-1071

Hawaii

Adolfi, Jr., Frank J.
1427 Akamai Place
Kailua, HI 96734
(808) 262-7730

Glen, Mark
Glen & Associates
350 Ward Ave., Suite 106
Honolulu, HI 96814-4091
(808) 599-3888
FAX (808) 955-6769

Idaho

Fivecoat, Bill
4850 Umatilla
Boise, ID 83709
(208) 338-8051

Hossner, Lynn
Hossner Brothers
Auction Company
109 N. 2nd West St.
Anthony, ID 83445
(208) 624-3782
FAX (208) 624-3783

Jensen, Darrel M.
Great Western Auctions, Int'l.
825 W. 100th South
Blackfoot, ID 83221
(800) 227-8759
FAX (208) 684-4580

Illinois

Beck, William B.
RR 2, Box 258
Edinburg, IL 62531
(217) 325-3351
FAX (217) 325-3313

Bickers, Michael W.
Auction Liquidators
420 W. State
Charleston, IL 61920
(217) 348-0288

Bornheimer, Robert C.
P.O. Box 52
Whittington, IL 62897
(618) 629-2622

Clingan, Jim
P.O. Box 52, Royal, IL 61871
(217) 582-2868
FAX (217) 582-2861

Croisant, Darwin L.
3727 Rt. 251 South
Mendota, IL 61342
(815) 539-7903

Decker, Don
P.O. Box 11
Milford, IL 60953
(815) 889-5355
FAX (815) 889-4113

Decker, William, CAI
Decker Realtor-Auctioneer
Rt. 2, Box 29
Milford, IL 60953
(815) 889-4213
FAX (815) 889-4113

Draper, Robert D.
No. 1, Draper Lane
Ohio, IL 61349
(815) 376-2001

Fiscus, Robert W.
Mac Auctions
307 E. Main
Robinson, IL 62454
(618) 546-1550

Gaule, William L., CAI
114 E. Walnut
Chatham, IL 62629
(217) 483-2484
FAX (217) 483-2485

Geer, Roberta L.
55 White Oak Circle
St. Charles, IL 60174
(708) 377-4625
FAX (708) 377-4680

Goodman, David A.
Martin Goodman Associates
370 E. Kensington, Ste. 200
Mt. Prospect, IL 60056
(708) 253-3451
FAX (708) 253-9194

Hachmeister, Greg L.
425 W. 4th St., Box 171
Pecatonica, IL 61063
(815) 239-2714
FAX (815) 239-1436

Hachmeister, Henry, CAI
305 E. 3rd St., Box 296
Pecatonica, IL 61063
(815) 239-1436
FAX (815) 239-1436

Hannam, Rolland R.
805 E. Second St.
Galesburg, IL 61401-6115
(309) 342-5494

Hayunga, Phil
4482 Lamm Rd.
Freeport, IL 61032
(815) 235-2323

Holley, Otis D.
Barliant Auction Co.
4701 W. Augusta Blvd.
Chicago, IL 60651
(312) 378-7171
FAX (312) 378-5285

Jeffries, Timothy J.
2642 Vermont St.
Quincy, IL 62301
(217) 223-0017

Johnson, Earl, CAI
1543 Aberdeen St.
Chicago Heights, IL 60411
(312) 472-2176

Lane, Leon
316 E. Harrison
Sullivan, IL 61951
(217) 728-7132

Lenhart, Doyne, CAI
Route 2, Box 12
Georgetown, IL 61846
(217) 662-8644
FAX (217) 662-2484

Martin, Larry D., CAI
603 N. Jackson St.
Clinton, IL 61727
(217) 935-3873
FAX (217) 935-3795

McAnly, Howard
P.O. Box 602
Rochelle, IL 61068
(815) 562-6957

Mezo, Joseph
P.O. Box 218
McLeansboro, IL 62859
(618) 643-3176

Nestrick, Donald E., CAI
Nestrick Mid-West Appraisals
Box 206
Aledo, IL 61231
(309) 582-2469
FAX (309) 596-2124

Newton, John L.
P.O. Box 1412, Hwy. 45 North
Vienna, IL 62995
(618) 658-3141

Ollis, Joe D.
Joe Ollis Auction Service
Rt. 4, Box 293
Marion, IL 62959
(618) 964-1431

Parker, Gregory O., CAI
Dunnings Auction Service
755 Church Rd.
Elgin, IL 60123-9302
(708) 741-3483
FAX (708) 741-3589

Perschke, Walter
Auction USA
Perfection Bldg.
1423 W. Fullerton
Chicago, IL 60614
(312) 871-7200
FAX (312) 871-8010

Phillips, Ronald L.
301 N. State St.
Freeburg, IL 62243
(618) 539-3427

Plocar, Joseph M.
Antique Enterprises, Inc.
203 N. Water St.
Wilmington, IL 60481
(815) 476-9020

Rath, Marcy M.
Marcy Rath Auction Services
38 W. 196, Rt. 20
Elgin, IL 60123
(312) 695-0388

Rath, Mari Kaye
Marcy Rath Auction Service
38 W. 196th, RT. 20
Elgin, IL 60123
(708) 695-0375

Reid, Keith
Box 99, Albion, IL 62806
(618) 445-2233

Roth, Jim, and Norman, CAIs
RR #5
E. Peoria, IL 61611
(309) 266-6784

Schrage, Larry R., CAI
Complete Auction Service
RR 1, Box 60
Grant Park, IL 60940
(815) 465-6137

Tosetti, Jack E.
Tosetti & Associates
Auction Service
120 S. Cedar St.
Nokomis, IL 62075
(217) 563-8641

Windler, William H.
P.O. Box 516
Irvington, IL 62848-0516
(618) 249-8241

Indiana

Abernathy, Terry C., CAI
Abernathy Auctions
& Real Estate
21 W. Union St.
Liberty, IN 47353
(317) 458-5826

Baber, Steven J.
SSJB Associates, Inc.
P.O. Box 599
New Palestine, IN 46163
(317) 861-4495

Butts, Virgil W., CAI
600 W. National Ave.
Brazil, IN 47834
(812) 446-2322
FAX (812) 446-2322

Campbell, Harold L.
57105 Country Rd. 21
Goshen, IN 46526
(219) 294-1328

Chitwood, Fred
Chitwood Auctions
2775 West 1505
Lebanon, IN 46052
(317) 482-3528

Crum, Lincoln
Crum's Auction & Realty
4909 Hamburg Pike
Jeffersonville, IN 47130
(812) 282-6043

Crume, Roy L., CAI
3619 W. Sycamore Lane
Kokomo, IN 46901
(317) 452-6946

D'Amico, David
P.O. Box 594
Richmond, IN 47375
(317) 962-6310

Eberly, Luther
Eberly Auction Service
RR 2, Box A202
Silver Lake, IN 46982
(219) 982-8100

Ellenberger, Robert, CAI
130½ W. Market St.
Bluffton, IN 46714
(219) 824-2426
FAX (219) 824-1728

Evans, Larry
Route 1, Box 223
Mentone, IN 46539
(219) 353-7121

Frantz, R. D.
Frantz & Assoc.
Auction/Realty
P.O. Box 511
Warren, IN 46792-0511
(219) 375-2056

Harritt, Douglas A., CAI
4704 Corydon Pike
New Albany, IN 47150
(812) 944-0217

Hines, Beecher D.
M & H Auction Service
416 S. Main St.
Auburn, IN 46706
(219) 925-4366

Hixson, Larry J.
Hixson Auction Service
1600 Allison Blvd.
Auburn, IN 46706-3221
(219) 357-4477

Klein, Victor J.
Klein Realty, Auction Co.
404 North 7th St.
Vincennes, IN 47591
(812) 882-2202
FAX (812) 882-8777

Lacy, Phillip H.
Lacy Auction & Realty
Company
329 E. Division Rd.
Valparaiso, IN 46383
(219) 462-1402

Lambright, Harvey C., CAI
112 N. Detroit St.
LaGrange, IN 46761
(219) 463-2013

Mavis, Fred C.
M & H Auction Service
416 S. Main St.
Auburn, IN 46706
(219) 925-4366

Michael, Greg M., CAI
P.O. Box 7
Camden, IN 46917
(219) 686-2400

Muench, Ron
15229 Shoreway E.
Carmel, IN 46032
(317) 844-2929
FAX (317) 844-3699

Ott, Robert A., CAI
Ott Auctioneer
c/o 1st National Bank
800 Lincolnway, Rm. 311
LaPorte, IN 46350
(219) 362-3365

Ratts, Noble
2223A Rome Dr.
Indianapolis, IN 46208
(317) 431-0606

Rinehart, Bret R.
44 S. Center, Box 98
Flora, IN 46929
(219) 967-4195

Robinson, Fred
RR #1
Butlerville, IN 47223
(812) 873-6855

Shaffer, Lee, CAI
Kurtz Auction & Realty
101 SE 3rd St., Suite 38
Evansville, IN 47708
(812) 464-9308

Silke, Jr., Marlin C.
Silke Auction & Realty
RR #2, Box 97
Eberfeld, IN 47613
(812) 983-4548

Sipe, Stephen L.
5800 S. Fairfield, Suite 114
Fort Wayne, IN 46807
(219) 745-5469

Smith, Ralph D.
3209 Kratzville Rd.
Evansville, IN 47710
(812) 422-6586

Somers, Roger K.
Somers Brothers
4074 E. 400 North
Blufton, IN 46714
(219) 622-4600

Steinman, Orville G.
AAA Auction Service, Inc.
11210 State Rd. 4 East
New Haven, IN 46774

Strakis, Herman D., CAI
3333 W. Troy
Indianapolis, IN 46241
(317) 244-8063
FAX (317) 244-3767

Swalls, Johnny Lee
RR 1, Box 8AA
Lewis, IN 47858
(812) 495-6119

Swartzendruber, Homer
CAI, Swartzendruber Realty
P.O. Box 331
Shipshewana, IN 46565
(219) 768-4744

Taylor, David A., CAI
Taylor Auction Company
6804 Summertime Dr.
Indianapolis, IN 46226
(317) 547-7319

Vogel, Philip L., CAI
909 U.S. 24 East
Monticello, IN 47960

Wagner, C.T.
405 E. Main St.
P.O. Box 481
Washington, IN 47501
(812) 254-4186
FAX (812) 254-4088

Warren, William
119 First St.
Pierceton, IN 46562
(219) 594-2126

Wilson, William B., CAI
William Wilson
Auction/Realty
Main & Church Sts.
New Harmony, IN 47631
(812) 682-4686

Iowa

Arnold, Jay
Arnold Auction Service
RR 1, Box 18
Mallard, IA 50562
(712) 425-3538

Bousselot, Norman
Rt. 1, Box 18
Calamus, IA 52729
(319) 246-2628

Buckles, Howard
Buckles Auctioneering
Service
1002 Sixth
Keosauqua, IA 52565
(319) 293-3012

Burke, Donald
114 N. Elm
Creco, IA 52136

Claussen, Leroy
3611 Parkdale Dr.
Bettendorf, IA 52722
(319) 332-9341

Forristal, Pat
c/o McGuire Auction Co.
123 N. Main
Holstein, IA 51025
(712) 368-2635
FAX (712) 368-2784

Gilchrist, Kyle
Rt. #1, Box 259
Douds, IA 52551
(515) 936-4670

Hamilton, William W.
Hamilton Auctions
2216 N. Third St.
Clinton, IA 52732
(319) 243-5828
FAX (800) 222-8450

Hattermann, Todd J.
P.O. Box 162
Pauline, IA 51046
(712) 448-3602

Helgerson, Martin R.
Rt. 3, Box 151
Ottumwa, IA 52501
(515) 683-1915

Huff, Jim
RR #2
Keosauqua, IA 52565
(319) 293-3711

Johnson, Roy B., CAI
P.O. Box 405
Buffalo Center, IA 50424
(515) 562-2032

King, Jeff
King Auction
1700 Grandview
Miscatine, IA 51761-1548
(319) 264-8190

Langstraat, Jerry
Northside Sales Company
725 11th Avenue
Sibley, IA 51249
(712) 754-3213

Law, Donald G.
300 5th Avenue SW
LeMars, IA 51031-2163
(712) 546-8188

Moehle, Richard W.
RR 2, Box 66
Mediapolis, IA 52637
(319) 394-3666

Morehead, Gregory P., CAI
Morehead Auction Co.
25 S. Clinton St.
Albia, IA 52531
(515) 932-7129

Murphy, Mike
2019 Hwy. 375
Council Bluffs, IA 51501

Rogers, Jerry A.
Box 89
Union, IA 50258
(515) 486-2475

Ryan, Dale J.
RR #1, Box 197
Decorah, IA 52101
(319) 382-9533
FAX (319) 382-8785

Schultz, Clete
1310 Rapids, Box 101
Adel, IA 50003
(515) 993-4440

Sharar, Larry L.
124 Ellsworth
Dows, IA 50071

Smith, Dale E.
801 Third Avenue, NW
Pocahontas, IA 50574
(712) 335-4111
FAX (712) 335-3111

Starling, Dennis G.
RR 1, Box 101
Lost Nation, IA 52554

Stewart, Bill
3808 72nd Street
Urbandale, IA 50322
(515) 279-4434
FAX (515) 244-1170

Swartzendruber, John
RR 1, Box 60-A
Wellman, IA 52654
(319) 256-5772

Swenson, Dennis E.
RR 2, Box 75
Belmond, IA 50421

Taylor, Gordon E.
P.O. Box 949, Hwy. 65 North
Mason City, IA 50401
(515) 423-5242

Van Der Werff, Rich, CAI
Ven Der Werff
Auctioneers, Inc.
Box 529, 215 Main
Sanborn, IA 51248
(712) 729-3264

Wears, Brent, CAI
RR 1, Box 360
Solon, IA 52333
(319) 644-3779

Kansas

Berning, Russell
Berning Auction
Box 113
Marienthal, KS 67873
(316) 379-4446

Bertram, Jerry L.
Banbury Auction & Real
Estate
Box 8733
Pratt, KS 67124
(316) 672-7723

Bletscher, Chris
Route 1
Abilene, KS 67410
(913) 598-2385

Bloomer, Robert A., CAI
Auction One, Inc.
Box 386
Osborne, KS 67463
(913) 346-2856
FAX (913) 346-5554

Boesker, Leland W.
RR 2, Box 28
Moundridge, KS 67107
(316) 345-2603

Bushart, Lowell M.
Auction One, Inc.
1023 N. Kansas, #4, Box 188
Liberal, KS 67905-0188
(316) 624-3814
FAX (316) 626-4332

Carlin, Wayne E., CAI
Carlin's Auction/Real Estate
Box 310
Osborne, KS 67473
(913) 346-5778

Cochran, J.E.
RR 2, Box 23
Caldwell, KS 67022
(316) 845-2155

Cole, Curtis C., CAI
Cole Auction & Real Estate
1405 Main
Goodland, KS 67735
(913) 899-2683
FAX (913) 899-5563

Ediger, Richard W.
119½ N. Main
P.O. Box 488
Buhler, KS 67522
(316) 543-6633

Fair, William, CAI
Bill Fair & Company
637 Indiana
Lawrence, KS 66044
(913) 842-9999
FAX (913) 842-1733

Gehrer, Kory J.
Rt. #1, Box 123
Newton, KS 67114
(316) 283-5309

Gerdes, Harley
Gerdes Equipment and
Auction
Box 571
Lyndon, KS 66451
(913) 828-4476

Hartter, Roger
Hartter Auction Service
Rt. 4, Box 236
Sabetha, KS 66534
(913) 284-2643

Haskins, David
Haskins Auction & Realty
114 S. State
Norton, KS 67654-2142
(913) 877-3275

Hunt, Myron B.
1002-B East 23rd Street
Hutchinson, KS 67502-5652
(316) 663-7428

Johnson, Roger A.
2154 Wesley
Salina, KS 67401
(913) 825-9306

Kobbeman, Shawn
RR 3, Box 68
Lincoln, KS 67455
(913) 524-3041

Koch, Vern E.
Koch Auction Service
1822 Cow Palace Rd.
Newton, KS 67124
(316) 283-6700

Mugler, Harold R.
Route 1, Box 42
Clay Center, KS 67432
(913) 632-3994
FAX (913) 632-3994

Olson, Galen D.
Olson Realty & Auction
1109 Easter
Wakeeney, KS 67672
(913) 743-2774

Porter, Sr., Roger L., CAI
P.O. Box 8, 1036 Ironwood
Olathe, KS 66061
(913) 782-8009
FAX (913) 782-7767

Potter, Gary
1125 S. Summit
Arkansas City, KS 67005
(316) 442-4136

Scott, Ronald J.
1719 Belmont, Box 398
Garden City, KS 67846
(316) 275-0202

Shivers, Ronald L.
300 Summit Dr.
Abilene, KS 67410
(913) 263-7488

Showalter, Bud
Rte. 1, Box 101B
Easton, KS 66020
(913) 651-5233

Stricker, Jerry L.
Route 1, Box 137B
Gardner, KS 66030
(913) 884-7074

Van Sickle, Ralph, CAI
15 W. 5th Avenue
Emporia, KS 66801
(316) 342-6431

Wood, Tharon L.
RR 4, Box 141
Abilene, KS 67410
(913) 263-7161

Kentucky

Adams, Roy E., CAI
Ford Realty &
Auction Co., Inc.
P.O. Box 1435
Mount Vernon, KY 40456
(606) 256-4555

Birdwhistell, E. Glenn
154 S. Main St.
Lawrenceburg, KY 40342
(502) 839-3456

Blackford, Glen
Route 3, Box 29
Russellville, KY 42276
(502) 726-9238

Bush, J. Randall, CAI
2689 Red Mill Rd.
Elizabethtown, KY 42701
(502) 765-2298
FAX (502) 737-7787

Butler, Dwight
Box 194
Harned, KY 40144
(502) 756-5859

Conners, Jr., Andy J.
302 Tincher Dr.
Versailles, KY 40383
(606) 873-8429

Crain, Frank, CAI
1710 Pear Orchard Rd.
Elizabethtown, KY
42701-9410
(502) 765-7684
FAX (502) 737-7787

Deane, Silas E.
5785 Highway 144
Owensboro, KY 42303
(502) 926-8553
FAX (502) 926-8574

Durham III, John L., CAI
Durham & Durham
Realty/Auction
135 N. Third St.
Danville, KY 40422
(606) 236-2770

Edwards, W.G.
P.O. Box 573
Monticello, KY 42633
(606) 348-9583

Erler, Donald R.
Century 21-Hall Powell
& Associates
1850 S. Hwy. 53
LaGrange, KY 40031
(502) 222-1114
FAX (502) 222-3470

Freeman, S. D.
110 Hospital St.
Cadiz, KY 42211
(502) 522-3101

Gibson, William S., CAI
1708 N. Mayo
Pikeville, KY 41501
(606) 432-8181
FAX (606) 478-9838

Godby, Samuel R.
P.O. Box 391
Somerset, KY 42501
(606) 678-8189

Hungerford, Dennis L.
Col. D's Auction Service
P.O. Box 59
Eddyville, KY 42038
(502) 388-2985

Hunt, Thomas R., CAI
Hunt Realty & Auction Co.
66131 W. Bypass Ave.
Bowling Green, KY
42101-4968
(502) 782-2200
FAX (502) 843-8780

Kachler, Billy
P.O. Box 21, Main St.
Mays Licks, KY 41055
(606) 763-6140
FAX (606) 763-6100

Kessler, John M. and Wayne
P.O. Box 271
Campbellsville, KY 42718
(502) 465-7051

Kurtz, William B., CAI
Kurtz Auction Company
305 Frederica St.
Owensboro, KY 42301
(502) 926-8553

Ledbetter, Kay S.
Ledbetter & Stewart, Ltd.
Realtors & Auctioneers
1999 Richmond Rd., Suite 500
Lexington, KY 40502
(606) 268-1400
FAX (606) 268-2677

Levy, Stuart G.
5602 Harrods Cove
Louisville, KY 40059
(502) 228-5254

Lewis, Stephen D.
129 E. Main St.
Morehead, KY 40351
(606) 784-4168
FAX (606) 784-4160

Lynch, James D., CAI
Lynch Auction & Realty
1186 E. Broadway
Louisville, KY 40204
(502) 589-9822

Maddox, Alan
501 School St.
Beaver Dam, KY 42320
(502) 274-9672
FAX (502) 274-5610

Maglinger, Gary
Maglinger Auction & Realty
1331 West 5th Street
Owensboro, KY 42301
(502) 683-5923
FAX (502) 683-5923

Melloan, James M.
Kurtz Auction & Realty
305 Frederica St.
Owensboro, KY 42301
(502) 926-8553
FAX (502) 926-8574

Mills, Larry
P.O. Box 143
Greensburg, KY 42743
(502) 932-4998

Monarch, Miller, CAI
Monarch Auction & Realty
P.O. Box 188
Hardinsburg, KY 40143
(502) 756-2153
FAX (502) 547-2100

Riden, Billy F.
Riden Auction & Realty
114 W. Main St.
Providence, KY 42450
(502) 667-2570
FAX (502) 667-2097

Roy, Ralph D.
Box 578
W. Cumberland Ave.
Jamestown, KY 42649-0578
(502) 343-3334
FAX (502) 343-3033

Sexton, James C.
200 S. Main
Harrodsburg, KY 40330
(606) 734-7585
FAX (606) 734-9923

Stewart III, Daniel D.
Ledbetter & Stewart, Ltd.
Realtors & Auctioneers
1999 Richmond Rd., Suite 500
Lexington, KY 40502
(606) 268-1400
FAX (606) 268-2677

Sutton, Lewis R.
Box 209
Richmond, KY 40475
(606) 792-4277

Tabb, Cordell
319 S. Mulberry St.
Elizabethtown, KY 42701

Thomason, David B., CAI
216 Buckman St.
P.O. Box 722
Shepherdsville, KY 40165
(502) 955-7342
FAX (502) 543-5414

True, Rene F.
3350 Snaffle Rd.
Lexington, KY 40513
(609) 268-2533
FAX (606) 266-3699

Turner, Linda R.
1506 S. Virginia St.
Hopkinsville, KY 42240
(502) 885-6789

Watt, Gerald W.
609 N. Main St.
Tomplinsville, KY 42167
(502) 487-8569

Wells, Gary L., CAI
Gary Wells Auctioneers
Rt. 1
Owingville, KY 40360
(606) 674-2453

White, Dwain C., CAI
Thomas White & Sons
Auction & Real Estate
Box 355
Kuttawa, KY 42055
(502) 388-2420

Willett, Roscoe
Real Estate & Auction Sales
6720 Contest Rd.
Paducah, KY 42001
(502) 554-0065

Louisiana

Babb, Keith, CAI
P.O. Box 4222
Monroe, LA 71211-4968
(318) 343-6211
FAX (318) 343-6232

Hemphill, Don
11762 Darryl Dr.
Baton Rouge, LA 70815
(504) 272-9635
FAX (504) 272-6526

Wolfe, Lynn, CAI
2026 Pitch Pine
Shreveport, LA 71118
(318) 688-9466

Maine

Blair, Robert
R. Blair's Auction Service
P.O. Box 308
Wells, ME 04090
(207) 646-7475
FAX (207) 646-4144

Caprara, Victor A.
RFD #3, Box 3530
Winthrop, ME 04364
(207) 377-2080

Giquere, Gerald P., Jr.
P.O. Box 1272
Windham, ME 04062
(207) 892-3800

Keating III, James J.
J. J. Keating, Inc.
Rt. 1, North
Kennebunk, ME 04043
(207) 985-2097

Ward, Richard W.
RFD 1, Box 69
Limestone, ME 04750
(207) 325-4755

Maryland

Biser, Robert C.
8615 Opossumtown Pike
Frederick, MD 21702
(301) 662-7424

Bradstreet, Mark E.
Middletown Valley
Auction Service
P.O. Box 1
Tuscarora, MD 21790
(301) 874-2303

Campbell, Robert H.
121 Prince George St.
Annapolis, MD 21401
(301) 263-5808
FAX (301) 263-8427

Cox, Jimmy
9409 Marlboro Pike
Upper Marlboro, MD 20772
(301) 599-6285

Fitzgerald, William J.
W. J. Fitzgerald & Co.
P.O. Box 288
Mechanicsville, MD 20659
(800) 365-7031
FAX (301) 843-9656

Hartman, David P.
8703 Maravoss La.
Baltimore, MD 21234

Hunt, George C.
19521 Woodfield Rd.
Gaithersburg, MD 20879
(301) 948-3937

Hunter, Norman E., CAI
Hunters Sale Barn, Inc.
Route 276, P.O. Box 427
Rising Sun, MD 21911
(301) 658-6400
FAX (301) 658-3864

Martin, Clair L.
P.O. Box 499
Margansville, MD
21767-0499
(301) 797-4428

Richardson, Pete
Pete Richardson
Auction Sales
P.O. Box 51
Willards, MD 21874
(301) 546-2425
FAX (301) 835-8613

Rigdon, H. B., CAI
Rigdon Auctioneers
P.O. Box 625
Forest Hill, MD 21050
(301) 836-2787
FAX (301) 836-2738

Rudnick, Joseph
P.O. Box 190
Galena, MD 21635
(301) 648-5601
FAX (301) 648-5298

Thomas, Robert P., CAI
Arbor Realty &
Auction Company
Rt. 925N, Box 278
Waldorf, MD 20601
(301) 449-4444
FAX (301) 843-0513

Whitson, Guy M.
T. R. O'Farrell, Inc.
6 Quintal Dr.
Westminster, MD 21157
(301) 848-5533

Massachusetts

Hacobson, Harvey A., CAI
390 Main St.
Worcester, MA 01608
(508) 755-2550
FAX (508) 791-8994

Maynard, Ronald V.
Ron Maynard Auctioneers
258 Groton St.
Dunstable, MA 01827
(508) 649-4280

Monroe, Sandra F.
10 State St.
Woburn, MA 01801
(617) 933-3998
FAX (617) 932-0421

Moon, William F., CAI
William F. Moon & Company
12 Lewis Rd., RFD #1
N. Attleboro, MA 02760
(508) 699-4477
FAX (508) 651-9877

Paine, Stanley J.
1198 Boyleston St.
Chestnut Hill, MA 02167
(617) 731-4455
FAX (617) 566-0840

Santa Lucia, Frank
80 Upham St.
Melrose, MA 02176-3526
(617) 337-2931
FAX (617) 337-2933

Santos, Michael
Bristol Auctioneers
568 Washington St.
Wellesley, MA 02181
(617) 235-9035

Torteson, James R., CAI
10 Hope Ave.
Oxford, MA 01540
(508) 987-2277

Valyou, Leroy N., Jr.
12 Hilltop Circle
West Newbury, MA 01985
(508) 363-2946

Michigan

Albrecht, Herbert, CAI
Herb Albrecht, CAI, &
Associates
3884 Saginaw Rd.
Vassar, MI 48768
(517) 823-8835

Ballor, R. William, CAI
Bill Ballor Auction Service
201 N. First St., P.O. Box 249
Linwood, MI 48634
(517) 697-4212

Berg, Roger S., CAI
23675 N. Shore Dr.
Edwardsburg, MI 49112
(616) 699-5584
FAX (616) 699-5584

Boyk, John S., CAI
Boyk's Auction Service
7878 Cathro Rd.
Alpena, MI 49707
(517) 356-9589

Canfield, Melody Rae
Mel's Auction
P.O. Box 1103
Fowlerville, MI 48836
(517) 223-8707

Chase, Alfred C.
Chase Auction Service
239 State St.
Hesperia, MI 49421
(616) 854-6865

Dilyard, Roy
305 W. Silver St.
Reading, MI 49274
(517) 283-3085

Egnash, Ray
P.O. Box 184
Howell, MI 48843
(517) 546-7496

Freund, Ken
Auctionway Sales, Inc.
P.O. Box 3096, 2443 S. Old 27
Gaylord, MI 49735
(517) 732-7808

Glardon, Daniel G.
988 E. Henderson Rd.
Owosso, MI 48867
(517) 725-7756

Hecht, Gerald W., CAI
9849 Bradley Rd.
Frankenmuth, MI 48734
(517) 652-2242

Hinsdale, Larry D.
394 Copeland Rd.
Coldwater, MI 49036
(517) 238-2619

Juckette, Rollo A.
16241 Brewer Rd.
Dundee, MI 48131
(313) 529-2388

King, Edward G.
P.O. Box 375
Mason, MI 48854
(517) 223-7184

Kubesh, Dennis
P.O. Box 61
Maple City, MI 49664
(616) 228-6667

Landstra, Bill
13027 7-Mile Rd.
Belding, MI 48809

Norton, David A.
Norton of Michigan
50 W. Pearl St.
Coldwater, MI 49036
(517) 279-9063
FAX (517) 279-9191

Reeser, Steve, CAI
1465 N. Cedar
Mason, MI 48854
(517) 699-2219
FAX (517) 699-3064

Ringel, Ronald W.
11444 Big Four Rd.
Bear Lake, MI 49614

Stanton, Steve E.
Stanton's Auctioneers &
Realtors
144 S. Main
Vermontville, MI 49096
(517) 726-0181
FAX (517) 726-0060

Stutzman, David E.
1847 Pine Dr.
Traverse City, MI 49684
(616) 938-9761

Whalen, John M., CAI
5844 Gotfredson Rd.
Plymouth, MI 48170-5075
(313) 459-5144

Zieman, Joseph L.
1320 Crooks #7
Royal Oak, MI 48067-1342
(313) 545-2332

Minnesota

Baker, John E.
Rt. #3, Box 171
Appleton, MN 56208
(612) 394-2489

Carpenter, Michael W.
Carpenter Auction Company
104 Parkview Dr.
P.O. Box 245
Lake Benton, MN 56149
(507) 368-4307

Christian, David, CAI
Quickie Auction Service
22895 141st Avenue N.
Rogers, MN 55374
(612) 428-4217
FAX (612) 428-8355

Fahey, James D.
P.O. Box 370
Hutchinson, MN 55350
(612) 587-3510
FAX (612) 587-3255

Haas, Rich H.
Continental Auctioneers School
P.O. Box 346
Mankato, MN 56002-0346
(507) 625-5595

Houghton, Richard E., CAI
1967 Launa Ave.
Red Wing, MN 55066
(612) 388-5870

Imholte, Frank B.
8160 Country Rd. 138
St. Cloud, MN 56301
(612) 255-9398

Lampi, Thomas
Lampi Auction Equipment
RR 1, Box 76
Annandale, MN 55302
(612) 274-5393

Landgraff, Frederick D.
P.O. Box 326, 409 N. Jackson
Minneota, MN 56264-0457
(507) 872-5430

Marguth, Terry
1500 E. Bridge St.
Redwood Falls, MN 56283
(507) 644-8433
FAX (507) 644-2425

Mitchell, Cliff
Mitchell Auction Service
P.O. Box 390
Albany, MN 56307-0390
(612) 845-2244
FAX (612) 845-2187

Nord, Ronald D.
Box 3451, 215 Ruby St.
Mankato, MN 56002
(507) 625-7653

Pinske, Bill
325 West Main St.
Arlington, MN 55307
(612) 964-2250

Scheffler, Richard
Scheffler Auctioneering
Route 1, P.O. Box 67
Morton, MN 56270
(507) 697-6257

Schroeder, Orville M.
106 W. Adams St.
Caledonia, MN 55921
(507) 724-2874

Wiedemoth, E. H.
564 Clark St.
Hutchinson, MN 55350
(612) 587-2210

Mississippi

Johnson, Lannie E. and
Merry. K.
Rt. 3, Box 297A
Fulton, MS 38843
(414) 862-2835

Ozborn, Kline, Jr.
Box 651
Canton, MS 39046
(601) 859-3845
FAX (601) 859-7828

Missouri

Arnaman, H. Willard
1312 E. Main St., P.O. Box 123
Unionville, MO 63565
(816) 947-2883

Atterberry, Larry P., CAI
Atterberry & Assoc.
Auction Co.
79121-70 Drive SE
Columbia, MO 65201
(314) 474-9295

Bayless, Alan
P.O. Box 14068
Parkville, MO 64152
(816) 587-7575

Burger, Ron
Ron Burger Auction Service
Route 1, Box 1085
Scott City, MO 63780
(314) 264-2501

Easley, Randy
Easley Auction Co.
P.O. Box 176, Hwy. 210
Orrick, MO 64077
(816) 483-1167
FAX (816) 496-3423

Hamilton, Robert F.
P.O. Box 231
Kimberling City, MO 65686
(417) 739-2047

Howard, Duane
718 Manzanola La.
Smithville, MO 64089
(816) 532-0705

Kallmeyer, Joy
Hwy. 100 East, P.O. Box 223
Hermann, MO 65041
(314) 486-5714

Kelly, Pat E.
Kelly & Kelly
P.O. Box 926, J
Joplin, MO 64801-0926
(417) 781-4022

Lambert, Mike
Mike Lambert
Enterprise Inc.
Rt. #3, Box 181
Kirksville, MO 63501
(816) 665-7889
FAX (816) 665-1139

Long, Billy, CAI
Billy Long Auction & Realty
1950-L S. Glenstone
Springfield, MO 65804
(417) 882-5664
FAX (417) 882-7653

Marter, Gregory G.
#90 Country Life Dr.
O'Fallon, MO 63366
(314) 272-4890

Merry, Donald E.
5805 Sorrel Tree Ct.
St. Louis, MO 63129
(314) 487-5846

Merry, Robert
Robert Merry Auction Co.
5501 Milburn Rd.
St. Louis, MO 63129
(314) 487-3992

Montgomery, Richard
716 Beardsley Court
Ferguson, MO 63135
(314) 521-0768

Pickett, Eddie
Route 1, Box 162
Stewartsville, MO 64490
(816) 669-3433

Ratliff, Dennis W.
Rt. 1, Box 18-B
Easton, MO 64443
(816) 667-5411

Schroff, Roy
130 E. 1st
Hermann, MO 65041
(314) 486-2332

Stanger, Ed
ABC Auction Co.
905 N. Yuma
Independence, MO 64056-1954
(816) 796-3065

Voorheis, Brent, CAI
10877 N. Hwy. J
Harrisburg, MO 65256-9730
(314) 874-5988
FAX (314) 874-5988

Wells, Jim
Ace Auction Service
104 Friendship La.
Clinton, MO 64735
(816) 885-3725

Woolery, David R.
Woolery Auction Co.
P.O. Box 414
Branson, MO 65616
(417) 335-4242

Yancey, Gary J.
1800 S. Sneed
Sedalia, MO 65301
(816) 827-3668

Ytell, Wayne H.
Ytell Auction Service
1244 Glenwood Pl.
Carthage, MO 64836
(417) 358-7024
FAX (417) 358-7024

Montana

Ellis, Jerry, CAI
Ellis Auction Sales
P.O. Box 50310
Billings, MT 59105
(406) 245-3519

Gardner, Davar and Todd
Gardner Auction Service
Box 943
Kalispell, MT 59901
(406) 752-7682
FAX (406) 752-9674

Mandeville, John
1112 Mandeville La.
Bozeman, MT 59715
(406) 587-7832

Metzger, William
3150 W. Cameron Bridge Rd.
Manhattan, MT 59741
(406) 285-6511
FAX (406) 285-6514

Nebraska

Dolan, Jr., Thomas R.
102 N. Dewey
North Platte, NE 69101-6903
(308) 532-0342
FAX (308) 532-1463

Elting, Bradley K.
145 N. 44th Street
Hebron, NE 68370
(402) 768-7270
FAX (402) 768-6016

Garey, Marsden, CAI
1610 Parkview Dr.
Grand Island, NE 68801
(308) 384-9011

Green, Norm E., CAI
Norm Green
Realty & Auction
Box 563, 104 S. Lincoln Ave.
York, NE 68467
(402) 362-5595
FAX (402) 362-4875

Maly, John L.
Maly Auction Service
1636 N. Garfield St.
Fremont, NE 68025
(402) 721-8879

Marshall, Robin
Route 1, Box 26
Elm Creek, NE 68836
(308) 856-4102

Martin, Dean C.
P.O. Box 207
Lexington, NE 68850
(308) 324-4931

Stander, Earl E.
E & E Auction Service
RR #1, Box 180
Weeping Water, NE 68463
(402) 267-5435

Standley, Dale E., CAI
Standley Auction & Realty
P.O. Box 3186
Omaha, NE 68103-3186
(402) 345-1117
FAX (712) 366-6631

Starman, Steve
1240 Royal Dr.
Papillon, NE 68128
(402) 592-1933
FAX (402) 592-2327

Swanson, Lynn
Box 245
Wallace, NE 69169
(308) 387-4307

Thomsen, Charles, CAI
RR 2
Hooper, NE 68031
(402) 654-2464
FAX (402) 721-0109

Nevada

Britt, Don P.
5126 S. Somerset Dr.
Las Vegas, NV 89120
(702) 451-9075

Robinson, J. D., David K.
1500 E. Tropicana Ave.
Suite 102
Las Vegas, NV 89119
(702) 597-9845
FAX (702) 736-9192

Stewart, Hagan L.
6979 Mountain Moss Dr.
Las Vegas, NV 89117
(702) 794-3174
FAX (702) 369-7430

New Hampshire

Little, Michael G.
191 Silk Farm Rd.
Concord, NH 03301
(603) 225-6066
FAX (603) 225-2855

Michael, George
74 Wilson Hill Rd.
Merrimack, NH 03054-2903
(603) 424-7400

Reblin, Howard E.
Phoenix Auction Service
P.O. Box 136
Newton Junction, NH 03859
(603) 382-8122

Schofield, Stephen H., CAI
Rt. 1, Box 178
Concord Hill Rd.
S. Effingham, NH 03882
(603) 539-6619
FAX (603) 539-5123

New Jersey

Copeland II, Harrie E.
P.O. Box 389
Stockton, NJ 08559

Doerrmann, Benjamin A.
Garden State Auction Co.
Box 376 A Sherwin Rd., RD 2
Sewell, NJ 08080
(609) 478-2389
FAX (609) 478-6066

Dubin, David W.
30 Sandy Dr.
Newfield, NJ 08344
(609) 697-4847
FAX (609) 697-4255

Glembocki, Eugene B.
Gem Auctioneering Inc.
1 Kenton Ave.
Marlton, NJ 08053
(609) 983-6313

Patalano, Diane
Country Girls, Ltd. Inc.
Box 144
Saddle River, NJ 07458
(201) 391-6225

Schrager, Steven R.
S. R. Schrager, Inc.
13 Dobson Rd.
E. Brunswick, NJ 08816
(908) 613-1350

Schueler, George W.
Realty & Land Exchange
1315 Allaire Ave.
Wanamassa, NJ 07712
(201) 531-4488

Slatoff, Robert W.
Lester & Robert Slatoff, Inc.
777 W. State St.
Trenton, NJ 08618
(215) 736-8989

Swartz, Brian L.
Swartz Assoc.
66 Linwood Ave.
Dover, NJ 07801
(800) 545-3459
FAX (201) 328-1120

Walsh, Edward R.
Walsh Auction Service
38 Lynn Dr.
Ocean, NJ 07712
(201) 493-4518

New Mexico

Bailey, Connie L.
Rt. 1, Box 74
Alamogordo, NM 88310
(505) 437-0597

Dance, Joan & Steve, CAI
P.O. Box 72156
Albuquerque, NM 87195

Wimberly, Bill
Auction Services, Inc.
10100 Central SW
Albuquerque, NM 87121
(505) 831-3449
FAX (505) 831-8035

New York

Alestra, Dennis
Divine Wood
9724 3rd Ave.
Brooklyn, NY 11209
(718) 748-1345

Amodeo, Michael
Michael Amodeo Co., Inc.
799 Broadway
New York, NY 10003
(212) 473-6830
FAX (718) 645-9596

Benjamin, Alan J., CAI
A. J. Benjamin, Auctioneer
131 Sherwood Ave.
Binghamton, NY 13903
(800) 767-4725

Bergerson, Carl H.
80 Howard St.
Wellsville, NY 14895
(716) 593-3434

Bontrager, Alfred, CAI
Bontrager Realtor
13238 Broadway
Alden, NY 14004
(716) 937-3323
FAX (716) 937-9393

Bryce, Charles R.
Bryce's Auction Service
Rte 1, Box 157
Greene, NY 13778
(607) 656-8016

Cole, George W., CAI
George Cole Auctioneers
34 Stuyvesant St.
Kingston, NY 12401
(914) 876-5215

Cummins, Dean D.
RD Box 67
Cato, NY 13033
(315) 626-2248
FAX (315) 626-2666

Deuble, Carl G., Sr.
4030 E. River Road
Grand Island, NY 14072
(716) 773-1692

Doherty, Jill
P.O. Box 574M
Bayshore, NY 11706
(516) 666-9118
FAX (516) 666-1321

Dumas, Paul E.
RD 2, P.O. Box 135
Plattsburg, NY 12901
(518) 562-0561

Fratantoni, Anthony M.
P.O. Box 1424
Stoney Brook, NY 11790
(516) 689-2496
FAX (516) 689-2496

Gansz, Duane E., CAI
Gansz Auction & Realty
14 William St.
Lyons, NY 14489
(315) 946-6241
FAX (315) 946-6747

Haroff, Edward T.
Haroff's Auction Service
P.O. Box 71, Pine Lane
Schroon Lake, NY 12870
(518) 532-9600

Hazzard, George
93 Elm St.
Yonkers, NY 10701
(914) 968-3200
FAX (914) 968-4453

Howard, Peter S., CAI
Howard & Reimold
P.O. Box 496
Findley Lake, NY 14736-0496
(716) 769-7447
FAX (716) 769-7447

Kantor, Linda
1 Duncan Rd.
Staten Island, NY 10301
(718) 442-0326
FAX (718) 876-7987

Knapp, Michael W.
Auction by Knapp
RD #1, Box 62
Utica, NY 13502
(315) 732-2042

Koster, Randall G., Ronald J.,
and Russell
Koster Industries Inc.
555 Broadhollow Rd.
Melville, NY 11747
(212) 661-2550

Manasse, Charlie
P.O. Box 496
Whitney Point, NY 13862
(607) 692-3516

Manasse, Melvin J.
P.O. Box 738
Whitney Point, NY 13862
(800) 626-2773

Medow, Stuart L., CAI
Medow and Associates
2935 W. Fifth St.
Brooklyn, NY 11224
(718) 996-2405
FAX (718) 372-3344

Molloy, William J.
Realty & Auction Service
286 Columbia St.
Cohoes, NY 12047
(518) 235-9200

Monasky, Richard, CAI
Colonel Dick Monasky & Co.
34 Chenango St.
Binghamton, NY 13903
(800) 800-8243
FAX (607) 723-0466

Murray, Robert T.
124 Dean St.
Valley Stream, NY 11580
(516) 285-9385

Passonno, Hannelore, CAI
225 Pinewoods Avenue Rd.
Troy, NY 12180
(518) 274-6464
FAX (518) 272-7189

Passonno, Jr., Ralph F., CAI
Uncle Sam Auctions & Realty
225 Pinewoods Avenue Rd.
Troy, NY 12180
(518) 438-3189
FAX (518) 438-9159

Reisner, Fred
Auctions Plus, Inc.
535 Island Ave.
Woodmere, NY 11598
(516) 295-1300
FAX (516) 295-1301

Reynolds, John T., CAI
Reynolds Auction Co.
P.O. Box 508
Newark, NY 14513-0508
(315) 331-8815
FAX (315) 331-1053

Rosenbach, Simon
93-54 Queens Blvd.
Rego Park, NY 11374
(718) 459-2248

Rosner, Richard, A.
Tepper Galleries, Inc.
110 E. 25th Street
New York, NY 10010
(212) 677-5300
FAX (212) 673-3686

Rusciano, Anthony
1025 Post Rd.
Scarsdale, NY 10583
(914) 472-5010

Seipp, Frank E.
9 Park Lane
Rockville Center, NY 11570
(516) 764-7459
FAX (516) 764-7460

Smith, Marvin L., CAI
M. L. Smith Realty & Auctions
12049 Andell Rd.
Silver Creek, NY 14126
(716) 934-4875

Sullivan, John F.
Sullivan's Auctioneers-
Appraisers
Route 3, P.O. Box 114
Malone, NY 23953
(518) 483-1122

Teitsworth, Roy
Barber Hill Rd.
Geneseo, NY 14454
(716) 243-1563
FAX (716) 243-3311

Visscher, Howard W.
Rd. 1, Box 507
Nichols, NY 13812
(607) 699-7250

Vlasto, Lou
L & L Liquidators
166 Botsford St.
Hempstead, NY 11550
(516) 292-6770

Wheeler, Ronald L.
Family Auction Center
RR 5, Route 57, P.O. Box 327
Fulton, NY 13069
(315) 695-2059
FAX (315) 695-4745

Wilcox, Beatrice M.
141 Main St., P.O. Box 100
Dansville, NY 14437
(716) 335-8234
FAX (716) 335-6212

Wilcox, Carleton E.
141 Main St., P.O. Box 100
Dansville, NY 14437
(716) 335-8234
FAX (716) 335-6212

Wilcox, Harris
17 S. Lake Ave.
Bergen, NY 14416
(716) 494-1880
FAX (716) 494-1605

North Carolina

Batson, Leslie W.
142 Dogwood La.
Hampstead, NC 28443
(919) 270-3593

Burch, Thomas R.
Burch & Co.
P.O. Box 867
Roanoke Rapids, NC 27870
(919) 537-7126

Byers, Donald W., CAI
407 Sterling Rd.
Jacksonville, NC 28546
(919) 455-5640

Curlee, Ernest J., CAI
American Auction Associates, Inc.
9327-B Albemarle Rd.
Charlotte, NC 28227
(704) 535-1724

Deal, Robert W.
403 Highway 10 East
Newton, NC 28658
(704) 464-3635
FAX (704) 465-6263

Faison, Ronald W., CAI
Ron's Auction & Realty Co.
215 N. Arendell Ave.
Zebulon, NC 27597
(919) 269-6700
FAX (919) 269-4536

Gallimore, Charles D., CAI
AMC Auction & Appraisal Co., Inc.
P.O. Box 306
160 Glendale Ave. SE
Concord, NC 28025
(800) 782-3011
FAX (704) 782-7979

Glenn, Samuel D.
P.O. Box 787
Monroe, NC 28111
(704) 289-6704

Gray, Curtis H., CAI
Curtis Gray Auction
Real Estate
5342 N. Roxboro Rd.
Durham, NC 27712
(919) 471-0133

Johnson III, James W.
Johnson Properties
120 E. Depot St.
Angier, NC 27501
(919) 639-2231
FAX (919) 639-2232

King, John D., CAI
J. D. King Realty & Auction
529-A S. Church St.
Asheboro, NC 27203
(919) 626-4400

Lilly, William B., CAI
Iron Horse Auction Co.
P.O. Box 938
Norwood, NC 28128
(919) 997-2248
FAX (919) 895-1530

Marshall, Gail Y., CAI
Auctions by Marshall
6500 Sharon Hills Rd.
Charlotte, NC 28210
(704) 553-0029

Mendenhall, Forrest A., CAI, and Wayne, CAI
Mendenhall Auction Co.
P.O. Box 7344
High Point, NC 27264
(919) 887-1165

Miller, Jack W.
Jack Miller Auction Co.
9 W. 5th Street
Tabor City, NC 28463
(919) 653-5252

Mullis, Harry E.
Route 11, Box 10
Reidsville, NC 27320
(919) 349-6577

Pierce, Keith J., CAI
P.O. Box 5215
5500 S. Main St.
Winston-Salem, NC
27113-5215
(919) 764-5338
FAX (919) 764-8642

Propst, Clyde
P.O. Box 563
Concord, NC 28026-0563

Rogers, R. Bracky, CAI
P.O. Box 729
Mt. Airy, NC 27030
(919) 789-2926
FAX (919) 789-2310

Smith, Robert M.
Smith Auction Co.
P.O. Box 1255
Graham, NC 27253
(919) 228-8842

Tate, Harvey L., CAI
Route 2, Box 208
Burlington, NC 27217
(919) 421-3282

Troutman, Jr., Lonnie J.,
CAI
150 E. Water St.
Statesville, NC 28677
(704) 873-5233

Wooten, W. Douglas, CAI
Wooten Realty & Auction Co.
221 Clarendon Crescent
Raleigh, NC 27610
(919) 832-7251

North Dakota

Atteberry, Earl
Professional Auction Service
930 11th Avenue SW
Valley City, ND 58072
(701) 845-5857

Haugen, Dale B.
RR #1, Box 74
Lisbon, ND 58054
(701) 683-4637
FAX (701) 683-4637

Lauf, Lyle
Missouri River Auction
RR 1, Box 15
Washburn, ND 58577
(701) 462-8210

Merfeld, Doug
RR 1, Box 135
Grand Forks, ND 58201
(701) 746-1378
FAX (701) 746-1379

Merfeld, Tracy
Curt D. Johnson Auction Co.
RR 1, Box 135
Grand Forks, ND 58201
(701) 746-1378
FAX (701) 746-1379

Penfield, Bob
P.O. Box 111
Bowman, ND 58623
(701) 523-3652

Smykowski, James
RR #1, Box 34
Cayuga, ND 58013
(701) 538-4466

Steffes, Robert, CAI
827 28th St. S, Suite D
Fargo, ND 58103
(701) 967-8927
FAX (701) 237-0976

Steffes, Scott, CAI
Steffes Auctioneers, Inc.
827 28th St. S, Suite D
Fargo, ND 58103-2324
(701) 237-9173

Vogel, Steve
SRV Auction Co.
P.O. Box 417
Casselton, ND 58012
(701) 347-5485

Ohio

Andrews, Stephen E.
51-7 S. Jefferson Rd.
Wooster, OH 44691
(216) 262-9186

Aspacher, Kenneth W.
2333 Belvedere Dr.
Toledo, OH 43614
(419) 385-9428

Aspacher, Linda S.
American Gold
Realty & Auction
2333 Belvedere Dr.
Toledo, OH 43614
(419) 385-9428
FAX (419) 385-6834

Baier, Thomas A., CAI
2719 Fulton Dr. NW, Ste C
Canton, OH 44718
(216) 455-1911
FAX (216) 455-1859

Baker, Michael, D., CAI
Mid-West Auctioneers
5376 Bishop Rd.
Greenville, OH 45331
(513) 548-7451

Baker, William
William Baker Auctioneer
4488th St., Rt. 412
Vickery, OH 43464
(419) 547-9218

Bambeck, Herb, CAI
Route 1, Box 392
Dover, OH 44622
(216) 343-1437
FAX (216) 343-1437

Basinger, J. Paul, CAI
7039 Bishop Rd.
Poland, OH 44514
(216) 757-1169
FAX (216) 757-1292

Bayman, Anthony M.
1200 Nicklin Ave.
Piqua, OH 45356
(513) 778-8017

Beitzel, Herbert L.
RFD 2, P.O. Box 2228
New Philadelphia, OH 44663
(216) 339-5197

Bonnigson, Kenneth J., CAI
1834 W. McPherson Hwy.
Clyde, OH 43410
(419) 547-9313

Brough, Chad W.
3653 S. Harris-Salem Rd
Oak Harbor, OH 43449
(419) 898-0290

Cain, Brad L., CAI
Box 116
East Springfield, OH 43925
(614) 266-2246
FAX (614) 266-6925

Colman, Thomas E.
Colman Realty
1411 S. Zane Hwy.
Martins Ferry, OH 43935
(614) 633-9874

Davy, Thomas A.
Tom Davy Auction Service
8945 Jasper Dr.
Hopewell, OH 43746
(614) 454-1495

Duvall, Donald D.
7450 Linnville Rd. SE
Newark, OH 43055
(614) 323-1436

Farnsworth, Harold R., CAI
8003 River Styx Rd.
Wadsworth, OH 44281
(216) 336-6057

Frey, Robert G.
Route 3, Box 47B
Archbold, OH 43502
(419) 445-0015
FAX (419) 445-8888

Gill, James D., CAI
5770 Courtland Ave. NW
Massillon, OH 44646-1133
(216) 832-2605
FAX (216) 453-1765

Hoyle, William L.
7068 Dunstans La.
Toledo, OH 43617
(419) 841-9892
FAX (419) 385-6834

Hudson, Jr. Harry
7103 4-Mile State Line Rd.
Eaton, OH 45320

Jones, David L., CAI
High St., Box 467
Flushing, OH 43977
(614) 968-3710

Kaspar, Robert J.
5718 Little Portage Rd.
Port Clinton, OH 43452
(419) 734-2930

Kessler, Dave
P.O. Box 100
New Paris, OH 45347
(513) 437-7071

Kramer, Horace J.
108 W. Main St.
Eaton, OH 45320-1906
(513) 456-1101

Lentz, Jeffrey M.
Lentz Auction Service
P.O. Box 28
Botkins, OH 45306
(513) 693-3100

Luggen, Jerome A.
Cincinnati Industrial Auction
6252 Hamilton Ave.
Cincinnati, OH 45224
(513) 471-5100

Luoma, Wayne
P.O. Box 308
Geneva, OH 44041
(216) 466-8383
FAX (216) 466-6305

Marino, James T., CAI
Whipple Auctioneer
Association
1219 Ardmore SW
Canton, OH 44710
(216) 452-7653
FAX (216) 477-9365

McCarty, Kenneth D.
Nationwide Auctions
901 Congress Park Dr.
Dayton, OH 45459
(513) 433-0039
FAX (513) 435-5128

McCullough, Frank E.
1666 Rudyard La.
Cincinnati, OH 45230
(513) 732-6301

Retcher, Sr., William H.
11693 Rd. 1
Montpelier, OH 43543
(419) 485-8141

Robinson, Jerry D.
Robinson Auction Service
523 Adrien St.
Delta, OH 43515
(418) 822-3555

Rucker, Randall K.
8113 Ohio River Rd.
Wheelersburg, OH 45694
(614) 820-2651

Semple, Brent T.,
and Garth, CAIs
Semple & Associates
278 N. 3rd Street
Williamsburg, OH 45176
(513) 724-1133
FAX (513) 724-1286

Sheridan, Keith
3644 Wilberforce-
Clifton Rd.
Cedarville, OH 45314
(513) 766-2021

Smith, Jack E.
2264 C.R. 141
Lindsey, OH 43442
(419) 665-2115

Stanley III, Henry, CAI
Stanley & Son
Auctioneer/Realtor
126 E. 4th Street
Chillicothe, OH 45601
(614) 775-3330
FAX (614) 775-3330

Stanley Jr., Henry M.
126 E. 4th Street
Chillicothe, OH 45601
(614) 775-3330
FAX (614) 775-3330

Stanley Sr., Henry M.
126 E. 4th Street
Chillicothe, OH 45601
(614) 775-3330
FAX (614) 775-3330

Straley, William C., CAI
Straley Realtors & Auctioneers
323 E. Main St.
Van Wert, OH 45891
(419) 238-9733
FAX (419) 238-3506

Vannatta, Richard M.
975 W. Broad St.
Columbus, OH 43222
(614) 621-2897
FAX (614) 621-0329

Wagner, Robert J., CAI
B. Wagner & Assoc., Inc.
1444 N. Main St.
N. Canton, OH 44720
(216) 499-9922
FAX (216) 499-5864

Wallick, Don R.
81 E. Iron Ave.
Dover, OH 44622
(216) 343-6734
FAX (216) 343-3655

Wilson, Marvin L.
Wilson National
Real Estate, Inc.
652 N. High St.
Hillsboro, OH 45133
(513) 393-3440
FAX (513) 393-3442

Oklahoma

Anderson, Adrian E.
Anderson & Associates
Auctioneers
114 S. Rock Island
El Reno, OK 73036
(405) 262-8600
FAX (405) 262-8601

Brink, Terry H., CAI
Kent & Brink
422 N. 14th
Frederick, OK 73542
(405) 335-5732

Bristol, R. W., CAI
Bristol & Associates
5508 Spitz
Oklahoma City, OK 73135
(405) 672-0114

Bruce, Joe D.
Bruce Auction
RR 2, Box 470
Welch, OK 74369
(918) 233-7074

Campbell, Lewis W.
Lewis Campbell & Associates
Auctioneers
Box 220
Wyandotte, OK 74370
(918) 678-2355

Donley, Gary L.
Rt. 1, Box 540
Ramona, OK 74061
(918) 534-0342

Dulaney, Sue, CAI
Rte. 4, Box 273
Claremore, OK 74017
(918) 342-5176
FAX (918) 342-5187

Godfrey, Donald D.
5105 NW 19th Street
Oklahoma City, OK 73127

Haynes, T. Eddie, CAI
Eddie Haynes
Auction & Realty
901 N. MacArthur
Oklahoma City, OK 73127
(405) 495-7653
FAX (405) 495-7657

Hines, Les
C & H Auctions
P.O. Box 521
Temple Hill, OK 73568
(405) 342-5133
FAX (405) 353-6109

McCracken, Richard D.
Rt. #1, Box 354
Cleveland, OK 74020
(918) 358-2020

Miller, DVM, Sterling, CAI
Sterling Miller
Realty & Auction
Route 3, Box 129-A
Perry, OK 73077
(405) 336-2030

Myers, Cecil D.
Cecil Myers Auction Service
Box 86
Felt, OK 73937
(405) 426-2447

Myers, Clay
Cecil Myers Auction Service
Box 181
Felt, OK 73937
(405) 426-2283

Spitler, Paul D.
Spitler Auction, Inc.
P.O. Box 685
Prague, OK 74864
(405) 567-3523

Stallings, Joey G.
502 N. Sheridan Rd.
Lawton, OK 73505
(405) 355-8302
FAX (405) 355-3550

Steen, Ben D., CAI
1201 Arlington Blvd.
Ada, OK 74820
(405) 332-4456

Wells, V. Paul, CAI
Wells Commercial Auctions
27428 E. 71st Street
Broken Arrow, OK 74014
(918) 357-1003

Wiggins, C. Perry, CAI
4720A W. Owen K.
Garriott Road
Enid, OK 73701
(405) 233-3066
FAX (405) 237-4915

Wilkinson, W. W. Buck
923 S. 85th E Avenue
Tulsa, OK 74112
(918) 838-3279

Wolfe, Michael E.
200 W. 12th Street
Ada, OK 74820
(405) 436-1281
FAX (405) 436-1578

Oregon

Cox, J. T., CAI, and
Cox, Jay S.
Cox Auctions
P.O. Box 6770
Portland, OR 97228
(503) 282-5027

O'Keefe, Arthur J.
11733 Hwy 62
Eagle Point, OR 97524
(503) 826-2192

Voorhees, Sidney I.
Sidco Management Inc.
P.O. Box 10205
Eugene, OR 97440
(503) 485-8885

Pennsylvania

Beamesderfer, Calvin E.
471 Weavertown Rd.
Myerstown, PA 17067
(717) 866-2998

Bechtold, Claude E., CAI
Bechtold Auctioneers
1928 Creek Hill Rd.
Lancaster, PA 17601
(717) 397-9240

Boswell, James M., CAI
P.O. Box 3073
West Chester, PA 19381
(215) 692-2226
FAX (215) 692-2042

Camelleri, Charles S.
Camelleri Auctioneering
P.O. Box 511
Birdsboro, PA 19508
(215) 582-1110

Charnego, Michael R., CAI
1 S. Main St.
Homer City, PA 15748
(412) 479-2481

Clayton, James A.
Clayton Auctions
RD 1, Box 73
Jefferson, PA 15344-9618
(412) 883-2885

Clemmer, Lon M.
Sanford Alderfer
Auction Co.
Box 640-501
Fairgrounds Rd.
Hatfield, PA 19440
(215) 368-5477
FAX (215) 368-9055

Cox, Alan D.
18551 Elgin Rd.
Corry, PA 16407
(814) 664-7526

Cunningham, Dale E.
RR 1, Box 366
Ellwood City, PA 16117
(412) 924-2836

Davis, Jr., James S.
Barr Davis Auctioneers
P.O. Box 7
Gap, PA 17527
(717) 442-3198

Deibert, George N., CAI
P.O. Box 72
Klingerstown, PA 17941
(717) 425-3313

Dobozynski, Joe, CAI
AAA Auction Service Inc.
RD 1, Box 420
Mifflintown, PA 17059
(717) 436-9594

Dreibelbis, Thomas G.
420 Gerald St.
State College, PA 16801-7485
(814) 238-1017
FAX (814) 238-1749

Gilbert, Jacob A.
Rt. #1
Wrightsville, PA 17368
(717) 252-3591

Gladd, Robert E.
103 McClung Blvd.
Butler, PA 16001
(412) 287-3827

Harriger, Emery L.
Harriger Auctioneer's
419 N. 4th Street
Reynoldsville, PA 15851
(814) 653-8610

Hostetter, Lee W., CAI
Lee Hostetter Real Estate
124 Blackhawk Rd.
Beaver Falls, PA 15010
(412) 847-1880
FAX (412) 847-3415

Hostetter, Jr., Sherman, CAI
Hostetter Auctioneers/Real
Estate
124 Blackhawk Rd.
Beaver Falls, PA 15010
(412) 847-1880
FAX (412) 847-1881

Hubscher, Christian, CAI
P.O. Box 500
Souderton, PA 18964
(215) 257-3001
FAX (215) 257-2717

Keller, Mark K.
RD #1, Box 64
Landisburg, PA 17040
(717) 789-3616

Kistler, Mark W.
753 Lawrence Dr.
Emmaus, PA 18049
(215) 967-3584

Krall, Peter H., CAI
Willow Brook Farms
Catasauqua, PA 18032
(215) 264-1088

McAloose, Robert L.
14 W. Broad St.
Tamaqua, PA 18252
(717) 668-5755

McKeown, Michael J.
956 North 9th Street
Stroudsburg, PA 18360
(717) 424-2762

Morrison, Arthur W., CAI
1004 N. McKean St.
Kittanning, PA 16201
(412) 545-9775

Nicolls, W. Bruce
733 Terrace St.
Meadville, PA 16335
(814) 333-1989
FAX (814) 333-1988

Niebauer, Joseph P.
Rd. 1, Box 130
Irvona, PA 16656
(814) 672-5541

Peters, Fred A., CAI
215 Lynn Rd.
Brownsville, PA 15417
(412) 785-8954
FAX (412) 785-8954

Randazzo, Salvatore A.
1030 Linden Ave.
Erie, PA 16505
(814) 838-2437

Rentzel, Blaine N.
Box 222
Emigsville, PA 17318
(717) 764-6412
FAX (717) 764-5492

Rentzel, Nevin B.
70 Knoll La.
York, PA 17402
(717) 764-6412

Slosberg, Barry S.
232 N. 2nd St.
Philadelphia, PA 19106
(215) 925-8020
FAX (215) 925-8047

Smith, Bradley K., CAI
RD #2, Box 483
Brogue, PA 17309
(717) 927-6949

Spataro, Anthony J.
Bennett Williams Inc.
1891 Santa Barbara Dr., #208
Lancaster, PA 17601
(717) 560-5611
FAX (717) 560-5625

Tedrow, Charles E.
Chuck's Auction Services
248 Wyoming Ave.
Wyoming, PA 18644
(717) 288-6089
FAX (717) 288-9185

Wagner, Dennis F.
100 Skyline Dr.
Shoemakersville, PA 19555
(215) 562-7445

Rhode Island

Loebenberg, Theodore F.
Box 2535
Providence, RI 02906
(401) 274-1930
FAX (401) 521-7845

Resnick, Bob
P.O. Box 9
Providence, RI 02901

Scott, Nino D.
15 Westminster St. #603
Providence, RI 02903-2417

South Carolina

Davis, W. Angus
Davis Auction Service
510 Dellwood Dr.
Greenville, SC 29609
(803) 268-6781
FAX (803) 268-6781

Hernandez, Calixto, A., CAI
P.O. Box 3086
Greenville, SC 29602
(803) 243-4858

Leonardi II, Robert J.
P.O. Box 1417
Easley, SC 29641-1417
(803) 233-3615

Meares, Larry J., CAI
P.O. Box 57
Pelzer, SC 29669
(803) 277-0504
FAX (803) 277-3255

Smith, Frank O., Jr.
524 Clinkscales Rd.
Anderson, SC 29624
(803) 832-6655

South Dakota

Hubner, Gregg C.
Gregg Hubner Auction Co.
RR 1, Box 174
Avon, SD 57315
(605) 286-3205

Payne, James T., CAI
Payne Auctioneers &
Appraisers
111 Cedar St.
Yankton, SD 57078
(605) 665-3889
FAX (605) 665-6478

Sutton, Charles A.
Kuhle-Sutton Agency
P.O. Box 325
Flandreau, SD 57028
(605) 997-3777
FAX (605) 997-3038

Wingler, Terry
Wingler's Furniture/Auction
611 N. Main Ave.
Sioux Falls, SD 57102
(605) 332-5682

Tennessee

Ayers, Haskel, CAI
2201 Jackson Pike
P.O. Box 1467
LaFollette, TN 37766
(615) 562-4941
FAX (615) 562-8148

Cayce, Clinton R.
Beck & Beck Realty & Auction
1450 Janie Ave.
Nashville, TN 37216
(615) 226-6915
FAX (615) 227-7053

Cole, David L.
Blue Ridge Properties Inc.
1337 Magnolia Ave.
Kingsport, TN 37664
(615) 378-4411

Cook, John W., CAI
P.O. Box 450
Troy, TN 38260
(901) 536-6424

Gregory, Jerry C., CAI
P.O. Box D, 805 Willow St.
Springfield, TN 37172
(615) 384-5557

Hall, Jerry E.
1141 Tusculom Blvd.
Greeneville, TN 37743
(615) 639-7162
FAX (512) 639-1116

Hamilton, Jr., George, CAI
P.O. Box 536
Dunlap, TN 37327
(615) 554-3999

Hines, Harry L.
1500 Bluff City Hwy.
Bristol, TN 37620
(615) 669-6385

Hobbs, Fred R.
P.O. Box 126, 131 N. Main St.
Eagleville, TN 37060
(615) 274-6826

Johns, Royce G., CAI
Royce Johns
Realty/Auctions
236 3rd Ave. North
Franklin, TN 37064
(625) 790-0414

Kennon, Joe D.
201 Jane St.
Paris, TN 38242
(901) 642-3750
FAX (901) 642-3750

Lynch, Tom P.
Carlton Lynch
Realty & Auction
1215 Dinah Shore Blvd.
Winchester, TN 37398
(615) 967-0678
FAX (615) 967-0694

Miller, William A.
302 Wesley St., Suite 2
Johnson City, TN 37601
(615) 283-4178
FAX (615) 283-4132

Murphy, James R.
2304 Memorial Blvd.
Springfield, TN 37172
(615) 384-7919
FAX (615) 384-7884

Orr, George C., CAI
Lewis-Orr Realty
Auction Sales
123 S. Jackson St.
Tullahoma, TN 37388
(615) 455-3447

Redenbaugh, Richard G.
Redenbaugh Auction
RR 3, Box 286
Tellico Plains, TN 37385
(615) 253-2666

Roebuck, John, CAI
River City Auction
3143 Carrier St.
Memphis, TN 38116
(901) 346-8644
FAX (901) 346-8669

Shepard, Tom
Nashville Auction &
Realty Co., Inc.
1407 Lebanon Rd.
Nashville, TN 37210
(615) 255-4933
FAX (615) 255-8052

Taggart, Raymond E., CAI
Delta Auction Co.
151 Walnut Creek
Cordova, TN 38018
(800) 592-2288
FAX (901) 382-5729

Texas

Alley, Lesley, R.
P.O. Box 1092
Del Rio, TX 78841
(512) 774-4255
FAX (512) 774-1222

Archer, William C.
Box 802635
Dallas, TX 75380
(214) 458-9781

Bates, Rene
Rene Bates Auctioneers, Inc.
Rt 4., McKinney, TX 75070
(214) 548-9636
FAX (214) 542-1604

Burlin, Morris L., CAI
Burlin's
2302 Matthew Dr.
Mt. Pleasant, TX 75455
(903) 572-3142

Caraway, Billy
P.O. Box 174
Denton, TX 76202
(817) 565-1487

Cleghorn, Michael L.
Cleghorn & Assoc.
P.O. Box 90065
Austin, TX 78709
(512) 892-0109

Cuthbert, Dale
#9 Manchester
Amarillo, TX 79106
(806) 376-9607
FAX (806) 374-7474

DeVore, Russell
DeVore Marketing
Auct./Rltrs.
P.O. Box 61872
San Angelo, TX 76906-1872
(915) 942-6666

Dickson, David J.
Dickson Diversified Services
16402 Mill Dr., P.O. Box 280
Rosharon, TX 77583
(713) 595-2337

Espensen, K. L., CAI
Espensen Co., Realtor-
Auctions
2212 Primrose St. #C
McAllen, TX 78504
(512) 687-5117
FAX (512) 687-7967

Flusche, Donald J.
P.O. Box 417
Muenster, TX 76252-0417
(817) 759-2832
FAX (817) 759-4288

Foster, Paul M.
15618 Highfield Dr.
Houston, TX 77095-2030
(713) 855-8686

Harlien, Cecil M., Jr.
2914 Euell Rd.
Crosby, TX 77532
(713) 328-3683

Henry, Paul N.
Federal Auction Co.
713 Lehman
Houston, TX 77018
(713) 688-6688
FAX (713) 694-8717

Henson, Roy P.
Alph Int'l Mktg Services, Inc.
Rt. 3, Box 3786
Chandler, TX 75758
(903) 849-2221
FAX (903) 849-2883

Jones, J. Michael
Box 1113
Gainesville, TX 76240
FAX (817) 668-6339

Kaddatz, Alvin
Kaddatz Auctioneering
Box 972
Hillsboro, TX 76645
(817) 582-3071

Keeping, Jim, CAI
Jim Keeping Auctions
5115 Lawnview
Dallas, TX 75227
(800) 527-7693
FAX (214) 388-8789

Lawless, Ed
RR 2, Box 52
Linden, TX 75563
(214) 756-5733

Meadows, Forres
P.O. Box 1287
Boerne, TX 78006
(512) 249-3403

Moore, Ronald G.
Plant & Machinery, Inc.
8705 Katy Fwy., #300
Houston, TX 77024-1710

Moses, Dwayne
Moses & Zuber Auctioneers
Rt. 1, Box 311
Ralls, TX 79357
(806) 253-2945

Ogle, Jack V., CAI
Ogle Auction & Realty
Rt. 2, Box 66A
Greenville, TX 75401
(903) 454-1091

Rudd, Charles D.
13214 Holly Park
Houston, TX 77015
(713) 453-2912

Slate, Sr., Kenneth D.
Slate Auction Service
1822 Cliffcrest
Duncanville, TX 75137
(214) 780-9118

Thomas, Brett R.
Rt. 6, Box 420
Mt. Pleasant, TX 75455
(903) 572-4517

Van Hauen, Jack W.
17 Rancho Dr.
Keller, TX 76248-5002
(817) 431-1712
FAX (817) 831-4465

Walker, Homar
Homar Walker
Auction & Realty
P.O. Box 5846
San Antonio, TX 78201
(512) 698-1155

Wiley, R. C., CAI
616 W. Cameron
Rockdale, TX 76567
(512) 446-3197
FAX (512) 446-5243

Utah

Earl, Scott C., CAI
3371 El Serrito Dr.
Salt Lake City, UT 84109
(801) 486-7910

Taylor, Doug
921 W. Riverdale Rd.
Ogden, UT 84405
(801) 392-2214

Tiedemann, Arthur H.
345 W. 6400 South
Murray, UT 84107
(801) 262-9920

Vermont

Manchester, Jean, CAI
Green Mountain Auctions
6 Beachcrest Dr.
Burlington, VT 05401
(802) 863-4153

Matteis, Vincent
American Auction Center
Box 1196 Finney Hill
Lyndonville, VT 05851
(802) 626-8589

Merrill, Duane
Merrill's Auction Gallery
32 Beacon St.
S. Burlington, VT 05401
(802) 862-1624

Stevenson, Frederick A.
Fred's Auction Service
HCR 30, Box 56
Barnet, VT 05821
(802) 592-3202

Whittaker, Tom P.
Box 157
Brandon, VT 05733
(802) 247-6633

Virginia

Bennett, Kendall J.
American Real Estate
525 Thornrose Ave.
P.O. Box 2487
Staunton, VA 24401
(703) 885-7231
FAX (703) 886-7566

Brown, James M.
J & J Realty
3302 Amherst Hwy
Madison Heights, VA 24572
(804) 929-5551

Cole, A. Barry, CAI
Rt. #1, Box 182
Callaway, VA 24067
(703) 483-4539

Counts, David C., CAI
Counts Auction Co.
Route 2
Abingdon, VA 24210

Des Roches, Jim
5100 Hingham Dr.
New Kent, VA 23124
(804) 932-3717

Gilbert, Marcus A.
Lambert & Gilbert,
Auction Company
P.O. Box 1287
N. Tazewell, VA 24630
(703) 988-9468

Green, Donnie G.
Green Auction & Realty
Rt. 1, Box 636
S. Boston, VA 24592
(804) 575-7924
FAX (804) 575-7926

Hilton, Paul S.
Rte. 1, Box 203
Newport, VA 24128
(703) 544-7214

Horney, Jr., J. C.
P.O. Box 73
Wytheville, VA 24382
(703) 228-4131
FAX (703) 228-6175

Kelley, C. Roy
3810 Atlantic Ave. #901
Virginia Beach, VA 23451
(804) 461-6867
FAX (804) 462-2147

Lyons, Dorothy R.
Jackass Flats, Rt. 1, Box 44B
Rapidan, VA 22733
(703) 825-3798

Moore, George H.
P.O. Box 1330
Mathews, VA 23109
(804) 725-7890

Peoples, Jack W.
1328 Head of River Rd.
Chesapeake, VA 23322
(804) 421-2525

Rall, Tom
5720 Wilson Blvd.
Arlington, VA 22205
(703) 525-1629

Sellars, Douglas V.
6174 Pattie Court
Haymarket, VA 22069
(703) 754-0328

Sheets, Stephen G., CAI
15 S. Jefferson St.
Roanoake, VA 24011
(703) 345-8885

Smith, Grayson L.
Rt. 2, Box 255A
Warsaw, VA 22572
(804) 333-4894

Tull, Ronald I., CAI
Tull Realty & Auction Co.
3912 Woodburn Rd.
Annandale, VA 22003
(703) 280-5555

Updike, Buddy
P.O. Box 330
King George, VA 22485
(703) 371-5965

Williams, Frederick J.
F. J. Williams Realty &
Auction Company
P.O. Box 201
Winchester, VA 22601
(703) 662-3539

Washington

Burnham, Elmer L.
658 Road L NE
Moses Lake, WA 98837
(509) 766-9100
FAX (509) 766-9925

Ehli, Randall L.
Ehli Auctions Inc.
2042-112th Street
South Tacoma, WA 98444
(206) 537-7255
FAX (206) 537-7302

Ehli, William, A.
Ehli & Sons Auction
2042 S. 112th Street
Tacoma, WA 98444-1537
(206) 537-7255
FAX (206) 537-7302

Hill, I. Andrew
Andy's Auction Service
2312 174th Street E.
Tacoma, WA 98445
(206) 531-7398

Hodges, Ken
Ken Hodges & Associates
Box 91
Bothell, WA 98011
(206) 363-4086

Honey, Jr., George P.
Northwest Auction Service
P.O. Box 397, 2003 Mac Place
Entlat, WA 98822
(509) 784-1938

Murphy, James G.
James G. Murphy, Inc.
P.O. Box 82160
18226 68th Avenue NE
Kenmore, WA 98028
(206) 486-1246

Stalheim, David L.
7117 44th Avenue E.
Tacoma, WA 98443-1925
(206) 531-9404

West Virginia

Belmont, Gary R.
Belmont Auction Co.
1252 Dorsey Ave.
Morgantown, WV 26505
(304) 292-4314

Frio, James W.
RD 2, Box 206
Valley Grove, WV 26060
(304) 336-7462
FAX (304) 843-1518

Meadows, Monroe B.
Meadows Auction & Realty
P.O. Box 23
Meadow Bridge, WV 25976
(304) 484-7043

Woofter, Danny
Dansco Auctioneers
226 Tenth Ave., S.
Charleston, WV 25303-1129
(304) 744-4197

Wisconsin

Barg, William H.
117 W. Fulton St.
Waupaca, WI 54981
(715) 258-8116

Berkshire, Gerald & Rita
Colonel's Auction Service
1117 Bushnell St.
Beloit, WI 53511
(608) 365-5089

Cassiani, Daniel
20810 W. Barton Rd.
New Berlin, WI 53146
(414) 744-9060
FAX (414) 744-9084

Dodge, Chris
Dodge Auction Service
24 Sinclair St.
Janesville, WI 53545
(608) 756-3154

Donahoe, Joseph
627 Harriett St., Box 133
Darlington, WI 53530
(608) 776-2156

Fisher, Gordon
Bear & Associates
718 Broadview Dr.
Green Bay, WI 54301
(414) 336-7672

Gillen, Melville
Gillen Auction Service
P.O. Box 45
Pound, WI 54161

Gonnering, Donald P.
11550 Birch Trail
Woodland Subdivision
Kaukauna, WI 54130
(414) 788-3332

Gonnering, Keith M.
Gonnering Auction & Real
Estate
126 E. Main St.
Little Chute, WI 54140-1413
(414) 788-4447

Hager, Barry J.
R. 3, Box 73
Ellsworth, WI 54011
(715) 273-4638

Hager, Norman J.
Route 3
Ellsworth, WI 54011
(715) 273-5729

Hazlewood, William J., CAI
935 Model Railroad
Rice Lake, WI 54868
(800) 345-2040

Lust, Richard O., CAI
Lust Auction Services
P.O. Box 4421
Madison, WI 53711
(608) 833-2001
FAX (608) 833-9593

Mantz, C. A.
Archie Mantz Auctioneer
7085 Winnebago
Fond Du Lac, WI 54935
(414) 921-1528

Massart, Pat, CAI and Robert
J., CAI
Massart Auctioneers Inc.
2545 Finger Rd.
Green Bay, WI 54302
(414) 468-1113

Morgan, Pete
Auction Associates
Box 335
Rosendall, WI 54974
(414) 872-2204
FAX (414) 748-3048

Murray, Lee A., CAI
Dells Auction Service
P.O. Box 212
Wisconsin Dells, WI 53965
(608) 254-8696

Ranft, Richard D.
Beloit Auction Service
534 W. Grand Ave.
P.O. Box 842
Beloit, WI 53511-5311
(608) 364-1965

Schomisch, Arthur
Schomisch Auction Service
1817 S. Jefferson St.
Appleton, WI 54915
(414) 734-9382

Schomisch, Michael R.
1326 Wild Rose La.
Neenah, WI 54956
(414) 734-9382

Spies, John R.
184 S. Washington St.
Waterloo, WI 53594
(414) 478-3365

Stewart, Laverne L.
5902 Michier Rd.
Eau Claire, WI 54701
(715) 834-6664

Stockwell, Randy J.
R. J. Stockwell Auctions
5340 County Line Rd.
Dorchester, WI 54425
(715) 654-5162

Temkin, Julius
910 S. Spring St.
Beaver Dam, WI 53916
(414) 623-2280

Theorin, Carl, CAI
Wausau Sales Corp.
2500 Rio Grande Dr.
Merrill, WI 54452
(715) 536-8694

Varney, Scott, CAI
Accredited Auctioneers
207 N. Livingston St.
Madison, WI 53703
(608) 255-7630

Voigt, Victor V., CAI
Voigt Auction Service
Route 2
Reedsville, WI 54230
(414) 772-4235

Wagner, Jim
American Auction
Rt. 4, Box 217
Wantoma, WI 54982
(414) 787-2680

Wagner, Thomas J.
Wagner Auction Service
428 W. Washington St.
Dodgeville, WI 53533
(608) 935-5131

Walla, Willia, L.
Walla's Auction &
Real Estate
1723 County J
Little Suamico, WI 54141
(414) 826-5472

Weisensel, Taylor W.
3016 Vercauteren Dr.
Green Bay, WI 54313-5896
(414) 336-3050

Wildermuth, Craig
12775 W. Silver Spring
Butler, WI 53007
(414) 781-1706
FAX (414) 781-7570

Wyoming

Brown, Kenneth R.
Kenneth Brown Enterprises
P.O. Box 133
Riverton, WY 82501
(307) 347-3408

Casteel, Roger A.
700 Foothills Blvd.
Rock Springs, WY 82901
(307) 362-8361

Frome, L. D.
RFD Box 47
Afton, WY 83110
(800) 433-1595

Hamilton, Thomas W.
10831 Powderhouse Rd.
Cheyenne, WY 82009
(307) 637-4447

Hughs, Lee D.
Action Auctioneers
808 Range Rd.
Rock Springs, WY 82901
(307) 382-5442
FAX (307) 382-5442

Olson, Lavar D.
347 Broadacres
Riverton, WY 82501
(309) 856-9347

Smith, Clark
415 W. Lincolnway
Cheyenne, WY 82001
(307) 635-4181
FAX (307) 634-6817

32

Real Estate Auctioneers

★★★

Real estate auctions are the hottest auctions going. Auctioneers can't get enough of them and *they want more!* Why? Real estate auctions pay well. Auctioneers get 6%–7% commissions on real estate sales they conduct. Real estate sales mean big dollars spent at an auction.

Selling a $100,000 home can mean $6,000 or more in commissions for a day's work. Now, what about those auctions where 5, 10, or 20 properties are all sold in the same day? That's healthy income for that auction company.

Real estate auctions present an interesting puzzle: How come the house couldn't sell at $115,000 after 180 days on the market and then sells for $145,000 at auction in one day? Auc-

tioneers know the answer. And when real estate brokers fully understand why, we'll have more auctioneers and fewer brokers.

Watch and see if this prediction holds true: real estate auctions are going to become as common as listings by the end of this century. That's exactly how hot they are. Buyers like them because of the excitement. Sellers love them because their house gets sold fast. And auctioneers are thrilled because of the fat paychecks.

Call a few auctioneers from the directory that follows and get a few mailings. Heck, you'll probably start going to them regularly instead of visiting brokers.

REAL ESTATE AUCTIONEERS DIRECTORY

Alabama

Acton, Mike F.
Acton & Associates
P.O. Box 43028
Birmingham, AL 35243
(205) 823-2330

Behel, Don, CAI
Don Behel Realty &
Auction, Inc.
Rt. 4, Box 505
Killen, AL 35645
(205) 757-4100
FAX (205) 757-4087

Brown, Richard
7595 Highway 72 West
Madison, AL 35758
(205) 837-6229
FAX (205) 830-9653

Farmer, David
Farmco Auctioneers
& Liquidations
P.O. Box 1725
Albertville, AL 35950
(800) 445-4608

Faulkner, William F.
2222 E. Arbor Dr.
Huntsville, AL 35811

Gonder, John A.
American Real Estate &
Auction Co., Inc
1206-20th St. S.
Birmingham, AL 35205
(205) 933-2580
FAX (205) 252-3838

Hancock, Greg
11 Red Fox Dr.
Pelham, AL 35124
(205) 663-7611

King, J. Craig, CAI
J.P. King Auction Company
108 Fountain Avenue
Gadsden, AL 35901
(205) 546-5217
FAX (205) 543-8036

Knotts, Edward V., CAI
Knotts R.E. & Auction Co.
411 E. 2nd St.
Sheffield, AL 35660
(205) 386-7048
FAX (205) 386-0110

Mayfield, Truman M.
P.O. Box 955
Alexander City, AL 35010
(205) 329-1863
FAX (205) 234-6329

Montgomery, John H.
613 Memorial Dr., SW
Decatur, AL 35601
(205) 350-6959

Perrin, Joyce L.
Vintage Auctions
Route 1, Box 388C
Guntersville, AL 35976
(205) 586-5784

Puckett, Harry C.
Puckett Realty & Auction Co.
P.O. Box 457
Hartselle, AL 35640
(205) 773-2685

Rudder, Robert R.
P.O. Box 3062
Montgomery, AL 36109
(205) 277-5099

Arizona

Amble, Leon J.
1804 Pony Soldier Rd.
Prescott, AZ 86303
(602) 776-1100
FAX (602) 776-4131

Bradley, Rex V.
Valley Auctioneers
8560 E. Cortez St.
Scottsdale, AZ 85260
(602) 948-2323
FAX (602) 274-2069

Hatcher, Dayle F.
Auction Realty USA
6201 E. Justine Rd.
Scottsdale, AZ 85254-1946
(602) 483-1467
FAX (602) 948-1403

Hiple, Timothy
American West Auction Inc.
HCR Box 4640
Benson, AZ 85602
(602) 586-2859
FAX (602) 325-2608

Kane, C.R. Kip
SW R.E. Auctioneers
1121 E. Missouri, #100
Phoenix, AZ 85014-2723
(602) 263-0050
FAX (602) 263-0085

Moubry, Robert J.
4624 E. Cortez St.
Phoeniz, AZ 85028
(602) 953-1285
FAX (602) 996-6113

Poulsen, Gary L., CAI
15220 N. 51 Place,
Scottsdale, AZ
85254-2281
(602) 996-6201
FAX (602) 971-6144

Smisek, Pamela S.
Larry Latham Auctioneers
10304 N. Hayden Rd., Ste. 6
Scottsdale, AZ 85258
(602) 998-1168

Arkansas

Gideon, Jess A.
718 Treasure Isle Rd.
Hot Springs, AR 71913
(501) 767-6221
FAX (501) 767-0657

Guthery, Donnie
20th Century Collectibles
Rte 8, Box 236
Fayetteville, AR 72701
(501) 839-3274

Hermann, Clay
Rte 7, P.O. Box 233
Hot Springs, AR 71901
(501) 623-0107

Hightower, Ray A.
308 Rock Street, P.O. Box 388
Little Rock, AR 72203
(501) 376-2361
FAX (501) 376-3776

Jenkins, Clifford W.
1505 Forest Hills Blvd.
Bella Vista, AR 72714
(501) 855-3709

Knight, William H.
Route 1
Manila, AR 72442
(501) 562-2405
FAX (501) 562-6552

Mooneyham, Jimmy S.
PO Box 1457
617 W. Conway
Benton, AR 72015
(501) 778-1448
FAX (501) 776-2253

Shepard, James
RR #1, Box 301
Corning, AR 72422
(501) 276-5351

Sullivan, Connie P.
Connie Sullivan Auction Co.
15610 VineyWoods Rd.
Mabelvale, AR 72103
(501) 847-8545

Wilson, Lonnie C.
P.O. Box 2507
Alma, AR 72921
(501) 474-9100

Wooley, Brad H., CAI
Brad H. Wooley Auction Inc.
9 Lombardy Lane
Little Rock, AR 72207
(501) 664-3826
FAX (501) 664-3826

California

Brewer, Allen
Allen Brewer
8301-5 Mission Gorge Rd.
Santee, CA 92071
(619) 448-8866

Burtzlaff, Jr., Paul G., CAI
1229-690 Vienna Dr.
Sunnyvale, CA 94089
(408) 745-7070

Daly, Jr., James, CAI,
International Auction
Service & Antiques
6320 Monterey St.
Gilroy, CA 95020
(408) 847-4038

Dorfman, Joseph
1730 Bodega Ave.
Petaluma, CA 94952
(707) 765-1944

Fern, Don
1718 N. McClelland
Santa Maria, CA 93454
(805) 922-2522

Gamson, Milton
Gamson & Associates
16133 Venuta Blvd.
Penthouse
Encino, CA 91436

Gulla, Michael A.
5244 Reseda Blvd.
Tarzana, CA 91356
(818) 345-0755

Hansen, Maurice N.
P.O. Box 3610
San Clemente, CA 92674
(714) 661-8020
FAX (714) 661-8083

Hather, Don
1729 Marine Ave.
Wilmington, CA 90744
(213) 834-2268
FAX (213) 834-4440

Hitchcock, Greg
5151 Robin Wood Rd. #21
Bonita, CA 92002
(619) 472-5278

Hochman, Jr., S.M.
P.O. Box 429,
Templeton, CA 93465
(805) 434-3400
FAX (805) 434-3389

Holloway, Tipton M.
P.O. Box 356
Live Oaks, CA 95953
(916) 695-1423
FAX (916) 695-1378

Jung, John P.
P.O. Box 1559
Fallbrook, CA 92028
(619) 728-4642
FAX (619) 728-4642

Kilner, Melvin E.
520 E. Terrace Ave.
Fresno, CA 93704
(209) 222-8898
FAX (209) 224-9809

Macon, Mike, CAI
Macon Brothers Auctioneers
558 S. Washington St.
Sonora, CA 95370
(209) 532-0112
FAX (209) 532-1594

Main, Robert W.
7640 Benbow Dr.
Garberville, CA 95440
(707) 923-2311
FAX (707) 923-2767

McEnerney, Gary A.
13331 Alabama Rd.
Galt, CA 95632
(916) 685-6500
FAX (916) 686-8504

Meyer, D.D., CAI
DD Meyer Realty
& Auction Co.
4275 Executive Square
Suite 800
La Jolla, CA 92037
(619) 282-8466
FAX (619) 453-2812

Mulrooney, Jim
Mulrooney Auction Co.
P.O. Box 748
Galt, CA 95632
(209) 745-4542

Nestel, Stephen
210 Porto St.
Manhattan Beach, CA 90266
(213) 545-3743
FAX (213) 546-7105

Nuss, Carol A.
R & P Auctioneers Inc.
14311 Newport Ave., Ste 1
Tustin, CA 92680
(714) 832-8628
FAX (714) 832-9548

Reinders, Wm. R. Bill
Van Tassell Realty & Auction
735 W. Middle Ave.
Morgan Hill, CA 95037
(408) 779-5868
FAX (408) 444-2981

Rogers, Ferris
1640 E. Branham Lane
San Jose, CA 95118
(408) 266-4203

Slavkin, Murray
19510 Ventura Blvd., #212
Tarzana, CA 91356
(213) 873-6871
FAX (818) 609-1616

Vantassell, Vance J.
917 G St.
Sacramento, CA 95814
(916) 444-8633

Vistica, Jerrold F.
P.O. Box 193002
San Francisco, CA 94119-3002
(415) 921-4529

Williams, Frank J.
United Auction Services
P.O. Box 107
Crescent Mills, CA 95934
(916) 284-6176
FAX (916) 284-6178

Colorado

Bohn, Charles F., CAI
Chuck Bohn & Assoc.
P.O. Box 3275
Littleton, CO 80161-3275
(303) 220-8729
FAX (303) 220-8729

Cumberlin, Charles E., CAI
P.O. Box 248
Brush, CO 80723
(303) 842-2822

Dickensheet, W.J.
Dickensheet & Assoc.
2021 S. Platte River Dr.
Denver, CO 80223
(303) 934-8322

Robbins, Matt
998 County Rd. 730
Gunnison, CO 81230
(303) 641-1900

Van Berg, E.S.
P.O. Box 647
Sterling, CO 80751
(303) 522-1950

Connecticut

D'Ausilio, David P.
Vantage Aucitoneers
612 White Plains Rd.
Trumbull, CT 06611
(203) 261-8080
FAX (203) 452-7303

Einhorn, Joseph
Einhorn Associates, Inc.
380 Boston Post Rd., Box 973
Orange, CT 06477
(203) 795-3545

Kaoud, Isam F.
27 Danbury Rd. Rt. 7
Wilton, CT 06897
(203) 762-0376

Keenan, Kelly R.
USAuction, Inc.
P.O. Box 120041
Stamford, CT 06912-0041
(203) 964-3657
FAX (203) 964-3606

Manheimer, Seymour
P.O. Box 421
New London, CT 06320
(203) 443-5942
FAX (203) 444-0759

Schafer, David J.
82 Bradley Rd.
Madison, CT 06443
(203) 245-4173

Sweedler, Norman I.
830 Grand Ave.
New Haven, CT 06511
(203) 865-8294

Zetomer, Arthur
Park City Auction Service
P.O. Box 6314
Bridgeport, CT 06604
(203) 333-5251

Delaware

Conley, Larry W.
RD 3, Box 215-D
Bridgeville, DE 19933
(302) 337-8601

Green, John G.
1104 Middletown/
Warrick Rd.
Middletown, DE 19709
(302) 378-4722

Hechter, Charles
19 Indian Rd.
Newark, DE 19711
(302) 738-9918
FAX (302) 994-3567

Pope, James C.
P.O. Box 81
Lewes, DE 19958
(302) 645-7722
FAX (302) 645-7718

Tindall, Vic
Shore Auctions
P.O. Box 86
Seaford, DE 19973
(302) 856-6739
FAX (301) 860-2257

District of Columbia

Evans, W. Ronald, CAI
Capital City Enterprise, Ltd.
407 H Street NE,
Washington, DC 20002
(202) 543-2828
FAX (202) 547-2545

Florida

Albritton, Kale
1023 Euclid Ave.
Lakeland, FL 33801
(813) 687-3938
FAX (813) 687-0610

Arey, Chester M., CAI
Arey's Auction Team, Inc.
P.O. Box 1953
Deland, FL 32721-1953
(904) 738-0050

Brandenburger, Paul W.
2959 Mercury Rd.
Jacksonville, FL 32207-7912
(904) 730-2911
FAX (904) 730-2911

Campbell, David
Campbell Auctioneers
1047 Bayshore Dr.
Englewood, FL 34223-2302
(813) 475-7166

Campen, Ben, CAI
Ben Campen Auctioneers
P.O. Drawer 1209
Gainesville, FL 32602
(904) 375-6600
FAX (904) 371-1990

Cappella, Joseph A.
404 W. Lantana Rd.
Lantana, FL 33462
(407) 585-5512
FAX (407) 585-6888

Castner, Donald L., CAI
Castner Estate Service
1008 Cimarron Circle NW
Bradenton, FL 34209
(813) 794-6033

Chana, Kurt E.
413 Willow Brook
Longwood, FL 32779
(407) 869-8519

Christenson, Warner T.
18529 SE Heritage Dr.
Tequesta, FL 33469
(407) 624-3882

Coakley, John W.
540 E. Compton Court
Deland, FL 32724
(904) 738-7974

Coburn, Joe E.
7545 N. Palm Oak Dr.
Hernando, FL 32642
(904) 344-5818

Croom, Dan R.
P.O. Box 3262
Longwood, FL 32779
(407) 788-3040

Dietch, Donald R.
Dietch & Company
6302 Manatee Ave.
Suite 6
Bradenton, FL 34209
(813) 798-9966
FAX (813) 798-9926

Dietrich, George T.
2156 Seminole Trail
Orlando, FL 32833
(407) 568-2351

Driggers III, Walter J.
AAPT Realty Inc.
7800 N. Carl G. Rose Hwy.
Hernando, FL 32642-2102
(904) 726-0275
FAX (904) 726-0235

Eggleston, Bernie
Eggleston Auctioneers
4601 W. Kennedy Blvd.
Suite 214
Tampa, FL 33609
(813) 282-0057

Ellis, Ronald L.
Ron Ellis,
Realtor & Auctioneer
3600 S. Atlantic Ave.
New Smyrna Beach,
FL 32169
(904) 423-8866

Faflak, Daniel P.
5950 SW 21st Avenue Rd.
Ocala, FL 32674-5945
(904) 873-3643

Fisher, Lamar P. and Louis
B. Jr. & III, CAI
Fisher Auction
Company, Inc.
431 NE First St.
Pompano Beach, FL 33060
(305) 942-0917

Fisher, Mitzi A., CAI
Fisher Auction
Company, Inc.
431 NE First St.
Pompano Beach, FL 33060
(305) 942-0917

Fullom, Cliff K.
Land & Sea Auctions, Inc.
P.O. Box 1062
Marathon, FL 33050
(800) 654-1889

Garner, Thomas L., CAI
First Coast Auction
P.O. Box 7878
5562-2 Timuquana Rd.
Jacksonville, FL 32238
(904) 772-0110
FAX (904) 777-7873

Gould, David M.
6600 SW 122 St.
Miami, FL 33156
(305) 284-8129

Graham, Jim, CAI
Jim Graham Inc.
Auctioneers-Realtors
204 US 1
N. Palm Beach, FL 33408
(407) 842-7605
FAX (407) 844-2100

Harwig, Anton H.
P.O. Box 282
Flagler Beach, FL 32126
(904) 439-2765

Higgenbotham, Martin, CAI
Higgenbotham Realty Inc.
1666 Williamsburg Square
Lakeland, FL 33803
(813) 644-6681

Hoopingarner, Neil
5121 US 41 North
Palmetto, FL 34221
(813) 722-1984

Huebner, Max
P.O. Box 1444
Ocala, FL 32678
(904) 732-6991

Jacobson, Roger
P.O. Box 2666
Fort Pierce, FL 33454
(407) 466-1930
FAX (407) 461-7563

Janacek, Rod
Janacek Auctioneers
P.O. Box 475
Fort White, FL 32038
(904) 497-1509

Johnson, Ray
701 S. Bumby Ave.
Orlando, FL 32806
(407) 896-1399

Kazaleh, Freddie S.
Professional Auctioneers, Inc.
P.O. Box 24465
Jacksonville, FL 32241-4465
(904) 733-9260

King, Hellen B.
AAPT Realty Inc.
7800 N. Carl G. Rose Hwy.
Hernando, FL 32642-2102
(904) 726-0275
FAX (904) 726-0235

Kirkland, Carol J.
Kirkland Auction Gallery
1907 Wahalaw Court
Tallahassee, FL 32301
(904) 877-6180

Kratschman, Joseph C.
26 Lone Oak Rd.
Spring Hill, FL 34610
(904) 799-7102

Marcovitch, Allen J.
Anaheim Realty & Auctions
1155 SW 25th Avenue
Boynton Beach, FL 33426
(407) 734-8029

McGerity, Francis C.
5386 Countryfield Circle
Ft. Myers, FL 33905
(813) 694-0510

Melburg, Charles D.
4306 Devonshire Lane
Orlando, FL 32812
(407) 898-3975

Messer, Ed
AAPT Realty Inc.
7800 N. Carl G. Rose Hwy.
Hernando, FL 32642-2102
(904) 726-0275
FAX (904) 726-0235

Moates, Robert C.
4082 Belair La. #20
Naples, FL 33940
(813) 262-4921

Myers, Lenny A.
Richard Myers Auction
& Realty
P.O. Box 2062
Winter Park, FL 32790-2062
(407) 644-7295
FAX (407) 644-7380

Myers, Richard L., CAI
Myers Real Estate
Auction Service
PO Box 2062
Winter Park, FL 32790-2062
(407) 644-7295
FAX (407) 644-7380

Neiswander, John, CAI
5115 N. Socrum Loop Rd.
#43
Lakeland, FL 33809-4213
(813) 859-7633

New, Gary C.
Auction Associates, Inc.
4823 Silver Star Rd.
Suite 160
Orlando, FL 32808
(407) 297-7695
FAX (407) 297-7695

Parfitt, Patricia S.
7611 S. Orange Blossom
Terr. #315
Orlando, FL 32809
(813) 644-6681
FAX (813) 644-6686

Passonno, Ralph F.
6141 Bay Isles Dr.
Boynton Beach, FL 33437
(407) 738-9055

Porter, Gordon
Panhandle Realty & Auction
Rt. 1, Box 399
Crestview, FL 32536
(904) 892-4050

Regenhold, Rick H.
Regenhold Auctions
611 S. Myrtle
Clearwater, Fl 34616
(813) 461-1666

Richards, George L.
National Auction Sales
10671 NW 20th St.
Pembroke Pines, FL 33026
(407) 364-8361
FAX (407) 364-8803

Sanders, Virgil
P.O. Box 5517
Ocala, FL 32678-5517

Selby, Brent L.
1013 W. Camino Real
Boca Raton, FL 33486
(407) 391-9145
FAX (407) 391-0139

Shuler, Cliff
422 Julia St.
Titusville, FL 32780
(407) 267-8563
FAX (407) 383-3147

Sklarey, Seth, CAI
Box K, Coconut Grove
Miami, FL 33233-0140
(305) 374-1166
FAX (305) 379-0653

Smith, Charles
The Place For Real
Estate, Inc.
2 El Camino Real
Boca Raton, FL 33432
(407) 383-6570

Smith, Donald J.
4925 University Dr.
Leesburg, FL 34748
(904) 787-5486

Smith, Robert K.
National Auction Sales
10671 NW 20th St.
Pembroke Pines, FL 33026
(407) 364-8361
FAX (407) 364-8803

Stampler, Harry
7875 NW 77th Ave.
Miami, FL 33166
(305) 883-5618
FAX (305) 884-4474

Strait, Harold
4159 Hidden Branch Dr. N.
Jacksonville, FL 32257
(904) 260-0516

Terry, Lanny
Rt. 5, Box 1057
Lake City, FL 32055
(904) 755-0723

Thompson, Judy
411 NE 25th Avenue
Ocala, FL 32670
(904) 732-7101,
FAX (904) 732-8525

Weise, Timothy J.
525 SW Buswell Ave.
Port St. Lucie, FL 34983-8736
(407) 878-6217,
FAX (407) 878-6394

Williams, Dixie L.
8329 Allen Dr.
Brooksville, FL 34613
(904) 596-4801

Williams, Richard M.
1556 Hwy. 97 So.
Cantonment, FL 32533
(904) 623-0141

Georgia

Ansley, Hershel P.
Ansley Realty
323-B East Jackson St.
Thomasville, GA 31792
(912) 228-4456

Barfield, Maurice, CAI
Southeastern Auction Inc.
Rt. 2, P.O. Box 323
Doerun, GA 31744
(812) 985-5700

Dixon, Joh, CAI
Hudson & Marshall Inc.
717 North Ave.
Macon, GA 31211
(800) 841-9400
FAX (912) 743-6110

Grant III, P.T., CAI
Hudson & Marshall Inc.
717 North Ave.
Macon, GA 31211
(800) 841-9400
FAX (912) 743-6110

Hudson, Jr., B.G.
Hudson & Marshall Inc.
717 North Ave.
Macon, GA 31211
(800) 841-9400
FAX (912) 743-6110

Lane, Larry
Brent Lane & Assoc., Inc.
717 North Ave.
Macon, GA 31298
(912) 743-8120
FAX (912) 742-3877

Ling, Jerry R.
Alco Auction & Properties
1739 Tullie Circle NE
Atlanta, GA 30329-2379
(404) 325-1447
FAX (404) 325-5691

Marshall III and IV, Asa M.
Hudson & Marshall Inc.
717 North Ave.
Macon, GA 31211
(912) 743-1511

Register, Jr., L.E.
Auctions Unlimited
Watkinsville, GA 30677
(404) 769-5561

Strickland, John S., CAI
Strickland Realty & Auction
P.O. Box 429
Moultrie, GA 31776
(912) 985-7730

Tarpley, T.J., CAI
J.L. Todd Auction Co.
531 Broad St.
Rome, GA 30161
(800) 241-7591
FAX (404) 291-0335

Whitney, Chuck, CAI
Hudson & Marshall, Inc.
4751 Best Rd., Suite 240
Atlanta, GA 30337
(404) 763-0211
FAX (404) 763-1071

Williams, Dow W.
446 Green St. NE
Gainesville, GA 30501
(800) 955-8881
FAX (404) 532-7546

Hawaii

Glen, Mark
Glen & Associates
350 Ward Ave., Suite 106
Honolulu, HI 96814-4091
(808) 599-3888
FAX (808) 955-6769

Idaho

Hossner, Lynn
Hossner Brothers
Auction Company
109 N. 2nd West
St. Anthony, ID 83445
(208) 624-3782
FAX (208) 624-3783

Lockhert, Bob
1407 Powers
Lewiston, ID 83510
(208) 743-7886

Illinois

Anderson, Dwayne R.
4130 W. Hollow Creek Dr.
#1011
Peoria, IL 61615
(309) 693-2019

Beck, William B.
RR 2, Box 258
Edinburg, IL 62531
(217) 325-3351
FAX (217) 325-3313

Burke, Don S.
RR 2, Box 191
McLeansboro, IL 62859
(618) 643-4527

Clingan, Jim
P.O. Box 52
Royal, IL 61871
(217) 582-2868
FAX (217) 582-2861

Decker, Don
P.O. Box 11
Milford, IL 60953
(815) 889-5355
FAX (815) 889-4113

Decker, William, CAI
Decker Realtor-Auctioneer
Rt. 2, Box 29
Milford, IL 60953
(815) 889-4213
FAX (815) 889-4113

Draper, Robert D.
No. 1, Draper Lane
Ohio, IL 61349
(815) 376-2001

Estes, Maurice W.
5426 Pierce Lane
Godfrey, IL 62035
(618) 466-1986

Gaule, William L., CAI
114 E. Walnut
Chatham, IL 62629
(217) 483-2484
FAX (217) 483-2485

Geer, Roberta L.
55 White Oak Circle
St. Charles, IL 60174
(708) 377-4625
FAX (708) 377-4680

Hachmeister, Greg L.
425 W. 4th St., Box 171
Pecatonica, IL 61063
(815) 239-2714
FAX (815) 239-1436

Hachmeister, Henry, CAI
305 E. 3rd St., Box 296
Pecatonica, IL 61063
(815) 239-1436
FAX (815) 239-1436

Hayunga, Phil
4482 Lamm Rd.
Freeport, IL 61032
(815) 235-2323

Hertenstein, Roger G., CAI
Hertenstein Auctions
P.O. Box 23
Wayne City, IL 62895
(618) 895-2663
FAX (618) 895-2663

Jeffries, Timothy J.
2642 Vermont St.
Quincy, IL 62301
(217) 223-0017

Josko, John A., CAI
Phillip Pollack & Co. Inc.
3000 Dundee Rd. Suite 320
Northbrook, IL 60062
(708) 480-0040
FAX (708) 480-1036

Lane, Leon
316 E. Harrison
Sullivan, IL 61951
(217) 728-7132

Lenhart, Doyne, CAI
Route 2, Box 12
Georgetown, IL 61846
(217) 662-8644
FAX (217) 662-2484

McAnly, Howard
P.O. Box 602
Rochelle, IL 61068
(815) 562-6957

Mezo, Joseph
P.O. Box 218
McLeansboro, IL 62859
(618) 643-3176

Newton, John L.
P.O. Box 1412, Hwy 45 North
Vienna, IL 62995
(618) 658-3141

Perschke, Walter
Auction USA
Perfection Bldg.
1423 W. Fullerton
Chicago, IL 60614
(312) 871-7200
FAX (312) 871-8010

Phillips, Ronald L.
301 N. State St.
Freeburg, IL 62243
(618) 539-3427

Rath, Mari Kaye
Marcy Rath Auction Service
38 W. 196th RT 20
Elgin, IL 60123
(708) 695-0375

Roth, Jim, and Norman, CAIs
R #5
E. Peoria, IL 61611
(309) 266-6784

Schrage, Larry R., CAI,
Complete Auction Service
RR 1, Box 60
Grant Park, IL 60940
(815) 465-6137

Smalley, Gregory R.
Smalley & Associates
Real Estate
11772 Hayloft Lane
Roscoe, IL 61073
(815) 623-7777

Swanson, Swanie, CAI
144 E. Church St.
Sandwich, IL 60548
(815) 786-2363

Tosetti, Jack E.
Tosetti & Associates
Auction Service
120 S. Cedar St.
Nokomis, IL 62075
(217) 563-8641

Windler, William H.
P.O. Box 516
Irvington, IL 62848-0516
(618) 249-8241

Indiana

Abernathy, Terry C., CAI
Abernathy Auctions
& Real Estate
21 W. Union St.
Liberty, IN 47353
(317) 458-5826

Baber, Steven J.
SSJB Associates, Inc.
P.O. Box 599
New Palestine, IN 46163
(317) 861-4495

Brown, Liston L.
100 J St.
La Porte, IN 46350
(219) 326-6066
FAX (219) 362-7653

Butts, Virgil W., CAI
600 W. National Ave.
Brazil, IN 47834
(812) 446-2322
FAX (812) 446-2322

Chitwood, Fred
Chitwood Auctions
2775 West 1505
Lebanon, IN 46052
(317) 482-3528

Craig, Roger W.
Craig Auction Service
RR 1
Petersburg, IN 47567
(812) 354-6045

Crume, Roy L., CAI
3619 W. Sycamore Lane
Kokomo, IN 46901
(317) 452-6946

Curtis, Terry W., CAI
6218 Conservation Dr.
Jeffersonville, IN 47130
(812) 283-8586

Ellenberger, Robert, CAI
130½ W. Market St.
Bluffton, IN 46714
(219) 824-2426
FAX (219) 824-1728

Evans, Larry
Rt. 1, Box 223
Mentone, IN 46539
(219) 353-7121

Frantz, R.D.
Frantz & Associates
Auction Realty
P.O. Box 511
Warren, IN 46792-0511
(219) 375-2056

Hixson, Larry J.
Hixson Auction Service
1600 Allison Blvd.
Auburn, IN 46706-3221
(219) 357-4477

Klein, Victor J.
Klein Realty, Auction Co.
404 North 7th Street
Vincennes, IN 47591
(812) 882-2202
FAX (812) 882-8777

Koontz, Stephanie L.
2600 WE. 16th Street
Bedford, IN 47421
(812) 275-4401
FAX (812) 279-4504

Lacy, Phillip H.
Lacy Auction & Realty
Company
329 E. Division Rd.
Valparaiso, IN 46383
(219) 462-1402

Lawson, Jack
Lawson Bros. Auctioneers
P.O. Box 327
Danville, IN 46122
(317) 745-6405
FAX (317) 745-6406

Michael, Greg M., CAI
P.O. Box 7
Camden, IN 46917
(219) 686-2400

Ness, Kurt J.
Ness Brothers
18 W. Washington St.
Huntington, IN 46750
(219) 356-3911

Ratts, Noble
2223A Rome Drive
Indianapolis, IN 46208
(317) 431-0606

Silke, Jr., Marlin C.
Silke Auction & Realty
RR #2, Box 97
Eberfeld, IN 47613
(812) 983-4548

Sprunder, Edward F.
RR 3
Decatur, IN 46733
(219) 724-3606

Taylor, David A., CAI
Taylor Auction Company
6804 Summertime Dr.
Indianapolis, IN 46226
(317) 547-7319

Wagner, C.T.
405 E. Main St., P.O. Box 481
Washington, IN 47501
(812) 254-4186
FAX (812) 254-4088

Winger, Loren E., CAI
Schrader Real Estate
& Auction
P.O. Box 404
Converse, IN 46919
(317) 395-3351
FAX (317) 395-3351

Iowa

Arnold, Jay
Arnold Auction Service
RR 1, Box 18
Mallard, IA 50562
(712) 425-3538

Bousselot, Norman
Route 1, Box 18
Calamus, IA 52729
(319) 246-2628

Collins, Warren
1155 6th St.
Jessup, IA 50648
(319) 827-1066

Forristal, Pat
McGuire Auction Co.
126 N. Main
Holstein, IA 51025
(712) 368-2635
FAX (712) 368-2784

Hattermann, Todd J.
P.O. Box 162
Pauline, IA 51046
(712) 448-3602

Huff, Jim
RR 2
Keosauqua, IA 52565
(319) 293-3711

King, Jeff, King Auction
1700 Grandview
Muscatine, IA 51761-1548
(319) 264-8190

Law, Donald G.
300 5th Avenue SW
LeMars, IA 51031-2163
(712) 546-8188

Ryan, Dale J.
RR #1, Box 197
Decorah, IA 52101
(319) 382-9533
FAX (319) 382-8785

Schultz, Clete
1310 Rapids, Box 101
Adel, IA 50003
(515) 993-4440

Smith, Dale E.
801 Third Ave., NW
Pocahontas, IA 50574
(712) 335-4111
FAX (712) 335-3111

Starling, Dennis G.
RR 1, Box 101
Lost Nation, IA 52554

Stewart, Wayne, CAI
P.O. Box 265
417 S. Park Pl.
Audubon, IA 50025
(712) 563-4288
FAX (712) 563-2111

Thies, Earl
Box 309
Ames, IA 50010
(515) 232-3322

Wears, Brent, CAI
RR 1, Box 360
Solon, IA 52333
(319) 644-3779

Kansas

Albertson, James L., II
P.O. Box 8573
Prairie Village, KS 66208
(913) 362-8049

Bannon, Jeff W., CAI
Jeff Bannon Auction/
Realty, Inc.
946 N. West St.
Wichita, KS 67203
(316) 945-0491

Bertram, Jerry L.
Banbury Auction
& Real Estate
Box 8733
Pratt, KS 67124
(316) 672-7723

Bletscher, Chris
Route 1
Abilene, KS 67410
(913) 598-2385

Cole, Curtis C., CAI
Cole Auction & Real Estate
1405 Main
Goodland, KS 67735
(913) 899-2683
FAX (913) 899-5563

Evenson, Charles S.
Charles Evenson
Auctioneers
260 N. Rock Rd., Ste. 140
Wichita, KS 67206
(316) 683-7733

Frederick, J.D.
JD Frederick & Associate
P.O. Box 3531
Wichita, KS 67201
(316) 267-1191

Hartter, Roger
Hartter Auction Service
Rt. 4, Box 236
Sabetha, KS 66534
(913) 284-2643

Horigan, Dan D.
P.O. Box 56
Frankfort, KS 66427
(913) 292-4977

Hunt, Myron B.
1002-B E. 23rd Street
Hutchinson, KS 67502-5652
(316) 663-7428

Koch, Vern E.
Koch Auction Service
1822 Cow Palace Rd.
Newton, KS 67114
(316) 283-6700

McCurdy, Lonny R.
7008 E. 14th
Wichita, KS 67206
(316) 683-0612
FAX (316) 683-8822

Olmsted, Timothy
Box 207
Beattle, KS 66406
(913) 353-2487

Olson, Galen D.
Olson Realty & Auction
1109 Easter
Wakeeney, KS 67672
(913) 743-2774

Porter, Sr., Roger L., CAI
P.O. Box 8, 1036 Ironwood
Olathe, KS 66061
(913) 782-8009
FAX (913) 782-7767

Potter, Gary
1125 S. Summit
Arkansas City, KS 67005
(316) 442-4136

Sherlock, Frederick
PO Box 926
St. Francis, KS 67756

Shivers, Ronald L.
300 Summit Dr.
Abilene, KS 67410
(913) 263-7488

Showalter, Bud
Rt. 1, Box 101B
Easton, KS 66020
(913) 651-5233

Van Sickle, Ralph, CAI
15 W. 5th Avenue
Emporia, KS 66801
(316) 342-6431

Veal, Stan R.
Box 56, Route #4
Abilene, KS 67410
(913) 263-7787

Kentucky

Adams, Roy E., CAI
Ford Realty &
Auction Co., Inc.
P.O. Box 1435
Mount Vernon, KY 40456
(606) 256-4555

Birdwhistell, E. Glenn
154 S. Main St.
Lawrenceburg, KY 40342
(502) 839-3456

Brewer, John C.
P.O. Box 579
105 N. Main St.
Stanton, KY 40380
(606) 663-4663
FAX (606) 663-4588

Bush, J. Randall, CAI
2689 Red Mill Rd.
Elizabethtown, KY 42701
(502) 765-2298
FAX (502) 737-7787

Claycomb, James E.
1131 Hopi Trail
Frankfort, KY 40601
(502) 695-3755

Conder, Jim
P.O. Box 368
Leitchfield, KY 42755
(502) 259-3114

Crain, Frank, CAI
1710 Pear Orchard Rd.
Elizabethtown, KY
42701-9410
(502) 765-7684
FAX (502) 737-7787

Cundiff, Marvin
1008 Springside Way
Louisville, KY 40223
(502) 245-3618

Darlin, John R., CAI
Main Auction Inc.
3540 Winding Dr.
Lexington, KY 40517
(606) 273-3133
FAX (606) 273-3133

Deane, Silas
5785 Hwy. 144
Owensboro, KY 42303
(502) 926-8553
FAX (502) 926-8574

Downs, Larry
4421 Santa Paula Lane
Lexington, KY 40219
(502) 589-3342

Dunnington, Ronald G., CAI
Mid-America Realty & Auction
Rt. 4, Unit 19
Monticello, KY 42633
(606) 348-9359

Durham III, John L., CAI
Durham & Durham,
Realty/Auction
135 N. Third St.
Danville, KY 40422
(606) 236-2770

Freeman, S.D.
110 Hospital St.
Cediz, KY 42211
(502) 522-3101

Fries, Richard D.
Butcher Auction & Realty
RR 2, Box 392
Butler, KY 41006
(606) 635-3197

Gibson, William S., CAI
1708 N. Mayo
Pikeville, KY 41501
(606) 432-8181
FAX (606) 478-9838

Godby, Samuel R.
P.O. Box 391
Somerset, KY 42501
(606) 678-8189

Gribbins, Jr., Aleck, CAI
Gribbins Auction House
2712 Crums La.
Louisville, KY 40216
(502) 447-9572

Helm II, Harold H., CAI
River Realty & Auction Co.
215 Breckenridge La.
Louisville, KY 40207
(502) 893-6611
FAX (502) 893-2181

Helm, II, Harold H., CAI
River Realty & Auction Co.
215 Breckenridge Lane
Louisville, KY 40207
(502) 893-6611
FAX (502) 893-2181

Hunt, Thomas R., CAI
Hunt Realty & Auction Co.
66131 W. Bypass Ave. W, #A
Bowling Green, KY
42101-4968
(502) 782-2200
FAX (502) 843-8780

Jones, Harvey M.
Wilkerson Realty & Auction
1224 E. Bryant St.
Corbin, KY 40701
(606) 528-1157

Kessler, John M. and Wayne
P.O. Box 271
Campbellsville, KY 42718
(502) 465-7051

Kirby, Ron, CAI
Ron Kirby Realty
& Auction, Inc.
P.O. Box 285
Franklin, KY 42134
(502) 586-8288
FAX (502) 586-8823

Ledbetter, Kay S.
Ledbetter & Stewart, Ltd.
Realtors & Auctioneers
1999 Richmond Rd.
Suite 500,
Lexington, KY 40502
(606) 268-1400
FAX (606) 268-2677

Levy, Stuart G.
5602 Harrods Cove
Louisville, KY 40059
(502) 228-5254

Lewis, Stephen D.
129 E. Main St.
Morehead, KY 40351
(606) 784-4168
FAX (606) 784-4160

Lynch, James D., CAI
Lynch Auction & Realty
1186 E. Broadway
Louisville, KY 40204
(502) 589-9822

Maddox, Alan
501 School St.
Beaver Dam, KY 42320
(502) 274-9672
FAX (502) 274-5610

Maglinger, Gary
Maglinger Auction & Realty
1331 West 5th Street
Owensboro, KY 42301
(502) 683-5923
FAX (502) 683-5923

Mattox, Mark T.
Mattox Real Estate & Auction
107 Locust St.
Carlisle, KY 40311
(606) 289-5720

Price, Jim, CAI
Price Realty & Auction Co.
12211 Old Shelbyville Rd.
Suite D
Louisville, KY 40243
(502) 244-1509

Riden, Billy F.
Riden Auction & Realty
114 W. Main St.
Providence, KY 42450
(502) 667-2570
FAX (502) 667-2097

Roy, Ralph D.
Box 578
W. Cumberland Ave.
Jamestown, KY 42629-0578
(502) 343-3334
FAX (502) 343-3033

Stewart III, Daniel D.
Ledbetter & Stewart, Ltd.
Realtors & Auctioneers
1999 Richmond Rd.
Suite 500
Lexington, KY 40502
(606) 268-1400
FAX (606) 268-2677

Sutton, Lewis R.
Box 209
Richmond, KY 40475
(606) 792-4277

Tabb, Cordell
319 S. Mulberry St.
Elizabethtown, KY 42701

Thomason, David B., CAI
216 Buckman St.
P.O. Box 722
Shepherdsville, KY 40165
(502) 955-7342
FAX (502) 543-5414

True, Rene F.
3350 Snaffle Rd.
Lexington, KY 40513
(609) 268-2533
FAX (606) 266-3699

Turner, Linda R.
1506 S. Virginia St.
Hopkinsville, KY 42240
(502) 885-6789

Waltrip, Michael J.
Best Auctions, Inc.
1660 W. Hill St.
Louisville, KY 40210
(502) 778-5500
FAX (502) 778-3000

Wells, Gary L., CAI
Gary Wells Auctioneers
Rt. 1
Owingville, KY 40360
(606) 674-2453

White, Dwain C., CAI
Thomas White & Sons
Auction & Real Estate
Box 355
Kuttawa, KY 42055
(502) 388-2420

Willett, Roscoe
Real Estate & Auction Sales
6720 Contest Rd.
Paducah, KY 42001
(502) 554-0065

Louisiana

Babb, Keith, CAI
P.O. Box 4222
Monroe, LA 71211-4968
(318) 343-6211
FAX (318) 343-6232

Baudry, Thomas P., CAI
Suite 1930
One American Place
Baton Rouge, LA 70825
(504) 344-2640
FAX (504) 336-9208

Corby, Peter C.
Jere M. Daye Inc
11914 Towering Oaks Dr.
Baton Rouge, LA 70810
(504) 344-2640

Daye, II, Jere M.
Jere M. Daye, Inc.
Suite 1930
One American Place
Baton Rouge, LA 70825
(504) 344-2640
FAX (504) 336-9208

Gilmore, David E., CAI
Gilmore Auction &
Realty Co.
2110 I-10 Service Rd.
Suite 203
Kenner, LA 70065
(504) 443-1280
FAX (504) 937-3387

Nelson, Ragan K.
P.O. Box 12360
Alexandria, LA 71315-2360
(318) 473-0510
FAX (318) 473-8914

Wolfe, Lynn, CAI
2026 Pitch Pine
Shreveport, LA 71118
(318) 688-9466

Maine

Blair, Robert
R. Blair's Auction Service
P.O. Box 308
Wells, ME 04090
(207) 646-7475
FAX (207) 646-4144

Caprara, Victor A.
RFD #3, Box 3530
Winthrop, ME 04364
(207) 377-2080

Giquere, Gerald P., Jr.
P.O. Box 1272
Windham, ME 04062
(207) 892-3800

Keating III, James J.,
J.J. Keating, Inc.
Rt. 1 North
Kennebunk, ME 04043
(207) 985-2097

Keenan, Richard J., CAI
Keenan Auction Company
P.O. Box 288
Kingfield, ME 04947
(207) 265-2011
FAX (207) 265-2607

Weinstein, King H.
King Real Estate
198 Saco Avenue
Old Orchard Beach, ME 04064
(207) 934-7622
FAX (207) 934-1566

Maryland

Biser, Robert C.
8615 Opossumtown Pike
Frederick, MD 21702
(301) 662-7424

Bradstreet, Mark E.
Middletown Valley
Auction Service
P.O. Box 1
Tuscarora, MD 21790
(301) 874-2303

Burkheimer, Robert C.
R.C. Burkheimer & Assoc.
P.O. Box 551
North East, MD 21901-0551
(800) 233-4169
FAX (301) 287-2029

Campbell, Robert H.
121 Prince George St.
Annapolis, MD 21401
(301) 263-5808
FAX (301) 263-8427

Campbell, II, Robert H., CAI
229 Garden Gate Lane
Annapolis, MD 21403
(301) 263-5808
FAX (301) 263-8427

Fitzgerald, William J.
W.J. Fitzgerald & Co.
P.O. Box 288
Mechanicsville, MD 20659
(800) 365-7031
FAX (301) 843-9656

Fox, David S.
Michael Fox
Auctioneers, Inc.
3835 Naylors Lane
Baltimore, MD 21208
(301) 653-4000
FAX (301) 653-4069

Fox, William Z., CAI
Michael Fox
Auctioneers, Inc.
3835 Naylors Lane
Baltimore, MD 21208
(301) 653-4000
FAX (301) 653-4069

Griffin, Jim
E.J.'s Auction Sales
202 West Street
Berlin, MD 21811
(301) 641-4448

Hartman, David P.
8703 Maravoss La.
Baltimore, MD 21234
(410) 661-7220

Hunt, George C.
19521 Woodfield Rd.
Gaithersburg, MD 20879
(301) 948-3937

Isennock, Sr., Robert L.
Isennock Auction
Services, Inc.
4203 Norrisville Rd.
White Hall, MD 21161
(301) 557-8052

Koelbel, John D.
P.O. Box 9804
Towson, MD 21204
(301) 823-0047
FAX (301) 823-0048

Martin, Clair L.
P.O. Box 499
Margansville, MD
21767-0499
(301) 797-4428

Nelson, Edward N., CAI
US Route 50
P.O. Box 95
Trappe, MD 21673
(301) 476-3140

Reedy, Jack
1631 N. Main St.
Hampstead, MD 21074-3006
(301) 239-8110
FAX (301) 239-4551

Pete Richardson
Auction Sales
P.O. Box 51
Willards, MD 21874
(301) 546-2425
FAX (301) 835-8613

Rigdon, H.B., CAI
Rigdon Auctioneers
P.O. Box 625
Forest Hill, MD 21050
(301) 836-2787
FAX (301) 836-2738

Thomas, Robert P., CAI
Arbor Realty & Auction Co.
Route 925N, Box 278
Waldorf, MD 20601
(301) 449-4444
FAX (301) 843-0513

Whitson, Guy M.
T.R. O'Farrell, Inc.
6 Quintal Dr.
Westminster, MD 21157
(301) 848-5533

Massachusetts

Berman, Myron
Harry A. Berman & Sons
80 Tarrytown La.
Worcester, MA 01602
(508) 753-2549
FAX (508) 755-9364

Caddigan, Jeremy J.
Caddigan Auctioneers Inc.
1130 Washington St.
Hanover, MA 02339
(617) 826-8648
FAX (617) 826-2438

Caddigan, Joan F., CAI
Caddigan Auctioneers Inc.
1130 Washington St.
Hanover, MA 02339
(617) 826-8648
FAX (617) 826-2438

Goldstein, Abe
Abe Goldstein Auctioneers
156 Lincoln St.
Brighton, MA 02135
(617) 787-4433
FAX (617) 789-5893

Healey, Garrett D.
Garrett Auctioneers
76 High Street
Danvers, MA 01923
(617) 233-7227

Herrick, Paul J.
P.J. Herrick Co., Inc.
Ste. 204, 8 Martin St.
Essex, MA 01929
(508) 768-6102
FAX (508) 768-6156

Hurwitz, Joel B.
Hurwitz Associates
P.O. Box 193
Boston, MA 02126
(617) 323-2700
FAX (617) 296-9588

Hyte, Barton K.
Barton K. Hyte Company
15 Court Square
Boston, MA 02108
(617) 720-0939
FAX (617) 720-0275

Jacobson, Harvey A., CAI
390 Main St.
Worcester, MA 01608
(508) 755-2550
FAX (508) 791-8994

Kaminski, Frank C.
Frank Kaminski Co., Inc.
193 Franklin St.
Stoneham, MA 02180
(617) 438-7595
FAX (617) 665-7418

MacIntyre, John R.
Speedi Auctioneers
10 Bryant St.
Dedham, MA 02026
(617) 329-3882

Manning, Jerome J.
45 Broad St.
Boston, MA 02109
(800) 521-0111
FAX (617) 451-9640

Maynard, Ronald V.
Ron Maynard Auctioneers
258 Groton St.
Dunstable, MA 01827
(508) 649-4280

Monroe, Sandra F.
10 State St.
Woburn, MA 01801
(617) 933-3998
FAX (617) 932-0421

Moon, William F., CAI
William F. Moon & Company
12 Lewis Rd., RFD #1
N. Attleboro, MA 02760
(508) 699-4477
FAX (508) 651-9877

Paine, Stanley J.
1198 Boylston St.
Chestnut Hill, MA 02167
(617) 731-4455
FAX (617) 566-0840

Potvin, Robert L., CAI
Potvin Auction & Realty
Box 808, Blair House
West Brookfield, MA 01585
(508) 867-3346

Regan, James E.
Regan Auctioneers
100 Hammond St.
Waltham, MA 02154
(617) 893-1181

Russo, George T.
78 Perry Ave.
Lynnfield, MA 01940
(617) 334-2747

Santa Lucia, Frank
80 Upham St.
Melrose, MA 02176-3526
(617) 337-2931
FAX (617) 337-2933

Santos, Michael
Bristol Auctioneers
568 Washington St.
Wellesley, MA 02181
(617) 235-9035

Stead, Robert A.
64 Pumpkin La., RFD 1
Southbridge, MA 01550
(508) 248-3120

Taylor, Richard H.
Auction Marketing
Group, Inc.
4 Bellows Rd.
P.O. Box 693
Westboro, MA 01581
(508) 835-3275

Torteson, James R., CAI
10 Hope Ave.
Oxford, MA 01540
(508) 987-2277

Michigan

Albrecht, Herbert, CAI
Herb Albrecht, CAI &
Associates
3884 Saginaw Rd.
Vassar, MI 48768
(517) 823-8835

Ballor, R. William, CAI
Bill Ballor Auction Service
201 N. First St., P.O. Box 249
Linwood, MI 48634
(517) 697-4212

Beyer, Nick & Sherry
Beyer Auction Service
7704 St. Huberts
Hesperia, MI 49421
(616) 894-7628

Bogdan, Thomas
939 W. Crescent St.
Marquette, MI 49855
(906) 228-3952

Boyk, John S., CAI
Boyk's Auction Service
7878 Cathro Rd.
Alpena, MI 49707
(517) 356-9589

Chase, Alfred C.
Chase Auction Service
239 State St.
Hesperia, MI 49421
(616) 854-6865

Dean, Ed
6693-28th Ave.
Hudsonville, MI 49426-9701
(616) 669-3716

Freund, Ken
Auction Way Sales, Inc.
P.O. Box 3096
2443 S. Old 27
Gaylord, MI 49735
(517) 732-7808

Glardon, Daniel G.
988 E. Henderson Rd.
Owosso, MI 48867
(517) 725-7756

Good, Arthur L., CAI
321 N. Cedar
Mason, MI 48854
(517) 676-4433
FAX (517) 676-4371

Juckette, Rollo A.
16241 Brewer Rd.
Dundee, MI 48131
(313) 529-2388

Kleiman, Ben
P.O. Box 2355
Grand Rapids, MI 49501
(616) 949-1900

Krol, Bernedia
K & K Auction Services
2020 Hunter Rd.
Brighton, MI 48116
(313) 227-8040
FAX (616) 229-2204

Kubesh, Dennis
P.O. Box 61
Maple City, MI 49664
(616) 228-6667

Norton, David A.
Norton Of Michigan
50 W. Pearl St.
Coldwater, MI 49036
(517) 279-9063
FAX (517) 279-9191

Reeser, Steve, CAI
1465 N. Cedar
Mason, MI 48854
(517) 699-2219
FAX (517) 699-3064

Ringel, Ronald W.
11444 Big Four Rd.
Bear Lake, MI 49614

Sheridan, William L., CAI
3175 W. Sitts Rd.
Mason, MI 48854
(517) 676-2503
FAX (517) 676-5400

Stanton, Steve E.
Stanton's Auctioneers
& Realtors
144 S. Main
Vermontville, MI 49096
(517) 726-0181
FAX (517) 726-0060

Stutzman, David E.
1847 Pine Dr.
Traverse City, MI 49684
(616) 938-9761

Whalen, John M., CAI
5844 Gotfredson Rd.
Plymouth, MI 48170-5075
(313) 459-5144

Minnesota

Baker, John E.
Rt. #3, Box 171
Appleton, MN 56208
(612) 394-2489

Barta, Wesley L.
Wagon Wheel Auctioneering
904 5th Avenue SE, Box 5
Barnesville, MN 56514
(218) 354-2440

Berens, Richard A.
Alliance Auction &
Realty Service
Twelve Oaks Center
15500 Wayzata Blvd. Ste. 768
Wayzata, MN 55391
(612) 475-3322
FAX (612) 475-2384

Burt, Quinten I., CAI
RR #1, Box 60
Long Prairie, MN 56347
(612) 732-6320

Carpenter, Michael W.
Carpenter Auction Company
104 Parkview Dr.
P.O. Box 245
Lake Benton, MN 56149
(507) 368-4307

Christian, David, CAI
Quickie Auction Service
22895 141st Avenue N.
Rogers, MN 55374
(612) 428-4217
FAX (612) 428-8355

Fahey, James D.
P.O. Box 370
Hutchinson, MN 55350
(612) 587-3510
FAX (612) 587-3255

Haas, Rich H.
Continental Auctioneers
School
P.O. Box 346
Mankato, MN 56002-0346
(507) 625-5595

Houghton, Richard E., CAI
1967 Launa Ave.
Red Wing, MN 55066
(623) 388-5870

Imholte, Frank B.
8160 Country Rd. 138
St. Cloud, MN 56301
(612) 255-9398

Kiefer, Kurt
Kiefer Auction Companies
P.O. Box 745
417 Stanton
Fergus Falls, MN 56537
(218) 739-4408
FAX (218) 736-7474

Lampi, Thomas
Lampi Auction Equipment
RR 1, Box 76
Annandale, MN 55302
(612) 274-5393

Landgraff, Frederick D.
P.O. Box 326, 409 N. Jackson
Minneota, MN 56264-0457
(507) 872-5430

Marguth, Terry
1500 E. Bridge St.
Redwood Falls, MN 56283
(507) 644-8433,
FAX (507) 644-2425

Mitchell, Cliff
Mitchell Auction Service
P.O. Box 390
Albany, MN 56307-0390
(612) 845-2244
FAX (612) 845-2187

Norling, Lefty
Norling Auction Service
Box 141
Kandiiyohi, MN 56251
(612) 382-6566

Pinske, Bill
325 West Main St.
Arlington, MN 55307
(612) 964-2250

Rehbein, Kenneth E.
426 Pine St.
Lino Lakes, MN 55014
(612) 429-1234
FAX (612) 429-1234

Reinhardt, Carol, CAI
Rte. 2, P.O. Box 1790
Palisade, MN 56469
(218) 845-2260
FAX (218) 845-2728

Reinhardt, Steve, CAI
Rt. 2, P.O. Box 1790
Palisade, MN 56469
(218) 845-2260
FAX (218) 845-2728

Scheffler, Richard
Scheffler Auctioneering
Route 1, P.O. Box 67
Morton, MN 56270
(507) 697-6257

Schroeder, Orville M.
106 W. Adams St.
Caledonia, MN 55921
(507) 724-2874

Spanier, David E.
Spanier Auction Service
5128 Julien St.
St. Peter, MN 56082
(507) 931-4259

Mississippi

Johnson, Lannie E.
Route 3, Box 297A
Fulton, MS 38843
(601) 862-2835

Johnson, Merry K.
Route 3, Box 297A
Fulton, MS 38843
(601) 862-2835

Ozborn, Kline Jr.
Box 651
Canton, MS 39046
(601) 859-3845
FAX (601) 859-7828

Missouri

Arnaman, H. Willard
1312 E. Main St.
P.O. Box 123
Unionville, MO 63565
(816) 947-2883

Atterberry, Larry P., CAI
Atterberry & Assoc.
Auction Co.
79121-70 Dr. SE
Columbia, MO 65201
(314) 474-9295

Bayless, Alan
Box 14068
Parkville, MO 64152
(816) 587-7575

Breckenridge, R. Bruce
P.O. Box 97
Theodosia, MO 65761-0097
(417) 273-4267

Burger, Ron
Ron Burger Auction Service
Rt 1, Box 1085
Scott City, MO 63780
(314) 264-2501

Easley, Randy
Easley Auction Co.
P.O. Box 176, Hwy. 210
Orrick, MO 64077
(816) 483-1167
FAX (816) 496-3423

Hall, Clarence
P.O. Box 113
Pleasant Hill, MO 64080
(816) 987-3246

Hamilton, Robert F.
P.O. Box 231
Kimberling City, MO 65686
(417) 739-2047

Kallmeyer, Joy
Hwy. 100 East, P.O. Box 223
Hermann, MO 65041
(314) 486-5714

Lambert, Mike
Mike Lambert
Enterprise Inc.
Rt. #3, Box 181
Kirksville, MO 63501
(816) 665-7889
FAX (816) 665-1139

Long, Billy, CAI
Billy Long Auction & Realty
1950-L S. Glenstone
Springfield, MO 65804
(417) 882-5664
FAX (417) 882-7653

Marter, Gregory G.
#90 Country Life Dr.
O'Fallon, MO 63366
(314) 272-4890

McBaine, F.F. Pete
2205 S. Country Club Drive
Columbia, MO 65201
(314) 449-3770

McFadden, Leslie J.
Leslie McFadden
Auction Service
8025 Route W
Jefferson City, MO 65101
(314) 635-6003

Merry, Donald E.
5805 Sorrel Tree Ct.
St. Louis, MO 63129
(314) 487-5846

Merry, Robert
Robert Merry Auction Co.
5501 Milburn Rd.
St. Louis, MO 63129
(314) 487-3992

Moore, Orval R.
P.O. Box 638
Branson, MO 65616
(800) 441-2261

Pickett, Eddie
Rt. 1, Box 162
Stewartsville, MO 64490
(816) 669-3433

Ratliff, Dennis W.
Rt. 1, Box 18-B
Easton, MO 64443
(816) 667-5411

Schroff, Roy
130 E. 1st
Hermann, MO 65041
(314) 486-2332

Voorheis, Brent, CAI
10877 N. Hwy. J
Harrisburg, MO 65256-9730
(314) 874-5988
FAX (314) 874-5988

Walker, E. Lance, CAI
Walker Auctions
202 S. 3rd Street
Hayti, MO 63851
(314) 359-1202
FAX (314) 359-1319

Wells, Jim
Ace Auction Service
104 Friendship La.
Clinton, MO 64735
(816) 885-3725

Woolery, David R.
Woolery Auction Co.
P.O. Box 414
Branson, MO 65616
(417) 335-4242

Yancey, Gary J.
1800 S. Sneed
Sedalia, MO 65301
(816) 827-3668

Montana

Ellis, Jerry, CAI
Ellis Auction Sales
P.O. Box 50310
Billings, MT 59105
(406) 245-3519

Gardner, Davar and Todd
Gardner Auction Service
Box 943
Kalispell, MT 59901
(406) 752-7682
FAX (406) 752-9674

Goggins, Pat
Box 30758
Billings, MT 59107
(406) 259-4589
FAX (406) 259-6888

Mandeville, John
1112 Mandeville La.
Bozeman, MT 59715
(406) 587-7832

Metzger, William
3150 W. Cameron Bridge Rd.
Manhattan, MT 59741
(406) 285-6511
FAX (406) 285-6514

Nebraska

Billups, Susan J.
Rehmeier & Billups Auction
RR 1, Box 220
Nebraska City, NE 68410
(402) 873-7111

Dolan, Jr., Thomas R.
102 N. Dewey
North Platte, NE 69101-6903
(308) 532-0342
FAX (308) 532-1463

Elting, Bradley K.
145 N. 44th Street
Hebron, NE 68370
(402) 768-7270
FAX (402) 768-6016

Garey, Marsden, CAI
1610 Parkview Dr.
Grand Island, NE 68801
(308) 384-9011

Green, Norm E., CAI
Norm Green
Realty & Auction
Box 563, 104 S. Lincoln Ave.
York, NE 68467
(402) 362-5595
FAX (402) 362-4875

Martin, Dean C.
P.O. Box 207
Lexington, NE 68850
(308) 324-4931

Meusch, Monty
Farmers National Company
11516 Nicholas St.
Omaha, NE 68154
(402) 496-3276
FAX (402) 496-7956

Rudolph, Harry
15719 S. 99th
Papillion, NE 68128
(402) 339-8129

Sanders, Harry
1107 N. Broad St.
Fremont, NE 68025
(402) 721-0860
FAX (402) 727-7818

Starman, Steve
1240 Royal Dr.
Papillon, NE 68128
(402) 592-1933
FAX (402) 592-2327

Nevada

Britt, Don P.
5126 S. Somerset Dr.
Las Vegas, NV 89120
(702) 451-9075

Chadwick, George H.
1325 S. Maryland Pkwy
Las Vegas, NV 81904
(702) 387-8980
FAX (702) 384-3552

Robinson, J.D., David K.
1500 E. Tropicana Ave.
Suite 102
Las Vegas, NV 89119
(702) 597-9845
FAX (702) 736-9192

White, Burton J.
Select Service/Burton White
5319 W. Tara Ave.
Las Vegas, NV 89102
(702) 566-9200
FAX (702) 564-3589

New Hampshire

Constantine, Lawrence
P.O. Box 5812
Manchester, NH 03108
(603) 644-5492

Fox, Martin
P.O. Box 173
Portsmouth, NH 03802-0173
(603) 433-3360

Lago, Robert W.
Hammond & Lago, Inc.
212 Pembroke Rd.
Concord, NH 03301
(603) 224-1942
FAX (603) 224-9558

Levin, Harv
142 Portsmouth Ave.
Stratham, NH 03885
(603) 772-8488
FAX (603) 772-4363

Liff, Walter H.
Action Auctions Inc.
P.O. Box 96
New Castle, NH 03801
(603) 431-6317

Little, Michael G.
191 Silk Farm Rd.
Concord, NH 03301
(603) 225-6066
FAX (603) 225-2855

Martin, Douglas C.
Martin Associates
P.O. Box 505
Wakefield La.
Hampstead, NH 03841
(603) 329-6758

McInnis, Paul, CAI
356 Exeter Rd.
Hampton Falls, NH 03844
(603) 778-8989
FAX (603) 772-7452

Michael, George
74 Wilson Hill Rd.
Merrimack, NH 03054
(603) 424-7400

Miller, John H.
P.O. Box 344
Portsmouth, NH 03802
(603) 436-3256

Phillips, Matk C.
1 Durgin Lane
Portsmouth, NH 03801
(603) 433-1566

Reblin, Howard E.
Phoenix Auction Service
P.O. Box 136
Newton Junction, NH 03859
(603) 382-8122

Reidy, Daniel F.
Daniel F. Reidy, Auctioneer
44 High St.
Golfstown, NH 03045
(603) 497-4812

Schofield, Stephen H., CAI
Rt. 1, Box 178
Concord Hill Rd.
S. Effingham, NH 03882
(603) 539-6619
FAX (603) 539-5123

Shanley, Joseph J.
J. Shanley Auction Services
75 Pleasant Street
Portsmouth, NH 03801
(603) 436-4808

Spaulding, Irene M.
Babylon Antiques Co.
3 Tiffany Lane
Bedford, NH 03102
(603) 472-8230

Tremblay, Thomas
Lin-Wood Real Estate
P.O. Box 700
Lincoln, NH 03251
(603) 745-3621

New Jersey

Barbiere, Charles J., CAI
Chestnut Realty
2 Gordon Court
Port Monmouth, NJ 07758
(201) 495-9383

Copeland II, Harrie E.
P.O. Box 389
Stockton, NJ 08559

Doerrmann, Benjamin A.
Garden State Auction Co.
Box 376 A Sherwin Rd., RD 2
Sewell, NJ 08080
(609) 478-2389
FAX (609) 478-6066

Fagans, Donn
8 Knowlton Drive
Marlton, NJ 08053
(609) 983-8841

Glembocki, Eugene B.
Gem Auctioneering Inc.
1 Kenton Ave.
Marlton, NJ 08053
(609) 983-6313

Hall, Wendell L.
469 Ramayso Valley Rd.
Oakland, NJ 07436
(201) 337-7766
FAX (201) 337-4919

Patalano, Diane
Country Girls Ltd, Inc.
Box 144
Saddle River, NJ 07458
(201) 391-6225

Schueler, George W.
Realty & Land Exchange
1315 Allaire Ave.
Wanamassa, NJ 07712
(201) 531-4488

Spann, Max E., CAI
RD 3, Box 318A
Washington, NJ 07882
(201) 735-8866
FAX (201) 735-8937

Swartz, Brian L.
Swartz Assoc.
66 Linwood Ave.
Dover, NJ 07801
(800) 545-3459
FAX (201) 328-1120

Walsh, Edward R.
Walsh Auction Service
38 Lynn Dr.
Ocean, NJ 07712
(201) 493-4518

Wilbert, Timothy P.
T. Paul Wilbert & Assoc.
1763 Lanemill Rd.
Lakewood, NJ 08701
(201) 840-2222

Zidek, Joseph M.
Schlott Realtors
RD 3, Box 546
Branchville, NJ 07826

New Mexico

Cramer, Ronald C.
Cramer & Associates,
World Wide
P.O. Box 2021
Clovis, NM 88101
(505) 769-6006
FAX (505) 389-1236

New York

Benjamin, Alan J., CAI
A.J. Benjamin, Auctioneer
131 Sherwood Ave.
Binghamton, NY 13903
(800)767-4725

Birbach, Steven
Carlton Brokerage Inc.
305 Northern Blvd.
Great Neck, NY 11021
(516) 829-4024

Bontrager, Alfred, CAI
Alfred Bontrager Realtor
13238 Broadway
Alden, NY 14004
(716) 937-3323
FAX (716) 937-9393

Bryce, Charles R.
Bryce's Auction Service
Rt. 1, Box 157
Greene, NY 13778
(607) 656-8016

Cole, George W., CAI
George Cole Auctioneers
34 Stuyvesant St.
Kingston, NY 12401
(914) 876-5215

Corsale, Joseph N. Jr.
107 Walnut St.
Saratoga Springs, NY 12866

Doherty, Jill
P.O. Box 574 M
Bayshore, NY 11706
(516) 666-9118
FAX (516) 666-1321

Doyle, Robert A., CAI
Doyle Auction & Appraisers
137 Osborne Hill Rd.
Fishkill, NY 12524
(800) 243-0061
FAX (914) 896-5874

Figman, Harry
Harry Figman & Co., Inc.
26 W. 225th Street
New York, NY 10010
(212) 929-1866
FAX (212) 645-2813

Frank, E. Rene
International
Property Counsel
654 Madison Ave.
New York, NY 10021
(212) 223-1354

Fratantoni, Anthony M.
P.O. Box 1424
Stony Brook, NY 11790
(516) 689-2496
FAX (516) 689-2496

Fuller, Jeb S.
Allstar Auctions
RD 5, Scotch Ridge Rd.
Schenectady, NY 12306
(518) 356-7053

Gansz, Duane E., CAI,
Gansz Auction & Realty
14 William St.
Lyons, NY 14489
(315) 946-6241
FAX (315) 946-6747

Gerard, Lloyd A.
Box 214, Main St.
Eastport, NY 11941
(516) 325-1819

Hagan, Thomas J.
T.J.'s Auctions
41-71 249 Street
Little Neck, NY 11363
(718) 225-1224
FAX (718) 224-3390

Haroff, Edward T.
Haroff's Auction Service
P.O. Box 71, Pine Lane
Schroon Lake, NY 12870
(518) 532-9600

Hazzard, George
93 Elm St.
Yonkers, NY 10701
(914) 968-3200
FAX (914) 968-4453

Howard, Peter S., CAI
Howard & Reimold
P.O. Box 496
Findley Lake, NY 14736-0496
(716) 769-7447
FAX (716) 769-7447

Jackson, Abbott R.
Jackson Hecht Assoc., Inc.
10 E. 21st St.
New York, NY 10010

Jensen, John J.
20 Madison Ave.
Batavia, NY 14020
(716) 343-5922

Kantor, Linda
1 Duncan Rd.
Staten Island, NY 10301
(718) 442-0326
FAX (718) 876-7987

Knapp, Michael W.
Auction by Knapp
RD #1, Box 62
Utica, NY 13502
(315) 732-2042

Koster, Randall G., Ronald J.,
and Russell
Koster Industries Inc.
555 Broadhollow Rd.
Melville, NY 11747
(212) 661-2550

Lambrecht, Dale A., CAI
RD 3, Box 307
Walton, NY 13856

Manasse, Melvin J.
P.O. Box 738
Whitney Point, NY 13862
(800) 626-2773

Mapes, David W.
1600 Vestal Pkwy. West
Vestal, NY 13850
(607) 754-9193

Matson, David I., CAI
Matson Auction &
Real Estate
147 Main St.
Randolph, NY 14772
(716) 358-6752
FAX (716) 358-6753

Medow, Stuart L., CAI
Medow and Associates
2935 W. Fifth St.
Brooklyn, NY 11224
(718) 996-2405
FAX (718) 372-3344

Molloy, William J.
Realty & Auction Service
286 Columbia St.
Cohoes, NY 12047
(518) 235-9200

Monasky, Richard, CAI
Colonel Dick Monasky & Co.
34 Chenango St.,
Binghamton, NY 13903
(800) 800-8243
FAX (607) 723-0466

Munson, Glenn & and
Munson, Glenn P.
Glenn H. Munson & Son
Box 127
Groton, NY 13073
(607) 898-3739

Murray, Robert T.
124 Dean St.
Valley Stream, NY 11580
(516) 285-9385

O'Sullivan, Jack
Jack O'Sullivan
Professional Auctioneer
2626 Kings Hwy.
Brooklyn, NY 11229
(718) 252-5167
FAX (718) 951-0340

Passonno, Hannelore, CAI
and Ralph F. Passonno, Jr. CAI
Uncle Sam Auctions & Realty
225 Pinewoods Ave Rd.
Troy, NY 12180-7246
(518) 274-6464
(800) 332-SOLD
FAX (518) 272-7189

Pepper, Ray
401 W. State
Olean, NY 14760
(716) 372-7100
FAX (716) 372-7126

Pinchasick, Steven W.
305 Northern Blvd. Ste. 204
Great Neck, NY 11021
(516) 829-4020
FAX (516) 487-9757

Plotsker, Glenn A.
Commercial Liquidators
60-20 59th Place
Maspeth, NY 11378
(212) 349-4447
FAX (718) 456-6579

Reisner, Fred
Auctions Plus, Inc.
535 Island Ave.
Woodmere, NY 11598
(516) 295-1300
FAX (516) 295-1301

Reynolds, John T., CAI
Reynolds Auction Co.
P.O. Box 508
Newark, NY 14513-0508
(315) 331-8815
FAX (315) 331-1053

Rusciano, Anthony
1025 Post Rd.
Scarsdale, NY 10583
(914) 472-5010

Scherrer, Russ
206 Brinkman St.
Buffalo, NY 14211
(716) 894-5731

Seipp, Frank E.
9 Park Lane
Rockville Centre, NY 11570
(516) 764-7459
FAX (516) 764-7460

Smith, Marvin L., CAI
M.L. Smith Realty
& Auctions
12049 Andell Rd.
Silver Creek, NY 14126
(716) 934-4875

St. George, Vincent
822 Palmer Rd.
Bronxville, NY 10708
(914) 793-7092

Tuck, John R.
950 Bowen Rd.
Elma, NY 14059
(716) 652-9310

Visscher, Howard W.
Rd. 1, Box 507
Nichols, NY 13812
(607) 699-7250

Wheeler, Ronald L.
Family Auction Center
RR 5, Route 57, PO Box 327
Fulton, NY 13069
(315) 695-2059
FAX (315) 695-4745

Wilcox, Beatrice M. &
Carleton E.
141 Main St., P.O. Box 100
Dansville, NY 14437
(716) 335-8234
FAX (716) 335-6212

Wilcox, Harris
17 S. Lake Ave.
Bergen, NY 14416
(716) 494-1880
FAX (716) 494-1605

Worsoe, Tor J., CAI
P.O. Drawer T
Holtsville, NY 11742
(516) 289-0555

Zientek, Anthony H.
Zientek Realty & Auction
4759 Route 98
North Java, NY 14113
(716) 457-3497

North Carolina

Burch, Thomas R.
Burch & Co.
P.O. Box 867
Roanoke Rapids, NC 27870
(919) 537-7126

Curlee, Ernest J., CAI
American Auction
Associates, Inc.
9327-B Albemarle Rd.
Charlotte, NC 28227
(704) 535-1724

Deal, Robert W.
403 Highway 10 East
Newton, NC 28658
(704) 464-3635
FAX (704) 465-6263

Faison, Ronald W., CAI
Ron's Auction & Realty Co.
215 N. Arendell Ave.
Zebulon, NC 27597
(919) 269-6700
FAX (919) 269-4536

Gallimore, Charles D., CAI
AMC Auction &
Appraisal Co., Inc.
P.O. Box 306
160 Glendale Ave. SE
Concord, NC 28025
(800) 782-3011
FAX (704) 782-7979

Gray, Curtis H., CAI
Curtis Gray Auction/
Real Estate
5342 N. Roxboro Rd.
Durham, NC 27712
(919) 471-0133

Johnson III, James W.
Johnson Properties
120 E. Depot St.
Angier, NC 27501
(919) 639-2231
FAX (919) 639-2232

King, John D., CAI
J.D. King Realty & Auction
529-A S. Church St.
Asheboro, NC 27203
(919) 626-4400

Lawing, W. Craig, CAI
Lawing Auction Company
5521 Brookshire Rd.
Charlotte, NC 28216
(800) 632-3043

Lawson, Dilmon B.
P.O. Box 411
Pilot Mountain, NC 27041
(919) 368-4412

Lilly, William B., CAI
Iron Horse Auction Co.
P.O. Box 938
Norwood, NC (919) 997-2248
FAX (919) 895-1530

Marshall, Gail Y., CAI
Auctions by Marshall
6500 Sharon Hills Rd.
Charlotte, NC 28210
(704) 553-0029

Mendenhall, Forrest A., CAI,
and Wayne, CAI
Mendenhall Auction Co.
P.O. Box 7344
High Point, NC 27264
(919) 887-1165

Miller, Jack W.
Jack Miller Auction Co.
9 W. 5th St.
Tabor City, NC 28463
(919) 653-5252

Mullis, Harry E.
Route 11, Box 10
Reidsville, NC 27320
(919) 349-6577

Pierce, Keith J., CAI
P.O. Box 5215
5500 S. Main St.
Winston-Salem, NC
27113-5215
(919) 764-5338
FAX (919) 764-8642

Propst, Clyde
P.O. Box 563
Concord, NC 28026-0563

Rogers, R. Bracky, CAI
Business Center, P.O. Box 729
Mt. Airy, NC 27030
(919) 789-2926
FAX (919) 789-2310

Smith, Robert M.
Smith Auction Co.
P.O. Box 1255
Graham, NC 27253
(919) 228-8842

Troutman, Jr.,
Lonnie J., CAI
150 E. Water St.
Statesville, NC 28677
(704) 873-5233

Wooten, W. Douglas, CAI
Wooten Realty & Auction Co.
221 Clarendon Crescent
Raleigh, NC 27610
(919) 832-7251

North Dakota

Atteberry, Earl
Professional Auction
Service
930 11th Ave. SW
Valley City, ND 58072
(701) 845-5857

Haugen, Dale B.
RR #1, Box 74
Lisbon, ND 58054
(701) 683-4637
FAX (701) 683-4637

Lauf, Lyle
Missouri River Auction
RR 1, Box 15
Washburn, ND 58577
(701) 462-8210

Merfeld, Doug
RR 1, Box 135
Grand Forks, ND 58201
(701) 746-1378
FAX (701) 746-1379

Merfeld, Tracy
Curt D. Johnson Auction Co.
RR 1, Box 135
Grand Forks, ND 58201
(701) 746-1378
FAX (701) 746-1379

Penfield, Bob
P.O. Box 111
Bowman, ND 58623
(701) 523-3652

Smykowski, James
RR #1, Box 34
Cayuga, ND 58013
(701) 538-4466

Steffes, Robert, CAI
827 28th Street S., Suite D
Fargo, ND 58103
(701) 967-8927
FAX (701) 237-0976

Steffes, Scott, CAI
Steffes Auctioneers, Inc.
827 28th Street S., Suite D
Fargo, ND 58103-2324
(701) 237-9173

Vogel, Steve
SRV Auction Co.
P.O. Box 417
Casselton, ND 58012
(701) 347-5485

Ohio

Andrews, Stephen E.
51-7 S. Jefferson Rd.
Wooster, OH 44691
(216) 262-9186

Aspacher, Kenneth W.
2333 Belvedere Dr.
Toledo, OH 43614
(419) 385-9428

Aspacher, Linda S.
American Gold
Realty & Auction
2333 Belvedere Dr.
Toledo, OH 43614
(419) 385-9428
FAX (419) 385-6834

Baier, Thomas A., CAI
2719 Fulton Dr. NW, Ste C.
Canton, OH 44718
(216) 455-1911
FAX (216) 455-1859

Baker, Michael, D., CAI
Mid-West Auctioneers
5376 Bishop Rd.
Greenville, OH 45311
(513) 548-7451

Bambeck, Herb, CAI
Route 1, Box 392
Dover, OH 44622
(216) 343-1437
FAX (216) 343-1437

Basinger, J. Paul, CAI
7039 Bishop Rd.
Poland, OH 44514
(216) 757-1169
FAX (216) 757-1292

Bates, Don L.
7010 Ragland Rd.
Cincinnati, OH 45244
(513) 421-4525
FAX (513) 561-8880

Bayman, Anthony M.
1200 Nicklin Ave.
Piqua, OH 45356
(513) 778-8017

Beitzel, Herbert L.
RFD 2, P.O. Box 2228
New Philadelphia, OH 44663
(216) 339-5197

Bonnigson, Kenneth J., CAI
1834 W. McPherson Hwy.
Clyde, OH 43410
(419) 547-9313

Brandly, Michael E.
Box 09732
Columbus, OH 43209
(614) 461-9229
FAX (614) 464-1466

Brough, Chad W.
3653 S. Harris-Salem Rd
Oak Harbor, OH 43449
(419) 898-0290

Cain, Brad L., CAI
Box 116
East Springfield, OH 43925
(614) 266-2246
FAX (614) 266-6925

Canterbury, Gerald R., CAI
5999 Avon-Belden Rd.
North Ridgeville, OH 44039
(216) 327-9394
FAX (216) 327-9394

Colman, Thomas E.
Colman Realty
1411 S. Zane Hwy.
Martins Ferry, OH 43935
(614) 633-9874

Cox, Gilbert, CAI
Semple & Associates
Auctioneers
5645 Bramble Ave.
Cincinnati, OH 45227
(513) 271-4085

Deatley, Herbert
413 Jefferson St.
Greenfield, OH 45123
(513) 981-4560

Duvall, Donald D.
7450 Linnville Rd. SE
Newark, OH 43055
(614) 323-1436

Farnsworth, Harold R., CAI
8003 River Styx Rd.
Wadsworth, OH 44281
(216) 336-6057

Flatter, Joe W., CAI
Joe W. Flatter, Auctioneer
1503 N. Broad St.
Fairburn, OH 45324
(513) 878-6445

Frey, Robert G.
Route 3, Box 47B
Archbold, OH 43502
(419) 445-0015
FAX (419) 445-8888

Gaisser, Michael F., CAI
P.O. Box 456
Maumee, OH 43537-0456
(800) 776-1755

Garner, Sr., Larry W., CAI
L.W. Garner
Realty/Auctioneers
332 S. Lisbon St. Box 323
Carrollton, OH 44614
(800) 452-8452
FAX (216) 627-3788

Gill, James D., CAI
5770 Courtland Ave., NW
Massillon, OH 44646-1133
(216) 832-2605
FAX (216) 453-1765

Hoyle, William L.
7068 Dunstans La.
Toledo, OH 43617
(419) 841-9892
FAX (419) 385-6834

Hurless, Herbert E.
Herbert E. Hurless Auction
61438 Greenbriar Dr.
Cambridge, OH 43725
(614) 432-4608

Jay, Kenneth
Mickelson Real Estate
US Rt. 127 N.
Paulding, OH 45879
(419) 399-5359

Jones, David L., CAI
High St., Box 467
Flushing, OH 43977
(614) 968-3710

Kaspar, Robert J.
5718 Little Portage Rd.
Port Clinton, OH 43452
(419) 734-2930

Kessler, Dave
P.O. Box 100
New Paris, OH 45347
(513) 437-7071

Kiko, James R., CAI
811 Fox Ave.
Paris, OH 44669
(216) 445-9357
FAX (216) 453-1765

Kiko, John D., CAI
Russ Kiko Assoc., Inc.
2805 Fulton Dr. NW
Canton, OH 44718
(216) 455-9357
FAX (216) 453-1765

Kramer, H. John, CAI
Kramer & Kramer
Auction Co.
108 W. Main St.
Eaton, OH 45320-1906
(513) 456-1101

Kramer, Horace J.
108 W. Main St.
Eaton, OH 45320-1906
(513) 456-1101

Lentz, Jeffrey M.
Lentz Auction Service
P.O. Box 28
Botkins, OH 45306
(513) 693-3100

Luggen, Jerome A.
Cincinnati Industrial
Auction
6252 Hamilton Ave.
Cincinnati, OH 45224
(513) 471-5100

Luoma, Wayne
P.O. Box 308
Geneva, OH 44041
(216) 466-8383
FAX (216) 466-6305

Marino, James T., CAI
Whipple Auctioneer
Association
1219 Ardmore SW
Canton, OH 44710
(216) 452-7653
FAX (216) 477-9365

McCarty, Kenneth D.
Nationwide Auctions
901 Congress Park Dr.
Dayton, OH 45459
(513) 433-0039
FAX (513) 435-5128

McCullough, Frank E.
1666 Rudyard La.
Cincinnati, OH 45230
(513) 732-6301

Rhoades, Floyd B.
125 W. Warren St.
Germantown, OH 45327
(513) 855-2240

Robinson, Jerry D.
Robinson Auction Service
523 Adrien St.
Delta, OH 43515
(418) 822-3555

Roush, S. David
Rt. 1, Roush Rd.
Shelby, OH 44875
(419) 347-4024

Semple, Brent T.,
and Garth, CAIs
Semple & Associates
278 N. 3rd Street
Williamsburg, OH 45176
(513) 724-1133
FAX (513) 724-1286

Sheridan, Keith
3644 Wilberforce-
Clifton Rd.
Cedarville, OH 45314
(513) 766-2021

Smith, Jack E.
2264 C.R. 141
Lindsey, OH 43442
(419) 665-2115

Stanley III, Henry, CAI
Stanley & Son
Auctioneer/Realtor
126 E. 4th St.
Chillicothe, OH 45601
(614) 775-3330
FAX (614) 775-3330

Stanley Jr., Henry M.
126 E. 4th Street
Chillicothe, OH 45601
(614) 775-3330
FAX (614) 775-3330

Stanley Sr., Henry M.
126 E. 4th Street
Chillicothe, OH 45601
(614) 775-3330
FAX (614) 775-3330

Straley, William C., CAI
Straley Realtors &
Auctioneers
323 E. Main St.
Van Wert, OH 45891
(419) 238-9733
FAX (419) 238-3506

Vannatta, Richard M.
975 W. Broad St.
Columbus, OH 43222
(614) 621-2897
FAX (614) 621-0329

Wagner, Robert J., CAI
B. Wagner & Assoc., Inc.
1444 N. Main St.
N. Canton, OH 44720
(216) 499-9922
FAX (216) 499-5864

Wallick, Don R.
81 E. Iron Ave.
Dover, OH 44622
(216) 343-6734
FAX (216) 343-3655

Walton, Max K.
3860 Paradise Rd.
Medina, OH 44256
(216) 725-8958

Wilson, Joel T.
Joel T. Wilson Co.
10 S. Third, Ste. 3
Batavia, OH 45103
(513) 732-6300
FAX (513) 732-6300

Wilson, Marvin L.
Wilson National
Real Estate, Inc.
652 N. High St.
Hillsboro, OH 45133
(513) 393-3440
FAX (513) 393-3442

Wistner, John R.
RR #1, Box 4
Haviland, OH 45841
(419) 622-6821

Oklahoma

Anderson, Adrian E.
Anderson & Associates
Auctioneers
114 S. Rock Island
El Reno, OK 73036
(405) 262-8600
FAX (405) 262-8601

Brock, William L.
Brock Auctioneers, Inc.
210 E. Main, Suite 200
Norman, OK 73069
(405) 329-6491

Bruce, Joe D.
Bruce Auction
RR 2, Box 470
Welch, OK 74369
(918) 233-7074

Dakil, Louis M.
Dakil Auctioneers Inc.
3441 W. Memorial Rd.
Oklahoma City, OK 73134
(405) 751-6179
FAX (405) 752-9669

Dulaney, Sue, CAI
Rt. 4, Box 273
Claremore, OK 74017
(918) 342-5176
FAX (918) 342-5187

Godfrey, Donald D.
5105 NW 19th Street
Oklahoma City, OK 73127

Haynes, T. Eddie, CAI
Eddie Haynes
Auction & Realty
901 N. MacArthur
Oklahoma City, OK 73127
(405) 495-7653
FAX (405) 495-7657

Hines, Les
C & H Auctions
P.O. Box 521
Temple Hill, OK 73568
(405) 342-5133
FAX (405) 353-6109

Karns, Robert D.
Route 1, Box 186
Watonga, OK 73772
(405) 623-2186

McCracken, Richard D.
Rt. #1, Box 354
Cleveland, OK 74020
(918) 358-2020

Miller, DVM, Sterling, CAI
Sterling Miller
Realty & Auction
Route 3, Box 129-A
Perry, OK 73077
(405) 336-2030

Spitler, Paul D.
Spitler Auction, Inc.
P.O. Box 685
Prague, OK 74864
(405) 567-3523

Stallings, Joey G.
502 N. Sheridan Rd.
Lawton, OK 73505
(405) 355-8302
FAX (405) 355-3550

Steen, Ben D., CAI
1201 Arlington Blvd.
Ada, OK 74820
(405) 332-4456

Wells, V. Paul, CAI
Wells Commercial Auctions
27428 E. 71st Street
Broken Arrow, OK 74014
(918) 357-1003

Wiggins, C. Perry, CAI
4720A W. Owen K.
Garriott Rd.
Enid, OK 73701
(405) 233-3066
FAX (405) 237-4915

Wilkinson, W.W. Buck
923 S. 85th E. Ave.
Tulsa, OK 74112
(918) 838-3279

Williams, Thomas L.
Williams & Williams
7666 E. 61st, Ste. 135
Tulsa, OK 74133
(918) 250-2012
FAX (918) 250-1916

Wolfe, Michael E.
200 W. 12th Street
Ada, OK 74820
(405) 436-1281
FAX (405) 436-1578

Oregon

Van Gordon, Steve, CAI
Team Van Gordon
52694 Ammon Rd.
LaPine, OR 97739
(503) 476-1551

Voorhees, Sidney I.
Sidco Management, Inc.
P.O. Box 10205
Eugene, OR 97440
(502) 485-8885

Pennsylvania

Alderfer, Sanford L., CAI
P.O. Box 1
Harleysville, PA 19438
(215) 368-5477
FAX (216) 368-9055

Beamesderfer, Calvin E.
471 Weavertown Rd.
Myerstown, PA 17067
(717) 866-2998

Bechtold, Claude E., CAI
Bechtold Auctioneers
1928 Creek Hill Rd.
Lancaster, PA 17601
(717) 397-9240

Behm, III, Charles J.
RD 1, Box 267
Wind Ridge, PA 15380
(412) 428-3664

Blum, George F., CAI
Blum's Inc.
2500 West End Ave.
Pottsville, PA 17901
(717) 622-3089

Boswell, James M., CAI
P.O. Box 3073
West Chester, PA 19381
(215) 692-2226
FAX (215) 692-2042

Brown, Jeffie L.
1 Graystone Lane
Levittown, PA 19055
(215) 336-8800
FAX (215) 336-8804

Camelleri, Charles S.
Camelleri Auctioneering
P.O. Box 511
Birdsboro, PA 19508
(215) 582-1110

Charnego, Michael R., CAI
1 S. Main St.
Homer City, PA 15748
(412) 479-2481

Clayton, James A.
Clayton Auctions
RD 1, Box 73
Jefferson, PA 15344-9618
(412) 883-2885

Clemmer, Lon M.
Sanford Alderfer
Auction Co.
Box 640-501
Fairgrounds Rd.
Hatfield, PA 19440
(215) 368-5477
FAX (215) 368-9055

Comly, Andrew J. & Daniel
F., Jr. & Stephen E. (CAI)
1825 E. Boston Ave.
Philadelphia, PA 19125
(215) 634-2500
FAX (215) 634-0496

Cox, Alan D.
18551 Elgin Rd.
Corry, PA 16407
(814) 664-7526

Cunningham, Dale E.
RR 1, Box 366
Ellwood City, PA 16117
(412) 924-2836

Davis, Jr., James S.
Barr Davis Auctioneers
P.O. Box 7
Gap, PA 17527
(717) 442-3198

Deibert, George N., CAI
P.O. Box 72
Klingerstown, PA 17941
(717) 425-3313

Dobozynski, Joe, CAI
AAA Auction Service Inc.
RD 1, Box 420
Mifflintown, PA 17059
(717) 436-9594

Dockey, Lee D.
P.O. Box 164
Pillow, PA 17080
(717) 758-6004
FAX (717) 758-6004

Dotta, James M.
412 N. Jerome St.
Allentown, PA 18103
(215) 759-7389

Dreibelbis, Thomas G.
420 Gerald St.
State College, PA 16801-7485
(814) 238-1017
FAX (814) 238-1749

Finkel, Arnold
3425 Iron Bridge Rd.
Allentown, PA 18104
(215) 395-0808

Geyer, Kenneth A.
Geyer Auction Co., Inc.
Suite 102, 661 W.
Germantown Pike
Plymouth Mtg., PA 19462
(215) 834-1854

Gilbert, Jacob A.
Rt. #1
Wrightsville, PA 17368
(717) 252-3591

Gladd, Robert E.
103 McClung Blvd.
Butler, PA 16001
(412) 287-3827

Hahn, Wil, CAI
Wil Hahn Auction Company
102 West Main St.
Bath, PA 18014
(215) 837-7140
FAX (215) 837-9451

Hansell, Kenneth A., Jr.
Geyer Auction Co., Inc.
P.O. Box 617, Rd. 1
Green Lane, PA 18054

Harriger, Emery L.
Harriger Auctioneer's
419 N. 4th Street
Reynoldsville, PA 15851
(814) 653-8610

Hock, Donald E.
205 Dutch Hill Rd.
Bloomburg, PA 17815

Hostetter, Lee W., CAI
Lee Hostetter Real Estate
124 Blackhawk Rd.
Beaver Falls, PA 15010
(412) 847-1880
FAX (412) 847-3415

Hostetter, Jr., Sherman, CAI
Hostetter Auctioneers
& Real Estate
124 Blackhawk Rd.
Beaver Falls, PA 15010
(412) 847-1880
FAX (412) 847-1881

Hubscher, Christian, CAI
P.O. Box 500
Souderton, PA 18964
(215) 257-3001
FAX (215) 257-2717

Keller, Harold K., CAI
Keller Auctioneers
268 Marietta Ave.
Mount Joy, PA 17552
(717) 653-8871

Keller, Mark K.
RD #1, Box 64
Landisburg, PA 17040
(717) 789-3616

Kistler, Mark W.
753 Lawrence Dr.
Emmaus, PA 18049
(215) 967-3584

Koser, Paris E.
RD #2, Box 492
Everett, PA 15537
(814) 735-3300

Krall, Peter H., CAI
Willow Brook Farms
Catasauqua, PA 18032
(215) 264-1088

McAloose, Robert L.
14 W. Broad St.
Tamaqua, PA 18252
(717) 668-5755

McKeown, Michael J.
956 North 9th Street
Stroudsburg, PA 18360
(717) 424-2762

Morrison, Arthur W., CAI
1004 N. McKean St.
Kittanning, PA 16201
(412) 545-9775

Murphy, Judith E.
1030 Cloudcrest Dr.
Tanglewood
Greentown, PA 18426

Myers, Roger
29 Plymouth Dr.
Jonestown, PA 17038
(717) 865-6656

Nicolls, W. Bruce
733 Terrace St.
Meadville, PA 16335
(814) 333-1989
FAX (814) 333-1988

Porter, Ross E.
Porter of Pennsylvania
P.O. Box 773
Smethport, PA 16749
(800) 828-4525
FAX (814) 887-5107

Randazzo, Salvatore A.
1030 Linden Ave.
Erie, PA 16505
(814) 838-2437

Reed, Jr., Kenneth, CAI
Ken Reed & Co.
401 Main St.
Royers Ford, PA 19468
(215) 948-4871
FAX (215) 327-8092

Rentzel, Blaine N.
Box 222
Emigsville, PA 17318
(717) 764-6412
FAX (717) 764-5492

Sitar, Steven M., CAI
P.O. Box 779
Waverly, PA 18471
(717) 586-1397
FAX (717) 586-6058

Slosberg, Barry S.
232 N. 2nd St.
Philadelphia, PA 19106
(215) 925-8020
FAX (215) 925-8047

Smith, Bradley K., CAI
RD #2, Box 483
Brogue, PA 17309
(717) 927-6949

Spataro, Anthony J.
Bennett Williams Inc.
1891 Santa Barbara Dr.
#208
Lancaster, PA 17601
(717) 560-5611
FAX (717) 560-5625

Tedrow, Charles E.
Chuck's Auction Services
248 Wyoming Ave.
Wyoming, PA 18644
(717) 288-6089
FAX (717) 288-9185

Vilsmeier, Frederick R., CAI
Vilsmeier Auction Co.
1044 Bethlehem Pike
Montgomeryville, PA 18936
(602) 762-5091

Wagner, Dennis F.
100 Skyline Dr.
Shoemakersville, PA 19555
(215) 562-7445

Young, James C.
P.O. Box 186
Dewart, PA 17730
(717) 538-1620

Rhode Island

Hurley, Patrick J.
3 Frances Court
Coventry, RI 02816
(401) 822-2040

Loebenberg, Theodore F.
Box 2535
Providence, RI 02906
(401) 274-1930
FAX (401) 521-7845

Mattera, Steve A.
3750 Quaker Lane
P.O. Box 1480
N. Kingston, RI 02852
(401) 295-0051
FAX (401) 295-8478

Phillips, Edward F.
1049 Greenwich Ave.
Warwick, RI 02886
(401) 737-9060

South Carolina

Davis, W. Angus
Davis Auction Service
510 Dellwood Dr.
Greenville, SC 29609
(803) 268-6781
FAX (803) 268-6781

Hernandez, Calixto A., CAI
P.O. Box 3086
Greenville, SC 29602
(803) 243-4858

Leonardi II, Robert J.
P.O. Box 1417
Easley, SC 29641-1417
(803) 233-3615

Meares, Larry J., CAI
P.O. Box 57
Pelzer, SC 29669
(803) 277-0504
FAX (803) 277-3255

Smith, Frank O., Jr.
524 Clinkscales Rd.
Anderson, SC 29624
(803) 832-6655

South Dakota

Hubner, Gregg C.
Gregg Hubner Auction Co.
RR 1, Box 174
Avon, SD 57315
(605) 286-3205

Sutton, Charles A.
Kuhle-Sutton Agency
P.O. Box 325
Flandreau, SD 57028
(605) 997-3777
FAX (605) 997-3038

Wingler, Terry
Wingler's Furniture/Auction
611 N. Main Ave.
Sioux Falls, SD 57102
(605) 332-5682

Tennessee

Ayers, Haskel, CAI
2201 Jackson Pike
P.O. Box 1467
LaFollette, TN 37766
(615) 562-4941
FAX (615) 562-8148

Blackford, Robert L.
3937 Gallatin Rd.
Nashville, TN 37216
(615) 228-2541
FAX (615) 227-6106

Caffey, Dan E.
1615 Haynes Dr.
Murfreesboro, TN 37129
(615) 896-1500

Carman Jr., Harold G.
R#1, Box 635
Castalian Springs, TN 37031
(615) 374-9326
FAX (615) 255-4939

Cayce, Clinton R.
Beck & Beck Realty &
Auction
1450 Janie Ave.
Nashville, TN 37216
(615) 226-6915
FAX (615) 227-7053

Cole, David L.
Blue Ridge Properties Inc.
1337 Magnolia Ave.
Kingsport, TN 37664
(615) 378-4411

Colson, William M., CAI
Colson Auction & Realty
2012 Beech Ave.
Nashville, TN 37204
(615) 292-6619

Cook, John W., CAI
P.O. Box 450
Troy, TN 38260
(901) 536-6424

Ducker, Herman M., CAI
Signal Auction/Realty
184 E. Ducker Rd.
Signal Mountain, TN 37377
(615) 886-2265

Durham, Albert
316 W. Lytle St.
Murfreesboro, TN 37130
(615) 896-2917

Durham, Tim J.
316 W. Lytle St.
Murfreesboro, TN 37130
(615) 896-2917

Edwards, Dr. Hugh F.
Route 12, Box 438
Greeneville, TN 37743
(615) 639-6781
FAX (615) 639-0851

Gaw, Monte
P.O. Box 1275
Cookeville, TN 38503
(615) 526-2307

Gregory, Jerry C., CAI
P.O. Box D, 805 Willow St.
Springfield, TN 37172
(615) 384-5557

Hall, Jerry E.
1141 Tusculom Blvd.
Greeneville, TN 37743
(615) 639-7162
FAX (512) 639-1116

Hamilton, Jr., George, CAI
P.O. Box 536
Dunlap, TN 37327
(615) 554-3999

Hines, Harry L.
1500 Bluff City Hwy.
Bristol, TN 37620
(615) 669-6385

Hobbs, Fred R.
P.O. Box 126
131 N. Main St.
Eagleville, TN 37060
(615) 274-6826

Johns, Royce G., CAI
Royce Johns
Realty/Auctions
236 3rd Ave. North
Franklin, TN 37064
(615) 790-0414

Kennon, Joe D.
201 Jane St.
Paris, TN 38242
(901) 642-3750
FAX (901) 642-3750

Lynch, Tom P.
Carlton Lynch
Realty & Auction
1215 Dinah Shore Blvd.
Winchester, TN 37398
(615) 967-0678
FAX (615) 967-0694

Mathis, Larry D.
Mathis Auction & Realty
Rt. 4, Box 898
Waynesboro, TN 38485
(615) 722-9408

Miller, William A.
302 Wesley St., Suite 2
Johnson City, TN 37601
(615) 283-4178
FAX (615) 283-4132

Murphy, James R.
2304 Memorial Blvd.
Springfield, TN 37172
(615) 384-7919
FAX (615) 384-7884

Orr, George C., CAI
Lewis-Orr Realty
Auction Sales
123 S. Jackson St.
Tullahoma, TN 37388
(615) 455-3447

Orr, John W.
610 Stone Blvd.
Tullahoma, TN 37388-3001
(615) 455-3447

Redenbaugh, Richard G.
Redenbaugh Auction
RR 3, Box 286
Tellico Plains, TN 37385
(615) 253-2666

Roebuck, John, CAI
River City Auction
3143 Carrier St.
Memphis, TN 38116
(901) 346-8644
FAX (901) 346-8669

Shepard, Tom
Nashville Auction &
Realty Co., Inc.
1407 Lebanon Rd.,
Nashville, TN 37210
(615) 255-4933
FAX (615) 255-8052

Slyman, James, CAI
Slyman Auction Co.
411 S. Gay St., Ste. A.
Knoxville, TN 37902
(615) 521-7416
FAX (615) 521-7417

Smith, IV, Oliver A.
Oliver Smith Auction
& Realty
F28 Westtown Mall
7600 Kingston Pike
Knoxville, TN 37919
(615) 693-0772
FAX (612) 693-1919

Taggart, Raymond E., CAI
Delta Auction Co
151 Walnut Creek
Cordova, TN 38018
(800) 592-2288
FAX (901) 382-5729

Texas

Alley, Lesley R.
P.O. Box 1092
Del Rio, TX 78841
(512) 774-4255
FAX (512) 774-1222

Archer, William C.
Box 802635
Dallas, TX 75380
(214) 458-9781

Cleghorn, Michael L.
Cleghorn & Assoc.
P.O. Box 90065
Austin, TX 78709
(512) 892-0109

Cuthbert, Dale
#9 Manchester
Amarillo, TX 79106
(806) 376-9607
FAX (806) 374-7474

DeVore, Russell
DeVore Marketing
Auct./Rltrs.
P.O. Box 61872
San Angelo, TX 76906-1872
(915) 942-6666

Downey, Tony
4630 50th Street #10
Lubbock, TX 79414
(806) 791-2628
FAX (806) 791-6429

Espensen, K.L., CAI
Espensen Co.,
Realtor-Auctions
2212 Primrose St. #C
McAllen, TX 78504
(512) 687-5117
FAX (512) 687-7967

Flusche, Donald J.
P.O. Box 417
Muenster, TX 76252-0417
(817) 759-2832
FAX (817) 759-4288

Foster, Paul M.
15618 Highfield Dr.
Houston, TX 77095-2030
(713) 855-8686

Henson, Roy P.
Alph Int'l Mktg Services, Inc.
Rt. 3, Box 3786
Chandler, TX 75758
(903) 849-2221
FAX (903) 849-2883

Jones, J. Michael
Box 1113
Gainesville, TX 76240
FAX (817) 668-6339

McClellan, Jerry
P.O. Box 9240449
Houston, TX 77292-4049
(713) 863-1001

McDonald, Dennis W.
11906 Four Colonies
San Antonio, TX 78249
(512) 699-0260

Mitchell, Larry
4 Dorchester Circle
Longview, TX 75601
(903) 753-7925

Moore, Ronald G.
Plant & Machinery, Inc.
8705 Katy Fwy., #300
Houston, TX 77024-1710

Moses, Dwayne
Moses & Zuber Auctioneers
Rt. 1, Box 311
Ralls, TX 79357
(806) 253-2945

Ogle, Jack V., CAI
Ogle Auction & Realty
Rt. 2, Box 66A
Greenville, TX 75401
(903) 454-1091

Owen Jr., James L., CAI
100 Spicewood Court
Irving, TX 75063
(214) 401-2472
FAX (214) 404-9685

Ray, Robert F.
Wright Realtors
230 W. Parker Rd., Ste. 380
Plano, TX 75075
(214) 422-7000
FAX (214) 881-7000

Ritchie, James R.
Asset Liquidators, Inc.
2611 N. Beltline Rd, Ste. 138
Sunnyvale, TX 75182
(214) 226-2303
FAX (214) 226-7542

Rudd, Charles D.
13214 Holly Park
Houston, TX 77015
(713) 453-2912

Segars, Ralph
10925 Estate Lane # 105
Dallas, TX 75238
(214) 343-4055
FAX (214) 343-8252

Short, Jim W.
7417 Maplecrest Dr.
Dallas, TX 75240
(800) 777-8142
FAX (214) 980-1618

Smith, Joe M.
5618 Bent Bough Lane
Houston, TX 77088
(713) 683-7368
FAX (713) 445-5904

Stall, Dorothy
1202 Saxony Lane
Houston, TX 77058
(713) 333-1000
FAX (713) 333-3020

Stall, Harold
1202 Saxony Lane
Houston, TX 77058
(713) 333-1000
FAX (713) 333-3020

Storey, Henry R.
Rt 4, Box 182
Brownwood, TX 76801
(915) 646-3956

Thomas, Brett R.
Rt. 6, Box 420
Mt. Pleasant, TX 75455
(903) 572-4517

Walker, Homar
Homar Walker
Auction & Realty
P.O. Box 5846
San Antonio, TX 78201
(512) 698-1155

Webster, William I.
14463 Luthe St.
Houston, TX 77039
(713) 442-2351
FAX (713) 442-8248

Wiley, R.C., CAI
616 W. Cameron
Rockdale, TX 76567
(512) 446-3197
FAX (512) 446-5243

Williams, E.C.
Auctioneers Unlimited, Inc.
4721 Bonner, #103
Corpus Christi, TX 78411
(512) 855-1886
FAX (512) 855-3295

Utah

Parker, Dean H.
P.O. Box 3266
Logan, UT 84321
(801) 752-7701
FAX (801) 752-7701

Vermont

Hirchak, Jr., Thomas, CAI
Thomas Hirchak Company
RD #3, Box 2430
Morrisville, VT 05661
(802) 888-4662

Manchester, Jean, CAI
Green Mountain Auctions
6 Beachcrest Dr.
Burlington, VT 05401
(802) 863-4153

Matteis, Vincent
American Auction Center
Box 1196 Finney Hill
Lyndonville, VT 05851
(802) 626-8589

Merrill, Duane
Merrill's Auction Gallery
32 Beacon St.
S. Burlington, VT 05401
(802) 862-1624

Stevenson, Frederick A.
Fred's Auction Service
HCR 30, Box 56
Barnet, VT 05821
(802) 592-3202

Whittaker, Tom P.
Box 157
Brandon, VT 05733
(802) 247-6633

Virginia

Bennett, Kendall J.
American Real Estate
525 Thornrose Ave.
P.O. Box 2487
Staunton, VA 24401
(703) 885-7231
FAX (703) 886-7566

Boone, John D.
J.D. Boone Auction & Realty
Route 2, Box 10
Speedwell, VA 24374
(703) 621-4811

Bowman, George M.
P.O. Box 212
Clifton Forge, VA 24422
(703) 362-4411

Brown, James M.
J & J Realty
3302 Amherst Hwy
Madison Heights, VA 24572
(804) 929-5551

Cole, A. Barry, CAI
Rt. #1, Box 182
Callaway, VA 24067
(703) 483-4539

Counts, David C., CAI
Counts Auction Co.
Route 2
Abingdon, VA 24210

De Loach, Greg, CAI
P.O. Box 165
Stephens City, VA 22655
(800) 274-6020
FAX (703) 869-6020

Des Roches, Jim
5100 Hingham Dr.
New Kent, VA 23124
(804) 932-3717

Dickenson, Gaines W., CAI
Gaines Dickenson
RT 3, Box 83
Castlewood, VA 24224
(703) 738-9230

Gilbert, Marcus A.
Lambert & Gilbert
Auction Company
P.O. Box 1287
N. Tazewell, VA 24630
(703) 988-9468

Green, Donnie G.
Green Auction & Realty
Rt. 1, Box 636
S. Boston, VA 24592
(804) 575-7924
FAX (804) 575-7926

Harlowe, William W., CAI
William Harlowe Ltd.
Box 120
Troy, VA 22974
(804) 293-2904

Heatwole, George R., CAI
169 Pleasant Hill Rd.
Harrisonburg, VA 22801
(703) 433-2929

Henson, Michael E.
123 Eberly Terrace
Hampton, VA 23669
(804) 723-3440
FAX (804) 485-2227

Hines, Larry N.
Hines Real Estate & Auction
P.O. Box 302
Jonesville, VA 24263
(703) 346-3657
FAX (703) 346-0151

Horney, Jr., J.C.
P.O. Box 73
Wytheville, VA 24382
(703) 228-4131
FAX (703) 228-6175

Kelley, C. Roy
3810 Atlantic Ave. #901
Virginia Beach, VA 23451
(804) 461-6867
FAX (804) 462-2147

Lyons, Dorothy R.
Jackass Flats, Rt. 1, Box 44B
Rapidan, VA 22733
(703) 825-3798

Moore, George H.
P.O. Box 1330
Mathews, VA 23109
(804) 725-7890

Peoples, Jack W.
1328 Head of River Rd.
Chesapeake, VA 23322
(804) 421-2525

Rall, Tom
5720 Wilson Blvd.
Arlington, VA 22205
(703) 525-1629

Sellars, Douglas V.
6174 Pattie Court
Haymarket, VA 22069
(703) 754-0328

Sheets, Stephen G., CAI
15 S. Jefferson St.
Roanoke, VA 24011
(703) 345-8885

Sheets, Garland
15 S. Jefferson St.
Roanoke, VA 24011
(703) 345-8885

Smeltzer, Don P., CAI
Smeltzer's Auction & Realty
1316 E. Main St.
Luray, VA 22835
(703) 743-4747
FAX (703) 743-9380

Smith, Grayson L.
Rt. 2, Box 255A
Warsaw, VA 22572
(804) 333-4894

Summs, William J.
Atlantic Auctions, Ltd.
1195 Lance Rd.
Norfolk, VA 23502
(804) 461-6887
FAX (804) 461-2147

Tull, Ronald I., CAI
Tull Realty & Auction Co.
3912 Woodburn Rd.
Annandale, VA 22003
(703) 280-5555

Updike, Buddy
P.O. Box 330
King George, VA 22485
(703) 371-5965

Williams, Frederick J.
F.J. Williams Realty &
Auction Company
P.O. Box 201
Winchester, VA 22601
(703) 662-3539

Washington

Hodges, Ken
Ken Hodges & Associates
Box 91
Bothell, WA 98011
(206) 363-4086

Honey, Jr., George P.
Northwest Auction Service
P.O. Box 397, 2003 Mac Place
Entlat, WA 98822
(509) 784-1938

McConkey, Bob
3006 Northrup Ways
Ste. 101
Bellevue, WA 98004
(206) 889-1181
FAX (206) 822-9393

Mroczek, Lawrence C., CAI
Mroczek Auctioneers
700 SW 4th Place
Renton, WA 98055
(206) 329-6138
FAX (206) 277-1684

Murphy, James G.
James G. Murphy, Inc.
P.O. Box 82160
18226 68th Ave. NE
Kenmore, WA 98028
(206) 486-1246

Sutter, Errold R., CAI
Auctions Inc.
P.O. Box 5587
Lynnwood, WA 98046
(206) 771-4232
FAX (206) 775-2052

West Virginia

Belmont, Gary R.
Belmont Auction Co.
1252 Dorsey Ave.
Morgantown, WV 26505
(304) 292-4314

Cooper, Jerry L.
1008 Summers St.
Hinton, WV 25951
(304) 466-3760

Felosa, Joseph A., CAI
Felosa Auction/Realty, Inc.
Box 179
77 Felosa Drive
Haywood, WV 26366-0179
(304) 592-0738
FAX (304) 592-0738

Frio, James W.
RD 2, Box 206
Valley Grove, WV 26060
(304) 336-7462
FAX (304) 843-1518

Meadows, Monroe B.
Meadows Auction & Realty
P.O. Box 23
Meadow Bridge, WV 25976
(304) 484-7043

Woofter, Danny
Dansco Auctioneers
226 Tenth Ave. S.
Charleston, WV 25303-1129
(304) 744-4197

Wisconsin

Barg, William H.
117 W. Fulton St.
Waupaca, WI 54981
(715) 258-8116

Berkshire, Gerald & Rita
Colonel's Auction Service
1117 Bushnell St.
Beloit, WI 53511
(608) 365-5089

Boge, R. Jerome, CAI
219 S. 21st Street
La Crosse, WI 54601
(608) 784-3952

Donahoe, Joseph
627 Harriett St., Box 133
Darlington, WI 53530
(608) 776-2156

Gonnering, Keith M.
Gonnering Auction &
Real Estate
126 E. Main St.
Little Chute, WI 54140-1413
(414) 788-4447

Hazlewood, William J., CAI
935 Model Railroad
Rice Lake, WI 54868
(800) 345-2040

Keul, Jonathan
Black Horse Auction
1610 Fremont Ave.
Madison, WI 53704
(608) 244-5801

Laszewski, Robert H.
Wausau Sales Co.
P.O. Box 3
Wausau, WI 54402
(715) 675-3824

Lust, Richard O., CAI
Lust Auction Services
P.O. Box 4421
Madison, WI 53711
(608) 833-2001
FAX (608) 833-9593

Massart, Pat, CAI and
Robert J., CAI
Massart Auctioneers Inc.
2545 Finger Rd.
Green Bay, WI 54302
(414) 468-1113

Morgan, Pete
Auction Associates
Box 335
Rosendall, WI 54974
(414) 872-2204
FAX (414) 748-3048

Murray, Lee A., CAI
Dells Auction Service
P.O. Box 212
Wisconsin Dells, WI 53965
(608) 254-8696

Naue, Thomas H.
2800 Royal Avenue
Madison, WI 53713
(800) 238-4646
FAX (608) 223-2721

Robbins, William W., CAI
Auction Way Realty
12217 W. St. Martins Rd.
Franklin, WI 53132
(414) 425-7160

Schuster, Jon S.
708 2nd Ave.
Onalaska, WI 54650
(608) 783-7653
FAX (608) 783-6079

Spies, John R.
184 S. Washington St.
Waterloo, WI 53594
(414) 478-3365

Stewart, Laverne L.
5902 Michier Rd.
Eau Claire, WI 54701
(715) 834-6664

Stockwell, Randy J.
R.J. Stockwell Auctions
5340 County Line Rd.
Dorchester, WI 54425
(715) 654-5162

Theorin, Carl, CAI
Wausau Sales Corp.
2500 Rio Grande Dr.
Merrill, WI 54452
(715) 536-8694

Thiel, R.A.
Box 189
Chilton, WI 53014
(414) 439-1666

Varney, Scott, CAI
Accredited Auctioneers
207 N. Livingston St.
Madison, WI 53703
(608) 255-7630

Walla, William L.
Walla's Auction &
Real Estate
1723 County J
Little Suamico, WI 54141
(414) 826-5472

Weisensel, Taylor W.
3016 Vercauteren Dr.
Green Bay, WI 54313-5896
(414) 336-3050

Wildermuth, Craig
12775 W. Silver Spring
Butler, WI 53007
(414) 781-1706
FAX (414) 781-7570

Wyoming

Brown, Kenneth R.
Kenneth Brown Enterprises
P.O. Box 133
Riverton, WY 82501
(307) 347-3408

Frome, L.D.
RFD Box 47
Afton, WY 83110
(800) 433-1595

Hughs, Lee D.
Action Auctioneers
808 Range Rd.
Rock Springs, WY 82901
(307) 382-5442
FAX (307) 382-5442

Smith, Clark
415 W. Lincolnway
Cheyenne, WY 82001
(307) 635-4181
FAX (307) 634-6817

33

Aircraft Auctioneers

★★

Many people have asked me about aircraft auctions. Few people know about them, where they are held and when. The government occasionally has them, particularly U.S. Customs and the Department of Defense. Occasionally, the GSA or private auctioneers hold them for the U.S. Marshals Service.

Now you can find out about aircraft auctions directly from auctioneers, by using the directory that follows. Many of these auctioneers also hold sales for other equipment and merchandise. Let the auctioneer know specifically what types of aircraft you wish to purchase. If you sketch him a broad picture, you may end up receiving a large amount of unnecessary mailings. The more specific your description, the fewer auction notices you will receive.

Aircraft dealers and other professionals usually attend these auctions, so caution is advised. Preparation, inspection, and a professional appraisal is particularly demanded at these auctions.

AIRCRAFT AUCTIONEERS DIRECTORY

California

McCormack, James K., CAI
McCormack Auction Co.
743 El Cajon Blvd.
El Cajon, CA 92020-4905
(619) 447-1196

Florida

Coburn, Joe E.
7545 N. Palm Oak Dr.
Hernando, FL 32642
(904) 344-5818

Regenhold, Rick H.
Regenhold Auctions
611 S. Myrtle Ave., Suite B.
Clearwater, FL 34616
(813) 461-1666

Illinois

Fiscus, Robert W.
Mac Auctions
307 E. Main
Robinsons, IL 62454
(618) 546-1550

Toppel, Edward A.
222 E. Pearson St., Apt. 1904
Chicago, IL 60611
(312) 944-0930

Indiana

Mavis, Fred C.
M & H Auction Services
416 S. Main St.
Auburn, IN 46706
(219) 925-4366

Kansas

Sherlock, Frederick
P.O. Box 926
St. Francis, KS 67756

Kentucky

Deane, Silas E.
5785 Hwy. 144
Owensboro, KY 42303
(502) 926-8553
FAX (502) 926-8574

Massachusetts

Paine, Stanley J.
1198 Boylston St.,
Chestnut Hill, MA 02167
(617) 731-4455
FAX (617) 566-0840

Stead, Robert A.
64 Pumpkin La., RFD 1,
Southbridge, MA 01550
(508) 248-3120

Michigan

Levy, David
Norman Levy Associates
21415 Civic Center Dr.
Southfield, MI 48075
(313) 353-6640
FAX (313) 353-1442

Missouri

Fischer, Ken
Business Network Corp.
501 N. Lindbergh
St. Louis, MO 63141
(314) 993-4500
FAX (314) 993-4437

Woolery, David R.
Woolery Auction Co.
P.O. Box 414
Branson, MO 65616
(417) 335-4242

Nebraska

Starman, Steve
1240 Royal Dr.
Papillion, NE 68128
(402) 592-1033
FAX (402) 592-2327

Nevada

Britt, Don P.
5126 S. Somerset Dr.
Las Vegas, NV 89120
(702) 451-9075

New Hampshire

Michael, George
74 Wilson Hill Rd.
Merrimack, NH 03054
(603) 424-7400

New Mexico

Cramer, Ronald C.
Cramer & Associates—World
Wide
P.O. Box 2021
Clovis, NM 88101
(505) 769-6006
FAX (505) 389-1236

New York

Molloy, William J.
Realty & Auction Service
286 Columbia St.
Cohoes, NY 12047
(518) 235-9200

North Dakota

Merfeld, Tracy
Curt D. Johnson Auction Co.
RR #1, Box 135
Grand Forks, ND 58201
(701) 746-1378
FAX (701) 746-1379

Ohio

Polakovic, John F.
40 Applewood Dr.
Oregon, OH 43616
(419) 691-5862

Oregon

Voorhees, Sidney I.
Sidco Management, Inc.
P.O. Box 10205
Eugene, OR 97440
(502) 485-8885

Texas

Bates, Rene
Rene Bates Auctioneers, Inc.
Rt. 4
McKinney, TX 75070
(214) 548-9636
FAX (214) 542-1604

Stall, Dorothy
1202 Saxony La.
Houston, TX 77058
(713) 333-1000
FAX (713) 333-3020

Weaver, Bill
HCR 3, Box 47
Del Rio, TX 78840
(512) 774-4408

Utah

Parker, Dean H.
P.O. Box 3266
Logan, UT 84321
(801) 752-7701
FAX (801) 752-7701

Vermont

Manchester, Jean, CAI
Green Mountain Auctions
6 Beachcrest Dr.
Burlington, VT 05401
(802) 863-4153

Matteis, Vincent
American Auction Center
Box 1196 Finney Hill
Lyndonville, VT 05851
(802) 626-8589

West Virginia

Belmont, Gary R.
Belmont Auction Co.
1252 Dorsey Ave.
Morgantown, WV 26505
(304) 292-4314

Wisconsin

Gonnering, Keith M.
Gonnering Auction &
Real Estate
126 E. Main St.
Little Chute, WI 54140-1413
(414) 788-4447

Hazlewood, William J., CAI
935 Model Railroad
Rice Lake, WI 54868
(800) 345-2040

34

Heavy Equipment and Construction Auctioneers

★★

Many small companies and contracting firms need good equipment to stay in business or expand. There are a large number of equipment and construction auctions taking place across America.

Why lease when you can buy? That should become a new policy for many firms. By going to an auction, a company might purchase equipment for one job, and then resell it at another auction later. Additionally, if a small company purchases office equipment to help it grow, it can then sell the old office equipment at auction, while purchasing new equipment to meet its growth.

The directory that follows contains a large number of equipment firms. Start-ups are going to need office and other equipment. Such auctions often have out-of-context merchandise and equipment as part of their sales. As dealers and professional buyers attend these types of auctions, they are not generally interested in fringe equipment. Bidders are scarce for that sort of machinery. This may bring a few lucky bargains to you.

Contact the auctioneers in the directory that follows and get a few auction fliers to see if such out-of-context equipment is available. It might be the source of good deals on vehicles, computers, fax machines, or whatever else might be offered as part of the auction.

HEAVY EQUIPMENT AND CONSTRUCTION AUCTIONEERS DIRECTORY

Alabama

Behel, Don, CAI
Don Behel Realty &
Auctions, Inc.
Rt. 4, Box 505
Killen, AL 35645
(205) 757-4100
FAX (205) 757-4087

Brown, Richard
7595 Highway 72 West
Madison, AL 35758
(205) 837-6229
FAX (205) 830-9653

Puckett, Harry C.
Puckett Realty & Auction Co.
P.O. Box 457
Hartselle, AL 35640
(205) 773-2685

Alaska

Arizona

Harms, Bernard D., CAI
4527 E. Devonshire
Phoenix, AZ 85018
(602) 840-2492
FAX (602) 261-3561

Kane, C.R. Kip
SW R.E. Auctioneers
1121 E. Missouri, #100
Phoenix, AZ 85014-2723
(602) 263-0050
FAX (602) 263-0085

Knuth, Dan
41656 Rattlesnake Rd.
Queen Creek, AZ 85242
(602) 987-9083

Poulsen, Gary L., CAI
15220 N. 51 Place
Scottsdale, AZ 85254-2281
(602) 996-6201
FAX (602) 971-6144

Vieu, Theodore R.
3350 E. Wetstones
Vail, AZ 85641
(602) 762-5091

Arkansas

Knight, William H.
Route 1
Manila, AR 72442
(501) 562-2405
FAX (501) 562-6552

Shoe, Alvin
Box 97
Delaplaine, AR 72425
(501) 249-3207

Stafford, David K.
Route 1, P.O. Box 1317
Donaldson, AR 71941
(501) 384-5352

Sullivan, Connie P.
Connie Sullivan Auction Co.
15610 Viney Woods Rd.
Mabelvale, AR 72103
(501) 847-8545

Vanover, Tommy
Vanover & Tucker
P.O. Box 1762
Springdale, AR 72765
(501) 756-6785

California

Daly, Jr., James, CAI
International Auction
Service & Antiques
6320 Monterey St.
Gilroy, CA 95020
(408) 847-4038

Hansen, Maurice N.
P.O. Box 3610
San Clemente, CA 92674
(714) 661-8020
FAX (714) 661-8083

Hather, Don
1729 Marine Avenue
Wilmington, CA 90744
(213) 834-2268
FAX (213) 834-4440

Holloway, Tipton M.
P.O. Box 356
Live Oak, CA 95953
(916) 695-1423
FAX (916) 695-1378

Isett, Greg
Pacific Coast
Auction Service
6001 - 88th St. Ste D.
Sacramento, CA 95828
(916) 381-6088
FAX (916) 381-3548

Macon, Mike, CAI
Macon Brothers Auctioneers
558 S. Washington St.
Sonora, CA 95370
(209) 532-0112
FAX (209) 532-1594

Main, Robert W.
7640 Benbow Dr.
Garberville, CA 95440
(707) 923-2311
FAX (707) 923-2767

McCormack, James K., CAI
McCormack Auction Co.
743 El Cajon Blvd.
El Cajon, CA 92020-4905
(619) 447-1196

Mulrooney, Jim
P.O. Box 748
Galt, CA 95632
(209) 745-4542

Vantassell, Vance J.
917 G St.
Sacramento, CA 95814
(916) 444-8633

Colorado

Bohn, Charles F., CAI
Chuck Bohn & Assoc.
P.O. Box 3275
Littleton, CO 80161-3275
(303) 220-8729
FAX (303) 220-8729

Cumberlin, Charles E., CAI
P.O. Box 248
Brush, CO 80723
(303) 842-2822

Dickensheet, W.J.
Dickensheet & Assoc.
2021 S. Platte River Dr.
Denver, CO 80223
(303) 934-8322

Rundell, E. W.
1521 E. Hwy. 50, P.O. Box 237
Salida, CO 81201
(719) 539-3262

Smith, Randell N., CAI
0151 Mel Rey Rd.
Glenwood Springs, CO 81601
(303) 945-9723

Delaware

Conley, Larry W.
RD 3, Box 215-D
Bridgeville, DE 19933
(302) 337-8601

District of Columbia

Evans, W. Ronald, CAI
Capital City Enterprise, Ltd.
407 H Street NE
Washington, D.C. 20002
(202) 543-2828
FAX (202) 547-2545

Florida

Banks, William S.
Banks Auction
2577 SE Madison St.
Stuart, FL 34996
(407) 287-5334
FAX (407) 287-1570

Brandendurger, Paul W.
2959 Mercury Rd.
Jacksonville, FL
32207-7912
(904) 730-2911
FAX (904) 730-2911

Campbell, David
Campbell Auctioneers
1047 Bayshore Dr.
Englewood, FL 34223-2302
(813) 475-7166

Campen, Ben, CAI
Ben Campen Auctioneers
P.O. Drawer 1209
Gainesville, FL 32602
(904) 375-6600
FAX (904) 371-1990

Chana, Kurt E.
413 Willow Brook
Longwood, FL 32779
(407) 869-8519

Coburn, Joe E.
7545 N. Palm Oak Dr.
Hernando, FL 32642
(904) 344-5818

Eggleston, Bernie
Eggleston Auctioneers
4601 W. Kennedy Blvd.
Suite 214
Tampa, FL 33609
(813) 282-0057

Johnson, Edward
9920 Steven Dr.
Polk City, FL 33868
(813) 984-3228

McGerity, Francis C.
5386 Countryfield Circle
Ft. Myers, FL 33905
(813) 694-0510

Moates, Robert C.
4082 Belair La. #20
Naples, FL 33940
(813) 262-4921

Myers, Richard L., CAI
Myers Real Estate
Auction Service
P.O. Box 2062
Winter Park, FL 32790-2062
(407) 644-7295
FAX (407) 644-7380

Passonno, Ralph F.
6141 Bay Isles Dr.
Boynton Beach, FL 33437
(407) 738-9055

Shuler, Cliff
422 Julia St.
Titusville, FL 32780
(407) 267-8563
FAX (407) 383-3147

Sklarey, Seth, CAI
Box K, Coconut Grove
Miami, FL 33233-0140
(305) 374-1166
FAX (305) 379-0653

Smith, Donald J.
4925 University Dr.
Leesburg, FL 34748
(904) 787-5486

Georgia

Arwood, David G., CAI
Arwood Auction Co., Inc.
P.O. Box 4485
Marietta (Atlanta), GA 30061
(404) 423-0110
FAX (404) 424-5200

Ledbetter, Gary B.
315 15th St. SE
Georgetown, Apt. G-6
Moultrie, GA 31768
(912) 890-2550

Register, Jr., L.E.
Auctions Unlimited
Watkinsville, GA 30677
(404) 769-5561

Toles, Bobby J.
Atlas Auction Co.
617 Shorter Avenue
Rome, GA 30161
(800) 992-2155
FAX (404) 235-5571

Whitney, Chuck, CAI
Hudson & Marshall, Inc.
4751 Best Rd., Suite 240
Atlanta, GA 30337
(404) 763-0211
FAX (404) 763-1071

Hawaii

Adolfi, Jr., Frank J.
1427 Akamai Place
Kailua, HI 96734
(808) 262-7730

Idaho

Hossner, Lynn
Hossner Brothers
Auction Company
109 N. 2nd West
St. Anthony, ID 83445
(208) 624-3782
FAX (208) 624-3783

Ralls, Ronald R.
11985 S. Cloverdale
Kuna, ID
83634
(208) 362-5132

Illinois

Bornheimer, Robert C.
P.O. Box 52
Whittington, IL 62897
(618) 629-2622

Burke, Don S.
RR 2, Box 191
McLeansboro, IL 62859
(618) 643-4527

Draper, Robert D.
No. 1, Draper Lane
Ohio, IL 61349
(815) 376-2001

Hertenstein, Roger G., CAI
Hertenstein Auctions
P.O. Box 23
Wayne City, IL 62895
(618) 895-2663
FAX (618) 895-2663

Honnold, Carl E.
14 N. Central
P.O. Box 44
Casey, IL 62420
(217) 932-4015

Johnson, Earl, CAI
1543 Aberdeen St.
Chicago Heights, IL 60411
(312) 472-2176

Martin, Larry D., CAI
603 N. Jackson St.
Clinton, IL 61727
(217) 935-3873
FAX (217) 935-3795

Mezo, Joseph
P.O. Box 218
McLeansboro, IL 62859
(618) 643-3176

Nelson, William J.
USA Auctioneers Inc.
P.O. Box 5444
Rock Island, IL 61204
(309) 787-2929
FAX (309) 788-8180

Swing Jr., Paul L.
RR #1, Box 362
Lawrenceville, IL 62439
(618) 943-2794

Winternitz, Stephen L.
235 Anthony Trail
Northbrook, IL 60062
(708) 272-0440
FAX (708) 272-0604

Indiana

Butts, Virgil W., CAI
600 W. National Avenue
Brazil, IN 47834
(812) 446-2322
FAX (812) 446-2322

Lambright, Harvey C., CAI
112 N. Detroit St.
LaGrange, IN 46761
(219) 463-2013

Steinman, Orville G.
AAA Auction Service, Inc.
11210 State Rd. 4 East
New Haven, IN 46774

Taylor, David A., CAI
Taylor Auction Company
6804 Summertime Dr.
Indianapolis, IN 46226
(317) 547-7319

Iowa

Hamilton, William W.
Hamilton Auctions
2216 N. Third St.
Clinton, IA 52732
(319) 243-5828
FAX (800) 222-8450

Langstraat, Jerry
Northside Sales Company
725 11th Ave.
Sibley, IA 51249
(712) 754-3213

Moehle, Richard W.
RR 2, Box 66
Mediapolis, IA 52637
(319) 394-3666

Murphy, Mike
2019 Hwy. 375
Council Bluffs, IA 51501

Starling, Dennis G.
RR 1, Box 101
Lost Nation, IA 52254

Taylor, Gordon E.
P.O. Box 949, Hwy. 65 North
Mason City, IA 50401
(515) 423-5242

Van Der Werff, Rich, CAI
Ven Der Werff
Auctioneers, Inc.
Box 529, 215 Main
Sanborn, IA 51248
(712) 729-3264

Zaugg, Martin
Zaugg Farms Inc.
1115 Birch Ave.
Ottosen, IA 50570-9708
(515) 379-1693

Kansas

Carlin, Wayne E., CAI
Carlin's Auction/Real Estate
Box 310
Osborne, KS 67473
(913) 346-5778

Cochran, J.E.
RR 2, Box 23
Caldwell, KS 67022
(316) 845-2155

Fair, William, CAI
Bill Fair & Company
637 Indiana
Lawrence, KS 66044
(913) 842-9999
FAX (913) 842-1733

Haskins, David
Haskins Auction & Realty
114 S. State
Norton, KS 67654-2142
(913) 877-3275

Porter, Sr., Roger L., CAI
P.O. Box 8, 1036 Ironwood
Olathe, KS 66061
(913) 782-8009
FAX (913) 782-7767

Showalter, Bud
Rt. 1, Box 101B
Easton, KS 66020
(913) 651-5233

Kentucky

Darlin, John R., CAI
Main Auction Inc.
3540 Winding Dr.
Lexington, KY 40517
(606) 273-3133
FAX (606) 273-3133

Deane, Silas
5785 Hwy. 144
Owensboro, KY 42303
(502) 926-8553
FAX (502) 926-8574

Gibson, William S., CAI
1708 N. Mayo
Pikeville, KY 41501
(606) 432-8181
FAX (606) 478-9838

Jones, Harvey M.
Wilkerson Realty & Auction
1224 E. Bryant St.
Corbin, KY 40701
(606) 528-1157

Ledbetter, Kay S.
Ledbetter & Stewart, Ltd.
Realtors & Auctioneers
1999 Richmond Rd.
Suite 500
Lexington, KY 40502
(606) 268-1400
FAX (606) 268-2677

Lewis, Stephen D.
129 E. Main St.
Morehead, KY 40351
(606) 784-4168
FAX (606) 784-4160

Lynch, James D., CAI
Lynch Auction & Realty
1186 E. Broadway
Louisville, KY 40204
(502) 589-9822

Maddox, Alan
501 School St.
Beaver Dam, KY 42320
(502) 274-9672
FAX (502) 274-5610

Melloan, James M.
Kurtz Auction & Realty
305 Frederica St.
Owensboro, KY 42301
(502) 926-8553
FAX (502) 926-8574

Mills, Larry
P.O. Box 143
Greensburg, KY 42743
(502) 932-4998

Stewart III, Daniel D.
Ledbetter & Stewart, Ltd.
Realtors & Auctioneers
1999 Richmond Rd.
Suite 500
Lexington, KY 40502
(606) 268-1400
FAX (606) 268-2677

Wells, Gary L., CAI
Gary Wells Auctioneers
Rt. 1, Owingville, KY 40360
(606) 674-2453

Louisiana

Babb, Keith, CAI
P.O. Box 4222
Monroe, LA 71211-4968
(318) 343-6211
FAX (318) 343-6232

Baudry, Thomas P., CAI
Suite 1930
One American Place
Baton Rouge, LA 70825
(504) 344-2640
FAX (504) 336-9208

Maine

Giquere, Gerald P., Jr.
P.O. Box 1272
Windham, ME 04062
(207) 892-3800

Maryland

Campbell, Robert H.
121 Prince George St.
Annapolis, MD 21401
(301) 263-5808
FAX (301) 263-8427

Cox, Jimmy
9409 Old Marlboro Pike
Upper Marlboro, MD 20772
(301) 599-6285

Richardson, Pete
Pete Richardson
Auction Sales
P.O. Box 51
Willards, MD 21874
(301) 546-2425
FAX (301) 835-8613

Massachusetts

Maynard, Ronald V.
Ron Maynard Auctioneers
258 Groton St.
Dunstable, MA 01827
(508) 649-4280

Monroe, Sandra F.
10 State St.
Woburn, MA 01801
(617) 933-3998
FAX (617) 932-0421

Michigan

Berg, Roger S., CAI
23675 N. Shore Dr.
Edwardsburg, MI 49112
(616) 699-5584
FAX (616) 699-5584

Freund, Ken
Auctionway Sales, Inc.
P.O. Box 3096, 2443 S. Old 27
Gaylord, MI 49735
(517) 732-7808

Glardon, Daniel G.
988 E. Henderson Rd.
Owosso, MI 48867
(517) 725-7756

King, Edward G.
P.O. Box 375
Mason, MI 48854
(517) 223-7184

Norton, David A.
Norton Of Michigan
50 W. Pearl St.
Coldwater, MI 49036
(517) 279-9063
FAX (517) 279-9191

Reeser, Steve, CAI
1465 N. Cedar
Mason, MI 48854
(517) 699-2219
FAX (517) 699-3064

Stutzman, David E.
1847 Pine Dr.
Traverse City, MI 49684
(616) 938-9761

Minnesota

Fahey, James D.
P.O. Box 370
Hutchinson, MN 55350
(612) 587-3510
FAX (612) 587-3255

Houghton, Richard E., CAI
1967 Launa Ave.
Red Wing, MN 55066
(623) 388-5870

Imholte, Frank B.
8160 Country Rd. 138
St. Cloud, MN 56301
(612) 255-9398

Wiedemoth, E. H.
564 Clark St.
Hutchinson, MN 55350
(612) 587-2210

Mississippi

Johnson, Lannie E.
& Merry K.
Rt. 3, Box 297A
Fulton, MS 38843
(601) 862-2835

Ozborn, Kline, Jr.
Box 651
Canton, MS 39046
(601) 859-3845
FAX (601) 859-7828

Missouri

Merry, Donald E.
5805 Sorrel Tree Ct.
St. Louis, MO 63129
(314) 487-5846

Merry, Robert
Robert Merry Auction Co.
5501 Milburn Rd.
St. Louis, MO 63129
(314) 487-3992

Ratliff, Dennis W.
Rt. 1, Box 18-B
Easton, MO 64443
(816) 667-5411

Ytell, Wayne H.
Ytell Auction Service
1244 Glenwood Pl.
Carthage, MO 64836
(417) 358-7024
FAX (417) 358-7024

Montana

Metzger, William
3150 W. Cameron Bridge Rd.
Manhattan, MT 59741
(406) 285-6511,
FAX (406) 285-6514

Nebraska

Green, Norm E., CAI
Norm Green
Realty & Auction
Box 563, 104 S. Lincoln Ave.
York, NE 68467
(402) 362-5595
FAX (402) 362-4875

Marshall, Robin
Rte 1, Box 26
Elm Creek, NE 68836
(308) 856-4102

Martin, Dean C.
P.O. Box 207
Lexington, NE 68850
(308) 324-4931

Rudolph, Harry
15719 S. 99th
Papillion, NE 68128
(402) 339-8129

Standley, Dale E., CAI
Standley Auction & Realty
P.O. Box 3186
Omaha, NE 68103-3186
(402) 345-1117
FAX (712) 366-6631

Nevada

Britt, Don P.
5126 S. Somerset Dr.
Las Vegas, NV 89120
(702) 451-9075

Robinson, J.D., David K.
1500 E. Tropicana Ave.
Suite 102
Las Vegas, NV 89119
(702) 597-9845
FAX (702) 736-9192

New Hampshire

Lago, Robert W.
Hammond & Lago, Inc.
212 Pembroke Rd.
Concord, NH 03301
(603) 224-1942
FAX (603) 224-9558

New Jersey

Schrager, Steven R.
S.R. Schrager, Inc.
13 Dobson Rd.
E. Brunswick, NJ 08816
(908) 613-1350

Schueler, George W.
Realty & Land Exchange
1315 Allaire Ave.
Wanamassa, NJ 07712
(201) 531-4488

Slatoff, Robert W.
Lester & Robert Slatoff, Inc.
777 W. State St.
Trenton, NJ 08618
(215) 736-8989

Walsh, Edward R.
Walsh Auction Service
38 Lynn Dr.
Ocean, NJ 07712
(201) 493-4518

New Mexico

Bailey, Connie
Rt. 1, Box 74
Alamogordo, NM 88310
(505) 437-0597

New York

Amodeo, Michael
Michael Amodeo Co., Inc.
799 Broadway
New York, NY 10003
(212) 473-6830
FAX (718) 645-9596

Doherty, Jill
P.O. Box 574 M
Bayshore, NY 11706
(516) 666-9118
FAX (516) 666-1321

Hazzard, George
93 Elm St.
Yonkers, NY 10701
(914) 968-3200
FAX (914) 968-4453

Koster, Randall G., Ronald J.,
and Russell
Koster Industries Inc.
555 Broadhollow Rd.
Melville, NY 11747
(212) 661-2550

Manasse, Charlie
P.O. Box 496
Whitney Point, NY 13862
(607) 692-3516

Murray, Robert T.
124 Dean St.
Valley Stream, NY 11580
(516) 285-9385

Reisner, Fred
Auctions Plus, Inc.
535 Island Ave.
Woodmere, NY 11598
(516) 295-1300
FAX (516) 295-1301

Reynolds, John T., CAI
Reynolds Auction Co.
P.O. Box 508
Newark, NY 14513-0508
(315) 331-8815
FAX (315) 331-1053

Rusciano, Anthony
1025 Post Rd.
Scarsdale, NY 10583
(914) 472-5010

Visscher, Howard W.
Rd. 1, Box 507
Nichols, NY 13812
(607) 699-7250

Wilcox, Harris
17 S. Lake Ave.
Bergen, NY 14416
(716) 494-1880
FAX (716) 494-1605

North Carolina

Keeter, James T.
Keeter Auction Company,
International
Rt. 5, Box 291
Forest City, NC 28043
(704) 245-5020
FAX (704) 245-5020

Lawing, W. Craig, CAI
Lawing Auction Company
5521 Brookshire Rd.
Charlotte, NC 28216
(800) 632-3043

Lilly, William B., CAI
Iron Horse Auction Co.
P.O. Box 938
Norwood, NC 28128
(919) 997-2248
FAX (919) 895-1530

Marshall, Gail Y., CAI
Auctions by Marshall
6500 Sharon Hills Rd.
Charlotte, NC 28210
(704) 553-0029

Mendenhall, Forrest A., CAI,
and Wayne, CAI
Mendenhall Auction Co.
P.O. Box 7344
High Point, NC 27264
(919) 887-1165

Pierce, Keith J., CAI
P.O. Box 5215
5500 S. Main St.
Winston-Salem, NC
27113-5215
(919) 764-5338
FAX (919) 764-8642

Propst, Clyde
P.O. Box 563
Concord, NC 28026-0563

Smith, Robert M.
Smith Auction Co.
P.O. Box 1255
Graham, NC 27253
(919) 228-8842

Wooten, W. Douglas, CAI
Wooten Realty & Auction Co.
221 Clarendon Crescent
Raleigh, NC 27610
(919) 832-7251

North Dakota

Steffes, Robert, CAI
827 28th St. S., Suite D
Fargo, ND 58103
(701) 967-8927
FAX (701) 237-0976

Steffes, Scott, CAI
Steffes Auctioneers, Inc.
827 28th St. S., Suite D
Fargo, ND 58103-2324
(701) 237-9173

Ohio

Baker, William
William Baker Auctioneer
4488 St. Rt. 412
Vickery, OH 43464
(419) 547-9218

Bambeck, Herb, CAI
Route 1, Box 392
Dover, OH 44622
(216) 343-1437
FAX (216) 343-1437

Frey, Robert G.
Route 3, Box 47B
Archbold, OH 43502
(419) 445-0015
FAX (419) 445-8888

Garner, Sr., Larry W., CAI
L.W. Garner
Realty/Auctioneers
332 S. Lisbon St. Box 323
Carrollton, OH 44614
(800) 452-8452
FAX (216) 627-3788

Gill, James D., CAI
5770 Courtland Ave., NW
Massillon, OH 44646-1133
(216) 832-2605
FAX (216) 453-1765

Luggen, Jerome A.
Cincinnati Industrial Auction
6252 Hamilton Ave.
Cincinnati, OH 45224
(513) 471-5100

Luoma, Wayne
P.O. Box 308
Geneva, OH 44041
(216) 466-8383
FAX (216) 466-6305

McCarty, Kenneth D.
Nationwide Auctions
901 Congress Park Dr.
Dayton, OH 45459
(513) 433-0039
FAX (513) 435-5128

Semple, Brent T.
and Garth, CAIs
Semple & Associates
278 N. 3rd St.
Williamsburg, OH 45176
(513) 724-1133
FAX (513) 724-1286

Ux, Dan B.
137 First St.
New London, OH 44851
(419) 929-1148

Vannatta, Richard M.
975 W. Broad St.
Columbus, OH 43222
(614) 621-2897
FAX (614) 621-0329

Oklahoma

Brink, Terry H., CAI
Kent & Brink
422 N. 14th
Frederick, OK 73542
(405) 335-5732

Wolfe, Michael E.
200 W. 12th St.
Ada, OK 74820
(405) 436-1281
FAX (405) 436-1578

Oregon

Voorhees, Sidney I.
Sidco Management Inc.
P.O. Box 10205
Eugene, OR 97440
(503) 485-8885

Pennsylvania

Bechtold, Claude E., CAI
Bechtold Auctioneers
1928 Creek Hill Rd.
Lancaster, PA 17601
(717) 397-9240

Camelleri, Charles S.
Camelleri Auctioneering
P.O. Box 511
Birdsboro, PA 19508
(215) 582-1110

Clemmer, Lon M.
Sanford Alderfer
Auction Co.
Box 640-501
Fairgrounds Rd.
Hatfield, PA 19440
(215) 368-5477
FAX (215) 368-9055

Dobozynski, Joe, CAI
AAA Auction Service Inc.
RD 1, Box 420
Mifflintown, PA 17059
(717) 436-9594

Harriger, Emery L.
Harriger Auctioneer's
419 N. 4th Street
Reynoldsville, PA 15851
(814) 653-8610

Hostetter, Jr., Sherman, CAI
Hostetter Auctioneers/Real
Estate
124 Blackhawk Rd.
Beaver Falls, PA 15010
(412) 847-1880
FAX (412) 847-1881

Nicolls, W. Bruce
733 Terrace St.
Meadville, PA 16335
(814) 333-1989
FAX (814) 333-1988

Peters, Fred A., CAI
215 Lynn Rd.
Brownsville, PA 15417
(412) 785-8954
FAX (412) 785-8954

Randazzo, Salvatore A.
1030 Linden Ave.
Erie, PA 16505
(814) 838-2437

Slosberg, Barry S.
232 N. 2nd Street
Philadelphia, PA 19106
(215) 925-8020
FAX (215) 925-8047

Spataro, Anthony J.
Bennett Williams Inc.
1891 Santa Barbara Dr.,
#208
Lancaster, PA 17601
(717) 560-5611
FAX (717) 560-5625

Rhode Island

Loebenberg, Theodore F.
Box 2535
Providence, RI 02906
(401) 274-1930
FAX (401) 521-7845

Phillips, Edward F.
1049 Greenwich Ave.
Warwick, RI 02886
(401) 737-9060

South Carolina

Hernandez, Calixto A., CAI
P.O. Box 3086
Greenville, SC 29602
(803) 243-4858

South Dakota

Wingler, Terry
Wingler's Furniture/Auction
611 N. Main Ave.
Sioux Falls, SD 57102
(605) 332-5682

Tennessee

Alexander, Marvin E., CAI
239 University St.
P.O. Box 129
Martin, TN 38237-0129
(901) 587-4244
FAX (901) 587-2698

Blackford, Robert L.
3937 Gallatin Rd.
Nashville, TN 37216
(615) 228-2541
FAX (615) 227-6106

Hamilton, Jr., George, CAI
P.O. Box 536
Dunlap, TN 37327
(615) 554-3999

Hobbs, Fred R.
P.O. Box 126, 131 N. Main St.
Eagleville, TN 37060
(615) 274-6826

Miller, William A.
302 Wesley St., Suite 2
Johnson City, TN 37601
(615) 283-4178
FAX (615) 283-4132

Shepard, Tom
Nashville Auction &
Realty Co., Inc.
1407 Lebanon Rd.
Nashville, TN 37210
(615) 255-4933
FAX (615) 255-8052

Taggart, Raymond E., CAI
Delta Auction Co.
151 Walnut Creek
Cordova, TN 38018
(800) 592-2288
FAX (901) 382-5729

Texas

Archer, William C.
Box 802635
Dallas, TX 75380
(214) 458-9781

Bates, Rene
Rene Bates Auctioneers, Inc.
Rt. 4
McKinney, TX 75070
(214) 548-9636
FAX (214) 542-1604

Burlin, Morris L., CAI
Burlin's
2302 Matthew Dr.
Mt. Pleasant, TX 75455
(903) 572-3142

Foster, Paul M.
15618 Highfield Dr.
Houston, TX 77095-2030
(713) 855-8686

Harlien, Cecil M., Jr.
2914 Euell Rd.
Crosby, TX 77532
(713) 328-3683

Henson, Roy P.
Alph Int'l Mktg Services, Inc.
Rt. 3, Box 3786
Chandler, TX 75758
(903) 849-2221
FAX (903) 849-2883

Kaddatz, Alvin
Kaddatz Auctioneering
Box 972
Hillsboro, TX 76645
(817) 582-3071

Moore, Ronald G.
Plant & Machinery, Inc.
8705 Katy Fwy., #300
Houston, TX 77024-1710

Moses, Dwayne
Moses & Zuber Auctioneers
Rt. 1, Box 311
Ralls, TX 79357
(806) 253-2945

Ogle, Jack V., CAI
Ogle Auction & Realty
Rt. 2, Box 66A
Greenville, TX 75401
(903) 454-1091

Slate, Sr., Kenneth D.
Slate Auction Service
1822 Cliffcrest
Duncanville, TX 75137
(214) 780-9118

Stommel, Thomas J.
1607 Deerfield Court
Richmond, TX 77469
(713) 667-9351

Thomas, Brett R.
Rt. 6, Box 420
Mt. Pleasant, TX 75455
(903) 572-4517

Weaver, Bill
HCR 3, Box 47
Del Rio, TX 78840
(512) 774-4408

Utah

Parker, Dean H.
P.O. Box 3266
Logan, UT 84321
(801) 752-7701
FAX (801) 752-7701

Tiedemann, Arthur H.
345 W. 6400 South
Murray, UT 84107
(801) 262-9920

Vermont

Hirchak Jr., Thomas J.,
CAI
Thomas Hirchak Company
RD #3, Box 2430
Morrisville, VT 05661
(802) 888-4662

Matteis, Vincent
American Auction Center
Box 1196 Finney Hill
Lyndonville, VT 05851
(802) 626-8589

Merrill, Duane
Merrill's Auction Gallery
32 Beacon St.
S. Burlington, VT 05401
(802) 862-1624

Stevenson, Frederick A.
Fred's Auction Service
HCR 30, Box 56
Barnet, VT 05821
(802) 592-3202

Virginia

Cole, A. Barry, CAI
Rt. #1, Box 182
Callaway, VA 24067
(703) 483-4539

Counts, Ted, CAI
Realty & Auction Co.
8314 Timberlake Rd.
Lynchburg, VA 24502
(804) 237-2991
FAX (804) 239-1333

Peoples, Jack W.
1328 Head of River Rd.
Chesapeake, VA 23322
(804) 421-2525

Tull, Ronald I., CAI
Tull Realty & Auction Co.
3912 Woodburn Rd.
Annandale, VA 22003
(703) 280-5555

Williams, Frederick J.
F.J. Williams Realty
& Auction Company
P.O. Box 201
Winchester, VA 22601
(703) 662-3539

Washington

Burnham, Elmer L.
658 Road L NE
Moses Lake, WA 98837
(509) 766-9100
FAX (509) 766-9925

Ehli, Randall L.
Ehli Auctions Inc.
2042-112th St.
South Tacoma, WA 98444
(206) 537-7255
FAX (206) 537-7302

Hodges, Ken
Ken Hodges & Associates
Box 91
Bothell, WA 98011
(206) 363-4086

Honey, Jr., George P.
Northwest Auction Service
P.O. Box 397, 2003 Mac Place
Entlat, WA 98822
(509) 784-1938

West Virginia

Felosa, Joseph A., CAI
Felosa Auction/Realty, Inc.
Box 179
77 Felosa Drive
Haywood, WV 26366-0179
(304) 592-0738
FAX (304) 592-0738

Frio, James W.
RD 2, Box 206
Valley Grove, WV 26060
(304) 336-7462
FAX (304) 843-1518

Wisconsin

Barg, William H.
117 W. Fulton St.
Waupaca, WI 54981
(715) 258-8116

Cassiani, Daniel
20810 W. Barton Rd.
New Berlin, WI 53146
(414) 744-9060
FAX (414) 744-9084

Dodge, Chris
Dodge Auction Service
24 Sinclair St.
Janesville, WI 53545
(608) 756-3154

Hazlewood, William J., CAI
935 Model Railroad
Rice Lake, WI 54868
(800) 345-2040

Mantz, C. A.
Archie Mantz Auctioneer
7085 Winnebago
Fond Du Lac, WI 54935
(414) 921-1528

Massart, Pat, CAI and
Robert J., CAI
Massart Auctioneers Inc.
2545 Finger Rd.
Green Bay, WI 54302
(414) 468-1113

Schomisch, Michael R.
1326 Wild Rose La.
Neenah, WI 54956
(414) 734-9382

Stockwell, Randy J.
R.J. Stockwell Auctions
5340 County Line Rd.
Dorchester, WI 54425
(715) 654-5162

Varney, Scott, CAI
Accredited Auctioneers
207 N. Livingston St.
Madison, WI 53703
(608) 255-7630

Voigt, Victor V., CAI
Voigt Auction Service
Route 2
Reedsville, WI 54230
(414) 772-4235

Walla, William L.
Walla's Auction &
Real Estate
1723 County J
Little Suamico, WI 54141
(414) 826-5472

Wyoming

Casteel, Roger A.
700 Foothills Blvd.
Rock Springs, WY 82901
(307) 362-8361

Frome, L.D.
RFD Box 47
Afton, WY 83110
(800) 433-1595

Hamilton, Thomas W.
10831 Powderhouse Rd.
Cheyenne, WY 82009
(307) 637-4447

Hughs, Lee D.
Action Auctioneers
808 Range Rd.
Rock Springs, WY 82901
(307) 382-5442
FAX (307) 382-5442

35

The Directory of the Certified Auctioneers Institute

★★

The Certified Auctioneers Institute (CAI) comprises the most highly regarded auctioneers in the industry. To join, auctioneers must first become members of the National Auctioneers Association. For certification, a member must go through a series of business and legal courses. These are held in cooperation with Indiana University and take three years to complete.

They are taught by both CAI and Indiana University faculty. CAI will bring in outside specialists to provide them with the most advanced auction education available. Their curriculum will include the professional aspects of commercial and residential properties, antiques, agriculture, and business liquidations. Additionally, these auc-

tioneers will take courses in accounting, law, finance, real estate law, advertising, and marketing. It's like business school for auctioneers.

While average annual income for auctioneers ranges from $50,000 to $75,000, some CAI members make well into the six figures. This caliber of auctioneer is the top of his profession. They are also the most seasoned, with an average of 17.5 years experience behind them.

Expect the government to single out CAI members for future auctions. The entire CAI membership directory has been printed here for your use and reference. These auctioneers are likely to be very active, in the thick of auctions. Some of the industry's prestigious names are included.

CERTIFIED AUCTIONEERS EDUCATION INSTITUTE
1991–1992 MEMBERS

Alabama

DECATUR

Ornburn, Bill
Bill Ornburn Auctions
Route 2, Box 494C (35603)
(205) 350-5305

FAIRFIELD

McCrary, Camille B.
McCrary Auctioneers & Realty
5116 Valley Road (35064)
(205) 785-4131
Real Estate; Personal Prop.;
Antiques

McCrary, J. Rex
McCrary Auctioneers & Realty
5116 Valley Road (35064)
(205) 785-4131
Real Estate; Personal Prop.;
Antiques

GADSDEN

King, J. Craig
J.P. King Auction Company
108 Fountain Ave. (35901)
(205) 546-5217
(800) 662-5464
Fax: (205) 543-8036
Condominiums; Town-Houses;
Acreage; Multi Property

King, J. Polk
J.P. King, Auction Co
108 Fountain Ave. (35901)
(205) 546-5217
Fax: (205) 543-8036
Real Estate

HUNTSVILLE

Horton, Pete
John Horton Realty & Auction
111 Fourth St. (35805)
(205) 536-7497
(800) 548-0130
Fax: (205) 539-3941
Real Estate; Bus. Liquid.

JACKSONVILLE

Motes, Gene
Gene Motes Auctioneers Inc.
104 Church Avenue,
S.E. (36265)
(205) 435-4287
FAX: (205) 435-4287
Real Estate; Construction;
Farm Equipment; Bankruptcy;
Business Liquidation; Special
Sales

KILLEN

Behel, Don
Don Behel Realty & Auction
Rt. 4, Box 505 (35645)
(205) 757-4100
(205) 757-3573
Fax: (205) 757-4087
Real Estate; Farm Equipment;
Liquidations; Antiques;
Livestock

LAFAYETTE

Ray, William D.
Ray Realty & Auction Co.
P.O. Box 57 (36862)
(205) 864-8380
Real Estate; Personal Prop.;
Estates; Antiques; Farm
Equipment; Livestock

LEIGHTON

Smith, Thomas G.
Holland Realty and Auctions
Rt. 1, Box 432 (35646)
(205) 446-6480
Real Estate; Personal Property;
Farm Equipment; Business
Liquidation

MOBILE

Rainey, Bratton III
Bratt Rainey Realty & Auction
2560 Dauphin Island
Parkway (36605)
(205) 479-1017
Real Estate; Commercial;
Equipment; Estates

Rainey, L.B., Jr.
Bratt Rainey Realty & Auction
2560 Dauphin Island Parkway
(36605)
(205) 479-1017
(205) 471-5692
Real Estate; Commercial Inv.;
Equipment; Estates Liq.;
Boats; Liquidations

ROGERSVILLE

Holland, Daniel R.
Holland Realty & Auction
356 E. Lee Street (35652)
(205) 247-0700
Real Estate; Antiques;
Liquidations; General

SHEFFIELD

Knotts, Edward V.
Knotts Real Estate
& Auction Co.
411 E. 2nd St. (35660)
(205) 386-7074
Fax: (205) 386-0110
Real Estate; Estates;
Liquidations; Guns;
Farm Equipment;
Consignments

TONEY

Fowler, John (Mickey)
Fowler Auction Service Inc.
8710 Highway 53 (35773)
(205) 420-4454

Fax: (205) 852-3022
Real Estate; Farm Equipment;
Farm; Heavy Equipment;
Estates; General

Alaska

ANCHORAGE

Hess, James S.
Anchorage Auction Co.
424 North Klevin (99508)
(907) 345-3180
(907) 272-7734
Industrial; Oil Equipment;
Bankruptcy; Automobiles; Real
Estate

Arizona

GOODYEAR

Cadzow, John C.
Western Sales Management
Inc.
Box 330 (85338)
(602) 272-7759
(602) 932-2028
Farm; Farm Equipment;
Antiques; Liquidations;
General

MESA

Holmes, Philip R.
Holmes Auction Co.
137 East University Dr.
(85201)
(602) 844-1221
Fax: (602) 649-1584
Real Estate

PHOENIX

Harms, Bernard D.
Bernard D. Harms & Assoc.
4527 E. Devonshire (85018)
(602) 840-2492
Estates; Commercial; Heavy
Equipment; General

Kane, Christopher R.
Southwest Real Estate
Auctioneers
1211 E. Missouri
Suite 100 (85014)
(602) 263-0050
(602) 246-1122
Fax: (602) 263-0085
Real Estate; Business Liq.

Poulsen, Gary L.
R.E.A.M.S.
16042 N. 32nd St (85032)
(602) 971-6360
Fax: (602) 971-6144
Real Estate; Farm Machinery;
Equipment; Liquidations

PRESCOTT VALLEY

Boone, Robert R.
Robert R. Boone Auction &
Realty Co.
P.O. Box 26479 (86312)
(602) 772-1720
Fax: (602) 772-7837
Real Estate; Heavy
Equipment; Commercial;
Industrial; Farm Machinery

SCOTTSDALE

Latham, Larry W.
Larry Latham Auctioneers, Inc.
10304 N. Hayden Rd.
Suite 6 (85258)
(602) 998-1168
Fax: (602) 991-8554
Real Estate

TUCSON

Coleman, Richard C.
Southwest Liquidators, Inc.
220 E. Los Reales (85706)
(602) 889-4664
Fax: (602) 889-0116
Tools; Machinery; Electronics; On Site Sales;
Bankruptcies

Arkansas

BLYTHEVILLE

Shields, Sammy K.
Sammy Shields RE &
Auction, Inc.
505 Park St. (72316)
(501) 763-2000
Real Estate; Estate;
Complete Liq.; Const. Co.

CARLISLE

Chudy, Frank
Chudy Auction & Realty
P.O. Box 1110 (72024)
(501) 552-3038
Farm Equipment; Real
Estate; Estates; Commercial;
Appraisals

LITTLE ROCK

Wooley, Brad H.
Brad H. Wooley
Auctioneers, Inc.
9 Lombardy Lane (72207)
(501) 664-3826
Fax: (501) 663-7420
Real Estate; Industrial;
Commercial; Business Liq.;
Machinery; Bankruptcies

MOUNTAINBURG

Murdoch, Warren
Murdoch Realty & Auction
Route 2, Box 434 (72946)
(501) 369-4305
Real Estate, Farm
Equipment, General

ROGERS

Hiett, Jerry
Fred Hiett, Auctioneer
1320 Monte N.E.
Road (72756)
(501) 636-3946
Antiques; Estates; Household;
Liquidations; Farm

RUSSELLVILLE

Spear, Richard L.
Spear Auction & Realty
Company
P.O. Box 1052 (72801)
(501) 968-2028
(501) 968-2764
Real Estate; Liquidations;
Estates; Farms; Household

SPRINGDALE

Callaway, Harold D.
Callaway Auctions & Real
Estate
Rt. 7, Box 17 (74764)
(501) 751-2220
(501) 631-1822
Estates; Business Liquidations;
Real Estate

California

EL CAJON

McCormack, Ken
K. McCormack Auction Co.,
Inc.
743 El Cajon Blvd. (92020)
(619) 447-1196
Fax: (619) 447-9358
Commercial; Industrial;
Bankruptcy; Vehicles;
Heavy Equipment; Retail
Liquidations

FREMONT

Hayward, Thomas
Liquidation Station Auctioneers
43198 Christy St. (94538)
(415) 770-1234
(415) 790-2414
Fax: (415) 770-1431
Estate; Personal Prop; Sm.
Businesses; Moving/Storage;
Furnishings

Sellner
P.O. Box 308 (94536)
(415) 745-9463
Fine & Rare Wines; Indian
Art/Artifacts; Western Art/
Artifacts; Bars & Restaurants;
Estates; Charity

GALT

Huisman, David W.
Huisman Auction Service
5420 E. Jahant Rd. (95632)
(916) 682-3338
Farm Equipment; Industrial;
Heavy Equipment

GILROY

Daly, James P., Jr.
Daly's International Auction
Serv.
6310 Monterey Street (95020)
(408) 847-4038
Commercial; Estate;
Equipment; Electronics;
Real Estate

HEALDSBURG

Bain, John C.
9625 Chalk Hill Rd. (95448)
(707) 838-0150
(707) 578-9222
Antiques; Estates;
Automobile; Real Estate;
Livestock; Charity

LA JOLLA

Meyer, D.D.
D. D. Meyer Realty &
Auction Co.
4275 Executive Square
Suite 800 (92037)
(619) 282-8466
Fax: (619) 272-0040
RE Auctions

MODESTO

Ernst, Roger
Ernst & Associates
P.O. Box 3251 (95353)
(209) 527-7399
Industrial; Commercial

REDONDO BEACH

Bishop, Bernie W.
Bishop Auctioneers
International
P.O. Box 561 (90277-0561)

(213) 372-8031
Fax: (213) 372-9590
Industrial; Commercial;
Antiques

SACRAMENTO

Geiger, Nelson A.
Geiger Auction Sales
9479 Mira Del Rio (95827)
(916) 368-0130
Fax: (916) 368-0514
Real Estate; Indust. Plants;
Bankruptcy; Govt. Liquid.;
Heavy Equipment; Vehicles

SANTA CRUZ

Sydes, Tom
A&A Auction Galleries
925 41st Ave. (95062)
(408) 464-2323
Fax: (408) 476-1713
Estates; Business/Commercial

SONORA

Macon, Mike
Macon Brothers Auctioneers
558 S. Washington St. (95370)
(209) 532-0112
(209) 532-5418
Fax: (209) 532-1594
Real Estate; Estate Settle-
ments; RTC Assets; Gov't
Surplus; Commercial;
Heavy Equipment

TRACY

Cardoza, John A.
Cardoza Auctioneering
1288 W. 11th St., Suite 286
(95376)
(209) 832-0260
Fund Raising; Estate

TUSTIN

Bendis, Jan T.
Bendis Co. Auctioneers
17300 17th Street
Suite J-212 (92680)
(213) 694-4308
(714) 354-0511
Fax: (714) 780-4431
Real Estate; Industrial;
Commercial; Construction;
Estate Sales; Appraisal Serv.

VAN NUYS

Sass, Robert
ABE'S Auctions
5531 Fulton Ave. (91401)
(818) 909-9408
(213) 626-5423
Antiques & Jewelry;
Collectibles; Movie/Sport
Memorabilia; Dolls & Toys;
General Oil Painting; Charity
& Estates

Colorado

AURORA

Behr, Paul C.
Paul C. Behr & Associates
4704 South Jasper St. (80015)
(303) 680-1855
Fax: (612) 452-3006
Livestock; Real Estate
Farm; Automobile; Antique;
Household

BRUSH

Cumberlin, Charles
Cumberlin Auctioneers
P.O. Box 248
1215 West Edison (80723)
(303) 842-2822
Real Estate; Farm Equipment;
Heavy Equipment; Livestock;
Trucks; Trailer; Industrial

CANON CITY

Ely, Dale D.
Dale Ely and Associates
575 Ash (81212)
(719) 275-5703
(719) 275-6135
Commercial; Liquidations;
Real Estate; Estates; Vehicles

COMMERCE CITY

McCrea, Steve L.
McCrea & Co.
5895 E. 72nd Ave. (80022)
(303) 289-4437

DENVER

Lockhart, Cookie
Lockhart Auction & Realty Co.
P.O. Box 37287 (80237)
(303) 771-4111
(800) 521-5275
Fax: (303) 733-0608
Real Estate; Commercial;
Farm/Ranch; Livestock;
Construction; Oil Equipment

FT. MORGAN

Doty, Eugene V.
Doty Auction & Realty Co.
531 W. Platte Ave. (80701)
(303) 867-6394
Real Estate; Estate;
Commercial; Antiques

GLENWOOD SPRINGS

Smith, Randell N.
AAA R & J Auction Service,
Inc.
0151 Mel Rey Rd. (81601)
(303) 945-9723
Heavy Equip; Estates;
General

GREELEY

Johnson, Robert L.
Bob Johnson Auction & Realty,
Inc.
2535 E. Hwy. 34 (80631)
(303) 356-2998
(303) 330-0912
Estates; Tools & Equip.;
General

LITTLETON

Bohn, Charles F.
Chuck Bohn & Associates
P.O. Box 3275 (80161)
(303) 220-8729
Fax: (303) 220-8729
Industrial; Commercial;
Business Liquidation;
Bankruptcy; Real Estate;
Private Collections

LONGMONT

Pratt, O.J.
Pacific Auction, Inc.
9138 N. 95th (80501)
(303) 772-9401
Antique; Estates; Liquidations;
Household; Real Estate

TIMNATH

Salisbury, Jack
Salisbury Auctions Ltd.
P.O. Box 190 (80547)
(303) 482-3404
Commercial; Industrial;
Restaurants

WOODLAND PARK

Gorman, Bob A.
Bob Gorman Auctioneering
780 Kelley Road (80863)
(719) 687-9554
Business Liq.; Estate; Real
Estate; Farm Machinery;
Livestock

Connecticut

MIDDLETOWN

Ferrara, Michael J., Jr. (Ret)
Hartford Auction Group
104 Grove Street (06457)
(203) 342-1699
Fax: (203) 342-0277
Industrial; Machinery; Tools;
Heavy Equipment; Trucks;
Real Estate

SOUTHPORT

Josko, David A.
P.O. Box 817 (06490)
(203) 255-1441
(203) 259-2300
Antiques; Liquidations;
General

STERLING

Glass, Gwendolyn
Robert H. Glass Associates,
Inc.
Box 237
Route 14 (06377)
(800) 933-3312
(203) 564-7318
Fax: (203) 564-8819
Antiques; Estates; Real Estate;
Commercial

Glass, Robert H., Jr.
Robert H. Glass Associates Inc.
Box 237
Route 14 (06377)
(800) 933-3312
(203) 564-7318
Fax: (203) 564-8819
Antiques; Estates; Art; Real
Estate; Commercial

Glass, Robert H.
Robert H. Glass Associates,
Inc.
Box 237, Route 14 (06377)
(800) 933-3312
(203) 564-7318
Fax: (203) 564-8819
Antiques; Estates; Real Estate;
Commercial

TRUMBULL

Pinto, A.C.
Richard Auction Specialist of
New England
P.O. Box 5 (06611)
(203) 268-0465
(203) 366-4085
Fax: (203) 876-9924
Restaurant Liq.; Vehicles;
Industrial; Realty; Estates;
General

District of Columbia Washington

Evans, W. Ronald
Capital City Enterprises, Ltd.
P.O. Box 60022 (20039)
202) 543-2828
Real Estate; Foreclosures;
Estate Auctions;
Liquidations; R.E. Personal
Prop. Appraisal; Fund Raisers

Florida

BRADENTON

Castner, Donald L.
Castner Estate Service
1008 Cimarron Circle W.
(34209)
(813) 794-6033
Estates; Real Estate; Municipal
Prop.; Appraisal Serv.

COCONUT GROVE

Sklarey, Seth
Capital Auction & Realty Co.
Box 33000K (33233)
(305) 374-1166
Fax: (305) 379-0653
Real Estate; Estates;
Business Liq.; Antiques;
Bankruptcies; Appraisals

CORAL SPRINGS

Puntolillo, Todd
Friendly Auctions, Inc.
10665 N.W. 42nd Dr. (33065)
(305) 755-1777
Fax: (305) 755-1637

Graphic Arts Mach.; Gen.
Personal Prop.;
Printing Machinery; Bindery
Machinery; Commercial
Auctions; Industrial Auctions

DAVIE

Vagi, Robert L.
Auctioneer Inc.
2140 S.W 114 Ave. (33325)
(305) 472-7653
Fax: (800) 333-7044
Real Estate; Estates; Marine;
Bus. Liquid.

DELAND

Arey, Chester M.
Arey's Auction Team Inc.
Box 1953 (32721)
(904) 738-0050
(904) 736-3438
Real Estate; Antiques;
Estates; Commercial Liq.;
Bankruptcy; General

DESTIN

King, J. Scott
J.P. King Auction Co.
P.O. Box 1588 (32541)
(904) 837-4717
Fax: (904) 837-7790
Resort Condos; Res. Condos;
Multi-Property; Acreage

GAINESVILLE

Campen, Ben
Ben Campen Auctioneers
P.O. Box 1209 (32602)
(904) 375-6600
Fax: (904) 375-1641
Real Estate; Antiques;
Machinery; Equipment

Wood, W.R.
Hometown Realty of Florida
Inc.
1002 NW 23rd Avenue (32609)
(904) 373-4490
Real Estate; Surplus; Personal
Prop.

HERNANDO

Driggers, Walter J., III
AAPT Realty, Inc.
7800 N. Carl G. Rose Hwy.
(32642)
(904) 726-0275
(904) 726-1047
Fax: (904) 726-0235
Real Estate; Business
Liquidation

King, Hellen B.
AAPT Realty, Inc.
7800 N. Carl G. Rose Hwy.
(32642)
(904) 726-0275
(904) 344-8142
Fax: (904) 726-0235
Real Estate; Business Liq.;
Charity

Messer, Ed
AAPT Realty, Inc.
7800 N. Carl G. Rose Hwy.
(32642)
(904) 726-0275
(904) 726-7533
Fax: (904) 726-0235

Real Estate; Store Liq.;
Equipment

JACKSONVILLE

Garner, Michael D.
First Coast Auction & Realty,
Inc.
P.O. Box 7878 (32238)
(904) 772-0110
Equipment; Real Estate;
Liquidations;
Estates; Antiques

Garner, Robert J.
First Coast Auction & Realty,
Inc.
P.O. Box 7878 (32238)
(904) 772-0110
(904) 783-8755
Fax: (904) 777-8387
Machinery; Real Estate;
Personal Prop.

Garner, Thomas
First Coast Auction & Realty,
Inc.
P.O. Box 7878 (32238)
(904) 772-0110
Fax: (904) 777-8387
Real Estate; Gov't Sales;
Commercial;
Estates; Equipment

Murray, Stephen P.
Mecca Properties, Inc.
2943 Forest Circle (32257)
(904) 739-0355
(800) 423-7687
Real Estate; Commercial;
Household; Estates;
Equipment; Bankruptcy

LAKE BUENA VISTA

Shearer, Donald
Walt Disney World Co.
P.O. Box 10,000 (32830)

(407) 847-3993
Machinery & Eq.; Business
Liq.; Estates; Commercial;
Benefits

LAKELAND

Cole, Phillip A.
Higgenbotham Realty &
Auction, Inc.
1666 Williamsburg Square
(33803)
(813) 644-6681
Fax: (813) 644-6686
Antiques; Coins; Estates;
Heavy Equipment;
Commercial; Land

Higgenbotham, Martin E.
Higgenbotham Realty Inc.
1661 Williamsburg
Square (33803)
(813) 644-6681
Fax: (813) 644-6686
Real Estate

Neiswander, John T.
Higgenbotham Realty Inc.
1661 Williamsburg
Square (33803)
(813) 644-6681
Fax: (813) 644-6686
Real Estate; Household; Farm;
Liquidations; General

MARATHON

Fullom, Cliff
Land & Sea Auctions Inc.
6805 Overseas Highway
(33050)
(800) 654-1889
Fax: (305) 743-6466
Real Estate; Estates; Marine;
Govt. & Municipal

MIAMI

Gall, Jim
Auction Company of America
100 N. Biscayne Blvd.
23rd Floor (33132)
(305) 577-3322
Fax: (305) 375-0932
Real Estate

Levine, Neal H.
Sold American Inc.
8175 S.W. 93 Ave. (33173)
(305) 235-7653
Benefit; Real Estate

NORTH MIAMI BEACH

Sugarman, Jay L.
Jay Sugarman Auctioneer
18500 N.E. 5th Avenue
(33179)
(305) 651-0101
(305) 651-0102
Fax: (305) 653-9669
R.T.C.-F.D.I.C. Sales

NORTH PALM BEACH

Graham, Jim
Jim Graham Inc. Auctrs. &
Realtors
204 US 1 (33408)
(407) 842-7605
Fax: (407) 844-2100
Real Estate; Heavy
Equipment; Autos; Boats;
Machinery; Gen. Inventory

PENSACOLA

Boyleston, Louis C.
Louis Boyleston Realty &
Auction
P.O. Box 12504 (32573)
(904) 434-0377

Farm; Bankruptcy; Farm
Equipment; Real
Estate; Goverment; Estate

POMPANO BEACH

Fisher, Benny B., Jr.
Fisher Auction Co., Inc.
431 Northeast 1st Street
(33060)
(305) 942-0917
Fax: (305) 782-8143
Real Estate; Bankruptcy;
Liquidations

Fisher, Lamar P.
Fisher Auction Co., Inc.
431 Northeast 1st Street
(33060)
(305) 942-0917
Fax: (305) 782-8143
Real Estate; Bankruptcy;
Liquidations

Fisher, Louis B. III
Fisher Auction Company
431 Northeast 1st Street
(33060)
(305) 942-0917
Fax: (305) 782-8143
Real Estate; Banrkuptcy;
Liquidations

Fisher, Mitzi A.
Fisher Auction Co., Inc.
431 Northeast 1st St. (33060)
(305) 942-0917
(800) 331-6620
Fax: (305) 782-8143
Real Estate; Bankruptcy;
Liquidations

Moore, Loren E.
Real Estate Auction Business
660 S. Federal Highway
(33062)
(305) 943-0301
Fax: (305) 943-0309
Real Estate

ST. PETERSBURG

Burchard, Jeffrey A.
Jeffrey Burchard & Assoc.
2528 30th Avenue North
(33713)
(813) 821-1167
(813) 823-4156
Fax: (813) 821-1814
Antiques; Fine Arts; Estate
Liquidation;
Business Liquidation; Real
Estate; On Site & Gallery Sale

TAMPA

Kuhn, P.D., Jr.
Waters Business Center
14189 Fennsbury Dr. (33624)
(813) 960-8911
General; Commercial;
Antiques; Real
Estate; Livestock; Dealer

VENICE

Van De Ree, Neal
Neal Van De Ree Auctioneers
205 E. Base Avenue (34285)
(813) 488-1500
(813) 488-7849
Fax: (813) 488-7849
Residential RE; Commercial
RE; Business Liq.; Jewelry;
Estates; Boats & Equip.

WINDERMERE

Manor, Dave
Dave Manor Auctioneers Inc.
P.O. Box 610 (32786)
(305) 282-8466
Fax: (407) 291-1411
Commercial; Real Estate;
Bankruptcies; Estates; Comm.
Equip.; Inventories

WINTER PARK

Myers, Richard L.
Higgenbotham Realty, Inc.-
Orlando
1850 Lee Road Suite 127
(32789)
(407) 644-5666
Fax: (407) 628-4255
Real Estate; Heavy
Equipment;
Comm./Bus. Liq.; Machinery;
Estates; Statewide

Georgia

ALBANY

Durham, Joseph P.J.
Durham & Assoc., Inc.
1216 Dawson Road Suite 102
(31707)
(912) 439-2733
Fax (912) 439-7823
Real Estate; Condominiums;
Commercial;
Resort Property; Farm Land;
Farm Equipment

AMERICUS

Gay, Carlus D., Jr.
Carlus D. Gay Auction Service
P.O. Box 665
1501 E. Forsyth St. (31709)
(800) 342-6973

Fax: (912) 924-0627
Construction Equip.; Farm
Equipment;
Industrial Liq.; General

ATLANTA

Dixon, John L.
Hudson & Marshall Inc.
4751 Best Rd., Suite 240
(30337)
(404) 763-0211
Fax: (404) 763-1071
Real Estate

COLLEGE PARK

Miller, Arvil W.
Miller Auction Co.
1635 Liberty Road (30337)

COLUMBUS

Evans, Wayne
Wayne Evans Auction Co.
P.O. Box 4600 (31904)
(404) 324-0344
Heavy Equipment; Auto &
Trucks; Business Liq.; Real
Estate; Machinery;
Farm Equipment

FAIRBURN

Harris, Bruce R.
Harris Auction Service Ltd.
99 Bay Street (30213)
(404) 969-1315
Real Estate; Heavy
Equipment; Estates;
Machinery; Antiques; Jewelry

Harris, Ronald C.
Harris Auction Service
99 Bay Street (30213)
(404) 969-1315
Commercial; Real Estate;
Appraisals;

Heavy Equipment;
Automobiles; Antiques

LAKELAND

Patten, Donald
Zenith Auction & Realty Inc.
P.O. Box 98 (31635)
(912) 482-2116
Fax: (912) 482-2116
Real Estate; Business
Liquidation; Estates; Farm
Equipment

MACON

Childs, Billy J.
Hudson & Marshall Inc.
717 North Avenue (31298)
(912) 474-2578
Fax: (912) 743-6110
Real Estate; Heavy
Equipment; Livestock

Grant, P.T.
Hudson & Marshall Inc.
717 North Avenue (31298)
(912) 743-1511
(912) 836-3744
Fax: (912) 743-6110
Farm Equipment; Heavy
Equip.; Real Estate

Marshall, Asa M., IV
Hudson & Marshall Inc.
717 North Ave.
Macon, GA 31298
(912) 743-1511
Fax: (912) 743-6110
Foreclosure; Equipment; Farm

MADISON

Rowell, Carew F., III
Cambridge Associates, Inc.
1910 Buckhead Rd. (30650)
(404) 342-7749
Fax: (404) 952-5272
Real Estate; Personal prop.

MARIETTA

Arwood, David, G., II
P.O. Box 4485 (30061)
(404) 423-0110
Fax: (404) 424-5200
Heavy Equip.; Trucks/Trailers;
Real Estate; Mfg. Factories;
Ind. Appraisals; Machinery

MOULTRIE

Barfield, Maurice
Southeastern Auctioneers Inc.
Box 1803, 411 S Main St.
(31776)
(912) 985-5700
Real Estate; Equipment

Green, Jerry W.
Southeastern Auctioneers Inc.
P.O. Box 1803 (31768)
(912) 985-5700
Real Estate; Commercial;
Estates; Farm
Equipment; Antiques

Rowell, Thomas W.
Rowell Realty & Auction
P.O. Box 1846 (31766)
(912) 985-8388
Fax: (912) 890-9567
Real Estate; Farm Equipment;
Commercial; Mobile Houses

Strickland, John S.
Strickland Realty & Auction
P.O. Box 429 (31776)
(912) 985-7730

Real Estate; Equipment;
Business Liq.;
Machinery

Whitney, Chuck
Hudson & Marshall, Inc.
3 Old Tram Road (31768)
(912) 985-2223
(800) 922-9401
Fax: (912) 985-1029
Real Estate; Personal Prop.

ROCK SPRING

Potts, Ben R.
Robert Potts Land & Auction,
Inc.
P.O. Box 38
Hwy 27 South (30739)
(404) 764-1226
(404) 375-3631
Fax: (404) 764-1149
Real Estate; Farm Equipment;
Antiques; Livestock

ROME

Land, Randy
J.L. Todd Auction Company
P.O. Box 553 (30161)
(404) 291-7007
(404) 295-4801
Fax: (404) 291-0335
Real Estate; Estate Sales;
Personal property; Equipment

Loftin, Mike
Loftin Auction
P.O. Box 1198 (30162-1198)
(404) 232-3631
Fax: (404) 295-4386
Real Estate; Machine Tools;
Woodworking Machinery;
Business Equipment; Trucks/
Trailers; Const. Equipment

Tarpley, Joe T.
J.L. Todd Auction Co.

531 Broad St. (30161)
(800) 241-7591
(404) 291-7007
Fax: (404) 291-0335
Real Estate; Equipment;
Antiques

Todd, John L.
J.L. Todd Auction Company
531 Broad St. (30161)
(404) 291-7007
Real Estate; Equipment;
Antiques

THOMASVILLE

DeSantis, Pete, Jr.
DeSantis Auction Company
Inc.
P.O. Box 487 (31799)
(912) 226-8849
Tobacco; Antiques; Real Estate

Idaho

TWIN FALLS

Henry, Don
Henry's Realty & Auction Co.
191 Addison Ave. (83301)
(800) 325-1431
(208) 734-3930
Fax: (208) 736-7263
Bankruptcy/Gov.; Farm
Equipment; Heavy
Equip.; Estates; Household;
Real Estate

Illinois

ALEDO

Nestrick, Donald E.
Don Nestrick Auction
& Realty
P.O. Box 206 (61231)
(309) 582-2469
Fax: (309) 596-2124
Real Estate; Farms;
Commercial; Heavy
Equip.; Estates

ALLERTON

Smith, Raymond L.
Smith Auction Service
101 Walnut
Box 232 (61810)
(217) 834-3314
Farm Equipment; Real Estate;
Household; Estates; Livestock

ARLINGTON HEIGHTS

Josko, John A.
Max Rouse & Sons, Inc.
3800 North Wilke Road
Suite 300
(60004-1267)
(800) 334-8032
(708) 255-6115
Fax: (708) 255-6187
Industrial; Liquidations;
Commercial;
Furniture

BELLEVILLE

Geolat, Norman J.
Geolat Auction Co.
2608 East B Street (62221)
(618) 234-6967
Land; Real Estate;
Commercial; Farm
Sales; Liquidations; Estates

Prindable, James G.
Prindable Auction Service
1432 East Main St. (62220)
(618) 277-6975
Estates; Real Estate;
Construction Eq;
Liquidations; Farm Sales; On
or Off Site

CHATHAM

Gaule, William L.
Wm L. Gaule Auction Serv.
144 E. Walnut (62629)
(217) 483-2484
(217) 483-2913
Real Estate; Farm Machinery;
Antiques; Commercial;
General; Liquidations

CHICAGO HEIGHTS

Johnson, Earl
Johnson Auction Service
1543 Aberdeen (60411)
(708) 755-1083
Antiques; Dir. Wholesale;
Commercial

CHICAGO

Dziedzic, John
Auction Service Inc.
5338 N. Lotus Ave. (60630)
(312) 631-2255
Machinery; Equipment;
Restaurants; Retail Liq.;
Real Estate; Vehicles

CLINTON

Martin, Larry D.
Rt. 51 S.
P.O. Box 343 (61727)
(217) 935-8211
Farm Equipment; Farm Land;
Construction

ELGIN

Dunning, C. P. (Terry)
Dunning's Auction Service
755 Church Road
Box 866 (60121)
(708) 741-3483
Fax: (708) 741-3589
Antiques; Art; Real Estate;
Jewelry; Business Liquidation

Parker, Greg O.
Dunning's Auction Service Inc.
212 Lovell St. (60120)
(708) 741-3483
(708) 695-6418
Fine Art; Antiques; Decorative
Art; Personal Property

FARMINGTON

Goldring, Marcy
Marcy Goldring Auctioneers
147 East Fort Street (61531)
(309) 245-4528
(309) 245-4023
Fax: (309) 245-5100
Estates; Real Estate; Bid
Assistant

GEORGETOWN

Lenhart, Doyne
Lenhart Auction Service
221 S. Main Street (61846)
(217) 662-8644
Fax: (217) 662-2484
Real Estate; Antiques; Estates;
Commercial; Farm Equipment

GRANT PARK

Schrage, Larry R.
Complete Auctioneering
Service RR 1
Box 60 (60940)
(815) 465-6137
Household; Antique; Farm;
Commercial;
Business Liq.

INGLESIDE

Obenauf, William M., Sr.
Obenauf Auction Service
25691 W. Old Grand Ave.
(60041)
(708) 587-8306
Antique; Farm; Household;
Estate; Charity; Real Estate

LYNWOOD

Buiter, Albert
Buiter's Auction Company
Route 1, Box 264 E (60411)
(312) 895-4745
Farm Equipment; Estates;
Antiques; Commercial; Real
Estate

MILFORD

Decker, William R.
Decker Real Estate/
Auctioneers
Route 2, Box 29 (60953)
(815) 889-4113
Real Estate; Antique;
Household; Farm
Machinery; Livestock

MORO

Henke, Homer R.
Homer Henke Auction
Service Route 1
Box 30 (62067)

(618) 377-6444
Real Estate; Farm; Household;
Estate; Antiques; Commercial

MT. PULASKI

Maske, Michael E.
Mike Maske, Auction/
Appraisal Srv.
Rt. 2, Box 70 (62548)
(217) 792-3959
Farm Machinery; Antiques;
Personal property

NEWTON

Schackmann, Arthur F.
Art Schackmann Auction
Service
307 N. Church St. (62448)
(618) 783-2084
Farm Equipment; Real Estate;
Antiques; General

NOKOMIS

Aumann, Nelson E.
Nelson Aumann Auction &
Realty
107 East State Street (62075)
(217) 563-2523
(217) 563-7528
Fax: (217) 563-2111
Real Estate; Antiques; Farm
Equipment; Guns

PECATONICA

Hachmeister, Henry L.
Hack's Auction and Realty
417 Main Street
Box 296 (61063)
(815) 239-1436
Real Estate; Antiques; General;
Farm; Commercial;
Liquidation

SANDWICH

Swanson, John (Swanie)
Swanson Auction Service
144 E. Church Str. (60548)
(815) 786-2363
Autos; Antiques; Household;
Real Estate; Commercial;
Farm

STAUNTON

Ahrens, Dennis W.
Ahrens Auction & Realty, Inc.
Route 1, Box 695 (62088)
(618) 459-3445
Personal Prop.; Real Estate

Ahrens, Edward H.
Ahrens Auction & Realty, Inc.
RR 1, Box 695 (62088)
(618) 459-3620
Real Estate; Farm Sales;
Antiques

WATERLOO

Kueker, Edmund E.
Kueker's Action
Auction Associates
Route 1, Box 302 (62298)
(618) 939-7273
General; Farm Equipment;
Real Estate; Antiques;
Liquidations; Horses

WAYNE CITY

Hertenstein, Roger
Hertenstein Auction Co.
Box 23, West Section
Line Road (62895)
(618) 895-2663
Fax: (618) 895-2663
Real Estate; Farm Equipment;
Antiques; Liquidations; Estate;
Consignment

Indiana

ANDERSON

Jackson, Dennis
Jackson's Auction Gallery
5330 Pendleton Ave. (46013)
(317) 642-7563
Fax: (317) 642-3550
Antiques; Estates; Household;
Real Estate; Art; Liquidations

Stevens, Donald R.
Don Stevens Professional
Services
3105 E. 10th Street
(46012)
(317) 644-8822
(317) 644-8847
Real Estate; Household;
Commercial

Webb, Claudean
Claudean Webb Auction &
Realty
2110 Columbus (46014)
(317) 643-1725
Farm; Estates; Antiques;
Appraisals

AUBURN

Kruse, Dennis K.
Ambassador Associates
Box 627 (46706)
(219) 925-0000
Fax: (219) 925-3152
Real Estate; General; Classic
Auto; Estates; Antiques;
Mobile Homes

BERNE

Lehman, Emerson
Lehman's Auction
120 S. Fulton Street (46711)
(219) 589-2261
General

Lehman, Maynard
Miz Lehman Realtor
P.O. Box 43 (46711)
(219) 589-2903
Real Estate

Yoder, Chris J.
Miz Lehman Realtor-
Auctioneer
P.O. Box
43 (46711)
(219) 589-2903
Real Estate; Antiques

BLUFFTON

Ellenberger, Kenneth J.
Ellenberger Brothers
Auctioneers
130 ½ W Market St. (46714)
(219) 824-2426
Real Estate; Machinery;
Antiques

Ellenberger, Robert
Ellenberger Brothers
Auctioneers
130 ½ W Market St. (46714)
(219) 824-2426
(219) 747-3189
Farm; Household; Antiques;
Estates; Residential;
Commercial

Frauhiger, Rudy G.
Ellenberger Brothers Inc.
130½ W Market Street
(46714)
(219) 824-2426
Real Estate; Farm Machinery;
Antiques

Holloway, Jody M.
Ellenberger Brothers Inc.
130½ W Market St. (46714)
(219) 824-2426
Antiques; Real Estate

BOONVILLE

Yager, John E., Jr.
Yager Auctioneers & Associates
944 W. Main St. (47601)
(812) 922-5502
Household; Estates; Real
Estate; Farm; Horses;
Commercial

BRAZIL

Butts, Virgil W.
Butts/Pell & Associates
600 W. National Ave. (47834)
(812) 466-2322
Industrial; Farm Machinery;
Estates; Real Estate; Specialty;
Household Antiques

Pell, Bradley R.
Butts-Pell & Associates
R.R. #15, Box 497A (47834)
(812) 448-8290
Household; Real Estate; Farm

Pell, Chris D.
Butts-Pell & Associates
600 W. National Ave. (47834)
(812) 448-3697
Estates; Real Estate; Farm
Equipment

CAMDEN

Michael, Greg M.
Craft & Michael Auctioneers
P.O. Box 7 (46917)
(219) 686-2615
Fax: (219) 686-9001
Farm Machinery; Household;
Antiques; Real Estate;
Liquidations

CAYUGA

Morgan, Brian K.
Lenhart Auction & Real Estate
RR1, Box 215 (47928)
(317) 492-3244
General; Estates; Real Estate

COLUMBIA CITY

Klingaman, Eugene
Schrader Real Estate &
Auction Co.
209 W. Van Buren Street
(46725)
(219) 244-7606
(219) 799-4415
Fax: (219) 244-4431
Farm RE; Farm Equipment;
Fertilizer Eq.; Grain Equip.

CONNERSVILLE

Koons, Michael J. and Roger
E. Koons
Koons & Koons Auctioneers
1324 East 5th St.
P.O. Box 617 (47331)
(317) 825-3594
Real Estate; Farm Machinery;
Antiques; Collectibles; Business
Liquidators; Estates

CONVERSE

Winger, Loren E.
Schrader Real Estate &
Auction Co.
Box 527 (46919)
(317) 395-3351
Fax: (317) 395-3351
Farms; Farm Equipment;
Consultation; Tax
Deferred; Industrial; Estates

CRAWFORDSVILLE

Sayler, John L.
The Town Crier Agency
3749 Old State Rd 32 W.
(47933)
(317) 362-4465
Antiques; Real Estate; Estates;
Farm Equipment; Household;
Commercial

ELWOOD

Wittkamper, Marvin B.
Wittkamper Bros. Auction RE/
Apprs.
Box 33, RR 3 (46036)
(317) 552-7977
Farm Equipment; Antiques;
Real Estate; Household

EVANSVILLE

Horral, Bradley R.
Curran Miller Auction/Realty,
Inc.
13020 N. State Hwy. 57
(47711)
(812) 867-2486
Farm Equipment; Agricultural
Ln; Real Estate

Marshall, John W., Jr.
Marshall Auction & Realty
623 Westchester Dr. (47110)
(812) 422-2331
Commercial Liq.; Estate;
Residential RE;
Commercial RE; Automobiles;
Aircraft/Boats

Miller, Hugh B.
Curran Miller Auction &
Realty
13020 N. State Hwy, 57
(47711)
(812) 867-2486
Fax: (812) 867-4091

Real Estate; Farm;
Commercial;
Antiques; Estates

Shaffer, Lee H.
Kurtz Auction & Realty
Company
101 SE Third St.
Suite 38 (47708)
(812) 464-9308
Res. Real Estate; Multi-tract
Auc; Estate Sales; Bankruptcy;
Machinery; Personal Property

Shon, Donald M.
Curran Miller Auction &
Realty
13020 N. State Hwy, 57
(47711)
(812) 867-2486
Real Estate; Antiques; Estates;
Commercial; Farm

FORT WAYNE

Bauermeister, Thomas D.
Bauermeister Auction & Realty
7415 Maples Road (46816)
(219) 447-9206
Real Estate; Farm; Residential;
Antiques; Specialty

Frecker, Kenneth E.
Ken Frecker Auctioneers
809 West Coliseum Blvd.
(46808)
(219) 462-9094
(219) 623-2202
General Mdse.; Real Estate;
Antiques; Industrial

Smith, Edward S.
Ellenberger Brothers Inc.
7410 Bluffton Road (46809)
(219) 747-3189
Personal Prop.; Farm
Equipment; Real
Estate; Antiques

GALVESTON

Johnson, Carl R.
Johnson Auctions
Box 657 (46932)
(219) 699-6756
Real Estate; Farm Equipment;
General

GREENCASTLE

Eilar, De
Eilar Auction & Real Estate
RR#1, Box 662 (46135)
(317) 653-8806
(317) 653-0738
Estate; Antiques; Household;
Farm; Real Estate

HUNTINGTON

Ness, Kurt J.
Ness Brothers
18 W. Washington St. (46750)
(219) 356-3911
Real Estate; Personal Prop.;
Liquidations

Ness, Stephen A.
Ness Brothers Realtors
18 W. Washington St. (46750)
(219) 356-3911
Real Estate; Estates; Farm;
Farm Equipment; Antiques;
Liquidations

INDIANAPOLIS

Adams, Bob
Allied Auctioneers Inc.
P.O. Box 39072 (46239)
(317) 763-6622
Farm Equipment; Livestock;
Real Estate;
Estate; Personal Prop.

Fife, Jack
Fife Real Estate & Auct.
Service

6414 Ferguson St. (46220)
(317) 251-9402
Real Estate; Commercial

King, Ronald E.
Ronald King and Associates
5610 Crawfordsville Rd.,
Suite 801
(46224)
(800) 359-1875
(317) 243-2139

Spurgeon, Don (Retired)
Don Spurgeon & Associates
609 E. 96th Street (46240)
(317) 844-2452
Real Estate; All Types

Strakis, Herman D.
Herman D. Strakis Auction
3333 W. Troy Av. (46241)
(317) 244-8063
Commercial; Real Estate;
Equipment; Farm; Estates;
Household

Taylor, David A. (Retired)
Taylor Auction Co.
6804 Summertime Drive
(46226)
(317) 547-7319
Industrial; Commercial; Heavy
Equipment; Bankruptcies; Real
Estate; Liquidations

JEFFERSONVILLE

Crum, Richard
Crum's Auction & Realty, Inc.
4909 Hanburg Pike (47130)
(812) 282-6043
Real Estate; Estate; Business
Liq.

Curtis, Terry W.
Curtis Auction Service
6218 Conservation Dr. (47130)
(812) 283-8586

General; Home; Farm;
Industry

KOKOMO

Crume, Roy L. (Retired)
3619 W. Sycamore Lane
(46901)
(317) 452-6946
Real Estate; Farm; Household

Ellis, R. Cartwright
Crume/Ellis Auctrs. &
Appraisers
115 S. Dixon Road (46901)
(317) 457-8238
Real Estate; Liquidations;
General; Appraisals

LAFAYETTE

Knop, David A.
Knop Corporation
627 N. Earl Avenue (47904)
(317) 447-9411
Bankruptcy Liq.; Commercial;
Real Estate; Farm Equipment;
Antiq. & Estates; Restaurant

LAGRANGE

Bollinger, Kirby L.
Lewis and Lambright Inc.
112 N. Detroit St. (46761)
(219) 463-2013
(219) 562-3027
General; Real Estate; Furs

Lambright, Harvey C.
Lewis and Lambright
112 N. Detroit (46761)
(219) 463-2013
(219) 562-3012
General; Real Estate; Antiques;
Indian Artifacts

LAPORTE

Ott, Robert V.
Ott Auction Service
800 Lincolnway, Suite 311
(46350)
(219) 362-3365

LEBANON

Summerville, James R.
Summerville Auction and
Appraisal
218 E. Washington St. (46052)
(317) 482-7923
Antiques; Farm Equipment;
Real Estate; Household

LIBERTY

Abernathy, Terry C.
Abernathy Auction & Real
Estate
21 W. Union St. (47353)
(317) 458-5826
(317) 458-5448
Real Estate; Farm Machinery;
Personal Prop.; Antiques;
Collectibles;
Commercial Liq.

Campbell, Harry
Campbell Auction Team
19 South Market (47353)
(317) 732-3372
(317) 458-6441
Real Estate; Farm Machinery;
Antiques; Business; General

LYNNVILLE

Yager, David R.
Yager Auctioneers & Assoc.
Rt. 1, Box 69 (47619)
(812) 749-5434
General

MONTGOMERY

Wittmer, Amos M.
A.M. Wittmer Auction &
Realty
Route 2, Box 456 (47558)
(812) 486-3700
Farm; Household; Real Estate

MONTICELLO

Vogel, Philip L.
Vogel Real Estate
1001 N. Main Street (47960)
(219) 583-3981
Fax: (219) 583-6925
Real Estate; Farm;
Commercial; Antiques; Estates;
Household

NEW ALBANY

Grose, Sherman R.
Grose-A-Sales
3504 Green Valley Road
(47150)
(812) 944-8046
Real Estate; Estates;
Commercial

Harritt, Douglas A.
Douglas Harritt Auction
Services
4704 Corydon Pike (47150)
(812) 944-0217
(812) 923-3631
Estates; Household; Farms;
Antiques; Real Estate

NEW HARMONY

Wilson, William B.
William Wilson Auction/
Realty
Church & Main Streets
(47631)

(812) 682-4686
Real Estate; Farm Equipment;
Antiques

OXFORD

Schultze, Curtis
Farmcraft Service Inc.
Box 65 (47971)
(317) 385-2266
Fax: (317) 385-2670
Real Estate; Farm Machinery;
Antiques; Liquidation;
Household

PLYMOUTH

Goebel, Samuel W.
Oak Crest Realty
440 E. Jefferson St.
P.O. Box 395 (46563)
(219) 936-7616
(219) 936-7159
Real Estate; Estates; Farm;
Antiques; Liquidations;
General Household

QUINCY

Sutherlen, Verbia
Sutherlen Auction Service
Route 1, Box 84 (47456)
(317) 795-3169
Antique Glass; Antique China;
Linens

SALEM

Fletcher, Floyd M.
Fletcher RE Agency & Auction
Serv.
202 W. Market St. (47167)
(812) 883-4727
Antiques; Estates; Farm
Equipment; Household; Real
Estate; Commercial

SEYMOUR

Pollert, Fred M.
Pollert's Inc.
404 N. Chestnut St. (47274)
(812) 522-2112
(812) 523-8025
Fax: (812) 522-2192
Farm; Real Estate; Household

SHELBYVILLE

Scott, John R.
Route 8, Box 328A (46176)
(317) 729-5304
Farm Equipment; Household;
Antique

SHIPSHEWANA

Swartzentruber, Homer
Swartzentruber Realty
P.O. Box 331 (46565)
(219) 768-4621
(219) 768-4744
Quilts; Real Estate; Colctbles/
Antqs; Household; Estates;
Appraisals

STILESVILLE

Vaughn, J. Eric
P.O. Box 260 (46180)
(317) 539-2885
Construction Equip.; Land
Lease; Farm Equipment

VALPARAISO

Lacy, Phillip H.
Lacy Auction & Realty Co.
329 East Division Rd. (46383)
(219) 462-1402
Antiques; Real Estate; Estates;
Guitars; Tools

Iowa

ALBIA

Morehead, Gregory P.
Morehead Auction Company
25 South Clinton St. (52531)
(515) 932-7129
Real Estate; Estates; Farm;
Bus. Liquid.; Household

AUDUBON

Stewart, Wayne
Southwest Iowa Real Estate
Co.
417 S. Park
P.O. Box 265 (50025)
(712) 563-4288
(712) 563-2316
Fax: (712) 563-2111
Real Estate; Antiques;
Commercial

BUFFALO CENTER

Johnson, Roy B.
Mid Continent Auction
105 Circle Drive (50424)
(515) 562-2032
Real Estate; Liquidation;
Commercial; Industrial; Farm
Machinery; Antiques

CLINTON

Hamilton, William W.
Hamilton Auctions
2216 North Third Street
(52732)
(800) 222-8450
Fax: (319) 243-5828
Horticulture; Agriculture;
Estates; Real Estate; Bus.
Liquid.; Antiques

COUNCIL BLUFFS

DeWitt, Georges G.
DeWitt Auction Service
Rt. 3, Box 174E (51501)
(712) 328-8716
Farm; Business Liq.; Antique

CRESCO

Cummings, Richard L.
Erickson-Prochaska Inc.
Box 239 (52136)
(319) 547-3700
Real Estate; Livestock; Farm
Machinery

Erickson, Lyle (Retired)
Erickson-Prochaska Inc.
Box 239 (52136)
(319) 547-3700
Real Estate; Machinery;
Antiques; Dairy;
General

DES MOINES

Stewart, Bill A.
Bill Stewart Auctioneer
2405 Ingersol Ave. (50322)
(515) 244-1060
(515) 278-5153
Fax: (515) 244-1170
Real Estate; Antiques;
Household;
Business Liq.

FORT DODGE

Donnelly, James N.
Iowa Auction Sales Co., Inc.
RRD 2 F (50501)
(515) 573-5992
Fax: (515) 573-7296
Commercial; Real Estate;
Antiques &
Household

HEDRICK

Helgerson, Martin R.
Messerschmitt R.E. & Auction
Box 56 (52563)
(515) 653-4947
(515) 683-1915
Personal Prop.; Farm
Dispersion; Real
Estate

Messerschmitt, Wallace
Messerschmitt Real Estate &
Auction
107 W. Second St. (52563)
(515) 653-4947
Farm Equipment; Real Estate;
Household; Antiques

KEOSAUQUA

Huff, Jim D.
Howard Buckles Auctioneering
Serv.
1002 6th Street
Box 267 (52565)
(319) 293-3012
(319) 293-3711
Farm; Agricultural; Household;
Antique; Quilt; Real Estate

SANBORN

Vander Werff, Rich
Vander Werff Auctioneers, Inc.
Box 529, 215 Main (51248)
(712) 729-3264
Real Estate; Farm Equipment;
Commercial; Household

SOLON

Wears, Brent
Wears Auctioneering
R.R. 1, Box 360 (52333)
(319) 644-3779

Estates; Antique; Collectible;
Farm Sales; Real Estate; Bus.
Liquid.

Kansas

GOODLAND

Cole, Curtis C.
Cole Auction & Real Estate
1405 Main (67735)
(913) 899-2683
Farm Equipment; Real Estate;
Antiques; Commercial;
Bankruptcies; Household

HAYS

Legere, Don R.
Legere Auction & Realty, Inc.
1013 Main St. (67601)
(913) 625-2545
(913) 625-4411
Fax: (913) 625-8188
Real Estate; Farm, Ranch;
Liquidations;
Benefit Charity

HOLTON

Pagel, Wayne
Pagel, Inc. Realty & Auction
Box 6, No. Hwy 75 (66436)
(913) 364-2456
(913) 933-2233
Real Estate; Farm Equipment;
Antiques; Liquidations

JUNCTION CITY

Brown, Earl M.
Earl M. Brown RE & Auction
Service
709 N. Madison

Box 68 (66441)
(913) 762-2266
(913) 238-3432
Antiques; Farm Liq.; Business
Liq.

KANSAS CITY

Fair, Bill
Bill Fair & Company
903 W. 20th Terr. (66046)
(913) 842-9999
Fax: (913) 842-7133
Real Estate; Commercial Eq.;
Business Liq.

LAWRENCE

Gentry, Kathleen A.
Bill Fair & Company
903 W. 20th Terr. (66044)
(913) 842-9999
(913) 887-6448
Fax: (913) 842-1733
Commercial Equipment;
Business Liquidation;
Bankruptcy; Real Estate

LONGTON

Persinger, Ernest E.
Frontier Auction & Realty
Route 1
P.O. Box 18 (67352)
(316) 642-6665
Real Estate; Estates; Farm
Equipment; Antiques;
Livestock; Liquidations

MANHATTAN

Anderson, Milton D.
Anderson Realty and Auction
121-A S. 4th (66502)
(913) 776-4834
Real Estate; Farm Machinery;
Antiques; Commercial/Ind.;
Liquidations; Appraiser

Gannon, Vern A.
Gannon Auction Service
2917 Karen (66502)
(913) 539-2316
Real Estate; Antiques; General

OLATHE

Hampton, Richard W.
Traban Auction
517 Valley Road (66061)
(913) 764-0643
Commercial; Real Estate;
Estates

Porter, Roger L.
Cable Car Auction & Realty
Co.
P.O. Box 8 (66061)
(913) 782-8009
Industrial; Machinery; Personal
Prop.; Real Estate

OSBORNE

Bloomer, Robert A.
Auction One
P.O. Box 386 (67473)
(913) 346-2856
Fax: (913) 346-5554
Real Estate; Estates; Farm
Equipment; Antiques; Business
Liq.

Carlin, Wayne E.
Carlin's Auction & Real Estate
Box 310 (67473)
(913) 346-2687
(913) 346-5778
Real Estate; Farm Machinery;
Household; Antiques

SHAWNEE

Lindsay, Thomas J.
Lindsay Auctioneer Service
24375 W. 63rd (66226)
(913) 441-1557

Liquidations; Farm; Estate;
Real Estate; Antiques;
Specialty

ST. GEORGES

Wilson, Robert G.
Wilson Realty & Auction
Rt. 3 Box 276 (66535)
(913) 776-9237
Fax: (913) 776-9238
Real Estate; Farm Equipment;
Antiques; Commercial;
Household; Bus. Liquid.

WELLINGTON

Theurer, Larry J.
Theurer Auction Realty
318 N. Washington
P.O. Box 601 (67152)
(316) 326-7315
Fax: (316) 326-5357
Farm Land; Farm Equipment;
Residential RE; Antiques;
Business Liquidation;
Household & Estate

WICHITA

Bannon, Jeff W.
Jeff Bannon Auction & Realty
Inc.
946 North West Street (67203)
(316) 945-0491
Res/Com Farm RE; Appraisals;
Liquidations; Estates; RE
Buyer; Sales

Loveall, Rick L.
Loveall Auction Company
211 S. Illinois (67213)
(316) 943-5489
Com. Re. Estate; Res. Re.
Estate; Investments;
Appraisals; Consultants;
Liquidations

Weed, Jim W.
Jim Weed Auction-Real Estate
Assoc.
8100 South Bernice (67233)
(316) 524-7343
Real Estate; Commercial;
Estates; Business Liq.; Farm
Sales; Bankruptcy

Kentucky

ALBANY

Haddix, Walton R.
Clearfork Realty Company
Box 435
144 Cross Street (42602)
(606) 387-6456
(606) 387-5016
Fax: (606) 387-5775
Oil & Gas Properties;
Commercial Dev.;
Lake Property

BOWLING GREEN

Branstetter, Robert J.
Auction Concepts USA
66131 W. Ave. W, Bypass A
(42101)
(502) 782-2200
(502) 782-3843
Fax: (502) 843-8780
Real Estate; Farm Equipment;
Personal Prop.; Livestock

Hunt, Thomas R.
Thomas R. Hunt Auction &
Realty
66131 W. Ave. W, Bypass A
(42101)
(502) 782-2200
Fax: (502) 843-8780
Real Estate; Commercial;
Industrial; Farm; Specialty;
Estate Liquid.

BRANDENBURG

Howard, Bill
Bill Howard Realty & Auction
Route 2, Box 223 (40108)
(502) 422-2168
Estates; Real Estate; Farm
Machinery;
Livestock; Antiques;
Liquidations

BROOKSVILLE

Poe Wanda J.
Poe Auction Service
Box 208 (41004)
(606) 735-3173
Antiques; Collectibles;
Household;
Liquidations; Farm Equipment

DANVILLE

Durham, Johnny L.
Durham & Durham Realty &
Auction
135 N. Third Street (40422)
(606) 236-2770
(606) 332-7368
Real Estate; Antiques; Farm;
Estates; Bankruptcy;
Commercial

ELIZABETHTOWN

Bush, Randy
Crain Auction Co., Inc.
Joey Lee Bldg.
Public Square (42701)
(502) 765-7684
Fax: (502) 737-7787
Boats Marine Eq.; Real Estate;
Agri-Business; Farm
Machinery; Estates; Antiques

Crain, Frank N.
Crain Auction Co., Inc.
Public Square (42701)

(502) 765-7684
Fax: (502) 737-7787
Real Estate; Commercial RE;
Farmland RE; Industrial Liq.;
Boats & Marine Sales;
Antiques

FALMOUTH

Butcher, David L.
Butcher Realty & Auctions
114 Courthouse Square
(41040)
(606) 654-3628
Real Estate; Farm Equipment;
Antiques; Household

Sullivan, Marvin K.
Butcher & Sullivan Auctions
Courthouse Square
Rt. 4 (41040)
(606) 654-6065
Real Estate; General; Farm
Equipment; Antiques;
Collectibles

FLEMINSBURG

Lytle, Terry
Lytle Auctions & Real Estate
Rt. 2, Box 273A (41041)
(606) 845-3110
Real Estate; Estates; Farm
Machinery

FRANKLIN

Kirby, Ronald R. and Ron
Kirby, Jr.
Ron Kirby Auction & Realty
P.O. Box 285
518 N. Main Street (42134)
(502) 586-8288
Fax: (502) 586-8823
Real Estate (Commercial,
Industrial, Residential); Heavy
Equipment; Condominium;
Farm Division;

Automobiles; Heavy Trucks

Layne, Chuck
Layne Real Estate
P.O. Box 2814 (42134)
(502) 586-7171
Fax: (502) 586-1718
Real Estate; Commercial RE;
Industrial RE; Timberland;
Hotel/Motel; Residential RE

HARDINSBURG

Butler, Roy, Jr.
Roy Butler Auction & Realty
Co.
P.O. Box 365 (40143)
(502) 756-5859
Bankruptcy; Farm Land; Farm
Machinery; Residential;
Commercial; Livestock

Monarch, Miller
Monarch Auction & Realty
P.O. Box 188;
Old US Hwy. 60 East (40143)
(502) 756-2153
FAX: (502) 547-2100
Real Estate; Estates; Farm
Equipment; Bus. Liquid.

KUTTAWA

White, Dwain C.
Thomas White & Sons Auction
& RE
Box 355 (42055)
(502) 388-2420
Real Estate; Estates; Antiques;
Business Liq.; Farm Dispersal

White, Todd
Thomas White & Sons Auction
& RE
Box 355 (42055)
(502) 362-4033
Real Estate; Primitives

LEXINGTON

Blair, Bruce B.
Rector-Hayden Realtors
P.O. Box 13187 (40503)
(606) 274-4811
(606) 271-6909
Fax: (606) 277-3856
Real Estate; Pesonal Prop.;
Autos; Heavy
Equipment; Miscellaneous

Darlin, John
Main Auction Inc.
3540 Winding Drive (40517)
(606) 273-3133
Estates; Commercial;
Industrial; Real
Estate; Antiques; Heavy
Equipment

LONDON

Humfleet, Ray
Ray Humfleet Real Estate
P.O. Box 39 (40741)
(606) 878-7111
Real Estate; Constr. Equip.;
Farm Machinery

LOUISVILLE

Gribbins, Aleck
Gribbins, Inc.-Auctions/Real
Estate
2712 Crums Lane (40216)
(502) 447-9572
Estates; Real Estate; Bus.
Liquid.

Haley, Robert D.
River Realty & Auction Co.
215 Breckinridge Lane (40207)
(502) 893-6611
Fax: (502) 893-2181
Res. Real Estate; Commercial
RE; Estates; Antiques;
Business Liquidation

Helm, Harold H., II
River Realty & Auction Co.
215 Breckinridge Lane (40207)
(502) 893-6611
FAX: (502) 228-3515
Fax: (502) 893-2181
Real Estate

Lynch, Jim
Lynch Auction & Appraisal
Service
1186 East Broadway (40204)
(502) 589-9822
(502) 589-2242
Business Liq.; Real Estate;
Estates; Antiques

Price, Jim
Price Auction Co.
12211 Old Shelbyville Rd.
(40243)
(502) 244-1509
Real Estate; Personal Prop.

MONTICELLO

Dunnington, B.G.
Mid-America Realty & Auction
Route 5
Box 4 Unit 19 (42633)
(606) 348-9359
Fax: (606) 348-8820
Real Estate; Business
Liquidation;
Commercial RE; Timberland;
Antiques; Estates

Dunnington, Ronald G.
Mid-America Realty & Auction
Route 5
Box 4 Unit 19 (42633)
(606) 348-9359
Fax: (606) 348-8820
Real Estate; Business
Liquidation;
Commercial RE; Timberland;
Antiques; Personal Prop.

MT. VERNON

Ford, Sammy L.
Ford Brothers, Inc.
P.O. Box 1435 (40456)
(606) 256-4545
(800) 435-5454
Fax: (606) 256-4555
Real Estate; Business
Liquidation; Farm
Machinery; Dairy Cattle;
Antiques

MT. WASHINGTON

Wigginton, John
P. Wigginton Realty & Auction
Box 639-982 Bardstown Rd.
(40047)
(502) 955-6578
(502) 538-8362
Fax: (502) 955-6515
Real Estate; Personal Prop.;
Estates

NICHOLASVILLE

Watts, Kenneth E.
Watts Realtors & Auctioneers
908 South Main St. (40356)
(606) 885-3355
Real Estate; Antiques; Farm
Equipment; Estates

OWENSBORO

Daniel, Karlin K.
Kurtz Auction & Realty
Company
305 Frederica Street (42301)
(502) 926-8553
Fax: (502) 926-8574
Real Estate; Industrial Sales;
On Site Estate Sales; Car Sales

Deane, Silas E.
Kurtz Auction & Realty Co.
305 Frederica
Street
(42301)
(502) 926-8553
Fax: (502) 926-8574
Farms; Land Divisions; Farm
Machinery

Grimsley, Robert G.
Kurtz Auction & Realty Co.
305 Frederica Street (42301)
(502) 926-8553
Fax: (502) 926-8574
Real Estate; Condominiums

Kurtz, William B.
Kurtz Auction & Realty Co.
305 Frederica Street (42301)
(502) 926-8553
Fax: (502) 926-8574
Multi-Parcel RE; Farm RE;
Com./Ind RE;
Res. RE; Farm Machinery;
Antiques

O'Connor, John P.
O'Connor's Auctions & Realty
1733 E. 18th Street (42301)
(502) 685-2000
Fax: (502) 685-2000
Real Property; Est. Liquid.;
Farm Machinery; Antiques

Prestigiacomo, Gary T.
O'Connor Auction & Realty
228 Crabtree Ave (42301)
(502) 685-2000
(502) 684-9881
Fax: (502) 685-2000
Real Estate; Bankruptcy;
Liquidations; Estates

OWINGSVILLE

Wells, Gary L.
Gary Wells Auctioneers & RE
Rt. 1 (40360)
(606) 674-2453
Real Estate; Estate;
Commercial Bus.;
Resort Prop.

Wells, Glenda
Gary Wells Auctioneers & RE
Rt. 1 (40360)
(606) 674-2453
Real Estate; Estate;
Commercial Bus.;
Resort Prop.

PIKEVILLE

Gibson, William S.
Action Auction & Realty
1708 North Mayo (41501)
(606) 432-8181
(606) 478-9987
Fax: (606) 478-9838
Real Estate; Industrial;
Construction;
Liquidations; Mining Equip.;
Estates

PROVIDENCE

Gibson, John M.
Gibson Realty & Auction
Wallace Street (42450)
(502) 667-2660
Real Estate; Antiques; Farm
Equipment

RICHMOND

Wright, Billy R.
Bill Wright Realty & Auction
115 Bel Air (40475)
(606) 723-4917
Real Estate; Personal Prop.;
Antiques

SALYERSVILLE

Patrick, Bill
Bill Patrick Auctioneer
P.O. Box 148 (41465)
(606) 349-2731
Real Estate; Commercial;
Equipment; Estates; Personal
Prop.

SHELBYVILLE

Smith, H.B. (Barry)
H.B. Smith Auction Co.
1004 Main Street (40065)
(502) 633-2746
Fax: (502) 633-3431
Dairy Cattle; Farm Machinery;
Real Estate

Willard, Jimmy H.
Barry Smith Co.
1004 Main Street (40065)
(502) 633-2746
Fax: (502) 633-3431
Real Estate; Agri Business;
Liquidations

SHEPERDSVILLE

Thomason, D. Bruce
Thomason/Sohm Realty &
Auction
P.O. Box 722 (40165)
(502) 955-7342
Fax: (502) 543-5414
Real Estate; Estates; Antiques;
Farm Equipment; Livestock;
Household

SOMERSET

Ford, Danny R.
Ford Brothers, Inc.
211-B South Hwy. 27 (42501)
(606) 679-2212
(800) 526-9430
Fax: (606) 678-0669
Real Estate; Business
Liquidation; Farm
Machinery; Dairy Cattle;
Antiques

STANTON

Briggs, James O.
J.O. Briggs & KY Land Auction
P.O. Box 395 (40380)
(606) 663-2519
Real Estate; Farm Equipment;
Household

Louisiana

BATON ROUGE

Baudry, Thomas P.
Daye Realtors & Auctioneers
4310 Highland Rd. (70808)
(504) 769-1157
Fax: (504) 769-0921
Real Estate; Liquidations;
Const. Equip.; Bankruptcy

Corby, Peter C.
Daye Realtors & Auctioneers
4310 Highland Rd. (70808)
(504) 769-1157
Fax: (504) 769-0921
Real Estate; Liquidations

Daye, Jerry M., II
Daye Realtors & Auctioneers
4310 Highland Rd. (70808)

(504) 769-1157
Fax: (504) 769-0921
Real Estate; Financial;
Institution; Liquidation

KENNER

Gilmore, Dave E.
Gilmore Auction & Realty Co.
2110 I-10 Service Rd.
Suite 203 (70065)
(504) 443-1280
(504) 465-0525
Fax: (504) 443-1289
Real Estate; Commercial RE;
Business Liq.

MONROE

Babb, Keith W.
Keith Babb & Associates, Inc.
P.O. Box 4968 (71211)
(318) 343-6211
(318) 343-1887
Fax: (318) 343-6232
Business Liq.; Machinery;
Commercial RE;
Reg. Livestock; Estates

NEW ORLEANS

Mutz, Penny
Sencore Auction Service
20391 Chef Menteur Hwy.
(70129)
(504) 254-1601
Fax: (504) 254-4861
Real Estate; Consumer Invtry;
Land Motor Veh.; Heavy
Equipment; Machine & Ind.;
Marine

Mutz, Timothy L.
Sencore Auction Service
20391 Chef Menteur Hwy.
(70129)

(504) 254-1601
Fax: (504) 254-4861
Shipyards; Vessels; Support
Equipment;
Machine/Fabrication;
Inventories;
Vehicles, Trucks

SHREVEPORT

Wolfe, Lynn A.
Lynn Wolfe & Assoc.
Auctioneers
2026 Pitch Pine (71118)
(318) 688-9466
Business; Estate; Real Estate;
Personal

Maine

KENNEBUNK

Keating, James J., III
J.J. Keating Inc.
Route 1 North (04043)
(207) 985-2097
(207) 985-3721
Estate; Antique; Household;
Real Estate;
Commercial RE

Murphy, Joseph D.
Oliver & Murphy Auction Co.
Post Road Center (04043)
(207) 985-3330
(207) 883-3939
Fax: (207) 985-7734
Real Estate; Business Assets

KINGFIELD

Keenan, Richard J.
Keenan Auction Company
Main Street (04947)
(207) 265-2011
Fax: (207) 265-2607
Condominiums; Real Estate;
Heavy Equipment; Forestry
Equip.; Business Liq.

MECHANIC FALLS

McMorrow, Jody P.
McMorrow Auction Co.
Rt. 1, Box 825 (04256)
(207) 345-9477
Antiques; Estates; Commercial;
Surplus

TENANTS HARBOR

Erickson, Steve
Steve Erickson Auctioneers
P.O. Box 329 (04860)
(207) 372-6462
Antiques; Estates; Real Estate;
Commercial; Farm; Industrial

Maryland

ANNAPOLIS

Campbell, Richard
Robert H. Campbell & Assoc.
121 Prince Georges St. (29041)
(301) 263-5808
Boats; Personal Prop.; Cars;
Real Estate

Campbell, Robert H., II
Robert H. Campbell & Assoc.
229 Garden Gate (21403)
(301) 263-5808

Fax: (301) 263-8427
Real Estate; Household;
Antiques; Marine; Vehicles;
Equipment

BALTIMORE

Billig, Andrew L.
A.J. Billig & Co. Auctioneers
16 E. Fayette St. (21202)
(301) 752-8440
Real Estate; Commercial;
Industrial; Restaurant;
Household; Automobiles

Billig, Daniel M.
A.J. Billig & Co.
16 E. Fayette St. (21202-1789)
(301) 752-8440
Fax: (301) 385-1841
Real Estate; Industrial; Heavy
Equipment; Commercial;
Automobiles; Household

Cooper, Joseph A.
Alex Cooper Auctioneers
908 York Road (21204)
(301) 828-4838
Res. Re. Estate; Com. Re.
Estate; Antiques & Art;
Machinery

Fox, David S.
Michael Fox Auctioneers Inc.
3835 Naylors Lane (21208)
(301) 653-4000
Fax: (301) 653-4069
Plant Machinery &
Equipment; Real
Estate; Radio/TV; Com. Assets;
Vehicles

Fox, William Z.
Michael Fox Auctioneers Inc.
3835 Naylors Lane (21208)
(301) 653-4000

Fax: (301) 653-4069
Real Estate; Plant Machinery
& Equipment; Radio/TV;
Comml. Assets; Vehicles

Levinson, Bruce P.
Alex Cooper Auctioneers
908 York Road (21204)
(301) 828-4838
Antiques; Art; Rugs;
Commercial RE;
Residential RE

Makowski, Larry A.
Express Auction Service Inc.
7500 Eastern Ave. (21224)
(301) 285-3333
Fax: (301) 285-3362
Real Estate Alltype; Machinery
& Equip.; Jewelry; Estate
Furnishings;
Construction Equip.; Office
Furnishings

Meinick, Jonathan A.
Jonathan Meinick Auction
721 E. 25th Street (21218)
(301) 366-5555
Fax: (301) 366-5576
Real Estate; Machinery;
Restaurants; Vehicles; Estates/
Jewelry; Art

DENTON

Roe, Michael A.
Curtis Andrew Auction, Inc.
Route 2, Box 143-E (21629)
(301) 479-0756
Fax: (301) 754-5201
Personal Prop.; Farm
Equipment; Real
Estate; Construction Eq.;
Antiques

FOREST HILL

Rigdon, H. Benjamin
Rigdon Auctioneers
P.O. Box 625 (21050)
(301) 836-2787
Fax: (301) 836-2738
Real Estate; Automobiles;
Estates; Machinery;
Equipment

FREDERICK

Gross, Anne-Lynn
The Singing Auctioneer
P.O. Box 1412 (21702)
(301) 662-6183
Furniture; Jewelry; Glassware;
Antiques; Coins; Baseball
Cards

HOLLYWOOD

Thompson, Rodney
Homestead Auction Co.
36 Commerce Ave. (20636)
(301) 373-3333
(301) 373-2916
Antiques; General; Coins;
Guns; Real Estate

OWINGS MILL

Harding, Grant I.
Reistertown Auction
P.O. Box 215 (21117)
(301) 833-8780
FAX (301) 833-2794
Real Estate; Estates; Antiques;
Commercial; General; Business
Liq.

REISTERTOWN

McKay, John L., Sr. & Assoc.
Inc.
602 Westminster Rd. (21136)
(301) 521-4466
Estate; Household; Industrial;
Auto

RISING SUN

Hunter, Norman E.
Hunter's Sale Barn Inc.
P.O. Box 427 (21911)
(301) 658-6400
Fax: (301) 658-3864
Antiques; Real Estate; Business
Liquidators; Weekly
Consignment

TIMONIUM

Opfer, Richard W., Jr.
Richard Opfer Auctioneering,
Inc.
1919 Grenn Spring Dr. (21093)
(301) 252-5035
Fax: (301) 252-5863
Estates; Collections; Antiques;
Real Estate; Horses

TOWSON

Dance, Lee H.
Dance Auctioneers, Inc.
611 Bosley Ave. (21204)
(301) 823-3993
Fax: (301) 823-0006
Real Estate; Estate;
Consignment;
Specialty; Appraisals

TRAPPE

Nelson, Edward N.
Nelson Auction Gallery
P.O. Box 95, US Route 50
(21673)
(800) 876-3140
Fax: (301) 820-4598
Antiques; Estates; Art; Guns;
Collectibles; Real Estate

WALDORF

Thomas, Robert P.
Arbor Real Estate & Auction
Co.
Route 925 North
Box 278 (20601)
(301) 449-4444
(301) 843-0442
Fax: (301) 248-6216
Real Estate; Estates;
Commercial

Massachusetts

CANTON

Gavrilles, Evan N.
Gabriel's Auction Co., Inc.
611 Neponset St. (02021)
(617) 821-2992
Fax: (617) 821-6084
Estates; Antiques;
Consignments;
Commercial; Real Estate;
Appraisals

HANOVER

Caddigan, Joan F.
Caddigan Auctioneers, Inc.
1130 Washington St. (02339)
(617) 826-8648
Fax: (617) 826-2438
Antiques; Antique Tools;
Vintage Clothes; Toys; Dolls

NORTH ATTLEBORO

Moon, William F.
William F. Moon & Co.
12 Lewis Rd.
RFD#1 (02760)
(508) 699-4477
Fax: (508) 761-9877
Antiques; Household; Real
Estate;
Storage; Equipment

NORTH EASTHAM

Fidalgo, Bill
Eastham Auction House
145 Holmes Rd. (02651)
(508) 255-9003
(508) 255-1344
Estate; Personal Prop.; Amer.
19, 20th century Art; Real
Estate

OXFORD

Torteson, James R.
10 Hope Avenue (01540)
(508) 987-2277
Estates; Commercial;
Appraisals;
Benefit; Marine; Real Estate

SOUTH DEERFIELD

Bilodeau, Doris A.
Douglas Auctioneers
Route 5 (01373)
(413) 665-2877
(413) 665-3530
FAX (413) 665-2877
Antiques; Estates; Real Estate;
Commercial

WORCESTER

Jacobson, Harvey A.
Harvey A. Jacobson Assoc., Inc.
390 Main St.

Suite 659 (01608)
(508) 755-2550
(508) 756-4708
Estate; Commercial Auctions;
Industrial Auctions

W. BROOKFIELD

Potvin, Robert L.
Potvin Auction & Realty
29 West Main Street (01585)
(508) 867-3346
Rare Coins U.S.; Antiques;
Real Estate; Postage Stamps;
Clocks; Houses

Michigan

ALPENA

Boyk, John S.
Boyks' Auctioneering Service
7878 Cathro Rd. (49707)
(517) 356-9589
Farm; Real Estate; Household

ANN ARBOR

Braun, Lloyd
Braun and Helmer
5155 Jennings Road (48105)
(313) 665-9646
Real Estate; Antiques;
Household; General

BELLEVUE

Spaulding, Larry R.
Belcher-Dingman-Spaulding
Auctrs.
124 N. Main (49021)
(616) 763-9494
Real Estate; Farm; Antiques;
General

BIRMINGHAM

Williams, Robert R.
Williams & Lipton Company
325 South Woodward Ave.
(48009)
(313) 646-7090
Fax: (313) 646-7093
Metalworking Mach.; Plastics
Equipment;
Earthmoving Machine;
Commercial Concerns

BRONSON

Wilber, Garth W.
Wilber Auction Service Inc.
211 Gilead Lake Rd. (49028)
(517) 369-5455
Industrial; Commercial; Real
Estate; Farm; Household;
Antiques

CHARLOTTE

Stanton, Christopher F.
Stanton's Real Estate &
Auctioneers
6462 W. Lawrence (48813)
(517) 726-0181
(517) 543-0598
Fax: (517) 726-0060
Antiques; Real Estate; Farm
Machinery; Heavy Machinery

CLINTON

Halchisbak, Steve
Halchisbak Auction Service
120 Clinton Street (49236)
(517) 456-7706

COMSTOCK PARK

Burns, Daniel
Burns Auction Service
500 Ten Mile Road N.E.
(49321)
(616) 887-7237
Real Estate; Antiques; Estates;
Farms

EDWARDSBURG

Berg, Roger S.
23675 North Shore Drive
(49112)
(616) 699-5584
Industrial; Commercial;
Liquidations; Estates

ESSEXVILLE

Van Sumeren, Dan
Dan Van Sumeren & Assoc.
519 W. Center Road (48732)
(517) 894-2859
Industrial; Commercial; Real
Estate; Liquidations; Farm;
Appraisals

FRANKENMUTH

Hecht, Gerald W.
Hecht Auction Service
9849 Bradley Road (48734)
(517) 652-2242
Farm Equipment; Household;
Estate; Commercial

GALESBURG

Schowalter, John D.
Schowalter/Horton Auctioneers
1541 N. 30th Street
(49053)
(616) 349-9400
Antiques; Real Estate; Farm;
General

HEMLOCK

Besner, Gwyn
Besner Auction Team
13785 Swan Creek (48626)
(517) 642-8158
Antique; Ind./Commercial;
Railroadiana;
Estate; Real Estate;
Consignment

KALAMAZOO

Horton, E.J. (Doc)
Schowalter/Horton Auctioneers
1541 North 30th Street
(49053)
(616) 349-9400
Real Estate; Estates; Apt.
Rental; Industrial; Commercial

LINWOOD

Ballor, Bill
Bill Ballor Auction Service
210 N. First St.
P.O. Box 249 (48634)
(517) 697-4212
(517) 893-7368
Fax: (517) 697-3355
Antiques; Estates; Asset
Recovery;
Personal Property

MASON

Good, Arthur L. (Retired)
Coldwell Banker Cedar
321 N. Cedar Street (48854)
(517) 676-4433
Fax: (517) 676-4371
Real Estate

Reeser, Steve L.
Steve Reeser Associates
1465 N. Cedar (48854)
(517) 699-2210
Fax: (517) 699-3064

Commercial; Construction;
Real Estate; Estates

Sheridan, Bill
Sheridan Auction Service Inc.
3175 Sitts Rd. (48854)
(517) 468-3500
(517) 676-2503
Fax: (517) 676-5400
Livestock; Machinery; Real
Estate; Antique

OKEMOS

Howe, Robert E., Jr.
Heritage Auction Firm
4256 Indian Glen (48864)
(517) 349-3553
Fax: (517) 349-7922
Jewelry; Antiques; Real Estate;
Coins; Estates

PLYMOUTH

Whalen, John
Whalen Real Estate & Auction
Co.
5844 Gotfredson Rd. (48170)
(313) 459-5144
Real Estate; Liquidations;
Estates; Farm

SAGINAW

Butler, Rodney G.
Butler Auction Service
630 S. Frost Dr. (48603)
(517) 799-4181
(517) 799-2324
Industrial; Commercial;
Estates; Antiques

SALINE

Helmer, Jerry L.
Braun & Helmer Auction
Service
7171 E. Michigan Ave. (48176)
(313) 944-6309
Real Estate; Farm; Antiques;
Household; General

TRAVERSE CITY

Bright, Fred
Woody's Auction
1190 North Carriage Hill
(49684)
(616) 922-2380
(616) 947-1351
Fax: (616) 938-9820
Real Estate

Horst, Devon A.
Woody's Auction Service
2751 N. US 31 South (49684)
(616) 946-0647
(616) 946-9663
Fax: (616) 947-7653
Baukruptcies; Antiques; Real
Estate; Estates

VASSAR

Albrecht, Herbert J.
Albrecht Auction Service Inc.
3884 Saginaw Road (48768)
(517) 823-8835
Farm Equipment; Commercial;
Real Estate; Antiques; Estates

Minnesota

ATWATER

Hawkinson, Gayle L.
Little Hawk Auction Co.
4600-165th St N.E. (56209)
(612) 974-8040

Estates; Real Estate;
Automobiles; Farm;
Household; Antiques

INVER GROVE HGTS.

Laumeyer, Wally
Wally Laumeyer Auction
3324 E. 75th Court
(55076)
(612) 455-9547
(813) 549-4955
Real Estate

JACKSON

Pike, Dan J.
Auctioneer Alley
Rt. 1, Box 39 (56143)
(507) 847-3468
Real Estate; Farm Equipment;
Const. Equipment; Fertilizer
Equip.; Antiques

LONG PRAIRIE

Burt, Quinten L.
Burt's Auction Service
RR 1, Box 60 (56347)
(612) 732-6320
Farm Equipment; Livestock;
Household; Antiques; Estates;
Real Estate

OSSEO

Christian, Greg J.
Quickie Auction House
19150 Territorial Road (55369)
(612) 428-2271
Fax: (612) 428-8355
Commercial; Industrial; Real
Estate; Food Service; Estate

PALISADE

Reinhardt, Carol E.
Reinhardt Auction Service

Route 2, Box 1790 (56469)
(218) 845-2260
Real Estate; Livestock;
Commercial;
Antiques

Reinhardt, Stephen R.
Reinhardt Auction Service
Route 2, Box 1790 (56469)
(218) 845-2260
Real Estate; Livestock;
Commercial; Antiques

PELICAN RAPIDS

Seifert, Loren M.
Seifert Auction & Realty Co.
Rt.#4 Box 111B (56572)
(218) 863-5936
(218) 863-1555
Farm; Antique-Household;
Business Liquidation; Real
Estate

PRINCETON

Pike, Wayne
Wayne Pike Auction Co.
P.O. Box 387 (55371)
(612) 389-2700
Fax: (612) 389-1767
Heavy Equipment; Farm;
Livestock; Real
Estate; Auto; Antiques

RED WING

Houghton, Richard E.
Houghton's Auction Service
1967 Launa Ave. (55066)
(612) 388-5870
General Auction; Farms &
Livestock; Household; Pottery;
Coins; Real Estate

ROCHESTER

Kruesel, John
John Kruesel's Gnl Mdse/Auct.
Co.
22 3rd Street S.W. (55902)
(507) 289-8049
Fax: (507) 288-4412
Antiques; Estates; Lighting;
Jewelry; Real Estate; Military
& Ant. Veh.

ROGERS

Christian, David
Quickie Auction House
22895 141st Ave. N. (55374)
(612) 428-4217
Fax: (612) 428-8355
Furniture; Food Service;
Commercial Bus.; Art (Indian);
Consignment; Farm

ST. CLOUD

Imholte, Frank B.
Black Diamond Auctions
8160 Co. Rd. 138 (56301)
(612) 255-9398
(612) 251-8208
Fax: (612) 363-4706
Farm Equip.; Real Estate;
Estate; Household;
Commercial Liq.

UPSALA

Schultz, Michael K.
Schultz Auctioneers
Box 306 (56384)
(612) 573-2468
Farm Machinery; Livestock;
Real Estate;
Antique; Estate

Mississippi

GULFPORT

Mozingo, John C. Jr.
Mozingo Real Estate, Inc.
549 E. Pass Road
P.O. Box 6641 (39507)
(601) 896-3400
(800) 874-2761
Fax: (601) 896-1927
Real Estate; Asset Recovery;
ORE Mult-Prop.

HOLLY SPRINGS

Utley, Stephen A.
Utley Realty Service
105 Van Dorn Ave. (Court
Square)
(38635)
(601) 252-5200
(800) 542-5666
Farm/Ranch RE; Small
Acreage; Houses

Utley, Walter A.
Utley Realty Service
105 Van Dorn Avenue (38635)
(601) 252-5200
(800) 542-5666
Real Estate; Appraisals; Farm
Equipment;
Resort Property; Commercial

Missouri

ASHLAND

Sapp, Glen E.
Sapp Auction Co.
Route 2, Box 429 (65010)
(314) 657-9072
Automobiles; Real Estate;
Antiques; Horses; Household;
Farm

COLUMBIA

Atterberry, Larry P.
Atterberry & Assoc. Auct. Co.
7912 I-70 Drive S.E. (65201)
(314) 474-9295
(314) 474-6457
Real Estate; Antiques; Estates;
Farm Equipment; Commercial;
Liquidation

Cornell, Larry J.
Kirskville Auto Auction
309 Bingham Rd. (65203)
(314) 474-7006
(314) 449-3991
Automobiles; Real Estate;
Personal Prop.

EXCELSIOR SPRINGS

Ryther, Gary D.
Gary Ryther Auctioneers, Inc.
1745 W. Jesse James Rd.
(64024)
(816) 637-4044
Fax: (816) 637-5545
Real Estate; Industrial;
Commercial;
Antiques; Farm; Household

HARRISBURG

Voorheis, Brent
Voorheis & Auction Realty
10877 North Route J (65256)
(314) 874-5988
Real Estate; Machinery;
Antiques; Commercial

HAYTI

Walker, E. Lance
Walker Auctions
202 S. Third St. (63851)
(901) 758-1621
Fax: (314) 359-1319
Charity/Fund Raising; Real
Estate; Estate; Business
Liquidation

HIGGINSVILLE

Campbell, John M.
Campbell Enterprises, Inc.
15 W. 21st (64037)
(816) 584-7653
Antiques; Estates; Farm
Machinery; Real
Estate; Household;
Commercial

KANSAS CITY

Dewees, Paul J.
Missouri Auction School
1600 Genessee (64102)
(816) 421-7117
Fax: (816) 421-4444
Auctioneer/Attorney;
Nationwide;
Auction Referral

LEBANON

Coleman, Bennie O.
Coleman Auction, Realty &
Insurance
Rt. 3, Box 416 (65536)
(417) 532-3208
Real Estate; Farm; Household;
Livestock;
Business Liquidation;
Consignments

MADISON

Johnston, James L.
Johnston Auction & Real
Estate
RR 2, Box 266 (65263)
(816) 291-5921
Antiques; Real Estate; Business
Liq.; Machinery

SPRINGFIELD

Brown, Gary
Bestway Auctions
6260 W. Hwy. 60 (65619)
(417) 865-0566
Fax: (417) 865-0596
Real Estate; Bus. Liquid.;
Industrial; Commercial

Kollmeier, Robert L.
Billy Long Auctioneers &
Realtors
4128 S. Broadway (65807)
(417) 882-5664
Real Estate; Antiques;
Machinery;
Household

Long, Billy
Billy Long Auctioneers &
Realtors
1950-L S. Glenstone (65804)
(417) 882-5664
Fax: (417) 882-7653
Real Estate; Estates; Antiques;
Farm; Business Liquidation;
Commercial

ST. LOUIS

Wilber, Garth
Burdette National Industrial
Services Inc.

5585 Pershing Suite 200
(63112)
(314) 454-1300
Industrial; Commercial; Real
Estate

Montana

BILLINGS

Ellis, Jerry R.
Ellis Auction Sales
P.O. Box 50310 (59105)
(406) 245-3519
Farm; Real Estate; Heavy
Equipment

Nebraska

ATKINSON

Fleming, Dean W. (Retired)
Fleming Realty & Auction
Company
East Highway 20, Box 337
(68713)
(402) 925-2802
Real Estate; Livestock; Farm;
Antiques

AUBURN

Caspers, Marvin
Marvin Caspers Real Estate/
Auction
RFD 1, Box 104 (68305)
(402) 274-5660
Real Estate; Farm Equipment;
Antiques; Furniture;
Household; Liquidations

COLUMBUS

Baum, Ted
Elgin Livestock Sales
RR2-7 Clearlake (68601)
(402) 563-3600
(402) 843-8875
Livestock; Auto; Farm; Estates;
Real Estate; Antiques

Morris, Wayne
Morris Auctioneers
P.O. Box 186 (68602)
(402) 564-6313
Industrial; Commercial

FREMONT

Nitz, Jack R.
Jack Nitz & Associates
Auctioneers
Box 1522, S. Hwy. 77 &
Ridgeland Rd.
(68025)
(402) 727-8800
Fax: (402) 727-8805
Farm Equipment; Real Estate;
Trucks; Commercial;
Industrial; Livestock

Nitz, Jay D.
Jack Nitz & Associates
Auctioneers
Box 1522, S. Hwy. 77 &
Ridgeland Rd.
(68025)
(402) 727-8800
Fax: (402) 727-8805
Farm Machinery; Real Estate;
Trucks; Commercial;
Industrial; Livestock

GRAND ISLAND

Garey, E.M.
The Garey Co. Real Estate &
Auction
1610 Parkview Dr. (68801)
(308) 384-9011
Household; Real Estate;
Antiques;
Commercial

HOOPER

Thomsen, Charles
Don Peterson & Associates
RR 2 (68031)
(402) 721-9700
(402) 654-2464
Fax: (402) 721-0109
Personal Prop.; Farm
Equipment; Real
Estate

LINCOLN

Fleming, Randy
Great Plains Realty-Auction
Co.
941 'O' St., Ste. 1020
Terminal Bldg (68508)
(402) 474-7324
Fax: (402) 474-0392
Com. Real Estate; Farmland;
Benefit Auction; Business Liq.

MADISON

Blank, Warren R.
Bill Blank Agency Inc.
117 S. Main Street (68748)
(402) 454-2500
Farm Machinery; Commercial;
Real Estate; Antiques

NEWMAN GROVE

Fowlkes, Dennis F.
Fowlkes Realty & Auction Co.
P.O. Box 471 (68758)
(402) 447-6113
Farm Equipment; Real Estate;
Automobiles; Antiques

OMAHA

Anderson, Steven B.
Anderson Auction Inc.
11662 Sunburst (68164)
(402) 397-5008
Commercial; Real Estate;
Estate

Hunter, Michael J.
Target Auctioneers, Inc.
4532 S. 24th Street
(68107)
(402) 733-9025
Fax: (402) 733-9121
Business Liquidation; Heavy
Equipment; Real Estate;
Trucks

Standley, Dale E.
Standley Auction & Realty
P.O. Box 3186 (68108)
(402) 345-1117
Real Estate; Commercial;
Estates; Vehicles; Antiques;
Heavy Equipment

YORK

Green, Norm
Norm Green Realty & Auction
P.O. Box 563
104 So. Lincoln Ave. (68467)
(402) 362-5595
Fax: (402) 362-4875
Real Estate; Farm Equipment;
Const. Equip.; Bankruptcy;
Antiques

Nevada

LAS VEGAS

Deiro, G. Robert
Robert Deiro & Associates
333 Rancho Dr. #626 (89106)
(702) 646-6077
Fax: (702) 648-9490
Real Estate; Gaming Eq.;
Construction; Aircraft;
Automobiles; Weapons

Nelson, Eric
Eric Nelson Auctioneering
4550 W. Oakey #111 (89102)
(702) 877-0878
(702) 871-4777
Fax: (702) 877-4570
Real Estate

New Hampshire

CHICHESTER

Martin, Kenneth, Jr.
Yankee School of
Auctioneering
RR2, Box 1335 Land Road
(03263)
(603) 798-4257
(800) 745-1257
Fax: (603) 798-4965
Real Estate; Antiques; Boats;
Benefit; RWO-Sealed Bid;
Comm. Indust.

CONCORD

Wallenstein, Christopher
Auctionworld, Inc.
5 South State St. (03301)
(603) 225-8808
(800) 521-7653
Fax: (603) 229-0078

Real Estate; Antiques;
Commercial;
Industrial; Estates

DOVER

Callioras, Peter C.
Circle Lee Real Estate
Calef Highway (Lee) (03820)
(603) 868-1070
(603) 868-7505
Fax: (603) 868-2695
Estates; Commercial; Real
Estate; Firearms; Automobiles;
Antiques

Maroney, Douglas E.
America's Auctioneer
P.O. Box 6110 (03820)
(603) 743-3100
(800) 272-7355
Fax: (603) 743-6559
Business Liquidation; Real
Estate; Restaurant Equip.;
Antiques; Appraiser; Estate
Settlements

EPSOM

Foster, Georges S., III
The Complete Auction Service
Route 28, Box 361 (03234)
(603) 736-9240
Estates; Antq/Collectibl; Real
Estate; Commercial; Industrial;
Appraisals

HAMPTON FALLS

McInnis, Paul
Paul McInnis Inc.
356 Exeter Road (03844)
(603) 778-8989
Fax: (603) 772-7452
Real Estate; Antiques; Estates;
Auction Gallery; Bus. Liq.

NEW LONDON

Sanders, Emory
Sanders & Mock Associates,
Inc.
Shaker Road (03257)
(603) 526-6326
Fax: (603) 526-6613
Real Estate; Institutional;
Commercial; Antiques

SO. EFFINGHAM

Byers, Deirdre G.
Scofield Auctions Inc.
Rt. 1, Box 178
Colcord Hill Rd. (03882)
(603) 539-6619
Fax: (603) 539-5123
Estates; Coins; Antiques;
Stamps; Orientalia; Jewelry

Scofield, Stephen H.
Scofield Auctions Inc.
Rt. 1, Box 178
Colcord Hill Rd. (03882)
(603) 539-6619
Fax: (603) 539-5123
Estates; Antiques; Coins;
Orientalia; Stamps;
Liquidations

TAMWORTH

Mock, Wayne
Sanders & Mock Associates
Box 37 (03886)
(603) 323-8749
Antiques; Art; Estates; Real
Estate; Commercial; Industrial

WILTON

Sanders, Rodney A.
Sanders Auctioneers, Inc.
Rt. 101 (03086)
(603) 654-6690
Antiques; Estates; Real Estate

New Jersey

CLINTON

Spann, Max E.
Max Spann Auction Company
12 Leigh Street
P.O. Box 5017 (08809)
(908) 735-8866
(908) 537-6110
Fax: (908) 735-8937
Land; Commercial;
Residential; Estates;
Farm; Industrial

FLEMINGTON

Kachmar, John P.
Kachmar Auction Service
101 Leffler Hill Rd. (08822)
(201) 782-4271
Antiques; Commercial;
Automobiles

FREEHOLD

Koty, Bob
Bob Koty Professional Auctrs./
Appr.
P.O. Box 625 (07728)
(908) 780-1265
Estates; Res. Contents;
Antiques; Moving/Storage;
Schools; Real Estate

LONG BRANCH

Costanzo, Peter
Peter Costanzo Auctioneers
Inc.
671 Broadway (07740)
(201) 229-2530
Rolling Stock; Equip./Machine;
Real Estate; Bldg. Materials;
Inventories;
Estate/Fine Art

MONROEVILLE

Dubin, David W.
Garden State Auction Co.
R2 Box 147B (08343)
(609) 358-8433
Fax: (609) 697-4255
Personal Property; Antiques;
Collectibles; Jewelry;
Hummels; Art

PORT MONMOUTH

Barbiere, Charles J.
Chestnut Realty
2 Gordon Court (07758)
(908) 495-9383
Racing Pigeons; Animals;
Music Stores;
Liquidations; General

New Mexico

ALBUQUERQUE

Dance, Joan (Retired)
P.O. Box 72156 (87195)
(505) 843-6587
Antiques; General; Real Estate

Dance, Steve (Retired)
P.O. Box 72156 (87195)
(505) 843-6587
Antiques; Personal Property,
Real Estate, Equipment

New York

ALDEN

Bontrager, Alferd
Alferd Bontrager Realtor
13238 Broadway (14004)
(716) 937-3323

Fax: (716) 937-9393
Real Estate; Household;
Estates; Antiques; Farm

AMENIA

Luther, David D.
David D. Luther Auctioneers
P.O. Box 77, East Main St.
(12501)
(914) 373-8215
(914) 373-9900
Farm; Real Estate; Antiques;
Estates; Commercial; Industrial

APO

Frame, John L.
10th MAS PSC
Box 944 (09860)
Real Estate; Farm Machinery;
Estates;
Commercial; Livestock

BAYSIDE

Altshuler, Mark
Tri-State Sales Co
35-28 209th (11361)
(718) 229-5812
Real Estate; Antiques; Jewelry

BERGEN

Wilcox, Craig H.
Harris Wilcox, Inc.
17 S. Lake St. (14416)
(716) 494-1880
Real Estate; Cattle; Farm
Machinery;
Business Liq.; Antique;
Household

BINGHAMTON

Benjamin, Alan J.
Col. Al Benjamin & Co.
131 Sherwood Ave. (13903)
(607) 722-2449
Commercial; Real Estate;
Liquidations

Monasky, Richard F.
Dick Monasky & Co.
34 Chenango St. (13902)
(607) 723-0466
Commercial; Industrial;
Municipal; Real
Estate; Estates

Walker, Andrew S.
Andy Walkers Auction
Unlimited
134 Elaine Dr. (13905)
(607) 775-1447
Antiques; Estates; Equipment;
Real Estate; Autos; Sporting
Goods

BROOKLYN

Medow, Stuart L.
Stuart L. Medow & Associates
2935 W. 5th St. (11224)
(718) 996-2405
Jewelry; Automobiles;
Antiques/Art;
Bankruptcy; Commercial Liq.;
Real Estate

ENDICOTT

DiLorenzo, Ron L.
Farrier & Ives Ltd.
P.O. Box 732 Union Station
(13760)

(607) 754-2277
Fax: (607) 754-2475
Commercial; Industrial;
Equipment;
Bankruptcies; Real Estate;
Liquidations

FALCONER

Ludwig, Charles L.
Ludwig Auction & Realty
Service
15 Cross Street (14733)
(716) 665-6614
Fax: (716) 665-6617
Estates; Antiques; Real Estate;
Business Liq.; Appraisals;
Consignments

FINDLEY LAKE

Howard, Peter S.
Howard/Reimold Comp.
Realty & Auction Service
P.O. Box 496 (14736-0496)
(716) 769-7447
Fax: (716) 769-7447
Real Estate; Industrial;
Commercial; Estates; Farms;
Nursery

FISHKILL

Doyle, Robert A.
Absolute Auction & Realty
137 Osborne Hill Rd. (12524)
(914) 896-9492
Fax: (914) 896-5874
Real Estate; Commercial; Liq.;
Estates; Appraisals; Antiques;
Bankruptcies

FULTON

Wheeler, Ronald L.
Family Auction Center
RD5, Route 57 South

Box 327 (13069)
(315) 695-2059
(315) 593-3738
Fax: (315) 695-4745
Liquidations; Personal
Property; Real
Estate; Vehicles; New
Merchandise; General

GENEVA

Hessney, Joseph D.
Hessney's Antique & Auction
Gallery
473 Exchange St. (14456)
(315) 789-9349
Estates; Antiques;
Liquidations;
Households; Collections

GROTON

Munson, Glenn P.
Glenn H. Munson & Son
Box 127
448 Locke Road (13073)
(607) 898-3739
(607) 898-3928
Fax: (607) 898-3323
Real Estate; Estate; Antiques

HOLTSVILLE-LONG ISLAND

Worsoe, Tor J.
Tor J. Worsoe Auctioneers
P.O. Box T
997 Waverly Ave. (11742)
(516) 289-0555
(516) 289-0201
Fax: (516) 289-0201
Commercial; Industrial;
Residential; Estates;
Real Estate; Appraiser

KINGSTON

Cole, George W.
Geo. Cole Auctioneers &
Appraisers
34 Stuyvesant St. (12401)
(914) 338-2367
(914) 876-5215
18th & 19th Century
Furniture; Furniture;
China; Glassware; R.E.;
Estates

LAKE GROVE

Slough, Marianne D.
Marianne D. Slough, Inc.
29 Moriches Rd. (11755)
(516) 467-0423
Estates; Jewelry; Household

LOCKPORT

Goldsmith, Robert
Goldsmith's Grand Auction
Gallery
6221 Fisk Rd. (14094)
(716) 625-9600
Inventories; Machinery;
Antiques; Art

LYONS

Gansz, Duane E.
Gansz Auction & Realty
14 William St. (14489)
(315) 946-6241
Fax: (315) 946-6747
Estates; Antiques; Farm;
Commercial; Real Estate

NEWARK

Reynolds, John T.
Reynolds Auction Co.
P.O. Box 508 (14513)
(315) 331-8815
Fax: (315) 331-1053

Business Liq.; Commercial;
Industrial; Municipal Dist.;
Real Estate; Estates

ONEONTA

Accurso, Rexford J.
Rex's Auction Service, Inc.
RD 2, Box 289A (13820)
(607) 433-1824
(607) 433-1220
Bankruptcies; Whls, used cars;
Antique cars; Collector cars;
Estates; Real Estate

PHOENIX

Brzostek, Bernard J.
Brzostek's Auction Srvc., Inc.
2052 Lamson Road (13135)
(315) 678-2542
(800) 562-0660
Fax: (315) 678-2579
Real Estate; Antiques; Estates;
Vehicles; Commercial; Liq.

RANDOLPH

Matson, David A.
Matson Auction & Real Estate
Co.
147 Main St. (14772)
(716) 358-6752
Real Estate; Machinery;
Equipment; Commercial;
Antiques; Benefit

Matson, Robert W.
Matson Auction & Real Estate
Co.
147 Main St. (14772)
(716) 358-6752
Real Estate; Machinery;
Equipment; Commercial;
Antiques; Benefit

SANDY CREEK

Janacek, Roland H.
Janacek Auction Sales
9298 N. Main St. (13145)
(315) 387-3194
Farm; Commercial; Real
Estate; Antiques

SARATOGA SPRINGS

Joki, Robert
Joki Auctioneers & Appraisers
674 Lake Ave. (12866)
(518) 584-5548
Antique; Estates; 19th C.
Furn.; Quilts;
Ephemera; Appl. Res. Content

TROY

Passonno, Hannelore
Uncle Sam Auctions
& Realty
225 Pinewoods Avenue Rd.
(12180)
(518) 274-6464
(518) 272-4143
Fax: (518) 272-7189
Real Estate; Estates;
Machinery & Eq.;
Antiques; Industrial; Farm/
Fund Raiser

Passonno, Ralph
Uncle Sam Auctions
& Realty
225 Pinewoods Avenue Rd.
(12180)
(518) 274-6464
(518) 272-4143
Fax: (518) 272-7189
Real Estate; Estates;
Machinery & Eq.;
Antiques; Industrial; Farm/
Fund Raiser

WALTON

Lambrecht, Dale
Lambrecht Auction Service
Rt 3, Box 307 (13856)
(607) 865-6951
Antiques; Real Estate;
Machinery; Household; Estates

WATERLOO

Cuddeback, Chester
Cuddeback's Auction Service
31 E. Main St. (13165)
(315) 539-9346
Estates; Real Estate; Antiques;
Household; Equipment;
Consignment

WEST NYACK

Knapp, Dorothy
Dorothy Knapp & Asso., Inc.
158 Germonds Road (10994)
(914) 623-5710
Estates; Antiques; Books;
Household; Jewelry; Silver

WILLIAMSVILLE

Cunningham, Cash
Cash Realty of NY, Inc.
22 Lafayette Blvd. (14221)
(716) 633-2274
(716) 836-4540
Fax: (716) 633-5209
Real Estate

North Carolina

ALBERMARLE

Boyd, John G., Jr.
Gary Boyd Auction & Real
Estate
P.O. Box 352 (28001)
(204) 982-5633

Fax: (704) 983-6929
Farm Equipment; Farm Liq.;
Business Liq.; Antiques;
Real Estate Auctions

ASHEBORO

King, John D., Jr.
J.D. King Realty & Auction
Co.
529-A S. Church St. (27203)
(919) 626-4400
Real Estate; Personal Prop.;
Liq.; Timber, Estates,
Appraisals

BAILEY

Stone, Tony R.
Stone Auction & Realty
Box 250 (27807)
(919) 235-4636
(919) 235-2200
Fax: (919) 235-2884
Real Estate; Farm Equip.;
Construction; Commercial

BURLINGTON

Tate, Harvey L.
Southern Caswell Auctioneers
Route 2, Box 208 (27215)
(919) 421-3282
Farm Equipment; Estates;
Personal Prop.; Real Estate

CHARLOTTE

Curlee, Ernest J.
American Auction Assoc. Inc.
9327-B Albermarle Road
(28227)
(704) 535-1724
(704) 537-5115
Estates; Office Furn.; Antiques;
Liq.; Real Estate; Gallery Sales

Lawing, W. Craig
Lawings Auction Company
5521 Brookshire Blvd. (28216)
(704) 399-6372
(800) 632-3043
Fax: (704) 399-1341
Vehicles; Heavy Equipment;
Real Estate;
Farm Equipment; Business
Equipment

Lilly, Bobby R.
Lilly Auction & Realty Co.
4500 Drifter Dr. (28227)
(704) 545-6377
Antiques; Estates, Real
Estate, Farm Equipment,
Business Equipment

Marshall, Gail Y.
Auctions By Marshall, Inc.
6500 Sharon Hills Road
(28210)
(704) 553-0029
Restaurants; Bank Equip.; Real
Estate; Heavy equip.; Textile
equip.; Art/Antiques

CONCORD

Gailimore, C.D.
AMC Auction & Appraisal Co.
160 Glendale Ave., S.E.
P.O. Box 306 (28025)
(800) 782-3011
(704) 782-3111
Fax: (704) 782-7979
Real Estate; Commercial;
Estates; Antique; Hosiery
Mills; Super Markets; Gen.

CRESWELL

Forbes, William R., Jr.
Bill Forbes & Assoc.
Auctioneers/Realty
Route 1, Box 130 (27928)
(919) 797-4528
Fax: (919) 797-4128
Farm Equipment; Real Estate;
Construction Equip.; Liq.;
Estates

DURHAM

Gray, Curtis H.
Gray's Auction & Real Estate
5342 N. Roxboro Rd. (27712)
(919) 471-0133
Real Estate; Estates;
Machinery; Antiques; Autos;
Surplus Goods

FAYETTEVILLE

Smith, H.B., Jr.
Col. H.B. Smith, Jr.
The Auctioneer
Rt. 5, Box 196 (28301)
(919) 483-1043
Commercial RE, Residential
RE, Business Liq.; Machinery;
Vehicles; Estates

FLETCHER

King, Jerry E.
King Auction & Realty Co.,
Inc.
P.O. Box 800 (28732)
(704) 684-6828
Bankruptcies; Heavy Equip.;
Real Estate; Farm Mach.;
Industrial; Sawmills

GRAHAM

Smith, Robert M.
Robert M. Smith Auction &
Realty Co.
P.O. Box 1255 (27253)
(919) 578-0355
Antiques & Estates; Farm
Equipment; Heavy
Equipment; Real Estate;
Business Liq.

GREENSBORO

Langley, William B.
Langley & Duncan Auction Srv
3703 Liberty Road (27406)
(919) 272-2262
Real Estate; Estates; Farm
Equip.; Liquidations; General

HIGH POINT

Mendenhall, Forrest A.
Mendenhall Auction Co.
P.O. Box 7344 (27264)
(919) 887-1165
Real Estate; Ind. Machinery;
Com. Machinery; Cars &
Trucks; Business Liq.

Mendenhall, F. Wayne
Mendenhall Auction Co.
P.O. Box 7344 (27264)
(919) 887-1165
(919) 887-8973
Business Liq.; Estates

JACKSONVILLE

Byers, Don W.
Don's Auction Barn
407 Sterling Road (28540)
(919) 455-5640
(919) 353-2524

Estates; Commercial;
Household; Antiques;
Bankruptcy; Consignment

MARION

Hollifield, Gilbert J.
Gilbert Hollifield Auction &
Real Estate
P.O. Box 939, Hwy 70W
(28752)
(704) 652-2510
(704) 652-3456
Antiques; Dolls; Toys; Estates;
General; Real Estate

MOCKSVILLE

Sheek, James L.
Jim Sheek Auction & Realty
Co.
P.O. Box 903 (27028)
(919) 998-3350
Estates; Real Estate; Comm.

MOORESVILLE

Horton, Donald L.
Don Horton Auctioneers
Hwy. 150 W., P.O. Box 1092
(28115)
(704) 663-1582
Real Estate; Business Liq.;
Estates; Farm Appraisals

MOUNT AIRY

Rogers, Bracky
Rogers Realty & Auction Co.
P.O. Box 729 (27030)
(919) 789-2926
(800) 442-7906
Fax: (919) 789-2310
Real Estate; Liq.; Estates;
Farm Equip.; Antiques; Gov't
Auctions

Rogers, B. Mark
Rogers Realty & Auction Co.
P.O. Box 729 (27030)
(800) 442-7906
Fax: (919) 789-2310
Real Estate; Liq.; Estates;
Farm Equip.

NEWTON GROVE

Hill, Edward J.
Hill Realty & Auction Co., Inc.
Rt 2, Box 14A (28366)
(919) 594-1751
Real Estate; Farm Equipment;
Timber; Estates

NORWOOD

Lilly, William B.
Iron Horse Auction Co.
P.O. Box 938 (28128)
(919) 997-2248
Fax: (919) 895-1530
Forest products; Transporta-
tion; Construction; Real
Estate; Livestock; Farm Mach.

OXFORD

Adcock, William T.
WM Adcock RE & Auction
Co.
912 College St.
P.O. Box 1185 (27565)
(919) 693-8000
Fax: (919) 693-4007
Estates; Farm Equipment; RE

PRINCETON

Worley, Jack D.
Worley Auction & RE Co.
Rt. 1, Box 108 (27569)
(919) 936-8281
Real Estate; Farm Equipment;
Estates; Tobacco

RALEIGH

Faison, Ronald W., Jr.
Ron's Auction & Realty Co.
Inc.
2828 Capital Blvd. (27504)
(919) 269-6700
Restaurants, Jewelry; Estates;
Farm Equipment; RE

Wooten, W. Douglas
Wooten Realty & Auction Co.
221 Clarendon Crescent
(27610)
(919) 832-7251
Industrl. Equip.; RE.; Business
Liq.; Farm Equipment;
Restaurants; Bankruptcy

ROCKINGHAM

McInnis, Tom
Iron Horse Auction Co.
Box 1267 (28379)
(919) 895-3871
Racing Equip.; Automobiles;
Forest Products; Real Estate;
Machine Tools; Mfg. Homes

STATESVILLE

Cline, M.B.
Piedmont Auction & Realty
703-A Sullivan Rd (28677)
(704) 872-8585
Real Estate; Sawmill Equip.;
Farm Mach.;
Business Liq.; Estate
Liquidations

Troutman, Lonnie
Troutman Realty
150 E. Water St. (28677)
(704) 873-5233
(704) 873-5234
Real Estate; Farm Mach.;
Household; Personal Prop.

WALKERTOWN

Mecum, David
Royal Realty & Auction
5510 Old Walkertown Rd.
(27051)
(919) 595-2181
(919) 595-3054
Real Estate; Estates; Liq.;
Personal Prop.;
Heavy Equip.; Farm
Machinery

WHISPERING PINES

Stout, Samuel B.
Sam Stout Auctioneers
272 B Pine Ridge Dr.
(28387)
(919) 944-3681
(919) 949-3845
Estate; Antique; Tools
Equipment; Real
Estate; Industrial

ZEBULON

Faison, Ronald W.
Ron's Auction & Realty
215 N. Arendell Ave. (27597)
(919) 269-6700
(800) 832-3534
Fax: (919) 269-4536
Business Liq.; RE; Farmland
Equip.; Industrial Liq.; Com.
Equip.; Gallery

North Dakota

BOWMAN

Penfield, Bert L.
Penfield Auction Service
Box 603 (58623)
(701) 523-3646
Real Estate; Farm Equip.;
Business Liq.; Antiques;
Household

FARGO

Steffes, Robert F.
Steffes Auctioneers
827 28th St. S., Suite D
(58103)
(701) 237-9173
Fax: (701) 237-0976
Farm; Commercial; Estates;
Real Estate

Steffes, Scott M.
Steffes Auctioneers
827 28th St. S., Suite D
(58103)
(701) 237-9173
Fax: (701) 237-0976
Farm; Commercial; Estates;
Real Estate

Ohio

ASHLAND

Dilgard, Byron E.
Dilgard & Associates, Inc.
135 Union Street (44805)
(419) 281-2122
(419) 289-2772
General; Bankruptcy; Liq.;
Real Estate

Donelson, Allen F.
Allen Donelson Auction & Rlty
1670 Co. Rd., 1095 (44805)

(419) 289-2484
Real Estate; Machinery/
Tools; Household Goods;
Construction Equip.; Farm
Equip.; Store Liq.

BERGHOLZ

Featheringham, Dale
Featheringham Realty &
Auction Co.
4th & Kennedy
Box 388 (43952)
(614) 264-7131
Personal Prop.; RE

BOWERSTON

Host, William H.
W. H. Host Broker/Auctioneer
215 Water Alley (44695)
(614) 269-2561
Farm/RE; Res. Real Estate;
Estates; Household; Antiques

BOWLING GREEN

Bradley, N. Keith
Bradley Real Estate & Auction
Co.
1037 N. Main St. (43402)
(419) 352-3268
(419) 352-3563
Real Estate; Commercial;
Farm Equipment; Estates; Bus.
Close-outs; Personal prop.

BRIDGEPORT

Smith, Robert C.
70961 Sharon Road (43912)
(614) 635-4397
Real Estate; Antiques;
Collectibles;
Commercial; Estates

BRYAN

Wilson, Wayne M.
Mohre-Wilson & Co.
102 W. Bryan St. (43506)
(419) 636-3187
(800) 489-7831
Fax: (419) 636-3850
Real Estate; Farm Equipment;
Antiques; Industrial
Equip.; Others

CANFIELD

Roman, Ronald L.
Roman Auctioneers
421 Dartmouth (44406)
(216) 533-4937
Fax: (216) 533-4071
Commercial; Industrial; Real
Estate; Estates

CANTON

Baier, Richard J.
Baier Realty & Auctioneers
2403 Cleveland Ave., N.W.
(44709)
(216) 452-6563
Real Estate; Commercial;
Farms; Liquidations; Antiques;
Livestock/Auto

Baier, Thomas A.
Tom Baier Auctioneers
2719 Fulton Dr. N.W.
Suite C (44718)
(216) 455-1911
Fax: (216) 455-1859
Real Estate; Antiques; Farm
Equipment

Dimmerling, Rodney C.
Tom Baier & Associates
2719 Fulton Dr. N.W.
Suite C (44718)
(216) 455-1911
Fax: (216) 455-1859
Real Estate; Antiques; Bus.
Liq.; Equipment; Livestock

Gill, Daniel P.
Russ Kiko Assoc. Inc. Auctions
2805 Fulton Dr. N.W. (44718)
(215) 488-0653
Real Estate; Farm Equipment;
Livestock; Antiques; Liq.;
Commercial

Gill, James D.
Russ Kiko Assoc. Inc. Auctions
2805 Fulton Dr. N.W. (44718)
(216) 832-2605
Real Estate; Farm Equipment;
Restaurant; Antiques; Liq.;
Commercial

Kiko, Eugene F.
Russ Kiko Assoc. Inc. Auctions
2805 Fulton Dr. NW (44718)
(216) 453-9187
Real Estate; Farm Equipment;
Household

Kiko, James R.
Russ Kiko Assoc. Inc. Auctions
2805 Fulton Dr. N.W. (44718)
(216) 862-3456
FAX (216) 453-1765
Farm Land; Real Estate; Farm
Equipment; Livestock;
Antiques; Bus. Liq.

Kiko, John D.
Russ Kiko Assoc. Inc. Auctions
2805 Fulton Dr. N.W. (44718)
(216) 453-9187
Real Estate; Farm Equipment;
Livestock; Antiques; Liq.;
Commercial

Kiko, Lawrence J.
Russ Kiko Assoc. Inc. Auctions
2805 Fulton Dr. N.W. (44718)
(216) 453-9187
(216) 455-9357
FAX (216) 453-1765
Real Estate; Farm; Antiques;
Household

Kiko, Richard T.
Russ Kiko Assoc. Inc. Auctions
2805 Fulton Dr. N.W. (44718)
(216) 453-9187
FAX (216) 453-1765
Farms; Lands; Residential;
Antiques; Commercial

Kiko, Russell T., Jr.
Russ Kiko Assoc. Inc. Auctions
2805 Fulton Dr. N.W. (44718)
(216) 525-7420
FAX (216) 453-1765
Real Estate; Farm; Estates;
Antiques; Household

Marino, James T.
Whipple Auction & Realty,
Inc.
1147 Whipple Ave., NW
(44708)
(216) 477-9365
(216) 477-7653
Real Estate; Commercial;
Gov't Sale; Grocery Equip.;
Heavy Equipment; Estates

Marino, Joe W., Jr.
Whipple Auction & Realty,
Inc.
1147 Whipple Ave., NW
(44708)
(216) 477-9365
(216) 477-7653

Real Estate; Commercial;
Gov't Sale; Restaurant Equip.;
Heavy Equipment; Estates

Marino, Scott I.
Whipple Auction & Realty,
Inc.
1147 Whipple Ave., NW
(44708)
(216) 477-9365
(216) 477-7653
Real Estate; Commercial Liq.;
Restaurant Equip.; Machinery
Farm Equipment

Marino, Tom A.
Whipple Auction & Realty,
Inc.
1147 Whipple Ave., NW
(44708)
(216) 477-9365
(216) 477-0004
Real Estate; Restaurant Equip.;
Commercial Liq.; Machinery
Antiques; Farm Equipment

Milano, Lennie E.
Russ Kiko Associates, Inc.
2805 Fulton Dr., NW (44718)
(216) 868-3483
Antiques; Collectibles; Farm
Equip.; Household; Residential
RE

CANTON (NORTH)

Wagner, Robert J.
Bob Wagner & Assoc, Inc.
1444 N. Main St. (44720)
(216) 499-9922
(216) 453-1188
Fax: (216) 499-5864
Real Estate; Household; Farm
Equip.

CARROLLTON

Garner, Larry W., Sr.
L.W. Garner Realty/
Auctioneers
332 S. Lisbon Street
Box 323 (44615)
(800) 452-8452
Real Estate; Com Equip.; Ind.
Equip.; Const. Equip.;
Fixtures; Firearms

Newell, Robert C.
Newell Realty & Auction Srvc.
550 Cantin Rd., N.W. (44615)
(216) 627-2350
Real Estate; Antiques;
Household; Farm

CHILLICOTHE

Stanley, Henry M., III
Stanley & Son Auction &
Realtors
126 E. Fourth St. (45601)
(614) 775-3330
(614) 773-5584
Real Estate; Automobiles

CINCINNATI

Cox, Gilbert L.
Semple & Associates
Auctioneers
5645 Bramble Ave. (45227)
(513) 271-4085
Liquidations; Real Estate;
General; Restaurant Equip.;
Equipment; Antiques

Mallette, Mark D.
Mark D. Mallette & Assoc. Inc
7901 Wild Orchard (45242)
(513) 984-0400
Commercial; Industrial; Fine
Art; Estates; Household

Semple, Brent T.
Semple & Associates, Inc.

P.O. Box 44006 (45244)
(513) 724-1133
Fax: (513) 724-1286
Supermarkets; Business Liq.;
Industrial; Vehicles; Real
Estate; Heavy Equipment

Semple, Garth
Semple & Associates, Inc.
P.O. Box 44006 (45244)
(513) 724-1133
Fax: (513) 724-1286
Com./Ind. Equip.; Business
Liq.; Bankruptcies; Lender
Assets; Real Estate; Liq.

CLEVELAND HEIGHTS

Hayes, Evelyn
Prosperity Productions
920 Beverly Rd. (44121)
(216) 381-3878
Antiques; Art; Quilts; Horses,
Benefit Auctions

CLYDE

Bonnigson, Kenneth
J. Baker Bonnigson
Auctioneers
1834 W. McPherson Hwy.
(43410)
(419) 547-9313
Farm Machinery; Antiques;
Real Estate; Estates

COSHOCTON

Rice, Greg J.
Peddicord & Rice Auction
Realty
125 S. 4th Street
(43812)
(614) 622-3111
Classic Autos; Farm Equip.;
Real Estate;
Household, Antiq.

DAYTON

Dice, William
David Bill Dice, CAI
P.O. Box 292961 (45429)
(513) 426-4425
Fax: (513) 426-4425
Industrial; Commercial; Hotels;
Real Estate

Wise, Karl
Wise & Associates
1428 W. Dorothy Lane
(45409)
(513) 298-4854
Fax: (513) 298-4854
Commercial; Industrial

DOVER

Bambeck, Herbert A.
Bambeck Auctioneers, Inc.
Rt 4, Box 405 (44622)
(216) 343-1437
(216) 343-1642
Real Estate; Estates; Farm;
Liq.; Commercial; Industrial

Brown, Jane B.
Bambeck Auctioneers, Inc.
Rt 4, Box 405 (44622)
(216) 343-1437
FAX (216) 343-1437
Real Estate; Plant Liq.;
Bus. Liq.

Triplett, Penny E.
Don R. Wallick Auction & Rlty
130 E. 17th Street (44622)
(216) 343-6734
(216) 343-6187
Real Estate; Household

EATON

Kramer, H. John
Kramer & Kramer, Inc.
108 W. Main Street (45320)
(513) 456-1101
Real Estate; Antiques; Farm;
Household; Hummels; General

FAIRBORN

Flatter, Joe W.
Joe W. Flatter Auctioneer
1503 N. Broad St (45324)
(513) 878-3444
Antiques; Real Estate;
Commercial; Farm
Chattels; Household;
Liquidations

FLUSHING

Jones, David
David Jones Auction Service
High St., Box 467 (43977)
(614) 968-3710
General Real Estate; Antiques;
Household; Farm

GERMANTOWN

Kuch, Charles (Chuck)
C-K Realty & Auction Service
38 W. Market St. (45327)
(513) 855-2164
Estates; Real Estate; General

GRAFTON

Murphy, John R.
1005 Plymouth Drive
(44044)
(216) 926-2932

GRANVILLE

Rhodeback, Ronald D.
Rhodeback Auctions

1077 Chestnut Hills Rd.
(43023)
(614) 587-2564
Salvage Auto Auction; Farm
Equipment; Livestock; Estates;
Tools; Machine Shop

GREENVILLE

Baker, Michael D.
Mid-West Auctioneers
7603 Celina Rd (45331)
(513) 548-2640
(513) 548-5464
Fax: (513) 548-0103
Real Estate; Antique; Farm;
Household

HAMILTON

Bowling, Myron
Myron Bowling Auctioneers,
Inc.
3901 Kraus Lane (45014)
(513) 738-3311
Fax: (513) 738-0221
Machine Tools; Metal Forming
Equip.; Material Handling
Equip.; Commercial RE

HILLSBORO

Chambers, Lowell
Chambers Realty & Auction
111 E. Main St. (45133)
(513) 393-1948
Real Estate; Farm Equip.;
Antiques; Timber; Livestock

KENT

Eberhart, Dennis C.
Yankee Trader Auction &
Realty Co.
1640 Franklin Ave., #4
PO Box 1776 (44240)
(800) 323-1876

Fax: (216) 677-1776
Antiques; Real Estate;
Commercial Liq.;
Fund Raiser

MAUMEE

Gaisser, Michael F.
Mikana Enterprises, Inc.
P.O. Box 456 (43537)
(419) 693-1756
(800) 776-1755
Fax: (419) 536-2888
Real Estate; Commercial;
Estates; Machinery;
Personal Property; Business
Liq.

MEDINA

Walton, Max K.
Walton & Assoc. Inc.
3860 Paradise Rd. (44256)
(216) 725-8958
Antique; Real Estate; Ind.
Equipment; Autos;
Commercial; Farm

MENTOR

Brown, Alan
Gallery One 7003
Center Street (44060)
(216) 255-1200
Art; Benefit

MIDDLETOWN

Anglin, John
John Anglin & Assoc.
Auctioneers
6577 Hamilton-Middletown
(45042)
(513) 422-4730
(513) 423-8555
Estates; Antiques; Real Estate;
Farm; Heavy Equip. Liq.

NORTH BEND

Beckmeyer, Maggie
Auctions By Maggie, Inc.
2191 Cliff Road (45052)
(513) 941-9519
(800) 745-3557
Real Estate; Complete Estates;
Antiques; Owner ready extras;
Consignments
Industrial

N. RIDGEVILLE

Canterbury, Jerry
Canterbury Auction Service
5999 Avon-Belden Rd.
(44039)
(216) 327-9394
Fax: (216) 327-5082
Business; Real Estate; Estates;
Antiques; Baseball Cards; Tools

Standen, Don W.
The Auctioneer
38146 Sugar Ridge Rd. (44039)
(216) 327-8141
Antiques; Household;
Commercial

PAULDING

Gorrell, Larry D.
Gorrell Brothers Auctioneer
105 W. Perry (45879)
(419) 399-4066
Fax: (419) 399-2999
Real Estate; Farm Land; Farm
Equip.; Antiques; Commercial

POLAND

Basinger, J. Paul
Basinger Auction Service
7039 Bishop Rd. (44514)
(216) 726-4120
Fax: (216) 726-4126

Oriental Rugs; Real Estate;
Heavy Equip.;
Household Goods; Antiques;
Store Liq.

RAVENNA

Cross, Jerry L.
Jerry Cross Auctioneer
5615 Lakewood Rd. (44266)
(216) 297-7990
Household/Ant.; Benefits; Real
Estate; Autos.; Farm Mach.

SANDUSKY

Keller, Perry E.
Keller Sales, Inc.
4203 Hayes Ave. (44870)
(419) 626-8655
(419) 627-8888
Estate Liq.; Auction Consignment; Real Estate; Vacation
Land; Farm Mach.; Livestock

SPRINGFIELD

Welch, Donald E.
Donald Welch Auctioneer
534 Sheffield Drive (45506)
(513) 325-0750
Estates; Antiques; Farm;
Commercial

STEUBENVILLE

Cain, Brad L.
Gary W. Cain Auctioneers
4237 Sunset Blvd. (43952)
(614) 266-2246
(614) 543-4019
Fax: (614) 266-6925
Real Estate; Antiques; Personal
Prop.

Cain, Gary W.
Gary W. Cain Auctioneers
4237 Sunset Blvd. (43952)

(614) 266-2246
Fax: (614) 266-6925
Real Estate; Liquidations;
Personal Prop.

Sponhaltz, Rick L.
Gary W. Cain Realtors &
Auctioneers
4237 Sunset Blvd. (43952)
(614) 266-2246
Fax: (614) 266-6925
Real Estate; Liquidations;
Personal Prop.

Westling, John
Westling's Auction Service
P.O. Box 792 (43952)
(614) 765-4276
Fax: (614) 282-4426
Real Estate; Restaurant Equip.;
Household; Store Equip.

SYCAMORE

Gregg, Ned F.
Ned F. Gregg Realty
6761 Crawford Wyandot Co.
Line Rd. (44882)
(419) 927-5492
Fax: (419) 927-5492
Real Estate; Estate Sales; Farm
Machinery; Antiques

Gregg, Scott L.
6761 Crawford Wyandot Co.
Line Rd. (44882)
(419) 927-5492
Fax: (419) 927-5492
Real Estate; Estate Sales; Farm
Machinery; Antiques

TORONTO

Swickard, Thomas D.
Swickard Auction Service
408 Knoxville Rd. (43964)
(614) 544-5446
Antiques; Ind. Mach.; Farm;
Household

TROY

Stichter, Jerry
Jerry Stichter, Auctioneer
467 Staunton Rd. W. (45373)
(513) 335-6758
Fax: (513) 339-5911
Antiques; Personal Prop.; Farm
Equip.; Real Estate; Business
Equipment

VAN WERT

Straley, William C.
Straley Realtors & Auctioneers,
Inc.
323 E. Main St. (45891)
(419) 238-9733
(800) 727-2021
Fax: (419) 238-3506
All type Real Estate; Farm
Equip.; Commercial Prop.;
Chattels; Restaurant Equip.;
Unique Items

WADSWORTH

Farnsworth, Harold R.
Harold R. Farnsworth—
Auctioneer
8003 River Styx Rd. (44281)
(216) 336-6057
Farm Machinery; Estate;
Antiques; Household, RE

WAUSEON

Newlove, Joe R.
Joe Newlove RE & Auctions

145 S. Fulton St. (43567)
(419) 337-8581
Real Estate; Antiques; Farm
Equip.; Household

Oklahoma

ADA

Steen, Ben D.
Big Ben Realty & Auction
1201 Arlington (74820)
(405) 332-0559
(405) 332-4456
Real Estate; Antiques; Estates;
Collectibles

BROKEN ARROW

Wells, V. Paul
Wells Commercial Auctions
27428 E. 71st Street (74014)
(918) 357-1003
Fax: (918) 357-2705
Commercial (food industry);
Business Liq.; Real Estate

BUFFALO

Crouch, Robert
Crouch Auction and Realty
Box 607 (73834)
(405) 735-2370
(405) 735-2621
Real Estate; Farm Equipment;
Household; General; Heavy
Equip.; Appraisals

CATOOSA

Vierheller, J. Edward
Mr. Ed's Auction Co.
21703 E. Admiral Pl.
(74015)
(918) 266-4218
Fax: (918) 266-4261

Estate Liq.; Real Estate;
Busines Liq.;
Const. Equip.; Farm Auctions;
In-House Facility

CLAREMORE

Dulaney, Sue
Sue Dulaney & Company
3900 S. Hwy 66
(The Red Barn) (74017)
(918) 342-5176
Fax: (918) 342-5187
Bus. Liq.; Farm; Antiques;
Coins; RE; Household

ENID

Wiggins, Cecil Perry, Jr.
Wiggins Auctioneers
4720 A W. Garriott Road
(73703)
(405) 233-3066
Farm Land; Farm Equipment

FREDERICK

Brink, Terry H.
Kent & Brink Auctioneers
422 N. 14th (73542)
(405) 335-5732
Farm Land; Farm Equip.;
Livestock; Estates; Antiques

GUYMON

Wilmeth, Norman C.
Wilmeth Realty & Auction
Box 877 (73942)
(405) 338-8148
Farm Land; Machinery;
Personal Prop;
Liq.; Estates

HYDRO

Entz, Roger
Roger Entz Auction & Realty
Rt 1, Box 47 (73048)
(405) 663-2200
Fax: (405) 663-2099
Farm Equip.; Real Estate;
Business Liq.

OKLAHOMA CITY

Bristol, Robert W.
558 Spitz (73135)
(405) 672-0114
Office Equip.; Institutional

Georgia, Roy (Retired)
Roy Georgia Realty & Auction
4808 Del View (73115)
(405) 677-3171
Real Estate; General; Antiques;
Collector Autos; Estates;
Commercial Liq.

Haynes, T. Eddie
Eddie Haynes, Inc. Auction &
Realty
901 N. MacArthur (73127)
(405) 495-7653
Fax: (405) 495-7657
Real Estate; Commercial;
Farm; Commercial Liq.

Kelly, Jim
Kelly Auction Inter., Inc.
9600 S. Sunny Lane (73160)
(405) 799-0814
(405) 364-6676
Fax: (405) 799-0855
Farm Equip.; Construction
Equip.; Trucks;
Trailers; Autos; Oil Field
Equipment;
Office Equipment

Tullis, Jerry W.
Tullis Auctioneering
11304 S. Villa (73170)

(405) 692-0077
(405) 692-0400
Real Estate; Commercial;
Estates

PERRY

Miller, Starling
Starling Miller RE & Auctions
Rt. 3, Box 129A (73077)
(405) 336-2030
Real Estate; Estates; Antiques;
Collectibles; Farm Equipment

STILLWATER

Voss, W.W. (Dutch) (Retired)
W.W. Voss Real Estate
Route 6, Box 90 (74074)
(405) 372-7631
Real Estate; General

VINITA

Robinson, J.B.
J.B. Robinson Auctioneers &
Realtors
P.O. Box 414 (74301)
(918) 256-6179
(918) 256-5524
Real Estate; Estates; Farm;
Antiques; Commercial

WAUKOMIS

Goodwin, Dwayne E.
Goodwin Real Estate &
Auction
P.O. Box 698 (73773)
(405) 758-3271
Estates; Farm/Ranch Land;
Farm Machinery; Commercial
RE; Residential RE

WESTVILLE

Dewey, Earl W., Sr. (Retired)
Outrigger Enterprises

RR 2 Box 409 (74965)
(515) 472-3816
Industrial; Machinery; RE;
Commercial Liq.; RE
Appraiser; Consultant

Oregon

BROWNSVILLE

Neagle, Mel
Mel Neagle Auctioneer
P.O. Box 8 (97327)
(503) 466-3068
Real Estate; Machine Shops;
Construction
Equip.; Computers;
Restaurant/Store
Equip.; Hardware Stores

CANBY

Van Gordon, Steve
Steve Van Gordon Auctioneer
P.O. Box 520 (97013)
(503) 266-1551
(800) 637-3140
Fax: (503) 266-7693
Real Estate; Commercial;
Industrial; Liq.;
Farm Equip.

FLORENCE

Free, William L.
Oregon West Auction Service
P.O. Box 57 (97439)
(503) 997-3263
Real Estate; Estate; Gov't
Surplus; Business Liq.;
Antiques; Firearms

GRANTS PASS

Morrison, Charles A.
C.A. Morrison Realty & Auct.
816 N.E. "E" St. (97526)
(503) 479-9761
Fax: (503) 474-5260
General; Estates; Real Estate;
Commercial; Liquidations

PORTLAND (WILSONVILLE)

Day, Gary H.
Gary Day Auctioneers
8288 SW Lafayette Way
(97070)
(503) 222-9000
Fax: (503) 694-2204
Industrial; Commercial; RE

RHODODENDRON

Cox, Jay Thomas
Cox Auctions
P.O. Box 187 (97049)
(503) 622-3397
Commercial; Industrial;
Equipment; Vehicles; Estates;
Real Estate

SILVERTON

Lang, Rick
Lang Sales Co.—Auctioneers
P.O. Box 255
405 N. Water St. (97381)
(503) 873-5289
Fax: (503) 873-8021
Commercial; Industrial; RE

Pennsylvania

ANNVILLE

Fortna, Michael R.
Fortna's Annville Auction Co.
18 E. Main St. (17003)

(717) 867-4451
General; Household; Antiques;
RE; Commercial; Liq.

BATH

Hahn, Wilbur E.
Wil Hahn Auction Company
102 West Main St. (18014)
(215) 837-7140
(215) 837-0208
Fax: (215) 837-9451
Real Estate; Estate Liq.;
Farms; Antiques;
Collections

BEAVER FALLS

Hostetter, Lee W.
Hostetter Realtors &
Auctioneers
124 Blackhawk Rd. (15010)
(412) 847-1880
Fax: (412) 847-3415
RE; Commercial; Industrial;
Machinery; Farm Equipment;
Estates

Hostetter, Sherman Jr.
Hostetter Realtors &
Auctioneers
124 Blackhawk Rd (15010)
(412) 847-1880
Fax: (412) 847-3415
RE; Business Liq.; Equipment;
Machinery; Estates; Household

BLOOMSBURG

Crawford, Robert J.
R.J. Crawford Auction Co.
Route 4 Box 70 (17815)
(717) 784-1690
Autos; Business Liq.; Estates

BROQUE

Smith, Bradley K.
Brad Smith Auction Co.
RD #2, Box 483 (17309)
(717) 927-6949
(717) 246-1770
RE; Antiques; Cars; Guns;
Coins; Household

BROWNSVILLE

Peters, Fred A.
Fred Peters Auctioneers
215 Lynn Road (15417)
(412) 785-8954
Industrial; S. Market/Rest.;
Bankruptcy;
Liq.; Res. RE; Antiques;
Collectibles; Estates

CATASAUQUA

Krall, Peter H.
Peter Krall Auction Co.
Willow Brook Farms (18032)
(215) 264-1088
General; Estate; RE; Farm
Equip.; Farm;
Municipal Surplus

COOPERSTOWN

Baker Auction Company
P.O. Box 155 (16317)
(814) 374-4508
Estates; Heavy Equip.; Farm;
Commercial; RE

DAUPHIN

Knosp, Jefrey L.
Kerry Pae Auctioneers
1311 La Carr Lane (17018)
(717) 236-3752

Pae, Kerry A.
Kerry Pae Auctioneers
P.O. Box 640 (17018)
(717) 236-3752
Real Estate; Bankruptcy;
Commercial; Estates

DOUGLASVILLE

Frey, George D.
Frey Auctioneers
RD 2, Box 377 (19518)
(215) 689-5269
Farm Machinery; Antiques;
Livestock; Real Estate

DUBOIS

Reed, Larry R.
Reed Auctioneers
RD #2, Box 69A (15801)
(814) 371-6605
Real Estate; Estates; Antiques;
Commercial

FOGELSVILLE

Zettlemoyer, Sherwood
Ralph W. Zettlemoyer
Auction Co.
P.O. Box 215 (18066)
(215) 395-8084
Fax: (215) 395-0227
Antiques; Primitives; Estates;
Farm Equipment; Commercial

GEORGETOWN

Anderson, Harry
Anderson Auctioneers, Inc.
Route 2, Box 50 (15043)
(412) 573-9533
Real Estate; Industrial

HARLEYSVILLE

Alderfer, Harold A.
Sanford A. Alderfer, Inc.

665 Harleysville Pike
Box 1 (19438)
(215) 256-9287
(215) 723-1171
Real Estate; Estates; Antiques;
Household; Commercial;
Industrial

Martin, Vernon L.
Sanford A. Alderfer Auction
Co.
Box 1 (19438)
(215) 723-1171
Fax: (215) 723-7945
Real Estate; Antiques; Estates;
Commercial; Farm Equipment

HATFIELD

Alderfer, Sanford L.
Sanford Alderfer Auction Co.
P.O. Box 640
501 Fairground Rd. (19440)
(215) 368-5477
Fax: (215) 368-9055
Real Estate; Antiques;
Firearms; Liquidations;
Commercial; Estate

HELLAM

Toomey, Frederick L.
Toomey Auction Service
241 E. Market St. (17406)
(717) 755-6105
Antiques; Real Estate; Coins;
Personal Property; Commercial

HOLSOPPLE

Holsopple, Ernest
Holsopple Auctioneers
RD #1, Box 47 (15935)
(814) 479-7682
RE, Commercial; Misc.

HOMER CITY

Charnego, Michael R.
Michael R. Charnego
Auctioneer
1 S. Main St. (15748)
(412) 479-2481
Real Estate; Estates; Coins;
Antiques; Collectibles;
Commercial

HONESDALE

Kinzinger, Gordon W.
The Country Auction
125 Shady Lane (18431)
(717) 253-6313
(717) 253-5967
Antiques; Estates; Consignment; Collectibles

HUNTINGDON

Schrack, Rob
Rob Schrack & Auctioneer
620 Washington St. (16652)
(814) 643-6600
Antiques; Liquidations; Bankruptcy; Household; Consignment; Sporting Goods

KITTANNING

Morrison, Arthur W.
Auctions By Morrison
1004 N. McKean St. (16201)
(412) 545-9775
Estates; Antiques; General;
Liquidations;
RE; Guns

KLINGERSTOWN

Deibert, George N.
Deibert RE & Auctions
P.O. Box 72 (17941)
(717) 425-3313
Real Estate; Estate Auctions;
Equip. Sales

LANCASTER

Bechtold, Claude F.
Bechtold Auctioneers
1928 Creek Hill Rd. (17601)
(717) 397-9240
Estates; Real Estate; Antiques;
Equip./Tools; Liquidations

Leaman, Sanford G.
Sanford G. Leaman Auction
Service
1000 N. Prince St. (17603)
(717) 393-2437
Fax: (717) 396-7143
Antiques; RE; Farm Equip.;
Livestock; Bankruptcy;
Liquidations

LANSDALE

Hunyady, Michael J.
Michael J. Hunyady, Inc.
Auction Co.
1909 S. Broad St. (19446)
(215) 699-8625
Fax: (215) 699-0485
Construction Equip.; Trucks
and Trailers; Mining Equip.;
Power Line Equipment;
Crushing & Aggregate;
Appraisals

LINDEN

Younkin, Scott
Scott Younkin & Associates
P.O. Box #69 (17744)

(717) 323-9011
Antiques; Collectibles; Estate;
Farm; Business Liq.; RE

LITITZ

Girvin, Thomas K.
Girvin Brothers Assoc.
859 Cindy Lane (17543)
(717) 627-1660
Autos; RE; Antiques

MESHOPPEN

Burke, Gerald E.
Shamrock Auction Service
P.O. Box 10 (18630)
(717) 833-5913
Fax: (717) 833-2186
Antiques; RE; Farm Equip;
Coins

MIFFLINTOWN

Dobozynski, Joe
AAA Auction Service, Inc.
Rd. 1, Box 420 (17059)
(717) 436-9594
Real Estate; Timber; Farm
Equip; Business Liq.;
Bankruptcies; Estates

MILLVILLE

Kapp, George S., Jr.
Derr & Kapp's Auction Srvc.
Rt. 1, Box 156 (17846)
(717) 458-4384
Gen.; Estates; Antiques; RE;
Farm Related; Bus. Liq.

MONTGOMERYVILLE

Hutchinson, Richard W.
Vismeier Auction Co., Inc.
P.O. Box 339 (18936)
(215) 699-5833
(215) 628-8031

Fax: (215) 628-8010
Utility; Const. Equip.; Indus.
Equip.; Appraisals

Vilsmeier, Frederick R.
Vilsmeier Auction Co., Inc.
1044 Bethlehem Pike (18936)
(215) 699-5833
Fax: (215) 628-8010
Const. Equip.; Utility Equip.;
Industrial Tool; Mechanical
Tool; Material; Automobiles

MOUNT JOY

Keller, Harold K.
Harold K. Keller, Auctioneers
268 Marietta Ave. (17552)
(800) 535-5372
(717) 653-8871
RE; Antiques; Estates

NEWPORT

Lesh, Ralph J., Jr.
Lesh Auction Co.
Route 2 (17074)
(717) 567-3182
RE; Liquidations; Estates;
Automotive;
Construction

NORTH EAST

Chesley, Todd
Chesley's Sales, Inc.
9372 Route 89 (16428)
(814) 725-1303
RE; Antiques; Estate, Heavy
Equip.; Farm
Equip.; Livestock

PHILADELPHIA

Clemens, Douglas
Traiman Real Estate
Auction
The Traiman Bldg.
1519 Spruce St. (19102)
(215) 545-4500
Fax: (215) 545-2462
RE Since 1924

Comly, Stephen E.
William F. Comly & Son, Inc.
1825 E. Boston Ave. (19125)
(215) 634-2500
Fax: (215) 634-0496
Commercial; Bankruptcies;
Construction; RE; General;
Restaurant

PLEASANT GAP

Marshall, Mike P.
Centre Auction Gallery
139 E. College Ave. (16823)
(814) 359-3030
Estate; RE; Appraisals

PLYMOUTH MEETING

Hansell, Kenneth A., Jr.
Kenneth A. Geyer Auction Co.,
Inc.
1 Plymouth Meeting
Suite 6 (19462)
(215) 834-1854
(215) 234-0955
Fax: (215) 834-1754
Autos; RE; Estates; Equipment

POTTSVILLE

Blum, George F.
Blum's
2500 West End Ave. (17901)
(717) 622-3089
Antiques; Collectibles; Estate;
Coins; Jewelry; RE

ROYERSFORD

Reed, R. Kenneth, Jr.
Ken Reed Auctioneer
401 Main St. (19468)
(215) 948-4871
Fax: (215) 327-8092
Personal Prop.; School
Property; Commercial;
Gov't.; Industrial; Real Estate

SLIPPERY ROCK

Huey, John R., II
John R. Huey, Auctioneer
Rt. 5, Box 9300 (16057)
(412) 794-6044
Commercial; Farm Equip.;
Livestock; Estates; Households;
Real Estate

SOUDERTON

Hubscher, Christian
Christian Hubscher Auctions
P.O. Box 500 (18964)
(215) 257-3001
Coins; Estates; Commercial;
Real Estate; Collections

VANDERBILT

Rittenhouse, Wylie S.
Rittenhouse Auctioneers
Rt. 1 Box 127 (15486)
(412) 438-0581
Real Estate; Estates; Industrial;
Commercial

WARREN

Erskine, Merrill F. (Retired)
P.O. Box 695 (16365)
(814) 726-2476
General

WAVERLY

Sitar, Steven M.
Col. Steve Sitar & Co.
P.O. Box 779 (18471)
(717) 586-1397
Commercial; Industrial, RE

WEST CHESTER

Boswell, James M.
Auction Marketing Assoc.
P.O. Box 3073 (19381)
(215) 692-2226
RE; Antiques; Machinery;
Tools; Estates; Household

Rhode Island

EXETER

Spicer, Bill
Spicer Auction Co., Inc.
Widow Sweets Rd. (02822)
(401) 295-0339
Real Estate; Estates

South Carolina

BELTON

Ashley, Allen L.
Double A Auction & Real
Estate
1032 Trail Rd. (29627)
(803) 338-9593
Estate Sales; Farm Equip.;
Antiques; Real Estate; General

BENNETTSVILLE

Shortt, Lee C.
Shortt Auction & Realty Co.,
Inc.
111 Market St. (29512)
(803) 479-6856
Fax: (803) 479-6856
Real Estate; Estates; Antiques

CHARLESTON

Roumillat, Ed
Roumillat's Auction & Realty
1238 Yeamans Hall Rd.
(29406)
(803) 744-9999
(803) 797-7318
Fax: (803) 566-0162
Estates; Real Estate;
Business Liq.; Antiques

COLUMBIA

Lee, Rodney H.
R H Lee & Co.
2305 Two Notch Road (29204)
(803) 254-7896
Commercial; Estates; Antiques;
Real Estate

FLORENCE

Younce, William M.
Bill Younce Auctioneers, Inc.
1702 S. Irby Street
P.O. Box 4867 (29502)
(803) 665-6060
(803) 662-9967
Fax: (803) 665-7601
Real Estate; Estates; Liq.

GREENVILLE

Hernandez, Calixto A.
Alicia Auction & Realty
P.O. Box 3086 (29602)
(803) 243-4858

Real Estate; General; Merchandise; Autos.; Farm Equip.;
Estates; Liquidations

Meares, Larry J., Jr.
Meares Auctions Inc.
P.O. Box 9124 (29604)
(803) 947-2000
Fax: (803) 947-6899
Real Estate; Industrial; Estates;
Farm Equipment; Autos;
Office Equipment

LANCASTER

Mullis, Fred
Mullis Bros. Auction Co.
28 N. Main
P.O. Box 727 (29720)
(803) 283-4574
Real Estate; Bus. Liquid.;
Estates; Super
Markets; Farm Equipment

Patterson, Richard L.
Cauthen & Patterson
P.O. Box 218 (29720)
(803) 286-6800
Automobiles; Real Estate;
Antiques; General

MAULDIN

Case, Edward C.
Century 21 Case & Assoc. Inc.
P.O. Box 692 (29662)
(803) 288-2121
Real Estate; Farms; Estates;
Personal Prop.; Business

SPARTANBURG

Lowe, Michael S.
Carolina Auction & Land Co.
P.O. Box 4125 (29305)
(803) 578-0784
(803) 578-6359

Fax: (803) 578-0383
Real Estate; Personal Prop.;
Machinery; Livestock

Pinckney, Carroll G.
Carolina Auction & Land Co.
P.O. Box 4125 (29305)
(803) 578-0784
(803) 536-4273
Fax: (803) 578-0383
Real Estate; Farm Machinery;
Const. Mach.; Estates

Smith, James R.
Carolina Auction Team, Inc.
P.O. Box 4125 (29305)
(803) 578-0784
Fax: (803) 578-0383
Real Estate

SUMMERVILLE

Stefani, Joseph R.
Joe Richard Auction Co.
1725 N. Main Street
Suite 101 (29483)
(805) 871-0400
Antiques; Gallery; Estates;
Jewelry; Real Estate; General

TIMMONSVILLE

Weatherly, Robert M.
Weatherly Auctioneers
Route 4, Box 59 (29161)
(803) 346-3345
Real Estate; Farm Equipment;
Construction

Weatherly, Teresa N.
Weatherly Auctioneers
Route 4, Box 59, Hwy. 76
(29161)
(803) 346-3345
Real Estate; Farm Land;
Resorts; Equipment; Personal
Prop.; Commercial

WALTERBORO

Blocker, James G.
J.G. Blocker Auction/Realty,
Inc.
Hwy. 15 N., P.O. Box 484
(29488)
(803) 538-2276
Fax: (803) 549-5134
Real Estate; Farm Equipment;
Bank Liquidations;
Bankruptcy; Livestock;
Personal Prop.

South Dakota

LONG LAKE

Fischer, Charles J.
Charles J. Fischer Auction Co.
Hay Wire Ave. R-239 (57457)
(605) 577-6600
Fax: (605) 577-6500
Heavy Equipment; Real
Estate; Ind. & Hospital Eq.;
Appraisals; Business Liq.; Farm
Equipment

Fischer, John C.
Charles J. Fischer Auction Co.
100 Main St. (57457)
(605) 577-6600
Fax: (605) 577-6500
Farm Equipment; Real Estate;
Heavy Equipment; Ind. &
Hospital Equip.; Appraisals;
Business Liq.

SIOUX FALLS

Wingler, Terry L.
Wingler's Furniture & Auction,
Inc.
611 N. Main (57102)
(605) 332-5682

Household; Antiques;
Collectibles;
Business Liq.

YANKTON

Payne, James T.
Payne Auctioneers
111 Cedar St. (57078-4331)
(605) 665-3889
(605) 665-8072
Fax: (605) 665-6478
Real Estate; Farm Equip.;
Trucks; Furn.; Antiques;
Industrial Equip.; Lake Prop.

Tennessee

CHATTANOOGA

Gravitt, Kenneth H.
Ken Gravitt Auction Co.
P.O. Box 71821 (37408)
(615) 267-7601
Fax: (615) 267-2403
Real Estate; Business Liq.;
Industrial Liq.;
Bankruptcy; Heavy
Equipment; Vehicles

CLINTON

Stephenson, William (Bear)
Stephenson Realty & Auction
123 Leinert Street (37716)
(615) 457-2327
Real Estate; Estate; Business
Liq.

DECATUR

Howard, Dean
Dean Howard & Daughters
Route 1, Box 236 (37322)
(615) 334-3335
Real Estate; Farm Equipment;
Gov't.; Household

DUNLAP

Hamilton, George, Jr.
George Hamilton Auction Co.
P.O. Box 536 (37327)
(615) 554-3999
Fax: (615) 277-3292
Real Estate; Estates;
Machinery

FRANKLIN

Johns, Royce
Royce Johns Realty & Auction
236 3rd Avenue North
(37064)
(615) 790-0414
Real Estate; Farm Mach.;
Farms; Estates; Cattle

GALLATIN

Carmen, Harold G., Jr.
Gene Carmen RE & Auction
137 Broadway (37066)
(615) 452-5341
Real Estate; Personal Prop.;
Farm Equipment; Cattle

KNOXVILLE

Furrow, Sam J.
Furrow Auction Company
P.O. Box 2087 (37901)
(615) 546-3206
(615) 584-0892
Fax: (615) 588-2588
Real Estate; Industrial Equip.

Slyman, James
Slyman Auction Co.
411 S. Gay St., Ste A (37902)
(615) 521-7416
Real Estate; Prop. Mgmt.; Bus
Liq.; Appraisals

LAFOLLETTE

Ayers, Haskel
Hack Ayers Auction & RE
P.O. Box 1467 (37766)
(615) 546-2296
(615) 562-4941
Real Estate; Estates

Dower, J. J.
Hack Ayers Auction & RE
P.O. Box 1467 (37766)
(615) 562-4941
(615) 562-7067
Fax: (615) 562-8148
Real Estate; Estates;
Equipment; Farms;
Liquidations; Commercial

LOUDON

Henderson, Joe E.
Auction Associates
Rt 2., Box 95 (37774)
(615) 637-8822
Farm Machinery; Personal
Prop.; Real Estate

MARTIN

Alexander, Marvin E.
Alexander Auctions & RE
Sales
239 University St.
Box 129 (38237)
(901) 587-4244
(901) 587-4568
Real Estate; Farm Equipment;
Dairy Cattle; Antiques

MEMPHIS

Roebuck, John
River City Auction & Realty
3143 Carrier St. (38116)
(901) 346-8644

Real Inv.; Real Estate;
Antiques; Farm
Equipment

Roebuck, Kenneth
River City Auction & Realty
3143 Carrier St. (38116)
(901) 346-8644
(901) 763-0942
Bus. Liq.; Real Estate; Farm
Machinery; Const. Equip.;
Antiques; Consignment

Taggart, Raymond E.
Delta Auction & RE Co., Inc.
2850 Austin Peay #E100
(38128)
(901) 382-5731

MURFREESBORO

Lamb, Earl
Comas Montgomery Realty &
Auction
727 S. Church St. (37130)
(615) 895-0078
Real Estate; Personal Prop.;
Farm Sales

Montgomery, Comas
Comas Montgomery Realty &
Auction
727 S. Church St. (37130)
(615) 895-0078
Real Estate; Personal Prop.;
Farm Sales

Slims, Larry
Jim Stevens Realty & Auction
300 E. Main #101 (37130)
(615) 893-3589
Fax: (615) 227-6106
Real Estate; Farm Equip.;
Restaurant Equip.; Antiques;
Liquidations; Manufacturers

NASHVILLE

Colson, Robert L.
Bill Colson Auction & Realty
2012 Beech Ave. (37204)
(615) 292-6619
Real Estate; Bankruptcies;
Commercial;
Personal Prop.

Colson, William M.
Bill Colson Auction & Realty
2012 Beech Ave. (37204)
(615) 292-6619
Real Estate; Autos; Estate
Sales; Bankruptcies;
Liquidations; Antiques

Ewing, John W.
Bill Colson Auction & Realty
2012 Beech Ave. (37204)
(615) 292-6619
(615) 356-6946
Real Estate; Autos; Estate
Sales; Commercial; Antiques

Hatcher, George A., Sr.
Top Bid, Inc.
50 Music Square West
Suite 200 (37203)
(615) 329-9466
Fax: (615) 329-9545
Bankruptcies; Foreclosures;
Commercial RE; Residential
RE; Financial Inst.

Kemmer, James Pit
Team Realty & Auction
506 Tanksley Ave. (37221)
(615) 333-3330
(615) 794-6953
Fax: (615) 833-7916
Real Estate; Livestock

Rutledge, Clayton
Rutledge Realty & Auction Co.
1012 Broadmoor Dr. (37216)
(615) 228-9507
Farm; Estates; Personal Prop.

RICEVILLE

Carter, Bobby
Dean Howard & Daughters
Rt 2., Box 200 (37370)
(615) 334-3335
Farm Mach.; Real Estate;
Cattle; Household; Autos

SIGNAL MOUNTAIN

Ducker, Herman M.
Signal Auction & Realty
194 E. Ducker Road (37377)
(615) 886-2265
Real Estate; Farms/Equip.;
Estate Sales; Hardware Stores;
Restaurants

SPRINGFIELD

Gregory, Jerry C.
Gregory Real Estate & Auction
805 Willow St.
P.O. Box D (37172)
(615) 384-5557
Real Estate; General; Estates;
Furniture; Antiques; Farm
Mach.

TEN MILE

Kimbel, John C.
Tri-State Auction Service
Rt 2., Box 729 (37880)
(800) 334-4395
(615) 376-7009
Sawmill Equip.; Logging
Equip.; Planning Mill;
Equipment

Kimbel, John C., Jr.
Tri-State Auction Service
Rt 2., Box 729 (37880)
(800) 334-4395
Lumber Equip.; Machine
Shops; Const. Equip.

TROY

Cook, John W.
Cook Auction & Real Estate
P.O. Box 450
Hwy 51 (38260)
(901) 536-6424
Real Estate; Farm Equip.;
Estates; Commercial

TULLAHOMA

Orr, George C.
Lewis-Orr Realty Auction Sales
123 S. Jackson St. (37388)
(615) 455-3447
Real Estate; Commercial;
Farm; Residential RE; Estates;
Liquidations

Texas

AMARILLO

Assiter, Tommy
Assiter & Associates
P.O. Box 8005 (79114-8005)
(806) 358-1000
(800) 283-8005
Fax: (806) 358-1067
Autos; Real Estate; Machinery;
Farm Equip.; Business Liq.

Gore, Bob L.
Bob Gore Auctioneers
1211 E. 27th St. (79103)
(806) 373-1379
(806) 353-4182
General; Antiques; Liq.; RE;
Bankruptcy; Heavy Equip.

Williams, Arvell
Williams & Webb, Inc.
228 Canyon Dr. (79109)
(806) 374-9387
Real Estate; Oil Equipment;
Commercial

AUSTIN

Pleasant, Ezra C.
Ezra Pleasant Auctioneers
400 E. Anderson Lane
Suite 494 (78752)
(512) 832-9006
Fax: (512) 837-9246
Gov. Surplus; Foreclosure;
Liquidation;
Police Confisct; Antiques;
Consignments

CROSBY

Walker, Rocky, Jr.
Old Texas Realty & Auction
Co.
5307–09 S. Main St. (77532)
(713) 328-4000
(713) 328-7000
Fax: (713) 328-1747
Real Estate; Estates; Fund
Raisers

DALLAS

Harvill, Patrick M.
Hudson & Marshall, Inc.
14901 Quorum Drive
#585 (75240)
(214) 458-8448
Real Estate; Farm Equipment;
Heavy Equip.; Fixtures; Autos

Keeping, Jim
Jim Keeping Auction
5193 Lawnview (75227)
(800) 441-0604
(800) 527-7653
Fax: (214) 388-8789
Auctions; Used Equip.; Liq.;
Appraisals

Small, Joe E.
Joe Small Auctioneers, Inc.
8231 Santa Clara Dr. (75218)
(214) 327-0606
(214) 321-1800
Charity Benefit

Thomas, Lanny G.
Lanny Thomas & Associates
4339 S. Capistrano (75287)
(214) 931-2380
Real Estate; Farm Equip.; Art;
Antiques; Construction

FREDERICKSBURG

Althaus, Dudley N.
Althaus Acres Auction & RE
Inc.
501 W. Main St. (78624)
(512) 997-7606
(512) 685-3226
Estates; Real Estate; Exotic
Game; Livestock; General

FT. WORTH

Smiley, Randy
Hudson & Marshall
3613 Stadium Dr. (76109)
(214) 458-8448
(817) 924-1482
Fax: (214) 934-2940
Real Estate; Charity

GARLAND

Autry, Miles T.
Miles Autry Auctioneers
3425 B Kingsley (75041)
(214) 272-7825
Antiques; Estates;
Liquidations;
Consignments

Bradford, Gary L.
Gary L. Bradford Auctioneer
2329 Bent Bow Dr. (75044)
(817) 481-9085
Estates; Commercial; RE

GREENVILLE

Ogle, Jack V.
Ogle Auction Service
Rt. 2, Box 66A (75401)
(903) 454-0910
(903) 455-3949
Real Estate; Farm Equip.;
Indus. Equip.;
Estate Liq.; Bus. Liq.

HOUSTON

Burnett, B. Randall
Houston Auction Exchange
4009 Piping Rock (77027)
(713) 961-5557
Bronzes; Estates; Rugs;
Orientals; Charity

Presswood, Joe T.
Joe Presswood Co., Inc.
1702 Washington Ave. (77007)
(713) 223-9453
Restaurants; Woodworking Plt;
Machine Shops; Industrial
Equipment

Sturgis, Bill
Great Southwest Auctions
P.O. Box 920980 (77292)
(713) 864-5430
Fax: (713) 864-5430
Commercial RE; Res. RE;
Fund Raising; Real Estate;
Agri-Business; Heavy Equip.

HUFFMAN

Gilbreath, Virginia A.
Huffman Horse Center
P.O. Box 530 (77336)
(409) 258-3093
(713) 324-3280
Fax: (409) 258-7988
Horses & Mules; Cattle;
Estates; Equipment

IRVING

Owen, James L., Jr.
Jim Owen Auctioneers, Inc.
100 Spicewood Ct. (75063)
(214) 401-2472
Real Estate; Construction
Equip.; Marine Equip.;
Trucks; Machine Shop Equip.;
Satellite Auctions

MCALLEN

Espensen, K.L., Sr.
Espensen Co. Realtor
Auctioneers
2212 Primrose St., #C (78504)
(512) 687-5117
Fax: (512) 687-7967
Real Estate; Gov't. Liq.;
General; RE Counsel; RE
Exchange

MT. PLEASANT

Burlin, Morris L.
Burlin's
2302 Matthew Dr. (75455)
(214) 572-3142
Commercial; General; Estates;
Bankruptcy; Antiques; Heavy
Equipment

QUITMAN

Cameron, Joe D.
Cameron & Assoc. Auctioneers
Route 3, 306 S. Main
(75783)
(214) 763-4691
Real Estate; Liquidations;
General

ROCKDALE

Wiley, R.C.
Wiley Auction Co.
616 W. Cameron St. (76567)
(512) 446-3197
Farm Equip.; Ind. Equip.; RE;
Liquidations

SAN ANTONIO

Kruse, Daniel
Superior Auctioneers & Mktg.
One Superior Plaza
Suite 200 (78230)
(512) 697-0700
Fax: (512) 697-9744
Antiques; Classic Autos; Heavy
Equip.; Oil/Gas Prop; Oilfield
Equip.

TOMBALL

Adkisson, Dan
Dan Adkisson Auction/Realty
106 N. Cherry (77375)
(713) 351-5289
Industrial; RE; Aircraft;
Commercial; Bankruptcy

UTOPIA

Bond, Pete
Bond & Bond Auctioneers &
Realty
Box 258 (78884)
(512) 966-6211

RE; Liquidations; Estates;
Heavy Equipment; Farm
Equipment

WHARTON

Speer, Sherrell
Speer's Country Auction &
Realty
Rt 3, Box 327-B (77488)
(409) 532-2417
Antiques; Estates;
Consignments

WOLFFORTH

Fletcher, Bobby
Bobby Fletcher Auctioneer
P.O. Box 609 (79382)
(806) 866-4201
Farm Equip.; RE; Livestock;
General

Utah

ELSINORE

Wood, C.R.
Diamond "W" Auctioneers
Box 328 (84724)
(801) 527-3808
Machinery; Livestock; Estate

SALT LAKE CITY

Earl, Scott C.
Olson Auction Galleries
3371 El Serrito Dr. (84109)
(801) 486-7910
Real Estate; Antiques; Estate;
Bankruptcy; Liquidation;
Furniture

Olson, Robert A.
Olson Auction Galleries
4303 So. Main St. (84107)
(801) 261-4258

Fine Furniture; Estates, Real
Estate; SBA; RTC;
Liquidations

Vermont

BURLINGTON

Manchester, Jean
Green Mountain Auctions
6 Beachcrest Dr. (05401)
(802) 863-4153
Real Estate; Estates; Antiques;
Appraisals

SHELBURNE

Hirchak, Thomas J., Jr.
Thomas Hirchak Company
1972 Shelburne Rd. (05482)
(802) 888-4662
(802) 985-9195
Fax: (802) 985-9196
Commercial; RE; Heavy
Equip; Vehicles; Antiques;
Estates; Liquidations

Virginia

ABINGDON

Counts, David C.
Counts Auction Company
843 W. Main St. (24210)
(703) 628-8123
RE; Farm Equip.; Commercial

ALEXANDRIA

Rasmus, Christopher R.
R.L. Rasmus Auctioneers, Inc.
6060 Tower Court
Suite LL-1 (22304)
(703) 370-2338
Fax: (703) 823-5587
Com./Ind. Assets; Hightech
Equip.; Computers; RE;
Intangibles

Rasmus, Ronald L.
R.L. Rasmus Auctioneers, Inc.
6060 Tower Court
Suite LL-1 (22304)
(703) 370-2338
Fax: (703) 823-5587
Com./Ind. Assets; Hightech
Equip.; Computers; RE;
Intangibles; Broadcasting

ANNANDALE

Tull, Ronald I.
Tull Realty & Auction Co.
3912 Woodburn Rd. (22003)
(703) 280-5555
RE; Est. Settlement;
Involuntary Auction;
Enforcement of Liens;
Business Liquidations

BERRYVILLE

Watkins, William B.
Wm. B. Watkins Auctioneer
RFD #3, Box 5445 (22611)
(703) 955-3606
Estate; Farm Mach.;
Household; Foreclosures;
Bus. Dispersals

BLACKSTONE

Daniel, George A.
Daniel Auction Service
Route 4, Box 261-A
(23824)
(804) 292-4609
Farm; Liquidations; RE;
Commercial;
Antiques; Livestock

BURKEVILLE

Elliott, Beau
Southside Auction Service
P.O. Box 396
Oak Street (23922)
(804) 767-4324
General RE; Antiques

CALLAWAY

Cole, A. Barry
Cole Brothers Auction Co.
Rt 1. Box 182 (24067)
(703) 483-4539
Personal Prop.; Antiques; RE;
Machinery; Auto

CASTLEWOOD

Dickenson, Gaines W.
Gaines Dickenson Auctioneers
Route 3, Box 83 (24224)
(703) 738-9230
Real Estate; Liquidations

CULPEPPER

Bennett, Lawrence
Bennett Realty & Auction Co.
700 Southridge Pkwy.
Suite 311 (22701)
(703) 825-4554
Fax: (703) 825-3171
Real Estate; Farm Equipment;
Estate Liq.; Charity Auction;
Foreclosures

HAMPTON

Bluestone, Herb
Auctions by Bluestone
727 Little Back River Rd.
(23669)
(804) 851-6411
(804) 851-7752
General; RE; Fund Raising;
Gov't. Autos; Estates

HARRISONBURG

Heatwole, G.R.
Heatwole Auction Team
169 Pleasant Hill Road
(22801)
(703) 433-2929
Commercial; RE; Estates;
Farm; Consignments

HILLSVILLE

Holder, John E.
Horney Bros. Land Auction
Co.
Rt. 1 Box 374 (24343)
(703) 228-4131
(703) 728-4452
Fax: (703) 228-6175
Real Estate; Indus. Liq.; Farm
Dispersal; Construction
Equipment; Business Liq.;
Antiques

HONAKER

Thomas, J.D.
J.D. Thomas Auctions, Inc.
Rt 3, Box 4 (24260)
(703) 873-5328
Livestock; Real Estate;
Machinery; General

KING GEORGE

Updike, S.K. (Buddy), Jr.
The Auction Man
Box 330 (22485)
(703) 371-5965
Real Estate; Estates; Antiques;
Car; Business Liq.

LAKE RIDGE

Bolton, Donna Blake
Just For Fund
2540 Kingswood Ct. (22192)
(703) 494-2388
Benefit; Estate; Liq.; RE;
Consignment

LURAY

Baldwin, Roderick
Smeltzer's Auction & Realty
RFD #4, Box 261 (22835)
(703) 743-4747
Fax: (703) 743-9380
Real Estate; Personal Prop.;
General

Smeltzer, Don P.
Smeltzer's Auction & Realty
1316 E. Main St. (22835)
(703) 743-4747
Fax: (703) 743-9380
Real Estate; Personal Prop.;
Farm

LYNCHBURG

Counts, Ted F.
Ted Counts Realty & Auction
Co., Inc.
8314 Timberlake Road (24502)
(804) 237-2991
(804) 525-1344
RE; Heavy Equip.; Farm
Equip.; Dairy Cattle

MADISON HEIGHTS

Brown, James
MJ & J Realty & Auctioneers
Rt. 1, Box 326 (24572)
(804) 929-5551
(804) 384-1382
Real Estate; Personal Prop.;
Farm Equip.; Estate; Sales

MANASSAS

Laws, H. Layton "Sonny", Jr.
Laws Auction Co.
7209 Centreville Rd. (22111)
(703) 361-3148
Fax: (703) 361-4308
Antiques; Estates; General

Reger, Fred H.
Laws Auction Co.
9924 Loudoun Ave. (22110)
(703) 361-3148
Fax: (703) 361-4308
General Auctions; Lien
Storage; Asset Recovery;
Commercial; Real Estate

MECHANICSVILLE

Timbrook, Larry J.
605 Ewell Rd. (23111)
(304) 822-4683
RE; Livestock; Farm Equip.;
Sawmills

PITTSVILLE

Reynolds, Lionel L.
Reynolds Auction Co.
Rt. 1, Box 600 (24139)
(804) 656-1097
General

RADFORD

Farmer, Kenneth W., Jr.
Ken Farmer Realty & Auction
1122 Norwood St. (24141)

(703) 639-0939
Fax: (703) 639-1759
RE; Antiques; Personal Prop.;
Commercial; Fund Raisers

RICHMOND

Davidson, John A.
Davidson Auction Co.
8612 Claypool Rd (23236)
(804) 276-3221
General; Household; Real
Estate; Estate Sales

ROANOKE

Sheets, Stephen G.
J. G. Sheets & Sons, Inc.
15 S. Jefferson St., S.W.
(24011)
(703) 345-8885
RE; Estates; Antiques;
Commercial

ROCKY MOUNT

Goodman, James E.
Goodman Realty & Auction
Co.
106 Forest Hill Lane (24151)
(703) 362-0866
General; Estates; Livestock;
Court Sales

SPOTSYLVANIA

DeBruhl, Ted
DeBruhl Auction Company
7927 Courthouse Rd. (22553)
(703) 898-2518
Autos; RE; Estates, Liq.;
General

SPRINGFIELD

Combs, Margaret H.
Auctions Unlimited
P.O. Box 2697 (22152-0697)
(703) 569-6521
Residential Contents; Estates;
Antiques; Moving & Storage;
Charity Fund Raisers

STANDARDSVILLE

Herring, Richard H.
Herring Auction Realty
Star Route, 33, Box B
(22973)
(804) 985-3906
Farm Equipment; Estates; RE;
Commercial

STEPHENS CITY

DeLoach, Greg
Auctioneer Greg DeLoach
P.O. Box 265 (22655)
(703) 869-6020
Estate Liquid.; RE; Antiques;
Commercial

TROY

Harlowe, William W.
Harlowe Auction Ltd.
Rt. 1, Box 895 (22974)
(804) 293-2904
Antiques; Estates; Autos; Bus.
Liq.; Farm Equipment; Land

VERONA

Craig, Roger L.
Roger L. Craig Auctioneers
Rt 1, Box 186 (24482)
(703) 363-5132
Estate Auctions; Farm Equip.;
RE; Liq.; Consignment

WOODSTOCK

Pangle, Mark E.
Pangle Real Estate & Auction
Company
933 S. Main St. (22664)
(703) 459-2113
RE; Estates; Antiques; Farm
Machinery

Pangle, Robert F., Jr.
Pangle Real Estate & Auction
Company
933 S. Main St. (22664)
(703) 459-2113
RE; Estates; Antiques; Farm
Machinery

Washington

BELLEVUE

Harris, Keith A.
Harris & Harris Commercial/
Industrial Auctioneers
P.O. Box 5657 (98006)
(206) 451-8922
Commercial; Industrial

CONNELL

Booker, Merle D.
Booker Auction Co.
11000 Coyan (99326)
(509) 488-3331
Fax: (509) 488-6584
Farm Equip.; Const. Equip.;
Trucking Equip.; Commercial/
Ind.; RE; Estate/Antique

ENUMCLAW

Anderson, Duane D.
Anderson Auction Service
P.O. Box 695 (98022)
(206) 825-5375
Classic Autos; Farm; Estates

KENMORE

Murphy, Tim
James G. Murphy Co., Inc.
P.O. Box 82160 (98028)
(206) 486-1246
Fax: (206) 483-8247
Metal Shops; Heavy Mach.;
Mfg. Plants; Mills; Wood
Shops; Real Estate

LYNNWOOD

Sutter, Errold R.
Auctions Incorporated
P.O. Box 5587 (98046)
(206) 771-4232
Fax: (206) 775-2052
Real Estate; Commercial;
Industrial

MOSES LAKE

Yarbro, Charles E., Sr.
Chuck Yarbro Auctioneers
3501 Hiawatha Rd., NE
(98837)
(509) 765-6869
Farm Machinery; RE; Business
Liq.; Estates; Antiques

OAK HARBOR

Witzel, Earl L. (Retired)
Witzel's Auction Company
761 E. Lefty Lane (98277)
(206) 675-6262
Estates; Commercial

PORT ORCHARD

Stokes, Jeff
Stokes Auction
2740 Spring Creek Road
(98366)
(206) 876-5123
(206) 876-0236
Fax: (206) 895-0550
Autos; Livestock; RE; Fund
Raising

Stokes, Larry S.
Stokes Auction
8398 Spring Creek Road
(98366)
(206) 876-0236
Fax: (206) 876-0236
RE; Estates; Commercial;
Industrial; Antiques;
Household

RENTON

Mroczek, Lawrence C.
Mroczek Brothers Auctioneers
& Associates
700 S.W. 4th Pl. (98055)
(206) 329-6138
RE; Commercial; Industrial;
Estates; Appraisals

SEATTLE

Bloss, Richard L.
The Boeing Co.
P.O. Box 3707 M/S 3T-10
(98124)
(206) 393-4043
Fax: (206) 393-4050
Industrial Liq.; Surplus
Capital; Assets

WALLA WALLA

Macon, Doug
Macon Brothers Auctioneers
728 Rees Ave. (99362)

(509) 529-7770
Fax: (509) 529-5606
RE; Estates; Industrial Equip;
Aviation Equip; Court Orders;
Asset Conversion

West Virginia

BRIDGEPORT

Millad, Carlyle
Diversified Marketing Inc.
413 High Street (26330)
(304) 842-2946
Fax: (304) 842-5826
Ind/Commercial; RE; Farm
Equipment; Estates; Antiques;
Appraisals

HAYWOOD

Felosa, Tony A.
Joseph A. Felosa Auction
Realty
P.O. Box 1373 (26366)
(304) 592-0738

WEST HAMLIN

Thompson, Albert L.
Resource Marketing
Route 1, Box 180 (25571)
(304) 824-5904
Construction; RE;
Commercial; Museums;
Liquidations; Appraisals

Wisconsin

BURLINGTON

Sevick, Robert J.
Times Past Estate Services
8110 400th Avenue (53105)
(414) 539-3198
Estates; Commercial; Antiques

FRANKLIN

Robbins, William W.
Auctionway Realty
12217 W. St. Martins Rd.
(53132)
(414) 425-1227
Real Estate

GREENBAY

Massart, Pat
Massart Auctioneers, Inc.
2545 Finger Rd. (54302)
(414) 468-5656
Household Est.; Antiques;
Farms, Real Estate; Liquidations; Commercial

Massart, Robert J.
Massart Auctioneers, Inc.
2545 Finger Rd. (54302)
(414) 468-1113
Farm; Commercial; Antiques;
Estates; RE; Construction

LACROSSE

Boge, R. Jerome
Action Sales By Auction
219 S. 21st St. (54601)
(608) 784-3952
RE; Household; Estate;
Commercial; Benefit

MADISON

Lust, Richard O.
Lust Auction Services
P.O. Box 44421 (53744-0421)
(608) 833-2001
Fax: (608) 833-9593
Restaurants; Commercial;
Retail Inventory; Real Estate;
Industrial; Grocery/Bakery

Varney, Scott
Accredited Auctioneers
207 N. Livingston St. (53703)
(608) 255-7630
RE; Estates; Small Business;
Restaurants/Grocery; Vehicles
& Equip.; Charities

MONDOVI

Heike, Dan J.
Heike Auction & Realty
135 E. Main St. (54755)
(715) 926-5005
(715) 926-5318
Farm; Real Estate; Machinery;
Antiques

Heike, James
Heike Auction & Realty
135 E. Main St. (54755)
(715) 926-5005
Dairy Cattle; Farm
Equipment; Household;
Antiques

REEDSBURG

Gavin, Robert J.
Gavin Bros., Inc.
296 Main St. (53959)
(608) 524-6416
Farm; Antiques; Household;
Real Estate

REEDSVILLE

Voigt, Victor V.
Voigt Auction Service
Route 2 (54230)
(414) 772-4235
Estates; Household; Farm;
Livestock; Equipment;
Antiques

RICE LAKE

Hazelwood, William J.
Hazelwood Auction & Realty
935 Model Railroad (54868)
(800) 345-2040
(715) 234-2040
Fax: (715) 234-2040
Real Estate; Antiques; Farm;
Commercial; Estates; Gov't
Dispersal

WAUSAU

Theorin, Carl
Wausau Sales Corporation
P.O. Box 1311 (54402)
(715) 675-9494
Loggin; Sawmill; Business Liq.;
Dairy Cattle; Farm Dispersals;
Construction

WAUTOMA

Wagner, James R.
American Auction
Box 975 (54982)
(414) 787-2680
Estate; Farm; Business Liq.;
Real Estate; Household

WILDROSE

Bieri, Bruce A.
Wild Rose Auction Co.
545 Main St. (54984)
(414) 622-4000
(414) 622-4686
Real Estate; Antiques; Farm;
Coin; Printing Equip.; Estates

WISCONSIN DELLS

Murray, Lee A.
Dells Auction Service
P.O. Box 212 (53965)
(608) 254-8696

Ind. Food Equip.; Commercial;
Real Estate; Farm Equip.;
Estates

Wyoming

BUFFALO

Carpenter, Thomas K.
Thomas Carpenter
Auctioneers
P.O. Box 607 (82834)
(307) 684-9222
Benefit; Real Estate;
Household; Art

KAYCEE

Addy, Dave
Dave Addy's Auctioneers
2075 Barnum Rd. (82639)
(307) 738-2312
Commercial Liq.; Oilfield Liq.;
RE; Personal Prop.

Canada

Alberta

EDMONTON

Victor, Ronald A.
Danbury Sales
10418–80 Avenue
(T6B 0E2)
(403) 439-8000
(403) 465-0284
Fax: (403) 433-3888
Liquidations; Industrial;
Equipment; Appraisals

WARBURG

Zajes, Karl S.
Zajes Auctions Ltd.
Box 157 (T0C 2T0)
(403) 848-2508
Aircraft; Industrial;
Liquidations; RE;
Farm; Lumber

British Columbia

KELOWNA

Niessen, Gerald E.
Hi-Bid Auction Co.
1525 Gordon Drive
(V1Y 3G6)
(604) 862-1388
Real Estate; Equipment;
Estates

Manitoba

BRANDON

Sumida, Guy
Prairie Auction Services Ltd.
155 9th Street (R7A 4A6)
(204) 725-2698
Real Estate; Farm Equipment;
Liquidations

Newfoundland

ST. JOHNS

Fitzpatrick, John J.
Fitzpatrick's Auction Service,
Ltd.
P.O. Box 8263 (A1B 3N4)
(709) 722-5865
(709) 739-5603
Fax: (709) 722-9612

Household; Heavy Equipment;
Autos; Real Estate; Antiques;
Ind. Equipment

Ontario

COURTRIGHT

Stephens, John W.
Great West Auction Co.
51 Thompson St. (N0N 1H0)
(519) 867-2908
Farm Auctions; Estates;
Household; Real Estate

KINGSTON

Gordon, Alicia Y.
Gordon Auctioneers and
Realty, Inc.
RR #6 (K7L 4V3)
(613) 542-0963
Fax: (613) 542-7520
Real Estate; Antiques; Estates;
Farm Machinery; Liquidations

Gordon, Barry F.
Gordon Auctioneers and
Realty, Inc.
RR #6 (K7L 4V3)
(613) 542-0963
Fax: (613) 542-7520
Real Estate; Antiques; Estates;
Farm Machinery; Liquidations

LONDON

Storey, Dennis N.
Storey Auctions
530 1st St. (N5V 1Z3)
(519) 455-5415
Fax: (519) 455-2763
Machine Shops; Restaurants;
Garage Equip.; Mfg. Plants;
Estates; RE; Vehicles

Quebec

MONTREAL

Peterson, Gary J.
Goldsmith & Peterson
Auctioneers
2945 Rue Diab (H4S 1M1)
(514) 331-6668
(514) 386-1718
Fax: (504) 331-6664
Commercial; Industrial;
Metals; Woodworking; Heavy
Equip.

Stein, Jerry
AAI Associated Auctioneers
ENR.
P.O. Box 40 Ahuntsic
(H3L 3N5)
(514) 335-0221
Fax: (514) 681-8912
Apparel Equipment; Antiques;
Bankruptcy; Commercial;
Construction; Industrial

36

Conclusion

★★

Everyone lives by selling something.
— ROBERT LOUIS STEVENSON

The auction business is going to grow faster during the 1990s than in any previous decade. Expect to see explosive and continued growth in bankruptcies and in the sale of government-repossessed real estate. The hype and excitement of drug auctions in the mid and late 1980s has died down considerably. While the titles change, the merchandise should stay about the same. Instead of buying a drug baron's Porsche you might be offered an ex-bank president's Mercedes.

This is going to be the decade of real estate auctions. More property will change hands via a real estate auctioneer than ever before. Should economic activity remain stagnant, or get worse throughout the 1990s, it may come to pass that auctioneers will replace real estate brokers as the prime purveyors of real estate, not only for government agencies but for the majority of real estate sales.

Government auctions, themselves, are changing cataclysmically. By the end of this century virtually all government agency auctions could be in the hands of private sector auctioneers. Private auctioneers already sell a large share of real estate and personal property. Budget cuts and incompetence have forced many government agencies to subcontract their auctions to professional auctioneers.

Only the General Service Administration, the Department of Defense, and the Internal Revenue Service steadfastly hold out and insist on playing auctioneer themselves. While the GSA often obtains a fair price at their auctions, Defense and IRS auctions are an industry-wide joke. Auctioneers and professional auction-goers ridicule both. Great for the bargain-hunter, deadly for the taxpayer. Since no amount of bad media publicity has changed Defense auctions, you might as well benefit from your tax dollars by attending their auctions.

Because many private auctioneers are not licensed, some auctions are going to place the novice auction-goers at risk. Fraud, in its various disguises, continues at many private auctions, especially bankruptcy auctions. The larger the auction, the less likely you will see fraud (but then again, you are not likely to find incredible steals at highly-promoted, well-attended auctions). States that are not now licensing auctioneers should adopt the National Auctioneers Association model licensing law and protect their consumers from dishonest auctioneers. This will give everyone connected with auctions a fair shake.

For you, the auction-goer, there will be a few requirements to keep pace with the auction industry. Anyone who is unwilling to educate himself on the subject of auctions yet insists on bidding at them without knowledge places himself at considerable risk. No doubt you will attend an auction only after fully understanding and being able to use the golden rules for auction-goers.

As government agencies place larger shares of their auction business into the hands of seasoned professionals, it will be expected of you more than ever to study what you are purchasing, and bid without losing your head. Veteran auction-goers are prepared to expect the unexpected. Knowing the auction basics and familiarizing yourself with the auctioneer's tactics and strategies reduces your risks and increases your potential rewards.

The name of the game at auctions is finding great bargains. Don't deny yourself that opportunity by not fully understanding each aspect of the auction, from the initial promotion of the event to the knockdown of the hammer and possession of your purchase.

Auctions are going to get even more exciting throughout the 1990s. Auctioneers have reported land-office business throughout 1991 and expect the next few years to grow by leaps and bounds. One thing to be said about auctions, and especially about government auctions, over the next few years is that auctions are going to be in the news. The question placed to you is this: Will you be merely reading about them or will you be actively and profitably buying at them as well?

Glossary

★★

This glossary consists of the legal and specialized terms found in this book. It has been set up in the back of this book for easy access. Refer to this glossary frequently as you study and restudy the book. Terms are listed alphabetically for your easy use.

Abandoned   Deserted. To abandon is to leave, to forsake completely and finally, to discontinue, give up, withdraw from. As in "abandon a sinking ship."

Absolute   Free from any restriction, limitation, or exception.

Absolute Auction   Strictly to the highest bidder, regardless of price.

Adjudication   The determination of a controversy and a pronouncement of a judgment based on evidence presented; implies a final judgment of the court. To adjudicate, for a court, is to make a decision on something.

Ad Valorum   Based on a rate percent of the value of something, as in a property tax. From Latin for "according to the value."

Agency   An organization that provides some service.

Agent   A person or thing that acts or has the power to act. A person authorized by another to act on his behalf.

Attorney   This is one of a class of persons admitted by the state's highest court or by a federal court to practice law in that jurisdiction.

Auction   A public sale to the highest bidder; the sale of real property or goods by public outcry and competitive bidding.

Auction Block   The place from which goods are sold or the table or podium that the auctioneer uses to strike his hammer. In Roman times this was an actual block of stone.

Auctioneer   A person who conducts sales by auction.

Auction Without Reserve   The Uniform Commercial Code retains the common law rule for sales "without reserve" in that once the auctioneer calls for a bid, the article for sale cannot be withdrawn unless there is no bid within a reasonable time. See "reserve".

Bankrupt   The state or condition of one who is unable to pay his debts as they are, or become, due. The term includes a person against whom an involuntary petition has been filed, or who has filed a voluntary petition.

Bankruptcy A legal process under federal law intended to not only ensure fairness and equality among creditors but also to help the debtor by enabling him to start anew with property he is allowed to retain as exempt from his liabilities, unhampered by pressure and discouragement of preexisting debts.

Bankruptcy Code A federal law for the benefit and relief of creditors and their debtors in cases in which the latter are unable or unwilling to pay their debts.

Bankruptcy Court The forum in which most bankruptcy proceedings are conducted.

Bankruptcy Discharge The order of bankruptcy court that discharges the bankrupt from all dischargeable obligations and debts.

Bankruptcy Trustee The person who takes legal title to the property of the debtor and holds it "in trust" for equitable distribution among the creditors. In most districts, the trustee is appointed by the bankruptcy judge or selected by the creditors and approved by the judge. In a limited number of "pilot districts," a United States Trustee, appointed by the attorney general, serves as or supervises the trustee.

Bid The amount someone offers to pay for something.

Bidding The activity of making offers for something at an auction.

Bidding Paddle A hand-held instrument, shaped like a Ping-Pong or table tennis paddle, with a number that is used to identify the bidder.

Certificate of Title A statement of opinion on the status of title to a parcel of real property based on an examination of specified public records.

Chapter Eleven (Bankruptcy) Petitions for relief under Chapter Eleven permit the debtor to undertake a reorganization to pay his debts.

Chapter Seven (Bankruptcy) Most assets of the debtor are liquidated as quickly as possible to pay off his creditors to the extent possible and to free the debtor to start anew. The debtor receives a discharge from most debts incurred prior to the time he filed for relief.

Claim The assertion of right to money or property.

Creditor One to whom money is owed by the debtor; or to whom an obligation exists. A creditor is one who voluntarily trusts or gives credit to another for money or other property. In its more general and extensive sense, it is one who has the right by law to demand and recover from another a sum of money on any account whatever.

Confirmation For a sale to be complete, the seller must accept the bid.

Conventional Loan A loan that is not insured or guaranteed by a government or private source.

Conveyance Every instrument in writing by which an estate or interest in realty is created. Also, transfer of title of land by deed, or assignment, lease, mortgage, or encumbrance of land.

Court The branch of government responsible for the resolution of disputes arising under the laws of government. A court system is usually divided into various parts that specialize in hearing different types of cases.

Court Hearings Proceedings of relative formality (though generally less formal than a trial), generally public, with definite issues of fact or law to be tried, in which witnesses are heard and parties proceeded against have the right to be heard, and is much the same as a trial and may terminate in final order.

Custody   Not ownership. A keeping, guarding, care, watch, inspection, preservation, or security of a thing.

Debt   Money, goods, or services owing from one person to another. An absolute promise to pay a certain sum on a certain date, or any obligation of one person to pay or compensate another.

Debtor   One who has the obligation of paying a debt; one who owes a debt; one who owes another anything, or is under any obligation arising from express agreement, implication of law, or from the principles of natural justice, to render and pay a sum of money.

Default   A failure of the mortgagor to pay mortgage installments when due. An omission or failure to perform a legal or contractual duty.

Defendant   One who is sued and called upon to make satisfaction for a wrong complained of by another.

Deficiency Judgment   A court order stating that the borrower still owes money when the security for a loan does not entirely satisfy a defaulted debt.

Deposit   Money paid in good faith to assure performance of a contract. Deposits are commonly used with sales contracts and leases. If the person who put up the deposit fails to perform, the deposit is forfeited, unless conditions of the contract allow for a refund.

Down Payment   The amount one pays for property in addition to the debt incurred.

Earnest Money   A deposit made by a purchaser of real estate to evidence good faith. It is customary for the buyer to give the seller earnest money at the time a sales contract is signed. The earnest money is generally credited to the down payment at closing.

Encumbrance   A lien, such as mortgage, tax, or judgment lien, an easement, a restriction on use of the land, or an outstanding dower right that may diminish the value of the property.

Equitable   According to natural right or natural justice, marked by due consideration for what is fair, unbiased, or impartial.

Execution   The process of carrying into effect a court's judgment, decree or order. It is the end of the law. It gives the successful party the fruits of his judgment.

Fair-Market Value   The price that goods or property would bring in a market of willing buyers and willing sellers in the ordinary course of trade.

Forced Sale   A sale that the vendor must accept immediately, without the opportunity to find a buyer who will pay a price representing a sum approaching the reasonable worth of the property sold.

Foreclosure   The cutting off or termination of a right to property; specifically, an equitable action to compel payment of a mortgage or other debt secured by a lien. As to real property, it is precipitated by nonpayment of the debt, and leads to selling of the property to which the mortgage or lien is attached in order to satisfy that debt.

Forfeiture   The permanent loss of property for failure to comply with the law.

Government   That form of fundamental rules and principles by which a nation or state is governed, or by which individual members of a body politic are to regulate their social actions.

Government Agency   A subordinate creature of federal, state, or local government created to carry out a government function or to implement a statute or statutes.

Government Agents   Those performing service and duty of a public character for benefit of all citizens of the community.

Insolvency   A financial condition in which one is unable to meet his obligations as they mature in the ordinary course of business or in which one's liabilities exceed his assets in any given time.

Instrument   A formal or legal written document, such as a deed, contract, lease, will, etc.

Involuntary Proceedings   An equitable proceeding for the purpose of impounding all the debtor's nonexempt property to distribute it equally among creditors, and to release the debtor from liability.

Judgment   The determination of a court of competent jurisdiction upon matters submitted to it; a final determination of the rights of the parties to a lawsuit.

Judicial   Pertaining to courts of law or to judges; or to the administration of justice; giving or seeking judgment, as in dispute or contest.

Judicial Sale   Sale conducted under a judgment, order, or supervision of a court as in a sale under a petition for partition of real estate or an execution. A "judicial sale" is one that must be based upon an order or decree of a court directing the sale.

Jurisdiction   The power to hear and determine a case. In addition to the power to adjudicate, a valid exercise of jurisdiction requires fair notice and an opportunity for the affected parties to be heard. Without jurisdiction, a court's judgment is void.

Law   The legislative pronouncement of the rules that should guide one's actions in society.

Law of the Land   Due process of law. By the law of the land is most clearly intended the general law that hears before it condemns, that proceeds upon inquiry, and renders judgment only after trial. The meaning is that every citizen shall hold his life, liberties, and property and immunities under protection of general rules that govern society.

Legal   Conforming to the law; according to the law; required or permitted by law; not forbidden or discountenanced by law; good, effectual in law. Created by law. Lawful.

Levy   To raise or collect; to seize; to assess, as to levy a tax. When one levies, or places a levy upon some property, it is seized and may be sold to satisfy a judgment.

Liabilities   Signifies monies owed. A liability is an obligation to do something; an obligation to pay money.

Lien   A charge, hold claim or encumbrance upon the property of another as security for some debt or charge; not a title to property but rather a charge upon it; the term connotes the right that the law gives to have a debt satisfied out of the property, by the sale of the property if necessary.

Lien Sale   Comes after a judgment lien on a judgment debtor's property in favor of a judgment creditor. When a judgment has been entered in a civil case, and the party liable for the judgment fails to pay it, the judgment creditor may file a lien against the property of the party liable, to give notice that the property is subject to sale in satisfaction of judgment. The judgment creditor may enforce the lien by having the sheriff seize the property and sell it at a sheriff's sale.

Lis Pendens A pending suit. A notice of lis pendens may be required in some jurisdictions to be placed in the public records to warn persons (such as prospective purchasers or others having an interest in the property under suit) that the title to the property is in litigation and that they will be bound by the possibly adverse judgment.

Liquidate To settle; to determine the amount due, and to whom due, and, having done so, to extinguish the indebtedness.

Lode Claims Deposits subject to lode claims include classic veins or lodes having well-defined boundaries. They also include other rock-in-place bearing valuable minerals and may be broad zones of mineralized rock. An applicant applying for patent to a lode claim is required to furnish a full description of vein or lode, and to state whether ore has been extracted, and, if so, the amount and value.

Lot A distinct portion or parcel of anything, such as merchandise. The manner in which articles, items, equipment or real estate is sold at an auction.

Mailing List A compilation of possible customers prepared as for use in direct mail solicitation. Through the use of these specially prepared lists, the direct mail advertiser is able to pinpoint almost exactly the target market for the advertised product.

Marshal An officer of the peace, appointed by authority of city or borough, who holds himself in readiness to answer such calls as fall within the general duties of a constable or sheriff. An office in each federal district that performs the same duties as the sheriffs do for the states. Federal marshals also execute writs and orders issued by the Federal Courts.

Minimum Bid The least or smallest offer that will be accepted by the government agency or auctioneer at a public sale, spot-bid, or sealed-bid auction. To bid successfully and have your offer accepted you must bid higher than the minimum bid in most cases.

Mortgage A written instrument that creates a lien upon real estate as security for the payment of a specified debt. The borrower gives the mortgage, which pledges the property as collateral. The lender gives the loan.

Mortgagee One who holds a lien on property or title to property as security for a debt, usually the bank or mortgage company.

Mortgagor One who pledges property as security for a loan, usually the homeowner.

Negotiated Sale The way merchandise or property is sold by discussion, with a small number of buyers or a single buyer, a price and arranging the sale in that manner, avoiding a public auction. A series of offers and counteroffers until both parties are satisfied with the price.

Open-Bidding Auctions Public auctions or public sales where bids are accepted from the auction-goers in person and are done vocally or in some similar manner.

Opening Bid The first offer made by an auction-goer to the auctioneer.

Oral Auction A voice auction where bids can be made to the auctioneer by stating the bid, raising one's hand or paddle or numbered card, or in some other obvious and accepted manner until a winning bid is made, the bid accepted, and the merchandise sold.

Patent Conveyance of title to government land. A grant of some property, authority, or right made by the government to (an) individual(s).

Patent a Claim In mining, the locator or owner of a valid mining location has the right to its exclusive posession for mining purposes if he performs certain work on the claim. If not, the claim is open to others on the condition that they patent a claim (follow procedures of the Bureau of Land Management). An application for a patent must be made and approved, showing discovery and qualification of the applicant. See also "Lode claim," and "Placer claim."

Personal Property   Things movable, as distinguished from real property or things attached to the realty. In a broad and general sense, everything that is the subject of ownership, not coming under denomination of real estate. Generally, all property other than real estate.

Petition   A formal written application to a court requesting judicial action on a certain matter.

Placer Claim   In mining, an applicant applying for patent to a placer claim must show that the land applied for is placer ground (containing mineral- or ore-rich sand or gravel deposits, or which is not a lode). An applicant for patent to a placer claim must show that the land applied for is placer ground containing valuable deposits not in vein or lode formation, and that the title is sought because of the mineral therein and not to control water courses or obtain valuable timber.

Plaintiff   A person who brings an action; the party who complains or sues in a civil action and is so named on the record. A person who seeks remedial relief for an injury to rights.

Possessions   Those things that a person has, holds, or maintains in his own power or command.

Possessory Lien   A lien is possessory where the creditor has the right to hold possession of the specific property until satisfaction of the debt or performance of an obligation.

Proceedings   The succession of events constituting the process by which judicial action is invoked and utilized. The form in which actions are to be brought and defended, the manner of intervening in suits and of conducting them, the mode of deciding them, opposing them, and of executing judgments.

Property   Ownership. The exclusive and unrestricted right to a thing. The right to dispose of a thing in every legal way, to possess it, to use it, and to exclude every one else from interfering with it.

Property Taxes   Taxes (based on the assessed value of a home) paid by homeowners for community services such as schools, public works, and other costs of local government. Paid usually as part of the monthly mortgage payment.

Public Auction   A sale upon notice to the public and in which members of the public may bid.

Public Outcry   Another way of saying public auction. Also known as public outcry auction, oral auction, voice auction, or open-bidding auction. All bids are out in the open as opposed to spot bid or sealed bid auctions.

Public Sale   The legal phrase most commonly used to describe a public auction and that distinguishes it from a private auction house's auction. With notice to general public.

Quit Claim Deed   A conveyance by which the grantor transfers whatever interest he or she has in the real estate without warranties or obligations.

Real Estate   Land and everything more or less attached to it. Ownership below to the center of the earth and above to the heavens.

Real Property   Land, including the surface, whatever is attached to the surface such as minerals and the area above the surface.

Repossession Seizure or foreclosure. The method by which a secured creditor satisfies a debtor's obligation after the debtor has defaulted.

Reserve Price The minimum selling price fixed by the auctioneer and the seller, often unknown to the bidders. If bidding does not reach this price, the auctioneer may withdraw the merchandise or property from the auction sale. A reserve auction refers to the minimum selling price for each item being sold at auction. Each item will have its own distinct minimum selling price. Nearly all government auctions currently have a reserve price on that which is up for sale.

Retailer A merchant whose primary activity is to sell directly to the consumers.

Retail Price The price at which goods are identified for sale or are sold for final consumption, as opposed to for resale or processing.

Sale A contract or agreement by which property is transferred from the seller (vendor) to the buyer (vendee) for a fixed price of money, paid or agreed to be paid by the buyer.

Satisfaction A discharge and subsequent release of obligation by the payment thereof. Discharging an obligation by paying a party what is due him (as on a mortgage, lien or contract).

Sealed Bid Each interested party submits a bid by a specific date and time by mail to a central location in a sealed envelope, often labeled in a certain way. All such bids are opened at the same time and the highest acceptable bid wins. Many auctioneers do not consider this an auction but instead refer to it as a sealed-bid sale.

Section 341 Meeting Also called the first meeting of creditors. In bankruptcy proceedings, during the first few weeks, a meeting of creditors occurs for informal negotiations including a discussion of postbankruptcy financing between debtors and creditors. This meeting may determine which companies will continue to do business with the debtor.

Seizure The act of forcibly dispossessing an owner of property under actual or apparent authority of law. Also, the taking of the property into the custody of the court for the satisfaction of a judgment.

Sheriff The chief executive and administrative officer of a county, being chosen by popular election.

Sheriff's Sale A sale of property by the sheriff under authority of a court's judgment and writ of execution in order to satisfy an unpaid judgment, mortgage lien, or other debt of the owner.

Spot Bid An auction where attendees write in their bid on a form and submit it to the auctioneer. It is done, generally, in person at the auction and in writing and is signed by the bidder.

Surplus That which remains above what is used or needed. An amount, quantity, greater than needed.

Straight Bankruptcy In this form of bankruptcy most assets of the debtor are liquidated as quickly as possible to pay off his creditors to the extent possible and to free the debtor to start anew.

Statute An act of legislature, adopted pursuant to its constitutional authority, by prescribing means and in certain forms such that it becomes the law governing conduct within its scope.

Subject to Seller's Approval The seller must accept the bid for the sale to be finalized.

Tax   A rate or sum of money assessed on a person or property for the support of the government, and commonly levied upon assets or real property, or income derived from wages, or upon the sale or purchase of goods.

Tax Sale   A sale of land for the nonpayment of taxes.

Title   Ownership. Having title to something means having the right to possess the thing.

Title Insurance   A policy insuring the owner or the mortgagee against loss by reason of defects in the title to a parcel of real estate, other than encumbrances, defects, and matters specifically excluded by the policy.

Trustee   One who holds legal title to property "in trust" for the benefit of another person, and who is required to carry out specific duties with regard to the property, or who has been given power affecting the disposition of the property for another's benefit.

Unclaimed   That which has been forgotten or abandoned.

Upset Price   The price at which any subject, as lands or goods, is exposed to sale by auction and below which it is not to be sold.

VA Loan   A loan guaranteed by the Department of Veterans Affairs against loss to the lender, and made through a private lender. (HUD homes may be purchased with a VA loan.)

Voluntary Proceedings   Proceedings whereby any debtor entitled to the benefits of the Bankruptcy Act may file a petition to be adjudged a voluntary bankrupt.

Warranty   A written statement arising out of a sale to the consumer of a consumer good, pursuant to which the manufacturer, distributor, or retailer undertakes to preserve or maintain the utility or performance of the consumer good or provide compensation if there is a failure in utility or performance. A promise contained in a contract.

Warranty Deed   A deed in which the grantor fully warrants good clear title to the premises. Used in most real estate deed transfers, a warranty deed offers the greatest possible protection of any deed.

Wholesale   To sell goods in gross to retailers, who then sell the merchandise to customers.

Wholesaler   An individual who buys and sells goods to retailers and other users but does not sell in significant amounts to the consumer.

Writ   An order issued from a court requiring the performance of a specified act, or giving authority to have it done.

Writ of Execution   A writ to put in force the judgment or decree of a court.